Congratulations, Ben! Good luck with all your upcoming adventures... come back + visit. Abby Allen

# CONGRATULATIONS

This book has been awarded by the Department of Psychology for the

Psychology Major Award

On April 27, 2018

to

Benjamin Ertman

Congratulations! Rick Platt

Congratulations, Ben - you have a very promising future ahead! It has been a pleasure to work with you. Dr. K

Congratulations!

Congrats, Ben! It's been a pleasure, keep in touch! - Prof Scott

Congratulations!

Stay Super! - James Maintell

# The Wiley Handbook of Developmental Psychopathology

# The Wiley Handbook of Developmental Psychopathology

Edited by

**Luna C. Centifanti**
**David M. Williams**

WILEY Blackwell

This edition first published 2017


*Registered Offices*
John Wiley & Sons, Inc., 111 River Street, Hoboken, NJ 07030, USA

John Wiley & Sons Ltd, The Atrium, Southern Gate, Chichester, West Sussex, PO19 8SQ, UK

*Editorial Office*
The Atrium, Southern Gate, Chichester, West Sussex, PO19 8SQ, UK

For details of our global editorial offices, customer services, and more information about Wiley products visit us at www.wiley.com.

Wiley also publishes its books in a variety of electronic formats and by print-on-demand. Some content that appears in standard print versions of this book may not be available in other formats.



*Library of Congress Cataloging-in-Publication Data*

Names: Centifanti, Luna C., 1974– editor. | Williams, David M., 1980– editor.
Title: The Wiley handbook of developmental psychopathology / [edited by] Luna C. Centifanti, David M. Williams.
Description: Hoboken, NJ : John Wiley & Sons, 2017. | Includes bibliographical references and index.
Identifiers: LCCN 2016055391 (print) | LCCN 2017001686 (ebook) | ISBN 9781118554555 (cloth) | ISBN 9781118554548 (pdf) | ISBN 9781118554531 (epub)
Subjects: LCSH: Psychology, Pathological–Handbooks, manuals, etc. | Developmental psychology–Handbooks, manuals, etc.
Classification: LCC RC454.4 .W544 2017 (print) | LCC RC454.4 (ebook) | DDC 616.89–dc23
LC record available at https://lccn.loc.gov/2016055391

Cover Image: © alepvfoto/Fotolia
Cover Design: Wiley

Set in 10/12pt Galliard by SPi Global, Pondicherry, India

Printed in Singapore by C.O.S. Printers Pte Ltd

10 9 8 7 6 5 4 3 2 1

# Contents

# List of Contributors

**Nathalie M. G. Fontaine**, School of Criminology, University of Montreal

**Isaac T. Petersen**, Department of Psychological and Brain Sciences, Indiana University

**Henrik Larsson**, Department of Medical Epidemiology and Biostatistics, Karolinska Institute, Stockholm, Sweden

**Brian M D'Onofrio**, Department of Psychological and Brain Sciences, Indiana University, Bloomington, IN, USA

**Madeleine J. George**, Duke University

**Michael A. Russell**, Penn State University

**Candice L. Odgers**, Duke University

**Nicola Shaughnessy**, School of Arts, University of Kent

**Cynthia S. Peng**, Department of Speech, Language, and Hearing Sciences, George Washington University, USA

**Gregory L. Wallace**, Department of Speech, Language, and Hearing Sciences, George Washington University, USA

**Nicola Botting**, Division of Language and Communication Science, School of Health Sciences, City, University of London

**Chloë Marshall**, UCL Institute of Education, University College London

**Jarla Pijper**, Adolescent Development, Utrecht University & Clinical Child and Adolescent Studies, Leiden University

**Minet de Wied**, Adolescent Development, Utrecht University

**Stephanie van Goozen**, Clinical Child and Adolescent Studies, Leiden University & School of Psychology, Cardiff University

**Wim H. J. Meeus**, Adolescent Development, Utrecht University & Developmental Psychology, Tilburg University

**Stefanie Hoehl**, 1. Max Planck Institute for Human Cognitive and Brain Sciences, Leipzig, Germany; 2. Department of Applied Psychology: Health, Development, Enhancement and Intervention, University of Vienna

**Emily J.H. Jones**, Brain and Cognitive Development, Birkbeck, University of London

**Mark H. Johnson**, Brain and Cognitive Development, Birkbeck, University of London

**Dr Alice Jones Bartoli**, University of London

**Prof Alice M. Gregory**, Goldsmiths, University of London

**Kostas A. Papageorgiou**, 1. School of Psychology, Queen's University Belfast, UK; 2. Department of Psychology, Tomsk State University, Russia

**Angelica Ronald**, Department of Psychological Sciences, Birkbeck, University of London

**Yulia Kovas**, (1) Goldsmiths, University of London; (2) Tomsk State University

**Maria Grazia Tosto**, Tomsk State University

**David M. Williams**, School of Psychology, University of Kent

**David J. Hawes, PhD**, School of Psychology, The University of Sydney

**Luna C. Muñoz Centifanti**, University of Liverpool, UK

**Scott Risser**, Montana Tech, USA

**Bethany Little**, Durham University, UK & Vrije Universiteit, Netherlands

**Hedwig Eisenbarth**, University of Southampton

**Dale M. Stack**, Concordia University, Department of Psychology and Centre for Research in Human Development

**Lisa A. Serbin**, Concordia University, Department of Psychology and Centre for Research in Human Development

**Célia Matte-Gagné**, Concordia University, Department of Psychology and Centre for Research in Human Development

**Danielle Kingdon**, Concordia University, Department of Psychology and Centre for Research in Human Development

**Kelly Doiron**, Concordia University, Department of Psychology and Centre for Research in Human Development

**Alex E. Schwartzman**, Concordia University, Department of Psychology and Centre for Research in Human Development

**Amanda Sheffield Morris**, Oklahoma State University

**Benjamin J. Houltberg**, Fuller Theological Seminary

**Michael M. Criss**, Oklahoma State University

**Cara D. Bosler**, Oklahoma State University

**Carl F. Weems**, Iowa State University

**Brandon G. Scott**, Arizona State University

**Jacob A. Burack**, Department of Educational and Counselling Psychology, McGill University, Montreal, Quebec, Canada

**Ashley Reynolds,** Department of Psychology, Concordia University, Montreal, Quebec, Canada

**Oriane Landry**, School of Psychology and Public Health, La Trobe University Melbourne, VIC, Australia

**Gillian Klassen**, Department of Educational and Counselling Psychology, McGill University, Montreal, Quebec, Canada

**Natalie Russo**, Department of Psychology, Syracuse University, Syracuse, New York, USA

**Stephanie A. Fryberg,** Department of Psychology and American Indian Studies, University of Washington, Seattle, Washington, USA

**Valsamma Eapen**, School of Psychiatry, Faculty of Medicine, University of New South Wales, Australia

**Rudi Črnčec**, School of Psychiatry, Faculty of Medicine, University of New South Wales, Australia

**William Mandy** Department of Clinical, Educational and Health Psychology, Division of Psychology & Language Sciences, Faculty of Brain Sciences, University College London

**Paul J. Frick**, Louisiana State University & Australian Catholic University

**Laura C. Thornton**, Boys Town, Omaha, Nebraska USA

**Kathryn L. Modecki**, Griffith University, Brisbane, Australia

**Bep Norma Uink**, Murdoch University, Western Australia

# Section I

# Developmental Psychopathology: An up-to-date Historical and Methodological Overview

# Part 1

# Methods for Studying Developmental Psychopathology

# 1

# Developmental Trajectories of Psychopathology

## *An Overview of Approaches and Applications*

Nathalie M. G. Fontaine and Isaac T. Petersen

## Introduction

Developmental psychopathology concerns the study of the development of psychological disorders (e.g., depression, anxiety, schizophrenia, conduct problems), risk and protective factors, as well as outcomes, through a lifecourse perspective (Cicchetti, 1989; Rutter, 1990). Longitudinal studies, which involve repeated measures of the same variables from the same individuals, are crucial to investigate change (increases or decreases), but also stability, of psychopathology over time. Indeed, unlike cross-sectional studies, in which different individuals are compared at one time point, longitudinal studies allow for (1) the exploration of within-individual change (or stability)—that is, how each individual develops over time—and (2) between individual differences—including the investigation of distinct patterns of change (or stability) over time across individuals and factors associated with these distinct patterns (Singer & Willett, 2003).

More specifically, longitudinal data enable testing hypotheses about the development of behaviors, the developmental association between different, yet related behaviors (e.g., hyperactivity and physical aggression) and the factors associated with stability or change of behaviors over time. The identification of factors associated with persistence or change in behavior (increasing or decreasing patterns) can shed light on the vulnerabilities associated with severe and persistent psychopathology. In turn, a better understanding of risk processes in the development of psychopathology can help in the development of effective intervention strategies that target protective factors associated with desistance or decreased levels of psychopathology. Longitudinal data can therefore be useful for testing developmental theories about psychopathology as well as the effectiveness of prevention and treatment programs (Cicchetti & Toth, 1992).

New advances in statistical approaches over the last decades help in maximizing what we can learn using longitudinal data in the field of psychopathology (Nagin, 2005). Methodologists have developed various statistical approaches, which include and are known variously as growth curve models (GCMs), random coefficient models, multilevel models, mixed models, mixed-effects models, hierarchical linear models,

*The Wiley Handbook of Developmental Psychopathology*, First Edition. Edited by Luna C. Centifanti and David M. Williams.

group-based trajectory models (GBTMs), latent class growth models (LCGMs), and growth mixture models (GMMs) (Muthén, 2004; Nagin, 2005; Singer & Willett, 2003). The approaches have been applied with a rapid rise in many areas of developmental psychopathology research (Curran, Obeidat, & Losardo, 2010; Nagin & Odgers, 2010), including conduct problems (Nagin & Tremblay, 1999), depression/anxiety (Côté et al., 2009), callous-unemotional traits (Fontaine, Rijsdijk, McCrory, & Viding, 2010), and substance use problems (Hu et al., 2008). These approaches have also been applied to assess heterogeneity in treatment responses to clinical trials (Muthén et al., 2002).

Statistical approaches for longitudinal data can be complex in terms of selecting the optimal approach, fitting the models to the data and interpreting the findings with respect to hypothesis and theory (Curran et al., 2010). In this chapter, we introduce some of the approaches and applications, particularly to non-technical readers, including researchers, clinicians, and graduate students, who may not have yet received an extensive training in this area. References to more detailed and complete technical developments on these approaches are offered for interested readers. We first provide an overview of the approaches, with a focus on GCM, GBTM and GMM, namely approaches focusing on developmental trajectories (Muthén, 2004; Nagin & Odgers, 2010). Next, we present selected examples of applications of these models in the field of developmental psychopathology and clinical psychology. Finally, we discuss methodological considerations when applying these models and interpreting the findings.

## Overview of the Approaches

This section presents an overview of three approaches applied to longitudinal data, and more specifically to trajectory modeling: GCM, GBTM and GMM. We selected these three approaches because they share a common analytical goal, namely to examine differences or variability across members of a population in their developmental trajectories (Nagin & Odgers, 2010). A developmental trajectory can be defined as the course of a behavior over time or age (Nagin, 1999). Because these trajectory analyses examine longitudinal data with more than two measurement occasions, they have key advantages over analytical approaches that do not examine trajectories (Beauchaine, Webster-Stratton, & Reid, 2005; Gueorguieva & Krystal, 2004). First, trajectory analyses tend to have better reliability and greater power to detect behavioral change than simple pre–post or difference score designs. Second, trajectory analyses have greater flexibility with unbalanced designs, unequal spacing of time points, and tolerate missing data, unlike repeated measures analysis of variance (ANOVA). Third, trajectory analyses are less likely to inflate the Type I error rate than are repeated measures ANOVA analyses, which have more strict assumptions (e.g., sphericity). Fourth, trajectory analyses often allow multiple outcomes to be examined in the same analysis. Although these approaches share a common goal, they make distinct assumptions about the distribution of trajectories in the population. Figure 1.1 presents hypothetical trajectories according to the GCM, GBTM, and the GMM approaches. In a nutshell, it is assumed with GCM that all individuals come from the same population and can be described by the same parameters of change. It is not assumed, however, that individuals' change is identical—the model captures the average developmental trend and person-specific variations around the average trend using the same parameters of

| Approach | Trajectories | Description |
|---|---|---|
| **GCM** | 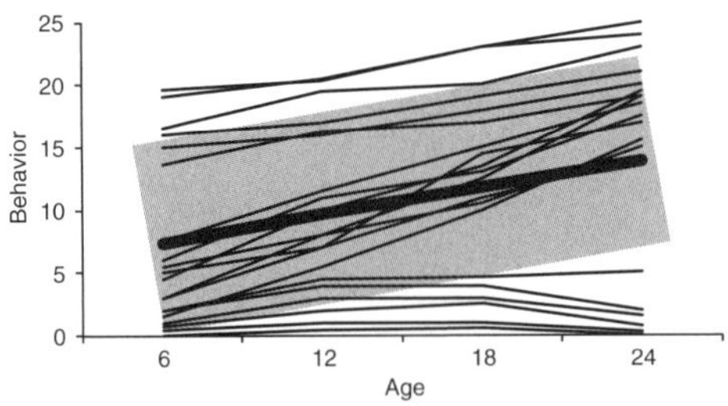 | Assumes that all individuals come from the same population, but allows individuals' change to differ—that is, the model captures the variations that are specific to each individual (random effects). The thin black lines denote the observed data points, the thick solid black line denotes the average trajectory of change and the shaded gray area around the line denotes the individual variations (Shiyko et al., 2012). |
| **GBTM** | 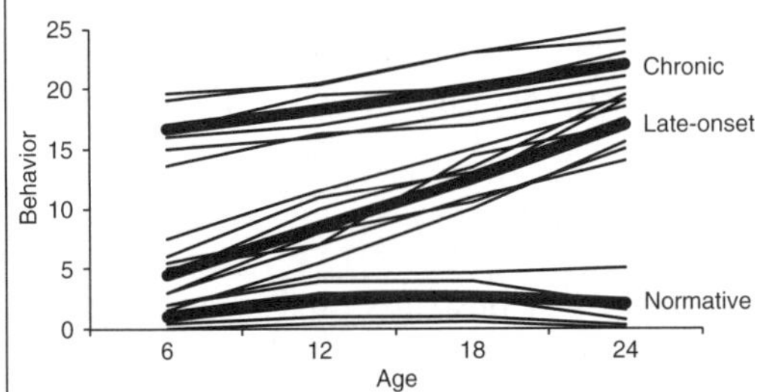 | Assumes that some individuals come from distinct subpopulations, as captured by different subgroups. The subgroups are assumed to be homogenous regarding change—that is, that all individuals on a particular trajectory have the same pattern of behavior over time. The thin black lines denote the observed data points. For each trajectory, the thick solid black line denotes the average trajectory of change (Shiyko et al., 2012). |
| **GMM** | 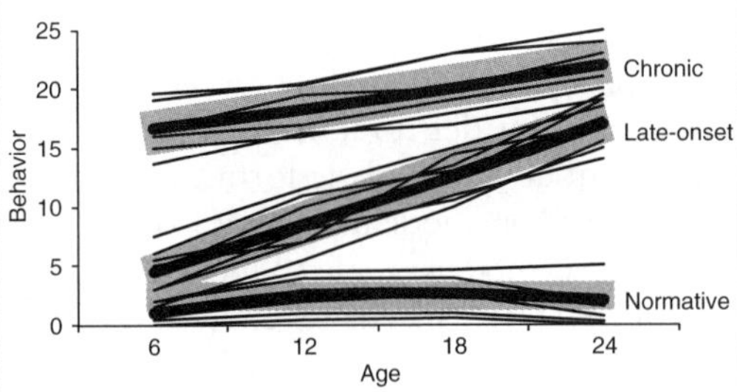 | Assumes that some individuals come from distinct subpopulations, as captured by different subgroups. However, contrary to GBTM, heterogeneity within each subgroup is also considered in GMM—that is, variations that are specific to each individual (random effects) like in GCM can also be modeled. The thin black lines denote the observed data points. For each trajectory, the thick solid black line denotes the average trajectory of change and the shaded gray area around the line denotes the individual variations (Shiyko et al., 2012). |

**Figure 1.1** Hypothetical Trajectories According to the GCM, GBTM, and the GMM Approaches.

change. GBTM and GMM, by contrast to GCM, assume that some individuals come from distinct subpopulations, as captured by different subgroups. These subgroups can be described by different parameters of change. In other words, the models allow different individuals to follow different trajectories, but only GBTM and GMM allow

**Table 1.1** Summary of the key outputs of the GCM, GBTM, and the GMM approaches.

| | *GCM* | *GBTM* | *GMM* |
|---|---|---|---|
| Intercept and slope of development | ✔ | ✔ (for each trajectory) | ✔ (for each trajectory) |
| Individual-specific effects (random effects) | ✔ | | ✔ (for each trajectory) |
| Proportion of the population following each developmental trajectory | | ✔ | ✔ |

subgroups (that are not captured by model predictors) of individuals with qualitatively different forms of change.

A number of differences exist between GCM, GBTM and GMM approaches. Researchers in developmental psychopathology often have to decide what approach they should apply. We present below a brief summary of the assumptions underlying each approach to help readers decide the optimal strategy for a given research question or hypothesis. Table 1.1 presents a summary of the key outputs of the three different approaches.

## GCM

In their simplest form, GCMs typically fit a best-fit straight line to each individual's trajectory of change over time. Each individual's line is allowed to have a different starting point (intercept) and direction and steepness of change (slope). Each individual's best-fit line is slightly adjusted to take into account the trajectories of the other individuals in the sample—a phenomenon known as shrinkage because individuals' GCM estimates are shrunk towards the mean estimate for the sample, making the GCM estimates more reliable (i.e., having less measurement error) than estimates from simple regression (Hox, 2010). Based on theory and/or how well the model fits the data, the modeler can decide whether each parameter (intercept, slope) is the same (fixed effect) or allowed to differ (random effect) between individuals. GCM can be extended to consider nonlinear forms of change, such as polynomial (e.g., quadratic), exponential, and logistic forms.

GCM can be fit in a structural equation modeling (SEM) or hierarchical linear modeling (HLM; also known as multilevel modeling, mixed modeling, or mixed-effects modeling; Raudenbush & Bryk, 2002) framework. In general, SEM is more advanced and flexible than HLM. SEM, unlike HLM, allows specifying latent variables that represent the common variance among observed (manifest) variables, and have less measurement error. Unlike HLM, SEM also allows specifying multiple outcomes in the same analysis and more flexibility in specifying correlated residuals (which, if residuals covary, would violate assumptions if unspecified). However, SEM typically requires a larger sample size than does HLM. In addition, HLM is more flexible when participants are not sampled at the same time points because HLM uses data in long form (rather than wide form in SEM). In long form, each row represents a combination of participant and measurement occasion (i.e., 100 participants × 3 measurement occasions = 300 rows, 100 variables = 100 columns). In wide form, each row represents one participant, with columns representing combinations of variable and measurement occasion (i.e., 100 participants = 100 rows, 100 variables × 3

**Table 1.2** Example of data in wide form and in long form. Data on externalizing problems in wide and long forms for three participants and four time points.

| *Wide form* | | | | | | *Long form* | | | |
|---|---|---|---|---|---|---|---|---|---|
| *ID* | *Sex* | *Ext_1* | *Ext_2* | *Ext_3* | *Ext_4* | *ID* | *Sex* | *Time* | *Ext* |
| 1 | F | 1 | 0 | 2 | Missing | 1 | F | 1 | 1 |
| 2 | F | 2 | 6 | 8 | Missing | 1 | F | 2 | 0 |
| 3 | M | 4 | 7 | 6 | 8 | 1 | F | 3 | 2 |
| | | | | | | 2 | F | 1 | 2 |
| | | | | | | 2 | F | 2 | 6 |
| | | | | | | 2 | F | 3 | 8 |
| | | | | | | 3 | M | 1 | 4 |
| | | | | | | 3 | M | 2 | 7 |
| | | | | | | 3 | M | 3 | 6 |
| | | | | | | 3 | M | 4 | 8 |

Abbreviations: ID = identification number; Ext = externalizing problems.

measurement occasions = 300 columns). If participants are not sampled at the same time points, however, wide form can be computationally cumbersome because it can result in too many columns where most participants have missing values (see Table 1.2 for an example of data in wide form and in long form). HLM (which uses long form—a more efficient data structure with less missingness when participants are sampled at different time points) can be advantageous in these circumstances. See Curran (2003) and Bauer (2003) for further discussion of similarities and differences between the two approaches, and when to use each.

GCM assumes that all individuals in the sample come from the same population and can be described by the same parameters of change (e.g., everyone could be described with a quadratic trajectory—a U-shaped trajectory—in which scores of psychopathology would first decrease and then increase over time). GCM does not necessarily assume, however, that all individuals show identical change. For example, a polynomial GCM can allow each individual to have different intercepts, slopes, and curvatures. GCM grasps the average developmental trend and person-specific variation around the average trend (random effect) using the same parameters of change for the population. Furthermore, GCM can also allow subgroups (e.g., males and females) with different trajectories, but the subgroups have to be described by the same parameters of change. Thus, individual or subgroup differences in GCM trajectories are assumed to reflect quantitative differences in degree rather than qualitative differences in kind. To examine qualitative differences between subgroups of individuals that are not captured by model predictors, however, one must use another type of model such as GBTM or GMM.

## GBTM

GBTM has been developed by Nagin and colleagues (Nagin, 1999, 2005; Nagin & Tremblay, 1999). With this approach, the population under study is considered to be composed of qualitatively distinct subgroups that are not detectable using measured characteristics (Nagin & Odgers, 2010). For instance, in a study on depressive symptoms, two different subgroups of individuals could compose the population, hypothetically one subgroup with a genetic vulnerability for depression and one without the vulnerability. If the subgroups are not distinguishable based on measured characteristics, we could assume that the dataset is composed of a combination of two different subgroups (Nagin & Odgers, 2010). Using GBTM, distinct statistical processes would be involved to explain the development of depressive symptoms in the two subgroups. Owing to distinct etiologies, the different subgroups might show different trajectories, which is the qualitative heterogeneity we seek to capture with subgroups in GBTM (as opposed to quantitative heterogeneity in GCM). The distinct subgroups are assumed to be homogeneous regarding change—that is, that all individuals on a particular trajectory have the same pattern of psychopathology (e.g., depressive symptoms) over time. Whether or not the trajectories really differ qualitatively as hypothesized may be subject to interpretation (Bauer & Reyes, 2010). In some instances, the trajectories may reflect points on a continuum as if a continuous variable was divided into different ordered-categorical levels (e.g., low levels, moderate levels and high levels of psychopathological symptoms). Still, the subgroups' trajectories could be distinguished by different predictors (e.g., childhood maltreatment) or be associated with different outcomes (e.g., job dissatisfaction).

Key outputs of GBTM are the proportion of the population following each trajectory and each individual's probability of being classified in each trajectory (probability of membership in each trajectory). GBTM takes into account uncertainty in group assignment. Table 1.3 presents, as an example, hypothetical scores of conduct problems between ages 6 to 12 for four participants. Based on their scores and assuming that the GBTM estimated four trajectories (i.e., stable high, increasing, decreasing and stable low), the model should most likely classify with a high probability (e.g., 0.75 and above) Sam as following a stable high trajectory, Gabby as following an increasing trajectory, and Max as following a decreasing trajectory. Fred's assignment to a group may be more challenging. For instance, Fred may have 0.51 probability to follow the stable high trajectory, 0.20 probability to follow the stable low trajectory, 0.10 probability to follow the increasing trajectory, and 0.19 probability to follow the decreasing trajectory (the probabilities sum to 1). Based on the probabilities, Fred would be classified in the stable high trajectory. Although using the trajectory membership (i.e., the assignment to trajectories according to the probabilities of each individual's most likely group membership) can be clinically relevant, it is important to consider that the trajectories are most likely approximations of a more complex reality (Nagin & Odgers, 2010).

**Table 1.3** Hypothetical scores of conduct problems from 6 to 12 years old for four participants.

| | *Scores of conduct problems between 6 to 12 years old* | | | | | | |
|---|---|---|---|---|---|---|---|
| *Participants* | *6* | *7* | *8* | *9* | *10* | *11* | *12* |
| Sam | 9 | 8 | 6 | 10 | 8 | 6 | 7 |
| Gabby | 2 | 4 | 5 | 4 | 6 | 8 | 10 |
| Max | 10 | 7 | 7 | 6 | 4 | 2 | 1 |
| Fred | 7 | 2 | 6 | 3 | 8 | 4 | 6 |

### GMM

GMM has been developed by Muthén and colleagues (Muthén & Shedden, 1999). This approach allows both qualitatively different patterns of change and quantitative differences within each pattern (Bauer & Reyes, 2010). Similarly to GBTM, the population under study is assumed to be composed of qualitatively distinct subgroups. However, heterogeneity within each subgroup is also considered—that is, variations that are specific to each individual (random effects) as in GCM can also be modeled within each subgroup. In GMM, the subgroups could not be explained by the between-individual variability accounted for by individual-specific effects in a single GCM (random effects). Instead, different single GCMs capture the population variability across time. In GMM, two or more GCMs are used to estimate the population variability in developmental trajectories. Key outputs of such an approach are two or more GCMs and estimates of the proportion of the population following each GCM.

Both GBTM and GMM provide helpful information about the shape and levels of the trajectories. The main difference between the two approaches is that GMM includes random effects (i.e., individual-specific effects) in each trajectory, whereas GBTM does not. Adding random effects can lead to a fewer number of trajectories because it allows for more within-group variability in individual-level trajectory (Nagin & Odgers, 2010).

## Examples of Applications

### Studying Externalizing and Internalizing Problems Using GCM

In the following section, we present examples of how GCM can be used to study externalizing and internalizing problems across ages. We discuss linear (i.e., linear trend over time) and nonlinear (e.g., quadratic trend over time) models.

*Linear Growth Curves* The most common GCMs fit linear growth curves. Owens and Shaw (2003) examined linear trajectories of mother-reported externalizing problems of children ($n$ = 299) from 2 to 6 years of age from low-income families. On average, children showed decreases in externalizing problems over time. Children with more externalizing problems at age 6 were characterized by more negative emotionality as infants and having depressed mothers, mothers who were less accepting of the child's behavior, and parents with more inter-parental conflict. Keiley, Bates, Dodge, and Pettit (2000) used SEM to simultaneously examine linear growth curves of mothers' and teachers' reports of children's ($n$ = 405) internalizing and externalizing problems from 5 to 12 years of age. Demonstrating the developmental comorbidity between internalizing and externalizing problems, intercepts and slopes of internalizing problems were positively correlated with the intercepts and slopes, respectively, of externalizing problems. In other words, the higher one's initial level of internalizing problems, the higher one's initial level of externalizing problems (and the greater one's increases in internalizing problems, the greater one's increases in externalizing problems). Children with higher intercepts of externalizing problems included children rejected by peers, children from lower socioeconomic status (SES) families, and European American (compared to African American) children. Children with greater increases of externalizing problems included boys, rejected children, and African American (compared to European American) children. In summary, GCMs can test the effect of risk and protective factors on intercepts (initial level) and slopes (growth/change) of developmental trajectories, and can fit multiple behaviors simultaneously to understand their codevelopment.

*Nonlinear Growth Curves* In addition to linear growth curves, previous studies using GCMs have examined nonlinear growth curves. Studies have examined polynomial trajectories of externalizing problems, including quadratic (e.g., Bongers, Koot, van der Ende, & Verhulst, 2003), cubic (e.g., Nærde, Ogden, Janson, & Zachrisson, 2014), and quartic (e.g., Petersen, Bates, Dodge, Lansford, & Pettit, 2014) trajectories. Bongers and colleagues (2003) examined quadratic trajectories of parent-reported externalizing problems (in addition to other behavior problems) in 2,076 Dutch children from ages 4 to 18 years. The sample showed curvilinear decreases in externalizing problems over time, on average. Boys had higher intercepts and steeper slopes (greater decreases) than girls, yet were reported to show more externalizing problems than girls across time. Nærde and colleagues (2014) examined cubic trajectories of parent-reported physical aggression in 1,159 Norwegian children from 8 to 26 months of age. Aggression increased from 8 months, with a peak around 20 to 22 months, followed by a decrease to 26 months. Higher intercepts were found among boys (compared to girls), those having a same-age sibling, higher levels of parental distress, lower parental education, more difficult child temperament, and higher levels of child activity. Slopes of aggression were predicted by the presence of a same-age sibling and high child-activity level. It is worth noting that it can be quite difficult to interpret the predictors of polynomial terms (Grimm, Ram, & Hamagami, 2011). In any case, GCMs can fit nonlinear trajectories and estimate the effects of risk and protective factors on the level and growth of these trajectories.

## Joint Development of Related yet Different Behaviors Using GBTM

In this section, we present an example of trajectory modeling of two related yet different behaviors. This type of model (referred to as a dual or joint model) allows examining the developmental relations between two behaviors of interest (Nagin, 2005; Nagin & Tremblay, 2001). The joint model has three key outputs: (1) the developmental trajectories for each type of behavior; (2) the probability of membership in each joint trajectory (which reflects the proportion of individuals belonging simultaneously to trajectories of both types of behaviors (e.g., being classified in the high trajectory of one type of behavior and in the low trajectory of the second type of behavior); and (3) the probabilities linking membership in trajectories across behaviors (e.g., the probability of following a high trajectory of one type of behavior given the trajectory membership of the other behavior).

In a study of girls from a population-based sample ($n$ = 881), Fontaine and colleagues (2008) examined the joint developmental trajectories of physical aggression and hyperactivity between 6 to 12 years old (teachers assessed the behaviors yearly) using GBTM. They identified four trajectories of hyperactivity (None/Low, Moderate declining, Moderate stable and High declining) and three trajectories of physical aggression (None/Low, Moderate, and High declining) (first key output). They also found that about 10% of the girls belonged to the high trajectory of hyperactivity without high levels of physical aggression, that a small proportion of the girls (less than 1% of the sample) belonged to the high trajectory of physical aggression without high levels of hyperactivity, that about 9% of the girls belonged to the high trajectory of hyperactivity *and* the high trajectory of physical aggression, and that the remainder of the sample encompassed all other trajectory combinations (second key output). Finally, they found an asymmetric developmental association between hyperactivity and physical aggression; in other words, girls with high levels of physical aggression were highly likely to have high levels of hyperactivity (probability = 0.96), but girls with high levels of hyperactivity were only moderately likely to have high levels of physical aggression (probability = 0.45). In addition, girls who were not hyperactive were likely not to be physically aggressive (probability = 0.91), but girls who were not physically aggressive could show moderate levels of hyperactivity (probability = 0.28 for moderate declining levels and probability = 0.20 for moderate stable levels). Figure 1.2 illustrates

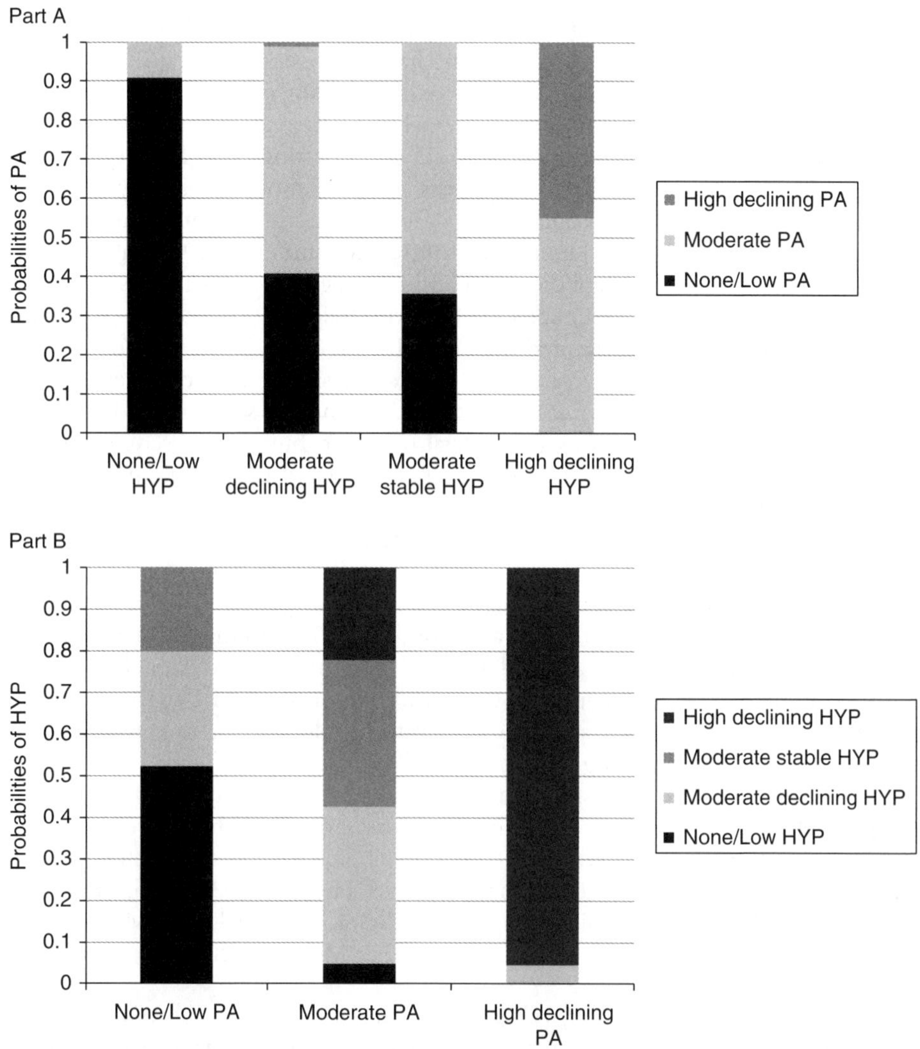


**Figure 1.2** Linking Probabilities between the Trajectories of Hyperactivity and Physical Aggression (Based on Fontaine et al., 2008). Part A: Probabilities of Physical Aggression (PA) Conditional on Hyperactivity (HYP); Part B: Probabilities of Hyperactivity (HYP) Conditional on Physical Aggression (PA).

these linking probabilities (third key output). In sum, GBTM allows for the study of the joint development of related yet different behaviors, including the probabilities linking membership in trajectories across behaviors.

## Testing Developmental Taxonomical Theories or Theoretical Models

Trajectory modeling can be useful to test taxonomical theories or theoretical models. In this section, we present studies that focused on testing theoretical models, such as Moffitt's taxonomical theory of antisocial behavior.

*The Example of Moffitt's Developmental Taxonomy* Moffitt (1993) postulated that antisocial behavior can follow two distinct trajectories, each with a unique etiology and prognostic: a small group of individuals engaging in antisocial behavior at an early age and persistent throughout their lifespan (lifecourse-persistent trajectory) and a larger group of individuals engaging in antisocial behavior only during adolescence (adolescence-limited trajectory). According to her theory, the interaction between childhood neuropsychological problems and adverse environments could lead to life-course-persistent antisocial behavior, whereas a contemporary maturity gap and involvement with deviant peers could lead to adolescence-limited antisocial behavior.

Odgers and colleagues (2008) used GMM to test Moffitt's (1993) taxonomic predictions regarding developmental course of antisocial behavior, risk factors and adult consequences. They identified four antisocial behavior trajectories: lifecourse-persistent, adolescence-onset, childhood-limited and low. In line with Moffitt's theory, their findings supported the existence of both lifecourse-persistent and adolescence-onset antisocial trajectories. However, contrary to the taxonomy, some individuals were identified with an adolescence-onset antisocial behavior, but also subsequent persistence into adulthood. Although Moffitt's theory predicted that variability in age at desistence could be explained by the cumulative number and type of ensnaring life events that entangle individuals in an antisocial lifestyle, methodological issues could also explain the findings by Odgers and colleagues (e.g., spacing of measurement occasions during adolescence and the challenges of mapping such transient behavioral pattern using trajectory modeling). In addition, a childhood-limited trajectory, not anticipated by the taxonomy, was identified. The individuals engaging in the childhood-limited trajectory appeared to desist from antisocial behavior, however, they were likely to experience small to moderate problems that were restricted to internalizing disorders, smoking and financial difficulties.

The examples above demonstrate that trajectory modeling has implications for testing developmental theories, which could at the same time inform research and clinical practice. For instance, given the different developmental course of each trajectory, as well as their associated risk factors and outcomes, targeted interventions that best address the profiles of vulnerabilities and strengths of individuals following distinct trajectories could be developed (Viding, Fontaine, & McCrory, 2012).

*A Dimensional Alternative to Moffitt's Developmental Taxonomy* There is a growing body of research showing that externalizing problems are dimensional rather than categorical in nature (Coghill & Sonuga-Barke, 2012; Krueger, Markon, Patrick, & Iacono, 2005; Markon & Krueger, 2005; Walton, Ormel, & Krueger, 2011). Recent findings also suggest that trajectories of externalizing problems are more accurately modeled dimensionally than with Moffitt's (1993) subgroups (Walters, 2011, 2012; Walters & Ruscio, 2013; for a review, see Fairchild, van Goozen, Calder, & Goodyer, 2013). The dimensional nature of the development of externalizing problems suggests that GCM may be useful when modeling trajectories of externalizing problems because GCM seeks to capture quantitative variation in individuals' trajectories.

However, one difficulty in measuring change in externalizing problems across long developmental periods is that the meaning of externalizing behaviors changes with development. For instance, physical aggression is more common in young children than adolescents (Miller, Vaillancourt, & Boyle, 2009), so physical aggression may likely represent a more severe trait level of externalizing behaviors in adolescence than it does in early childhood. Because the meaning of externalizing behaviors changes with development (known as heterotypic continuity), the same measure may have a different meaning at different ages. Thus, developmental changes in the construct of externalizing behavior may necessitate changes in measurement. A widely used measurement system for externalizing behavior, the Achenbach System of Empirically Based Assessment (ASEBA; Achenbach, 2009) accommodates changes in the construct of externalizing behaviors by including different items at different ages in development. A key challenge is ensuring that differences across time reflect actual change rather than differences in the meaning of the measure. One approach to make scores on different measures statistically comparable is to use a proportion score (Little, 2013), where the child's problem sum is divided by the total possible score on the measure.

Petersen and colleagues (2015) examined GCMs of externalizing problems from 5 to 27 years of age ($n = 585$) using proportion scores of ratings by mothers, fathers, teachers, peers and self-report on the ASEBA. Quartic (fourth-degree polynomial) trajectories were the best-fitting form of change. On average, externalizing problems decreased from early childhood to preadolescence (ages 5–11), increased during adolescence (11–16), and decreased from late adolescence to adulthood (16–27). Yet there were great individual differences in intercepts and slopes that were predicted by risk factors reflecting family process, peer process, stress, and individual characteristics. The quartic model with these risk factors as predictors was fairly accurate, and accounted for 70% of the variability in the development of externalizing problems. In sum, GCMs can accurately capture dimensional individual differences in the development of externalizing problems over long developmental spans with changing measures.

## Testing the Effectiveness of Interventions Using Trajectory Modeling

Trajectory modeling can be applied to assess the effects of intervention strategies nested in longitudinal studies, such as longitudinal randomized trials. In the following section, we present studies in which GBTM, GMM and GCM were applied to examine interventions' effects in longitudinal randomized trials.

*GBTM and GMM to Test the Effectiveness of Randomized Preventive Interventions* GBTM and GMM can be used to examine the impact of interventions on subgroups characterized by different growth trajectories, that is the effects on populations that include individuals who have normative and non-normative patterns. The strength of such analysis is that it allows the assessment of intervention effects on the different trajectories rather than focusing on overall intervention effects at a specific time point.

Lacourse and colleagues (2002) used GBTM to assess the effects of a randomized multimodal preventive intervention in boys ($n = 909$). Boys with high levels of disruptive behavior (based on the teachers' assessment in kindergarten) were randomly assigned to the intervention group ($n = 42$) or the control group ($n = 115$). The rest of the sample was considered to be at low risk (based on the teacher's assessment of disruptiveness in kindergarten). The intervention took place when the boys were aged between 7 and 9 years old. GBTM was used to identify the trajectories for three different outcomes between 11 and 17 years old, that is physical aggression, vandalism and theft (based on self-reports). For each outcome, six trajectories were identified (i.e., Low 1, Low 2, Low rising, Low decline, Medium decline, and High rising). The authors examined the probabilities of following the trajectories of physical aggression, vandalism, and theft depending on whether the participants were in the intervention group, the control group or the low-risk group. Results suggested that the intervention changed the course of antisocial behavior throughout adolescence, especially physical aggression. Boys in the intervention group compared to those in the control group were more likely to follow the lowest-level trajectory of physical aggression and were less likely to follow high-level trajectories of physical aggression.

Using GMM, Muthén and colleagues (2002) examined the effects of a randomized intervention aimed at reducing aggressive behavior in children (119 boys were in the intervention group and 80 boys were in the control group). The intervention was applied during the first and second grade, and the children were followed from the first to seventh grade with respect to the course of aggressive behavior. The authors notably tested whether or not intervention effects differed across trajectories. They found that the estimated four-trajectory model fitted the data well (e.g., High, Medium, Low and Late-starters), and that the benefits from the intervention were more evident for boys who were initially more aggressive (i.e., the rate of change over time for the boys in the High trajectory was greater for the ones in the intervention group compared to their counterparts in the control group).

According to Muthén and colleagues (2002), trajectory-modeling techniques should not be used as a substitute for examining significant overall effects of an intervention (e.g., when the group that received the experimental treatment is compared with the control group on the outcomes of interest regardless of the trajectory membership). Reliance on trajectory modeling in the absence of overall effects of an intervention could result in spurious findings given the multiple comparisons issue (as more comparisons are performed, it becomes more likely that the treatment and control groups will appear to differ on at least one aspect by random chance alone). They recommended that trajectory modeling should be carried out by comparing the estimated trajectories with those from existing empirical data or theory. Still, the identification of different intervention effects for individuals following distinct trajectories can be clinically useful. For instance, this information could be used for designing intervention studies where specific interventions could be implemented to address the strengths and vulnerabilities of individuals following different trajectories based on longitudinal screening procedures (Muthén et al., 2002).

*GCM to Test Predictors, Moderators and Mediators of Treatment Response* Beauchaine and colleagues (2005) examined predictors, moderators, and mediators of treatment response among 514 3–8-year-old children treated for conduct problems. Children were randomly assigned to a waitlist condition or to one or more combinations of parent, child, or teacher training. The study examined children's response to treatment using a latent GCM fit to three time points: (1) pre-treatment, (2) post-treatment, and (3) 1-year follow-up, where steeper negative slopes reflected greater improvement over time. The authors tested three questions: (1) For whom (or under what conditions) was treatment *in general* most effective (i.e., predictors of treatment response)? (2) For whom was a *particular* treatment most effective (i.e., moderators of treatment response)? (3) Why (by what mechanisms) did treatment work (i.e., mediators of treatment response)?

Regarding question 1 (predictors that described for whom treatment in general was most effective), the authors identified the following cases that were associated with better treatment response: older mother, father or mother with history of substance use, child with higher levels of anxiety/depression, and more treatment components. Regarding question 2 (moderators indicating for whom particular treatments were most effective), the authors identified the following cases for whom parent training was particularly effective: parents with lower marital satisfaction, depressed or single mother, father with history of substance use, and child with lower levels of anxiety/depression or from a lower SES family. The following cases for whom child training was particularly effective were: depressed mother, father with history of substance use, and a lower-SES family. Teacher training was particularly effective when the child was higher in attention problems. Regarding question 3 (mediators explaining treatment response), the authors identified reductions in the following parenting factors that explained why treatment worked: verbal criticism, harsh parenting, and ineffective parenting. In sum, GCMs can identify predictors, moderators, and mediators of treatment response.

## Methodological Considerations

The next section provides an overview of relevant methodological considerations to take into account when applying trajectory modeling.

### Measures of Behavior

Psychopathological disorders are often composed of different measured components. For instance, Conduct Disorder (American Psychiatric Association, 2013) is composed of criteria assessing aggression, destruction of property, deceitfulness or theft, and serious violations of rules. Aggregating these different types of behavior while modeling developmental trajectories may blur the analysis and mask etiological differences associated with the development of distinct types of behaviors. For instance, the emergence of physically aggressive behavior may be observed before theft and vandalism, which may emerge and show important growth during adolescence (Séguin, Sylvers, & Lilienfeld, 2007). Data suggest that physical aggression peaks during the second year of birth and then decreases (Tremblay, 2000). Let us consider Moffitt's taxonomy (Moffitt, 1993), which includes a lifecourse-persistent trajectory and an adolescence-limited trajectory. The identification of an adolescence-limited trajectory may depend on the items under investigation. For instance, if a scale of physically aggressive behavior is used, the likelihood of finding an adolescence-limited trajectory may be low, whereas if a global measure of antisocial behavior (including physical aggression, but also other behaviors that may emerge later in development such as theft, vandalism, and drug use), the likelihood of finding an adolescence-limited trajectory may be high (Vitaro, Brendgen, & Barker, 2006). Developmental trajectories can vary across different types of behaviors (e.g., physical aggression, opposition, property violations and status violations; Bongers, Koot, van der Ende & Verhulst, 2004). This should be considered when modeling developmental trajectories of psychopathology.

Still, the best level of analysis is the most useful one for the researcher's goal. There are many ways to parse out behavior, which is heterogeneous by nature. For instance, externalizing problems can be split into aggression and non-aggression phenotypes. Aggression can further be reduced into physical, verbal, and relational. Physical aggression can be further reduced into proactive and reactive. Proactive physical aggression can be further reduced into targeting peers versus siblings. One could further reduce to the different brain mechanisms involved. At each level, the behaviors likely consist of heterogeneous mechanisms (and therefore combine behaviors with different developmental trajectories). One can always reduce to a lower level (more basic) unit, but the question is: what is the most useful level of analysis for the goal? This reflects the classic tension between lumpers and splitters. There are advantages of focusing on more specific behaviors, but there can also be benefits of accounting for the co-occurrence of different behaviors. For instance, there may be usefulness in examining the construct of general externalizing behavior because it is an efficient summary of many cases of psychopathology, the subdimensions tend to co-occur, and similar developmental processes appear to be involved with the different subdimensions (Olson, Bates, Sandy, & Lanthier, 2000). Alternatively, Insel (2014) has argued that instead of focusing on behavior to define syndromes (because behavior is imprecise and provides little information about the underlying mechanisms), we should focus on the developmental trajectories of underlying brain mechanisms. In sum, the researcher should consider his or her goal when choosing which levels of analysis to examine.

## Number of Trajectories and Model Fit

An important aspect with regard to using GBTM or GMM concerns the determination of the number of trajectories that best represents or fits the data. As we previously mentioned, the use of GMM, compared to GBTM, could lead to a fewer number of trajectories, because adding random effects allows for more within-group variability in individual-level trajectory (Nagin & Odgers, 2010). Still, for both types of models, researchers should rely on criteria and theory to make their decision about the optimal number of groups.

Common criteria to assess the model fit include the Bayesian information criterion (BIC; Raftery, 1995), the Akaike information criterion (AIC; Akaike, 1974), the Lo–Mendell–Rubin likelihood ratio test (LMR-LRT; Lo, Mendell, & Rubin, 2001), and entropy (Muthén, 2004). The BIC and the AIC are indices that assess the model fit by balancing the goodness of fit to the sample data and the complexity of the model. They can be used to identify the best model from all the models considered (e.g., from a two-trajectory model to a six-trajectory model). That is, from the estimated models, the one with the lowest AIC (or the lowest BIC) would be selected as best fitting the data. The LMR-LRT is an indicator to determine the ideal number of trajectories; a low *p*-value ($p < .05$) indicates that the k trajectory model is a better fit to the data compared to the k-1 trajectory model). Entropy is a measurement of classification accuracy, with values closer to 1 suggesting that the classes are well separated (range 0 to 1). Other tests of adequacy have been proposed such as verifying that the average of the posterior probabilities of trajectory membership for individuals assigned to each trajectory surpasses a minimum threshold (i.e., at least 0.70) (Nagin, 2005). Further information about the fit indices can be found in prior work (e.g., Nagin, 2005; Nylund, Asparouhov, & Muthén, 2007).

Model selection should also be based on the research questions/hypotheses under investigation, as well as extant relevant theories and prior empirical research. Although the identification of trajectories through GBTM or GMM can be clinically relevant, it is important to note that the identified trajectories only approximate the developmental course of subgroups in the population (Nagin & Odgers, 2010). Extant theories about the number and the shapes of trajectories for a given research question may not be available. In this case of a more exploratory framework, it becomes especially important to communicate and justify the decisions associated with the model selection. In addition, one strategy to verify if the identified trajectories appear meaningful is to test whether or not the trajectories can be differentiated from each other in terms of risk factors, response to treatment or outcomes. Replications of the findings using different datasets could also help to ascertain whether or not the trajectories identified represent meaningful subgroups of individuals in the population.

Although GCM does not involve the identification of distinct trajectory groups, it is still essential to establish the adequacy of fit for the growth models assessed (see Curran et al., 2010). The appropriate fit indices to be considered depend on the specific analytic strategy used to estimate the models (e.g., SEM or multilevel modeling). Examples include the RMSEA (root mean squared error of approximation) and the CFI (comparative fit index). Further information can be found in more technical references (e.g., Raudenbush & Bryk, 2002; Schreiber, Nora, Stage, Barlow, & King, 2006).

## Data Sources

The types of data sources may impact the identification of the trajectories because of differences in the raters' assessments. For instance, teachers' ratings may be associated with higher independence in assessments (e.g., if there is a different teacher at each assessment) and are less likely to be influenced by the characteristics of any one rater (e.g., a parent's mental health problems; Côté, Zoccolillo, Tremblay, Nagin, & Vitaro, 2001). In addition, teachers and parents may underestimate certain behaviors, such as youth antisocial conduct (especially for teenagers), but self-reports can be affected by biases including problems recalling relevant information and social desirability. Self-reports may have the advantage of providing information that is unknown to adults or official services (e.g., police). For example, in a study on the links between self-reported and official offending behavior, GBTM was used to estimate trajectories of violent and nonviolent offending from self-reports collected between 11 and 17 years from a sample of 969 boys (Fontaine, Lacourse, Vitaro, & Tremblay, 2014). The researchers selected a five-trajectory model for violent offending (i.e., Chronic, 3%; Desisting, 12%; Delayed, 6%; Moderate, 47%; and Low, 32%) and a three-trajectory model for nonviolent offending (Chronic, 8%; Moderate, 45%; and Low, 47%). Although they found that self-reports were associated with official records, especially for violent offending behavior, they could not perform meaningful trajectory analyses using the official offending data due to a low prevalence and frequencies of these behaviors, despite the use of an at-risk sample (i.e., boys from disadvantaged environments).

Indeed, the types of samples (e.g., population-based, at-risk, or clinical) should also be taken into account when performing the analyses and interpreting the findings, as it could influence the trajectories identified and the proportion of individuals assigned to each trajectory. For instance, the percentage of individuals following an early-onset/persistent trajectory of antisocial behavior has been found to be higher in at-risk or clinical samples compared to population-based samples (Fontaine, Carbonneau, Vitaro, Barker, & Tremblay, 2009).

## Developmental Periods

To model trajectories (GCM, GBTM, and GMM), a minimum of three time points (usually as a function of age) is needed for proper estimation, but four or more time points are preferable to estimate more complex models, such as trajectories following quadratic or cubic trends (Curran & Muthén, 1999). This does not imply that all individuals need to have data on all time points (see the section on missing data management, p. 22). However, several time points across different developmental periods may be necessary to address certain research questions. For instance, if a researcher aims to test a developmental theoretical model, such as Moffitt's taxonomy (i.e., to test whether or not lifecourse-persistent and adolescence-limited trajectories can be identified; Moffitt, 1993), data collected at different time points from childhood to adulthood would be necessary. A number of published studies on the developmental trajectories of antisocial behavior were based on data collected at the end of childhood or during adolescence (i.e., where a proportion of individuals already manifested behavioral problems) and did not include data in adulthood (e.g., Broidy et al., 2003; Fontaine et al., 2014). Thus, the empirical validation of such a model on the development of individuals' antisocial behavior may be limited due to restrictive ranges of the ages considered.

The number and the shape of each trajectory are not fixed certainties. The number of time points or periods for which the individuals are monitored can have an impact on the number and shapes of the trajectories, although this remains an understudied topic (Nagin, 2005). For instance, Eggleston, Laub, and Sampson (2004) tested whether or not length of follow-up affected trajectory number, shape and group membership. Using a sample of 500 delinquent boys and their official crime counts from ages 7 to 70, their findings suggested that the length of follow-up (7 to 25 vs. 7 to 32 vs. 7 to 45 vs. 7 to 70) influenced trajectory number, shapes, and group membership, but that groups were differentially affected. The high rate-chronic group, for example, was not identified when the analysis was restricted to the shortest age range (i.e., 7 to 25). Eggleston and colleagues (2004) also reported that variables such as incarceration and mortality could affect the estimation of offending patterns over time. For instance, individuals who are incarcerated may be classified in a desisting offending trajectory because they would not show up in official records. Similarly, trajectory analyses on depressive symptoms may classify participants who passed away as desisters.

Therefore, it appears important to take into account the length of follow-up, the type of variables under investigation (e.g., offending behavior) and to consider that the trajectories are not immutable. In addition, it appears that more data allow for more refined statistical inferences (Nagin, 2005). For instance, in clinical research, failing to identify trajectories because of too few time points could lead to errors in intervention effectiveness given that heterogeneity may wash out effects for some or identify positive effects for others. Further research is needed to test further the influence of temporal length of studies on the trajectory estimation, as well as other design features such as spacing of temporal retest intervals and sample size.

## Sample Size

The sample size, that is the number of individuals included in the analysis, can also have an impact on the estimation of the trajectories. It seems that a clear consensus has not been established about the minimum number of individuals needed to perform trajectory analysis. In GCM, sample sizes approaching at least 100 are often preferred (Curran et al., 2010). However, we should expect that large samples of individuals followed throughout several years (and developmental periods), allow for greater capacity to identify meaningful trajectories (Hertzog, Lindenberger, Ghisletta, & von Oertzen, 2006; Nylund et al., 2007). Indeed, one may question the meaningfulness of having one or two trajectories with a very small number of participants (e.g., a high chronic trajectory including five participants when using GBTM or GMM). Using GBTM, D'Unger, Land, McCall, and Nagin (1998) tested whether or not the number of trajectories in the selected model was influenced by the number of individuals included in the analysis (i.e., samples of 500, 1,000 and 2,000 individuals). They found that their selected model (i.e., the model with five trajectories of offenders) was robust to sample size. Sampson, Laub, and Eggleston (2004) varied their sample size from 25 men to almost 500 to model trajectories of offending behavior. They reported that the number of trajectories varied from five to eight, with the eight-trajectory model derived only for sample sizes of 200 and higher. Sampson and colleagues (2004) suggested that the sample size problem is relatively modest. Theories and previous empirical research could be used to inform design decisions when planning a longitudinal study, including the required sample size that may best allowed to test the hypotheses under investigation, such as the number and shapes of trajectories.

## Missing Data

When using longitudinal data, researchers and clinicians are often confronted with missing information and attrition. Several reasons can lead to missing data across assessments, including participants' refusal to respond to specific questions of the assessment and participants dropping out of clinical experimentations and being lost within longitudinal studies (because of refusal to continue to participate, disappearance, or death). The impact of missing data when performing trajectory analysis can be particularly problematic if missingness is related to the variables of interest. For instance, in research on antisocial behavior, individuals with the highest levels of adjustment problems may also tend to have the highest levels of missing data (e.g., adolescents with antisocial behavior may be unwilling to continue participation in a study into which their parents initially enrolled them, and initially cooperative parents may drop out at later ages of their children even if their children remain in the study; Asendorpf, van de Schoot, Denissen, & Hutteman, 2014). Biases can be introduced if individuals with incomplete data are excluded from the analyses, especially if they differ on key characteristics from those who are included.

One important step when applying trajectory modeling is to document and understand both the type and the quantity of missing data across assessments (Nagin & Odgers, 2010). Missing data can be classified into different categories. They can be characterized as missing completely at random (data are truly missing at random), as missing at random (data are missing as a function of measured characteristics, such as sex) or as missing not at random (data are missing as a function of unmeasured characteristics such as the very value that is missing) (Curran et al., 2010). The statistical importance and complexity of the missing data management will depend on the type of missing data (Little & Rubins, 1987; Schafer & Graham, 2002). A detailed discussion of the different methods of missing data management would go beyond the scope of the present chapter. However, it should be noted that missing data issues can be addressed using statistical techniques either outside of the trajectory modeling framework (e.g., multiple imputation) or when performing the trajectory analysis (e.g., when using the full-information maximum likelihood estimation) (for more information, see Enders, 2001; Nagin & Odgers, 2010).

## Conclusions

In this chapter, we presented an overview of three trajectory modeling approaches, namely GCM, GBTM, and GMM. These approaches share a common analytical goal: they allow the modeling of differences or variability across members of a population in their developmental trajectories (Nagin & Odgers, 2010). We also presented examples of applications of these trajectory modeling approaches in the field of developmental psychopathology and clinical psychology, such as studies that focused on the development of externalizing and internalizing problems, on the validation of theoretical models and on the examination of intervention effects. Finally, we discussed methodological considerations when applying these models and interpreting the findings, such as issues related to the measurement of behavior, the determination of the number of trajectories that best represents or fits the data, the potential impact of data sources, the influence of the developmental periods considered, the requirement in terms of sample size and the management of missing data.

Numerous research questions about the developmental trajectories of psychopathology can be addressed using these approaches. Researchers need to select the approach that will allow them to address appropriately their hypotheses given the data to be analyzed. For instance, if they expect that all individuals in their sample come from the same population and can be described by the same parameters of change, then GCM could be appropriate. Alternatively, if they expect that some individuals come from distinct subpopulations, which can be captured by different subgroups, GBTM (with the assumption that the subgroups are homogeneous regarding change) and GMM (if heterogeneity within each subgroup is considered) could be more appropriate. Researchers should clearly articulate their rationale for using the approach they have selected and they should also justify their final model (e.g., choice of the number of trajectories) based on a combination of formal statistical criteria as well as extant empirical data and theory.

Several software packages for fitting these models are available, including SAS (PROC TRAJ, for GBTM; Nagin, 2005), Mplus (e.g., GMM and GCM; Muthén & Muthén, 2012), and R (SEM, Boker et al., 2011; HLM, Pinheiro, Bates, DebRoy, Sarkar, & the R Core team, 2009). Tutorials and workshops that focus on the theory and technical applications of these models are also available and could be useful to get started or to acquire more advanced knowledge. We presented an overview of these approaches and applications. Several recent published articles, chapters, and textbooks cover more comprehensive and technical aspects of these approaches and their applications (e.g., Hox, 2010; Little, 2013; McArdle & Nesselroade, 2014; Muthén, 2004; Nagin, 2005; Nylund et al., 2007; Raudenbush & Bryk, 2002; Shiyko, Ram, & Grimm, 2012; Singer & Willett, 2003). Statistical models are constantly evolving; collaborations between researchers, clinicians and developers of these models should lead to enhanced tools for testing hypotheses in the domains of developmental psychopathology and clinical psychology.

## Acknowledgments

We thank Mr. Alain Girard, statistician, for the helpful comments on this chapter. Dr. Nathalie Fontaine is a Research Scholar, Junior 1, Fonds de recherche du Québec–Santé.

## References

Achenbach, T. M. (2009). *Achenbach System of Empirically Based Assessment (ASEBA): Development, findings, theory, and applications.* University of Vermont, Research Center of Children, Youth & Families.

Akaike, H. (1974). New look at statistical-model identification. *IEEE Transactions on Automatic Control, 19*, 716–723.

American Psychiatric Association. (2013). *Diagnostic and statistical manual of mental disorders* (5th Ed.). Washington, DC: Author.

Asendorpf, J. B., van de Schoot, R., Denissen, J. J. A., & Hutteman, R. (2014). Reducing bias due to systematic attrition in longitudinal studies: The benefits of multiple imputation. *International Journal of Behavioral Development, 38*, 453–460. doi:10.1177/0165025414542713

Bauer, D. J. (2003). Estimating multilevel linear models as structural equation models. *Journal of Educational and Behavioral Statistics, 28*, 135–167. doi:10.3102/10769986028002135

Bauer, D. J., & Reyes, H. L. M. (2010). Modeling variability in individual development: Differences of degree of kind? *Child Development Perspectives, 4*, 114–122. doi:10.1111/j.1750-8606.2010.00129.x

Beauchaine, T. P., Webster-Stratton, C., & Reid, M. J. (2005). Mediators, moderators, and predictors of 1-year outcomes among children treated for early-onset conduct problems: A latent growth curve analysis. *Journal of Consulting and Clinical Psychology, 73*, 371–388. doi:10.1037/0022-006X.73.3.371

Boker, S., Neale, M., Maes, H., Wilde, M., Spiegel, M., Brick, T., Spies, J., Estabrook, R., Kenny, S., Bates, T., Mehta, P., & Fox, J. (2011). OpenMx: An open source extended structural equation modeling framework. *Psychometrika*, *76*, 306–317. doi:10.1007/s11336-010-9200-6

Bongers, I. L., Koot, H. M., van der Ende, J., & Verhulst, F. C. (2003). The normative development of child and adolescent problem behavior. *Journal of Abnormal Psychology*, *112*, 179–192. doi:10.1037/0021-843x.112.2.179

Bongers, I. L., Koot, H. M., van der Ende, J., & Verhulst, F. C. (2004). Developmental trajectories of externalizing behaviors in childhood and adolescence. *Child Development*, *75*, 1523–1537. doi:10.1111/j.1467-8624.2004.00755.x

Broidy, L. M., Nagin, D. S., Tremblay, R.E., Bates, J. E., Brame, B., Dodge, K. A., Fergusson, D., Horwood, J. L., Loeber, R., Laird, R., Lynam, D. R., Moffitt, T. E., Pettit, G. S., & Vitaro, F. (2003). Developmental trajectories of childhood disruptive behaviors and adolescent delinquency: A six-site, cross-national study. *Developmental Psychology*, *39*, 222–245. doi:10.1037/0012-1649.39.2.222

Cicchetti, D. (1989). Developmental psychopathology: Some thoughts on its evolution. *Development and Psychopathology*, *1*, 1–4. doi:10.1017/S0954579400000201

Cicchetti, D., & Toth, S. L. (1992). The role of developmental theory in prevention and intervention. *Development and Psychopathology*, *4*, 489–493. doi:10.1017/S0954579400004831

Coghill, D., & Sonuga-Barke, E. J. S. (2012). Annual research review: Categories versus dimensions in the classification and conceptualisation of child and adolescent mental disorders: implications of recent empirical study. *Journal of Child Psychology and Psychiatry*, *53*, 469–489. doi:10.1111/j.1469-7610.2011.02511.x

Côté, S. M., Boivin, M., Liu, X., Nagin, D. S., Zoccolillo, M., & Tremblay, R. E. (2009). Depression and anxiety symptoms: Onset, develomental course and risk factors during early childhood. *Journal of Child Psychology and Psychiatry*, *50*, 1201–1208. doi:10.1111/j.1469-7610.2009.02099.x

Côté, S., Zoccolillo, M., Tremblay, R. E., Nagin, D., & Vitaro, F. (2001). Predicting girls' conduct disorder in adolescence from childhood trajectories of disruptive behaviors. *Journal of the American Academy of Child and Adolescent Psychiatry*, *40*, 678–684. doi: 10.1097/00004583-200106000-00013

Curran, P. J. (2003). Have multilevel models been structural equation models all along? *Multivariate Behavioral Research*, *38*, 529–569. doi:10.1207/s15327906mbr3804_5

Curran, P. J., & Muthén, B. O. (1999). The application of latent curve analysis to testing developmental theories in intervention research. *American Journal of Community Psychology*, *27*, 567–595. doi:10.1023/A:1022137429115

Curran, P. J., Obeidat, K., & Losardo, D. (2010). Twelve frequently asked questions about growth curve modeling. *Journal of Cognition and Development*, *11*, 121–136. doi:10.1080/15248371003699969

D'Unger, A. V., Land, K. C., McCall, P. L., & Nagin, D. S. (1998). How many latent classes of delinquent/criminal careers? Results from mixed Poisson regression analyses. *American Journal of Sociology*, *103*, 1593–1630.

Eggleston, E. P., Laub, J. H., & Sampson, R. J. (2004). Methodological sensitivities to latent class analysis of long-term criminal trajectories. *Journal of Quantitative Criminology*, *20*, 1–26. doi:10.1023/B:JOQC.0000016696.02763.ce

Enders, C. K. (2001). A primer on maximum likelihood algorithms available for use with missing data. *Structural Equation Modeling*, *8*, 128–141. doi:10.1207/S15328007SEM0801_7

Fairchild, G., van Goozen, S. H. M., Calder, A. J., & Goodyer, I. M. (2013). Research review: Evaluating and reformulating the developmental taxonomic theory of antisocial behaviour. *Journal of Child Psychology and Psychiatry*, *54*, 924–940. doi:10.1111/jcpp.12102

Fontaine, N., Carbonneau, R., Barker, E. D., Vitaro, F., Hébert, M., Côté, S. M., Nagin, D. S., Zoccolillo, M., & Tremblay, R. E. (2008). Girls' hyperactivity and physical aggression during childhood and adjustment problems in early adulthood: A 15-year longitudinal study. *Archives of General Psychiatry, 65*, 320–328. doi:10.1001/archgenpsychiatry.2007.41

Fontaine, N., Carbonneau, R., Vitaro, F., Barker, E. D., & Tremblay, R. E. (2009). Research review: A critical review of studies on the developmental trajectories of antisocial behavior in females. *Journal of Child Psychology and Psychiatry, 50*, 363–385. doi:10.1111/j.1469-7610.2008.01949.x

Fontaine, N. M. G., Lacourse, E., Vitaro, F., & Tremblay, R. E. (2014). Links between trajectories of self-reported violent and nonviolent offending and official offending during adolescence and adulthood. *Criminal Behaviour and Mental Health, 24*, 277–290. doi:10.1002/cbm.1935

Fontaine, N. M. G., Rijsdijk, F. V., McCrory, E. J. P., & Viding, E. (2010). Etiology of different developmental trajectories of callous–unemotional traits. *Journal of the American Academy of Child and Adolescent Psychiatry, 49*, 656–664. doi:10.1016/j.jaac.2010.03.014

Grimm, K. J., Ram, N., & Hamagami, F. (2011). Nonlinear growth curves in developmental research. *Child Development, 82*, 1357–1371. doi:10.1111/j.1467-8624.2011.01630.x

Gueorguieva, R., & Krystal, J. H. (2004). Move over ANOVA: Progress in analyzing repeated-measures data and its reflection in papers published in the archives of general psychiatry. *Archives of General Psychiatry, 61*, 310–317. doi:10.1001/archpsyc.61.3.310

Hertzog, C., Lindenberger, U., Ghisletta, P., & von Oertzen, T. (2006). On the power of multivariate latent growth curve models to detect correlated change. *Psychological Methods, 11*, 244–252. doi:10.1037/1082-989X.11.3.244

Hox, J. J. (2010). *Multilevel analysis: Techniques and applications* (2nd Ed.). New York, NY: Routledge.

Hu, M.-C., Muthén, B., Schaffran, C., Griesler, P. C., & Kandel, D. B. (2008). Developmental trajectories of criteria of nicotine dependence in adolescence. *Drug and Alcohol Dependence, 98*, 94–104. doi:10.1016/j.drugalcdep.2008.04.017

Insel, T. R. (2014). Mental disorders in childhood: Shifting the focus from behavioral symptoms to neurodevelopmental trajectories. *JAMA: Journal of the American Medical Association, 311*, 1727–1728. doi:10.1001/jama.2014.1193

Keiley, M. K., Bates, J. E., Dodge, K. A., & Pettit, G. S. (2000). A cross-domain growth analysis: externalizing and internalizing behaviors during 8 years of childhood. *Journal of Abnormal Child Psychology, 28*, 161–179. doi:10.1023/A:1005122814723

Krueger, R. F., Markon, K. E., Patrick, C. J., & Iacono, W. G. (2005). Externalizing psychopathology in adulthood: A dimensional-spectrum conceptualization and its implications for DSM-V. *Journal of Abnormal Psychology, 114*, 537–550.

Lacourse, E., Côté, S., Nagin, D. S., Vitaro, F., Brendgen, M., & Tremblay, R. E. (2002). A longitudinal-experimental approach to testing theories of antisocial behavior development. *Development and Psychopathology, 14*, 909–924. doi:10.1017/S0954579402004121

Little, R. J. A., & Rubin, D. B. (1987). *Statistical analysis with missing data.* New York: Wiley.

Little, T. D. (2013). *Longitudinal structural equation modeling.* New York, NY: The Guilford Press.

Lo, Y., Mendell, N. R., & Rubin, D. B. (2001). Testing the number of components in a normal mixture. *Biometrika, 88*, 767–778. doi:10.1093/biomet/88.3.767

Markon, K. E., & Krueger, R. F. (2005). Categorical and continuous models of liability to externalizing disorders: A direct comparison in NESARC. *Archives of General Psychiatry, 62*, 1352–1359. doi:10.1001/archpsyc.62.12.1352

McArdle, J. J., & Nesselroade, J. R. (2014). *Longitudinal data analysis using structural equation models.* Washington, DC: American Psychological Association.

Miller, J., Vaillancourt, T. & Boyle, M. (2009). Examining the heterotypic continuity of aggression using teacher reports: Results from a national Canadian study. *Social Development, 18*, 164–180. doi:10.1111/j.1467-9507.2008.00480.x

Moffitt, T. E. (1993). Adolescence-limited and life-course-persistent antisocial behavior: A developmental taxonomy. *Psychological Review*, *100*, 674–701. doi:10.1.1.314.783

Muthén, B. (2004). Latent variable analysis: Growth mixture modeling and related techniques for longitudinal data. In D. Kaplan (Ed.), *The Sage handbook of quantitative methodology for the social sciences* (pp. 345–368). Thousand Oaks, CA: Sage.

Muthén, B., Brown, C. H., Masyn, K., Jo, B., Khoo, S. T., Yang, C. C., Wang, C. P., Kellam, S. G., Carlin, J. B., & Liao, J. (2002). General growth mixture modeling for randomized preventive interventions. *Biostatistics*, *3*, 459–475. doi:10.1093/biostatistics/3.4.459

Muthén, B. & Shedden, K. (1999). Finite mixture modeling with mixture outcomes using the EM algorithm. *Biometrics*, *55*, 463–469. doi:10.1111/j.0006-341X.1999.00463.x

Muthén, L. K., & Muthén, B. O. (2012). *Mplus user's guide* (7th Ed.). Los Angeles, CA: Muthén & Muthén.

Nærde, A., Ogden, T., Janson, H., & Zachrisson, H. D. (2014). Normative development of physical aggression from 8 to 26 months. *Developmental Psychology*, *50*, 1710–1720. doi:10.1037/a0036324

Nagin, D. S. (1999). Analyzing developmental trajectories: A semiparametric, group-based approach. *Psychological Methods*, *4*, 139–157. doi:10.1037/1082-989X.4.2.139

Nagin, D. S. (2005). *Group-based modeling of development*. Cambridge, MA: Harvard University Press.

Nagin, D. S., & Odgers, C. L. (2010). Group-based trajectory modeling in clinical research. *Annual Review of Clinical Psychology*, *6*, 109–138. doi:10.1146/annurev.clinpsy.121208.131413

Nagin, D. & Tremblay, R. E. (1999). Trajectories of boys' physical aggression, opposition, and hyperactivity on the path to physically violent and nonviolent juvenile delinquency. *Child Development*, *70*, 1181–1196. doi:10.1111/1467-8624.00086

Nagin, D. S. & Tremblay, R. E. (2001). Analyzing developmental trajectories of distinct but related behaviors: A group-based method. *Psychological Methods*, *6*, 18–34. doi:10.1037/1082-989X.6.1.18

Nylund, K. L., Asparouhov, T., & Muthén, B. O. (2007). Deciding on the number of classes in latent class analysis and growth mixture modeling. A Monte Carlo simulation study. *Structural Equation Modeling*, *14*, 535–569. doi:10.1080/10705510701575396

Odgers, C. L., Moffitt, T. E., Broadbent, J. M., Dickson, N., Hancox, R. J., Harrington, H., Poulton, R., Sears, M. R., Thomson, W. M., & Caspi, A. (2008). Female and male antisocial trajectories: From childhood origins to adult outcomes. *Development and Psychopathology*, *20*, 673–716. doi:10.1017/S0954579408000333

Olson, S. L., Bates, J. E., Sandy, J. M., & Lanthier, R. (2000). Early developmental precursors of externalizing behavior in middle childhood and adolescence. *Journal of Abnormal Child Psychology*, *28*, 119–133. doi:10.1023/A:1005166629744

Owens, E. B., & Shaw, D. S. (2003). Predicting growth curves of externalizing behavior across the preschool years. *Journal of Abnormal Child Psychology*, *31*, 575–590. doi:10.1023/a:1026254005632

Petersen, I. T., Bates, J. E., Dodge, K. A., Lansford, J. E., & Pettit, G. S. (2015). Describing and predicting developmental profiles of externalizing problems from childhood to adulthood. *Development and Psychopathology*, *27*, 791–818. doi: 10.1017/S0954579414000789

Pinheiro, J., Bates, D., DebRoy, S., Sarkar, D., & the R Core team. (2009). nlme: Linear and nonlinear mixed effects models. *R package version 3*.1–93. Retrieved December 9, 2016 from http://cran.r-project.org/web/packages/nlme/index.html.

Raftery, A. E. (1995). Bayesian model selection in social research. In P. V. Marsden (Ed.), *Sociological methodology* (Vol. 25, pp. 111–163). Washington, DC: American Sociological Association.

Raudenbush, S. W., & Bryk, A. S. (2002). *Hierarchical linear models: Applications and data analysis method* (2nd Ed.). Thousand Oaks, CA: Sage Publications.

Rutter, M. (1990). Psychosocial resilience and the protective mechanisms. In J. Rolf, A. S. Masten, D. Cicchetti, K. H. Nuechterlein, & S. Weintraub (Eds.), *Risk and protective factors in the development of psychopathology* (pp. 181–214). Cambridge: Cambridge University Press.

Sampson, R. J., Laub, J. H., & Eggleston, E. P. (2004). On the robustness and validity of groups. *Journal of Quantitative Criminology*, *20*, 37–42. doi:10.1023/B:JOQC.0000016698.36239.91

Schafer, J. L., & Graham, J. W. (2002). Missing data: Our view of the state of the art. *Psychological Methods*, *7*, 147–177. doi:10.1037/1082-989x.7.2.147

Schreiber, J. B., Nora, A., Stage, F. K., Barlow, E. A., & King, J. (2006). Reporting structural equation modeling and confirmatory factor analysis results: A review. *Journal of Educational Research*, *99*, 323–337. doi:10.3200/JOER.99.6.323-338

Séguin, J. R., Sylvers, P., & Lilienfeld, S. O. (2007). The neuropsychology of violence. In D. J. Flannery, A. T. Vazsonyi, & I. D. Waldman (Eds.), *The Cambridge handbook of violent behavior and aggression* (pp. 187–214). Cambridge: Cambridge University Press.

Shiyko, M., Ram, N., & Grimm, K. J. (2012). An overview of growth mixture modelling: A sample nonlinear application in OpenMx. In R. H. Hoyle (Ed.), *Handbook of structural equation modelling* (pp. 532–546). New York: The Guilford Press.

Singer, J. D., & Willett, J. B. (2003). *Applied longitudinal data analysis: Modeling change and event occurrence.* New York: Oxford University Press.

Tremblay, R. E. (2000). The development of aggressive behaviour during childhood: What have we learned in the past century? *International Journal of Behavioral Development*, *24*, 129–141. doi:10.1080/016502500383232

Viding, E., Fontaine, N. M. G., & McCrory, E. J. (2012). Antisocial behaviour in children with and without callous–unemotional traits. *Journal of the Royal Society of Medicine*, *105*, 195–200. doi:10.1258/jrsm.2011.110223

Vitaro, F., Brendgen, M., & Barker, E. D. (2006). Subtypes of aggressive behaviors: A developmental perspective. *International Journal of Behavioral Development*, *30*, 12–19. doi:10.1177/0165025406059968

Walters, G. D. (2011). The latent structure of life-course-persistent antisocial behavior: Is Moffitt's developmental taxonomy a true taxonomy? *Journal of Consulting and Clinical Psychology*, *79*, 96–105. doi:10.1037/a0021519

Walters, G. D. (2012). Developmental trajectories of delinquent behavior: One pattern or several? *Criminal Justice and Behavior*, *39*, 1192–1203. doi:10.1177/0093854812443645

Walters, G. D., & Ruscio, J. (2013). Trajectories of youthful antisocial behavior: Categories or continua? *Journal of Abnormal Child Psychology*, *41*, 653–666. doi:10.1007/s10802-012-9700-1

Walton, K., Ormel, J., & Krueger, R. (2011). The dimensional nature of externalizing behaviors in adolescence: Evidence from a direct comparison of categorical, dimensional, and hybrid models. *Journal of Abnormal Child Psychology*, *39*, 553–561. doi:10.1007/s10802-010-9478-y

# 2

# Family-based Quasi-experimental Designs for Studying Environmental Risk Factors

Henrik Larsson and Brian M. D'Onofrio

Recent research that has found correlations between early environmental risk factors and psychopathology (Bale et al., 2010; Beydoun & Saftlas, 2008; Buss, Davis, Muftuler, Head, & Sandman, 2010; A. C. Huizink, Robles de Medina, Mulder, Visser, & Buitelaar, 2003; O'Connor, Heron, Golding, Beveridge, & Glover, 2002; O'Connor, Heron, Golding, Glover, & ALSPAC study team, 2003) has led to great excitement about the developmental origins of disease hypothesis, which emphasizes the significant role of early stressors for later functioning (Barker, 1998; Gluckman & Hanson, 2007; Gluckman, Hanson, Cooper, & Thornburg, 2008). Yet, many researchers have expressed concern of such strong causal inferences because most of the studies have not been able to rigorously test causal inferences by ruling out plausible alternative explanations for the associations between the risk factors and outcomes (Kramer, 2000; O'Connor, 2003; Thapar & Rutter, 2009).

Because we cannot randomly assign individuals to most of the early risk factors for psychopathology, researchers must rely on alternatives to randomized controlled trials for ruling out plausible competing explanations for the associations (Kraemer et al., 1997; Shadish, Cook, & Campbell, 2002). Given that it is impossible to identify and accurately measure every important confounding factor, there is a growing push in medicine (Academy of Medical Sciences Working Group, 2007; British Academy of Science Working Group, 2010), psychiatry (Kendler, 2005; Lahey, D'Onofrio, & Waldman, 2009), statistics (Shadish, 2010), sociology (Freese, 2008), psychology (Rutter, Pickles, Murray, & Eaves, 2001; Shadish et al., 2002), family studies (D'Onofrio & Lahey, 2010), epidemiology (Donovan & Susser, 2011; Gilman & Loucks, 2012), basic sciences (Smith, 2008), and economics (Duncan, 2012), to use quasi-experimental designs, approaches that rely on design features to help rule out alternative hypotheses, such as unmeasured environmental confounding factors (Rutter, 2000), unmeasured genetic confounding factors (due to gene–environment correlations) (Kendler & Baker, 2007; Plomin & Bergeman, 1991), and reciprocal influences/child effects (Bell & Harper, 1997). And, reviews have specifically called for more quasi-experimental studies of early environmental risk factors for

*The Wiley Handbook of Developmental Psychopathology*, First Edition. Edited by Luna C. Centifanti and David M. Williams.

psychopathology because of the limitations of existing studies (Duncan, 2012; O'Connor, 2003; Pluess & Belsky, 2011; Rutter, 2005; Rutter, 2007; Shonkoff, Boyce, & McEwen, 2009).

In this context, this chapter stresses the advantages of using family-based, quasi-experimental research designs when studying early environmental risk factors for psychopathology because the approaches allow strong tests of causal inferences that are critical for advancing the understanding of the etiology of psychopathology. We use recent quasi-experimental studies on the association between maternal smoking during pregnancy (SDP) and Attention Deficit Hyperactivity Disorder (ADHD) as an exemplar.

ADHD is a stable (Faraone, Biederman, & Mick, 2006) neurodevelopmental disorder with an early onset that predicts important social outcomes later in life (Biederman et al., 2010). Even though the secular trend in ADHD (Singh, 2008) has been debated, current estimates of the prevalence of ADHD during childhood (≈5%) (Polanczyk, de Lima, Horta, Biederman, & Rohde, 2007) further underscore their large societal impact. Understanding the etiology of this disorder, therefore, is of critical importance. In addition to a strong genetic component, quantitative genetic studies highlight that environmental factors are important (Faraone et al., 2005; Larsson, Anckarsater, Rastam, Chang, & Lichtenstein, 2012). The early onset of ADHD and early emerging structural and functional brain abnormalities suggest a prenatal and early postnatal origin of ADHD (Swanson et al., 2007). Recent research has indeed identified several early risk factors for ADHD (Halperin & Schulz, 2006; Thapar, Cooper, Eyre, & Langley, 2013), consistent with the developmental origins of health and disease hypothesis that emphasizes the significant role of early stressors for later functioning (Bale et al., 2010; Szatmari, 2011). Among these putative environmental risk factors maternal smoking during pregnancy (SDP) is probably the most commonly cited risk factor for ADHD (Froehlich et al., 2009; Galera et al., 2011; Mick, Biederman, Faraone, Sayer, & Kleinman, 2002; Milberger, Biederman, Faraone, & Jones, 1998; C. Obel et al., 2009; Rodriguez & Bohlin, 2005b).

SDP is associated with various offspring problems, including pregnancy-related and perinatal outcomes (Cnattingius, 2004) and later developmental outcomes, such as cognitive deficits (Lambe, Hultman, Torrang, MacCabe, & Cnattingius; Lundberg et al., 2010), obesity (Iliadou et al., 2010) and social and behavioural difficulties (Glantz & Campbell Champers, 2006; Wakschlag, Pickett, Cook, Benowitz, & Leventhal, 2002). Several reviews have concluded that fetal exposure to maternal SDP causes these problems (Cnattingius, 2004; M. Y. Glantz & Campbell Champers, 2006; Slotkin, 2013; Wakschlag et al., 2002) because the statistical associations (a) have been replicated in numerous studies, (b) are independent of the effects of measured covariates that are used to account for confounding, and (c) and consistent with basic neuroscience research on SDP in animals (Ernst, 2001; Shea & Steiner, 2008). Based in this body of literature researchers have hypothesized mediating mechanisms through which maternal SDP influences offspring psychopathology (Cornelius, Ryan, Day, Godschmidt, & Willford, 2001). For instance, researchers suggest that maternal SDP alters fetal development of brain systems related to stress reactivity (Koob, 1999), reward sensitivity (Ferriero & Dempsey, 1999; M. D. Glantz & Chambers, 2006), and decision-making (Lotfipour et al., 2009), which could subsequently influence offspring psychopathology, including ADHD. Yet, SDP is correlated with numerous risk factors, such as maternal and paternal intellectual abilities, psychopathology (including ADHD), substance use problems, and socioeconomic status that also predict offspring ADHD (Huizink & Mulder, 2006). As such, an association between SDP and offspring psychopathology could be explained by unmeasured background factors rather by casual effects of SDP. Quantitative genetic research has also found that maternal SDP is influenced by genetic factors (Agrawal et al., 2008; D'Onofrio et al., 2003; Ellingston, Rickert, Lichtenstein, Långström, & D'Onofrio, 2012). The genetic factors that influence SDP are correlated with both nicotine dependence problems (Agrawal et al., 2008) and criminality (Ellingston et al., 2012). The fact that genetic factors influence SDP, therefore, raises the possibility that genetic confounds also could account for the association between SDP and offspring psychopathology, including ADHD (Rutter et al., 2001; Scarr & McCartney, 1983). Given these alternative explanations and the fact that few human studies are able to account for all environmental and genetic confounds, several researchers have explicitly cautioned against drawing strong causal inferences related to the consequences of maternal SDP (D'Onofrio et al., 2003; Fergusson, 1999; Maughan, Taylor, Caspi, & Moffitt, 2004; Silberg et al., 2003; Wakschlag et al., 2002).

## Confounding in Observational Studies

Most observational studies use unrelated individuals (i.e., one person per family). This means that environmental risk factors can be confounded with genetic factors and environmental influences that are shared within the family. Confounds between genetic variants and environments, which are pervasive (Jaffee & Price, 2012; Kendler & Baker, 2007; Plomin & Bergeman, 1991), can arise systematically through two basic types of gene–environment correlation (rGE) (Eaves, Last, Martin, & Jinks, 1977; Plomin, DeFries, & Loehlin, 1977; Scarr & McCartney, 1983):

1. *Passive rGE.* This occurs because parents provide both their children's segregating genes and home environments. When an allele (version) of a genetic variant in parents is associated with their childrearing, the same allele in the offspring is passively correlated with their experienced childrearing.
2. *Active and evocative rGE.* Genes and environments also become correlated when the genetically influenced behavior and characteristics of individuals actively select them into, or evoke changes in, their environments.

## Family-Based Quasi-Experimental Designs for Environmental Risk Factors

Although there are numerous designs that can strengthen causal inferences by ruling out different forms of confounding (Rutter et al., 2001), including confounding due to genetic factors, this chapter focuses on family-based quasi-experimental designs. In general, quasi-experiments are based on studies in which individuals are not randomly assigned to conditions but that use *design features* to rule out confounding factors instead of solely using statistical controls for measured covariates (Shadish et al., 2002). Family-based quasi-experimental designs in particular are based on comparing family members who vary in their exposures and outcomes (D'Onofrio, Lahey,

Turkheimer, & Lichtenstein, 2013). The approaches provide rigorous tests of causal inferences by delineating among different plausible explanations for statistical associations between risk factors and outcomes. It is important to note that each approach has assumptions and limitations that influence their ability to make strong causal inferences (internal validity) and generalize to other samples (external validity). As such, using multiple family-based quasi-experimental designs can help researchers identify the mechanisms underlying the statistical associations between risk factors and outcomes. We briefly review several designs, including sibling-comparison, offspring of siblings/twins, adoptions, and the *in vitro* fertilization designs here; in-depth reviews of the designs and others are available elsewhere (D'Onofrio et al., 2013; Eaves, Last, Young, & Martin, 1978; Lawlor & Mishra, 2009; Rutter et al., 2001). We will also briefly review the possibilities when researchers includes *multiple* family relationships that differ in their environmental exposure and genetic risk in the same study because quantitative genetic models can be used to further test competing causal hypotheses (D'Onofrio et al., 2003; Heath et al., 1993; Schermerhorn et al., 2011).

## Sibling-comparison Designs

Instead of comparing unrelated individuals who vary in their exposure to a risk (e.g., SDP), which is the typical design in developmental psychopathology studies, sibling-comparison studies explore differences among siblings who were differentially exposed (e.g., one sibling was exposed to SDP but his/her sibling was not). These comparisons help account for certain types of confounding because siblings share familial factors that could confound the associations between the risk and outcome. For example, the comparisons of siblings raised in the same family account for all environmental confounds that are shared by siblings, such as early life shared environmental factors. Furthermore, sibling-comparisons help rule out some forms of genetic confounding (when genetic factors influence exposure to the risk and outcome) (Donovan & Susser, 2011; Lahey & D'Onofrio, 2010; Rutter, 2007). The process of meiosis, the type of cell division that produces eggs and sperm, randomly distributes alleles from parents to each of their offspring. As such, this random process rules out the *systematic* genetic confounding due to passive rGE. For example, the comparison of full-siblings (siblings who share 50% of their genes), rules out the possibility that genetic factors passively passed down from both parent could account for the association between the exposure and the outcome. The design does not rule out genetic confounding arising from active or evocative rGE, which occurs when a child's genotype influences the exposure to the risk (and can vary within siblings). To completely rule out all genetic factors researchers can compare identical twins who share 100% of their genetic sequences (McGue, Osler, & Christensen, 2010). It is important to note that the design cannot be used to examine exposures that are shared by twins, such as SDP (Purcell & Koenen, 2005; Turkheimer, D'Onofrio, Maes, & Eaves, 2005). However, if the probability of exposure cannot be influenced by the genetic characteristics of the offspring (e.g., the risk occurred before conception, such as maternal or paternal age at childbearing), the combination of the temporal ordering and sibling-comparisons can rule out all genetic confounding.

Like all research designs, sibling-comparisons have a number of assumptions and limitations. First, the designs cannot rule out environmental confounds that vary within siblings. Second, the comparison of full-siblings cannot always identify which confounding factors responsible for associations between risk factors and outcomes (Donovan & Susser, 2011; Lahey & D'Onofrio, 2010). It is important to note however, that researchers can combine different sibling-comparison designs (e.g., full- *and* half-siblings) (Tierney, Merikangas, & Risch, 1994) or fraternal *and* identical twins (Neale & Cardon, 1992)) and quantitative genetic models to explore the degree to which an association is due to genetic and shared environmental confounds or environments that make siblings unique. If the association was due to environments that make siblings unique the results would be consistent with a causal inference (Turkheimer & Harden, 2014).

Third, researchers have to consider whether the results from the comparison of differentially exposed siblings generalize to other populations (Frisell, Oberg, Kuja-Halkola, & Sjolander, 2012; Lahey & D'Onofrio, 2010). Fourth, sibling-comparisons rely on the assumptions that there are no carry-over effects, which occurs when the exposure of one sibling influences the outcome of another (Donovan & Susser, 2011; Frisell et al., 2012; Lahey & D'Onofrio, 2010; Rutter, 2007; Susser, Eide, & Begg, 2010). Fortunately, researchers can test these assumptions by using different quasi-experimental approaches. For instance, researchers can conduct bidirectional case-cross studies, which explore differential exposure within sibling pairs based on their birth order (i.e., when the mother smoked more during the first versus the second pregnancy), to test the assumption of no carry-over effects (Meyer, Williams, Hernandez-Diaz, & Cnattingius, 2004).

## Offspring of Siblings/Twins

Instead of comparing differentially exposed siblings, the offspring of siblings/twins compare differentially exposed cousins to help account for unmeasured genetic and environmental selection factors. The comparisons account for environmental effects that make cousins similar. Cousin-comparisons also can help account for genetic selection, although cousins share much less of their genetic makeup than siblings. For example, offspring of half-siblings (6.25% of genetic variants), offspring of full-siblings and fraternal twins (12.5%), and offspring of identical twins (25%) share less genetic makeup than full siblings. Interestingly, the offspring of identical twins design share the same amount of genetic makeup as half-siblings, so that socially the offspring are cousins, while genetically they are half-siblings (D'Onofrio et al., 2003; D'Onofrio et al., 2005; Gottesman & Bertelsen, 1989; Heath, Kendler, Eaves, & Markell, 1985; Nance & Corey, 1976; Rutter et al., 2001; Silberg & Eaves, 2004).

Cousin-comparisons enable researchers to examine risk factors that are almost always shared by siblings, like parental divorce, or by twins (e.g., SDP). The design also has different assumptions and limitations from sibling-comparisons, which makes them important because researchers need commensurate findings from multiple designs to draw strong causal inferences. Plus, cousin-comparisons can help researchers test assumptions in sibling-comparisons. For example, the comparison of differentially exposed first-born offspring of siblings/twins can be used to study a environmental risk free of the effects of birth order, which could confound sibling-comparison studies (Donovan & Susser, 2011; Lahey & D'Onofrio, 2010; Susser et al., 2010). Yet, cousin comparisons also have a number of limitations. Most importantly, the design cannot account for all genetic and environmental confounds, especially the genetic and environmental influences passed down from the spouses of the twin parents (Eaves, Silberg, & Maes, 2005). When studying individual-level risk factors, such as SDP, the design, in fact, rules out fewer confounds than sibling-comparisons (e.g., cousin-comparisons do not account for as much genetic confounding as the comparison of full-sibling).

When offspring of multiple types of adult siblings are included in a study (e.g., offspring of full- *and* half-siblings and/or identical *and* fraternal twins) researchers can use quantitative-genetic models to specify the genetic and shared environmental sources of the familial confounding; that is, to estimate the extent to which environmental and genetic influences confound the statistical associations between risk factors and outcome (D'Onofrio et al., 2003; D'Onofrio et al., 2005; Gottesman & Bertelsen, 1989; Heath et al., 1985; Rutter et al., 2001; Silberg & Eaves, 2004). For instance, researchers can combine use offspring of siblings/twins to specify the familial background factors that confound sibling-comparisons (D'Onofrio et al., 2008; Harden et al., 2007; Kuja-Halkola et al., 2010). This is an important advantage because sibling-comparisons cannot identify the source of familial confounding when the comparison of differentially exposed siblings suggests no causal influence (Donovan & Susser, 2011; Lahey & D'Onofrio, 2010).

## Adopted-at-birth Design

The children adopted-at-birth design can be used to explore whether the associations between prenatal factors and psychopathology are confounded by postnatal environmental factors. This is because the biological mothers provide genetic and prenatal environmental factors, but not the postnatal environment to the children. Thus, the design cannot remove effects of genetic confounding from prenatal environmental influences on children, such as SDP (Gaysina, Fergusson, Leve, et al., 2013).

By using a sample of children adopted-at-birth and their genetically unrelated rearing parents it is, on the other hand, possible to control for genetic confounding when examining the association between postnatal environmental factors (e.g., parenting) and child outcomes (Harold et al., 2013). This is because adoptive mothers provide postnatal environmental factors, but not genetic or prenatal environmental factors to children

## *In Vitro* Fertilization Design

The *in vitro* fertilization (IVF) design is a special type of adoption study that relies new reproductive technologies to conduct "cross-fostering" studies. The design typically includes both offspring who are genetically related to mothers (e.g., when IVF is conducted on a woman's own egg) and not genetically related to their birth mothers (e.g., when there was an embryo donation) (Thapar et al., 2007). The design enables researcher to test whether a putative risk is associated with an offspring outcome in families where the offspring is not related to mother—the design rules out passive rGE. When IVF studies include offspring who are genetically related to their mothers *and* offspring who are not genetically related, researchers can explore the extent to which the statistical association between the risk and outcome is due to genetic confounding.(Thapar et al., 2007) Although the design has high internal validity, there are concerns about the generalizability of findings from a sample of women who have had IVF (e.g., how representative are women who become pregnant through IVF and then smoke during pregnancy?).

## Family-Based Quasi-Experimental Studies of SDP and ADHD

Clinical and epidemiological studies based on unrelated individuals show a consistent association (pooled analyses estimate the odds ratio as 2.36) and also dose–response relationships between maternal SDP and offspring ADHD (Langley, Rice, van den Bree, & Thapar, 2005b). In these studies, the associations between SDP and ADHD remained after controlling for measured covariates (e.g., maternal age at childbirth and parental psychopathology), which may therefore indicate a causal effect (Banerjee, Middleton, & Faraone, 2007; Langley, Rice, van den Bree, & Thapar, 2005a; Linnet et al., 2003; Motlagh et al., 2010; Rodriguez & Bohlin, 2005a). However, given that it is impossible to identify or accurately measure all the potential confounders, unmeasured confounding might also explain the observed associations.

Sibling-comparison studies of SDP and ADHD (D'Onofrio et al., 2008; Obel et al., 2011) have all reached the opposite conclusion—familial unmeasured familial factors account for all of the association. Although there is a robust correlation between maternal SDP and ADHD in studies using unrelated individuals, differentially exposed siblings do not differ in the rate of ADHD. There were concerns about the outcome measurement in some early sibling-comparison studies because they were based on maternal report or extreme cases(Rutter, 2007; Talati & Weissman, 2010), but all published sibling-comparison studies of ADHD to date, including studies predicting continuous trait measures (e.g., parent-ratings of offspring ADHD) and categorical measures (e.g., clinically diagnosed) of ADHD, have concluded that familial selection factors, not exposure to maternal SDP, account for the associations. These sibling-comparison results have been questioned by researchers who have explicitly hypothesized that women who vary in their smoking status across pregnancies are not comparable to all smoking women (Talati & Weissman, 2010). To address concerns about the generalizability of the findings from previous sibling-comparison and limitations inherent in the design (Talati & Weissman, 2010), a recent study included full-siblings, as well as full-cousins (Skoglund, Chen, D'Onofrio, Lichtenstein, & Larsson, 2013). This study found that the association between maternal SDP and ADHD gradually attenuated towards the null when adjusting for measured confounders, unmeasured confounders shared within the extended family (i.e., cousin comparison), and unmeasured confounders within the nuclear family (i.e., sibling comparison), suggesting that familial confounding accounts for the association between SDP and ADHD. Those results are also consistent with an offspring of twins study of SDP and offspring attention-deficit/hyperactivity problems (Knopik et al.). Thus, previous research suggest converging evidence across sibling and cousin comparison (offspring of full-siblings and offspring of twins), which provide strong support for the familiar confounding hypothesis.

A recent adoption study that suggests that postnatal genetic factors (e.g., the children's genetic factors influencing the adoptive parents behaviors) do not account for the association between SDP and offspring conduct problems (Gaysina et al., 2013).

The only available IVF study on SDP and offspring ADHD likewise suggests that genetic factors passed down from women account for the observed statistical associations (Thapar et al., 2009). This study included both offspring who were genetically related to (i.e., the mother's own egg was fertilized) and not genetically related to their birth mothers (i.e., the birth mother became pregnant through an embryo donation). SDP was significantly associated with offspring ADHD in the genetically related mother-offspring pairs, but not in the genetically unrelated mother-offspring pairs, which suggest inherited factors explain the associations. The importance of unmeasured familial factors is also supported by a recent study that compared the offspring ADHD risk between maternal and paternal SDP (Langley, Heron, Smith, & Thapar, 2012). Offspring ADHD symptoms were associated with exposure to both maternal and paternal SDP, which do not support a causal inference. Furthermore, when paternal smoking was examined in the absence of maternal smoking the associations remained and did not appear to be due to passive smoking exposure in utero. These findings together suggest that the association between maternal SDP and child ADHD may be due to unmeasured familial confounding. The converging evidence from studies using multiple quasi-experimental designs, therefore, provides strong evidence that unmeasured familial factors, including genetic confounds, account for the statistical associations between SDP and offspring ADHD.

## Implications of Quasi-Experimental Research for Developmental Psychopathology

Family-based quasi-experimental designs have profound implications for developmental psychopathology research. First, quasi-experimental studies have important ramifications for research studying putative risk factors using epidemiological or convenience samples. It has become clear from recent quasi-experimental research, including studies that are based on comparing differentially exposed family members, that relies solely on including measured covariates in an analysis to control for confounds does not rule out all plausible alternative hypotheses. We encourage researchers to follow the scientific approach of identifying plausible alternative explanations for statistical associations ahead of time and using multiple designs to test competing causal hypotheses (Rutter et al., 2001; Shadish et al., 2002). This framework will often require researchers to stop the standard practice of conducting observational designs using one person from each family.

Second, quasi-experimental research has profound implications for basic science research on biological mechanisms related to psychopathology, an example of translational epidemiology (Hiatt, 2010; Talge, Neal, & Glover, 2007; Weissman, Brown, & Talati, 2011). As we have argued elsewhere (D'Onofrio & Lahey, 2010; D'Onofrio, Lahey, Turkheimer, & Lichtenstein, 2013), family-based quasi-experimental studies can greatly inform which mechanisms basic research should be exploring.

Third, the use of family-based quasi-experimental designs has important implications for research exploring biological moderating factors, such as gene by environment interaction (G×E) (Dick, 2011; Duncan & Keller, 2011). Studies that explore the interactions among specific genes and putative environmental risk factors are based on strong causal assumptions about the environmental influence (Conley & Rauscher,

2010; Dick, 2011; Moffitt, Caspi, & Rutter, 2005). As we illustrated above, many putative environmental risk factors may not have a specific influence on psychopathology; rather, the associations are due to confounding factors. As such, recent $G \times E$ studies of maternal SDP and psychopathology (Becker, El-Faddagh, Schmidt, Esser, & Laucht, 2008; L. S. Wakschlag et al., 2010), therefore, may have incorrectly interpreted the statistical interaction. Instead of a $G \times E$ interaction the statistical interaction could represent gene-by-gene interactions.

Finally, quasi-experimental designs are of great value in designing and testing preventions/interventions, a key aim of the field. Designing the best scientifically based interventions and prevention efforts relies on etiological studies that support strong causal inference regarding environmental exposures (Cicchetti, 1993; Coie et al., 1993; National Research Council & Institute of Medicine, 2009). Family-based quasi-experimental research can specify which environmental risk factors are associated with psychopathology independent of many environmental and genetic confounds. Interventions and preventative efforts, thus, aimed at decreasing these risk factors (or increasing these protection factors) could subsequently be studied using randomized controlled studies. It is also quite important to emphasize that quasi-experimental research can also identify risk factors that do not have a causal influence on psychopathology.

## Summary

Researchers have identified environmental risk factors that are correlated with psychopathology. Based on these findings, researchers have developed complex developmental models and have tested biological moderating factors for these outcomes. We still know little about the true causes of psychopathology, however, because the extent to which the environmental risk factors are truly causal or due to familial confounding remains unclear (Academy of Medical Sciences Working Group, 2007; British Academy of Science Working Group, 2010). It is important to stress that this is true of both social science research, which has typically focused on environmental risk factors, and genetic research with susceptibility genes or other biomarkers (Turkheimer, 2012).

In this paper, we describe how family-based quasi-experimental methods can help inform our understanding of the true environmental causes of psychopathology. We argue that studies employing quasi-experimental methods play a unique position in bridging gaps between basic research and social science research because the approaches rigorously test causal hypotheses (Gaziano, 2010; Hiatt, 2010; Khoury, Gwinn, & Ioannidis, 2010; Weissman et al., 2011). We exemplified these principles using studies on maternal SDP and ADHD.

## Acknowledgment

The writing of this chapter was supported by grants from the National Institute of Child Health and Human Development (HD061817 and HD061384), Swedish Research Council (Medicine), and Swedish Prison and Probation Services.

## References

Academy of Medical Sciences Working Group. (2007). *Identifying the Environmental Causes of Disease: How should we decide what to believe and when to take action?* London: Academy of Medical Sciences.

Agrawal, A., Knopik, V. S., Pergadia, M. L., Waldron, M., Bucholz, K. K., Martin, N. G., et al. (2008). Correlates of cigarette smoking during pregnancy and its genetic and environmental overlap with nicotine dependence. *Nicotine and Tobacco Research, 10*, 567–578

Bale, T. L., Baram, T. Z., Brown, A. S., Goldstein, J. M., Insel, T. R., McCarthy, M. M., et al. (2010). Early life programming and neurodevelopmental disorders. *Biological Psychiatry, 68*(4), 314–319.

Banerjee, T. D., Middleton, F., & Faraone, S. V. (2007). Environmental risk factors for attention-deficit hyperactivity disorder. *Acta Paediatr, 96*(9), 1269–1274.

Barker, D. J. P. (1998). *Mothers, Babies and Health in Later Life* (2nd ed.). Edinburgh: Churchill Livingstone.

Becker, K., El-Faddagh, M., Schmidt, M. H., Esser, G., & Laucht, M. (2008). Interaction of dopamine transporter genotype with prental smoke exposure on ADHD symptoms. *Journal of Pediatrics, 152*, 263–269.

Bell, R. Q., & Harper, L. V. (1997). *Child Effects on Adults.* Hillsdale NJ: Lawrence Erlbaum.

Beydoun, H., & Saftlas, A. F. (2008). Physical and mental health outcomes of prenatal maternal stress in human and animal studies: A review of recent evidence. *Paediatric and Perinatal Epidemiology, 22*, 438–466.

Biederman, J., Petty, C. R., Monuteaux, M. C., Fried, R., Byrne, D., Mirto, T., et al. (2010). Adult psychiatric outcomes of girls with attention deficit hyperactivity disorder: 11-year follow-up in a longitudinal case-control study. *The American Journal of Psychiatry, 167*(4), 409–417.

British Academy of Science Working Group. (2010). *Social Science and Family Policy.* London: British Academy Policy Center.

Buss, C., Davis, E. P., Muftuler, L. T., Head, K., & Sandman, C. A. (2010). High pregnancy anxiety during mid-gestation is associated with decreased gray matter density in 6-9-year-old children. *Psychoneuroendocrinology, 35*, 141–153.

Cicchetti, D. (1993). Developmental psychopathology: Reactions reflections projections. *Developmental Review, 13*, 471–502.

Cnattingius, S. (2004). The epidemiology of smoking during pregnancy: Smoking prevalence, maternal characteristics, and pregnancy outcomes. *Nicotine and Tobacco Research, 6*, S125–S140.

Coie, J. D., Watt, N. F., West, S. G., Hawkins, J. D., Asarnow, J. R., Markman, H. J., et al. (1993). The science of prevention: A conceptual framework and some directions for a national research program. *American Psychologist, 48*, 1013–1022.

Conley, D., & Rauscher, E. (2010). *Genetic Interactions with Prenatal Social Environment: Effects on Academic and Behavioral Outcomes.* Cambridge, MA: National Bureau of Economic Research.

Cornelius, M. D., Ryan, C. M., Day, N. L., Godschmidt, L., & Willford, J. A. (2001). Prenatal tobacco effects on neuropsychological outcomes among preadolescents. *Journal of Developmental and Behavioral Pediatrics, 22*, 217–225.

D'Onofrio, B. M., & Lahey, B. B. (2010). Biosocial influences on the family: A decade review. *Journal of Marriage and Family, 72*, 762–782.

D'Onofrio, B. M., Lahey, B. B., Turkheimer, E., & Lichtenstein, P. (2013). Critical need for family-based, quasi-experimental designs in integrating genetic and social science research. *American Journal of Public Health, 103* Suppl 1, S46–55.

D'Onofrio, B. M., Lahey, B. B., Turkheimer, E., & Lichtenstein, P. (2013). The critical need for family-based, quasi-experimental research in integrating genetic and social science research. *American Journal of Public Health, 103*, S46–S55.

D'Onofrio, B. M., Turkheimer, E., Eaves, L. J., Corey, L. A., Berg, K., Solaas, M. H., et al. (2003). The role of the Children of Twins design in elucidating causal relations between parent characteristics and child outcomes. *Journal of Child Psychology & Psychiatry, 44*, 1130–1144.

D'Onofrio, B. M., Turkheimer, E. N., Emery, R. E., Slutske, W., Heath, A., Madden, P. A. F., et al. (2005). A genetically informed study of marital instability and its association with offspring psychopathology. *Journal of Abnormal Psychology, 114*, 570–586.

D'Onofrio, B. M., Van Hulle, C. A., Waldman, I. D., Rodgers, J. L., Harden, K. P., Rathouz, P. J., et al. (2008). Smoking during pregnancy and offspring externalizing problems: An exploration of genetic and environmental confounds. *Development and Psychopathology, 20*, 139–164.

Dick, D. M. (2011). Gene-environment interaction in psychological traits and disorders. *Annual Review of Clinical Psychology, 7*, 383–409.

Donovan, S. J., & Susser, E. (2011). Commentary: Advent of sibling designs. *International Journal of Epidemiology, 40*, 345–349.

Duncan, G. J. (2012). Give us this day our daily breadth. *Child Development, 83*(1), 6–15.

Duncan, L. E., & Keller, M. C. (2011). A critical review of the first 10 years of candidate gene-by-environment interaction research in psychiatry. *American Journal of Psychiatry, 168*, 1041–1049.

Eaves, L. J., Last, K., Martin, N. G., & Jinks, J. L. (1977). A progressive approach to non-additivity and genotype-environmental covariance in the analysis of human differences. *British Journal of Mathematical and Statistical Psychology, 30*, 1–42.

Eaves, L. J., Last, K. A., Young, P. A., & Martin, N. G. (1978). Model-fitting approaches to the analysis of human behaviour. *Heredity, 41*, 249–320.

Eaves, L. J., Silberg, J. L., & Maes, H. H. (2005). Revisiting the children of twins: Can they be used to resolve the environmental effects of dyadic parental treatment on child behavior? *Twin Research, 8*, 283–290.

Ellingston, J. M., Rickert, M. E., Lichtenstein, P., Långström, N., & D'Onofrio, B. M. (2012). Disentangling the relationships between maternal smoking during pregnancy and co-occurring risk factors. *Psychological Medicine, 42*, 1547–1557.

Ernst, M. (2001). Behavioral and neural consequences of prental exposure to nicotine. *Journal of the American Academy of Child and Adolescent Psychiatry, 40*, 630–642.

Faraone, S. V., Biederman, J., & Mick, E. (2006). The age-dependent decline of attention deficit hyperactivity disorder: a meta-analysis of follow-up studies. *Psychological Medicine, 36*(2), 159–165.

Faraone, S. V., Perlis, R. H., Doyle, A. E., Smoller, J. W., Goralnick, J. J., Holmgren, M. A., et al. (2005). Molecular genetics of attention-deficit/hyperactivity disorder. *Biological Psychiatry, 57*(11), 1313–1323.

Fergusson, D. M. (1999). Prenatal smoking and antisocial behavior. *Archives of General Psychiatry, 56*, 223–224.

Ferriero, D. M., & Dempsey, D. A. (1999). Impact of addictive and harmful substances on fetal brain development. *Current Opinion in Neurology, 12*(2), 161–166.

Freese, J. (2008). Genetics and the social science explanation of individual outcomes. *American Journal of Sociology, 114*, S1–S35.

Frisell, T., Oberg, S., Kuja-Halkola, R., & Sjolander, A. (2012). Sibling comparison designs: Bias from non-shared confounders and measurement error. *Epidemiology, 23*, 713–720.

Froehlich, T. E., Lanphear, B. P., Auinger, P., Hornung, R., Epstein, J. N., Braun, J., et al. (2009). Association of tobacco and lead exposures with attention-deficit/hyperactivity disorder. *Pediatrics, 124*(6), e1054–1063.

Galera, C., Cote, S. M., Bouvard, M. P., Pingault, J. B., Melchior, M., Michel, G., et al. (2011). Early risk factors for hyperactivity-impulsivity and inattention trajectories from age 17 months to 8 years. *Archives of General Psychiatry, 68*(12), 1267–1275.

Gaysina, D., Fergusson, D. M., Leve, L. D., et al. (2013). Maternal smoking during pregnancy and offspring conduct problems: Evidence from 3 independent genetically sensitive research designs. *JAMA Psychiatry, 70*(9), 956–963.

Gaziano, J. M. (2010). The evolution of population science. *JAMA: The Journal of the American Medical Association, 304*(20), 2288–2289.

Gilman, S. E., & Loucks, E. B. (2012). Invited commentary: Does the Childhood environment influence the association between every *x* and every *y* in adulthood? *American Journal of Epidemiology, 176*(8), 684–688.

Glantz, M. D., & Chambers, J. C. (2006). Prenatal drug exposure effects on subsequent vulnerability to drug abuse. *Development and Psychopathology, 18*(3), 893–922.

Glantz, M. Y., & Campbell Champers, J. (2006). Prenatal drug exposure effects on subsequent vulnerability to drug abuse. *Development and Psychopathology, 18*, 893–922.

Gluckman, P. D., & Hanson, M. A. (2007). Developmental plasticity and human disease: Research directions. *Journal of Internal Medicine, 261*(5), 461–471.

Gluckman, P. D., Hanson, M. A., Cooper, C., & Thornburg, K. L. (2008). Effect of *in utero* and early-life conditions on adult health and disease. *New England Journal of Medicine, 359*, 61–73.

Gottesman, I. I., & Bertelsen, A. (1989). Confirming unexpressed genotypes for schizophrenia. *Archives of General Psychiatry, 46*, 867–872.

Halperin, J. M., & Schulz, K. P. (2006). Revisiting the role of the prefrontal cortex in the pathophysiology of attention-deficit/hyperactivity disorder. *Psychological bulletin, 132*(4), 560–581.

Harden, K. P., Lynch, S. K., Turkheimer, E., Emery, R. E., D'Onofrio, B. M., Slutske, W. S., et al. (2007). A behavior genetic investigation of adolescent motherhood and offspring mental health problems. *Journal of Abnormal Psychology, 116*, 667–683.

Harold, G. T., Leve, L. D., Barrett, D., Elam, K., Neiderhiser, J. M., Natsuaki, M. N., et al. (2013). Biological and rearing mother influences on child ADHD symptoms: revisiting the developmental interface between nature and nurture. *Journal of Child Psychology and Psychiatry, 54*(10), 1038–1046.

Heath, A. C., Kendler, K. S., Eaves, L. J., & Markell, D. (1985). The resolution of cultural and biological inheritance: Informativeness of different relationships. *Behavior Genetics, 15*, 439–465.

Heath, A. C., Kessler, R. C., Neale, M. C., Hewitt, J. K., Eaves, L. J., & Kendler, K. S. (1993). Testing hypotheses about direction of causation using cross-sectional data. *Behavior Genetics, 23*, 29–50.

Hiatt, R. A. (2010). Invited commentary: The epicenter of translational science. *American Journal of Epidemiology, 172*(5), 525–527.

Huizink, A. C., & Mulder, E. J. H. (2006). Maternal smoking, drinking or cannabis use during pregnancy and neurobehavioral and cognitive functioning in human offspring. *Neuroscience and Biobehavioral Reviews 30* 24–41.

Huizink, A. C., Robles de Medina, P. G., Mulder, J. H., Visser, G. H. A., & Buitelaar, J. K. (2003). Stress during pregnancy is associated with developmental outcome in infancy. *Journal of Child Psychology & Psychiatry, 44*(6), 810–818.

Iliadou, A. N., Koupil, I., Villamor, E., Altman, D., Hultman, C., Långström, N., et al. (2010). Familial factors confound the association between maternal smoking during pregnancy and young adult offspring overweight. *International Journal of Epidemiology, 39*, 1193–1202.

Jaffee, S. R., & Price, T. S. (2012). The implications of genotype–environment correlation for establishing causal processes in psychopathology. *Development and Psychopathology, 24*(Special Issue 04), 1253–1264.

Kendler, K. S. (2005). Psychiatric genetics: A methodological critique. *American Journal of Psychiatry, 162*, 3–11.

Kendler, K. S., & Baker, J. H. (2007). Genetic influences on measures of the environment: A systematic review. *Psychological Medicine, 37*, 615–626.

Khoury, M. J., Gwinn, M., & Ioannidis, J. P. A. (2010). The emergence of translational epidemiology: From scientific discovery to population health impact. *American Journal of Epidemiology, 172*(5), 517–524.

Knopik, V. S., Sparrow, E. P., Madden, P. A. F., Bucholz, K. K., Hudziak, J. J., Reich, W., et al. (2005). Contributions of parental alcoholism, prenatal substance exposure, and genetic transmission to child ADHD risk: A female twin study. *Psychological Medicine, 35*, 625–635.

Koob, G. F. (1999). Stress, corticotropin releasing factor, and drug addiction. *Annals of the New York Academy of Sciences, 897*(1), 27–45.

Kraemer, H. C., Kazdin, A. E., Offord, D. R., Kessler, R. C., Jensen, P. S., & Kupfer, D. J. (1997). Coming to terms with the terms of risk. *Archives of General Psychiatry, 54*, 337–343.

Kramer, M. S. (2000). Inivited commentary: Association between restricted fetal growth and adult chronic disease: Is it causal? Is it important? *American Journal of Epidemiology, 152*(7), 605–608.

Kuja-Halkola, R., D'Onofrio, B. M., Illiadou, A., Pawitan, Y., Langstrom, N., & Lichtenstein, P. (2010). Prenatal smoking exposure and stress coping in late adolescence: No causal link. *International Journal of Epidemiology, 39*, 1531–1540.

Lahey, B. B., & D'Onofrio, B. M. (2010). All in the family: Comparing siblings to test causal hypotheses regarding environmental influences on behavior. *Current Directions in Psychological Science., 19*, 319–323.

Lahey, B. B., D'Onofrio, B. M., & Waldman, I. D. (2009). Using epidemiologic methods to test hypotheses regarding causal influences on child and adolescent mental disorders. *Journal of Child Psychology and Psychiatry, 50*, 53–62.

Lambe, M., Hultman, C., Torrang, A., MacCabe, J., & Cnattingius, S. (2006). Maternal smoking during pregnancy and school performance at age 15. *Epidemiology, 17*, 524–530.

Langley, K., Heron, J., Smith, G. D., & Thapar, A. (2012). Maternal and paternal smoking during pregnancy and risk of ADHD symptoms in offspring: Testing for intrauterine effects. *American Journal of Epidemiology, 176*(3), 261–268.

Langley, K., Rice, F., van den Bree, M. B., & Thapar, A. (2005a). Maternal smoking during pregnancy as an environmental risk factor for attention deficit hyperactivity disorder behaviour. *A review. Minerva Pediatr, 57*(6), 359–371.

Langley, K., Rice, F., van den Bree, M. B., & Thapar, A. (2005b). Maternal smoking during pregnancy as an environmental risk factor for attention deficit hyperactivity disorder behaviour. *A review. Minerva pediatrica, 57*(6), 359–371.

Larsson, H., Anckarsater, H., Rastam, M., Chang, Z., & Lichtenstein, P. (2012). Childhood attention-deficit hyperactivity disorder as an extreme of a continuous trait: a quantitative genetic study of 8,500 twin pairs. *Journal of Child Psychology and Psychiatry, and Allied Disciplines, 53*(1), 73–80.

Lawlor, D. A., & Mishra, G. D. (2009). *Family Matters: Designing, Analysing, and Understanding Family-Based Studies in Life Course Epidemiology.* Oxford: Oxford University Press.

Linnet, K. M., Dalsgaard, S., Obel, C., Wisborg, K., Henriksen, T. B., Rodriguez, A., et al. (2003). Maternal lifestyle factors in pregnancy risk of attention deficit hyperactivity disorder and associated behaviors: review of the current evidence. *American Journal of Psychiatry, 160*(6), 1028–1040.

Lotfipour, S., Ferguson, E., Leonard, G., Perron, M., Pike, B., Richer, L., et al. (2009). Orbitofrontal cortex and drug use during adolescence: Role of prenatal exposure to maternal smoking and BDNF genotype. *Archives of General Psychiatry, 66*(11), 1244–1252.

Lundberg, F., Cnattingius, S., D'Onofrio, B., Altman, D., Lambe, M., Hultman, C., et al. (2010). Maternal smoking during pregnancy and intellectual performance in young adult Swedish male offspring. *Pediatric and Perinatal Epidemiology, 24*, 79–87.

Maughan, B., Taylor, A., Caspi, A., & Moffitt, T. E. (2004). Prenatal smoking and early childhood conduct problems. *Archives of General Psychiatry, 61*, 836–843.

McGue, M., Osler, M., & Christensen, K. (2010). Causal inference and observational research: The utility of twins. *Perspectives on Psychological Science, 5*, 546–556.

Meyer, K. A., Williams, P., Hernandez-Diaz, S., & Cnattingius, S. (2004). Smoking and the risk of oral clefts: Exploring the impact of study designs. *Epidemiology, 15*, 671–678.

Mick, E., Biederman, J., Faraone, S. V., Sayer, J., & Kleinman, S. (2002). Case control study of attention deficit hyperactivity disorder and maternal smoking, alcohol use, and drug use during pregnancy. *Journal of the American Academy of Child and Adolescent Psychiatry, 41*, 378–385.

Milberger, S., Biederman, J., Faraone, S. V., & Jones, J. (1998). Further evidence of an association between maternal smoking during pregnancy and attention deficit hyperactivity disorder: findings from a high-risk sample of siblings. *Journal of Clinical Child Psychology, 27*(3), 352–358.

Moffitt, T. E., Caspi, A., & Rutter, M. (2005). Strategy for investigating interactions between measured genes and measured environments. *Archives of General Psychiatry, 62*, 473–481.

Motlagh, M. G., Katsovich, L., Thompson, N., Lin, H., Kim, Y. S., Scahill, L., et al. (2010). Severe psychosocial stress and heavy cigarette smoking during pregnancy: an examination of the pre- and perinatal risk factors associated with ADHD and Tourette syndrome. *European Child and Adolescent Psychiatry, 19*(10), 755–764.

Nance, W. E., & Corey, L. A. (1976). Genetic models for the analysis of data from the families of identical twins. *Genetics, 83*, 811–826.

National Research Council & Institute of Medicine. (2009). *Preventing Mental, Emotional, and Behavioral Disorders Among Young People: Progress and Possibilities.* Washington, DC: National Academies Press.

Neale, M. C., & Cardon, L. R. D. (1992). *Methodology for Genetic Studies of Twins and Families.* Dordrecht, The Netherlands: Kluwer Academic Press.

O'Connor, T. G. (2003). Natural experiments to study the effects of early experience: Progress and limitations. *Development and Psychopathology, 15*, 837–852.

O'Connor, T. G., Heron, J., Golding, J., Beveridge, M., & Glover, V. (2002). Maternal antenatal anxiety and children's behavioural/emotional problems at 4 years. *British Journal of Psychiatry, 180*, 502–508.

O'Connor, T. G., Heron, J., Golding, J., Glover, V., & ALSPAC study team. (2003). Maternal antenatal anxiety and behavioural/emotional problems in children: a test of a programming hypothesis. *Journal of Child Psychology & Psychiatry, 44*(7), 1025–1036.

O'Connor, T. G. (2003). Natural experiments to study the effects of early experience: Progress and limitations. *Development and Psychopathology, 15*, 837–852.

Obel, C., Linnet, K. M., Henriksen, T. B., Rodriguez, A., Jarvelin, M. R., Kotimaa, A., et al. (2009). Smoking during pregnancy and hyperactivity-inattention in the offspring–comparing results from three Nordic cohorts. *International Journal of Epidemiology, 38*(3), 698–705.

Obel, C., Olsen, J., Henriksen, T. B., Rodriguez, A., Järvelin, M.-R., Moilanen, I., et al. (2011). Is maternal smoking during pregnancy a risk factor for hyperkinetic disorder?—findings from a sibling design. *International Journal of Epidemiology, 40*, 338–345.

Plomin, R., & Bergeman, C. S. (1991). The nature of nurture: Genetic influences on "environmental" measures. *Behavioral and Brain Sciences, 10*, 1–15.

Plomin, R., DeFries, J. C., & Loehlin, J. C. (1977). Genotype–environment interaction and correlation in the analysis of human behavior. *Psychological Bulletin, 84*, 309–322.

Pluess, M., & Belsky, J. (2011). Prenatal programming of postnatal plasticity? *Development and Psychopathology, 23*, 29–38.

Polanczyk, G., de Lima, M. S., Horta, B. L., Biederman, J., & Rohde, L. A. (2007). The worldwide prevalence of ADHD: a systematic review and metaregression analysis. *The American Journal of Psychiatry, 164*(6), 942–948.

Purcell, S., & Koenen, K. C. (2005). Environmental mediation and the twin design. *Behavior Genetics, 35*, 491–498.

Rodriguez, A., & Bohlin, G. (2005a). Are maternal smoking and stress during pregnancy related to ADHD symptoms in children? *Journal of Child Psychology & Psychiatry, 46*(3), 246–254.

Rodriguez, A., & Bohlin, G. (2005b). Are maternal smoking and stress during pregnancy related to ADHD symptoms in children? *Journal of Child Psychology and Psychiatry, 46*(3), 246–254.

Rutter, M. (2000). Psychosocial influences: Critiques, findings, and research needs. *Development and Psychopathology, 12*, 375–405.

Rutter, M. (2005). Environmentally mediated risks for psychopathology: Research strategies and findings. *Journal of the American Academy of Child and Adolescent Psychiatry, 44*(1), 3–18.

Rutter, M. (2007). Proceeding from observed correlation to causal inference: The use of natural experiments. *Perspectives on Psychological Science, 2*, 377–395.

Rutter, M., Pickles, A., Murray, R., & Eaves, L. J. (2001). Testing hypotheses on specific environmental causal effects on behavior. *Psychological Bulletin, 127*, 291–324.

Scarr, S., & McCartney, K. (1983). How people make their own environments: A theory of genotype → environment effects. *Child Development, 54*, 424–435.

Schermerhorn, A. C., D'Onofrio, B. M., Turkheimer, E. N., Ganiban, J. M., Spotts, E. L., Lichtenstein, P., et al. (2011). A genetically informed study of associations between family functioning and child psychosocial adjustment. *Developmental Psychology., 47*, 707–725.

Shadish, W. R. (2010). Campbell and Rubin: A primer and comparison of their approaches to causal inference in field settings. *Psychological Methods, 15*, 3–17.

Shadish, W. R., Cook, T. D., & Campbell, D. T. (2002). *Experimental and quasi-experimental designs for generalized causal inference*. New York: Houghton Mifflin.

Shea, A. K., & Steiner, M. (2008). Cigarette smoking during pregnancy. *Nicotine and Tobacco Research, 10*, 267–278.

Shonkoff, J. P., Boyce, W. T., & McEwen, B. S. (2009). Neuroscience, molecular biology, and the childhood roots of health disparities: building a new framework for health promotion and disease prevention. *JAMA, 301*(21), 2252–2259.

Silberg, J. L., & Eaves, L. J. (2004). Analyzing the contribution of genes and parent-child interaction to childhood behavioral and emotional problems: A model for the children of twins. *Psychological Medicine, 34*, 347–356.

Silberg, J. L., Parr, T., Neale, M. C., Rutter, M., Angold, A., & Eaves, L. J. (2003). Maternal smoking during pregnancy and risk to boys' conduct disturbance: An examination of the causal hypothesis. *Biological Psychiatry, 53*, 130–135.

Singh, I. (2008). Beyond polemics: Science and ethics of ADHD. [Review]. *Nature Reviews. Neuroscience, 9*(12), 957–964.

Skoglund, C., Chen, Q., D'Onofrio, B., Lichtenstein, P., & Larsson, H. (2013). Familial confounding of the association between maternal smoking during pregnancy and ADHD in offspring. *Journal of Child Psychology & Psychiatry.*

Slotkin, T. A. (2013). Maternal smoking and conduct disorder in the offspring. *JAMA Psychiatry, 70*(9), 901–902.

Smith, G. D. (2008). Assessing Intrauterine influences on offspring health outcomes: Can epidemiological studies yield robust findings? *Basic & Clinical Pharmacology & Toxicology, 102*(2), 245–256.

Susser, E., Eide, M. G., & Begg, M. (2010). Invited commentary: The use of sibship studies to detect familial confounding. *American Journal of Epidemiology, 172*(5), 537–539.

Swanson, J. M., Kinsbourne, M., Nigg, J., Lanphear, B., Stefanatos, G. A., Volkow, N., et al. (2007). Etiologic subtypes of attention-deficit/hyperactivity disorder: brain imaging, molecular genetic and environmental factors and the dopamine hypothesis. [Review]. *Neuropsychology Review, 17*(1), 39–59.

Szatmari, P. (2011). Is autism, at least in part, a disorder of fetal programming? *Archives of General Psychiatry, 68*(11), 1091–1092.

Talati, A., & Weissman, M. M. (2010). *In utero* smoking exposure warrants further investigation. *Archives of General Psychiatry, 67*, 1094.

Talge, N. M., Neal, C., & Glover, V. (2007). Antenatal maternal stress and long-term effects on child neurodevelopment: How and why? *Journal of Child Psychology & Psychiatry, 48*(3/4), 245–261.

Thapar, A., Cooper, M., Eyre, O., & Langley, K. (2013). What have we learnt about the causes of ADHD? *Journal of Child Psychology And Psychiatry, And Allied Disciplines, 54*(1), 3–16.

Thapar, A., Harold, G., Rice, F., Ge, X., Boivin, J., Hay, D., et al. (2007). Do intrauterine or genetic influences explain the foetal origins of chronic disease? A novel experimental method for disentangling effects. *BMC Medical Research Methodology, 7*, 25.

Thapar, A., Rice, F., Hay, D., Boivin, J., Langley, K., van den Bree, M., et al. (2009). Prenatal smoking might not cause attention-deficit/hyperactivity disorder: evidence from a novel design. *Biological Psychiatry, 66*(8), 722–727.

Thapar, A., & Rutter, M. (2009). Do prenatal risk factors cause psychiatric disorder? Be wary of causal claims. *British Journal of Psychiatry, 195*, 100–101.

Tierney, C., Merikangas, K. R., & Risch, N. (1994). Feasibility of half-sibling designs for detecting a genetic component to a disease. *Genetic Epidemiology, 11*, 523–538.

Turkheimer, E. (2012). Genome wide association studies of behavior are social science. In K. S. Plaisance & T. A. C. Redydon (Eds.), *Philosophy of Behavioral Biology* (pp. 43–64). New York: Springer.

Turkheimer, E., D'Onofrio, B. M., Maes, H. H., & Eaves, L. J. (2005). Analysis and interpretation of twin studies with measured environments. *Child Development, 76*, 1217–1233.

Turkheimer, E., & Harden, K. P. (2014). Behavior genetic research methods: Testing quasi-causal hypotheses using multivariate twin data. In H. T. Reis & C. M. Judd (Eds.), *Handbook of Research Methods in Personality and Social Psychology* (2nd ed.) (pp. 159–187). Cambridge: Cambridge University Press.

Wakschlag, L. S., Kistner, E. O., Pine, D. S., Biesecker, G., Pickett, K. E., Skol, A. D., et al. (2010). Interaction of prenatal exposure to cigarettes and MAOA genotype in pathways to youth antisocial behavior. *Molecular Psychiatry, 15*(9), 928–937.

Wakschlag, L. S., Pickett, K. E., Cook, E., Benowitz, N. L., & Leventhal, B. L. (2002). Maternal smoking during pregnancy and severe antisocial behavior in offspring: A review. *American Journal of Public Health, 92*, 966–974.

Weissman, M. M., Brown, A. S., & Talati, A. (2011). Translational Epidemiology in Psychiatry: Linking Population to Clinical and Basic Sciences. *Archives of General Psychiatry, 68*(6), 600–608.

# 3

# Using Mobile Technologies to Advance the Study of Psychopathology among Children and Adolescents

Madeleine J. George, Michael A. Russell, and Candice L. Odgers

Mobile technologies have become an integral part of children and adolescents' daily interactions and activities. This generation, often referred to as 'digital natives,' have been exposed to technology since birth (Palfrey & Gasser, 2008). They have never known a world without the Internet or without access to devices such as mobile phones and tablets. The growing presence of mobile devices in the lives of children is illustrated by the recent finding that one in three children under the age of 2 have used a smartphone and 75% of all children under age 8 have access to a mobile device at home (Rideout, Saphir, Pai, Rudd, & Pritchett, 2013). Usage and ownership increases with age. Ninety-five percent of all adolescents in the US have regular access to the Internet (Lenhart, 2012) and 88% own or have access to a mobile phone (Lenhart, 2015). Text messaging has become one of the most common forms of daily communication between adolescents and their friends and families (Lenhart, 2012), with adolescents are spending, on average, about 4 hours per day interacting with mobile devices on a daily basis (Rideout, Pai, Saphir, Pritchett, & Herrick, 2015), and text messaging has become one of the most common forms of daily communication between adolescents and their friends and families (Lenhart, 2012).

Given the pervasiveness of mobile technologies in the lives of children and adolescents, researchers have begun to explore how new technologies may be used to capture, understand and, ideally, respond to, their emerging mental health problems. For example, the use of smartphones and tablets is opening up novel opportunities for the intensive study of symptoms of psychopathology in the daily lives of young people. In this chapter, we review the ways in which new technologies can be used by researchers to understand the etiology, daily triggers, contexts, and developmental course of psychopathology. Specific examples of the application of mobile technologies to the study of conduct problems in adolescence and ADHD symptoms in childhood are provided, alongside a discussion of how mobile devices can enhance existing

*The Wiley Handbook of Developmental Psychopathology*, First Edition. Edited by Luna C. Centifanti and David M. Williams.

methodologies, such as ecological momentary assessment. Special attention is paid to the unique fit—and potential misfit—between 21st-century children and the use of mobile technologies within research and intervention contexts. Finally, possible applications of mobile technologies in the study and treatment of psychopathology among young people are introduced, alongside a discussion of emerging fears regarding whether the (over)use of mobile technologies may be influencing children's mental health.

## Using Mobile Technologies to Study the Mental Health of Children and Adolescents in Daily Life

Mobile technologies offer a number of opportunities to capture, measure, predict, and potentially respond to symptoms of mental disorder among children and adolescents. First, mobile technologies provide an ideal platform for the delivery of diary-based studies, often referred to as ecological momentary assessment (EMA; Shiffman, Stone, & Hufford, 2008) or experience sampling methodologies (ESM; Csikszentmihalyi, Larson, & Prescott, 1977). Using mobile devices to deliver EMA protocols allows for real-time and repeated capture of individuals in their natural environments, a strategy with established value in the study of psychopathology (for a review see Myin-Germeys et al., 2009). Second, wireless sensors and other wearable devices are rapidly becoming available to capture unobtrusive physiological (e.g., sleep, heart rate), environmental (e.g., exposure to toxins, noise levels, location) and social (e.g., proximity to others and their devices) factors that may influence how and when psychological symptoms are experienced. Third, mobile technologies may provide new and potentially more effective ways to collect information from, and engage with, young people. In particular, these tools may be helpful in reaching typically marginalized adolescents who are adopting new technologies at unprecedented rates (Lenhart, 2015; Rice, Monro, Barman-Adhikari, & Young, 2010), but who have been more difficult to reach in traditional research and intervention contexts. Fourth, there is increasing evidence that these types of ambulatory measures of symptoms and experiences have stronger associations with physiological markers of stress and related biomarkers compared to retrospectively recalled information (for a review see Conner & Barrett, 2012). Thus, ambulatory measures may be best positioned to answer questions related the complex interplay between mental health symptoms and physiology among young people.

### Mobile Technologies Can Capture Symptoms in Real Time via EMA

Diary methods can provide repeated, and often momentary, assessments of symptoms, experiences and related events and are a valuable set of tools for studying 'life as lived' (Bolger, Davis, & Rafaeli, 2003). Diary methods have a rich history in the study of psychology and psychopathology (for reviews see Iida, Shrout, Laurenceau, & Bolger, 2012; Nezlek, 2012; Shiffman et al., 2008) and provide the type of data required to track rapid symptom changes and fluctuations over time (Odgers et al., 2009). The repeated assessment of an individual within their natural contexts also provides an opportunity to identify daily triggers of symptoms and test whether the presence of other individuals or involvement in certain activities may exacerbate or reduce the emergence of symptoms (Shiffman et al., 2008). Diary studies have traditionally been administered via pencil and paper assessments, pagers, phone calls, and palm pilots or handheld computers. More recently, mobile phones and tablets have been introduced as EMA data collection tools. EMA methods allow researchers to capture events and symptoms as they are experienced, rather than as they are remembered, thereby minimizing recall bias. That is, diary methods can help to minimize (but not necessarily eliminate) retrospective recall biases by shortening the window of recall to minutes or hours, which can result in more accurate self-reports (see for example Shiffman, 2009). Although diary methods may be burdensome on participants, feasibility of this approach has been demonstrated in a range of participants, including children as young as eight years old (Whalen et al., 2009) through to elderly participants (Keller-Cohen, Fiori, Toler, & Bybee, 2006).

Electronic response formats for diary data have been around since the early 1990s (for a review see Iida et al., 2012), and have become increasingly popular with the introduction of mobile phones. While there is some debate regarding the advantages of paper and pencil versus electronic response options for enhancing the accuracy of recall in diary studies, it is clear that electronic methods offer a number of advantages with respect to data entry, storage, and transfer and may provide unique ways to engage with and gather information from study participants (for a discussion of strengths and limitations of different diary formats see Iida et al., 2012). Along with participants' responses, mobile phones can capture data that have not been traditionally gathered in EMA studies, including geo-coded location information, video diaries, photos from the day, and/or information about participants' movements, communications, and online activities from the phone itself. All of this data can be synced immediately with a secure database and, in some cases, used to inform the content of future protocols and individualized assessments.

Mobile devices are also often carried by individuals throughout the day, increasing the likelihood that they will respond to surveys when prompted and providing the opportunity to capture other measures of the environment as the phone travels with the individual across settings. In addition, the ability to have two-way communication channels set up with the device allows researchers to adapt assessment protocols based on participants' responses and provides a direct line to study members via text messaging, voice and/or video. Information from the participant and/or device can also be used in a recursive loop to trigger data collection protocols that are tailored to capture specific behaviors or contexts. For example, the ohmage system, an open mobile system for activity and experience sampling, can prompt participants to complete a brief survey every time they enter a particular location (e.g., a pre-specified 'stressful' environment) or the phone itself can automatically capture information (e.g., time and location stamps) whenever a participant presses a 'stress button' (Hicks et al., 2011). These features can allow for more individualized and context-sensitive data collection, while maintaining survey consistency.

One potential advantage of using mobile devices versus traditional pen-and-paper assessments is the ability to provide researchers and clinicians with opportunities to administer 'just in time' interventions (for a discussion of ecological momentary interventions (EMI) see Heron & Smyth, 2010). By tracking momentary changes in children's symptoms and identifying contextual factors that may influence symptom onset throughout the day, can help researchers to create individualized prediction models and identify windows for intervention delivery. For example, if depressive symptoms typically onset at the end of the day for an individual, supports could be offered and targeted during that time period (e.g., prompts to call a friend, engage in physical activity, open a cognitive behavioral therapy app). Likewise, for researchers, adaptive testing protocols could be optimized to collect information only on relevant stimuli and symptoms (e.g., administering follow up questions to identify the level and types of depressive symptoms the individual is experiencing after they have passed an initial symptom screen or only when they are in a setting where symptoms are likely to onset).

Analytically, the intensive assessment of symptoms over time provides the opportunity to more accurately describe patterns of symptom onset, co-occurrence, and expression, while also facilitating causal inference by isolating the effects of specific (and time-varying) risk factors or 'triggers' in daily life *within individuals*. That is, stable characteristics such as genetic makeup, biological sex, and ethnicity are effectively held constant (Allison, 2005; Bolger & Laurenceau, 2013), providing a test of whether exposure to a specific event or context increases the risk of experiencing symptoms for a given individual (relative to their own baseline and to times when they are not 'exposed'). The analytic advantages of delivering EMA protocols on mobile phones also include the ability to conduct 'real-time' analyses of incoming data and to use those data to make decisions about: (1) adapting or revising surveys for participants, (2) stopping data collection, such as when estimates of effect sizes have stabilized, and (3) monitoring incoming data immediately for any errors in coding or lack of response from participants.

The use of mobile phones to collect information about psychological states, especially among vulnerable populations, also raises ethical issues around how and when to intervene in the lives of study participants as streaming information about their levels of distress are received by investigators. On one hand, the ability to capture a running film versus a snapshot of study member's symptoms is advantageous in terms of being able to effectively intervene if needed and to do so in a time-sensitive manner. In this case, extremely high levels of distress or calls for help (e.g. elevated depression or indications of self-harm) could trigger an immediate response and referral system (e.g. text or call from help-line). On the other hand, data are not always viewed by investigators in 'real time'. In this case specific safety protocols or alarms would need to be built into the data collection protocol to ensure that reports of distress and adverse incidents were immediately recorded and reported. It is likely that some forms of psychopathology may be more amenable to being captured and/or 'treated' using mobile platforms. For example, mobile technologies are being used to study and develop interventions to assist those with Autism Spectrum Disorders (e.g., using accelerometers and/or sensors to identify or monitor characteristic body movements: Goodwin, Intille, Albinali, & Velicer, 2011) and anxiety-related disorders (e.g., using text messages to deliver Cognitive Behavioral Therapy: Shapiro et al., 2010). However, given that most research and virtually all intervention efforts are still in their infancy, it is too early to tell where the most successful applications may be found.

In addition, study member confidentiality may be more easily compromised as information about their location, behaviors, and interactions are captured intensively over time and as data are transferred back and forth between devices and data warehousing servers. Creating and maintaining secure channels for the transfer of data and de-identified storage of data on both the device and 'in the cloud' are essential steps in study design, but one which traditional academic support units may not be equipped to adequately support. In short, there are a number of issues around participant safety and data confidentiality that are often not covered by traditional guidelines or research support mechanisms in psychology. In the field of medicine, using mobile technologies to administer assessments and deliver interventions has been called *mobile health* (or mHealth) by the National Institutes of Health (2015) and World Health Organization (Kay, Santos, & Takane, 2011). The mHealth movement has already begun to address many of these issues (e.g., ethical issues for research with persons with HIV/AIDS or substance use: Labrique, Kirk, Westergaard, & Merritt, 2013), and psychologists who intend to gather data via these new technologies will need to quickly and efficiently put these types of mechanisms for safety, privacy and technical support in place.

## Small Phones Gather 'Big Data' That Can Advance the Study of Psychopathology

Mobile phones and their associated sensors can capture an incredible amount of streaming, and often unobtrusive, data on individuals' behaviors, social interactions, location, and physiological state. Momentary assessment and monitoring of biomarkers and health status is often considered the gold standard in medical research and practice. Until recently, conducting ambulatory assessments of key markers of biological functioning, stress reactivity and physiological states has been a costly enterprise reserved primarily for high-risk patients or those managing acute phases of a disease. The growing and widespread availability of commercially available wireless sensors, many of which can be held in the palm of your hand and connect seamlessly with your smartphone, are providing researchers with the ability to monitor and record real time fluctuations in our health status, stress response and physiological state. At the same time, new methods for assessing our behaviors and experiences in real time are creating new possibilities for understanding the interplay between daily experiences, mental health symptoms and physiology. For example, strong momentary associations have been documented between ambulatory measures of self-reported stress and blood pressure and heart rate (Bhattacharyya, Whitehead, Rakhit, & Steptoe, 2008), as well as between affective state and heart rate variability (Kamarck et al., 2005). These types of studies are well positioned to trace the effects of daily triggers (events or experiences) on affect, symptoms and physiology in real time.

Self-report diaries comprise only one of many different types of assessments that can be gathered via mobile technologies. Mobile devices also have the capacity to collect more objective information from recording components (photo, video, and voice) and global positioning systems (GPS). These features not only capture information of a different type, but they also greatly increase the amount of data that can be captured as the study participant makes their way throughout the day. For example, photo and voice-recording capabilities of smartphones allow participants to more thoroughly document their daily behaviors and experiences compared to retrospective self-reports (see the Food Intake Visual and voice Recognizer or FIVR; Weiss, Stumbo, & Divakaran, 2010). GPS also provides researchers with an account of where adolescents are spending their time and the paths that they travel throughout the day. GPS features are quickly becoming standard on mobile phones, and have been used in conjunction with adolescents' self-reports to more fully measure their experiences and environments (Wiehe et al., 2008). Smart phones can also be used to capture features of the built or social environment that we believe are relevant for understanding behaviors such as smoking, alcohol use and other high-risk behaviors. For example, McClernon and Choudhury (2013) have developed a smart phone app called 'i see smoking', which allows smartphone users to discretely swipe their phone and record the coordinates of where they observe smoking and related behaviors as they move throughout the day. Maps can then be over-laid to test how these features of the built and social environment may predict behavior and symptoms. The geo-spatial information can then be probed via online tools, such as Google Street View, to code images of neighborhoods where adolescents spend their time and engage in risky behaviors and activities (see for example Odgers, Caspi, Bates, Sampson, & Moffitt, 2012).

As adolescents' social environments are moving into the virtual realm, mobile devices can also be used to more fully capture aspects of their social networks and relationships. Social network analysis is a rapidly evolving field that has produced important findings related to child and adolescent psychopathology (e.g., Ennett et al., 2006; Mouttapa, Valente, Gallaher, Rohrbach, & Unger, 2004). For example, a study of middle school students found that the characteristics of adolescents' peer networks (i.e., density, centrality, proximity to others) predicted how likely they were to use substances, such that adolescents with fewer friend connections, higher status in a group, and/or ties to a peer who used substances were the most likely to initiate substance use over the course of middle school (Ennett et al., 2006). Now as adolescents increasingly rely on text and online messaging to interact with their peers, many of these social network characteristics can be assessed by examining adolescents' peer-to-peer virtual communication patterns.

Social support and strong friendship ties are also important predictors of positive adjustment among children and adolescents and often serve as a buffer in the face of adversity, daily stressors, and other negative life events (e.g., Galambos, Sears, Almeida, & Kolaric, 1995; von Weiss et al., 2002). With the widespread use of mobile phones and texting among adolescents, the question of how online communication may be influencing children's mental health 'for better or for worse' has arisen (for a review see George & Odgers, 2015 and Underwood & Ehrenreich, 2017). To address this question, Underwood and colleagues (2012, 2014) examined the content of eighth-graders' text messages (over the course of 2 days among a sample of 175 adolescents they collected over 43,000 messages!). In this first study of its kind, the authors were able to describe the quantity and content of all the text messages exchanged between friends. The authors found that adolescents who sent a greater proportion of messages with negative or sexual content, also reported higher symptoms of internalizing disorders (Underwood et al., 2015). Similarly, adolescents who sent a higher proportion of messages about discussing antisocial behaviors were rated by parents and teachers as exhibiting higher externalizing behaviors (Ehrenreich, Underwood, & Ackerman, 2014). These types of studies can provide a unique view of adolescents' relationships, communication patterns, and the mapping of peer networks that influence adolescent psychopathology (e.g., identifying peers and peer groups that provide social support versus those that increase the risk for substance use initiation).

In addition, network analysis of adolescents' online or text messages can map adolescents' friendships across contexts and time. Reich et al (2012) used self-reports of adolescents' top online and offline friendships to see the overlap between the virtual and school contexts. The authors reported that, typically, online friendships are an extension of offline friendships and adolescents rarely have many strong, online-only friendships. Examining text messages versus relying solely on one-time self-report measures can supply greater information in terms of the strength of friendships, the quantity and quality of interactions, and the chain of interactions within groups of individuals. Developing reliable measures of children's and adolescents' online communications and activities are important given the central role that social support plays in determining mental health across the lifespan and young peoples' increasing reliance on mobile devices (in relation to traditional forms communication) for daily communication with friends and family.

In pairing message content with the network analyses of mobile communication, a great deal of new information can be derived about children and adolescents' relationships. Mobile phones can build upon prior EMA work by opening up the potential to examine communication patterns and social networks, so that we are able to 1) more fully describe adolescents' networks and online communication-including their linkages to others with mental health problems and health-seeking behaviors, 2) examine the role that social support and interactions can play in buffering contextual triggers of symptoms and 3) eventually leverage the strongest sources of social support or communication patterns in targeted interventions, some of which may involve virtual tools.

The integration of EMA surveys (described above) with sensors and ambulatory devices able to capture streaming information from the physical and social environment, as well as individuals' bodies, could provide a number of new opportunities for discovery. These tools also help to move data collection away from sole reliance on self-report information of both psychological (e.g., 'angry') and physiological (e.g., 'heart racing') states and provide opportunities to monitor key dimensions of mental health intensively over time. Indeed, one of the current claims in the mHealth space—an industry projected to be worth $58 billion by 2020 (Franco & Jeevane, 2014)—is that one day our phones will know that we are sick before we (or our doctors) do. By integrating EMA protocols with these types of sensors, we can begin exploring the potential of real-time assessments to predict mental health status, onset, and triggers. Taking these types of ambulatory assessment out of the lab and into real-life settings allows us to capture a continuous stream of data from the daily lives of children and adolescents, and in so doing, opens up new opportunities for scientific discovery.

By pairing EMA with passive measures of the environment, studies using mobile phones have the potential to collect 'big' health and network data that can describe adolescents' social and physical environments. Moving forward, the challenges in this domain will be developing efficient means of synthesizing and protecting vast amounts of data and developing tools that can uniquely identify behavioral and contextual signatures—based on streaming data from the environment and people. To this end, interdisciplinary collaborations between psychologists, computer scientists, engineers and those with related expertise and technical skills will be required.

## Digital Natives Love Their Phones and May Be More Willing to Share Information about Their Psychological States Using Them

"I love my phone. I love it enough to risk my life for it," hyperbolized Walia, an adolescent girl, when asked about what lengths she would go to retrieve her missing phone (Weber & Mitchell, 2008, p. 32). Mobile technologies have become an integral piece of children and adolescents' lives, and for some, their personal identities That is, adolescents report feeling that their online presence and devices are important pieces of their identity, because of the exploration, self-expression, and intimate communication they allow (see books by boyd, 2014; Buckingham, 2008). Phones have become a normal (bordering on essential) tool for communication in adolescent friendships. Outside of the school context, text messaging has overtaken face-to-face interactions as the most frequent form of daily communication among adolescents (Lenhart, 2012) to the point that adolescents often sleep with their phones to avoid missing a message. Among teens who own their own mobile phone, more than 80% sleep with the phone in or next to their bed (Lenhart, Ling, Campbell, & Purcell, 2010). While the average number of text messages sent per day hovers around 30 (Lenhart, 2015), some very active adolescent text messagers send upwards of 1000 messages per day (Lenhart, 2012) and will respond to message any time of the day or night, so their friends won't think they are angry (Lenhart et al., 2010).

In short, adolescents seem to be particularly motivated to use mobile technologies given the close fit between the emphasis on social relationships and communication at this stage of development. They are accustomed to always being in close reach of their mobile phone and responding to notifications promptly, which may increase the likelihood that adolescents will respond to surveys and queries when prompted (as in many EMA studies). Indeed, there is some evidence that individuals who use their phones regularly as part of their daily routine, have higher participation rates in mobile diary surveys than those who are not regular phone users (Hicks et al., 2011). Adolescents are likely then to have high compliance for even intensive diary studies. In our current work we observe rates of compliance that exceed 90%, even when adolescents are 'beeped' to respond to surveys multiple times per day (Russell, Wang, & Odgers, 2016). When needed, researchers can also provide additional incentives to enhance study compliance by, for example, installing popular games on the devices themselves or providing electronic gift cards and other types of rewards delivered through the phones.

Frequent mobile technology users may be easier to target for intensive research studies, but ownership and engagement rates suggest that capturing a broader range of adolescents may also be feasible. Most adolescents (upwards of 90%) go online on a daily basis (Lenhart, 2015) most typically with mobile phones or devices. Although a digital divide still exists, some of the largest rises in mobile technology usage have been among minority and low-income adolescents (Lenhart, 2015; Rideout et al., 2010). Like most of the population, adolescents from lower socioeconomic (SES) and minority groups are increasingly relying on mobile phones as their sole source of virtual access (Lenhart, 2015).

Mobile phone ownership is growing to near saturation in the population, especially among young people. As a result, new opportunities for intensively studying the lives and mental health of children and adolescents across development are emerging. Mobile-phone-based interventions are also coming online as a potentially effective, and increasingly affordable way to target and deliver support for children and adolescents who are traditionally understudied and hard to reach. The type of intensive assessment data gathered via EMA methods and mobile devices are also providing new opportunities to evaluate heterogeneity in the short and long-term effects of traditional treatment studies and to embed relatively low cost supplements or 'boosters' into standard therapies and interventions (e.g., electronic supplements or supports in cognitive behavior therapies).

## Applications Using Mobile Technologies in the Study of Child and Adolescent Psychopathology

Researchers in the field have started to put mobile devices into the hands of children, adolescents, and their parents to learn more about the developmental course, contextual triggers, and outcomes associated with various forms of psychopathology. A few examples of research using mobile devices with children and adolescents are provided below.

### Example 1: PalmPartners Study of Family Processes and Contextual Triggers among Children with and without ADHD

A number of researchers have used EMA approaches to study family processes in daily life (for a review see Laurenceau & Bolger, 2005). When used in familial or dyadic contexts, EMA designs allow for tests of how different members of a family system or relationship drive and/or respond to the behaviors of others through fine-grained, and time-ordered sequencing of assessments and shared interactions. One of the longest standing questions in the study of child psychopathology is the extent to which parenting behavior *per se* determines children's mental health and behavioral outcomes, versus the extent to which children (who also often share genetic information and predispositions towards behavioral and emotional problems) elicit parenting behaviors from their caregivers. EMA designs delivered via electronic methods can help disentangle this question by examining the interactions between parents and children intensively over time and testing: how, within dyad parenting, behavior predicts changes in children's behaviors and emotions in real-time and over time (and vice versa), while holding constant all stable characteristics of the parent and the child that may otherwise confound the interpretation of the parenting-to-child behavior link.

Whalen and colleagues (2006, 2001) used intensive assessments of mothers and their children (every 20 minutes!) via Palm Pilot devices to test how contextual or individual factors (e.g., time of day, prior risk, mothers' levels of psychopathology) may influence the ways that mothers responded to their children's behavior over the course of day. For example, the authors reported that children with an ADHD diagnosis had heightened behavioral problems, elevated maternal negative affect, and increased dyadic conflict during transition times (e.g., getting ready for school) compared to children without an ADHD diagnosis (Whalen et al., 2006). Similarly, parent-child dyads with ADHD (in comparison to non-ADHD comparison dyads) were more likely to enter into patterns of negative exchanges that persisted over time (Whalen et al., 2009) and were more likely to elicit negative reactions from each other over the course of the study (Whalen, Odgers, Reed, & Henker, 2011). In this case, parents and children were driving each other's behaviors across the week, with evidence of both parent-driven and child-elicited effects on behavior. This work was important as it provided a new window into the micro-level exchanges that ADHD children and their parents engage in throughout the day, while also establishing that children as young as eight years of age could provide reliable information about their symptoms and activities using a handheld devices.

## Example 2: miLife Study of Biological and Environmental Interactions in Adolescents' Daily Lives

More recently, our research team has followed a group of young adolescents using mobile phones to understand how exposure to violence and daily stressors influence mental health, substance use and related health-risk behaviors. Following baseline assessments, 151 adolescents were given mobile phones and tracked prospectively over a one-month period. Participants responded to three surveys per day during the initial 30 day assessment, and were then followed up 18 months later to assess the emergence or worsening of symptoms and behavioral problems during the transition from early to mid-adolescence. The use of mobile phones in this study allowed us to obtain multiple assessments of adolescents' mental health symptoms over the course of a day, alongside information about their activities and experiences. This high-resolution data allowed for tests of how daily and individual level factors (e.g., witnessing violence and genetic predispositions) were related to adolescents' same and next-day emotional health and risk-taking behaviors.

We are currently using the study's repeated measures of context, experience, and symptomatology in adolescents' daily lives to examine longstanding models of person-by-environment interaction, such as the diathesis–stress model. That is, we are estimating within- versus between-person comparisons of the effects of daily stressors on affect and behavior, guided by the hypothesis that those who carry the highest risk for psychopathology will also have heightened responses to stressful experiences in daily life. The diathesis–stress model suggests that some adolescents will be more vulnerable to stressful environments than others, by virtue of pre-existing characteristics such as their genetic makeup (Ingram & Price, 2010). The majority of research in this area, however, has relied on between-person comparisons, which cannot directly test an important implication of the diathesis–stress model (i.e., 'vulnerable' individuals will be more *reactive* to stressful or risky environments as they experience them).

Our results suggest that adolescents with versus without the 7-repeat allele of the dopamine receptor *D4* gene (*DRD4*-7R), a gene that has received attention for as a potential vulnerability factor, may be more reactive to risky environments in daily life. Adolescents with this allele showed greater increases in externalizing symptomatology compared to themselves on high versus low risk-exposure days. Additionally, we found no evidence that adolescents with versus without the *DRD4*-7R allele experienced greater levels of risk exposure, thus ruling out gene–environment correlation as a potential counter-explanation of these results (Russell, Wang, & Odgers, 2016). Because these results are based on within-person comparisons obtained through repeated naturalistic measurement of the same individuals, they cannot be explained away by stable individual difference factors (e.g., sex, ethnicity, current family socioeconomic status) that serve as potential confounds in studies relying on between-person comparisons. As such, we are able to move one step closer to causal inferences regarding how adolescents' everyday experiences interact with their pre-existing characteristics to influence their risk for psychopathology.

## Drawbacks and Limitations of Mobile Technologies for Researchers

Although mobile technologies can be valuable tools for capturing life as lived, monitoring treatment efficacy and heterogeneity effects, and delivering more individualized interventions, certain drawbacks and limitations do exist. First, there is growing concern that frequent or continuous use of mobile technologies may have negative effects on children's mental and physical health, yet the limited evidence for technology's negative impacts to date has been mixed or inconclusive (George & Odgers, 2015). It appears that adolescents' use of technology is likely to mirror their engagement in offline activity. For example, adolescents who report greater online communication also tend to have stronger in-person relationships (Valkenburg & Peter, 2007). Similarly, problems stemming from adolescents' usage of mobile technologies may also reflect pre-existing conditions and self-selection factors (e.g., poor offline social skills or high depressive symptoms). Adolescents' use of mobile technologies can also exacerbate or dampen psychopathology symptoms, depending on if it isolates or exposes adolescents to new dangers (e.g., cyberbullying), or provides new opportunities for adolescent coping (e.g., seek support from friends). Our research team has used daily EMA methods (i.e., miLife study) to examine the coupling between adolescents' daily technology usage and their same-day mental health symptoms. On days in which adolescents spent more time online (as compared to days when they used technology less) they experienced more externalizing symptoms, but they also reported fewer internalizing symptoms (George, Russell, Piontak, & Odgers (2017). Future research is required to fully understand how usage patterns, content, and online contexts amplify or dampen mental health symptoms among children and adolescents.

Second, the fast pace of the development of newer models and devices means that mobile technologies are constantly being updated or replaced, leading to obsolete devices or (if studying technology itself) behavior patterns. The devices themselves can allow for faster collection periods, but methods using mobile technologies should never be a substitute for a sound, theoretically driven study. Rather, mobile technologies should be thought of one of many tools that researchers have in fielding intensive assessment studies.

Lastly, EMA studies can be intensive or burdensome for participants, so attrition and compliance is a concern, especially in studies with long duration (see Christensen, Barrett, Bliss-Moreau, Lebo, & Cynthia, 2003 for an excellent review of these and other practical considerations inherent in diary research). However, engagement can be enhanced by designing an incentive system for children and adolescents for their continued involvement in responding to prompts. EMA studies can also place additional burdens on researchers with respect to ensuring the protection and privacy of participant data and through the generation of, at times, massive amounts of data that require advanced skills in data synthesis and analysis (for excellent overviews of state-of-the-art methods for analyzing diary data see Bolger et al., 2003; for intensive longitudinal methods see Bolger & Laurenceau, 2013; and for dyadic data analysis see Kenny, Kashy, & Cook, 2006).

## Conclusions and Future Directions

With over 6 billion cellular phones worldwide, our society and the daily lives of children and adolescents have become increasingly connected and dependent on mobile technologies. Mobile devices already keep children and adolescents in greater virtual contact with their friends and families, and may start to bring them closer to researchers as well.

The introduction and rapid evolution of mobile technologies is also transforming research opportunities, with new features that track location, monitor health and changes in affect, and provide quantitative and qualitative information about children's everyday lives. The introduction of wireless sensors, GPS tracking capabilities, and recording features into EMA studies allows for an added layer of information about the adolescents in context that would otherwise be difficult, and in some cases impossible, to gather. New tools for connecting commercially available wireless sensors and mobile phone applications to EMA protocols are now available for little to no additional cost (e.g., open source APIs in Apple‘s ResearchKit, 2015). Mobile technologies continue to evolve, providing researchers with more options regarding the types of data they can collect.

Mobile technologies may also offer new ways to reach study populations that have traditionally be difficult to engage in mental health related research and interventions. While not ideal for all research designs, mobile devices can be used to collect high-resolution data on children and adolescents. In addition, these technologies are providing researchers and health professionals with new opportunities for assessment and intervention. In the health field, mHealth methods have been embraced for intervention administration for disease prevention and management, and psychological researchers may be able to use similar methods to assess and intervene earlier in the course of psychopathology (for a review see Mohr, Burns, & Schueller, 2013).

Message-based interventions for psychopathology can incorporate EMA to test—and eventually disseminate—intervention content that might promote coping strategies or reduce ineffective or maladaptive habits. For example, mobile phone delivery of intervention content could be used to supplement cognitive behavioral therapy (CBT; Beck, 1991), an intervention known to be effective among children and adolescents (James, James, Cowdrey, Soler, & Choke, 2013; McCart, Priester, Davies, & Azen, 2006). Mobile phone interventions have been shown effective in reaching and helping diverse groups of participants, such as those from ethnic minority (Napolitano, Hayes, Bennett, Ives, & Foster, 2013) and/or from harder-to-reach populations, that may be at heightened risk for psychopathology. Continuous assessments obtained by mobile technologies facilitate the development of "just-in-time" intervention—or the delivery of interventions following environmental "cues". For example, when adolescents report stressors in their daily lives, such as an argument with a parent or conflict with a peer, intervention messages reminding youth to use positive coping strategies could be delivered via SMS messaging. Intervention messages could also be triggered using smartphone-based sensing of environments, without relying exclusively on participants' self-reports (see McClernon & Choudhury, 2013 for a discussion of these techniques in smoking research and treatment).

With respect to preventing and treating adolescents' mental health, intervention content could be delivered when smartphone sensors detect changes in stress markers (such as heart-rate variability), increases in the volume of speech sounds (possibly indicating yelling), or specific word choices suggestive of conflict or distress. In this way, the type and delivery of intervention content could be based on both the theoretical knowledge of psychopathology and the individual information provided about personal triggers of symptoms. Mobile devices could afford greater exchange between users and researchers or clinicians, so that users have greater control and input.

As mobile technologies are already providing new channels of communication between adolescents and their friends/families, researchers could explore the ways in which online communications or activities may buffer against (e.g., as a source of social support) or exacerbate (e.g., cyberbullying) the onset of major health problems, including depression, anxiety disorders, and substance use. An experimental study of 72 young adults and 51 young adolescents examined the benefits of online chatting with a stranger after a social exclusion task (Gross, 2009). Adolescents and young adults who had a conversation online, compared to those who played a solitary online game, had faster recoveries of their self-esteem and positive mood. These results suggest that virtual communication may provide avenues for intimate discussion and problem disclosure. However, adolescents' social media 'lurking' (i.e., browsing and comparing oneself to others) and vicitimization are also linked to poor adjustment and wellbeing (see Underwood & Ehrenreich, 2017). Researchers can simultaneously provide adolescents with virtual environments that allow informal disclosure of feelings, while measuring symptoms of psychopathology, such as depression and anxiety. Mobile technologies are already being utilized by adolescents to seek information and help about their mental health and well-being, and could be leveraged in ways that increase access to, or effectiveness of, these help seeking behaviors.

Mobile technologies are not a perfect fit for all research designs or intervention efforts; yet, they can offer new research opportunities and have already provided some key insights in areas of child and adolescent development. Although there are limitations, there are also exciting possibilities for understanding and improving the mental health of children and adolescents via mobile technologies. Mobile technologies have the potential to provide high-resolution information about children and their risk for psychopathology, both in the moment and over time. At the same time, they offer new platforms for broad dissemination of tailored interventions, including among youth who may be traditionally difficult to reach and engage. Mobile technologies can be best thought of as one of many tools that can be used to study and treat mental health problems among children and adolescents.

## References

Allison, P. D. (2005). *Fixed Effects Regression Methods for Longitudinal Data Using SAS.* Cary, NC: SAS Institute, Inc.

Apple Inc. (2015). ResearchKit. Retrieved December 12, 2016, from http://researchkit.org/

Beck, A. T. (1991). Cognitive therapy: A 30-year retrospective. *American Psychologist*, *46*(4), 368–375.

Bhattacharyya, M. R., Whitehead, D. L., Rakhit, R., & Steptoe, A. (2008). Depressed mood, positive affect, and heart rate variability in patients with suspected coronay artery disease. *Psychosomatic Medicine*, *70*(9), 1020–1027. doi: 10.1097/PSY.0b013e318189afcc

Bolger, N., Davis, A., & Rafaeli, E. (2003). Diary methods: Capturing life as it is lived. *Annual Reviews of Psychology*, *54*, 579–616. doi: 10.1146/annurev.psych.54.101601.145030

Bolger, N., & Laurenceau, J.-P. (2013). *Intensive longitudinal Methods: An introduction to diary and experience sampling research.* New York, NY: Guilford Press.

boyd, D. (2014). *It's Complicated: The social lives of networked teens.* New Haven, CT: Yale University Press.

Buckingham, D. (2008). *Youth, Identity, and Digital Media.* Cambridge, MA: MIT Press.

Christensen, T. C., Barrett, L. F., Bliss-Moreau, E., Lebo, K., & Cynthia, K. (2003). A practical guide to experience-sampling procedures. *Journal of Happiness Studies, 4,* 53–78. doi: 10.1023/A:1023609306024

Conner, T. S., & Barrett, L. F. (2012). Trends in ambulatory self-report: The role of momentary experience in psychosomatic medicine. *Psychosomatic Medicine, 74*(4), 327–337. doi: 10.1097/PSY.0b013e3182546f18

Csikszentmihalyi, M., Larson, R., & Prescott, S. (1977). The ecology of adolescent activity and experience. *Journal of Youth and Adolescence, 6*(3), 281–294. doi: 10.1007/bf02138940

Ehrenreich, S. E., Underwood, M. K., & Ackerman, R. A. (2014). Adolescents' text message communication and growth in antisocial behavior across the first year of high school. *Journal of Abnormal Child Psychology, 42*(2), 251–264. doi: 10.1007/s10802-013-9783-3

Ennett, S. T., Bauman, K. E., Hussong, A., Faris, R., Foshee, V. A., Cai, L., & DuRant, R. H. (2006). The peer context of adolescent substance use: Findings from social network analysis. *Journal of Research on Adolescence, 16*(2), 159–186.

Franco, J., & Jeevane, Y. (2014). *mHealth Market: Global share, size, industry analysis, trends, opportunities, growth and forecast 2013–2020.* Portland, OR: Allied Market Resaerch

Galambos, N. L., Sears, H. A., Almeida, D. M., & Kolaric, G. C. (1995). Parents' work overload and problem behavior in young adolescents. *Journal of Research on Adolescence, 5*(2), 201–223. doi: 10.1207/s15327795jra0502_3

George, M. J., & Odgers, C. L. (2015). Seven fears and the science of how mobile technologies may be influencing adolescents in the digital age. *Perspectives in Psychological Science, 10,* 832–851.

George, M. J., Russell, M. A., Piontak, J. R., & Odgers, C. L. (2017). Concurrent and subsequent associations between daily digital technology use and high-risk adolescents' mental health symptoms. *Child Development, (online),* 1–11. doi: 10.1111/cdev.12819

Goodwin, M. S., Intille, S. S., Albinali, F., & Velicer, W. F. (2011). Automated detection of stereotypical motor movements. *Journal of Autism and Developmental Disorders, 41,* 770–782. doi: 10.1007/s10803-010-1102-z

Gross, E. F. (2009). Logging on, bouncing back: An experimental investigation of online communication following social exclusion. *Developmental Psychology, 45*(6), 1787–1793. doi: 10.1037/a0016541

Heron, K. E., & Smyth, J. M. (2010). Ecological momentary interventions: Incorporating mobile technology into psychosocial and health behavior treatments. *British Journal of Health Psychology, 15*(1), 1–39. doi: 10.1348/135910709X466063

Hicks, J., Ramanathan, N., Falaki, H., Longstaff, B., Parameswaran, K., Monibi, M., … Estrin, D. (2011). *ohmage: An open mobile system for activity in experience sampling.* Los Angeles, CA: Center for Embedded Networked Sensing.

Iida, M., Shrout, P. E., Laurenceau, J.-P., & Bolger, N. (2012). Using diary methods in psychological research. In H. Cooper, P. M. Camic, D. L. Long, A. T. Panter, D. Rindskopf & K. J. Sher (Eds.), *APA Handbook of Research Methods in Psychology, Vol 1: Foundations, planning, measures, and psychometrics* (pp. 277–305). Washington, DC: American Psychological Association.

Ingram, R. E., & Price, J. M. (2010). *Vulnerability to psychopathology: Risk across the life-span* (2nd ed.). New York, NY: Guilford Press.

James, A. C., James, G., Cowdrey, F. A., Soler, A., & Choke, A. (2013). Cognitive behavioural therapy for anxiety disorders in children and adolescents. *Cochrane Database of Systematic Reviews, 2013*(6), 1–104. doi: 10.1002/14651858.CD004690.pub3

Kamarck, T. W., Schwartz, J. E., Shiffman, S., Muldoon, M. F., Sutton-Tyrrell, K., & Janicki, D. L. (2005). Psychosocial stress and cardiovascular risk: What is the role of a daily experience? *Journal of Personality, 73*(6), 1749–1774. doi: 10.1111/j.0022-3506.2005.00365.x

Kay, M., Santos, J., & Takane, M. (2011). mHealth: New horizons for health through mobile technologies. *Global Observatory for eHealth series* (Vol. 3). Geneva, Switzerland: World Health Organization.

Keller-Cohen, D., Fiori, K., Toler, A., & Bybee, D. (2006). Social relations, language and cognition in the 'oldest old.' *Ageing and Society, 26*(4), 585–605. doi: 10.1017/S0144686X06004910

Kenny, D. A., Kashy, D. A., & Cook, W. L. (2006). *Dyadic Data Analysis.* New York, NY: Guilford Press.

Labrique, A. B., Kirk, G. D., Westergaard, R. P., & Merritt, M. W. (2013). Ethical issues in mHealth research involving persons living with HIV/AIDS and substance abuse. *AIDS Research and Treatment, 2013*, 1–6. doi: 10.1155/2013/189645

Laurenceau, J.-P., & Bolger, N. (2005). Using diary methods to study marital and family processes. *Journal of Family Psychology, 19*(1), 86–97. doi: 10.1037/0893-3200.19.1.86

Lenhart, A. (2012). *Teens, Smartphones & Texting.* Washington, D.C.: The Pew Research Center Internet & American Life Project.

Lenhart, A. (2015). *Teens, Social Media & Technology Overview 2015.* Washington, DC: Pew Research Center.

Lenhart, A., Ling, R., Campbell, S., & Purcell, K. (2010). *Teens and Mobile Phones.* Washington, D.C.: University of Michigan Dept of Communication Studies; The Pew Research Center Internet & American Life Project.

McCart, M. R., Priester, P. E., Davies, W. H., & Azen, R. (2006). Differential effectiveness of behavioral parent-training and cognitive behavioral therapy for antisocial youth: A meta-analysis. *Journal of Abnormal Child Psychology, 34*(4), 527–543. doi: 10.1007/s10802-006-9031-1

McClernon, F. J., & Choudhury, R. R. (2013). I am your smartphone, and I know you are about to smoke: The application of mobile sensing and computing approaches to smoking research and treatment. *Nicotine & Tobacco Research, 15*(10), 1651–1654. doi: 10.1093/ntr/ntt054

Mohr, D. C., Burns, M. N., & Schueller, S. M. (2013). Behavioral intervention technologies: Evidence review and recommendations for future research in mental health. *General Hospital Psychiatry, 35*(4), 332–338.

Mouttapa, M., Valente, T., Gallaher, P., Rohrbach, L. A., & Unger, J. B. (2004). Social network predictors of bullying and victimization. *Adolescence, 39*(154), 315–335.

Myin-Germeys, I., Oorschot, M., Collip, D., Lataster, J., Delespaul, P., & van Os, J. (2009). Experience sampling research in psychopathology: Opening the black box of daily life. *Psychological Medicine, 39*(09), 1533–1547. doi: 10.1017/S0033291708004947

Napolitano, M. A., Hayes, S., Bennett, G. G., Ives, A. K., & Foster, G. D. (2013). Using Facebook and text messaging to deliver a weight-loss program to college students. *Obesity, 21*, 25–31. doi: 10.1038/oby.2012.107

National Institutes of Health. (2015). mHealth: Mobile Health Technologies. Retrieved June 12, 2015, from http://obssr.od.nih.gov/scientific_areas/methodology/mhealth/

Nezlek, J. B. (2012). *Diary Methods*: Thousand Oaks, CA: Sage.

Odgers, C., Mulvey, E., Skeem, J., Gardner, W., Lidz, C., & Schubert, C. (2009). Capturing the ebb and flow of psychiatric symptoms with dynamical systems models. *American Journal of Psychiatry, 166*(5), 575–582.

Odgers, C. L., Caspi, A., Bates, C. J., Sampson, R. J., & Moffitt, T. E. (2012). Systematic social observation of children's neighborhoods using Google Street View: a reliable and cost-effective method. *Journal of Child Psychology and Psychiatry, 53*(10), 1009–1017.

Palfrey, J. G., & Gasser, U. (2008). *Born Digital: Understanding the first generation of digital natives.* New York: Basic Books.

Rice, E., Monro, W., Barman-Adhikari, A., & Young, S. D. (2010). Internet use, social networking, and HIV/AIDS risk for homeless adolescents. *Journal of Adolescent Health, 47*(6), 610–613. doi: 10.1016/j.jadohealth.2010.04.016

Rideout, V. J., Foehr, U. G., & Roberts, D. F. (2010). *Generation M: Media in the lives of 8 to 18 year olds.* Menlo Park, CA: The Kaiser Family Foundation.

Rideout, V. J., Saphir, M., Pai, S., Rudd, A., & Pritchett, J. (2013). *Zero to eight: Children's media use in America 2013.* San Francisco, CA.: Common Sense Media.

Rideout, V. J., Pai, S., Saphir, M., Pritchett, J., & Herrick, D. (2015). *The Common Sense Census: Media use by tweens and teens.* San Francisco, CA: Common Sense Media.

Russell, M. A., Wang, L., & Odgers, C. L. (2016). Witnessing substance use increases same day antisocial behavior among at-risk adolescents: Gene–environment interaction in a 30-day ecological momentary assessment study. *Development and Psychopathology, 28*, 1441–1456.

Shapiro, J. R., Bauer, S., Andrews, E., Pisetsky, E., Bulik-Sullivan, B., Hamer, R. M., & Bulik, C. M. (2010). Mobile therapy: Use of text-messaging in the treatment of bulimia nervosa. *International Journal of Eating Disorders, 43*(6), 513–519. doi: 10.1002/eat.20744

Shiffman, S. (2009). How many cigarettes did you smoke? Assessing cigarette consumption by global report, time-line follow-back, and ecological momentary assessment. *Health Psychology, 28*(5). doi: 10.1037/a0015197

Shiffman, S., Stone, A. A., & Hufford, M. R. (2008). Ecological Momentary Assessment. *Annual Review of Clinical Psychology, 4*(1), 1–32. doi: 10.1146/annurev.clinpsy.3.022806.091415

Underwood, M. K., Ehrenreich, S. E., More, D., Solis, J. S., & Brinkley, D. Y. (2015). The BlackBerry Project: The hidden world of adolescents' text messaging and relations with internalizing symptoms. *Journal of Research on Adolescence, 25*(1), 101–117. doi: 10.1111/jora.12101

Underwood, M. K., & Ehrenrich, S. E. (2017). The power and pain of adolescents' digital communication: Cyber victimization and the perils of lurking. *American Psychologist, 72*(2), 144–158. doi: 10.1037/a0040429

Underwood, M. K., Rosen, L. H., More, D., Ehrenreich, S. E., & Gentsch, J. K. (2012). The BlackBerry project: Capturing the content of adolescents' text messaging. *Developmental Psychology, 48*(2), 295–302. doi: 10.1037/a0025914

Valkenburg, P. M., & Peter, J. (2007). Preadolescents' and adolescents' online communication and their closeness to friends. *Developmental Psychology, 43*(2), 267–277. doi: 10.1037/0012-1649.43.2.267

von Weiss, R. T., Rapoff, M. A., Varni, J. W., Lindsley, C. B., Olson, N. Y., Madson, K. L., & Bernstein, B. H. (2002). Daily hassles and social support as predictors of adjustment in children with pediatric rheumatic disease. *Journal of Pediatric Psychology, 27*(2), 155–165. doi: 10.1093/jpepsy/27.2.155

Weber, S., & Mitchell, C. (2008). Imaging, keyboarding, and posting identities: Young people and new media technologies. In D. Buckingham (Ed.), *Youth, Identity, and Digital Media* (pp. 25–47). Cambridge, MA: The MIT Press.

Weiss, R., Stumbo, P. J., & Divakaran, A. (2010). Automatic food documentation and volume computation using digital imaging and electronic transmission. *Journal of the American Dietetic Association, 110*(1), 42–44. doi: 10.1016/j.jada.2009.10.011

Whalen, C. K., Henker, B., Ishikawa, S. S., Floro, J. N., Emmerson, N. A., Johnston, J. A., & Swindle, R. (2009). ADHD and anger contexts: Electronic diary mood reports from mothers and children. *Journal of Pediatric Psychology, 34*, 940–953. doi: 10.1093/jpepsy/jsn138

Whalen, C. K., Henker, B., Ishikawa, S. S., Jamner, L. D., Floro, J. N., Johnston, J. A., & Swindle, R. (2006). An electronic diary study of contextual triggers and ADHD: Get ready, get set, get mad. *Journal of the American Academy of Child & Adolescent Psychiatry, 45*(2), 166–174. doi: 10.1097/01.chi.0000189057.67902.10

Whalen, C. K., Jamner, L. D., & Henker, B. (2001). Smoking and moods in adolescents with depressive and aggressive dispositions: Evidence from surveys and electronic diaries. *Health Psychology, 20*(2), 99–111. doi: 10.1037/0278-6133.20.2.99

Whalen, C. K., Odgers, C. L., Reed, P. L., & Henker, B. (2011). Dissecting daily distress in mothers of children with ADHD: an electronic diary study. *Journal of Family Psychology, 25*(3), 402–411. doi: 10.1037/a0023473

Wiehe, S. E., Carroll, A. E., Liu, G. C., Haberkorn, K. L., Hoch, S. C., Wilson, J. S., & Fortenberry, J. D. (2008). Using GPS-enabled cell phones to track the travel patterns of adolescents. *International Journal of Health Geographics, 7*(22), 1–11. doi: 10.1186/1476-072X-7-22

# 4

# Opening Minds

## *The Arts and Developmental Psychopathology*

Nicola Shaughnessy

## Introduction

***Sound Cue 4: Track 3— Counting & Items (voiceover)***

*I have a ring and a tiny pair of earrings. The earrings have to be exactly straight on top of my chest of drawers before I can get into bed. Sometimes I alter them 25 times before it feels right. I then have to make sure the ring is exactly perpendicular to the earrings. Again, I can move it over and over again ever so slightly before it feels right. The more I do it, the longer it takes for it to feel just right so I can stop touching it. I count to control it, at first. I can only touch my ring five times, or only five lots of five times. One two three four five. But then the counting becomes part of the compulsion, one two three four five. Over and over. I have to keep counting and tapping until it feels right. One two three four five, one two three four five.*

*One two three four five. One two three four five. One two three four five.*

*Clothes, window, jewellery, light switch, toilet, cooker, back door, tap, front door, wardrobe, knives, shoes, hairdryer, jewellery, window, plugs, door handle, ring.*

*One.two.three.four.five. One.two.three.four.five. One.two. One.two.three.four.five. One. two.three. Start again. One. And again, it doesn't feel right. Start again. One.two.three. four.five. Get in to bed. I can't, not yet. Leave the house. I can't, not yet. One.two.three.four. bed. No. One, two, three, four, fuck, start again. I don't want to. I'm too tired. I want to lie down. Just take my clothes off and lie down. And sleep. One.two.three.four.five. You don't need to do it. I can't not do it. If I don't do it something bad will happen. What if something bad happens? What if I do something? What if something happens to me? What if I get ill? What if I die? It makes no difference. I know. Get into bed. Go to sleep. I can't. Not yet. It doesn't feel right yet.*

*Jewellery, light switch, clothes, wardrobe, lamp, plug, window, lock, teddy, jewellery, ring. Touch my ring five times, four times, then twice, then four times, then four times, then four times, then four times, until it feels right. Then five times, five lots of five times, shut my eyes and count to five. Open my eyes and count to five, shut my eyes and count to five, breathe deeply, count again. ONE.TWO.THREE.FOUR.FIVE.*

These words describe the experience of Obsessive Compulsive Disorder (OCD). They transport us into the interior world of the sufferer, giving us a felt and affective insight into how intrusive thoughts invade the sufferer's consciousness and dominate their actions. The lines form part of the opening sequence of a play, *This Room* (2015), and

*The Wiley Handbook of Developmental Psychopathology*, First Edition. Edited by Luna C. Centifanti and David M. Williams.

are delivered as a recorded voice over so that we are hearing the words *as if* they are in our heads.[1] The voice that speaks them is that of the solo performer on stage, Laura Jane Dean, who wrote and performed this autobiographical one-woman show, describing it as "based on my own experiences of living with Obsessive Compulsive Disorder and receiving cognitive behavioral therapy (CBT) as treatment."[2] Prior to seeing this piece, I associated OCD with behavioral extremes such as the overzealous hygiene of frequent hand washing or obsessive checking rituals involving light switches and door locks. As an audience member, I gained new understanding of the condition. I felt projected into the mind space of this psychopathology, *as if* I was having an episode of OCD, wanting the nagging voices to stop as the cacophony became overwhelming. "I had no idea this was a such a tortuous condition," I observed to the psychologist I'd invited, hoping she'd find the piece informative and affecting. In so doing, it was also my intention to impress upon her the power of the arts to explore the hard-to-reach areas of human experience and their capacity to interact with science to enhance understanding of conditions such as OCD.

In this chapter I consider the role and value of the arts as a means of engaging with developmental psychopathology, with reference to three key aspects.. The first I define as **representation,** which refers to the potential to create an artefact whose form enables us to imaginatively engage with an experience that is other to our own. Third- and first-person perspectives engage in dialogue, enabling us to "walk in the shoes of the other." Secondly, I consider the **reparative** function of the arts as a therapeutic vehicle for those affected by psychopathology. The third function I define in terms of **realization** which I link to the concept of the **relational,** to describe a coming to an understanding of psychopathology as a process, moving beyond diagnostic fixity to conceptualize it as dynamic, embedded and temporal. This is allied to changing paradigms of disability as difference, rather than deficit, with recognition that a medical model of diagnois, treatment and cure might not be appropriate to the complexities of developmental psychopathology which is in flux throughout the lifespan. The value of the arts to this process is articulated by Olivia Sagan (2015) in her conceptualization of the "third space," with reference to Lynne Frogett's notion of the node she describes as the "aesthetic third": "[This] contains both something of the individual and something of the world, meaningfully conjoined. It is in the link—the experience of being meaningfully conjoined with a bit of the world—that well being resides" (Frogett, 2011, p. 98, cited in Sagan, 2015, p. 132).

This triangulation in Frogett's account is presented as a structure around which 'social relations and imaginative constructs are generated' with artwork helping people to 'create an embodied, sensual connection to the world outside themselves' (Frogett, 2011, p. 92). The artwork thus provides "a third object between themselves and others that can be shared. By animating, or re-animating, a link between an individual and the cultural field, it enhances their relational capacity" (p. 92). This has important implications for mental wellbeing, as Sagan explains:

> For if art (or its making) functions to provide a third, through which relations can be mobilized and energized, be they relations between one's self and wider cultural experience; between the artist and other(s); between the art work and the group; or the art work and the community—then community or relational (social) art has a further role to play with regard to human well being and flourishing communities (Sagan, 2015, 137).

The aim of this chapter is to elucidate the various ways in which the arts and humanities can complement and enrich scientific (neuropsychological) studies of psychopathology. I will address some of the issues in the study of (developmental) psychopathology that the arts provides insight into. I will use examples that refer to depression (visual art), schizophrenia (theatre) and autism (participatory drama and film) to illustrate a central and recurring point that arts-based activity is a medium through which complex interior worlds can be illuminated and engaged with, facilitating a dialogic and relational approach to psychopathology. The arts as process and as artefact offer a "third space" around which, to use Sagan's terms, "a problematic set of relationships [can] be symbolized and re-configured" (p. 137). The selected case studies are indicative of how the arts can benefit those affected as well as the networks of others who interact with these processes as carers, health professionals, educators or researchers.

## *Head Hand Head*: Embodying and Enacting OCD

In her response to *This Room*, neuroscientist, Emily Holmes describes the piece as:

> An affecting, sobering account of a life shaped by, yet transcending, a mental-health condition and treatment... Dean underwent a technique identified as graded exposure and response prevention. In one riveting scene, she faces her worst fears (standing on chairs placing stockings around her neck) and lets her obsessive thoughts (of hanging) occur, but without trying to neutralize them with compulsions (the checking). Crucially, this happens not on a couch in a clinic, but in Dean's bedroom, with her therapist. The episode movingly captures the bravery of the patient and the skill of the therapist (Holmes, 2015, p. 289).

What is also crucial, I suggest, is that this episode happens in a theatre, performed at Battersea Arts Centre as well as at the Cambridge Science Festival, reviewed in *Nature* and featured in a Horizon TV documentary. Dean developed the play in consultation with a scientific adviser, the neuroscientist Trevor Robbins, who is cited by Holmes: "Laura has interacted with our researchers studying OCD to bring their findings into register with her subjective experience." Having talked to her he feels "even more convinced that researchers should bring together psychological and neuroscientific experiences to improve treatments" (Robbins, cited in Holmes, 2015, p. 289). This is where theatre and performance have an important role to play, as Holmes recognizes, "Dean puts this call to action centre stage by drawing us into her mental world."

The double-voiced articulations of the performer on stage and her recorded and intrusive "unwanted thoughts" offer a harrowing insight into the experience of living with this condition. Supported by the Wellcome Trust and performed at the Maudsley Hospital as well as other arts venues, the piece is indicative of the various roles the arts can play in understanding and elucidating the phenomenology of developmental psychopathology. On one level, the work functions *recreatively* as a *representation* of mental illness, offering access to the mind space of OCD. This is its documentary function, blending the facts of the condition with the fiction of the art form. As an autobiographical piece, performed by the writer (and sufferer), moreover, it crosses boundaries and challenges dualisms, as the person who is physically present on stage is at once author/subject and performer. This creates an illusion of authenticity as the audience are invited to respond to Laura and her symptoms as a truth, rather than as a staged persona. What we see and hear, however, is, nevertheless a rehearsed and carefully crafted script, building upon an earlier version of the piece under a different title and shaped by the directorial, dramaturgical, and design contributions of the production team. Melanie Wilson's sound design contributes to the illusion of authenticity, transporting us into the mental landscape of Laura's condition which we experience "as if" it was real, hearing the voices with her as the intruders in her head. On another level, the piece can be seen to function as a form of therapy for the writer/performer, as the act of writing (and performance) is a means of asserting control over her condition; by giving it a voice, she positions herself as a witness, able to objectify her experience. This is evident in the research question Dean poses, to frame her application for funding: "The objective of this project, using myself as subject is to attempt to answer the question, where does the OCD end and where do I begin?" Indeed, people with mental illness often fight with identifying with the disorder, because they might lose sight of their "true" identity but also because this identity is associated with social stigma and a "spoiled identity" (Hinshaw, 2005, p. 715). Through the research, the writing and the performance, Dean positions herself in relation to the OCD; the theatre offers a means of self-expression, giving her a sense of agency, so that she is not defined by her condition and can see herself as other to it. This then, is the *reparative* role of the arts as a vehicle for *recovery*. For Jennings (1992, p. 1), the "overriding principle behind arts therapies generally and drama therapy in particular is that the arts have always existed to communicate those things which otherwise cannot be expressed." Art therapies (drama, music, visual arts, creative writing, and poetry) are used to access difficult-to-process emotions, enabling victims of trauma, for example, to find a means of engaging with and processing their experience by giving it expression through visual, physical, narrative or musical modalities.

The interplay between the arts as representation, reparation and realization describes the development of Dean's work as it progressed from its first incarnation *Head Hand Head* (2013)[3] to *This Room*. The earlier version presented Dean through a dramatic monologue as the victim who overcame her diagnosis through the intervention of CBT. Her experience of the voices in the head who govern her actions and rituals and the agony of their persistence, is movingly portrayed as Dean, seated for much of the performance, in close proximity to the audience, recounts her symptoms, the diagnosis and referral process and the dialogues with the psychologist who treated her. At the end of the performance, her symptoms have diminished, as evidenced by the diagnostic scores she reads out which confirm her responses as returning to the normal range. An accompanying installation which the audience walk through, contains case notes and associated documentary materials, verifying the documentary authenticity of the piece. In the longer version (*This Room*), the ending is more ambivalent, the symptoms return and the relapse leaves the audience with a more profound sense of the reality of mental health where recovery, is conceived in relational terms, as a process in which the individual positions themself in relation to their condition so they have agency in their movement beyond it, aware of the possibility of its return and knowing the strategies to address this. In this scenario, sickness and wellness are reconceptualized. Rather than being conceived as a linear narrative from illness to cure, *This Room* recognizes the iterative nature of conditions such as OCD and the importance of diagnosis not becoming self-defining.

As a play, Dean's work can be categorized in the context of contemporary performance practice, a form of theatre that is sometimes referred to as the "post dramatic" (Lehmann, 2006) and which emerges from experimental and conceptual art, with a text created through devised (improvisational) methods and which is often more abstract than mainstream dramatic theatre. Contemporary performance stresses liveness, challenging the barriers between performers and audience by emphasizing presence; being "in the moment" as spectators who are conscious of being physically present and actively engaged as partakers. This mode of theatre uses strategies that are non-illusionist, so not based on structures of pretence. Dean's form bears a close relation to her content, creating an immersive and experiential encounter, illustrating how performance art can make visible the phenomenology of the neurodivergent imagination.

## Theorizing Imagination: Blind Spots in Art and Science

The need to move beyond symbolic paradigms of creativity has been referred to by Gregory Minnisale as a "blind spot" in science:

> Conceptual art presents an important challenge for neuroaesthetics. Such art helps to stimulate complex psychological events—beyond the perceptual responses usually studied by neuroscience. If science is to engage meaningfully with art, scientists need to address the conceptual content of our experience of many different kinds of art (Minnisale, 2012, p. 43).

The distinction between the "creative" and "recreative imaginations," as defined by Currie and Ravenscroft, (2003) is indicative of the ways in which psychologists and philosophers engage with this experiential domain, theorizing and evaluating this aspect of cognitive functioning. "Imaginative creativity" is defined as doing things in a new way, whilst the "recreative imagination" is to put ourselves in place of another (theory of mind) and is associated with symbolization: "Let us call the imaginative capacity, whatever it is that underpins perspective-shifting, the recreative imagination. What the recreative imagination is, how it works and what functions it performs are the central questions of [*Recreative Minds*]" (p. 9). Thus autism and schizophrenia, in Currie and Ravenscroft's account, are considered as disorders of the imagination. Schizophrenia is regarded as a failure to introspectively monitor one's own acts of imagination, while autism is considered as a failure of the imagination per se. Both conditions are associated with art. The imagination is described by Roth (2007, p. 9) as a "theoretical and empirical lacuna," so much so that researchers in the cognitive sciences and psychology "have been reluctant to engage directly with the concept[s]." Roth's work on the neuropsychology of autism demonstrates that "much can be learned about the imagination from atypical cases."

"As a scientist," states Barnard (2004, p. 987), "I am challenged by a whole range of deep questions that arise when it come to thinking about cognition and creativity."[4] For Barnard, "our theoretical landscape [has been] dominated by micro-theories of restricted scope" tailored to deal with "particular laboratory phenomena"; theories that refer to separate mental functions that may be separated off in diagnosis but should not be. He warns that "to even approach a level of sufficient adequacy and applicability our theories must inevitably address that complexity [i.e. different mental functions] in one way or another." He suggests a strategy that involves seeking to develop "basic macro-theories of broader scope and a new means of applying them in real world contexts" (p. 987). Barnard challenges traditional dualisms to create a bridging model that conceives of mental architecture as interacting visual, auditory and bodily elements, a paradigm that can also be used as a bridge between neuropsychology and art.

Barnard's (2004) articulation of "bridging practices" between the real world and scientific theory describes not only the craft of clinical practice, but also the practice-based research that was the basis for his work with dancers, particularly Wayne McGregor and Scott deLahunta, whose collaboration with Barnard led to the development of a "choreographic thinking tool" to help dancers overcome habit (deLahunta, Clarke & Barnard, 2012). Interacting Cognitive Subsystems (ICS) provides a comprehensive framework for understanding cognitive–affective interaction and change. It recognizes qualitatively different kinds of information that have different relations to affect, distinguishing between two levels of meaning, one specific the other more holistic, and suggests that the more holistic one is linked to affect. This has been used in relation to conditions of mind including depression, schizophrenia, and eating disorders, helping us to understand how the negative cognitive biases and thought patterns associated with mental illness might be overcome—a remodeling of negative thought. ICS also explains the contrast between hot and cold cognition, "knowing with the head" versus "knowing with the heart," facilitating understanding of the central aspects of psychotherapeutic change. In terms of Barnard's ICS, there are a series of interacting information codes and internal loops contributing to meaning-making:

1. sensory codes (visual, acoustic and proprioceptive) that the audience register as body state sensory inputs, conveyed through the sights, sensors, and sounds of the staging;
2. intermediate codes for speech-level and object information (spoken and recorded text as well as the object information from the stage action);
3. propositional codes ("knowing with the head") arising from conceptual processing of 1 and 2 (meanings that can be expressed verbally and evidenced);
4. implicational codes ("knowing with the heart"), a more abstract level of meaning that is non-verbal and intuitive, the "felt" sense associated with emotional experience.

## Minding the Gaps: Participatory and Relational Approaches to Arts and Health

The emphasis on process, affect, action, and the role of the spectator in the aesthetic experience has been crucial to discussions of the role of the arts to health and wellbeing. Debates about contemporary art, its applications and participatory practices have been central to discussion of the value of the arts in the 21st century as aesthetic or utilitarian practices. Nicolas Bourriaud's concept of relational aesthetics (1998) has been used to challenge the binaries of aesthetics and ethics, art and instrumentalism (Bishop, 2004; Kester, 2004; Shaughnessy, 2012). The spectator becomes a critical component in relational aesthetics through art that concerns itself with creating encounters as non-scripted social interactions, lessening the importance of the author. Bourriaud defines relational aesthetics as "a set of artistic practices which take as their theoretical and practical point of departure the whole of human relations and their social context" (Bourriaud, 2002, p. 14). As we will see below, in my discussion of a drama project with autistic children ("Imagining Autism"), in participatory arts practices, the relations between artist and spectator are changed as the participants become coproducers. Informed by theories of cognitive neuroscience and understanding of cognition as embodied, embedded, extended, and enacted, the Imagining Autism project demonstrated how the multimodalities of performance (engaging interacting physical, auditory, and visual systems) led to insights about the imagination and creativity in autism.

The arts have an extensive and complex relationship with the study of psychopathology and hence play an important role in the context of the rapidly developing field of medical humanities. As Belinda Jack observes in her commentary on the rise of this interdisciplinary area, dialogues and synergies between arts, humanities, and science are evident in the writing of the ancient Greek physician Hippocrates whose statement: "wherever the art of Medicine is loved, there is also a love of Humanity," suggests "both that medicine is an 'art' and that there is a crucial association between medicine and the 'human' dimension of the humanities" (Jack, 2015). The representational function of the arts is often seen as that of a mirror, offering a window onto conditions that are "other" to normative experience. This two-way mirror function has the capacity to enhance understanding of the lived experience of psychopathology for carers/families, health professionals and the wider public, whilst it also provides a means of communication for those affected. Through this articulation it facilitates a potential repositioning in relation to the condition. Crucially, this involves the individual affected having agency in understanding the causes and effects of the condition, facilitated by the professionals who help them create the new scripts that chart the journey towards recovery. This recovery narrative, however, a dominant trope in arts/health contexts, comes with a health warning, as articulated by Sagan (2015), reflecting her interviews with artists who also have histories of mental illness. In her preface, Lynn Frogett draws attention to this aspect:

> The discourse of recovery is strongly normative at times, and can itself take on the aspect of an ideology. The responsibility to recover and be well may be experienced by some as an empowering spur to self-efficacy, but the suffering of those who fail will be stamped with desolation and futility. If the generalization of recovery discourse develops in the absence of a range of mental health resources that offer an individuated approach, including those which allow for the full expression of disturbance and despair, the recovery movement unwittingly aligns with the neo-liberalization of health care. In such a model the withdrawal of public provision demands of individuals an increasing ability to look after themselves and a re-construction of health-care subject as utility-maximizing rational chooser [...] It presupposes a health-care system in which there is little patience and even affordability for the expression of existential crisis and its working through. The re-symbolization of relationship between mind, body and world that art making allows is beyond its scope. Under these conditions arts provision will gain the support of health professionals and policy makers to the extent that it offers a cost-effective route to self-responsibility [...] [T]he voices recorded by Sagan remind us that individuals may frame their illness narratives as "quest" but rather than any simple quest for

> "recovery," or even meaning, *this maybe a quest for the kind of psychosocial integration that allows for a bearable co-existence with one's demons. It may even be here that creativity resides* (Frogett in Sagan, 2015, xvi, my emphasis).

A further function of the arts, then, in relation to developmental psychopathology, can be conceptualized in terms of *realization*, whereby the individual achieves an awareness of their condition as process, rather than diagnostic fixity. In this configuration, the individual is able to position themself in relation to their condition, locating and drawing upon creative resources to explore and articulate the uniqueness of their perceptual (and changing) experience.

At the time of the first approach to write this chapter, the suggested working title was "The Role of the Arts in Developmental Psychopathology," which, I suggest, placed emphasis on the instrumental function of arts practices as vehicles for representation or reparation. My final subtitle, "The Arts and Developmental Psychopathology," is indicative of changing conceptions of medicine as we move towards social and "asset"-based models of health and disability. The medical model is one which regards the individual and the disability as the problems to be addressed, focusing on causes and treatments, while the social model foregrounds society as playing a central role to the experience of disability, acknowledging the need to accommodate and make adjustments for different needs. The social model stresses difference rather than deficit.

In the 21st century, I suggest, the role of the arts is creative, whereby artists as well as art therapists contribute to arts in health practices and where artistry may productively and creatively coexist with psychopathology.

In the case studies below I will consider imaginative cognition within creative processes through selected examples of artistic practices associated with developmental psychopathology. I will discuss how the arts contribute to theoretical understanding of how individuals affected by these conditions express creativity and make meaning. The role of the arts is associated with agency and authorship, a means of moving between and beyond the different aspects of lived experience, harnessing creative resources to bring the cognitive and affective into dialogue. As such it addresses some of the tensions between scientific models of explanation and arts-based approaches that seek to understand first- and third-person perspectives of complex inner lives through creative expression.

## Health Warning: Madness and Creativity

In taking this approach, I am mindful of the risks of romanticizing the disputed relations between creativity and psychopathology. It is unusual for the journal *Nature* to foreground work of this kind, but Holmes's review of *This Room* (as discussed above) also featured in the magazine's editorial with a challenging subheading: "The public's distorted attitude towards mental health conditions hampers their treatment" (*Nature*, March 19, 2015).[5] Citing research published in *Social Science and Medicine* the editorial suggests "stories about people who were successfully treated for depression, schizophrenia and drug addiction reduced negative attitudes towards mental illness in those who heard them… Perhaps here is a way to tackle the stigma of mental illness." There follows, however, a health warning that qualifies this narratological invitation to the arts and humanities:

> In doing so, a powerful cultural myth must be challenged: that mental illness is a gift and comes with benefits. From the supposed enhanced creativity and meaningful visions of those with schizophrenia to the claimed cognitive wizadry and insight of people with autism, mental-health conditions are too often presented as just another way of seeing the world (*Nature,* 19 March 2015).

Whilst aware of the risks of romanticizing associations between creativity and psychological disorder, this chapter takes issue with the dualisms between the typical and atypical (that divide "normal" and "abnormal") to advocate reconceptualizing the complexities of these relationships. As Finlay (2014, p. 121) observes in her definition of the "phenomenological attitude": "the task remains profoundly dialectical: researchers need to straddle subjectivity and objectivity, intimacy and distance, being inside and outside, being a part of and a part from, bracketing the self and being self-aware, and so on." A related position is described by a systemic family therapist who coins the term "informed orienteering" to describe his experience of "navigating systemic positioning dilemmas within the field of anorexia" (Jacobs, 2015). He outlines a dialogic and relational approach in the negotiation of multiple discourses and perspectives that include psychomedical models, feminist perspectives, and the perspectives of the sufferer, with an emphasis on "withness" in the positioning between therapist and the person affected: "I find myself moving between two polarities, often holding more than one in a both/and manner (rather than an either/or dichotomy)." This dialogic therapeutic paradigm with its emphasis on relational contexts, agency, and perspective-taking has parallels with the development of participatory and relational arts approaches and their foregrounding of process and intersubjectivity, as I discuss below.

Three key points that can be taken from the autobiographical performance of *This Room* are firstly, the complexity of the human mind and the limitations of our knowledge of its functioning; secondly, the efficacy of performance for conveying something of the felt and perceptual experience of psychic distress and, finally, the role of the therapist in working with the sufferer, using techniques that have synergies with drama therapy as they involve an acting out of the fears and behaviors experienced by the affected individual in a safe and supported environment. Theatre, as both accounts in *Nature* indicate, offers a window into the mind, a visceral space for exploring identities in flux. The fictional space also offers a means to rehearse, to play with the imagined obsessions so that the sufferer can position herself differently *in relation* to the thoughts, recognizing the difference between the imagined and the real. In graded Exposure and Response Prevention (ERP), the individual gradually (step by step) confronts the problem:

> It works by breaking the link between your obsessional thoughts, images, urges or impulses and the compulsive things that you do to reduce the distress or anxiety that they cause. During ERP exercises you gradually expose yourself to situations that bring on or cue your obsessions, whilst not carrying out your compulsions (Chellingsworth, 2014, p. 5).

Questions that continue to dominate scientific discussion are concerned with how we understand the mind and our capacity to change thinking in conditions that cause psychological distress. In this chapter, I suggest that the arts have much to contribute to scientific understanding of the embodied mind and also have the capacity to change our thinking and perception through experience and action. For the neuroscientist Francisco Varela, the blind spot in the cognition sciences of the 20th century is that we do not have a method of properly accessing experience.[6] Developments in cognitive science have facilitated understanding of mental processes and representations, but accessing interior worlds continues to challenge scientists, and this is what has led researchers such as Holmes (2015) to turn to art.[7] She describes herself as a cognitive scientist and clinical psychologist who is curious about mental imagery. Indeed, there is evidence that that visual imagery can have a more powerful impact on emotion than its verbal counterpart. She works with drawing to explore, understand, and intervene in mental health conditions with particular reference to depression and trauma. Her work demonstrates that "an imagery focus" can open treatment innovations that help mood stability in bipolar disorder as well as generating new methods to prevent emotional images after trauma. Butler and Holmes (2009) describe pictures drawn at the start of therapy by clients who have experienced child abuse, enabling them to summarize, reconceptualize, and articulate their experience. Techniques such as Imagery Rescripting combine mental imagery with verbalization to help individuals transform their relation to and understanding of experiences, so that negative images can be recast as positive and new positive images can be constructed to rescript negative schemas.

Arts-based trauma therapies frequently draw upon psychoanalysis as a theoretical paradigm (and it is interesting to note recent efforts to integrate psychoanalysis into a neuroscientific framework; e.g., Damasio, 2012; Ramus, 2013). The experience is relegated to the unconscious as a failure of language and memory. By retrieving it through arts practice, the trauma is expressed and through its articulation there is release. In psychotherapeutic theoretical paradigms, the mind is conceived in relation to and arising from "the developmental experiences of the body" (Klin & Jones, 2007, p. 6) so that trauma can be held in the body. The paradox, however, as articulated by Klin and Jones, is that "although psychoanalysis focuses a great deal on instinctual needs and responses to the world, it shies away from dealing with the basic unit of its philosophy – that is how bodily sensations and experiences become symbolic tools" (p. 6). Klin and Jones explore the relations between psychodynamic theory and developmental science, areas that have rarely engaged in dialogue. In the arts, however, there is understanding of the dynamic interplay between mind and body, and of knowledge emerging through interactions between bodies and environments. Action and representation are similarly perceived as connected. In the so-called "cognitive turn," arts and humanities scholars have increasingly looked to cognitive neuroscience to conceptualize these processes (Buckland, 2007; Garrett, 2016; Shaughnessy, 2013a, b; Zunshine, 2015). The "4E" view of cognition as embodied, embedded, enactive, and extended (Menary, 2010; Ward & Stapleton, 2012) offers a useful formulation of the embodied mind-in-society, its inseparability from language and feeling (Lakoff & Johnson, 2003), and the key features that connect performance and theatre with cognitive science (Blair & Cook, 2016; Kemp, 2012; Lutterbie, 2011; McConachie, 2006).[8] Sensorimotor and semantic understanding are linked with body/action and language, through the physical (embodied), sensory interactions with environmental affordances and stimuli (embedded), connections beyond the individual to the social and interpersonal (extended and ecological) and the links between action and perception (enacted). As Cook (2007, p. 262) suggests, "language is less a system of *communicating* experience than actually *being* experience; we do not translate words into perceptions, we perceive in order to understand." This shifts our understanding beyond arts as representation or reparation towards the realization and relational paradigms of meaning-making as a process of dialogue and exchange rather than a "single instantaneous state of insight" (Kester, 2004, p. 12). As Rhonda Blair (in Levinson, 2005, p. 709) has observed, imagining, doing, and understanding use the same neural substrates: "The image points toward possibilities for action; they are physically, objectively linked in our brains [...]These images are not end points, but tools for creativity and experiencing." Blair's comments on the implications for the teaching of actor training are also pertinent to therapeutic approaches to neuropsychology; "it is about prompting creative responses, not about excavating the psychologically repressed from one's tiny 'cupboard' of personal history." "The '"I" may have begun with "you"' hypothesis provides an image, a touchstone to focus actors on the fact that what they do is fundamentally dependent upon by what those around them are doing." Connection is crucial as our minds and bodies affect each other. Andy Clark's work on the "extended mind" (Clark, 2008) similarly suggests that we should not treat creativity as a state of the mental interior; as Gerald Levinson has summarized, "The artist's sketch pad can extend her creativity in the same way that the diary entry extends her memory" (Levinson, 2005).

This means, as we will see in the examples below, that the arts can help to situate psychopathologies beyond individuals, rather than seeing them wholly as a manifestation of inner experience.

## Beyond Words: Bobby Baker

The potential of visual art and mental imagery to engage with complex interior worlds and psychological distress is evident in the work of the UK artist, Bobby Baker. Having trained as a fine artist, Baker was drawn to performance and live art as she sought to find appropriate forms for her explorations of identity, the body, and mental illness. Her use of food and domestic items as a feature of her artistic palette has attracted considerable interest and acclaim as she works with the found materials of everyday life to create live art in which thinking, feeling, and sensing are conjoined. Her work intuitively links perception and action, a manifestation of the 4E's view as representation becomes dependent on physical, perceptual systems through the hybridity of her art. In 1996, Baker was diagnosed with borderline personality disorder and alongside (and in dialogue with) her career as a performance artist, she turned to visual art as a documentation of her mental and physical suffering and recovery. Published as *Diary Drawings: Mental Illness and Me* (2010), these offer insights into an interior world in chaos and flux, a mind that is affected by and affects those around her. The drawings make visible the invisible, functioning as the "third space" Sagan and Froggett conceptualize (Sagan, 2015), an object through which relational connections can be made. To use the words of Baker's daughter, the psychologist Dora Whittuck, *Diary Drawings* demonstrate that "true collaboration" is a key to "great change" (Baker, 2010, p. 219). The drawings, as I discuss below, are a key to this collaboration, facilitating dialogue with Baker and understanding of her relationship to and experience of her condition. As such, the drawings function as an "aesthetic third." This is the basis for the cognitive and affective engagement with the subjective experience of psychopathology that takes us beyond the knowledge provided through scientific study:

> Her figure is arched so far backwards that her feet and head are on the same level. Her hands are clasped together as if in prayer, and the rest of the image is filled with tears, flooding up over her human hill. There is so much sorrow here that it almost makes us laugh. And as we absorb its full impact, like so many of these drawings, having been both wretched and funny, it maybe also strikes us as haunting, wise, moving, angry, loving (p. 1).

As her career as a performance artist flourished through her unique blend of autobiography, storytelling, stand-up comedy and live art, her eccentric professional persona masked the chaos of her private inner life, causing her to seek refuge or be hospitalized in a variety of psychiatric treatment centers. The account of her journey towards recovery is positioned in what is referred to as the "intersection between art and madness" so that it might be regarded as both a representation of psychopathology for those on the outside and a reparation for Baker herself, whose art served a therapeutic purpose as well as being an aesthetic medium. Whilst it is remarkable that Baker continued to devise and perform her one-woman shows as a live artist in the midst of severe mental health episodes, her drawings were not originally conceived as public art. Nevertheless, as is evident in Arnold's description, the diary drawings have a powerful poignancy that moves the viewer through images that operate on a number of levels, blending terrorizing mental trauma (self-harm, paranoia, severe depression) with comedy through her self-deprecating caricatures that objectify her condition/experience. The exaggeration of Baker's physical features (long face, prominent chin) that we associate with caricature intensifies, rather than diminishes the experience. The laughter generated, however, is shared *with* the artist, rather than directed at Baker's parodies of herself and the medical establishment.

The drawings are structured chronologically in seventeen stages, progressing from her first self-referral to a day care center in 1997, through multiple psychiatric admissions in a variety of settings. The final drawing, "The Daily Stream of Consciousness," dated August 25, 2008 is an image of serenity and empowerment: a bold head and shoulders portrait of a woman who has grown in stature and self-belief, her body supporting the tiny figures who play around and upon her shoulders and facial contours. The drawings begin with expressions of self imprisonment, isolation, entrapment, self mutilation, destructive fantasy, and despair. Day 7 is a severed ear with the handwritten caption "murder method 2" (p. 24), Day 8 is the poignant veil of blue tears (described above) concealing the hunched figure in "the start of the weeping" p. 25), while day 10 is "a tragic drawing" depicting the spread eagled nudity of Baker's body etched with blood red crosses, and a flesh-colored heart shape covering the vagina; "I love its simple beauty and it stopped me self-harming for a while" (p. 27). A series of self -portraits, contain repeated features such as two mouths, blood-drenched hallucinations and bodies splitting to convey fragmenting identity. The phantoms of mental illness are graphically depicted in various guises, the monster in the mirror (day 25, p. 35), the tiny demons that taunt her and, later, the paranoia of the women in purple fleeces who spy on her (day 574, p. 157 and day 575. p. 158). As the drawings progress, other figures become more frequent as Baker depicts the networks of relations (positive and negative) that contribute to her experience and to her recovery.

The drawings convey the complexity of these often fraught and tense relationships to include their breakdowns. "My Psychotherapist" has attracted particular attention for its representation of Baker's clinician as "a cartoon-style scary witch with long talons." This is not her attack on the NHS, she explains but "*was simply a way for me to make private fun of a frustrating situation*" (p. 211). The captions are important and revealing as contextualizations of the work. As the diary progresses, the moods and colors change, with the despair being more frequently accompanied by poignant, comic and positive representations and comments. There is anger and frustration; Day 561 is a head containing printed paper cut-outs, fragments of lines taken from her ten-page letter to the mental health trust (p. 154) while day 598 shows an oversize back overwhelmed by her huge shadow, as little green and purple men laugh and point in derision (p. 162). Her caption provides explanation, "*Thanks a bunch Dr—Off you go to your SENIOR JOB 'well we never thought medication was helping you.' 5 years of obesity as a result. Even my fucking shadow is fat.*" Baker's figure is frequently presented in stark and comic contrast to the health professionals working with her. She alternates from a huge monster facing a small but perfectly formed consultant, with coordinated suede shoes (Day 532, p. 135) to a diminutive green but baggy elf, cowering at the onslaught from a "big bully ward manager" (Day 547, p. 145). The captions are indicative that although Baker, on occasions, felt belittled, humiliated and objectified as a service user, she also experienced compassion, understanding and empathy from those who worked "with" her (rather than the experts who only observed her "patient" status, applying treatments "to" the behaviors and symptoms presented). The death of her mother and her experience of breast cancer are poignantly conveyed, as well as the changing face of her public persona as Baker's growing reputation as performance artist led to her experiencing a celebrity status as an icon of feminist performance art. The drawings reveal the split between the interior world of psychic distress and the public staged identity as a live art comedienne par excellence (p. 142). The diary is an iterative account, charting with honesty the nonlinear pathway towards "recovery" from mental illness, with each relapse and hospitalization, a progression towards the realization that no amount of medication or therapy can provide a cure: "I realized I had to take things into my own hands from now on" (p. 139). Baker holds the key to her imprisonment and release, as evidenced in the drawing of herself imprisoned, too big for the container that traps her, clutching in despair the bars that are constructed as mini versions of herself, standing one on top of the other. Stage 12, post-discharge is a series of furious and funny drawings of housework (a tumble drier body, hoover legs, broom arms and bin head, p. 150) a family holiday and exhaustion (in bed, p. 152 and at the gym, p. 155) as she fights and finds her way to health: "my planned major skills for recovery were to be exercise, a healthy diet and writing, writing, writing" (p. 150). Towards the end of the drawings as Baker's journey draws to an end, the images become more self-contained, the closed container images are replaced by the open scenes of peace and freedom as recovery from cancer also brings release. Stage 17 consists of only two drawings, simple and intimate, the one showing Baker in bed, "ill but happy" and the next, the penultimate image of two shadows, the figures of Baker and her husband holding hands on a beach (on the anniversary of her father's death), looking towards a sunset.

The empathy provoked by this work involves us being in a position of witness to the suffering represented, aware of it as "other" to us, but also aware of its relationship to ourselves through the felt responses it generates. The aesthetic experience is, I suggest, an important (and overlooked) feature of the arts and psychopathologies. Yet this affective capacity (the qualities that move us) is how knowledge is generated and embodied. Whittuck (Baker, 2010, p. 219), articulates this relational aspect of her mother's work: "in those early years I found the images of her work strangely comforting; they were a confirmation of what I suspected but wasn't meant to know. Despite the horror and pain that they often expressed, they also helped to stop my fears from spiraling[…] For me the drawings became a record, a basis for us to talk, and an antidote to isolation." In this configuration, the art is positioned in an intermedial space, between the m/other (as artist and as sufferer) and the daughter who is seeking to communicate and to understand. The art serves a relational function " the drawings are of course my mother's story, and they offer a window to eleven years of her life, but they also tell a story of us as a family (her, my father, my brother and me) and some of the events that significantly shaped our lives while she was unwell" (p. 216). This is a recovery narrative, but in the Bakhtinian sense (Bakhtin, 1981) whereby psychopathology can be regarded as a temporal, relational and changing process (in lifecourse, relationships, and environment). A dialogic approach involves three elements: an utterance, a reply, and the relationship between the two, where the relationship is the most important element. Each voice is equally valid, and the narratives are produced by multiple characters in accordance with Bakhtin's theory of polyphony (Bakhtin, 1984). For Baker, visual art was the "third object," to use Sagan's terms (2015), a dialogic encounter; and the concept of dialogism and the questions around the value of Baker's art as an aesthetic practice and/or therapeutic medium brings me to a consideration of these dualisms and the relations between them through a play that explores schizophrenia and dialogic therapy.

## Arts Applications and their Discontents: Aesthetic and Socially Engaged

Jan Cohen Cruz emphasizes the relational aspect of socially engaged theatre, as Gareth White summarizes:

> the engagement and the relational influences face in both directions, so that the art and artist are transformed by those they engage with, as well as being the catalyst for change themselves. And an understanding of aesthetics that serves this purpose needs to face in two directions too: it needs to show how art can be "'real' knowledge" in its own right, and at the same time remain a tool of social and personal change (White, 2015, p. 5).

This facing in two directions is aptly demonstrated in *The Eradication of Schizophrenia in Western Lapland* (Haynes & Woods, 2014), a play devised by the UK-based theatre company Ridiculusmus (Jon Haynes and David Woods) and which offers a particularly pertinent example of theatre interacting with neuropsychology. The novel staging creates a form appropriate to the content and determines the audience's experience, helping us to sense and make sense of the internal world of schizophrenia:

> *Setting*
>
> Audience members are arranged on either side of a wall. Acts One and Three of the play are performed on each side of the wall simultaneously. Each audience can hear both sides

> but can see only one. One of the sides—the "domestic side'—is set five to ten years in the past. Mum is presenting psychotic symptoms, her eldest son Richard has left for university and the younger son Rupert has become her nurse. The act on the other side, the "public side," takes place in the present and features a psychiatrist treating Richard at the same hospital in which Mum is a long-stay patient. The audiences change sides at the interval and acts one and three are repeated. The audience see the acts they have heard but not yet seen. The dividing wall changes into a transparent antechamber for the final act (act two), both audiences seeing what happens within simultaneously (p. 7).

Described as "the play that wants to change the way we view mental health," the production is informed by the Finnish "Open Dialogue" approach to therapeutic intervention for psychosis. Whilst the split staging and structure contribute to the audience's insight into the experience of psychic distress, the dialogic therapy that has transformed approaches to acute psychosis in Finland (a network-based language approach to psychiatric care) is endemic to the play's conceptualization. Form and content coalesce as the dramatization of Bakhtin's concepts of polyphony and dialogism facilitate understanding of psychosis in terms of relational factors, as process, in flux and enacted. The play explores the interactions between the family members (Rupert, Richard, Mum and Dad and the stepmother, Jade) and the Doctor treating Richard through a series of comic and absurd juxtapositions, plunging the audience into a hallucinatory world where any sense of reality is suspended in a staging that insists on the "tolerance of uncertainty," one of the principles of Open Dialogue theory and part of the contract between performers and audience. We are uncertain about whose reality we are witnessing, who is mad and who is sane, whether the sons are children or adults, whether the Doctor is or isn't a patient and, at the end of the play, who is dead or alive.

The systems theory informing this radical therapy and understanding of the dynamic relations between brain, body and environment are endemic to the principles and practices of cognitive approaches to performance. In *The Eradication of Schizophrenia*, we are witness to and find ourselves laughing at/with a staging of acute psychosis, something that would not normally be considered as a laughing matter. This, in itself, positions us differently towards the subject matter. The influence of the theoretical principles underpinning communication approaches to psychosis contributes to the "real" knowledge imparted by the play. Gregory Bateson's pioneering work on the concept of "double-bind" communication is played out in the paradoxical familial encounters and the reality of their unreality. As Bateson summarizes, "the most useful way to phrase double-bind description is not in terms of binder and a victim but in terms of people caught up in an ongoing system which produces conflicting definitions to the relationship and consequent subjective distress" (1962, p. 42). In the polyphonic uncertainty of Ridiculusmus's staging, there is no clear sense of family or patients being the cause of the psychosis or objects of treatment; the play constitutes an alternative reality (or realities), creating a "heteroglossia," to use Bakhtin's term:

> meaning is not fixed and intrinsic, although words carry traces and fragments of meanings from our diverse linguistic heritage. Since meaning occurs only in an ongoing exchange, the speaker and listener are intimately joined together in making sense of the psychotic episode. The therapeutic process requires creative participation in language that attends not only to what people say, but also to the existing feelings and sensuous responses that flow between them. Within the dialogical borderland where the person,

> the important others and the professionals meet, a language for suffering may be born that can give the suffering a voice (Seikkula & Olson, 2003, p. 409).

This goes to the heart (and mind) of contemporary arts practices in relation to neuropsychology as borne out in this example of a play's staging of schizophrenia and the multiple subjects and voices of the Open Dialogue therapeutic framework. The play's split staging is itself indicative of its facing in two directions (as appropriate to the subject matter), as aesthetic and ethical. At the centre, however, are the audience who physically move between the domestic and clinical settings, thereby shifting between the lived experience and "real world behavior" of the domestic environment and the clinical and therapeutic contexts of the psychiatric unit on the "public" side. It is the audience who crosses the boundaries between the two worlds to create meaning.

## "Imagining Autism"

In my final example, I focus on work that is categorized as "applied theatre," thereby more readily equated with the "ethical" as it is produced in educational, social and community contexts. This has led to debates about the role and purpose of the art and artists involved in creative practices where participants are co-producers. In settings where the arts are used to engage with neuropsychology, there are questions about how far the arts function therapeutically and whether or not this means renders them "non-aesthetic" (Shaughnessy, 2012; White, 2015). My discussion considers how drama and film have been used to engage with the psychopathology of autism with reference to a UK research project, "Imagining Autism" and an associated film documentary (2013).[9] In atypical cognitive functioning, as discussed above, there are differences in how individuals perceive and interpret their environments. It has been suggested that individuals on the autism spectrum perceive the world as it "really is" rather than as being imbued by prior experiences, and that "this could help to explain the range and idiosyncrasy of sensory sensitivities and their difficulties dealing with new experiences." Differences in perceptual processing have also been linked to areas of ability and special talent in autism. Ockelford (2013) advances the convincing thesis that autistic children are affected by what he defines as "an Exceptional Early Cognitive Environment, similar to that experienced by blind children, and with the same potential to promote high levels of musical interest and development." Citing the relatively high proportion of autistic children with perfect or absolute pitch (1 in 20), he suggests that variances in sensory input during early childhood development create different neural networks. This may well lead to higher levels of sensory awareness, which might then be nurtured as abilities in conjunction with support for areas of deficit. People with autism, Francesca Happé has suggested, have considerable potential for originality as they are not wired to "follow the herd" (Preface to Ockelford, 2013):

> It is notable that typically developing (TD) children lose aspects of originality in, for example, their art as a result of acquiring stereotyped forms from their peers (think, for example, of rays drawn on a sun or birds drawn as "ticks"), Without doubt, the obligatory and automatic recognition of others' mental states ... places blinkers on most TD young people.[...]Thus, individuals with ASC are, perhaps more able than TD individuals

> to think their own thoughts, regardless of what others think. Whilst this contributes to originality, in the sense of a unique "world view," however, it does not "guarantee talent" (Happé & Frith, 2010, p. 3).

The cognitive processes described by Armstrong and Detweiler-Bedell (2008), lend support to the "priors" theory, indicating that a-priori knowledge can inhibit imaginative thinking: "In 'ordinary' cognition [it is suggested] a person smothers uncertainty with a familiar concept to avoid confusion. During free play, a person contemplates a novel stimulus while holding prior understandings at bay, to expand his or her knowledge structures" (p. 320).

Autism is a complex and multifaceted condition that has attracted considerable scientific interest since its early definitions in the work of Kanner (1943) and Asperger (1944). It was first characterized by the Swiss psychiatrist Eugen Bleuler, who used the term in his study of schizophrenia to describe social isolation and withdrawal into a fantasy world. "Autistic thinking" in Bleuler's account is equated with an excess of imagination and hallucinations arising from the desire to escape from reality. The reconceptualization of autism through the work of Kanner and Asperger shifted understanding to focus on difficulties in social interaction and social imagination. Kanner describes what is often referred to as "classic autism," characterized by profound difficulties in language, communication, empathy, and socialization. Asperger's "autistic psychopathy" refers to what is now regarded as "high-functioning" autism where structural language capabilities are in the normal range, or even above average, but conversation will be one-sided (reflecting pragmatic language difficulties) in conjunction with associated traits such as obsessive interests, limited eye contact, unusual gait, and an absence of humor. Wing's (1996) concept of an autism spectrum reconceptualized the condition as multifaceted with areas of ability as well as deficit. Definitions of autism continued to shift through reformulations that were linked to diagnostic categories, rather than observing individual behavior, as Bonnie Evans has discussed (2013, 2016). In spite of several decades of research, autism attracts attention as continues to attract attention as a psychopathology that continues to perplex cognitive science and is arguably misunderstood. The potential of the arts to enhance understanding of autism is evident in the work of autistic artists such as the British savant Stephen Wiltshire, the animal scientist Temple Grandin (and her oft-cited "thinking in pictures"; 1995, 2006) as well as autistic contributions to the "outsider art" movement (Cardinal, 1972). More recently, collections such as *Drawing Autism* (2009) reveal imagination and creativity across the spectrum, offering insight into the rich interior lives of people experiencing this condition. Current research is seeking to draw attention to the phenomenology of the imagination in autism, the subjective experience of perceiving differently and the felt reality beyond the stereotypes (Loftis, 2015; Murray, 2008; Osteen, 2008; Roth, 2007).

"Imagining Autism" was an interdisciplinary collaboration between Drama and Psychology at the University of Kent. (2011–14).[10] The project investigated the potential of drama to be used as an intervention for autism to facilitate communication, social interaction, and imagination. How far could participatory performance practices impact upon these areas of deficit, often referred to as the "triad of impairments" in autism? As these three areas are fundamental to performance practice (what we refer to as the drama "triad" of communication, interaction and imagination), the central hypothesis was that exposure to a program of practical workshops could effect positive change, facilitating language, sociability, empathy (theory of mind), and creativity. Performance, we speculated (with interacting bodily, auditory, temporal, and spatial elements), was a means of accessing the cognitive, physical and perceptual processing involved in autism as an atypical neuropsychology. The embodied qualities of participatory, immersive performance create an opening into the autistic child's world. Since the highly visual, kinetic, and aural qualities of autistic perception are also the qualities of contemporary performance, the project also investigated how drama might help us to understand the imagination in relation to autism.

The psychologists led the evaluation of the project (Beadle-Brown et al., 2017), developing a range of measures to assess the responses of the participants (22 children with a diagnosis of autism) and to measure any changes in their behavior and autistic symptoms. As in other intervention evaluations, the main outcome variable was the Autism Diagnostic Observation Schedule (ADOS; Lord et al., 2000). In addition, the evaluation used measures of theory of mind, imitation, emotion recognition, as well as observations of spontaneous social activity and play and ratings by parents and staff of attention, social engagement, communication, and play-based activities. The practise-based methods involved a series of immersive installations, contained within the "pod," a portable tent like structure (functioning like an interactive multisensory room). The "environments" (forest, arctic, outer space, under water, under the city), were designed to facilitate communication (verbal and physical), social interaction (with practitioners and peers), imagination (participating in fictional frameworks), and creativity (through improvisation). Working in conjunction with performers, autistic participants (in groups of four, aged 7–12) encountered a range of stimuli, triggers, and responsive technologies including physical action, puppetry, lighting, sound, costume and masks, digital media (e.g. live feed), and responsive technologies. These elements were designed to help participants develop "felt" understanding through experiential, physical, and immersive media. The approach emphasized the importance of presence and "being" (rather than acting) as a means to work intuitively and creatively. The multisensory environments were highly stimulating (in contrast to the prevalence of low-arousal learning environments for autism), whilst the participatory and process based approaches emphasized autonomy, authorship, and offered a license to play creatively (often overlooked post-diagnosis). Psychologists were able to establish preliminary proof of concept that the methods positively impacted upon language, social interaction, empathy, and imagination. The research is leading to new understandings of the imagination in autistic children and of how it is differently inflected from the neurotypical child, particularly in terms of visual and auditory perceptual processes, awareness of time and space, physical and verbal modes of creative expression, and responses to objects and interactive media (Trimingham & Shaughnessy, 2016).

A further element of this practise-based research was the collaboration with a film artist, Sarah Turner, to create an experimental film documentary exploring the imagination in autism.[11] As the work developed, the participants emerged as codevisers and performers, authors and choreographers. This interaction between contemporary performance and film moved beyond an illustrative documentary project to find new perceptual vocabularies appropriate to the articulation of atypical cognitive experience. The dialogue between contemporary modes of participatory performance and experimental film produced a dynamic relationship between form and content, while the creative and conceptual process can be analysed in terms of Barnard's "bridging" model of the interactions between creative mental processes. As a model which bridges disciplines, particularly interactions between arts and science, Barnard's theorization is particularly pertinent to the practices engaged in "Imagining Autism." The film, like the "pod" (the tent structure containing the performance environments) is positioned in between the social realities of the neuro typical world and the atypical cognitive and perceptual experience of autism. Within the pod, we were situated in the now/here of nowhere, the special time of performance, conceptualized in terms of "presence" in contemporary theatre, whereby performance is about itself, spectators are participants and realist modes of representation are supplanted by alternative modes of perception. The film's aesthetic engages with the neurodivergent aesthetic as a piece that reflects upon itself.

The distinction between a theatre that merely reflects or imitates the world, and one that instead refashions or extends the world, offers one method for distinguishing categories of performance (Bailes, 2011, p. 27). Moreover, the collaboration between the multimodalities of experimental film and performance are particularly and peculiarly appropriate to exploring the strangeness of perception and imagination in autism. As Arthur P. Shimamura (2013) has summarized with reference to Rudolf Arnheim's pioneering insights in *Film and Art*, "[He] attempted to justify film as an art form because it alters our views of the world and thus *fails* to render an exact copy of the real world[...] Arnheim considered dissolves, cross cuts and point of view editing as ways of creating an illusion of space and time that was different from the way we perceive real space and time" (p. 11). The filmic techniques developed through avant-garde and experimental film, move beyond traditional "movie schema," Shimamura continues to "act as commentaries on the film process itself" and/or to "*offer interpretations of mental processes*[...] *through unorthodox narrative techniques.* These movies define and describe the movie process through the process itself" (my emphases). This describes the work of the film's auteur, Sarah Turner, whose immersive and durational vocabularies create experiential cinematics. The self-reflexive qualities Shimamura describes are fundamental to the aesthetics of the *Imagining Autism* film documentary as it explores and realizes the phenomenology of the autistic experience.

The Beckettian qualities of the film are part of its "beautiful otherness," to borrow the terminology used by Happe and Frith to refer to autism. The children climb in and out of dustbins in the Under the City environment, transforming objects from found materials in a post-apocalyptic urban wasteground as they interact with the strange human inhabitants of this underworld as well as its rats. Beckettian slapstick and clowning is performed by practitioner snowmen in the Arctic environment, a minimalist white landscape in which the strangeness of clown language and physical humor are the performance vocabularies used. Incongruity is also a defining feature of both the film and the process it is documenting. According to Todd Berliner, incongruity in film enables "creative insights that more unified narratives do not, insights that logic, scrutiny and the practicalities of the real world inhibit" (Berliner, 2013, p. 204). The film mimics the playful processes of the project, leaving the gaps Berliner identifies, to "encourage the viewer to imagine answers to questions posed" so that the audience for the film are creatively engaged as participants in an "attempt to understand [subjects] that elude understanding (p. 205)."

Structurally, the film has an exposition which contextualizes the work, a substantial middle movement in which filmed sequences interact with commentary taken from presentations in ways which create dialogues between different voices rather than film being used illustratively. In this middle section, the film seeks to immerse the audience, engaging them affectively through the voices and perspectives of the autistic participants; the camera focuses on the tactile aspects of the environments, looking through material gauze, snowflakes, and the rippling blue satin of the wave material that transports us into the underwater of the environments; shots from odd angles explore the children's point of view. The denouement is the revelation of the affect of the project on its participants, focusing on a twelve-year-old boy who becomes the film's protagonist, finding his voice through a microphone and rapping to the audience's applause in the climactic closing sequence.

What can be gleaned from the film is, I suggest, is an insight into the processes involved in perceiving differently and an articulation of the creative imagination as an aesthetic medium associated with the highest levels of original thinking. This involves challenging the hierarchies suggested by Currie and Ravenscroft (2003) between creative and recreative as we see language ("cognition at its most complex") and movement making meaning together, a "triangulation between the phenomenological, psychological and neurological" (Smith, 2011) and a synthesis that integrates the perspectives of psychodynamic theory (the "embodied psychoanalysis" advocated by Klin & Jones, 2007) with cognitive science. The interdisciplinary challenges articulated by Klin and Jones are precisely what Imagining Autism sought to address: "In mainstream science, we constrain experiments to simple variables in explicit designs that abstract and isolate capacities that otherwise could not be measured. The [enactive mind] framework would push us in the other direction. We should take the world as it is, embracing the individual's recreation of that world, while making a concerted effort to develop methods that capture and quantify that complexity" (2007, p. 29). They suggest the arts may have a role to play here: "By taking [an] artistic perspective, I think we'll begin to grasp just how different [autism's] internal world is" (Klin & Jones, 2007).

## Conclusion: Opening Dialogues between Neuropsychologies, the Arts and Neuroscience

The polyvocal and affective potential of contemporary arts vocabularies, as evident in the examples featured in this chapter, distribute perception across theoretical thinking and practice. Artistic discourses in relation to developmental psychopathology enable us to contextualize the developmental nature of these conditions as processes. Whilst the scientific stance is to observe and measure, arts-based approaches are a means to engage and interact, creating knowledge that is not possible through the science on its own. As Tim Ingold writes "whether our concern is to inhabit this world or to study it …and at root these are the same, since all inhabitants are students and all students inhabitants—our task is not to take stock of its contents but to *follow what is going on*, tracing the multiple trails of becoming, wherever they lead" (Ingold, 2011, p. 15). Cognitive neuroscience and the 4E's approach provide a theoretical framework in which to reconceptualize dynamic interactions between mind–body–world, to facilitate new understanding of the embodied mind-in-society and to rethink representational metaphors. Creative approaches to neuropsychologies through the arts facilitate new cross-disciplinary perspectives and positionings, such as those associated with the "Open Dialogue," model, placing symptoms "outside the person rather than seeing them as a manifestation of inner experience." This is part of the "realization" (and hence transportational or transformational) potential of the arts and is evident in Bobby Baker's work and the theatre of Ridiculusmus; the artwork helps to position the individual and their surrounding networks of relations in a different relationship to the condition and diagnosis, so that it ceases to be self-defining, becoming other to their personhood, thereby creating possibilities for change. As I have discussed, there are parallels between participatory and relational aesthetics and new approaches to treatment based on dialogic practices. The changing hierarchies between therapists and clients and relational understandings of family and patients as agents of change with a forum and language for their experience is analogous to the shifting relations between artist and spectator (elsewhere referred to as "spect/actor" or "partaker"). These practices address tensions between scientific models of explanation and arts approaches that seek to understand first- and third-person perspectives through creative expression, creating opportunities for "walking in the shoes of the other." Psychosis, from a social constructionist perspective is described by Seikkula & Olsen (2003, p. 409) as "a temporary, radical and terrifying alienation from shared, communicative practices: a 'no-man's land' where unbearable experience has no words and, thus, the patient has no voice and no genuine agency" (Seikkula and Olsen, 2003). A Bakhtinian dialogic approach is a "voice making, identity-making, agentic activity" occurring jointly between people. As evident in Bobby Baker's work in particular, creative practices also function dialogically, creating similar opportunities for remaking "the relationships that construct the self and social world" (Seikkula & Olson, 2003, p. 409). Open Dialogue is described as the "game without an author" with its emphasis on listening, analogous to some forms of participatory performance, as evident in the autism project where the concept of authorship is called into question; audiences and participants become coproducers. For Sikkula and Olson, "Open Dialogue allows every person to enter the conversation in his or her own way" and "with no attempt to uncover a particular truth"; this is also true of the participatory performance and the relational aesthetics associated with such practices: audiences have agency as creators of meaning with the capacity "to make changes and contribute to the work, which means that their experience and responses become part of the aesthetic of the performance" (Breel, 2015). Both contemporary art practices and Open Dialogue approaches are predicated upon postmodernist paradigms, informed by Derridean desconstructionist philosophical perspectives so that there is no "essence rigorously independent of that which transports it" (Derrida, 1971, p. 229) and hence "no conception of truth or reality that can be known as separate from and outside human expression" (Seikkula & Olson, 2003, p. 410). In the conclusion to their discussion of "the open dialogue approach to acute psychosis: its poetics and micropolitics," Seikkula and Olson cite Gregory Bateson: "if this pathology can be warded off or resisted, the total experience may promote creativity" (Bateson, 1962, p. 242). The Open Dialogue approach, they suggest "is a way of resisting the experience of "pathology." It builds a "transformative dialogue" within a social network (Gergen & McNamee, 2000). As the examples discussed above demonstrate, the arts function in related (and relational) ways, challenging the closure of traditional pathologizing discourse, giving voice to the inexpressible (polyphony, dialogism) and opening minds to more creative possibilities. I close with a final citation taken from Ridiculusmus's *Eradication of Schizophrenia*, as the arts have the last word:

> Act Three—Clarity
>
> FOUR VOICES: We are a polyphony of voices.
> We are who we are because
> We listen to all voices in the group
> And adhere to basic principles.
> Tolerance of uncertainty is one.
> A new approach to psychiatric care's emerged
> In which the basic elements of dialogue
> Can lead to healing or,
> If you don't like that word,
> To positive change.
> What we want to do is
> Open up the boundaries
> And integrate family perspectives
> Into psychotherapy

## Notes

1 *This Room* (2015), is a play by Laura Jane Dean (unpublished script), developed from an earlier piece, *Head Hand Head* and funded by the Wellcome Trust. It has been performed at various venues to include Battersea Arts Centre, the Maudsley Hospital and the Cambridge Festival of Science. See http://laurajanedean.com/thisroom

2 Dean's 2013 Wellcome Trust Arts Award Application. Correspondence with the author.

3 *Head Hand Head* (2013/14) was initially presented as a work in progress at the Aphra Theatre, University of Kent and subsequently performed at Battersea Arts Centre, London, March 21–22, 2014. See http://laurajanedean.com/head-hand-head.Retrieved December 12, 2016.

4 Philip Barnard, 'Bridging Art and Science: Little pictures and bigger ones.' Lecture presented to the University of Kent, May 28, 2013. This initiated an ongoing collaboration between Barnard and the author, informing the development of the research project, "Imagining Autism." Barnard's theories have been cited elsewhere in publications arising from this research (e.g. Trimingham & Shaughnessy, Autism in the Wild, in Peter Garrett (Ed.) (2016), *The Cognitive Humanities.*

5 *Nature,* March 18, 2015, "Hollow Humour."Retrieved December 12, 2016 from http://www.nature.com/news/hollow-humour-1.17126 .

6 Francesco Varela. (2000). Interview with Claus Otto Scharmer. See also Depras, Varela, & Vermersch (2003).

7 Holmes is Programme Leader for Emotion at the MRC Cognition and Brain Sciences Unit, Cambridge.

8 I am indebted to Rhonda Blair's discussion of the 4Es and performance in her unpublished paper for the American Society for Theatre Research, 2015.

9 The film documentary can be accessed at https://www.routledgeperformancearchive.com/multimedia/video/imagining-autism-now-i-see-the-world.(Retrieved December 213, 2016).

10 "Imagining Autism: Drama, Performance and Intermediality and Interventions for Autistic Spectrum Conditions" was an AHRC-funded project based at the University of Kent

(October 2011–March 2014). Investigators were Professor Nicola Shaughnessy (Drama), Dr. Melissa Trimingham (Drama), Dr. Julie Beadle-Brown (Tizard), and Dr. David Wilkinson (Psychology). Participating schools were St Nicholas School Canterbury (Spring term 2012), Laleham Gap, Broadstairs (Summer Term 2012) and Helen Allison School, Meopham (Autumn Term 2012). The schools covered a wide spectrum of ability. The project worked with between six and eight participants in each school, aged 7–11, with a diagnosis of autism. The intervention involved participants in weekly sessions (45 minutes) in a portable installation (the 'pod').

11 Sarah Turner is an experimental documentary film artist whose work includes explorations of memory, identity, fiction and autobiography in *Perestroika* (2010) and *Perestroika Reconstructed* (2013).

## References


Armstrong, T. & Detweiler-Bedell, B. (2008). Beauty as an emotion: The exhilarating prospect of mastering a challenging world. *Review of General Psychology, 12*, 305–329.

Asperger, H. (1944). Die "Autistischen Psychopathen" im Kindesalter. *Archiv für Psychiatrie und Nervenkrankheiten, 1*, 76–136.

Bailes, S. J. (2011). *Performance theatre and the poetics of failure.* London: Routledge.

Baker, B. (2010). *Diary drawings: Mental illness and me.* London: Wellcome.

Bakhtin, M. (1981). The Dialogic Imagination. Ed. Michael Holquist. Trans. Caryl Emerson and Michael Holquist. Austin and London: University of Texas Press.

Bakhtin, M. M. (1984). Problems of Dostoevsky's Poetics. Ed. and trans. Caryl Emerson. Minneapolis: University of Minnesota Press.

Barnard, P. (2004). Bridging between basic theory and clinical practice. *Behaviour Research and Therapy, 42*, 977–1000.

Bateson, G. (1962). A note on the double bind. In C. Sluzki & D. Ransom (Eds.), *Double bind: The foundation of the communicational approach to the family* (pp. 39–42). New York: Grune & Stratton.

Beadle-Brown, J. et al (2017 forthcoming), Imagining Autism: Feasibility of a Drama-Based Intervention on the Social, Communicative and Imaginative behaviour of Children with Autism. *Autism: International Journal of Research and Practice.*

Berliner, T. (2013). Hollywood storytelling and aesthetic pleasure. In A. Shimamura (Ed.), *Psychocinematics: exploring cognition at the movies* (pp. 195–213). Oxford: Oxford University Press.

Bishop, C. (2004) Antagonism and relational aesthetics. *October, 110*, Fall 2004, 51–79.

Blair, R. & Cook, A. (Eds.). (2016). *Theatre, performance, cognition: Languages, bodies, ecologies.* London: Bloomsbury Methuen.

Bourriaud, N. (1998). *Relational aesthetics.* Paris: Les Presses Du Reel.

Breel, A. (2015). Audience agency in participatory performance: A methodology for examining audience experience. *Participations: Journal of Audience and Reception Studies, 12*, 368–387.

Buckland, W. (2007). *The cognitive semiotics of film.* Cambridge: Cambridge University Press.

Butler, G. & Holmes, E. A. (2009). Imagery and the self following childhood trauma: Observations concerning the use of drawings and external images. In L. Stopa (Ed.), *Imagery and the threatened self: Perspectives on mental imagery and the self in cognitive therapy* (pp. 166–180). London: Routledge.

Cardinal, Roger (1972) *Outsider art.* London#; Routledge.

Chellingsworth, M. (2014). CEDAR clinical education development and research exposure and response prevention. Retrieved December 12, 2016 from http://cedar.exeter.ac.uk/

media/universityofexeter/schoolofpsychology/cedar/documents/Exposure_and_Response_Prevention_Recovery_Guide_Single_pages_Colour.pdf.

Clark, A. (2008). *Supersizing the mind: Embodiment, action and cognitive extension.* Oxford: Oxford University Press.

Cook, A. (2007). Cognitive interplay: How blending theory and cognitive science reread Shakespeare. In M. Ravassat & J. Culpeper (Eds.), *Stylistics and Shakespeare's language: Transdisciplinary approaches* (pp. 246–268). New York: Continuum.

Currie, G. & Ravenscroft, I. (2003) *Recreative minds: Imagination in philosophy and psychology.* Oxford: Oxford University Press.

Damasio, A. R. (2012). Neuroscience and psychoanalysis: A natural alliance. *Psychoanalytic Review, 99,* 591–594.

deLahunta, S., Clarke, G., & Barnard, P. (2012). A conversation about choreographic thinking. *Journal of Dance and Somatic Practices, 3,* 243–259.

Depras, N., Varela, F., & Vermersch, P. (Eds.). (2003). *On becoming aware: A pragmatics of experiencing.* Amsterdam: John Benjamins Publishing.

Derrida, Jacques (1971). *Margins of philosophy,* trans. Alan Bass. Chicago: Chicago University Press.

Evans, B. (2013). How autism became autism: The radical transformation of a central concept of child development in Britain. *History of the Human Sciences, 26,* 3–31.

Fauconnier, G., & Turner, M. (2002). *The way we think: Conceptual blending and the mind's hidden complexities.* New York: Basic Books.

Finlay, L. (2014). Engaging phenomenological analysis. *Qualitative Research in Psychology, 11,* 121–141.

Flaherty, A. (2005). Frontotemporal and dopaminergic control of idea generation and creative drive. *Journal of Comparative Neurology, 493,* 147–153.

Frogett, L. (2011). Artistic output as an intersubjective third. In S. Clarke, H. Hahn, & P. Hogget (Eds.), *Object relations and social relations: The implications of the relational turn in psychoanalysis,* (pp. 87107). London: Karnac Books.

Gallese, V., & Lakoff, G. (2005). The brain's concepts: The role of the sensory–motor system in conceptual knowledge. *Cognitive Neuropsychology, 2,* 455–479.

Garratt, P. (Ed.). (2016). *The cognitive humanities: Embodied mind in literature and culture.* Basingstoke: Palgrave Macmillan.

Gergen, Kenneth J. & McNamee, Sheila (2000) From disordering discourse to transformative dialogue. In Robert A. Neimeyer & Jonathan D. Raskin, (Eds.), *Constructions of disorder: Meaning-making frameworks for psychotherapy,* (pp. 333–349). Washington, DC: American Psychological Association.

Grandin, T. (1995, 2006). *Thinking in pictures.* London: Bloomsbury.

Hackman, A., Bennett-Levy, J., & Holmes, E. (2009). *Oxford guide to imagery in cognitive therapy.* Oxford: Oxford University Press.

Happé, F. & Frith, U. (Eds.). (2010). *Autism and talent.* Oxford: Oxford University Press.

Haynes, J. & Woods, D. (2014). *The eradication of schizophrenia in Western Lapland.* London: Oberon Books.

Hinshaw, S. P. (2005). The stigmatization of mental illness in children and parents: Developmental issues, family concerns, and research needs. *Journal of Child Psychology and Psychiatry, 46,* 714–734.

Holmes, E., (2015). Performing Rituals. *Nature. 19* March 519 (289). Retrieved December 12, 2016 from http://www.nature.com/nature/journal/v519/n7543/pdf/519289a.pdf.

Ingold, T (2011). *Being alive: Essays on movement, knowledge and description.* London: Routledge.

Jack, B.(2015). The rise of the medical humanities. *Times Higher Education,* January 22, 2015. Retrieved December 12, 2016 from https://www.timeshighereducation.com/features/the-rise-of-the-medical-humanities/2018007.article

Jacobs, N. (2015). *Informed orienteering: A study of navigating systemic positioning dilemmas within the field of anorexia*. Unpublished PhD thesis, University of London.

Jennings, S. (1992). *Dramatherapy:Theory and practice 2*. London: Routledge.

Kanner, L. (1943). Autistic disturbances of affective contact. *Nervous Child, 2*, 117–250.

Kemp, R. (2012). *Embodied acting: What neuroscience tells us about performance*. London: Routledge.

Kester, G. (2004). *Conversation pieces: Community and communication in modern art*. Berkeley: University of California Press.

Klin, A., & Jones, W. (2007). Embodied psychoanalysis? Or, on the confluence of psychodynamic theory and developmental science. In L. C. Mayes, P. Fonagy, & M. Target (Eds.), *Developmental Science and Psychoanalysis: Integration and Innovation* (pp. 5–38). London: Karnac Books.

Klin, A., & Jones, W. (2008). Melding art and science for autism. *Spectrum*. Retrieved December 12, 2016 from https://spectrumnews.org/news/profiles/ami-klin-warren-jones-melding-art-and-science-for-autism/.

Lakoff, G. & Johnson, M. (1980, 2003). *Metaphors we live by*. Chicago: Chicago University Press.

Lehmann, Hans-Thies. (2006). *Postdramatic theatre*. Trans. K. Jurs-Mundy. London: Routledge.

Levinson, G. (2005). *Oxford handbook of aesthetics*. Oxford: Oxford University Press.

Loftis, S. F. (2015). *Imagining autism :Fiction and stereotypes on the spectrum*. Bloomington: Indiana University Press.

Lord, C., Risi, S., Lambrecht, L., Cook, E. H., Leventhal, B. L., DiLavore, P. C., et al. (2000). The autism diagnostic observation schedule–generic: A standard measure of social and communication deficits associated with the spectrum of autism. *Journal of Autism and Developmental Disorders, 30*, 205–223.

Lutterbie, J. (2011). *Toward a general theory of acting: Cognitive science and performance*. Basingstoke: Palgrave Macmillan.

McConachie, B. (Ed.). (2006). *Performance and Cognition*. London: Routledge.

Menary, R. (2010). Introduction to the Special Issue on 4E Cognition. *Phenomenology and the Cognitive Sciences, 9*, 459–463.

Minissale, G. (2012). Conceptual art: A blind spot for neuroaesthetics? *Leonardo, 45*, 43–48.

Murray, S. (2008). *Representing autism: Culture, narrative, fascination*. Liverpool: Liverpool University Press.

Osteen, M. (Ed.). 2008. *Autism and representation*. London: Routledge.

Ockelford, A. (2013). *Music, language and autism: Exceptional strategies for exceptional minds*. London: Jessica Kingsley.

Pellicano, E. & Burrs, G. (2012). When the world becomes too real. *Trends in Cognitive Sciences, 16*, 504–510.

Ramus, F. (2013). What's the point of neuropsychoanalysis? *British Journal of Psychiatry, 203*, 170–171.

Roth, I. (Ed.). (2007) *Imaginative minds*. Oxford: Oxford University Press.

Sagan, O. (2015). *Narratives of art practice and mental well being: Reparation and connection*. London: Routledge.

Seikkula, J. & Olson, M. (2003). The Open Dialogue approach to acute psychosis: Its poetics and micropolitics. *Family Process, 42*, 403–418.

Shaughnessy, N. (2012). *Applying performance: Live art, socially engaged theatre and affective practice*. Basingstoke: Palgrave Macmillan.

Shaughnessy, N. (Ed.). (2013a). *Affective performance and cognitive science: Body, brain and being*. London: Bloomsbury Methuen.

Shaughnessy, N. (2013b). Imagining otherwise: Autism, neuroaesthetics and contemporary performance. *Interdisciplinary Science Reviews, 38*, 321–334.

Shimamura, A. (Ed.). (2013). *Psychocinematics: Exploring cognition at the movies.* Oxford: Oxford University Press.
Smith, M. (2011). Triangulating aesthetic experience. In A. Shimamura, & S. E. Palmer (Eds.), *Aesthetic Science: Connecting Minds, Brains, and Experience* (pp. 80–102). New York: Oxford University Press.
Trimingham, M. & Shaughnessy, N. (2016). Material Voices: Intermediality and Autism. *Research in Drama Education: The Journal of Applied Theatre and Performance, 21*(3), 293–308.
Varela, F. (2000) Dialog on Leadership. Francisco Varela Summary. Retrieved December 12, 2016 from http://www.iwp.jku.at/born/mpwfst/02/www.dialogonleadership.org/Varela.html
Ward, D. & Stapleton, M. (2012). E's are good. Cognition as enacted, embedded, affective and extended. In F. Paglieri (Ed.), *Consciousness in interaction: The role of the natural and social context in shaping consciousness* (pp. 89–104). Amsterdam: John Benjamins Publishing.
White, G. (Ed.). (2015) *Applied theatre: Aesthetics.* London: Bloomsbury Methuen.
Wing, L. (1996). *The autistic spectrum: A guide for parents and professionals.* London: Robinson.
Zunshine, L. (Ed.). (2015). *The Oxford handbook of cognitive literary studies.* Oxford: Oxford University Press.

# Section II

# Cognitive, Neurobiological, and Genetic Influences

# Part 1

# Cognition/Socioemotional Factors

# 5

# Profiles of Executive Control in Autism Spectrum Disorder, Attention Deficit Hyperactivity Disorder, and Tourette's Syndrome

## *Performance-Based versus Real-World Measures*

Cynthia S. Peng and Gregory L. Wallace

## Introduction

Executive function (EF) is broadly defined as a set of cognitive processes that subserve behavioral and cognitive regulation in goal-directed processes. As an umbrella term, it encompasses working memory, flexibility, generativity, monitoring, planning, and inhibition (Rogers & Bennetto, 2000). In measuring EF, performance-based tasks (PB) and real-world (RW) measures are commonly used as complementary approaches.

PB tasks are often designed to increase experimental control and to isolate one specific domain of EF, though many measures remain multifactorial in their cognitive demands. In essence, they aim for specificity by controlling the conditions under which data are collected and tapping into one domain at a time, with outcome variables such as accuracy or reaction time to be the dependent measure that distinguish between groups and highlights any potentially clinically relevant deficits. Though traditionally administered by an experimenter in a highly structured setting, there has been a more recent movement for computerized administration, homogenizing results by taking away the social demands and variability inherent in person-to-person testing (Kenworthy et al., 2008).

RW assessment tools prioritize ecological validity or the "representativeness" of the measure as well as its "generalizability" to everyday situations (Burgess et al., 2006; Kvavilashvili & Ellis, 2004). In other words, this approach seeks to maximize external validity while often sacrificing some degree of experimental control and/or EF domain specificity. RW EF measures are broadly divided into two categories: questionnaire-based approaches, such as the Behavior Rating Inventory of Executive Function

*The Wiley Handbook of Developmental Psychopathology*, First Edition. Edited by Luna C. Centifanti and David M. Williams.

(BRIEF), and task-based approaches, the most well-known of which is the Behavioral Assessment of Dysexecutive Syndrome (BADS). Executive functions are, by their nature, hard to capture in a controlled setting (e.g. the laboratory); with RW comes less directive and structured tasks or demands when EF is most taxed. Overall, the resemblance to everyday demands and the scope of those everyday demands they encompass give a broader picture of a given individual's EF over a wide range of experiences and in contexts representative of real-world functioning demands. Thus, when impairments are noted, there is added confidence that these deficits could be representative of real-world functioning, though isolating the exact cognitive demands that lead to that breakdown can be challenging.

Though previous studies have traditionally utilized either PB or RW measures alone, there are now a growing number of studies that employ both. When both PB and RW EF measures are used they often do not correlate strongly. Therefore, they provide a complementary approach to evaluating intact and impaired EF domains because they appear to be measuring different aspects of EF. (In the case of some RW questionnaires, behavior as it relates to EF.) As is consistent with their methodological approaches, PB EF tasks are thought to assess discrete cognitive functions, while RW measures tap into the multifactorial demands placed on individuals in their everyday decision-making. Here, we offer a comparison of disorder-specific EF impairments as a function of EF measurement approach. Historically, there has been a lack of consensus on the definition and component processes of EF. One of the as yet unresolved debates is whether EF is a unitary or fractionated construct in development (Isquith, Gioia, & Espy, 2004; Kenworthy et al., 2008; Miyake et al., 2000). Broadly, while some authors consider EF as a singular entity not unlike a general intelligence factor, *g*, most others in the field subscribe to the idea that there exist relatively independent subfunctions within the umbrella term of EF (Lehto, Juujarvi, Kooistra, & Pulkkinen, 2003).

While PB tasks aim to pinpoint categorical deficits by sampling different component processes, RW measures aim to contextualize those EF deficits in daily living across situations and with highly diverse demands. The investigation of both will aid in elucidating a comprehensive profile of EF in relation to everyday function. We recognize that PB tasks and RW tasks provide complementary information about EF; however, noting similarities and dissimilarities is crucial in determining profiles of intact and impaired EF across disorders.

Generally speaking, EF is crucial to everyday functioning for us all. Therefore, it is important to elucidate divergent EF profiles (and constituent deficits) across a range of neurodevelopmental disorders to determine how EF deficits manifest in the context of various forms of developmental psychopathology. Different EF profiles and their constituent deficits might uniquely impact behavioral, cognitive, and social functioning and require distinct intervention approaches.

## Methods

In focusing primarily on EF deficits across three neurodevelopmental disorders (NDD), we input the search terms "autism," "autism spectrum disorder," "Attention Deficit Hyperactivity Disorder," and "Tourette's syndrome" in tandem with "executive function" or "executive dysfunction" in PubMed. We chose these particular neurodevelopmental disorders, because executive dysfunction has been implicated in each of them on a frequent basis. Studies selected for inclusion in the review were determined using the following criteria: they included a comparison group of typically developing (TD) participants and they included sufficient quantifiable metrics (such as number of participants, age ranges, etc.). Because widespread utilization of RW EF measures is a relatively recent phenomenon, and because of the size of the extant literature, papers for consideration were studies published from 2010 to 2015, an apt period that picks up shortly after Kenworthy et al.'s (2008) review of this topic (in ASD only) leaves off.

In order to objectively evaluate past research by accounting for sample sizes employed in prior studies, study weights were computed via noting if the given measure in the study elicited differences between groups ("Yes" for significantly different; "No" for failing to reach the threshold for significant difference), multiplied by the number of subjects included in the sample. With this weight appropriately placed in each column (Tables 5.1–5.6), the total weighted sum of studies that found significant group differences and studies that did not can be computed for each EF assessment approach by domain and by measure, and they can be compared across and between disorders. This simple method prevents small studies from having an undue influence on conclusions drawn from this survey of the literature. Our classification of significant group differences is in accordance with each study authors' pre-existing methodology of determining statistical significance.

The calculation of study weights allows the aggregation of study findings beyond relying upon counts of the total number of studies that do and do not find significant group differences. Study weights can then be applied across several levels, such as comparisons made in a specific EF domain (e.g., Inhibition) or for a specific measure (e.g., studies that utilize the BRIEF). To assess the magnitude of group differences, we devised an Executive Function Deficit Metric (EFDM), computed as follows:

$$\text{EFDM} = \frac{\textit{Study weights finding significant differences between groups}}{\textit{Study weights finding non-significant differences between groups}}$$

When computed, an EFDM of 1 indicates that in the studies reviewed for a particular disorder, a significant group difference is as likely as not finding a significant group difference. An EFDM above 1 means that a greater proportion of studies as computed by study weights found significant group differences as opposed to not, with increasing EFDM indicating more robust group differences. Accordingly, ">> 1" is used when all studies within a particular category comparison found significant group differences. An EFDM below 1 means more often than not, group differences were not found using that measure. This ratio-based method serves as a transparent and concrete, quantitative measure to compare results across studies and methodologies.

In examining specific EF domains in PB tasks, we categorized all relevant tasks according to the five domains delineated in Pennington and Ozonoff's (1996) seminal review: fluency (the ability to generate different solutions to a problem), planning (the ability to plan the steps needed to reach a solution for a problem), working memory (the ability to store information in mind during concurrent processing/distraction), inhibition (the ability to inhibit or withhold one's actions), and set shifting (the ability to shift to another action or problem-solving set when necessary). We renamed "shifting" to "flexibility," in accordance with the domains set forth by

**Table 5.1** Summary of executive function studies (2010–2015) utilizing real-world measures among individuals with ASD.

| *Reference* | *Groups/ages (years)* | *Matching criteria* | *Real world measure* | *Impairments? (TD/others)** |
|---|---|---|---|---|
| Granader et al. (2014) | ASD (*n* = 411): 10.7<br>TD (*n* = 467): 10.2 | Age, gender | BRIEF | Y |
| Hovik et al. (2014) | ASD (*n* = 34): 11.9<br>TD (*n* = 50): 11.6<br>TS (*n* = 19): 11.8<br>ADHD-C (*n* = 33): 11.6<br>ADHD-I (*n* = 43): 11.6 | Age | BRIEF<br>Inhibit<br>Shift<br>Emotional Control<br>Initiate<br>WM<br>Plan/Organize<br>Org of Materials<br>Monitor<br>BRI<br>MI<br>GEC | Y:<br>TS, ADHD-C>ASD<br>Y:<br>ADHD-C, TS>ASD<br>Y/N/N/N<br>Y/N/N/N<br>Y/N/N/N<br>Y/N/N/N<br>Y/N/N/N<br>Y/N/N/N<br>Y/N/N/N<br>Y/N/N/N<br>Y/N/N/N<br>Y/N/N/N |
| Panerai et al. (2014) | Total ASD (*n* = 27): 9.82<br>Total non-ASD (*n* = 34): 11.32 | Age, gender, Raven's CPM score | BRIEF:<br>BRI<br>MI<br>GEC | Y<br>N<br>Y |
| Leung et al. (2016) | ASD (*n* = 70): 11.23<br>TD (*n* = 71): 11.69 | Age, gender | BRIEF:<br>BRI<br>MI | Y<br>Y |
| Samyn et al. (2011) | ASD (*n* = 27): 12.73<br>TD (*n* = 27): 12.91<br>ADHD (*n* = 27): 13.21 | Age, FSIQ | EATQ-R-p<br>ECS<br>EATQ-R-s | Y/N<br>Y/Y<br>Y/N |
| Samyn et al. (2015) | ASD (*n* = 31): 12.83<br>TD (*n* = 148): 12.73<br>ADHD (*n* = 30): 13.16 | Age, gender (all male) | ECS<br>EATQ-R-s<br>EATQ-R-p | Y/Y<br>Y/Y<br>Y/Y |
| Samyn et al. (2014) | ADHD (*n* = 20): 12.82<br>TD (*n* = 21): 13.58<br>ASD (*n* = 20): 12.61 | Age, FSIQ | ECS<br>EATQ-R-s<br>EATQ-R-p | Y/N<br>Y/N<br>Y/N |

Key: ADHD: Attention Deficit Hyperactivity Disorder; ADHD-C: Attention Deficit Hyperactivity Disorder-Combined; ADHD-I: Attention Deficit Hyperactivity Disorder-Inattentive subtype; ASD: Autism Spectrum Disorder; ASD-BID: Autism Spectrum Disorder—Borderline Intellectual Disability; ASD-MID: Autism Spectrum Disorder—Mild Intellectual Disability; BRIEF: Behavior Rating Inventory of Executive Function; BRI: Behavior regulation index; GEC: Global executive composite; MI: Metacognition index; BRIEF-P: Behavior Rating Inventory of Executive Function-Preschool; EATQ-R-p: Early Adolescent Temperament Questionnaire-Revised, parent report; EATQ-R-s: Early Adolescent Temperament Questionnaire-Revised, self-report; ECS: Effortful Control Scale; FSIQ: Full-scale intelligence quotient; HF-ASD: High-functioning Autism Spectrum Disorder.

* Note: "Y/Y," "Y/Y/Y," and "Y/Y/Y/Y" denote whether the ASD group is impaired (Y = Yes) or not (N = No) relative to the next group listed under the "Groups/ages" column.

**Table 5.2** Summary of executive function studies utilizing performance-based tasks (2010–2015) among individuals with ASD.

| *Reference* | *Groups/ages (years)* | *Matching criteria* | *EF Measures* | *EF Domains* | *Impairments? (TD/other)* * |
|---|---|---|---|---|---|
| Kimhi et al. (2014) | ASD ($n$ = 29): 4.95<br>TD ($n$ = 30): 4.61 | Sex, age, IQ | FIST cat error<br>FIST shifting error<br>ToL | Flexibility<br>Flexibility<br>Planning/multiple EF | N<br>Y<br>Y |
| Durrleman & Franck (2015) | ASD ($n$ = 17): 9.2<br>TD ($n$ = 17): 7.6 | Nonverbal IQ | DCCST | Inhibition/Flexibility | N |
| McLean et al. (2014) | ASD ($n$ = 175): 9.4<br>TD Sibling ($n$ = 114): 9.0 | Not stated | D-KEFS subtests | Flexibility<br>Inhibition<br>Monitoring | Y<br>Y<br>N |
| Panerai et al. (2014) | Total ASD ($n$ = 27): 9.82<br>Total non-ASD ($n$ = 34): 11.32<br>Subgroups:<br>HF-ASD ($n$ = 11): 8.99<br>TD ($n$ = 9): 9.73<br>ASD-BIF ($n$ = 8): 9.56<br>BIF ($n$ = 12): 11.86<br>ASD-MID ($n$ = 8): 9.99<br>MID ($n$ = 13): 12.77 | Raven's CPM score, age, gender | ToL<br>CDT<br>WCST<br>Stroop<br>Verbal fluency task | Planning/multiple EF<br>Planning<br>Flexibility<br>Inhibition<br>Generativity:<br>category fluency<br>phonemic fluency | Y/Y/Y/Y<br>Y/N/N/Y<br>Y/N/N/N<br>N/N/Y/N<br>Y/N/Y/Y<br>N/N/Y/Y |
| Matsuura et al. (2014) | ASD ($n$ = 11): 12.0<br>TD ($n$ = 19): 11.4<br>ADHD ($n$ = 15): 10.8 | Age, sex, FSIQ | CANTAB:<br>RVP<br>SWM<br>DMS<br>SSP | Inhibition<br>Working Memory<br>Working Memory<br>Working Memory | N/N<br>N/N<br>N/N<br>N/N |
| Vogan et al. (2014) | ASD ($n$ = 19): 11.05<br>TD ($n$ = 17): 11.12 | Age, sex, FSIQ | CMT | Working Memory | Y |
| Samyn et al. (2015) | ASD ($n$ = 31): 12.83<br>TD ($n$ = 148): 12.73<br>ADHD ($n$ = 30): 13.16 | Age, gender (all boys) | Go/No-go<br>Animal Stroop<br>FA<br>Shifting attention task-auditory | Inhibition<br>Inhibition<br>Inhibition<br>Flexibility | N/N<br>N/N<br>N/N<br>N/N |

(*Continued*)

Table 5.2 (Continued)

| *Reference* | *Groups/ages (years)* | *Matching criteria* | *EF Measures* | *EF Domains* | *Impairments? (TD/other)* * |
|---|---|---|---|---|---|
| Samyn et al. (2014) | ASD ($n$ = 20): 12.61<br>TD ($n$ = 21): 13.58<br>ADHD ($n$ = 20): 12.82 | Age, FSIQ | Eriksen flanker paradigm | Inhibition | N/N |
| Brunsdon et al. (2014) | ASD ($n$ = 181): 13.49<br>TD-Cotwins ($n$ = 73): 13.50<br>TD ($n$ = 160): 12.79 | None | Planning drawing task, part A<br>Sentence Completion task<br>FAS test Luria hand game<br>ID/ED | Planning<br>Generativity<br>Generativity<br>Inhibition<br>Flexibility | Y/Y<br>Y/Y<br>N/N<br>Y/Y<br>Y/Y |
| Alderson-Day (2014) | HFA ($n$ = 15): 14.74<br>TD ($n$ = 15): 14.05<br>AS ($n$ = 15): 12.93 | IQ | TQT<br>ACE-R<br>Letter<br>Semantic<br>SDT<br>RT category<br>RT exemplar<br>Acc category<br>Acc exemplar | Generativity/Planning<br>Generativity<br>Generativity | Y/Y<br>N/N<br>N/N<br>N/N<br>N/N<br>N/N<br>N/N |
| Sachse et al. (2013) | HFASD ($n$ = 30): 19.2<br>TD ($n$ = 28): 19.9 | Age, sex, verbal IQ | CANTAB:<br>SOC<br>ID/ED<br>SWM<br>Stroop | Planning<br>Flexibility<br>Working Memory<br>Inhibition | N<br>N<br>N<br>Y |
| Yasuda et al. (2014) | ASD ($n$ = 33): 26.1<br>TD ($n$ = 33): 26.8 | Sex, age, FSIQ | WCST<br>CPT-IP | Flexibility<br>Inhibition | Y<br>Y |
| Wilson et al. (2014) | ASD ($n$ = 89): 26<br>TD ($n$ = 89): 28<br>AS ($n$ = 55): 28<br>HFA ($n$ = 34): 24 | Age, verbal IQ | FAS test<br>NWR<br>Go/No-Go | Generativity<br>Working Memory<br>Inhibition | N<br>N<br>N |

| | | | | | |
|---|---|---|---|---|---|
| Johnston et al. (2011) | ASD ($n$ = 24): 27.8 | Verbal IQ, age, gender | Stroop | Inhibition | Y/N |
| | TD ($n$ = 14): 28.7 | | MFF | Inhibition | N/Y |
| | ADHD ($n$ = 24): 27.3 | | Hayling | Inhibition/ Generativity | Y/Y |
| Kretschmer et al. (2014) | ASD ($n$ = 27) 35.63 | Age, IQ | Virtual Week | Planning/Working Memory | N |
| | TD ($n$ = 27): 39.85 | | | | |
| Geurts & Vissers (2012) | ASD ($n$ = 23): 63.6 | Age, gender, IQ, education | SART | Inhibition | Y |
| | TD ($n$ = 23): 63.7 | | Commission err | Working Memory | N |
| | | | Omission err | Flexibility | Y |
| | | | Spatial | Planning/multiple EF | N |
| | | | Span from WMS-III | Generativity | N |
| | | | MCST | Working Memory | Y |
| | | | ToL-DX | Working Memory | N |
| | | | COWAT | | N |
| | | | Visual Memory from WMS-III | | |
| | | | RAVLT (Dutch version) | | |

Key: ACE-R: Addenbrooke's Cognitive Examination—Revised ; ANTP: Amsterdam Neuropsychological Tasks Program; AS: Articulatory Suppression; ASD-BIF: Autism Spectrum Disorder—Borderline intellectual functioning; ASD-MID: Autism Spectrum Disorder—Mild intellectual disability; CANTAB: Cambridge Neuropsychological Test Automated Battery; CDT: Clock drawing test; CMT: Color matching task; COWAT: Controlled Oral Word Association Test; CPM: Raven's Colored Progressive Matrices; CPT-IP: Continuous Performance Test—Identical Pairs version ; DCCST: Dimensional Change Card-Sorting Task; D-KEFS: Delis–Kaplan Executive Functioning System; DMS: Delayed match to sample (from CANTAB); FA: Focused attention task (from ANTP); FIST: Flexible Item Selection Task; HFA: High functioning autism; ID/ED: Intradimensional/Extradimensional task (from CANTAB); MCST: Modified Card Sorting Test; MFF: Matching familiar figures; NWR: Non-word repetition; PM: Prospective Memory; RAVLT: Rey Auditory Verbal Learning Task; RI: Response Inhibition; RVP: Rapid visual information processing (from CANTAB); SART: Sustained Attention to Response Test; SDT: Semantic decision task; SOC: Stockings of Cambridge Test (from CANTAB); SSP: Spatial span (from CANTAB); SWM: Spatial Working Memory (from CANTAB); ToL: Tower of London; ToL-DX: Tower of London—Drexel University; TQT: Twenty Questions Task; WMS-III: Wechsler Memory Scale-III.

* Note: "Y/Y," "Y/Y/Y," and "Y/Y/Y/Y" denote whether the ASD group is impaired (Y = Yes) or not (N = No) relative to the next group listed under the "Groups/ages" column.

**Table 5.3** Summary of executive function studies (2010–2015) utilizing real world measures among individuals with ADHD.

| *Reference* | *Groups/ages (years)* | *Matching criteria* | *Real world measure* | *Impairments? (TD/others)** |
|---|---|---|---|---|
| Crippa et al. (2014) | ADHD (*n* = 11): 9.00<br>TD (*n* = 68): 10.40<br>ADHD+ODD (*n* = 12): 10.00<br>ADHD+RD (*n* = 13): 9.46 | FSIQ, Age | BRIEF (parental rating)<br>Inhibit<br>Shift<br>Emotional Control<br>Initiate<br>WM<br>Plan/Organize<br>Org of Materials<br>Monitor<br>BRI<br>MI<br>GEC | Y/Y/N<br>Y/N/N<br>Y/N/N<br>Y/N/N<br>Y/N/N<br>Y/N/N<br>N/N/N<br>Y/N/N<br>Y/N/N<br>Y/N/N<br>Y/N/N |
| Skogli et al. (2014) | ADHD-C (*n* = 36): 11.84<br>ADHD-I (*n* = 44): 12.12<br>TD (*n* = 50): 12.00 | Sex, age | BRIEF<br>Monitor subsc.<br>Inhibition subs. | Y<br>ADHD-C<ADHD-I<br>ADHD-C<ADHD-I |
| Hovik et al. (2014) | ADHD-C (*n* = 33): 11.6<br>ADHD-I (*n* = 43): 11.6<br>TD (*n* = 50): 11.6<br>TS (*n* = 19): 11.8<br>ASD (*n* = 34): 11.9 | Age | BRIEF<br>Inhibit<br>Shift<br>Emotional Control<br>Initiate<br>WM<br>Plan/Organize<br>Org of Materials<br>Monitor<br>BRI<br>MI<br>GEC | Y:<br>ADHD-I = ASD>TD<br>Y on Inhibit subsc<br>ADHD-C = TS>ASD<br>N/Y/N/N<br>N/Y/N/N<br>N/Y/N/N<br>N/Y/N/N<br>N/Y/N/N<br>N/Y/N/N<br>N/Y/N/N<br>N/Y/N/N<br>N/Y/N/N |
| Samyn et al. (2014) | ADHD (*n* = 20): 12.82<br>TD (*n* = 21): 13.58<br>ASD (*n* = 20): 12.61 | Age, FSIQ | ECS<br>ACS<br>EATQ-R-s<br>EATQ-R-p | Y/N<br>Y/N<br>Y/N<br>Y/N |
| Samyn et al. (2015) | ADHD (*n* = 30): 13.16<br>TD (*n* = 148): 12.73<br>ASD (*n* = 31): 12.83 | Age, gender (all boys), Not on FSIQ | ECS<br>ACS<br>EATQ-R-s<br>EATQ-R-p | Y/Y<br>Y/N<br>Y/Y<br>Y/Y |
| Samyn et al. (2011) | ADHD (*n* = 27): 13.21<br>TD (*n* = 27): 12.91<br>ASD (*n* = 27): 12.73 | Age, FSIQ | EATQ-R-p<br>ECS<br>ACS<br>EATQ-R-s | Y/N<br>Y/Y<br>Y/N<br>Y/N |

**Table 5.3** (Continued)

| *Reference* | *Groups/ages (years)* | *Matching criteria* | *Real world measure* | *Impairments? (TD/others)** |
|---|---|---|---|---|
| Boyer et al. (2014) | TD (*n* = 34): 14.66<br>ADHD-I (*n* = 77): 14.40<br>ADHD-C (*n* = 38): 14.11 | Age, gender, IQ | Key Search<br>BADS<br>Zoo Map<br>BADS<br>BRIEF<br>Plan/Organize<br>MI<br>GEC | N<br>N<br>Y<br>TD<ADHD-I = -C<br>TD<ADHD-I = -C<br>TD<ADHD-I<-C |
| Martinussen & Mackenzie (2015) | ADHD (*n* = 22): 15.71<br>TD (*n* = 22): 15.55 | Gender. Matched post-recruitment on word identification from WJ-III subtest | EF subscale of Conners 3-T (teachers' report) | Y |
| Grane et al. (2014) | TD (*n* = 35): 32.2<br>ADHD (*n* = 36): 31.8 | Age, sex, years of education, FSIQ | BRIEF-A | Y |
| Bueno et al. (2014) | ADHD (*n* = 48):<br>[Nonmed (*n* = 14): 32.4<br>Medicated (*n* = 34): 30.2]<br>TD (*n* = 20): 28.4 | Age, nonverbal IQ, education | Zoo Map Test of BADS | N (N) |
| Stern and Maeir (2014) | ADHD (*n* = 81): 36.20<br>TD (*n* = 64): 29.29 | Education, sex | BRIEF-A:<br>Shift<br>EC<br>Self-monitor<br>BRI<br>Initiate<br>WM<br>Plan/Organize<br>Task Monitor<br>Org of<br>materials<br>MI<br>GEC | Y<br>Y<br>Y<br>Y<br>Y<br>Y<br>Y<br>Y<br>Y<br>Y<br>Y |

Key: AAQoL: Adult ADHD Quality-of-Life Scale; ACS: Attentional Control Scale; BADS: Behavioral Assessment of Dysexecutive Syndrome; BDEFS: Barkley Deficits in Executive Functioning Scale; BRIEF-A: Behavior rating inventory of executive function-Adult; [BRI: Behavioral Regulation Index; GEC: Global Executive Composite; MI: Metacognitive]; CD: Conduct disorder; EATQ-R-s/p: Early Adolescent Temperament Questionnaire—Revised, self or parent report; ECS: Effortful Control Scale; ODD: Oppositional Defiant disorder; RD: Reading disorder.

* Note: "Y/Y," "Y/Y/Y," and "Y/Y/Y/Y" denotes whether the ADHD group is impaired (Y = Yes) or not (N = No) relative to the next group listed under the "Groups/ages" column.

**Table 5.4** Summary of executive function studies (2010–2015) utilizing performance-based tasks among individuals with ADHD.

| *Reference* | *Groups/ages (years)* | *Matching criteria* | *EF Measures* | *EF Domains* | *Impairments? (TD/other)** |
|---|---|---|---|---|---|
| Salum et al. (2014) | ADHD ($n$ = 100): 9.6<br>TD ($n$ = 378): 9.7<br>Fear disorders ($n$ = 90): 9.8<br>Distress disorders ($n$ = 57): 10.5<br>ODD/CD ($n$ = 40): 10.0<br>ADHD+ODD-CD ($n$ = 39): 9.4 | Not specified | 2C-RT<br>CCT<br>GNG | Inhibition<br>Inhibition<br>Inhibition | T: Y/Y/Y/N/N<br>A: Y/N/N/Y/N<br>E: Y/Y/N/N/N<br>V: Y/Y/Y/Y/Y<br>T: Y/N/N/N/N<br>V: Y/Y/N/N/N<br>N/N/N/N/N |
| Crippa et al. (2014) | ADHD ($n$ = 11): 9.00<br>TD ($n$ = 68): 10.40<br>ADHD+ODD ($n$ = 12): 10.00<br>ADHD+RD ($n$ = 13): 9.46 | FSIQ, Age | Honk Test<br>Daily Planning Test<br>Sentence completion Test<br>Battersea Multitask Paradigm | Inhibition<br>Planning<br>Generativity<br>Flexibility/Planning<br>Across Measures:<br>Processing speed<br>Inhibition<br>Planning<br>Execution<br>Retrospective memory | Y<br>N<br>Y<br>Y<br>Y |
| Reck et al. (2010) | ADHD ($n$ = 17): 10.19<br>TD ($n$ = 21): 10.74 | Age, gender, FSIQ | Box task (specially designed) | Working Memory | N |
| Matsuura et al. (2014) | ADHD ($n$ = 15): 10.8<br>TD ($n$ = 19): 11.4<br>ASD ($n$ = 11): 12.0 | Age, sex, FSIQ | CANTAB:<br>SWM<br>DMS<br>SSP | Working Memory<br>Working Memory<br>Working Memory | Y/N<br>N/N<br>N/N |

| | | | | | |
|---|---|---|---|---|---|
| Gau & Huang (2014) | ADHD ($n$ = 438): 11.8 | Not on age, IQ, or gender, parents' age | CCPT | Inhibition | Y/Y |
| | TD ($n$ = 173): n = 12.6 | | RVP | Inhibition | Y/N |
| | ADHD-sib ($n$ = 180): 12.3 | | RTI | Inhibition | Y/N |
| | | | MTS | Working Memory | Y/Y |
| Skogli et al. (2014) Group 1 | ADHD-C ($n$ = 36): 11.84 | Sex, age | LN (from WISC-IV) | Working Memory | Y |
| | TD ($n$ = 50): 12.00 | | CWIT | Inhibition | N |
| | | | TMT | Flexibility | N |
| | | | Tower Test | Multiple EF | N |
| | | | Letter Fluency | Generativity | Y |
| | | | Hungry Donkey Test | Multiple EF | N |
| Skogli et al. (2014) Group 2 | ADHD-I ($n$ = 44): 12.12 | Sex, age | LN (from WISC-IV) | Working Memory | Y |
| | TD ($n$ = 50): 12.00 | | CWIT | Inhibition | Y |
| | | | TMT | Flexibility | Y |
| | | | Tower Test | Multiple EF | N |
| | | | Letter Fluency | Generativity | Y |
| | | | Hungry Donkey Test | Multiple EF | N |
| Samyn et al. (2014) | ADHD ($n$ = 20): 12.82 | Age, FSIQ | Erikson flanker paradigm | Inhibition | N/N |
| | TD ($n$ = 21): 13.58 | | | | |
| | ASD ($n$ = 20): 12.61 | | | | |
| Samyn et al. (2013) | ADHD ($n$ = 25): 13.16 | Age, FSIQ | ANT | Multiple EF | Acc: Y/N<br>RT: Y/N |
| | TD ($n$ = 25): 12.94 | | | | |
| | ASD ($n$ = 25): 12.75 | | | | |
| Samyn et al. (2015) | ADHD ($n$ = 30): 13.16 | Age, gender (all male) | Go/No-go | Inhibition | N/N |
| | TD ($n$ = 148): 12.73 | | Animal Stroop | Inhibition | N/N |
| | ASD ($n$ = 31): 12.83 | | Shifting attention task—auditory | Flexibility | N/N |

(*Continued*)

**Table 5.4** (Continued)

| *Reference* | *Groups/ages (years)* | *Matching criteria* | *EF Measures* | *EF Domains* | *Impairments? (TD/other)** |
|---|---|---|---|---|---|
| Boyer et al. (2014) | ADHD ($n$ = 115): 14.30 | Age, gender, IQ | Tower Test | Multiple EF | N |
| | TD ($n$ = 34): 14.66 | | TMT | Flexibility | N |
| Poon & Ho (2014) | ADHD ($n$ = 29): 14.93 | SES, non-medicated, language, IQ, age | Stroop | Inhibition | Y/N/N |
| | RD ($n$ = 24): 15.15 | | Backward digit span | Working Memory | Y/N/N |
| | AS+RD ($n$ = 35): 15.11 | | BVRT | Working Memory | Y/N/N |
| | TD ($n$ = 29): 14.52 | | CNT | Inhibition | N/Y/Y |
| | | | ToL | Multiple EF | Y/N/N |
| Van Rooij et al. (2015) | ADHD ($n$ = 185): 17.3 | None | Stop signal task | Inhibition | RT: Y/Y |
| | TD ($n$ = 124): 16.5 | | | | |
| | ADHD-sib ($n$ = 111): 17.3 | | | | |
| Johnston et al. (2011) | ADHD ($n$ = 24): 27.3 | Verbal IQ, age, gender | Stroop | Inhibition | Y/Y |
| | TD ($n$ = 14): 28.7 | | MFF | Inhibition | N/Y |
| | ASD ($n$ = 24): 27.8 | | Hayling | Inhibition/ Generativity | Y/Y |
| Grane et al. (2014) | ADHD ($n$ = 36): 31.8 | Age, sex, years of education, FSIQ | TOVA | Inhibition | Y–RT, omission & commission errors |
| | TD ($n$ = 35): 32.2 | | | | |
| Halleland et al. (2015) | ADHD ($n$ = 74): 34.0 | Gender | TMT | Flexibility | N |
| | TD ($n$ = 74): 28.9 | | Word Fluency Test | Generativity | N |
| | | | CWIT | Inhibition | Y |
| | | | Tower Test | Multiple EF | N |
| Bueno et al. (2014) | ADHD ($n$ = 48): | Age, nonverbal IQ, education | Plus-minus task | Flexibility | Y (N) |
| | [Nonmed ($n$ = 14): 32.4 | | Dual-task paradigm | Working Memory | N (Y-trend) |
| | Medicated ($n$ = 34): 30.2] | | Word fluency | Generativity | Y (phonetic) (N) |
| | TD ($n$ = 20): 28.4 | | RNG | Generativity | N (N) |

| | | | | | |
|---|---|---|---|---|---|
| Boonstra et al. (2010) | ADHD ($n$ = 49): 38.7<br>TD ($n$ = 49): 38.1 | Age, gender | Category fluency | Generativity | N |
| | | | COWAT | Generativity | N |
| | | | RFFT | Generativity | N |
| | | | ToL-R | Multiple EF | N |
| | | | CPT | Inhibition | Y |
| | | | ChT SST | Inhibition | Y |
| | | | CDT | Inhibition | N |
| | | | SCWT | Inhibition | Y |
| | | | ChT CR | Flexibility | Y |
| | | | WCST | Flexibility | N |
| | | | WAIS-III DS-B | Working Memory | Y |
| | | | WAIS-III LNS | Working Memory | Y |
| | | | VMS-B | Working Memory | N |
| | | | SOP | Working Memory | N |

Key: ADHD-C: Combined subtype; ADHD-I: Inattentive subtype; ADHD-PI: Predominantly Inattentive; ADHD-HI: Predominantly hyperactive-impulsive; ANT: Attention Network Test ; BVRT: Benton visual retention test; CANTAB: Cambridge automated neuropsychological testing battery; CCPT: Conner's Continuous Performance Test; CCT: Conflict Control Task; CE: Commission errors ; ChT: Change Task; CNT: Contingency naming test; CR: Change response; CWIT: Color–Word Interference Test (from D-KEFS); D-KEFS: Delis–Kaplan Executive Functioning System (9 subtests); DS-B: Digit Span-Backwards (from WAIS-III); GNG: Go/No-Go; LN: Letter–Number sequencing test (from WISC-IV); LNS: Letter and Number Sequencing (from WAIS-III); MFF: Matching familiar figures; MTS: Match to Sample Visual Search (from CANTAB); ODD: Opoositional defiant disorder; OE: Omission errors—failure to respond to target; RD: Reading disability; RI: Response inhibition; RNG: Random number generation; RTI: Reaction Time; RVP: Rapid Visual Information Processing; SOP: Self-Ordered Pointing Test; SSP: Spatial span (from CANTAB); SST: Stop signal test; TMT: Trail-Making Test (from D-KEFS); ToL: Tower of London; ToL-R: Tower of London—Revised ; TOVA: Test of Variables of Attention ; VMS-B: Visual Memory Span—Backwards (from WMS—Revised); 2C-RT: Two-Choice Reaction Time Task.

* Note: "Y/Y," "Y/Y/Y," and "Y/Y/Y/Y" denotes whether the ADHD group is impaired (Y = Yes) or not (N = No) relative to the next group listed under the "Groups/ages" column.

**Table 5.5** Summary of executive function studies (2010–2015) utilizing real world measures among individuals with TS.

| *Reference* | *Groups/ages (years)* | *Matching criteria* | *Real world measure* | *Impairments? (TD/others)** |
|---|---|---|---|---|
| Hovik et al. (2014) | TS ($n$ = 19): 11.8<br>TD ($n$ = 50): 11.6<br>ADHD-C ($n$ = 33): 11.6<br>ADHD-I ($n$ = 43): 11.6<br>ASD ($n$ = 34): 11.9 | Age | BRIEF:<br>Inhibit<br>Shift<br>Emotional Control<br>Initiate<br>WM<br>Plan/Organize<br>Org of Materials<br>Monitor<br>BRI<br>MI<br>GEC | Y/N/Y/Y<br>Y/Y/Y/Y<br>Y/N/N/N<br>Y/N/N/N<br>Y/N/N/N<br>Y/N/N/N<br>Y/N/N/N<br>Y/N/N/N<br>Y/N/N/N<br>Y/N/N/N<br>Y/N/N/N |

Key: BRI: Behavioral Regulation Index; BRIEF: Behavior rating inventory of executive function; GEC: Global Executive Composite; MMI: Metacognition Index.
* Note: "Y/Y," "Y/Y/Y," and "Y/Y/Y/Y" denotes whether the TS group is impaired (Y = Yes) or not (N = No) relative to the next group listed under the "Groups/ages" column.

Kenworthy et al. (2008). Findings for children (<18 years) and adults (18+) are presented separately to investigate any potential developmental differences in the pattern of group differences.

## Results and Discussion

### Autism Spectrum Disorder vs. Typically Developing Controls

Autism spectrum disorder (ASD) is a neurodevelopmental disorder affecting approximately 1.0% to 1.1% of the population, depending upon DSM diagnostic criteria utilized (Maenner et al., 2014), with males being affected nearly four times as frequently as females (APA, 2013). It is characterized by social-communication deficits as well as restricted interests and repetitive behavior. The studies reviewed here include individuals with ASD from childhood through adulthood and those with and without co-morbid intellectual disability.

*Real-world Measures* Robust EF impairments in ASD are found using RW measures. Overall, the weighted average of all RW measures produced an EFDM of 31.87. Given that an EFDM of 1 indicates a group difference is as likely as not finding a significant group difference, and an EFDM of >>1 indicates many more studies surveyed found significant differences than not, our EFDM of 31.87 demonstrates strong evidence for a significant EF difference between individuals with ASD and TD controls when assessed using RW measures. The most commonly utilized RW measure was the BRIEF, used in four of the seven studies. All of these four studies found differences in the overall Global Executive Composite (GEC) of the BRIEF. The BRIEF also consists of the Behavioral Regulation Index (BRI) and the Metacognition

**Table 5.6** Summary of executive function studies (2010–2015) utilizing performance-based tasks among individuals with TS.

| *Reference* | *Groups/ages (years)* | *Matching criteria* | *EF Measures* | *EF Domains* | *Impairments? (TD/other)** |
|---|---|---|---|---|---|
| Hovik et al. (2013) | TS ($n$ = 19): 11.8 | Age, ethnicity, educational background | CWIT | Inhibition | N/N |
| | TD ($n$ = 50): 11.6 | | CCPT-II | Inhibition | N/N |
| | ADHD ($n$ = 79): 11.7 | | | | |
| Eichele et al. (2010) | TS ($n$ = 20): 12.64 | Age, gender | Go/No-go | Inhibition | N |
| | TD ($n$ = 19): 13.16 | | | | |
| Jeter et al. (2015) | TS ($n$ = 30): 13.0 | Age, gender, IQ | 0-back (from N-back) | Working Memory | Y |
| | TD ($n$ = 29): 13.2 | | 1-back (from N-back) | Working Memory | Y |
| | | | Anti-saccade | Inhibition | Y |
| Drury et al. (2012) Experiment 1 | TS-alone ($n$ = 16): 13.44 | Age, gender, nonverbal IQ | CWIT | Inhibition | N/N |
| | TD ($n$ = 27): 14.12 | | | | |
| | TS+ADHD ($n$ = 15): 13.55 | | | | |
| Eddy et al. (2012) | TS ($n$ = 40): 32.00 | Age, years of education | FAS test | Generativity | Y |
| | TD ($n$ = 20): 27.35 | | DOT-A | Working Memory | Y |
| | | | Stroop | Inhibition | Y |
| Eddy & Cavanna (2014) | TS ($n$ = 27): 32.11 | Age, years of education | Verbal fluency | Generativity | N |
| | TD ($n$ = 25): 30.48 | | DOT-A | Working Memory | N |
| | | | Hayling test | Inhibition | Y |
| | | | TMT | Flexibility | Y-borderline |
| | | | WCST | Flexibility | N |
| | | | WAIS DSST | Generativity | Y |
| | | | WAIS Similarities | Multiple EF | N |
| | | | WAIS picture arr. | Planning | N |
| | | | WAIS matrix reas. | Multiple EF | N |
| Drury et al. (2012) Experiment 2 | TS-alone ($n$ = 23): 34.00 | Age, gender, years of education | CWIT | Inhibition | N |
| | TD ($n$ = 21): 32.23 | | LNS (from WMS-III) | Working Memory | N |
| Drury et al. (2013) | TS ($n$ = 20): 38.20 | Age, years of education, FSIQ | Automatic Cognitive Inhibition: Retrieval-Induced forgetting | Working Memory | N |
| | TD ($n$ = 21): 33.10 | | Effortful Cognitive Inhibition: Directed Forgetting | Working Memory | N |

Key: CCPT-II: Conners' Continuous Performance Test-II; CWIT: Color–Word Interference Test (Subtest of D-KEFS); DOT-A: Digit Ordering Test-Adapted; DSST: Digit Symbol Substitution Test; FAS: Verbal Fluency Test; LNS: Letter-Number Sequencing (from WMS-III); TMT: Trail Making Test; WAIS: Wechsler Adult Intelligence Scale; WCST: Wisconsin Card Sorting Test; WM: Working memory; WMS-III: Wechsler Memory Scale, 3rd edition

* Note: "Y/Y" and "Y/Y/Y" denotes whether the TS group is impaired (Y = Yes) or not (N = No) relative to the next group listed under the "Groups/ages" column.

Index (MI), each of which can be further subdivided into scales. The BRI includes the Inhibit, Shift, and Emotional Control scales, while MI includes the Initiate, Working Memory, Plan/Organize, Organization of Materials, and Monitor scales (see Table 5.7). In looking at BRI alone, all three studies that investigated this (Hovik et al., 2014; Leung, Vogan, Powell, Anagnostou, & Taylor, 2016; Panerai, Tasca, Ferri, D'Arrigo, & Elia, 2014) found ASD impairments compared to TD controls. Though not unanimous,

**Table 5.7** A sampling of real world executive function measures, including the associated age range and a brief description.

| *Name* | *Age range* | *Description* |
|---|---|---|
| **Questionnaires** | | |
| Attentional Control Scale (ACS) (Derryberry & Reed, 2002) | Adults | Self-report questionnaire that measures individual differences in voluntary attentional control on a four-point likert scale; comprising 20 items that fall under the attentional focusing and attentional shifting scales. |
| Barkley Deficits in Executive Functioning Scale (BDEFS) (Barkley, 2011) | 18–81 years | Self-report plus other-report (e.g. spouse, parent, sibling) rating scales of executive function measures such as time management, organization and problem-solving, self-restraint, self-motivation, and self-regulation of emotions. |
| Behavior Rating Inventory of Executive Function (BRIEF) (Gioia et al., 2000) | Informant report: 5–18 years<br>Self-report: 11–18 years | The BRIEF is an informant (86 items) or self-report (80 items) questionnaire that assesses everyday executive control and produces eight non-overlapping clinical scales, which can be collapsed into two broader indices, Behavior Regulation (BRI) and Metacognition (MI). The BRI includes Inhibit, Shift, and Emotional Control. The MI includes Monitor, Working Memory, Plan/Organize, Organization of Materials, and Initiate (or Task Completion in the self-report version) |
| BRIEF-Adult (BRIEF-A) (Roth et al., 2006) | 18–90 years | The BRIEF-A is an informant or self-report (75 items) questionnaire that assesses everyday executive control and produces nine non-overlapping clinical scales, which can be collapsed into two broader indices, Behavior Regulation (BRI) and Metacognition (MI). The BRI includes Inhibit, Shift, Emotional Control, and Self-Monitor. The MI includes Initiate, Working Memory, Plan/Organize, Task Monitor, and Organization of Materials. |
| Conners 3-Teacher (Conners 3-T) (Conners, 2008) | 6–18 years | Rating scale used by teachers in evaluating key areas of inattention, hyperactivity/impulsivity, learning problems, aggression, and peer relations; short and full-length versions available; when used in conjunction with the parent form, differences in school and home behavior are highlighted. |

**Table 5.7** (Continued)

| *Name* | *Age range* | *Description* |
|---|---|---|
| Early Adolescent Temperament Questionnaire-Revised, parent report (EATQ-R-p) (Ellis & Rothbart, 2001) | Parents of adolescents 10–16 years | 62-item questionnaire on a five-point scale (1 = almost always untrue; 5 = almost always true) that assesses nine areas of self-regulation of adolescents: activation control, affiliation, attention, fear, frustration, inhibitory control, shyness, aggression, and depressive mood. |
| Dysexecutive Questionnaire (DEX; part of BADS) (Wilson et al., 1996) | 16–87 years | 20-item questionnaire that evaluates areas that are susceptible to change over time: emotional or personality changes, motivational, behavioral or cognitive. |
| Early Adolescent Temperament Questionnaire-Revised, self-report (EATQ-R-s) (Ellis & Rothbart, 2001) | 10–16 years | 62-item questionnaire on a five-point scale (1 = almost always untrue; 5 = almost always true) that assesses 12 areas of self-regulation of adolescents: activation control, affiliation, attention, fear, frustration, high-intensity pleasure, inhibitory control, perceptual sensitivity, pleasure sensitivity, shyness, aggression, and depressive mood. |
| Effortful Control Scale (ECS) (Lonigan & Phillips, 2002) | | 24-item self-report questionnaire on a five-point scale indicating how much the item describes the individual "most of the time," tapping into the domains of persistence/low distractibility and impulsivity. |
| **Tasks** | | |
| Behavioral Assessment of Dysexecutive Syndrome (BADS) (Wilson et al., 1996) | 16–87 years | Series of six subtests designed to test everyday problems that come from dysexecutive syndrome, including problem solving, organizing and planning, continental scheduling system, and supervisory attention system; standardized against 216 UK controls and 92 patients. Subtests include:<br>• Rule shift card test<br>• Key search test (see below)<br>• Temporal Judgement Test<br>• Zoo Map Test (see below)<br>• Action program test<br>• Modified Six Elements Test |
| Key Search Test (from BADS) | 16–87 years | Participants are presented with a piece of paper with a 100-mm square in the middle and a small black dot 50 mm below it and are asked to draw a line indicating how they would walk to search the field for their keys. |
| Zoo Map Test (from BADS) | 16–87 years | Participants are presented with a map of a zoo and are asked how they would plan to visit a set of designated locations, following certain route rules. There are only four variations on a route in which none of the rules would be infringed; thus the maximum score is 4. |

the Metacognition Index (MI) was also found to be more impaired in individuals with ASD in two of the three studies (Hovik et al., 2014; Leung et al., 2014), with one study finding no ASD impairments (Panerai et al., 2014).

Overall, the near-unanimity of EF impairments when utilizing RW measures in ASD suggests excellent sensitivity to EF difficulties but does not address questions of specificity. The magnitude of the BRI finding is consistent with the well-established cognitive profile of ASD. The BRI includes Shift and Emotional Control, which are significant areas of impairment in ASD. Difficulties with cognitive flexibility, such as struggling to switch or shift attention between competing tasks (Maes, Eling, Wezenberg, Vissers, & Kan, 2011; Yerys et al., 2009), and behavioral flexibility, such as getting "stuck" in a pattern of behavior (Hill & Bird, 2006), are well established among individuals with ASD. Emotion regulation is another area of difficulty for individuals with ASD, in that they use cognitive reappraisal less frequently than their TD peers; thus allowing perseveration of negative emotions (Samson, Hardan, Lee, Phillips, & Gross, 2015). These two EF domains are encapsulated in, and thus drive the broader deficits in the BRI index as a whole.

The three other studies of RW EF in ASD utilized the Early Adolescent Temperament Questionnaire (EAT-Q) and Effortful Control Scale (ECS). They also unanimously reported significant EF impairments in ASD (Samyn et al., 2011, 2014, 2015). The Persistence subscale of the ECS was particularly prominent in demonstrating ASD deficits relative to TD groups (Samyn et al., 2015). Because there have been no adult studies of RW EF in adults with ASD since 2010, no age split can be performed.

Finally, one notable and potentially confounding variable when examining these studies as a whole is intellectual functioning. Only two out of seven studies matched groups on full-scale IQ. Even though EF and IQ are separate constructs that are only weakly to moderately correlated, IQ may nevertheless exert influence on other cognitive functions including EF, leaving open the question of the extent to which reported EF differences for some studies are due to IQ differences versus actual EF impairments. Future studies should carefully match on IQ to alleviate these potential confounding factors.

*Performance-Based Measures* Findings based on PB measures in ASD were much more mixed. In the overall weighted sums report, about half of the studies found significant deficits relative to TD controls; half did not. The pattern of findings reflected the established EF cognitive profile of individuals with ASD. The tasks on which ASD-related deficits were most likely to be found assessed flexibility, planning and multiple EF domains, consistent with the seminal review of EF in ASD (Pennington & Ozonoff, 1996). Deficits on multistep tower tasks, which are linked to planning, but also considered to tap multiple EF domains, were most consistently reported to reveal deficits in individuals with ASD (Kimhi, Shoam-Kugelmas, Ben-Artzi, Ben-Moshe, & Bauminger-Zviely, 2014; Panerai et al., 2014) with an EFDM of 2.61. Similarly, tasks of flexibility also consistently reveal more deficits than not, with an EFDM of 2.75. Tasks linked to generativity (EFDM = 0.83) (e.g., verbal fluency) and inhibitory control (EFDM = 1.37) (e.g., Stroop and Go/No-go tasks) are equivocal in the likelihood of finding ASD-related deficits relative to TD controls. Finally, one category, working memory, had an EFDM of 0.20, revealing the failure to demonstrate significant differences was more likely than finding significant ASD-related deficits. This failure to find significance may be due to the types of working-memory tasks administered—across our cohort of studies, their composite contents were variable, with some studies employing color matching (Vogan et al., 2014) while others employed spatial span (Geurts & Vissers, 2012) or even virtual reality (Kretschmer, Altgassen, Rendell, & Bolte, 2014). Broadly, when working memory tasks are split into verbal versus visual-storage requirements, a more distinctive pattern emerges. Visual tasks evinced significant group differences, whereas verbal tasks did not, corroborating the visual-domain-specific deficits elucidated by Williams, Jarrold, Grainger, & Lind (2014).

In order to examine possible developmental differences, studies were divided into child versus adult samples. Across all EF domains, when separated by age, the child studies ($n$ = 10) had an EFDM of 1.22, which is modestly over 1, reflecting largely equivocal results. On the other hand, the adult studies ($n$ = 6) had an EFDM of 0.42. This suggests that the adult studies are driving the failure to find significant group differences across EF PB tasks in ASD versus TD comparisons. However, the overall impaired profiles on flexibility, planning, and multiple EF warranted closer investigation into each respective category's developmental effects.

Flexibility showed a consistently robust EF deficit metric across both child (EFDM = 2.76) and adult (EFDM = 2.70) studies, indicating its relative stability throughout development as a significant EF problem. A trademark of poor flexibility in ASD is difficulty in modulating actions, indicating struggles with shifting to a dynamically changing set of demands (Hill, 2004). The most frequently used PB test to assess this is the Wisconsin Card Sorting Task. In performing the task, individuals with ASD have a higher rate of perseverative errors, in which participants continue to abide by previous card-sorting rules rather than switching to the new rule (e.g., Panerai et al., 2014).

All studies of planning in children showed significant deficits (EFDM>>1), but it was much diminished and equivocal in adults (EFDM = 1.07), suggesting that maturation, intervention, or both effects could be driving these findings. However, with only two studies in adults focused on measures of planning, a look into work prior to 2010 is warranted. The Kenworthy et al. (2008) review revealed two more studies on planning in adults: one study finding significant deficits while the other did not, corroborating our equivocal EFDM. The Hill (2004) review found significant differences in planning abilities between individuals with ASD and TD controls in just one of one adult study. Though there is a relative paucity of studies of planning in adults with ASD, it is fair to say that evidence thus far is equivocal for planning-related deficits in ASD during childhood, while deficits in this domain are more robust in childhood.

The profile of EF impairments obtained across the reviewed cohort of studies is highly consistent with findings from previous reviews/meta-analyses. Pennington and Ozonoff (1996) also reported deficits in planning and flexibility in ASD along with intact inhibition and working memory. This pattern was corroborated with the meta-analysis completed by Sergeant, Geurts, & Oosterlaan (2002) and the literature review performed by Hill (2004). Here, we have provided additional evidence for different developmental patterns across areas of EF difficulty in ASD. This is particularly important given that there is an increasing focus on adult outcomes in ASD. Particularly striking is that nearly nothing is known about aging in ASD, a time when normal declines in EF across PB and RW measures are observed. Much more research is needed to confirm and bring precision to these potential age-related and developmental dissociations in PB EF difficulties in ASD.

### Attention Deficit Hyperactivity Disorder vs. Typically Developing Controls

ADHD is a neurodevelopmental disorder characterized by the two main symptoms of hyperactivity and impulsivity (APA, 2013). First manifesting in childhood, about half of affected individuals continue to experience symptoms into adolescence and adulthood (Asherson, Manor & Huss, 2014), suggesting both continuity and change in the developmental profiles associated with ADHD. There are three main subtypes: ADHD-Inattentive, ADHD-Hyperactive/Impulsive, and ADHD-Combined, which combines ADHD-Inattentive and ADHD-Hyperactive/Impulsive (APA, 2013).

*Real-world Measures* Individuals with ADHD exhibited robust EF deficits on RW measures compared to TD controls, with an overall EFDM of 4.47. Across the board, the BRIEF and its constituent scales, as well as the EAT-Q and ECS all produced consistent significant ADHD-related deficits across studies. The only measure that failed to reveal significant deficits in RW EF in ADHD was the BADS. Interestingly, going beyond ADHD–TD group comparisons, specific RW EF measures also differ based on ADHD subtypes and medication status (i.e., on or off stimulants; Adler Clemow, Williams, & Durell, 2014). More specifically, those with ADHD-I show elevated scores on the Inhibition scale and children with ADHD-C subtype showed elevated scores on the Monitor scale (Hovik et al., 2014). However, neither scales nor index scores of the BRIEF could distinguish between ADHD alone and ADHD with comorbid conditions, in this case, Oppositional Defiant Disorder (ADHD + ODD) or Reading Disorder (ADHD + RD) (Crippa et al., 2015). Lastly, examining child versus adult groups separately did not reveal discrepancies in patterns of results as both age groupings exhibited consistently robust deficits in ADHD.

*Performance-Based Measures* Studies utilizing LB EF measures found robust ADHD-related deficits compared to TD controls (EFDM = 1.94), although they were not of the same magnitude as studies utilizing RW EF measures. The EF domains that were most consistently significantly impaired in ADHD were Inhibition (EFDM = 3.12) and Working Memory (EFDM = 3.29), which is highly consistent with previous studies examining the EF profile of individuals with ADHD (Miyake et al., 2000). In contrast, taken as a whole, studies utilizing LB measures of Generativity (EFDM = 0.56) produced largely equivocal results. The domains least likely to elicit ADHD-related impairments were Flexibility (EFDM = 0.46) and Multiple EF (EFDM = 0.25). There were not enough studies in the Planning domain to calculate a meaningful EFDM.

Additionally, PB tasks often reveal significant impairments among individuals with ADHD as compared to their unaffected siblings. Van Rooij and colleagues (2015) found that individuals with ADHD had longer reaction times as well as more errors on a stop-signal task than their unaffected siblings. Gau and Huang (2014) also found significantly reduced accuracy in a match-to-sample visual search task as well as higher omission and commission errors on the Continuous Performance Test among individuals with ADHD compared to their siblings.

Turning to developmental differences in ADHD, surprisingly, if anything, Inhibition deficits appear to be exacerbated for adults compared to children (Child EFDM = 2.96; Adult EFDM = 4.04). This could suggest that these difficulties are developmentally intransigent and thus do not disappear in some adults with ADHD; however, there is a likely recruitment bias in that only those maintaining an ADHD diagnosis were included in the adult studies. If, on the other hand, adults who lost their ADHD diagnosis were also included in these studies, the findings would likely be quite different and this developmental pattern might be flipped. For the domain of Working Memory, a very large discrepancy in findings between child (EFDM = 9.62) and adult (EFDM = 0.74) studies was noted; however, given that there were only two adult studies, this should be viewed with caution.

Since there is a dearth of studies among adults available to determine a tangible trend in both the Inhibition and Working Memory domains we look to the broader literature in this regard to corroborate our findings. In particular, Boonstra, Oosterlaan, Sergeant, Kooij, & Buitelaar (2005) examined 13 studies and reported a meta-analysis for both the Stroop test (a measure of inhibition) and the WAIS backward digit span task (a measure of working memory). They found very strong evidence for ADHD-related deficits in the Inhibition domain, which corroborates the assertion that deficits in Inhibition in ADHD pervade into adulthood. However, they also found deficits in working memory among adults with ADHD, which suggests that our small sample of studies did not capture the broader findings in the literature and that working memory continues to be a significant deficit in adulthood in ADHD. It is worth noting that verbal (as opposed to visuospatial) working memory, in particular, is most often impaired in ADHD, as corroborated by Boonstra et al.'s (2005) meta-analysis. Accordingly, all four tasks from three studies reviewed here were administered verbally (Boonstra et al., 2010; Poon & Ho, 2014; Skogli, Egeland, Andersen, Hovik, & Oie, 2013) and revealed ADHD-related working memory deficits as compared to their respective control groups.

Overall, PB tests failed to differentiate among ADHD subtypes and among individuals with ADHD and various comorbidities, (e.g., those with generalized vs. focal seizures (Kang, Yum, Kim, Kim, & Ko, 2005), ODD vs. RD (Crippa et al., 2014), ADHD-I vs. ADHD-C (Boyer, Geurts, & Van der Oord, 2014; Skogli et al., 2015) and medicated vs. unmedicated participants (Bueno, da Silva, Alves, Louza, & Pompeia, 2014). This stands in stark contrast to the ability of RW EF measures, particularly the BRIEF, to distinguish between medicated and unmedicated ADHD groups (Adler et al, 2014), for example.

## Autism Spectrum Disorder vs. Attention Deficit/Hyperactivity Disorder

Neither PB (EFDM = 0.33) nor RW (EFDM = 0.58) measures were able to reliably distinguish between ASD and ADHD. Among studies utilizing RW EF measures, there were only three that compared ASD to ADHD, limiting the ability to generalize. The BRIEF (whether looking at the global indices or the finer grain scales) did not reveal ASD–ADHD group differences (Hovik et al., 2014). However, two studies reported significant deficits utilizing a different measure, the Effortful Control Scale (ECS), for the ADHD group relative to the ASD group (Samyn et al., 2011; Samyn et al., 2015). This is consistent with the established cognitive profiles of both disorders since the ECS has two subscales: Persistence/Distractibility and Impulsivity, both of which are hallmark impairments for ADHD, not ASD.

The EAT-Q was equivocal, with one study revealed significant differences while the other did not. In the Samyn studies (2011, 2015), the authors utilized only relevant items from the Inhibitory control, Attentional control, and Activation control scale. However, it remains unclear how the results might change if the Inhibitory control and Activation control were decoupled. It could be that examining these scales separately might clarify the picture a bit given that Inhibition is the EF domain most likely to distinguish between ASD and ADHD.

Only four studies utilized PB measures to compare performance between groups. On the whole these studies suggest that distinctions between groups is relatively poor. When comparing ASD vs. ADHD, measures of inhibition are most widely utilized. Significant differences were found for two measures of inhibition (Stroop and MFF) and a generativity task (Hayling), two domains of EF in which individuals with ADHD often demonstrate deficits. However, these significant differences in Inhibition stand in contrast to three other studies (Matsuura et al., 2014; Samyn et al., 2015) that reported no significant differences in Inhibition when comparing ASD and ADHD groups. These inconsistencies should be framed against specific task demands. For example, when completing the Stroop task, the two groups appear to take distinct approaches. While individuals with ASD show slow and steady performance (i.e., generally focusing on accuracy at the expense of speed), individuals with ADHD demonstrate the opposite pattern whereby they favor speed at the expense of accuracy (Johnston, Madden, Bramham, & Russell, 2011).

## Tourette's Syndrome vs. Typically Developing Controls, Autism Spectrum Disorder, and Attention Deficit/Hyperactivity Disorder

Tourette's syndrome (TS) is a neurodevelopmental disorder characterized by vocal and motor tics. Vocal tics include grunting, throat clearing, sniffing, screaming, screeching, repeating words, and barking (Schwam, King, & Greenberg, 2015). Motor tics include eye blinking, facial grimacing, nose twitching, flexing, twirling, and jerking of appendages. These tics are associated with basal ganglia as well as frontostriatal dysfunction (Mazzone et al., 2010). Additionally, motor regions are activated when tics occur. Tic severity increases until 10–12 years and is then followed by an attenuation of symptoms during or after puberty (Hovik,Plessen, Skogli, Andersen, & Oie, 2013). TS patients generally have somewhat depressed IQ scores that fall within the normal range, and they exhibit educational difficulties (Singer, Schuerholz, & Denckla, 1995).

*Real-world Measures* There has been only one study including individuals with TS since 2010 that utilized RW EF measures (Hovik et al., 2014). It was found that individuals with TS were rated as having significantly more RW EF impairments than TD controls utilizing the BRIEF (at both the global index and scale levels). However, given that this is the only study, more evidence is needed before making strong conclusions about RW EF in TS. Because the Hovik et al., study included other neurodevelopmental disorders as well, comparisons of TS vs. ADHD and TS vs. ASD can be made. Individuals with TS scored lower on the Shift scale of the BRIEF than did participants with ADHD-I and ADHD-C, indicating that shifting or flexibility in the real world is more of an issue for individuals with TS than it is for participants with ADHD. Additionally, individuals with TS or ADHD-C were more impaired than those with ASD or ADHD-I on the Inhibit subscale, in line with previous literature pointing out the fact that excessive motor activity is present in both TS and ADHD-C and perhaps the underlying factor (Leckman, 2002). Moreover, individuals with TS appear to have significant interplay between emotional regulation and EF given that they show elevated scores on Emotional Control while individuals with ADHD-C have more difficulty inhibiting impulsive behaviors, indicating a potential double dissociation in EF deficit areas for the two groups. Overall, more studies are needed to assess RW EF in TS in order to ascertain the profile of deficits compared to the TD population and in comparison to other neurodevelopmental disorders. Finally, how the RW EF profile in TS is affected by commonly comorbid disorders such as ADHD or OCD needs to be investigated.

*Performance-Based Measures* PB measures proved to be equivocal to poor (EFDM = 0.73) in documenting EF deficits in TS compared to TD controls. These results largely corroborate studies completed prior to 2010. There are several explanations as to why significant differences are difficult to elicit. One may be due to the inability to distinguish true EF difficulties from decreased ability to focus on a task due to the experience of having distracting tics (Eddy & Cavanna, 2014). There is also the potential influence of comorbid conditions; only three of the six studies (Drury et al., 2013; Eddy, Rickards, & Cavanna, 2012; Hovik et al., 2014) explicitly indicate that individuals with TS do not have comorbid conditions. Lastly, PB measures have been reported to be ineffective in their ability to detect deficits in youth with an above-average to high-average IQ (Mahone et al., 2001). Accordingly, the IQs of the TS samples described here fall in the average to above-average range.

No single EF domain emerges as a prominent deficit in TS based on the EFDM. When examining across all EF domains, Inhibition is the highest with an EFDM of 1.02. Therefore, it is worth considering why an Inhibition deficit, a prominent characteristic of TS, fails to emerge consistently across studies. One explanation is perhaps the lack of comorbidity in sampling; two out of the three studies that included TS only groups reported no significant deficits on inhibition, which is likely due to the omission of any participants with comorbid ADHD. On the other hand, when Eichele and colleagues (2010) failed to find a difference between a TS and a TD control group on the go/no-go task, it was attributed to the fact while boys with TS perform comparably to TD controls on inhibition, the TS sample does not exhibit post-hoc corrective behavior, such as post-error slowing. Perhaps a measure that more encompasses a wider time period of a given trial in a task, taking into account non-decision time and time between trials, can more readily provide a comprehensive view of behavior.

An age split analysis revealed that there were three studies of youth and five adult studies of PB EF tasks in TS. Overall, results revealed equivocal evidence for PB EF deficits (EFDM = 1.0) while the adult subgroup had even weaker support (EFDM = 0.64). However, it is difficult to generalize given the limited number of EF domains assessed and the limited number of studies completed since 2010. Lastly, it is noteworthy that no other PB EF tasks revealed group differences between TS and ADHD (Drury et al., 2012; Hovik et al., 2013) and between medicated and non-medicated individuals with TS (Eddy & Cavanna, 2014). Unfortunately, there were no studies comparing PB EF in TS vs. ASD groups since 2010.

## General Discussion of Performance-Based vs. Real-world Measures

In examining the nature by which PB tasks and RW measures provide complementary information about EF, patterns emerged with respect to the three neurodevelopmental disorders (i.e., ASD, ADHD, and TS) discussed in this chapter. A broader cross-disorder analysis allowed for a comparison of disorder-specific EF impairments as a function of EF measurement approach, the efficacy of which is noted here (Table 5.8).

PB tasks typically aim to measure a particular cognitive process (Boonstra et al., 2005) through performance challenges that seek to isolate and identify specific process deficiencies (Sergeant & van der Meere, 1990). PB tasks tap into state-like information, providing information on an individual's capacities at a specific moment in time under specific circumstances. Some have proposed that no measures are 'pure' in that they rely upon and isolate only one domain of EF (Samyn et al., 2015). Moreover, these tasks are categorized under subdomains like "Inhibition" or "Generativity," suggesting that EF is not a unitary construct that can be separated into distinct processes. However, it is acknowledged that lower-level cognitive factors as well as contextual factors like motivation and fatigue play a role influencing outcomes, and that these distinctions may not be as singular as proposed (Samyn et al., 2015). They may not be as specific as intended; for example, there has been evidence that alternative processes may account for the Stroop effect; thus, it is not inhibitory control alone that accounts for task success (MacLeod, 1991).

On the other hand, RW measures are thought to tap into more trait-like information—information on behavior over a period of time (Samyn et al., 2015). As previously stated, they encompass a wider range of EF. PB tasks may be specific to the situation and thus susceptible to contextual effects, whereas RW measures, particularly questionnaires, reflect a more aggregate level of behavioral and attentional control (Samyn et al., 2015).

The differential nature in which PB and RW measures distinguish between the three neurodevelopmental disorders is worthy of examination. When comparing EF between individuals with ASD vs. TD controls the most prominent differences emerged between the two measurement approaches. There were various reasons why several studies did not find significant differences between these groups when EF was measured with PB tasks. Matsuura and colleagues (2014) postulated it was small sample sizes, while Alderson-Day (2014) posited that any task that is language-based is skewed because individuals with ASD may have atypical language development. Sachse and colleagues (2012) hypothesized that sensitivity of the different EF tasks has not been made comparable across the CANTAB battery since the CANTAB has not been standardized (Cambridge Cognition, 2016), while on a similar note, Geurts and Vissers (2011) also questioned if their tasks were sensitive enough. Some even allude to the extent of daily life-planning that PB tasks cannot capture, acknowledging that a "psychometrically defined" EF deficit does not exclude daily living difficulties, such as planning and daily tasks that involve a social component (Sachse et al., 2013.

One potential explanation why PB measures are not as potent as RW measures in detecting deficits in ASD relative to TD groups could be the social component of having an experimenter administer the task. A face-to-face administration imposes an inherently social demand to the task that individuals with ASD may have trouble internalizing in conjunction with performing the task (Ozonoff, 1995). Thus, whenever trying to isolate EF specific demands from social demands, one approach is to use

**Table 5.8** A sampling of performance-based executive function measures, including the associated age range and a brief description.

| *Name* | *Age range* | *Description* |
|---|---|---|
| Addenbrooke's Cognitive Examination–Revised (ACE-R) (Mioshi et al., 2006) | 50–75 years | 26-item dementia-screening test, sensitive to early cognitive dysfunction; includes five sub-domain scores of orientation/attention, memory, verbal fluency, and visuospatial function. |
| Amsterdam Neuropsychological Tasks Program (ANTP) (De Sonneville, 1999) | 4–15 years | Battery of assessments of speed and accuracy of visual and auditory information processing, executive function, visuomotor coordination, etc. Subtests include but are not limited to:<br>• Focused attention task (see below)<br>• Shifting attention task-auditory (see below) |
| Animal Stroop task (AS) (Wright et al., 2003) | 3–16 years | Modified version of the Stroop task to circumvent limited abilities on reading; participants are presented with four exemplar images of animals (cow, pig, sheep, duck), which can be oriented to the right or to the left. In congruent conditions, the head and body of the animal are matched; in incongruent conditions, each animal's head is replaced with the head of one of the other three animal prototypes. |
| Antisaccade task (Klein & Foerster, 2001) | 6–26 years | Computerized test in which participants are asked to stare at a fixation cross on a computer screen for a fixed duration, after which a peripheral target appeared randomly in four landmark boxes. Participants are asked to saccade to the target's mirror image location on the opposite side of the screen. |
| Attention Network Test (ANT) (Fan et al., 2002) | Children and adults | Task designed to test three attentional networks in children and adults: alerting, orienting, and executive control. Participants are presented with a central arrow surrounded by two congruent, incongruent, or neutral flankers, and are asked to press two keys indicating which direction the central arrow is pointing. Changes in reaction time between the congruent, incongruent, and neutral conditions are examined. |
| Automatic Cognitive Inhibition: Retrieval-Induced Forgetting (Anderson et al., 1994) | Adults | The study consisted of three phases: study, retrieval, and test. In the study phase, participants were presented with items from six categories (e.g., fruit) consisting of six exemplars (e.g., orange) each along with two filler categories with six items each as well. Participants were shown all 48 exemplar words paired with their category name (e.g., "fruit–orange"). In the retrieval phase, participants practiced completing fragments using three of the six exemplars from three of the six categories. After a delay, in the test phase, participants were provided with category names and asked to recall all exemplars from that category. The benefit of practice was examined as the main dependent measure. |

(*Continued*)

**Table 5.8** (Continued)

| *Name* | *Age range* | *Description* |
|---|---|---|
| Battersea Multitask Paradigm (Mackinlay et al., 2006) | Children | Participants were presented with three tasks: bead-sorting, counter-sorting, and caterpillar-sorting. The goal of the test is to achieve the most effective strategy to perform these three tasks simultaneously and score the most points in a time interval that is not sufficient to perform these tasks one at a time. |
| Benton Visual Retention Test (BVRT) (Sivan, 1992) | 8+ years | Assesses visual perception, memory, and visuoconstructive abilities via a series of designs. Participants view designs for a designated period of time (depending on method of administration; in increments of 5, 10, and 15 seconds) and reproduce it from memory; scoring is based on different types of errors committed, including but not limited to omissions, distortions, perseverations, rotations, misplacements, size errors; there are three alternative forms of ten designs each and four ways of administration |
| Box Task (Reck et al., 2010) | Children | Participants are presented with an open box with a bottom marked by 20 yellow dots. The experimenter places 20 various miniature objects on the dots and the participant learns their locations. The objects are then removed and the participant asked to re-place them in the box one at a time. |
| Cambridge Neuropsychological Test Automated Battery (CANTAB) (Cambridge Cognition, 1996; Robbins & Sahakian, 1994) | 4–90 years | Computerized and standardized battery of 22 tests divided into six main groups: motor and visual memory, executive function, working memory and planning, attention, verbal/semantic memory, and decision making and response control. CANTAB allows researchers to create their own battery by selecting tests for their research purpose. Subtests include but are not limited to:<br>• DMS (Delayed Match-to-Sample; see below)<br>• ID/ED (Intradimensional/Extradimensional; see below)<br>• MTS (Match to Sample Visual Search; see below)<br>• RTI (Reaction Time Task; see below)<br>• RVP (Rapid visual information processing; see below)<br>• SOC (Stockings of Cambridge; see below)<br>• SWM (Spatial Working Memory Task; see below)<br>• 2C-RT (Two-choice reaction time task; see below) |
| Category fluency test, Dutch version (Luteijn & van der Ploeg, 1983) | Children and adults | Participants were asked to name as many animals and professions as they could in one minute per category. |

| | | |
|---|---|---|
| Change Task (ChT) (Logan & Burkell, 1986) | Adults | Extension of the Stop Signal Task (see below), where participants are instructed to not only withhold response to a stimulus when an auditory stop-signal tone is presented, but perform an additional, different response (change response); main dependent measure is reaction time. |
| Circle Drawing Test (Bachorowski & Newman, 1990) | Children and adults | Measured number of seconds to trace a large circle under inhibition conditions, minus the number of seconds to trace in a neutral condition, with larger inhibition time indicating the participants' increased ability to inhibit the continuous tracing response. |
| Clock Drawing Test (CDT) (Kaplan, 1988) | Children, adult patients | Children are asked to draw hands on a previously drawn clock, indicating understanding of certain times. |
| Color Matching Task (CMT) (Arsalidou et al., 2010) | 7+ years | Children were presented with colored pictures of a clown and asked to ignore the clown's face and irrelevant colors (blue and green) and focus on other, relevant colors. Participants had to indicate whether or not the current target item had the same set of relevant colors as the previous criterion item. The number of '*n*' relevant colors (capacity) was increased with each increasing difficulty level. |
| Color-Word Interference Test (from DKEFS) (Delis, Kaplan & Kramer, 2001a, b) | 8–89 years | Participants are presented with a word page of words printed in black ink, a color page of Xs printed in color, and a color-word with words from the first page printed in colors from the second page (where the color and word do not match); participants are asked to go down each sheet reading the words or naming ink colors as quickly as possible without a time limit. |
| Conners' Continuous Performance Test (CCPT) (Conners, 2004) | 6+ years | Participants are presented with a repetitive array of visual stimuli on the computer screen and are asked to press the space bar each time a letter other than "X" appears, with presentation rates of 1, 2, and 4 second intervals throughout the task. |
| Conflict Control Task (CCT) (Hogan et al., 2005) | Children and adults | Similar to the 2C-RT but with an inhibitory component in which participants must occasionally suppress a tendency to respond to an arrow and respond in the other direction, as prompted by a change in color of the arrow; there were 75 congruent trials and 25 incongruent trials. |
| Contingency Naming Test (CNT) (Taylor et al., 1990) | Children and adults | Participants are presented with shapes outlined in black with solid color interiors and asked to name the color under different rules; Level A required naming the color or shape of the stimulus, Level B require switching between naming the stimuli by color or by shape depending on the attribute, thus presenting both working memory and inhibitory control demands |

(*Continued*)

**Table 5.8** (Continued)

| *Name* | *Age range* | *Description* |
|---|---|---|
| Continuous Performance Test –Identical Pairs (CPT-IP) (Cornblatt et al., 1988) | 12+ years | Computerized test of inhibition that requires the participant to focus on two, three, and four-digit numbers on a screen while pressing down on the mouse, lifting the finger press only if two identical stimuli appear on consecutive trials; measure of sustained attention that can be analyzed via signal detection theory. |
| Controlled Word Association Test (COWAT) (Benton & Hamsher, 1989) | 16–70 years | Test of letter fluency; dependent variable is total number of correct responses generated by the participant that start with a given letter, proper nouns excluded.<br>FAS test (subtest that can be administered independently): participants verbalized out loud as many words they could think of beginning with a certain letter; in this instance, one minute was given for each of the letters F, A, and S. |
| Delayed Match-to-Sample (DMS; from CANTAB) | 4–90 years | Participants are down a complex visual pattern (the sample) followed by four similar patterns after a brief delay and asked to select the pattern that matches the sample; outcome measures include but are not limited to accuracy and reaction time. |
| Delis-Kaplan Executive Functioning System (D-KEFS) (Delis et al., 2001a, b) | 8–89 years | Battery of tests assessing higher-level cognitive functions. Subtests include: Sorting, Trail Making, Verbal Fluency, Design Fluency, Color-Word Interference, Tower, 20 Questions, Word Context, and Proverb; scores based on normed population of 1,500 individuals. Subtests include but are not limited to:<br>• Color–Word Interference Test (CWIT)<br>• Trail-Making Test (TMT) |
| Digit Ordering Test-Adapted (DOT-A) (Cooper et al., 1991; Werheid et al., 2002) | Children and adults | Participants were presented with a series of six items of increasing length (three to eight digits) at a rate of one digit per second and are asked to repeat these digits immediately in ascending order. |
| Digit Span-Backward (DS-B; from WAIS-III) | 16–89 years | Participants are presented with a series of digits and asked to repeat them in backward order. |
| Digit Symbol Substitution Test (DSST; from WAIS-III) | 16–89 years | Participants are presented with a coding system (key) in which the digits 0 through 9 were matched to simple symbols along with a response form in which the top half of the rows were filled with digits from 0 to 9 and the bottom half of the rows were empty; participants are asked to match draw as many symbols in a span of two minutes, using the key, and moving right to left and without skipping any boxes. |

| | | |
|---|---|---|
| Dimensional Change Card-Sorting Task (Zelazo, 2006) | 3+ years | Children are required to sort a series of images in two dimensions. Children are presented on a computer screen with two boxes: one with a blue car and one with a red teddy bear. In Block 1 (12 trials), children are asked to sort objects by color; in Block 2 (12 trials), by shape; in Block 3 (24 trials), the sorting criterion varied across items and announced by a computer voice just before the object was presented. |
| Dual-task paradigm (Baddeley et al., 1997; Della Sala et al., 2010) | 18+ | Two tasks are presented to the participant. First, to assess participants' maximum digit span, lists of increasing number of digits are read aloud, with the participant asked to repeat the digits. Maximum digit span is taken to be the maximum digit length in which the participant correctly repeated 5 sequences. The other task consisted of linking a series of circles with arrows to create a path. Participants were asked to independently complete these two tasks, followed by their simultaneous presentation, with the percent loss in completing the dual task as compared to the single tasks as the dependent variable. |
| Effortful Cognitive Inhibition: Directed Forgetting (Conway & Fthenaki, 2003) | Adults | The task consisted of two different conditions (forget and remember) along with three phases (study, recall, old-new recognition). Participants were presented with 120 unrelated concrete nouns, assigned randomly to two pools of 60 words matched for frequency and concreteness, each divided into four lists of 15 words. Participants were asked to either remember all the words or remember on the to-be-remembered words. |
| Eriksen Flanker Paradigm (Eriksen & Eriksen, 1974) | Adults | Participants were presented with five horizontally-arranged arrows and asked to evaluate if the middle arrow was pointing left or right. Flankers could be congruent (pointing the same direction) or incongruent (pointing the opposite direction); a mean RT in the congruent condition was subtracted from the mean RT in the incongruent condition. |
| FAS Test-Letter Fluency (See COWAT) | Children and adults | Participants verbalized out loud as many words they could think of beginning with a certain letter; in this instance, one minute was given for each of the letters F, A, and S. |
| Flexible Item Selection Task (FIST) (Jacques & Zelazo, 2001) | 2–5 years | Participants were presented with 15 cards with three printed pictures of objects and asked to select two pictures that match each other on one category (object, color, or size) and then asked to select a different pair that matched on another category. |
| Focused attention task (FA; from ANTP) | 4–15 years | Participants are presented with a four-letter display arranged in two diagonals and instructed to attend to one diagonal only; participants were instructed to press a "yes" key if a target stimulus (defined as a stimulus that contains a letter from the relevant diagonal) is present, or a "no" key if the target stimulus is no present. |
| Go/No-Go (GNG) (Bitsakou et al., 2008) | Children and adults | Similar to the 2C-RT task (see below) but required participants on occasion to completely withhold a response to a stimulus when prompted with a certain color arrow; there were 75 "go" trials and 25 "no-go" trials. |

(*Continued*)

**Table 5.8** (Continued)

| *Name* | *Age range* | *Description* |
|---|---|---|
| Hayling Test (Burgess & Shallice, 1996) | 18–80 years | Participants are presented with ten sentences read aloud one at a time and asked to complete each sentence with a single word. In the first part of the test, participants were told to use a word choice best suited to complete the sentence; in the second part of the test, participants were asked to suppress the obvious word choice strongly primed by the corresponding cue sentence (the answers from the first part). Incorrect responses to both parts as well as reaction time were noted. |
| Honk Test (Oosterlaan & Sergeant, 1998) | Children and adults | Participants are presented with a visual stimulus (a red car) on a computer screen on either the left or right side. In the "Go" condition, participants had to press a key indicating which side the stimulus appeared; in the "Stop" condition, participants had to respond as per usual in the "Go" condition 75% of the time, but had to inhibit their response 25% of the time when a horn sounded; in the "Change" condition, participants responded as per usual in the "Go" condition 75% of the time but had to use a different response key 25% of the time during the sounding of the horn. |
| Hungry Donkey Test (Crone & van der Molen, 2004) | 8–18 years | Child version of the Iowa Gambling Task in which participants try to win as many apples for a hungry donkey by choosing one of four doors, with the amount of wins and losses varying between choices–Doors A and B represented disadvantageous choices (overall loss) while Doors C and D represented advantageous choices (overall gain). |
| Intradimensional/ Extradimensional (ID/ED; from CANTAB, see above) | 4–90 years | Participants are presented with a series of stimuli composed of colored lines and shapes and then learn through trial and error to respond to the shape and not lines. Once training is complete, two types of shifts take place. In an intradimensional shift, new stimuli are presented, but shape is still the relevant dimension; tests perceptual flexibility. In an extradimensional shift, the lines become the relevant dimension; tests conceptual flexibility. |
| Letter–Number Sequencing Test (LN; from WISC-IV) | 6–16 years | Participants are presented with a series of auditory numbers and letters and rearranges the numbers first, from lowest to highest, followed by the letters, in alphabetical order. The test consists of ten items, with the total correctly recalled trials as a dependent measure. |
| Letter and Number Sequencing (LNS; from WAIS-III, WMS-III) | 16–89 years | Participants are presented with a series of auditory numbers and letters and rearranges the numbers first, from lowest to highest, followed by the letters, in alphabetical order. The test consists of ten items, with the total correctly recalled trials as a dependent measure. |
| Luria hand game (Luria et al., 1964) | Children and patients | Participants first had to imitate a hand action. In the subsequent conflict test condition, participants had to produce a hand action that bore only arbitrary relation to the experimenter's hand action (e.g. make a fist when the experimenter pointed a finger). |

| | | |
|---|---|---|
| Non-word Repetition (NWR) (Gathercole et al., 1994) | 4–9 years | Participants hear a non-word aloud and repeated it verbally. |
| Match to Sample Visual Search (MTS; from CANTAB) | 4–90 years | Participants are presented with a complex visual pattern (the sample) in the middle of the screen; after a brief delay, a varying number of similar patterns is shown in a circle of boxes around the edge of the screen; participant must indicate which one matches the pattern in the center of the screen by touching it. |
| Matching Familiar Figures Test (MFF) (Kagan et al., 1964) | 4+ years | Participants are shown a target picture and asked to identify a picture that among with five distracter items; response latency for first item along with number of errors for each trial are recorded. |
| Modified Card Sorting Test (MCST) (Nelson 1976) | Patients | Simpler and less ambiguous version of the WCST with a new method of documenting perseverative errors. |
| N-back task (Jeter et al., 2011) | Children and adults | Variant of the classic N-back task; instead of a single continuous trial, discrete trials of 0-back and 1-back are presented to participants. Length of the sequence is varied from trial to trial; furthermore, each stimulus in the sequence is presented in the visual periphery, with the participant indicating their response by looking at the location of the stimulus. For the 0-back, participants must indicate the position of the last stimulus. For the 1-back, participants must indicate the position of the next-to-last stimulus. |
| Planning Drawing Task (Booth et al., 2003) | Children | Participants were presented with four pictures that needed completion: a snowman (add teeth), a clock (add numbers), a house (add four windows), and a ship (add people and portholes). The pictures and both local and global elements and required the participant to plan ahead in order to accurately depict the size and relation of each part of the picture to other parts. |
| Plus-minus task (Bueno et al., 2014; Miyake et al., 2000) | Children and adults | Participants are presented with three lists of two-digit numbers (10–99). On the first list, participants were asked to add three to each number; on the second list, subtract three. On the third list, participants were asked to switch between adding and subtracting three on each subsequent item. Dependent measures include list completion times as well as number of errors; the difference between the time needed to complete the alternating list and the sum of the addition and subtraction list represents the cost of shifting. |
| Random Number Generation (RNG; Miyake et al., 2000) | Adults | Participants are asked to generate numbers in a random order, using the digits 1 through 9 at 1-second intervals marked by a sound signal. Degree of randomness was assessed by software. |
| Rapid visual information processing (RVP; from CANTAB) | 4–90 years | Participants are presented with digits (from 2 to 9) appearing in the middle of a computer screen in random order and are asked to press a response pad when they detect any one of three number sequences (3–5–7, 2–4–6, 4–6–8). |

(*Continued*)

**Table 5.8** (Continued)

| *Name* | *Age range* | *Description* |
|---|---|---|
| Raven's Colored Progressive Matrices (CPM) (Raven et al., 2003) | 5–11 years, elderly, mentally and physically impaired persons | Paper-and-pencil untimed assessment of nonverbal mental abilities; requires the examinee to solve problems presented in abstract figures and designs, administered on three levels of difficulty. |
| Rey Auditory Verbal Learning Task (RAVLT) (Rey, 1964; van den Burg et al., 1985) | 16+ years | Participants memorize a list of 15 words; immediate recall tested along with delayed recall and recognition after 20 minutes. Dependent measure includes correct number of recalled words and correct number of recognized words. |
| Reaction Time (RTI; from CANTAB, see above) | 4–90 years | In the simple condition, participants must react as soon as a yellow dot appears. In the five-choice condition, participants respond by using a press-pad, touch screen, or both; the dot may appear in one of five locations on the screen. Outcome measures include reaction time and movement time. |
| Self-Ordered Pointing Task (SOP) (Petrides & Milner, 1982) | Children and adults | Participants are presented with four series of cards with 6, 8, 10, or 12 abstract designs. On each card within a series, the same designs are presented, but the position of the designs differs. The participant is asked to point to a different design on each card within the series. |
| Semantic Decision Task (SDT) (Alderson-Day et al., 2014) | Children and adults | Participants are presented with a single target word followed by three cue words and asked which of the cue words are associated with the target; three blocks of ten trials for the superordinate category and the exemplar category, respectively. |
| Sentence Completion Task (Happé et al., 2001) | 8–25 years | Participants are presented with ten question stems and asked to complete the sentence. The task is designed to pit demands for global sentence meaning against the tendency to give locally cued associative responses. Participants' responses were scored and local errors were noted if the response did not make sense in the context of the entire sentence. |
| Shifting attention task-auditory (from ANTP) | 4–15 years | Stimuli consisted of four auditory cues: high tone once, low tone once, high tone twice, and low tone twice. Depending on the pitch of the tone, participants were required to copy the tone (press once or twice) or mirror the tone (press once when a double tone is presented and twice when a single tone is presented). The pitch of the tone indicated whether copying or mirroring was to be performed. |
| Spatial Span Task (SSP; from CANTAB, see above) | 4–90 years | Participants are presented with a series of white squares on a screen, which briefly change color one at a time in a sequence. Participants are asked to touch the boxes that changed colors in the same order they were displayed (clinical mode) or reverse order (reverse mode). The number of boxes that change color begin at two and go up to nine. |

| | | |
|---|---|---|
| Spatial Working Memory Task (SWM; from CANTAB, see above) | 4–90 years | Participants are asked to search for a blue token hidden among boxes (sets of 4, 6, and 8 boxes presented); prevents serial search by noting the number of boxes searched where a blue token had already been found. |
| Stockings of Cambridge Task (SOC; from CANTAB, see above) | 4–90 years | Spatial planning test similar to Tower of London; participants are presented with a three different colored balls, which are located in three pockets that are able to hold one, two, and three balls, respectively. Participants are also presented with a target screen in the upper half of the screen, which shows the final positions of the balls. By manipulating the lower half of the screen, participants are asked to recreate the target screen, but by only able to move one ball at a time and only from the top of each pocket, in as few moves as possible ("plan and move" condition). Participants are then asked to recreate their own solution as quickly as possible ("follow" condition). |
| Stop-Signal Test (SST) (Logan et al., 1984) | Children and adults | Participants are presented with a sequential series of letter stimuli and instructed to press a key, except in the case of an auditory stop signal, in which they would withhold a response. |
| Stroop Test (Stroop, 1935) | 15–90 years | Participants are presented with a word page with color words printed in black ink, a color page with 'Xs' printed in color, and a color–word page with words from the first page printed in colors from the second page. Participants are asked to go down each sheet reading words or naming the ink colors as quickly as possible. |
| Sustained Attention to Response Task (SART) (Robertson et al., 1997) | Children and adults | Participants are presented sequentially with a series of digits (1 through 9) and are asked to press a key when each appears, except in the case of a no-go digit (e.g. "3"). |
| Test of Variables of Attention (TOVA) (Greenberg, 1991) | 4–80 years | Computerized test in which the participant learns to respond to two test conditions: target frequent and target infrequent; in the first half of the test, the target : non-target ratio is 1 : 3.5; thus the participant must pay close attention to responding to a target. In the second half of the test, the target : non-target ratio is 3.5 : 1; thus, participants respond most of the time but must occasionally inhibit the tendency to respond. Errors of commission (response to a non-target) and errors of omission (lack of response to a target) are noted. |
| Tower of London (Shallice, 1982) | 16–80 years | Participants are presented with two boards with three different colored beads and three levels of pegs, which can hold one, two, and three beads, respectively. The administrator arranges a target pattern on one board and the participant is asked to replicate the pattern on their own board in as few moves as possible while abiding by two rules: 1) only moving one bead at a time, and 2) not putting more beads on a peg than the peg can hold. Dependent measures collected are total correct trials, total moves, total initiation time, total execution time, total time, total time violations, and total rule violations. |

(*Continued*)

**Table 5.8** (Continued)

| *Name* | *Age range* | *Description* |
|---|---|---|
| Tower of London –Drexel University (ToL-DX) (Culbertson & Zillmer, 2001) | 16–80 years | Expansion of the traditional Tower of London task with the following differences: introduction of 6- and 7-move test problems, elimination of repeated trials for failed problems; normative data available for TD and ADHD subjects on this measure. |
| Tower of London–Revised (Schnirman et al., 1998) | Adults | Expansion of the traditional Tower of London task with the following differences: the number of items was increased from 15 to 69 (15 three-move items, 19 four-move items, 19 five-move items, and 16 six-move items) along with three start states. Participants were allowed up to 120 seconds per trial. |
| Trail Making Test (TMT; part of D-KEFS) | 8–89 years | Participants are presented with a series of letters and numbers on a page and asked to connect them in alphabetical and numerical order, switching between letters and numbers beginning with 1 and A, respectively. |
| Twenty Questions Task (TQT) (Mosher & Hornsby, 1966) | Children and adults | A measure of verbal problem-solving skills whereby the experimenter selects an object and the participant asks a series of questions to determine its identity; used to assess categorical hierarchy. |
| Two-choice reaction time task (2C-RT; from CANTAB) | 4–90 years | Participants are presented with an arrow-shaped stimulus on either the left or the right side of the computer screen and are asked to press the corresponding button (right or left) on the press pad. |
| Virtual Week Test (Rendell & Craik, 2000; Rendell & Henry, 2009) | Adults | Computer-based board game-like test in which participants are presented with a board that represents a waking day. Participants move around the board by rolling a dice and pick up cards that describe an activity relevant to the time of day, mimicking many features of daily living. |
| Visual Memory (from WMS-III) | 16–89 years | Participants were presented with five geometrical stimuli for 10 seconds and asked to reproduce them at two different time points: immediately after viewing the figures and 20 minutes after viewing. |
| Visual Memory Span–Backwards (VMS-B; from WMS—Revised) | 16–89 years | Participants were presented with colored squares on a sheet and asked to tap them in the reverse order as tapped by the experimenter |
| WAIS Matrix reasoning (from WAIS-III) | 16–89 years | Participants are presented with a sequence of geometric shapes where one section is missing and are asked to select the missing section from five possible response options. |
| WAIS picture arrangement (from WAIS-III) | 16–89 years | Participants are presented with a series of cards with simple drawings of characters in certain situations, carrying out simple to complex tasks. Participants are asked to arrange the cards from beginning to end so that they made a sensible story. The simplest trials were made out of three cards, while the most complex trials were made out of six cards. |

| | | |
|---|---|---|
| WAIS Similarities Task (from WAIS-III) | 16–89 years | Participants are presented with a pair of words verbally and are asked to explain how they were alike. Word pairs gradually increased in complexity, requiring more abstract thought. |
| Wisconsin Card Sorting Test (WCST) (Heaton et al., 1993) | 7–89 years | Participants are presented with a series of 64 stimulus cards along with four "key" cards. All cards contain four different shapes in one of four colors and one of four numerical formats. The participant is told to match each of the stimulus cards to one of the key cards. They are not explicitly told how to match, but rather, a verbal indication from the experimenter whether their match is correct or incorrect. Once the participant deduced the correct sorting rule and matched ten consecutive cards correctly, the experimenter would change the category without warning. |
| Wechsler Adult Intelligence Scale–3rd edition (WAIS-III) (Wechsler, 1997a) | 16–89 years | Battery of tests to measure an adult's intellectual ability. Subtests include but are not limited to:<br>• Digit Span-Backwards (DS-B; see above)<br>• Digit Symbol Substitution Test (DSST; see above)<br>• LNS (Letter and Number Sequencing; see above)<br>• WAIS matrix reasoning (see above)<br>• WAIS picture arrangement (see above)<br>• WAIS similarities (see above) |
| Wechsler Intelligence Scale for Children (WISC-IV) (Wechsler 2003, 2004) | 6–16 years | Battery of tests to measure a child's intellectual ability. Subtests include but are not limited to LN Letter–Number sequencing test (see above) |
| Wechsler Memory Scale–Revised (WMS-R) (Wechsler & Stone, 1987) | 16–89 years | Revision of original Wechsler Memory Scale, includes measures of nonverbal attention, learning, and short term and delayed recall Subtests include but are not limited to:<br>• VMS-B (Visual Memory Span–Backwards; see above) |
| Wechsler Memory Scale, 3rd edition (WMS-III) (Wechsler, 1997b) | 16–89 years | A battery of eight primary and four secondary tests of auditory and visual memory abilities. Subtests include but are not limited to:<br>• LNS (Letter, Number and Sequencing; see above)<br>• Visual Memory (see above) |

computerized versions of EF tasks when available. This should lessen interaction with the experimenter and therefore reduce the likelihood of a social confound influencing the results (Durrleman & Franck, 2015). Correspondingly, in a meta-analysis spanning 30 years' work on the Wisconsin Card Sorting Task, Landry and Al-Taie (2016) posited that the computerized version of the WCST is not necessarily equivalent to the manual administration, and that there were no significant differences in levels of impairment between the two modalities. One key point in the human-versus-computerized administration dichotomy is that many studies have not employed both in a single study for direct comparison across the same individuals. Williams and Jarrold (2013) were the first to do so in directly comparing performance on computerized and experimenter-administered tests among individuals with ASD, and they found equal levels of impairment for both, suggesting that the difficulties that children with ASD might experience engaging with experimenters was not a confound in performing (at least some) EF tasks. Accordingly, the authors call for further investigation to corroborate this result.

In comparing ADHD and TD groups, RW tasks appear to be particularly sensitive. When examining ADHD subgroup contrasts, it appears that only BRIEF Index scores, not individual scales, could differentiate between different subtypes of ADHD. PB tasks are also fairly sensitive in detecting deficits in ADHD as compared to TD controls, in contrast to findings from studies of ASD and TD groups. Even so, PB measures are known to be especially context-dependent in ADHD (Sonuga-Barke, Wiersema, van der Meere, & Roeyers, 2010). Additionally, a distinction is made between "hot" EF vs. "cold" EF tasks, with Skogli and colleagues (2014) postulating that they tap into different systems. When an emotional component is involved in a given test, the test is considered to be "hot" in the sense that decision-making processes are influenced by the experience of emotion (Damasio, 1994). It has been shown that between "hot" and "cold" EF tasks, individuals with ADHD are more impaired on "hot" EF, but only when using RW measures (Skogli et al., 2014). Overall, a robust profile of EF deficits in ADHD with inhibition and working memory showing the greatest degree of impairment is emerging.

When comparing individuals with TS vs. TD controls, one particularly relevant study (Hovik et al., 2014) that employed both RW measures and PB tasks found that RW measures were more sensitive to TS-related deficits. It is hard to generalize because while there were a handful of studies for PB, there was only one study in the RW category with a TD group comparison.

## Interchangeability of Real-world and Performance-Based Assessment of Executive Function

It is increasingly clear that RW and PB measures should not be used interchangeably, but should be used as complementary sources of information about EF. Nevertheless, to date many studies employ one or the other exclusively. In our current survey of the literature only a handful employed both simultaneously (Boyer et al., 2014; Crippa et al., 2014; Skogli et al., 2014) and a few used both and compare and contrast pattern of findings (Hovik et al., 2014; Samyn et al., 2014, 2015). Samyn and colleagues (2015) propose that effortful control (EC) as measured by questionnaires and EF as measured by neuropsychological tasks (i.e., PB) may tap into different domains.

When Samyn and colleagues explicitly compared EF tasks and EC questionnaires, they found no associations to modest relationships. This only serves to reinforce the value of employing both RW and PB tasks whether utilized clinically or in a research setting to assess intact and impaired EF domains.

Another important issue is if RW and PB tasks are able to distinguish between clinical groups and reveal similar patterns of deficits either independently or taken together. One important characteristic that separates the two is the aforementioned distinction in the literature between "hot" EF and "cool" EF; hot tasks involve regulation of emotions while cool tasks are more decontextualized and emotionally neutral. PB tasks are usually "cool," thus eliciting EF without emotional components. Previous research supports this; when "cool" EF tasks are contextualized in everyday situations, they interact and are influenced by affective and motivational processes (Sonuga-Barke et al., 2003, 2005). Furthermore, higher correlations were found between cold BRIEF scales (Inhibit, Initiate, Working Memory, Plan/Organize, Organization of Materials, and Monitor) and "cold" EF tests (e.g. Color–Word Interference Test, Letter Fluency Test) than "cold" BRIEF scales with "hot" BRIEF scales (Emotional Control, Shift) (Skogli et al., 2014).

## Developmental Differences in Executive Dysfunction

There are several explanations as to the difference in the EFDM between youth and adult when examining diagnostic group differences by EF domain. This was particularly prominent when analyzing by domain in ASD and ADHD. There may exist a developmental effect, whereby maturation or intervention bolsters decreasing executive dysfunction in adults. Of note is the Planning domain in ASDs; whereas the youth group evinced an EFDM of >>1, showing that all the studies in ASD youth found significant differences, the adult group had an EFDM of 1.07, showing an approximately equal number of studies that did and did not find significant differences. This dramatically reduced planning deficit in ASD during adulthood as compared to childhood might suggest that planning is an EF domain particularly susceptible to intervention, or it might represent a maturational effect whereby there is a developmental delay in planning in ASD. Similarly, among individuals with ADHD, Working Memory is a domain in which youth had severe deficits (EFDM = 9.22), but the impairment was dramatically less in adult studies (EFDM = 0.74). Similar factors to those described above could be playing a role here. Nevertheless, more work is needed to better understand the malleability of various EF domains, particularly as they are now commonly employed as primary treatment targets in various intervention and training programs (e.g., Kenworthy et al., 2014; Ziereis & Janson, 2015).

Another explanation for developmental effects lies in the measurement method. Though some standardized questionnaires have an adult and child version (i.e. BRIEF-A and BRIEF-P), therein lies the question of whether each measure is as sensitive among adults as it is in youth, or vice versa. This concern arises when considering that many measures were originally formulated exclusively for children or exclusively for adults, only to be later extended developmentally up (into adulthood) or down (into childhood). For example, it might be that adults are more apt to perform better and ceiling out on measures originally developed for children, thereby decreasing variance and the ability to detect potentially meaningful and significant group differences.

## Future Directions

Though our current cohort of studies from 2010 to 2015 reveals interesting patterns of deficits and developmental dissociations and demonstrates useful progress in the field, more task development is needed. For PB tasks, homogenization of existing tasks needs to continue. Previously, researchers have raised concerns that tasks are susceptible to variation across labs and even within the same lab. For example, there are many different difficulty levels (i.e. the number of 7- vs. 8- vs. 9- vs. 10-, etc. move problems varies) in tower tasks (Boonstra et al., 2005), and there are many dependent variables reported for various tasks—accuracy, reaction time, omission errors, commission errors, perseverative errors, etc. are selectively reported to differing degrees of comprehensiveness. Future studies should homogenize the reporting of outcome variables and not bias towards those that highlight significant (e.g. clinical vs. control) group differences.

Another valuable investment in task development is virtual reality (VR). There exists a gap in the field between PB tasks and RW, standardized questionnaires. Currently, the BADS is the only intermediate that exists between PB and RW tasks. Its construct lies in the fact that participants are performing tasks, but the outcomes of these tasks have been standardized and normalized (Wilson, Alderman, Burgess, Emslie, & Evans, 1996). Therein lies the need for more and similar kinds of instruments, acting as an intermediate between PB and RW measures. As a newly burgeoning methodology, virtual reality has already been employed in variety of settings and populations. A recent study investigated congruent vs. incongruent motor movement in adults with ASD and TD adults and discerned how the perception of biological motion differs between these groups (Cook et al., 2014). Other research includes the employment a supermarket virtual reality program to assess the ecological validity of the program to real-life grocery shopping in people with schizophrenia (Aubin et al., 2015) as well as a VR task to serve as a marker to detect Parkinson's Disease patients at risk for dementia (Cipresso et al., 2014). It would be beneficial to expand these EF VR tasks for administration to individuals with ASD, ADHD, and TS.

Lastly, a wider age range of participants across neurodevelopmental disorders (and TD control) groups is needed in order to delineate more refined developmental effects and trajectories. Only one study reviewed here tested preschoolers (Kimhi et al., 2014). Additionally, given that there is a relative lack of adult studies, an emphasis should be placed upon tracking EF development beyond childhood (when most individuals with these neurodevelopmental disorders are initially diagnosed). The need to examine EF across broader age ranges is exigently needed given that the majority of studies in the development of EF have focused primarily on young children and on fairly narrow age ranges. Part of the challenge lies in developing tasks appropriate for a wide age-range (i.e., both simple enough for young children and complex enough for adolescents and adults), given that some EF domain skills do not mature until adolescence or early adulthood (Best & Miller, 2010). This could be especially useful with respect to assessing and correlating these EF deficits with independent living outcomes and other factors related to quality of life. Additional work examining EF in older age groups and across child and adult development would rapidly advance our theoretical and clinical knowledge by offering a broader developmental view of EF across domains and assessment approach.

## References

Adler, L. A., Clemow, D. B., Williams, D. W., & Durell, T. M. (2014). Atomoxetine effects on executive function as measured by the BRIEF-A in young adults with ADHD: A randomized, double-blind, placebo-controlled study. *PloS One 9*(8): e104175.

Albert, D., & Steinberg, L. (2011). Age differences in strategic planning as indexed by the Tower of London. *Child Development, 82*, 1501–1517.

Alderson-Day, B. (2014). Verbal problem-solving difficulties in autism spectrum disorders and atypical language development. *Autism Research, 7*, 720–730.

American Psychiatric Association. (2013). *Diagnostic and statistical manual of mental disorders: DSM-5* (5th ed.). Arlington, VA: American Psychiatric Publishing.

Anderson, M. C, Bjork, R. A., & Bjork, E. L. (1994). Remembering can cause forgetting: Retrieval dynamics in long-term memory. *Journal of Experimental Psychology: Learning, Memory, & Cognition, 20*, 1063–1087.

Arsalidou, M., Pascual-Leone, J., & Johnson, J. (2010). Misleading cues improve developmental assessment of working memory capacity: The color matching tasks. *Cognitive Development, 25*, 262–277.

Asherson, P., Manor P., & Huss, M. (2014). Attention-deficit/hyperactivity disorder in adults: Update on clinical presentation and care. *Neuropsychiatry, 4*, 109–126.

Aubin, G., Béliveau, M. F., & Klinger, E. (2015). An exploration of the ecological validity of the Virtual Action Planning-Supermarket (VAP-S) with people with schizophrenia. *Neuropsychological Rehabilitation.*

Bachorowski, J. A., & Newman, J. P. (1990). Impulsive motor behavior: Effects of personality and goal salience. *Journal of Personality and Social Psychology, 58*, 512–518.

Baddeley, A., Della Sala, S., Gray, C., Papagno, C., & Spinnler, H. (1997). Testing central executive functioning with a pencil-and-paper test. In P. M. Rabbitt (Ed.), *Methodology of frontal and executive function* (pp. 61–80). Hove, UK: Lawrence Erlbaum.

Barkley, R. A. (2011). *Barkley deficits in executive functioning scale (BDEFS).* New York, NY: Guilford.

Benton, A. L., & Hamsher, K. D. (1989). *Multilingual aphasia examination.* Iowa City, IA: AJA Associates.

Best, J. R., & Miller, P. H. (2010). A developmental perspective on executive function. *Child Development, 81 (6)*, 1641–1660.

Bitsakou, P., Psychogiou, L., Thompson, M., & Sonuga-Barke, E. J. (2008). Inhibitory deficits in attention-deficit/hyperactivity disorder are independent of basic processing efficiency and IQ. *Journal of Neural Transmission, 115*, 261–268.

Blijd-Hoogewys, E. M. A., Bezemer, M. L., & van Geert, P. L. C. (2014). Executive functioning in children with ASD: an analysis of the BRIEF. *Journal of Autism and Developmental Disorders, 44*, 3089–3100.

Boonstra, A. M., Kooij, J. J. S., Oosterlaan, J., Sergeant J. A., & Buitelaar, J. K. (2010). To act or not to act, that's the problem: Primarily inhibition difficulties in adult ADHD. *Neuropsychology, 24(2)*, 209–221.

Boonstra, A. M., Oosterlaan, J., Sergeant, J. A., Kooij S., & Buitelaar, J. K. (2005). Executive functioning in adult ADHD: a meta-analytic review. *Psychological Medicine, 35*(8), 1097–1108.

Booth, R., Charlton, R., Hughes, C., & Happé, F. (2003). Disentangling weak coherence and executive dysfunction: Planning drawing in autism and attention-deficit/hyperactivity disorder. *Philosophical Transactions of the Royal Society B: Biological Sciences, 358*, 387–392.

Boyer, B. E., Geurts, H. M., & Van der Oord, S. (2014). Planning skills of adolescents with ADHD. *Journal of Attention Disorders.* doi: 10.1177/1087054714538658

Brunsdon, V. E. A., Colvert, E., Ames, C., Garnett, T., Gillan, N, Hallett, V., ... & Happé, F. (2015). Exploring the cognitive features in children with autism spectrum disorder, their co-twins, and typically developing children within a population-based sample. *Journal of Child Psychology and Psychiatry, 56(8)*, 893–902.

Bueno, V. F., da Silva, M. A., Alves, T. M., Louza, M. R., & Pompeia, S. (2014). Fractionating executive functions of adults with ADHD. *Journal of Attention Disorders.* doi: 10.1177/1087054714545537

Burgess, P. W., Alderman, N., Forbes, C., Costello, A., Coates, L., Dawson, D. R., & Channon, S. (2006). The case for the development and use of "ecologically valid" measures of executive function in experimental and clinical neuropsychology. *Journal of the International Neuropsychological Society, 12 (2)*, 1–16.

Burgess, P., & Shallice, T. (1996). Response suppression, initiation and strategy use following frontal lobe lesions. *Neuropsychologia, 34*, 263–273.

Cambridge Cognition. (1996). *CANTAB.* Cambridge, England: Cambridge Cognition.

Capaldi, D. M., & Rothbart, M. K. (1992). Development and validation of an early adolescent temperament measure. *Journal of Early Adolescence, 12*, 153–173.

Cipresso, P., Albani, G., Serino, S., Pedroli, E., Pallavicini, F., Mauro, A., & Riva, G. (2014). Virtual multiple errands test (VMET): a virtual reality-based tool to detect early executive functions deficit in Parkinson's disease. *Frontiers in Behavioral Neuroscience.*

Conners, C. K. (2004). *Conners' Continuous Performance Test (CPT II): Version 5 for Windows: Technical guide and software manual.* North Tonawanda, NY: Multi Health Systems.

Conners, C. K. (2008). *Conners 3rd edition manual.* Toronto: Multi-Health Systems.

Conway, M. A., & Fthenaki, A. (2003). Disruption of inhibitory control of memory following lesions to the frontal and temporal lobes. *Cortex, 39*, 667–686.

Cook, J., Swapp, D., Pan, X., Bianchi-Berthouze, N., & Blakemore, S. J. (2014). Atypical interference effect of action observation in autism spectrum conditions. *Psychological Medicine, 44*(4), 731–740.

Cooper, J. A., Sagar, H. J., Jordan, N., Harvey, N. S., & Sullivan, E. V. (1991). Cognitive impairment in early, untreated Parkinson's disease and its relationship to motor disability. *Brain, 114*, 2095–2122.

Cornblatt, B. A., Risch, N. J., Faris, G., Friedman, D., & Erlenmeyer-Kimling, L. (1988). The continuous performance test, identical pairs version (CPT-IP): I. new findings about sustained attention in normal families. *Psychiatry Research, 26(2)*, 223–238.

Crippa, A., Marzocchi, G. M., Piroddi, C., Besana, D., Giribone, S., Vio, C., … & Sora, M. L. (2015). An integrated model of executive functioning is helpful for understanding ADHD and associated disorders. *Journal of Attention Disorders, 19(6)*, 455–467.

Crone, E. A., & van der Molen, M. W. (2004). Developmental changes in real life decision making: Performance on a gambling task previously shown to depend on the ventromedial prefrontal cortex. *Developmental Neuropsychology, 25*(3), 251–279.

Culbertson, W. C., & Zillmer, E. A. (2001). *The Tower of London DX (TOLDX) manual.* North Tonawanda, NY: Multi-Health Systems.

Damasio, A. R. (1994). *Descartes' error: Emotion, reason, and the human brain.* New York, NY: Putnam.

Delis, D. C., Kaplan, E., & Kramer, J. H. (2001a). *The Delis–Kaplan Executive Function System: Examiner's manual.* San Antonio, TX: The Psychological Corporation.

Delis, D. C., Kaplan, E., & Kramer, J. H. (2001b). *The Delis–Kaplan Executive Function System: Technical manual.* San Antonio, TX: The Psychological Corporation.

Della Sala, S., Cocchini, G., Logie, R. H., & MacPherson, S. E. (2010). Dual task during encoding, maintenance and retrieval in Alzheimer disease and healthy ageing. *Journal of Alzheimer's Disease, 19*, 503–515.

De Sonneville, L. M. J. (1999). Amsterdam neuropsychological tasks: A computer-aided assessment program. In B. P. L. M. den Brinker, P. J. Brand, S. J. Maarse, & L. J. M. Mulder (Eds.), *Cognitive ergonomics, clinical assessment and computer-assisted learning: computers in psychology. 6*. 187–203. Lisse: Swets.

Derryberry, D., & Reed, M. A. (2002). Anxiety-related attentional biases and their regulation by attentional control. *Journal of Abnormal Psychology, 111*, 225–236.

Drury, H., Channon, S., Barrett, R., Young, M.-B., Stern, J. S., Simmons, H., & Crawford, S. (2012). Emotional processing and executive functioning in children and adults with Tourette's syndrome. *Child Neuropsychology, 18(3)*, 281–298.

Drury, H., Stern, J., Wilkinson, V., Parikh, N., & Channon, S. (2013). Effortful and automatic cognitive inhibition in adults with Tourette's Syndrome. *Neuropsychology, 27(1)*, 132–140.

Durrleman, S., & Franck, J. (2015). Exploring links between language and cognition in autism spectrum disorders: complement sentences, false belief, and executive functioning. *Journal of Communication Disorders, 54*, 15–31.

Dvorsky, M. R., & Langberg, J. M. (2014). Predicting impairment in college students with ADHD: the role of executive functions. *Journal of Attention Disorders.* doi: 10.1177/108705471458037

Eddy, C. M., & Cavanna, A. E. (2014). Set-shifting deficits: A possible neurocognitive endophenotype for Tourette syndrome without ADHD. *Journal of Attention Disorders.* doi: 10.1177/1087054714545536

Eddy, C. M., Rickards, H. E., & Cavanna, A. E. (2012). Executive functions in uncomplicated Tourette syndrome. *Psychiatry Research, 200 (1)*, 46–48.

Eichele, H., Eichele, T., Hammar, A., Freyberger, H. J., Hugdahl, K., & Plessen, K. J. (2010). Go/NoGo performance in boys with Tourette syndrome. *Child Neuropsychology, 16(2)*, 162–168.

Ellis, L. K., & Rothbart, M. K. (2001). Revision of the Early Adolescent Temperament Questionnaire. Poster presented at the biennial meeting of the Society for Research in Child Development, Minneapolis, MN.

Eriksen, B. A., & Eriksen, C. W. (1974). Effects of noise letters upon the identification of a target letter in a nonsearch task. *Perception and Psychophysics, 16*, 143–149.

Fan, J., McCandliss, B. D., Sommer, T., Raz, A., & Posner, M. I. (2002). Testing the efficiency and independence of attentional networks. *Journal of Cognitive Neuroscience, 14(3)*, 340–347.

Gathercole, S. E., Willis, C. S., Baddeley, A. D., & Emslie, H. (1994). The children's test of nonword repetition: A test of phonological working memory. *Memory, 2*, 103–127.

Gau, S. S. F., & Huang, W. L. (2014). Rapid visual information processing as a cognitive endophenotype of attention deficit hyperactivity disorder. *Psychological Medicine, 44*, 435–446.

Geurts, H. M., & Vissers, M. E. (2012). Elderly with autism: executive functions and memory. *Journal of Autism and Developmental Disorders, 42*, 665–675.

Gioia, G. A., Isquith, P. K., Guy, S. C., Kenworthy, L. (2000). Behavior rating inventory of executive function. *Clinical Neuropsychology, 6(3)*, 235–238.

Granader, Y., Wallace, G. L., Hardy, K. K., Yerys, B. E., Lawson, R. A., Rosenthal, M, … & Kenworthy, L. (2014) Characterizing the factor structure of parent-reported executive function in autism spectrum disorders: the impact of cognitive inflexibility. *Journal of Autism and Developmental Disorders, 44*, 3056–3062.

Grane, V. A., Endestad, T., Pinto A. F., & Solbakk, A. K. (2014) Attentional control and subjective executive function in treatment-I adults with attention deficit hyperactivity disorder. *PloS ONE 9(12):* e115227. doi: 10.1371/journal.pone.0115227

Greenberg, L. M. *Test of variables of attention.* Los Alamitos, CA: The Tova Company; 1991.

Halleland, H. B., Sorensen, L., Posserud, M. B., Haavik, J., & Lundervold, A. J. (2015). Occupation status is compromised in adults with ADHD and psychometrically defined executive function deficits. *Journal of Attention Disorders.* doi: 10.1177/1087054714564622

Happé, F., Briskman, J., Frith, U. (2001). Exploring the cognitive phenotype of autism: Weak "central coherence" in parents and siblings of children with autism: I. Experimental tests. *Journal of Child Psychology and Psychiatry, 42*, 299–307.

Heaton, R. K., Chelune, G. J., Talley, J. L., Kay, G. G., & Curtiss, G. (1993). *Wisconsin Card Sorting Test manual: Revised and expanded.* Odessa, FL: Psychological Assessment Resources.

Hill, E.L. (2004). Executive dysfunction in autism. *Trends in Cognitive Sciences, 8*, 26–32.

Hill, E., & Bird, C. (2006). Executive processes in Asperger syndrome: patterns of performance in a multiple case series. *Neuropsychologia, 44(14)*, 2822–2835.

Hogan, A. M., Vargha-Khadem, F., Kirkham, F. J., & Baldeweg, T. (2005). Maturation of action monitoring from adolescence to adulthood: an ERP study. *Developmental Science, 8*, 525–534.

Hovik, K. T., Egeland, J., Isquith, P. K., Gioia, G., Skogli, E. W., Andersen, P. N., & Oie, M. (2014). Distinct patterns of everyday executive function problems distinguish children with Tourette syndrome from children with ADHD or autism spectrum disorder. *Journal of Attention Disorders.* Advance online publication.

Hovik, K. T., Plessen, K. J., Skogli, E. W., Andersen, P. N., & Oie, M. (2013). Dissociable response inhibition in children with Tourette's Syndrome compared with children with ADHD. *Journal of Attention Disorders, 20(10)*, 825–835.

Isquith, P. K., Gioia, G. A., & Espy, K. A. (2004). Executive function in preschool children: Examination through everyday behavior. *Developmental Neuropsychology, 26*, 403–422.

Jacques, S., & Zelazo, P. D. (2001). The flexible item selection task (FIST): A measure of executive function in preschoolers. *Developmental Neuropsychology, 20*, 573–591.

Jeter, C. B., Patel, S. S., Morris, J. S., Chuang, A. Z., Butler, I. J., & Sereno, A. B. (2015). Oculomotor executive function abnormalities with increased tic severity in Tourette syndrome. *Journal of Child Psychology and Psychiatry, 56(2)*, 193–202.

Jeter, C. B., Patel, S. S., & Sereno, A. B. (2011). Novel n-back spatial working memory task using eye movement response. *Behavior Research Methods, 43*, 879–887.

Johnston, K., Madden, A. K., Bramham, J., & Russell, A. J. (2011). Response inhibition in adults with autism spectrum disorder compared to attention deficit/hyperactivity disorder. *Journal of Autism and Developmental Disorders, 41*, 903–912.

Kagan, J., Rosman, B. L., Day, D., Albert, J., & Phillips, W. (1964). Information processing in the child: Significance of analytic and reflective attitudes. *Psychological Monographs, 78*, (No. 578).

Kang, S. H., Yum, M. S., Kim, E. H., Kim, H. W., & Ko, T. S. (2015). Cognitive function in childhood epilepsy: importance of attention deficit hyperactivity disorder. *Journal of Clinical Neurology, 11(1)*, 20–25.

Kaplan, E. (1988). A process approach to neuropsychological assessment. In T. Boll, & B. K. Bryant (Eds.), *Clinical neuropsychology and brain function: Research, measurement, and practice.* Washington, D.C: American Psychological Association; 1988.

Kenworthy, L., Anthony, L. G., Naiman, D. Q., Cannon, L., Wills, M. C., Luong-Tran, C., … & Wallace, G. L. (2014). Randomized controlled effectiveness trial of executive function intervention for children on the autism spectrum. *Journal of Child Psychology and Psychiatry, 55*(4), 374–383.

Kenworthy, L., Yerys, B. E., Anthony, L. G., & Wallace, G. L. (2008). Understanding executive control in autism spectrum disorders in the lab and in the real world. *Neuropsychology Review, 18*(4), 320–338. doi: 10.1007/s11065-008-9077-7

Kimhi, Y., Shoam-Kugelmas, D., Ben-Artzi, G. A., Ben-Moshe, I., & Bauminger-Zviely, N. (2014). Theory of mind and executive function in preschoolers with typical development versus intellectually able preschoolers with autism spectrum disorder. *Journal of Autism and Developmental Disorders, 44*, 2341–2354.

Klein, C., & Foerster, F. (2001). Development of prosaccade and antisaccade task performance in participants aged 6 to 26 years. *Psychophysiology, 38*, 179–189.

Kretschmer, A., Altgassen, M., Rendell, P. G., & Bolte, S. (2014). Prospective memory in adults with high-functioning autism spectrum disorders: exploring effects of implementation intentions and retrospective memory load. *Research in Developmental Disabilities, 38*, 3108–3118.

Kvavilashvili, L., & Ellis, J. (2004). Ecological validity and twenty years of real-life/laboratory controversy in memory research: A critical (and historical) review. *History and Philosophy of Psychology*, *6*, 59–80.

Landry, O., & Al-Taie, S. (2016). A meta-analysis of the Wisconsin Card Sort Task in autism. *Journal of Autism and Developmental Disorders*, *46*, 1220–1235.

Leckman, J. F. (2002). Tourette's syndrome. *The Lancet*, *360*, 1577–1586.

Lehto, E. J., Juujarvi, P., Kooistra, L., & Pulkkinen, L. (2003). Dimensions of executive functioning: Evidence form children. *British Journal of Developmental Psychology*, *21*, 59–80.

Leung, R. C., Vogan, V. M., Powell, T. L., Anagnostou, E., & Taylor, M. J. (2016). The role of executive functions in social impairment in autism spectrum disorder. *Child Neuropsychology*, *22(3)*, 336–344.

Logan, G. D., & Burkell, J. (1986). Dependence and independence in responding to double stimulation: A comparison of stop, change, and dual-task paradigms. *Journal of Experimental Psychology: Human Perception and Performance*, *12*, 549–563.

Logan, G. D., Cowan, W. B., & Davis, K. A. (1984). On the ability to inhibit responses in simple and choice reaction time tasks: A model and a method. *Journal of Experimental Psychology: Human Perception and Performance*, *10*, 276–291.

Lonigan, C. J., & Phillips, B. M. (2001). Temperamental influences on the development of anxiety disorders. In M. W. Vasey, & M. R. Dadds (Eds.), *The developmental psychopathology of anxiety* (pp. 60–91). New York: Oxford University Press.

Lonigan, C. J. & Phillips, B. M. Longitudinal relations between effortful control, affectivity, and symptoms of psychopathology in children and adolescents. Unpublished raw data; Florida State University: 2002.

Luria, A. R., Pribam, K. H., & Homskaya, E. D. (1964). An experimental analysis of the behavioral disturbance produced by a left frontal arachnoidal endothelioma (meningioma). *Neuropsychologia*, *2*, 257–280.

Luteijn, F., & van der Ploeg, F. A. E. (1983). *Groninger Intelligentie Test [Intelligence Test from Groningen]*. Lisse: Swets & Zeitlinger.

Mackinlay, R., Charman, T., & Karmiloff-Smith, A. (2006). High-functioning children with autism spectrum disorder: A novel test of multitasking. *Brain and Cognition*, *61*, 14–24.

MacLeod, C. M. (1991). Half a century of research on the Stroop effect: an integrative review. *Psychological Bulletin*, *109*, 163–203.

Maenner, M. J, Rice, C. E., Arneson, C. L, Cunniff, C., Schieve, L. A., Carpenter, L. A., ... & Durkin, M. S. (2014). Potential impact of DSM-5 Criteria on autism spectrum disorder prevalence estimates. *JAMA Psychiatry*, *71(3)*, 292–300.

Maes, J., Eling, P., Wezenberg, E., Vissers, C., & Kan, C. (2011). Attentional set shifting in autism spectrum disorder: differentiating between the role of perseveration, learned irrelevance, and novelty processing. *Journal of Clinical Experimental Neuropsychology*, *33(2)*, 210–217.

Mahone, E. M., Koth, C. W., Cutting, L., Singer, H. S., & Denckla, M. B. (2001). Executive function in fluency and recall measures among children with Tourette syndrome or ADHD. *Journal of the International Neuropsychological Society*, *7*(1), 102–111.

Martinussen, R., & Mackenzie, G. (2015). Reading comprehension in adolescents with ADHD: exploring the poor comprehender profile and individual differences in vocabulary and executive functions. *Research in Developmental Disabilities*, *38*, 329–337.

Matsuura, N., Ishitobi, M., Arai, S., Kawamura, K., Asano, M., Inohara, K., ... & Kosaka, H. (2014). Distinguishing between autism spectrum disorder and attention deficit hyperactivity disorder by using behavioral checklists, cognitive assessments, and neuropsychological test battery. *Asian Journal of Psychiatry*, *12*, 50–57.

Mazzone, L., Yu, S., Blair, C., Gunter, B. C., Wang, Z., Marsh, R., & Peterson, B. S. (2010). An fMRI study of frontostriatal circuits during the inhibition of eye blinking in persons with Tourette syndrome. *American Journal of Psychiatry*, *167(3)*, 341–349.

McLean, R. L., Harrison, A. J., Zimak, E., Joseph, R. M., & Morrow, E. M. (2014). Executive function in probands with autism with average IQ and their unaffected first-degree relatives. *Journal of the American Academy of Child and Adolescent Psychiatry, 53(9)*, 1001–1009.

Mioshi, E., Dawson, K., Mitchell, J., Arnold, R., Hodges, J. R. (2006). The Addenbrooke's Cognitive Examination Revised (ACE-R): A brief cognitive test battery for dementia screening. *International Journal of Geriatric Psychiatry, 21*, 1078–1085.

Miyake, A., Friedman, N. P., Emerson, M. J., Witzki, A. H., Howerter, A., & Wager, T. D. (2000). The unity and diversity of executive functions and their contributions to complex "frontal lobe" tasks: A latent variable analysis. *Cognitive Psychology, 41*, 49–100.

Mosher, F. A., & Hornsby, J. R. (1966). On asking questions. In J. S. Bruner, R. R. Olver, & P. Greenfield (Eds.), *Studies in cognitive growth* (pp. 86–102). New York: John Wiley & Sons.

Nelson, H. (1976). A modified card sorting test sensitive to frontal lobe defects. *Cortex, 12*, 313–324.

Oosterlaan, J., & Sergeant, J. A. (1998). Response inhibition and response re-engagement in attention-deficit/hyperactivity disorder, disruptive, anxious and normal children. *Behavioral Brain Research, 94*, 33–43.

Ozonoff, S. (1995). Reliability and validity of the Wisconsin card sorting test in studies of autism. *Neuropsychology, 9*, 491–500.

Panerai, S., Tasca, D., Ferri, R., D'Arrigo, V. G., & Elia, M. (2014). Executive functions and adaptive behavior in autism spectrum disorders with and without intellectual disability. *Psychiatry Journal*, 2014, doi: 101155/2014/941809

Pennington, B. F., & Ozonoff, S. (1996). Executive functions and developmental psychopathology. *Journal of Child Psychological Psychiatry, 37(1)*, 51–87.

Petrides, M., & Milner, B. (1982). Deficits on subject-ordered tasks after frontal- and temporal-lobe lesions in man. *Neuropsychologia, 20*, 249–262.

Poon, K., & Ho, C. S. H. (2014). Contrasting deficits on executive functions in Chinese delinquent adolescents with attention deficit and hyperactivity disorder symptoms and/or reading disability. *Research in Developmental Disabilities, 35*, 3046–3056.

Raven, J., Raven, J. C., & Court, J. H. (2003, updated 2004) *Manual for Raven's Progressive Matrices and Vocabulary Scales.* San Antonio, TX: Harcourt Assessment.

Reck, S. G., Hund, A. M., & Landau, S. (2010). Memory for object location in boys with and without ADHD. *Journal of Attention Disorders, 13(5)*, 505–515.

Rendell, P. G., & Craik, F. I. M. (2000). Virtual Week and actual week: Age-related differences in prospective memory. *Applied Cognitive Psychology, 14(7)*, 43–62.

Rendell, P. G., & Henry, J. D. (2009). A review of Virtual Week for prospective memory assessment: Clinical implications. *Brain Impairment, 10(1)*, 14–22.

Rey, A. (1964). *L'examen clinique en psychologie.* Paris: Presses Universitaires de France.

Robbins, T. W, & Sahakian, B. J. (1994). Computer methods of assessment of cognitive function. In, J. R. M. Copeland, M. T. Abou-Saleh, & D. G. Blazers, (Eds.), *Principles and Practice of Geriatric Psychiatry*, pp. 205–209. Chichester: John Wiley & Sons.

Robertson, I. H., Manly, T., Andrade, J., Baddeley, B. T., & Yiend, J. (1997). "Oops!": Performance correlates of everyday attentional failures in traumatic brain injured and normal subjects. *Neuropsychologia, 35*, 747–758.

Rogers, S. J., & Bennetto, L. (2000). Intersubjectivity in autism: The roles of imitation and executive function. In A. P. Wetherby, & B. Prizant (Eds.), *Autism spectrum disorders: A transactional developmental perspective.* Baltimore: Brookes.

Rosenthal, M., Lawson, R., Dixon, E., Wallace, G. L., Wills, M. C., Yerys, B. E., & Kenworthy, L. (2013). Impairments in real-world executive function increase from childhood to adolescence in autism spectrum disorders. *Neuropsychology, 27(1)*, 13–18.

Roth, R.M., Isquith, P.K., & Gioia, G.A. (2005). *Behavior rating inventory of executive function – Adult Version (BRIEF-A).* Lutz, FL: Psychological Assessment Resources.

Russell-Smith, S. N., Comerford, B. J. E., Mayberry, M. T., & Whitehouse, A. J. O. (2014). Brief report: further evidence for a link between inner speech limitations and executive function in high-functioning children with autism spectrum disorders. *Journal of Autism and Developmental Disorders, 44*, 1236–1243.

Sachse, M., Schlitt, S., Hainz, D., Ciaramidaro, A., Schirman, S., Walter H., … & Freitag, C. M. (2013). Executive and visuo-motor function in adolescents and adults with autism spectrum disorder. *Journal of Autism and Developmental Disorders, 43*, 1222–1235.

Salum, G. A., Sergeant, J., Sonuga-Barke, E., Vandekerckhove, J., Gadelha, A., Pan, P. M., … & Rohde, L. A. P. (2014). Specificity of basic information processing and inhibitory control in attention deficit hyperactivity disorder. *Psychological Medicine, 44*, 617–631.

Samson, A. C., Hardan, A. Y., Lee, I. A., Phillips, J. M., & Gross, J. J. (2015). Maladaptive behavior in autism spectrum disorder: The role of emotion experience and emotion regulation. *Journal of Autism and Developmental Disorders, 45(11)*, 3424–3432.

Samyn, V., Roeyers, H., & Bijttebier, P. (2011). Effortful control in typically developing boys and in boys with ADHD or autism spectrum disorder. *Research in Developmental Disabilities, 32*(2), 483–490.

Samyn, V., Roeyers, H., Bijttebier, P., Rossel, Y., & Wiersema, J. R. (2015). Assessing effortful control in typical and atypical development: Are questionnaires and neuropsychological measures interchangeable? A latent-variable analysis. *Research in Developmental Disabilities, 36*, 587–589.

Samyn, V., Roeyers, H., Bijttebier, P., & Wiersema, J. R. (2013). Attentional networks in boys with ADHD or autism spectrum disorder and the relationship with effortful control. *Journal of Attention Disorders.*

Samyn, V., Wiersema, J. R., Bijttebier, P., & Roeyers, H. (2014). Effortful control and executive attention in typical and atypical development: an event-related potential study. *Biological Psychology, 99*, 160–171.

Schnirman, G. M., Welsh, M. C., & Retzlaff, P. D. (1998). Development of the Tower of London—Revised. *Assessment, 5*, 355–360.

Schwam, D. M., King, T. Z., & Greenberg, D. (2015). Characteristics of executive functioning in a small sample of children with Tourette syndrome. *Applied Neuropsychology: Child, 4(4)*, 297–308.

Sergeant, J. A., Geurts, H., & Oosterlaan, J. (2002). How specific is a deficit of executive function for attention-deficit/hyperactivity disorder? *Behavioural Brain Research, 130*, 3–28.

Sergeant, J. A., & van der Meere, J. (1990). Additive factor method applied to psychopathology with special reference to childhood hyperactivity. *Acta Psychologica, 74(2–3)*, 277–295.

Shallice, T. (1982). Specific impairments of planning. *Philosophical Transactions of the Royal Society of London B Series, 298*, 199–209.

Singer, H. S., Schuerholz, L. J., & Denckla, M. B. (1995). Learning difficulties in children with Tourette syndrome. *Journal of Child Neurology, Supplement 1*, S58–61.

Sivan, A. B. (1992). *Benton Visual Retention Test.* 5th Edition. San Antonio, TX: Psychological Corporation.

Skogli, E. W., Egeland, J., Andersen, P. N., Hovik, K. T., & Oie, M. (2014). Few differences in hot and cold executive functions in children and adolescents with combined and inattentive subtypes of ADHD. *Child Neuropsychology, 20(2)*, 162–181.

Sonuga-Barke, E. J. (2003). The dual pathway model of AD/HD: An elaboration of neurodevelopmental characteristics. *Neuroscience and Biobehavioral Reviews, 27(7)*, 593–604.

Sonuga-Barke, E. J. (2005). Causal models of attention-deficit/hyperactivity disorder: From common simple deficits to multiple developmental pathways. *Biological Psychiatry, 57(11)*, 1231–1238.

Sonuga-Barke, E. J., Wiersema, J. R., van der Meere, J. J., & Roeyers, H. (2010). Context-dependent dynamic processes in attention deficit/hyperactivity disorder: Differentiating common and unique effects of state regulation and delay aversion. *Neuropsychology Review, 20*, 86–102.

Stern, A., & Maeir, A. (2014). Validating the measurement of executive functions in an occupational context for adults with attention deficit hyperactivity disorder. *American Journal of Occupational Therapy, 68*, 719–728.

Stroop, J. R. (1935). Studies of interference in serial verbal reactions. *Journal of Experimental Psychology 18*, 643–662.

Taylor, H. G., Mills, E. L., Ciampi, A., DuBerger, R., Watters, G. V., Gold R., … & Michaels R. H. (1990). The sequelae of *Haemophilus influenzae* meningitis in school-age children. *New England Journal of Medicine, 323*, 1657–1663.

Van den Burg, W., Saan, R. J., & Deelman, B. G. (1985). *15- Woordentest. Provisional manual.* Groningen: University Hospital, Department of Neuropsychology.

Van Rooij, D., Hoekstra, P. J., Mennes, M., von Rhein, D., Thissen, A. J. A. M., Hesenfeld, D., … & Hartman C. A.(2015). Distinguishing adolescents with ADHD from their unaffected siblings and healthy comparison subjects by neural activation patterns during response inhibition. *American Journal of Psychiatry, 172(7)*, 674–683.

Vogan, V. M., Morgan, B. R., Lee, W., Powell, T. L., Smith, M. L., & Taylor, M. J. (2014). The neural correlates of visuo-spatial working memory in children with autism spectrum disorder: Effects of cognitive load. *Journal of Neurodevelopmental Disorders, 6*, 19. doi: 10.1186/1866-1955-6-19

Wechsler, D. (1997a). *Wechsler Adult Intelligence Scale.* 3rd edition. San Antonio: The Psychological Corporation.

Wechsler, D. (1997b). *Wechsler Memory Scale. 3rd edition manual.* San Antonio, TX: The Psychological Corporation.

Wechsler, D. (2003). *Wechsler Intelligence Scale for Children. 4th edition: Administration and Scoring Manual.* San Antonio, TX: Pearson.

Wechsler, D. (2004). Wechsler Intelligence Scale for Children. 4th edition: Norwegian version. Stockholm, Sweden: The Psychological Corporation.

Wechsler, D, & Stone, CP. (1987). *Wechsler Memory Scale—Revised*: New York: Psychological Corporation.

Werheid, K., Hoppe, C., Thone, A., Muller, U., Mungersdorf, M., & von Cramon, D. Y. (2002). The adaptive digit ordering test: Clinical application, reliability, and validity of a verbal working memory test. *Archives of Clinical Neuropsychology, 17*, 547–565.

Werling, D. M., & Geschwind, D. H. (2013). Sex differences in autism spectrum disorders. *Current Opinion in Neurology, 26(2)*, 146–153.

Williams, D. M., & Jarrold, C. (2013). Assessing planning and set-shifting abilities in autism: Are experimenter-administered and computerized versions of tasks equivalent? *Autism Research, 6*, 461–467.

Williams, D. M., Jarrold, C., Grainger, C., & Lind, S. E. (2014). Diminished time-based, but undiminished event-based, prospective memory among intellectually high-functioning adults with autism: Relation to working memory ability. *Neuropsychology, 28*, 30–42.

Wilson, B. A., Alderman, N., Burgess, P. W., Emslie, H., & Evans, J. J. (1996). *The behavioural assessment of the dysexecutive syndrome.* Bury St Edmunds: Thames Valley Test Company.

Wilson, C.E., Happé, F., Wheelwright, S.J., Ecker, C., Lombardo, M.V., Johnston, P., Daly, E., Murphy, C.M., Spain, D., Lai, M.C., Chakrabarti, B., Sauter, D.A., MRC AIMS Consortium, Baron-Cohen, S., & Murphy, D.G. (2014). The neuropsychology of male adults with high-functioning autism or Asperger syndrome. *Autism Research, 7*, 568–581. doi: 10.1002/aur.1394.

Wright, I., Waterman, M., Prescott, H., & Murdoch-Eaton, D. (2003). A new Stroop-like measure of inhibitory function development: Typical developmental trends. *Journal of Child Psychology and Psychiatry and Allied Disciplines*, *44*, 561–575.

Yasuda, Y., Hashimoto, R., Ohi, K., Yamamori, H., Fujimoto, M., Umeda-Yano, S., Fujino, H., & Takeda, M. (2014). Cognitive inflexibility in Japanese adolescents and adults with autism spectrum disorders. *World Journal of Psychiatry*, *4*(2), 42–48. doi: 10.5498/wjp.v4.i2.42

Yerys, B., Wallace, G., Harrison, B., Celano, M., Giedd, J., & Kenworthy, L. (2009). Set-shifting in children with autism spectrum disorders reversal shifting deficits on the intradimensional/extradimensional shift test correlate with repetitive behaviors. *Autism*, *13*(5), 523–538.

Zelazo, P.D. (2006). The dimensional change card sort (DCCS): A method of assessing executive function in children. *Nature Protocols*, *1*, 297–301.

Ziereis, S., & Jansen, P. (2015). Effects of physical activity on executive function and motor performance in children with ADHD. *Research in Developmental Disabilities*, *38*, 181–191.

# 6

# Domain-specific and Domain-general Approaches to Developmental Disorders

## *The Example of Specific Language Impairment*

Nicola Botting and Chloë Marshall

The specificity of impairments in development has been used historically in the theoretical study of developmental disorders to indicate that particular skills may dissociate, and to support domain-specific theories of cognition. In recent years, however, it has become apparent that traits in developmental disorders are often not as "specific" as once thought, and a more domain-general approach has become popular. These contrasting positions have been able to arise in part due to the challenges of specifying the phenotype in behaviorally defined disorders. Specific language impairment (SLI) is a developmental disorder in which language difficulties are seen in the absence of obvious causes. It has long fascinated cognitive scientists because it appears to provide evidence for dissociation between language and non-verbal cognition. SLI is a prime example of the way in which domain-general and domain-specific theories have been applied to the investigation of apparently specific difficulties. However, research from these two theoretical approaches has not always been complementary, and the way in which knowledge has been presented has, at times, worked in a counter-productive manner. Furthermore, an important recent debate has begun to question the usefulness of the term 'SLI' itself (see Bishop, 2014; Reilly et al., 2014). However, because no firm consensus has yet been reached on this issue, and because some of the arguments referred to here are directly linked to this terminology, we will use the term specific language impairment throughout this chapter.

Here we use SLI as an example to outline some ways the domain-specific and domain-general approaches have been used to describe clinical impairments. We provide counter-positions, and we argue that these strongly opposing traditions present a significant barrier to the advancement of knowledge about SLI and other developmental disorders. We then propose a way forward that builds on the strengths of the domain-specific and domain-general approaches, takes the process of development into account, and considers where the two approaches might usefully meet.

*The Wiley Handbook of Developmental Psychopathology*, First Edition. Edited by Luna C. Centifanti and David M. Williams.

## Specific Language Impairment

Specific language impairment (SLI) is a neurodevelopmental disorder that affects around 7 % of the preschool population (Tomblin et al., 1997) and lasts in some cases until adulthood (Tomblin, Freese, & Records, 1992). SLI diagnosed when a child's language does not develop normally and these difficulties cannot be accounted for by generally slow intellectual development, speech impairment, autism, acquired brain damage, hearing loss or impoverished input (Leonard, 1998). It has been identified in languages as typologically diverse as English (Rice & Wexler, 1996), French (Paradis & Crago, 2001), Greek (Stavrakaki, 2001), Finnish (Niemi, 1999), Hungarian (Lukács, Leonard, Kas, & Pléh, 2009), Hebrew (Leonard & Dromi, 1994), Inuktitut (Crago & Allen, 2001), Arabic (Abdalla & Crago, 2008), Cantonese (Wong, Leonard, Fletcher, & Stokes, 2004), British Sign Language (Mason et al., 2010) and American Sign Language (Quinto-Pozos, Singleton, & Hauser, 2017). It is heterogeneous in its presentation both within and across languages, varying in its severity and in which components of language are relatively worst affected. Overall, however, grammar (i.e. syntax and inflectional morphology) appears to be most severely impaired. SLI runs in families, and progress is being made in understanding its genetic etiology (see Newbury, Fisher, & Monaco, 2010, for a review).

Since its conception more than a hundred years ago (see Lorch & Hellal, 2011, for a historical overview), one of the most theoretically fascinating aspects of SLI has been its role in reflecting what by definition appears to be a selective cognitive deficit, i.e. one that affects just language (and, in particular, grammar), and by extension, therefore, potential evidence for the cognitive specialization of language as distinct from non-verbal abilities. However, vigorous and at times acrimonious debate surrounds just how "specific" the language impairment actually is, and, as we argue in this paper, research from two diametrically opposing positions has worked in a manner that has muddied, not clarified, our understanding of what causes SLI.

These two opposing positions, "domain-specificity" and "domain-generality", have radically different conceptualizations of cognitive architecture. By domain-specificity we mean one of the characteristics of Fodorian modules, namely that modules only operate on certain kinds of inputs, i.e. they are specialized for processing just certain types of information (Fodor, 1983). Relevant to SLI is the proposal that a language "module" processes just linguistic information. The distinction between language and non-language cognitive systems is sometimes termed "big" modularity. "Little" modularity has also been proposed, i.e. that language itself is modular because it, too, comprises distinct levels of representation and processing, with grammar separate from the lexicon and pragmatics (Levy & Kave, 1999). Under domain-general processing accounts the cognitive architecture is very different: mental activity is instead distributed across the brain and cannot be decomposed, even abstractly, into independent units (Rumelhart, McClelland, & the PDP Research Group, 1986).

With respect to language acquisition, the domain-specific and domain-general views are consistent with a polarization of the field of language acquisition more generally. The domain-specific approach is part of a wider set of views that fall under the nativist–generativist umbrella: "nativist" because the child is born with some innate knowledge of language, and "generativist" because the child's knowledge of grammar consists of knowledge of formal rules that operate on abstract linguistic categories and phrases (e.g. nouns, noun phrases, verbs and verb phrases) (Crain & Pietroski, 2001;

Pinker, 1999; Valian, 2009). In contrast, the domain-general approach fits in with constructivist, input-based and functional approaches, because they assume no innate knowledge of language. Knowledge of language is instead constructed by generalizing across the language input, and acquisition is driven by children's desire to use language to perform communicative functions (Ambridge, Rowland, & Pine, 2008; Tomasello, 2003). Ambridge and Lieven (2011) provide an excellent critical review of these two approaches with respect to typical language acquisition. There has long been a reciprocal relationship between the study of atypical and typical language development (Paul & Cohen, 1982), and the field of SLI does not escape the domain-specific versus domain-general dispute.

The territory that is being fought over here is not cognitive specialization in the adult brain, but rather how cognitive specialization develops. In the *adult* brain, the existence of functionally specialized cognitive systems, including those specialized for language, has strong support from neuropsychological studies of stroke patients, amongst whom different types of language loss (aphasia) are associated with lesions in different regions of the brain (for a review, see Denes, 2011). Broca's aphasia, which is characterized by non-fluent speech and difficulties with grammar, is associated with lesions in the posterior third of the left inferior frontal gyrus, whereas Wernicke's aphasia, characterized by a major impairment of language comprehension, while speech retains a natural-sounding rhythm and a relatively normal grammar, is associated with lesions in the left temporal lobe. In contrast, it is less clear that specific language impairment in *children* represents evidence for functional specialization of language (and, in particular, of grammar) from the start of life. Indeed, the very application of adult cognitive neuropsychology, a framework in which certain cognitive mechanisms can be considered impaired while others are essentially intact, to developmental disorders is now strongly debated (see Filippi & Karmiloff-Smith, 2013, for a recent review, and papers in Bishop, Nation, & Patterson, 2014). In recent years an alternative, domain-relevant, approach (termed "neuroconstructivism") proposes that the dichotomy between "impaired" and "unimpaired" cognitive abilities is not supported by the data, and that although certain cognitive processes become domain-specific over developmental time, they do not start that way (Filippi & Karmiloff-Smith, 2013). Nevertheless, this view has not propelled the field of SLI in the way one might expect. Significant barriers still remain, which prevent optimum research strategies and knowledge advancement from occurring, a topic which we will revisit later.

This chapter now turns to the areas of evidence which have been championed by the domain-specific and domain-general approaches respectively. We have identified key themes that epitomize the arguments, although these are intended to be neither exhaustive nor comprehensive reviews of the areas. Each section highlights three evidence bases that have been used to promote an approach, followed by a counter-argument from the alternative standpoint.

## Areas in SLI that have been Championed by Domain-specific Research

Since the 1990s, debate has raged over several pieces of key domain-specific evidence which potentially shed light on the underlying causes of SLI, three of which we discuss here: the existence of a language impairment in a three-generational family, the KE family; the double dissociation between language and non-language impairments demonstrated by SLI and Williams Syndrome; and the existence of a subgroup of children with SLI, the Grammatical-SLI subgroup. All three were hailed by proponents of domain-specificity as providing evidence for nativism/modularity/domain-specificity, but this interpretation was subsequently vigorously disputed by supporters of domain-generality. Yet despite this debate, we are still far from understanding the underlying causes of SLI. These are by no means the only pieces of key evidence that are disputed, but they serve to illustrate how the two approaches have interpreted the evidence, and the questions that still remain, so we focus on them here.

## Genetic Heritability of Specific Language Skills

If SLI is caused by an impairment to an innate and modular language system, it should be heritable. In the early 1990s, interest developed in a three-generational British family, the KE family. 16 of the 30 family members studied had a severe speech and language impairment with a very simple (autosomal dominant) inheritance pattern. The impairment appeared to be specific, in that non-verbal deficits could not be considered characteristic of the disorder because although the mean non-verbal IQ of affected members was lower than that of unaffected members, there were affected individuals in the family who had non-verbal ability close to the population average. The impairment was particularly striking in inflectional morphology. For example, in a test eliciting past tense forms of existing verbs from adults and children in the family (e.g. "*Every day he walks eight miles. Yesterday he* _____"), Gopnik and Crago (1991) reported that affected family members produced many uninflected verb forms, i.e. "*Yesterday he walk eight miles*". In another task participants were asked to pluralize nonsense nouns. Affected family members produced many bizarre responses, including *zack*→*zacko*, *sas*→*sasss* (i.e. the final "s" was lengthened), and *zoop*→*zoopez* (i.e. the participant used the syllabic suffix which would added to the real words *horses* and *benches*). One (adult), when given the first item on this task, was reported to repeat it "under her breath several times and then whisper to herself "add an 's'" (Gopnik & Crago, 1991, p. 18). This is a task that Berko (1958) had shown to be completed implicitly, quickly, accurately and effortlessly by the majority of typically developing seven-year-olds.

The language errors that the affected members of the family made could, according to Gopnik and Crago (1991, p. 33), "be accounted for by postulating that a part of the grammar, which for independent theoretical linguistic reasons is considered to be more or less autonomous, is selectively impaired." That part of the grammar was argued to be specifically the abstract morphological features that mark grammatical functions such as number, tense, and aspect. The KE family therefore became central to discussions regarding the innate aspects of language ability, and in particular the innateness of grammar. Interest in this family intensified during the 2000s with the discovery of the gene responsible for the impairment, *FOXP2* (Lai, Fisher, Hurst, Vargha-Khadem, & Monaco, 2001; Lai, Gerrelli, Monaco, Fisher, & Copp, 2003).

## Double Dissociations within Developmental Disorders

If language is domain-specific, then this would predict the existence of individuals with impaired language but intact non-verbal cognition, and vice versa. For nativists, the existence of SLI alongside developmental disorders with different cognitive profiles provides strong support for language being a domain-specific cognitive ability from the start, i.e. for "big" modularity. Pinker, for example, contrasts SLI with another developmental disorder, Williams syndrome, which is characterized by mild to moderate intellectual disability and by language abilities that are arguably relatively strong. He claims that the two provide evidence for a double dissociation between grammar and non-verbal intelligence.

> Overall, the genetic double dissociation is striking, suggesting that language is ... a specialization of the brain... The genes of one group [i.e. SLI] impair their grammar while sparing their intelligence; the genes of another group of children [i.e. Williams syndrome] impair their intelligence while sparing their grammar (Pinker, 1999, p. 262).

For Pinker, therefore, SLI "shows that there must be some pattern of genetically guided events in the development of the brain (namely, the events disrupted in this syndrome) that is specialized for the wiring in of linguistic computation" (Pinker, 1994, p. 324). The existence of SLI is therefore interpreted as supporting the domain-specific view of language and of cognition more generally.

## Highly Specific Subgroups of SLI

In addition, to "big modularity", i.e. the division between language and non-verbal cognition, is "little modularity", the proposal that language is itself made up of different modules (Levy & Kave, 1999). Several researchers of a nativist persuasion have proposed that the heterogeneity in SLI is caused by there being different subgroups with selective deficits in the different components of language. The most extensively studied group is Grammatical-SLI. Children with Grammatical-SLI have significant difficulty assigning thematic roles in passive sentences (van der Lely, 1996), forming and understanding wh-questions (Fonteneau & van der Lely, 2008; van der Lely & Battell, 2003), using the past tense correctly (Marshall & van der Lely, 2006; van der Lely & Ullman, 2001) and assigning reference to accusative and reflexive pronouns (e.g. *him*, *himself*; van der Lely & Stollwerck, 1997), with the impairment proposed to be in the computational syntactic system. Relatively less impaired in Grammatical-SLI are lexical and pragmatic aspects of language, for example derivational morphology (Marshall & van der Lely, 2007) and the use of referential expressions in narrative discourse (van der Lely, 1997). Friedmann and her colleagues have gone further and proposed four subgroups of SLI: syntactic, phonological, lexical and pragmatic, where the syntactic-SLI group show selective impairments on complex syntactic tasks, the lexical-SLI group show selective impairments in a range of lexical tasks, the phonological-SLI show selective impairments on phonological tasks, and the pragmatic-SLI group have a selective impairment at the level of discourse-pragmatic skills (Friedmann & Novogrodsky, 2008).

## Counter-arguments from a Domain-general Perspective

The claims of domain-specific proponents with respect to these three sets of evidence – the KE family, the double dissociation between SLI and Williams syndrome, and subgroups of SLI – were quickly challenged by the domain generalists. An immediate riposte to Gopnik (1990) and Gopnik and Crago's (1991) proposal that the KE family had a specific deficit in morphology came from Vargha-Khadem, Watkins, Alcock, Fletcher, and Passingham (1995). They drew attention to the severe speech dyspraxia that rendered many affected members of the family unintelligible to people who did not know them. Furthermore, they studied the family using not only a range of language tasks, but also non-verbal and orofacial praxis tasks, and discovered that the impairment did not appear to be specific to speech and language at all. Striking were the affected family members' difficulties imitating a range of oral and facial movements, including copying sequences such as closing the lips, opening the mouth and protruding the tongue. Rather, Vargha-Khadem and her colleagues argued that the speech and language difficulties constitute "only a part of the affected members' total syndrome" (Vargha-Khadem et al., 1995, p. 933). Consistent with this, Lai et al. (2003) measured *FOXP2* expression in the developing mouse and human embryonic/fetal brain and found expression in a number of related brain areas: the caudate nucleus, thalamus, inferior olives, and cerebellum. These are not "language areas," but rather are circuits related to movement. The authors conclude that "Our data suggest that *FOXP2* might be generally implicated in aspects of motor control in mammalian species, and was already playing a role in the development of motor-related brain regions in the human–mouse common ancestor" (Lai et al., 2003, p. 2461).

The flipside to the issue of the "specificity" of the language deficit in the KE family (and in other individuals with SLI) is the issue of how "intact" language is in Williams syndrome. The majority of children with WS have more limited vocabularies than typically developing children of the same age, whether measured experimentally (Paterson, Brown, Gsödl, Johnson, & Karmiloff-Smith, 1999), using standardized vocabulary tests (Mervis & Becerra, 2007) or by parental report (Mervis & Robinson, 2000). Furthermore, syntax is also generally poor, and below the level expected from vocabulary (Grant, Valian, & Karmiloff-Smith, 2002; Karmiloff-Smith, Grant, Berthoud, Davies, Howlin, & Udwin, 1997). Karmiloff-Smith, Mervis and their colleagues have argued that it does not make sense to think of language as a module that is unimpaired in WS. Language might be a "strength" relative to severe weaknesses in other areas such as visuo-spatial cognition and number skills, but in no way does it represent the development of an unimpaired language or grammar module. The strength of feeling in this debate can be seen in the following rebuttal of domain-specific claims: "The most extreme claims about the independence of language from cognition in Williams Syndrome are made by people who either have not studied the syndrome directly or who have tested very small samples" (Mervis & Beccera, 2007, p. 4).

Finally, what about the existence of subgroups of SLI that reflect underlying impairments in the different components of language? An obvious question is that if children with SLI are allocated to subgroups such as Grammatical-SLI and Lexical-SLI, how many children are actually left out because they do not fulfil those strict inclusion and exclusion criteria? How specific are the deficits within the language components? Bishop, Bright, James, Bishop, and van der Lely (2000) found very few cases of Grammatical-SLI when they used van der Lely's syntactic tests with a sample of 54 language-impaired children, and the majority of those who showed the syntactic errors characteristic of Grammatical-SLI showed impairments in other areas of language, e.g. word-finding difficulties. They therefore argued that a highly selective profile of language impairment is relatively rare. The same is the case for the subgroups studied by Friedmann and Novogrodsky (2008): although some children showed pure impairments in just one component of language, many children had more than one impairment. The authors acknowledge this and write that "The claim here is existential: *there are* children who have purely syntactic impairments, and there are children who have pure lexical, phonological, or pragmatic impairments, without syntactic deficits" (Friedmann & Novogrodsky, 2008, p. 214). That might be so, but when subgroups are based on arbitrary cut-offs on task performance, does it make sense to talk about subgroups (where sharp boundaries between impairment and non-impairment are implied)? Perhaps one should think instead in terms of multidimensionality (the direction in which the literature on reading impairments is progressing, for example: Snowling & Hulme, 2012). And as Bishop cautions in a commentary on (and in agreement with) Paterson et al.'s (1999) study: "We must be aware … of jumping to the conclusion that different language profiles reflect the status of specialized innate brain areas that mediate complex functions such as syntax. Different profiles could reflect the status of, for example, simple auditory memory" (Bishop, 1999, p. 2284).

Furthermore, Joanisse and Seidenberg (2003) have shown that the syntactic deficit in Grammatical-SLI can be modelled in a connectionist network through simulation of a phonological deficit, with no need to posit a specific grammatical impairment. In a more recent event-related potential study of language processing in Grammatical-SLI (Fonteneau & van der Lely, 2008), children and young adults were presented with sentences containing either syntactic or semantic violations. The syntactic violations failed to elicit the normal Early Left-Anterior Negative electrophysiological response, which is held to be specific to grammatical processing. Yet language processing appeared otherwise typical: the syntactic violations elicited a normal P600 response, which is associated with the re-analysis of syntactic structure or syntactic integration, and the semantic violations elicited a normal N400. Fonteneau and van der Lely (2008, p. 1) claimed that "grammatical neural circuitry underlying language is a developmentally unique system in the functional architecture of the brain, and this complex higher cognitive system can be selectively impaired." In contrast, Filippi and Karmiloff-Smith (2013, p. 198) argue that normal semantic processing by the time an individual reaches adolescence "does not constitute evidence of a lack of low-level perceptual problems at an earlier phase of development when such timing may have been critical, something that individuals could have overcome by adolescence." In their view, one cannot take data from language in adolescence to reconstruct the infant's starting state.

## Areas in SLI that have been Championed by Domain-general Research

### Phonological Memory Deficits as a Cause of SLI

Alongside linguistic models of SLI, research exploring the relationship between memory functioning and language has gathered pace since the 1990s. In a hugely influential series of studies, Gathercole and Baddeley reported findings regarding a phonological short-term memory task called non-word repetition (e.g., Gathercole & Baddeley, 1990). They found that children with SLI were particularly poor at repeating nonsense words, in comparison not only to age-matched peers, but also to language-ability-matched peers. Their conclusion was that SLI can be explained purely via a deficit in phonological short-term memory rather than in terms of a domain-specific language or syntactic impairment, providing a concrete domain-general explanation for language impairments. Since these original studies, the association between non-word repetition and language has been replicated many times not only with children who have SLI across many languages but also with typical children and children with other developmental disorders (see Coady & Evans, 2008, for a review). Non-word repetition is considerably poorer in those with SLI when compared even with younger language-age matched groups (Gallon, Harris, & van der Lely, 2007; Gathercole & Baddeley, 1990) and when executive function has been controlled for (Briscoe & Rankin, 2009). In short, poor non-word repetition is a highly reliable feature of language impairment.

## Wider Cognitive Difficulties as Evidence of a Domain-general Impairment in SLI

Following this surge of research in phonological short term memory, there was an increase in research examining wider memory deficits in SLI. In particular, studies showed deficits in non-verbal memory (Bavin, Wilson, Maruff, & Sleeman, 2005; Hick, Botting & Conti-Ramsden, 2005) and longer-term procedural memory (Ullman & Pierpont, 2005; Lum, Conti-Ramsden, Page, & Ullman, 2012). The Procedural Deficit Hypothesis (PDH) put forward by Ullmann and Pierpont (2005) has some particularly convincing evidence to support the idea that "proceduralization" or implicit learning is impaired more generally. This evidence of wider impairment meant that a strong domain-specific position was harder to maintain. At the very least, SLI could no longer be used to demonstrate a neat dissociation between language and other cognitive functions without some further explanation. More recent work has started to tease apart verbal and non-verbal elements of memory tasks (Botting, Psarou, Caplin, & Nevin, 2013). Indeed, recent work on executive functions by Henry, Messer, and Nash (2012) reveals more non-verbal differences between children with SLI and their typically developing controls than verbal ones.

As well as other types of memory difficulty, more general non-verbal skills have also been reported as being affected in children with SLI. Botting (2005) reported data showing a lag not just in memory, but in non-verbal IQ more generally. Hick et al. (2005) also showed that it was the *development* of non-verbal skills in those with SLI that was slower than a group with Down syndrome matched at recruitment, suggesting a more dynamic and domain-general picture of development rather than simply an impairment in a language/grammar module.

## Social and Emotional Difficulties in SLI

Another central issue to the domain-specificity of SLI is the evidence now available suggesting that children with language impairments experience a range of symptoms outside of language and cognition. As detailed above, these include non-verbal memory and general cognition, but recent studies have also shown that those with SLI have poorer social skills (Botting & Conti-Ramsden, 2008), and are more prone to anxiety, depression and other psychiatric disorders (Clegg, Hollis, Mawhood, & Rutter, 2005; Conti-Ramsden & Botting, 2008). Importantly, longitudinal work has started to highlight pathways in these wider issues that were previously unknown

(Botting, Toseeb, Pickles, Durkin & Conti-Ramsden, 2016; Wadman, Botting, Durkin & Conti-Ramsden, 2011). Evidence from the Manchester Language Study has failed to reveal clear and consistent longitudinal relationships between the degree of language difficulty and social skills including social cognition (Botting & Conti-Ramsden, 2008) and between language skill and emotional health (Conti-Ramsden & Botting, 2008). Domain-specific theories posit that the wide-ranging social difficulties in such children as "sequelae" of the specific language deficit (e.g., Rice, 1993), however this would lead logically to a prediction that severity of language impairment would directly associate with level of social limitations. Furthermore, this causal suggestion appears to be countered by the fact that 60 % of young people with severe speech and language difficulties experience no such problems (Durkin & Conti-Ramsden, 2007). Instead, the domain-general approach argues that the data point more convincingly to a domain-general neurological factor(s) which places both language and social skill (among other things) at risk, in a similar fashion to the overlap between increased visual and hearing problems in those with learning disabilities.

## Counter-arguments from a Domain-specific Perspective

Despite this expansion of evidence indicating that domain-general cognitive skills might be impaired alongside language in children with SLI, at least three key issues have been left relatively unaddressed by the domain-general approach.

Firstly, the assumption that language impairments are driven solely by reduced phonological memory capacity is more debatable than it first appeared. Since the early experiments, non-word repetition has been revealed to be much more than a "pure" phonological memory task. Crucially, short-term recall of non-words (especially for Gathercole and Baddeley's non-words) is affected by "word-likeness"—i.e., existing top-down lexical knowledge (Munson et al., 2005) as well as phonotactic frequency (Coady, Evans, & Kluender, 2010) and phonological structure (Gallon et al., 2007; Marshall & van der Lely, 2009). This means that the poor performance on this task could be at least in part explained by a language-specific deficit. Archibald and Gathercole (2007) also produced evidence that non-word repetition measures were more than the sum of short-term memory processes. Furthermore, the mechanisms linking poor phonological working memory to the particular difficulties in syntax seen in children with SLI have been difficult to establish. Although some models leading to these deficits have been proposed (for example the mapping hypothesis, Chiat 2001; the surface hypothesis, Leonard, 1998), these causal pathways remain poorly established in the evidence base.

Finally, the links between the *development* of language and non-word repetition are less convincing than sometimes expressed (Melby-Lervåg, Lervåg, Halaas-Lyster, Klem, Hagtvet, & Hulme, 2012) and although there is some evidence of this in very young children (Chiat & Roy, 2008) and in school-age children with language impairment (Botting & Conti-Ramsden, 2001), the amount of variance in expressive and receptive language that non-word repetition explains is conservative (12 % and 15 % respectively; Conti-Ramsden & Durkin, 2007, p. 150). Attempts have also been made to directly compare the predictive value of linguistic/syntactic impairment versus memory difficulties on language impairment status. Conti-Ramsden (2003) reported that when entered into regression analysis both past tense ability and non-word repetition serve equally as predictive markers for SLI.

Second, some of the "wider memory deficit" results need replication and scrutiny. Measurement continues to be a relevant confound in much of the research and remains one of the central barriers to attempts to disprove modular or domain-general predictions. For example, one apparent truth that has emerged is that little is known surrounding the domain-general skills of very young, or preverbal children who are developing typically. This clearly leads onto another central problem with the assessment of children with immature language either due to age or impairment. Without a reliable norm base, let alone information about developmental patterns, researchers have struggled to make robust empirical claims about how domain relevant skills and language (difficulties) might relate and have therefore relied heavily on theoretical or ideological arguments. Furthermore, domain-general skills have been shown to be highly sensitive to task specific effects. Of particular relevance here is that in many studies the tasks described as "non-verbal," a verbalizing strategy may be used effectively by typical children, but provide a source of disadvantage for those with SLI. This type of verbal advantage in typical development might be at a very subtle level, and this could explain results like those of Henry et al. (2012) in which the lower performance on non-verbal executive function tasks in comparison to verbal executive function tasks is counter-intuitive for a disorder that primarily affects language.

This seems to be supported by a recent paper investigating verbalizing strategies in SLI during a Tower of London task. SLI children were equally susceptible to articulatory suppression as their TD peers and clearly used a verbalizing strategy, however they remained poorer at the task *per se,* and, crucially, their inner speech was both less private and less "complex" (Lidstone, Meins, & Fernyhough, 2012). The authors suggest that the susceptibility to auditory suppression points to an "adequate function" of verbalization in non-verbal tasks, however it maybe that the focus of this verbalization was not as efficient as in TD children. In Botting et al. (2013) we show a clear disadvantage for short-term recall of verbalizable items in children with SLI even when the presentation and response are both non-verbal. The Procedural Deficit Hypothesis has some good evidence, however this theory suggests that declarative memory is intact, and there is some doubt as to whether that is the case. If it is, there is little explanation for the poor irregular vocabulary exhibited by children with SLI (Conti-Ramsden, Botting, Simkin, & Knox, 2001) and the limitations on declarative tasks that only dissipate once language is controlled for (Lum, Conti-Ramsden, Page, & Ullman, 2012).

Whilst emotional and behavioral difficulties seem to associate with language impairment in an indirect way, there are other explanations than a domain-general causal model. It is now established that SLI is somewhat heritable (Newbury et al., 2010). This means that children with SLI not only grow up with inherent language difficulties, but are also more likely to have parents and siblings with language limitations (see Stromswold, 1998 for a review) even when these skills are still in the normal range (Lindgren, Folstein, Tomblin, & Tager-Flusberg, 2009). This means that social experience and enjoyment is at risk of being more limited for the whole family and the opportunities for social practice reduced, regardless of the child's own particular language severity.

There are also wider considerations. An important unanswered question for domain-general approaches is why more widespread cognitive deficits are not seen from an earlier age in individuals later diagnosed with specific difficulties. For example, children with SLI do not generally present in the same way as a child with developmental delay, even though that might be expected if wide-ranging domain-general memory problems were present. As Filippi and Karmiloff-Smith (2013, p. 194) acknowledge, "the domain-general approach has difficulty in accounting for uneven cognitive profiles in which some domains are defective and others not". Furthermore, if language is not modular at early ages, why is it so vulnerable to deficit? One would expect a number of domain-general skills to be available for compensation in language learning. It may be that children referred for services and receiving an SLI diagnosis are simply those for whom this compensation does not readily develop. This may suggest an interaction between domain-general and domain-specific systems or between domain-general systems of cognition and more general ability to generalize and compensate.

Some researchers within the wider field of developmental cognitive psychology have returned to "microgenetic" (Siegler & Chen, 1998) or "dynamic assessment" approaches (see Hasson, Dodd, & Botting, 2012) in which even very small degrees of change over close time points are examined, to emphasize the gradual, interactive process of development which rarely if ever occurs in "stages" or in isolation. Nevertheless, this approach has been seldom used with children who have SLI. This may be in part influenced by the modular measurement tradition which sees language testing undertaken using static psychometric measures that guide the user to a minimum time between test occasions. The most widely recognized attempt to combine domain-specific and domain-general approaches, however, has been the "neuroconstructivist" approach, and we turn to this now.

## Combination of Approaches for Developmental Disorders: I Neuroconstructivism

Data thus far might suggest some sort of **combination** of domain-general and domain-specific inefficiency. Karmiloff-Smith was a major leader in neuroconstructivism, a proposal that a sequential combination of the two mechanisms exists, in which early domain-general skills lead to later domain-specific structures and skills (Karmiloff-Smith, 1992, 1998, 2009). In recent years Karmiloff-Smith referred to early domain-general skills as "domain-relevant" and proposed that the dichotomy between "impaired" and "unimpaired" cognitive abilities is not supported by the data. This school of thought suggests that although certain cognitive processes become domain-specific over developmental time, they do not start that way. Neuroconstructivism considers domain specificity to be the *outcome* of development rather than the start state. Thus in this approach "development is itself the key to change" (Karmiloff-Smith, 1998).

This position on developmental disorders has partly grown out of shifts in the available evidence. Not least is the expansion of developmental psychology in general. This has seen a move away from the application of adult models to childhood development (both typical and atypical) and a realization that the developing brain is a quite different entity to the adult one (Karmiloff-Smith, 1998). This has been supported by new technology allowing imaging studies in which typical and atypical children have been participants. Although these studies show some aspects of structural localization for language (for a review see Price, 2012), taken as a whole the findings suggest numerous loci related to language with differing and conflicting results across different children, and sometimes disperse brain activation noted within individuals, especially for receptive tasks (Pecini et al., 2005). The trend has meant that in cognitive psychology more generally, the process of maturation, whether typical or atypical, is the focus of study. This is quite different from the approach of clinical and theoretical linguistics, which seeks primarily to describe language and particularly syntax in detail at any given time point, using a static "adult model" as the target.

Nevertheless, neuroconstructivism has not propelled the field of SLI (and other developmental disorders) in the way one might expect. There are a number of possible reasons for this. One is simply that the above research positions are so entrenched that it has been difficult to take forward a neuroconstructivist approach. However, there may be other possibilities. Although neuroconstructivism explicitly combines domain-specific and domain-general theories, it also implicitly fails to use the more detailed analysis of domain-specific approaches (in the case of SLI the more linguistic elements) and keeps each approach separated in developmental time (i.e. domain-general development *followed by/leading to* domain-specificity). In some literature there is a lack of direct match between modelling neuroconstructivist data and the pattern seen in data from children (as noted by Ring & Clahsen, 2005), and in other work confusion may arise from cross-sectional "developmental trajectories" appearing to measure change (see Thomas et al., 2009 for a description of this method).

There is also little exposition of how domain-relevant skills become modularized or when this might occur. In addition, there still remain those significant barriers of diagnostic validity and measurement that prevent optimum research strategies and knowledge advancement from occurring.

## Combination of Approaches for Developmental Disorders: II A New Constructive Way Forward

Thus, two fairly robust positions have built up within the literature, both with distinct strengths: Domain-specific theories have enabled the examination of detailed theories on behavior; domain-general approaches have facilitated the search for wider causes and contributory factors and the exploration of development in a more focused way. The two approaches also raise issues that have not been resolved in a satisfactory way. In particular the use of static non-developmental models in many domain-specific approaches means that little can be assumed about atypical development of a modular system. For domain-general proponents there is widespread debate about the nature and even existence of SLI which does not feature in domain-specific accounts. Domain-general assumptions of generalized and transferable skills lead naturally to models of continuum and dimension in developmental disorders that are not as problematic for the strict diagnostic and dissociative view often evident in modularity or in adult neuropathology.

Attempts to combine these theories have been made at a sequential developmental level—i.e. the neuroconstructivist approach discussed above. However, before the adult brain develops, the domain-general and domain-specific theories outlined earlier argue for both typical and atypical development contained within their separate ideologies. From a logical point of view it does not necessarily need to be the case that

**Table 6.1** Differing theoretical stances on typical and atypical development.

| | *Domain-specific* | *Domain-general* |
|---|---|---|
| Typical development | (a) Individual cognitive skills and language are modular from start | (c) Individual cognitive skills and language are built from domain-relevant but generalized skills |
| Atypical development | (b) Specific impairments in cognition and language are the result of an impaired or poorly encapsulated module | (d) Specific impairments in cognition and language are the result of a particular combination of inefficient domain-general skills |

Strong domain-specific functioning would be signified above by (a) + (b).
Strong domain-general functioning would be signified above by (c) + (d).
Parallel combination theory 1, inefficient domain-general causes for specific impairments in the context of intact modular development, would be signified above by (a) + (d).
Parallel combination theory 2, inefficient modularization in the context of intact domain-general skills, would be signified above by (c) + (b).
Parallel combination theory 3, collective domain-general and domain-specific inefficiency interaction, would be signified above by (a), (b), (c), and (d) all being partly in evidence.

typical and atypical presentations are driven by the same systems. Rather, from the two differing perspectives, it is possible to construct a model of the ways in which both typical and atypical development might be viewed as a way forward to a possible combinatory or complementary model. Having evaluated the data against the claims made for them by the two positions, we propose a way forward that builds on the strengths of the two approaches, takes the process of development into account, and considers where the two approaches might usefully meet and interact *within the same chronological time frame.* We have termed this a "parallel combination" approach. Using Table 6.1 as a starting point, at least five different theories can be constructed.

The strong and mutually exclusive versions of domain-specific and domain-general functioning would be those signified above by (a) + (b) and (c) + (d) respectively. We will now consider the three other options.

## Parallel Combination Theory 1: Inefficient Domain-general Causes for Specific Impairments in the Context of Intact Modular Development

*(a) and (d) are the case*

In this scenario, the cognitive skill in question would indeed have some genetically determined triggers in typical development. These may even be in the form of an innate module. However in the context of a very inefficient wider system, this innate skill may not be able to function adequately. Over time one might speculate that this interaction could actually de-modularize or over-modularize language in terms of neural development, perhaps leading to the widespread and inconsistent brain imaging results in the population of children with developmental disorders.

## Parallel Combination Theory 2: Inefficient Modularization in the Context of Intact Domain-general Skills

*(c) and (b) are the case*:

For this configuration, a typically developing cognitive skill is built via a neuroconstructivist pathway from a number of other domain-relevant skills. Although no innate specialized structure exists, these generalized skills would lead relatively quickly to an increasingly modular architecture for that skill in typical development. However in some cases, despite inherent skills and input being adequate, the process of modularization itself, (and whatever might trigger this) is inefficient. One could speculate, in the example of SLI, that rather than developing increasing speed, efficiency and rules in language, the child would continually have to "build" language from scratch using as many domain-general cues as possible. This might lead to a pattern of good or excellent cognitive skill alongside slow and inefficient language processing, especially in the expressive domain, whereby the modularization is necessary for speed and relies less on domain general support. This combination has some potential overlap with the procedural deficit hypothesis.

## Parallel Combination Theory 3: Collective Domain-general and Domain-specific Inefficiency Interaction

(a), *(b), (c), and (d) are all partly in evidence*:

Is it possible that all parts of these approaches might have something to offer a theory of developmental disorder? One way of contemplating this would be to speculate the following, again using SLI as an example: Language is innate in the sense that children have an innate, genetic predisposition to fast-track the modularization of language (a), rather than having the sort of language knowledge ("universal grammar") that nativists propose. They do this by gathering a biased amount of information such as faces, social behavior and human speech (c). However this process can be interrupted by an impoverished source of data due to inefficient domain-relevant skills such as attention (d) which in turns leads to (or perhaps occurs comorbidly with/as part of (d)) an impairment in the actual process of implicitly learning/modularizing from this data (b). Alternatively, the process of modularization itself is impaired (b), and the skills at (d) are not impaired in their own right but are not strong enough to protect against this impairment. When this combination of events occurs we call it a "specific impairment."

The collective inefficiency model above starts to tackle some of the other key issues in the area:

1 *Heterogeneity.* The most severely affected children may have inefficient domain-general skills and poor modularization, giving them little chance for compensation. On the other hand, children with milder, or less wide ranging, difficulties may have problems mainly at (b) which will in turn affect (c). This will lead to such children showing some lag in wider cognitive skills as affected by lack of speed in the affected domain, but as this is supported by an unimpaired domain-general system, they do not show deficits at the severity of some their peers.

2 *Comorbidity.* Comorbidity of language, attention, memory, social, and emotional impairments are known to be more prevalent in more severely affected children.

This would be predicted by the model since these children have inefficient domain-general systems, affecting other areas of functioning, maybe as these are due to become modularized later in life.

3 *Differential neurological and genetic evidence for different parts of cognition and language*. The collective inefficiency seems to support early modularization of certain skills (such as expressive language processing) with a wider reliance on domain-general skills for others (e.g., receptive language). Genetic studies also suggest that the more specific impairments are more easily tracked through families. For SLI these are represented by phonological memory and expressive skills (e.g., Newbury et al., 2010).
4 *Disadvantage and socio-economic status (SES)*. Using a combined approach model such as those above, some effects of SES are predicted. Impoverished conditions may be the result of genetic factors, but the collective inefficiency model also predicts a double deficit for those in less rich environments whose domain-general skills in particular may not be supported as well as within a highly educated and financially secure family. The model may also help to explain the high rates of children with low language and cognition (many of whom "catch up") in socially disadvantaged areas: Children with low SES and impoverished environmental opportunities may need longer to get the encapsulation at (b) into action due to poorer input, but following that, some will basically have typically developing skills.
5 *Boundaries of disorder*. Outside of the individuals with clinically significant impairment, this model allows for a more dimensional approach to diagnosis whereby children who appear to be developing typically may nevertheless have problems with modularization (b) but compensate because these issues are supported by highly efficient typical domain-general processes to boost the process (c); or by children who have highly efficient modularization processes (a) that can encapsulate despite relatively poor input (either due to environmental or neurological factors) via other domain-general skills (d).

We hope that increased evidence will test the idea of a system consisting of *parallel* and *complementary* domain-specific and domain-general pathways. This should be achieved using multimethod approaches, including observation and assessment studies, intervention trials, and computational modelling.

## Summary: Keeping the Best of Both Approaches

In summary, these apparently opposing viewpoints initially defined important and differing approaches to the field of developmental disorders, but in recent years, and particularly for language acquisition and SLI, they have forced some inertia into empirical study. We propose that some of the divide is an illusion— a theoretical "Necker Cube" in which the same framework can be viewed one way and also in another, and yet still maintain the same shape in reality.

We argue that there are strong advantages to each approach within the context of developmental disorders. Domain-specific approaches bring depth: detailed analysis and a sense of careful measurement that is sometimes lacking in other work. This approach also recognizes explicitly that specific cognitive skills such as language are a primary developmental focus, and that a primary difficulty in a particular area is important. We do not see a random disordering of domain-general processes but a more salient difficulty with certain wider skills—in language impairment, this is particularly the case for syntax and inflectional morphology. On the other hand, domain-general frameworks push a more empirical and developmental agenda which is vital to progress in the field. These emphasize the fact that "pure" impairments are somewhat of a misnomer and remind us that development is key—the child brain is not the same as the adult one. They also highlight the likelihood of multifactorial etiology. For SLI, Bishop (2010) has introduced the idea of "phenomimicry" in which certain groups of symptoms/behaviors may appear like others but have different causes. Likewise Tomblin (2010) has speculated whether the diagnostic labels given to children with communication disorders are purely a creation of clinical practice—that is all children have different dimensions of different skills and only those with particular combinations of these are diagnosed into our pre-existing categories.

This issue of unnecessary mutual exclusivity between these two positions was recently picked up in the field of bilingualism by Peets and Bialystok (2011, p. 315), who comment that "the problem is in the attempt to dichotomize language ability as being controlled by either domain-specific or domain-general factors." They liken these two approaches to the distinction made between "crystallized" and "fluid" intelligence, that is, we should not be looking at which is "right," rather at which approach is best for which purpose, and at how elements of domain-specific or domain-general development can be measured sensitively over developmental time.

Nevertheless, it is important to acknowledge that in both these approaches empirical data depends to some extent on top-down ideologies—researchers will not be able to find data in areas that they do not measure. Instead, they tend to measure behaviors in ways that fit in with their own framework and interpret those data with considerable bias. One example is the assumption that impairment signifies cause. Thus, diagnostic labels also influence the two positions. None the less, we feel they may still have an important role to play at this point in the history of research into developmental disorders. Ultimately, human beings can only be described at the individual level. Work in support and intervention for families of children with developmental disorders benefits from some recognition of patterns across different *groups* of children, but it is important to recognize that these groupings are complex and dynamic. Equally, the underlying mechanisms of even specific impairments are likely to be multifactorial, and would benefit from a fresh approach to combining traditional theories.

## References

Abdalla, F., & Crago, M. (2008). Verb morphology deficits in Arabic-speaking children with specific language impairment. *Applied Psycholinguistics*, *29*, 315–340.

Ambridge, B., & Lieven, E. (2011). *Child language acquisition: Contrasting theoretical approaches*. Cambridge: Cambridge University Press.

Ambridge, B., Rowland, C. F. & Pine, J. M. (2008). Is structure dependence an innate constraint? New experimental evidence from children's complex question production. *Cognitive Science*, *32*, 222–255.

Archibald, L. M., & Gathercole, S. E. (2007). Nonword repetition in Specific Language Impairment: more than a phonological short-term memory deficit. *Psychonomic Bulletin & Review*, *14*, 919–924.

Bavin, E. L., Wilson, P., Maruff, P., & Sleeman, F. (2005). Spatio-visual memory of children with Specific Language Impairment: evidence for generalized processing problems. *International Journal of Language and Communication Disorders, 40*, 319–332.

Berko, J. (1958). The child's learning of English morphology. *Word, 14*, 150–177.

Bishop, D. V. M. (1999). Perspectives: cognition. An innate basis for language? *Science, 286*, 2283–2284.

Bishop, D. V. M. (2010). Overlaps between autism and language impairment: Phenomimicry or shared etiology? *Behavioral Genetics, 40*, 618–629.

Bishop D. V. M., Bright, P., James, C., Bishop, S., & van der Lely, H. K. J. (2000). Grammatical SLI: A distinct subtype of developmental language impairment? *Applied Psycholinguistics, 21*, 159–181.

Bishop, D. V. M., Nation, K. & Patterson, K. (Eds.). (2014). *Language in developmental and acquired disorders: Converging evidence for models of language representation in the brain. Special issue of Philosophical Transactions of the Royal Society, B.369 (1634).*

Bishop, D. V. M. (2014). Ten questions about terminology for children with unexplained language problems. *International Journal of Language & Communication Disorders, 49*(4), 381–415.

Botting, N. (2005). Non-verbal cognitive development and language impairment. *Journal of Child Psychology and Psychiatry, 46*, 317–326.

Botting, N., & Conti-Ramsden, G. M. (2008). The role of language, social cognition, and social skill in the functional social outcomes of young adolescents with and without a history of SLI. *British Journal of Developmental Psychology, 26*, 281–300.

Botting, N., Psarou, K., Caplin, T. & Nevin, L. (2013). Short-term memory skills in children with Specific Language Impairment: The effect of verbal and nonverbal task content. *Topics in Language Disorders, 33*, 313–327.

Botting, N., Toseeb, U., Pickles, A., Durkin, K., & Conti-Ramsden, G. (2016). Depression and anxiety change from adolescence to adulthood in individuals with and without language impairment. *PLoS One, 11*(7), e0156678.

Briscoe, J. & Rankin, P. M. (2009). Exploration of a "double-jeopardy" hypothesis within working memory profiles for children with specific language impairment. *International Journal of Language and Communication Disorders, 44*, 236–250.

Chiat, S. (2001). Mapping theories of developmental language impairment: premises, predictions and evidence. *Language and Cognitive Processes, 16*, 113–142.

Chiat, S. & Roy, P. (2008). Early phonological and sociocognitive skills as predictors of later language and social communication outcomes. *Journal of Child Psychology and Psychiatry, 49*, 635–645.

Clegg, J., Hollis, C., Mawhood, L., & Rutter, M. (2005). Developmental language disorders – a follow-up in later adult life. Cognitive, language and psychosocial outcomes. *Journal of Child Psychology and Psychiatry, 46*, 128–149.

Coady, J., & Evans, J. L. (2008). Uses and interpretations of non-word repetition tasks in children with and without specific language impairments (SLI). *International Journal of Language & Communication Disorders, 43*, 1–40.

Coady, J., Evans, J. L., & Kluender, K. R. (2010). Role of phonotactic frequency in nonword repetition by children with specific language impairments. *International Journal of Language and Communication Disorders, 45*, 494–509.

Conti-Ramsden G. (2003). Processing and linguistic markers in young children with specific language impairment (SLI). *Journal of Speech Language and Hearing Research, 46*, 1029–1037.

Conti-Ramsden, G. & Botting, N. (2004). Social difficulties and victimization in children with SLI at 11 years of age. *Journal of Speech, Language and Hearing Research, 47*, 145–161.

Conti-Ramsden, G. & Botting, N. (2008). Risk of affective disorders in adolescents with a history of SLI. *Journal of Child Psychology and Psychiatry, 49*, 516–525.

Conti-Ramsden, G., Botting, N., Simkin, Z. & Knox, E. (2001). Follow-up of children attending infant language units: Outcomes at 11 years of age. *International Journal of Language and Communication Disorders*, *36*, 207–220.

Conti-Ramsden, G., & Durkin, K. (2007). Phonological short-term memory, language and literacy: Developmental relationships in early adolescence in young people with SLI. *Journal of Child Psychology and Psychiatry*, *48*, 147–156.

Crago, M., & Allen, S. (2001). Early finiteness in Inuktitut: The role of language structure and input. *Language Acquisition*, *9*, 59–111.

Crain, S., & Pietroski, P. (2001). Nature, nurture and Universal Grammar. *Linguistics and Philosophy*, *24*, 139–185.

Denes, G. (2011). *Talking heads: The neuroscience of language*. Hove, UK: Psychology Press.

Durkin, K., & Conti-Ramsden, G. (2007). Language, social behavior and the quality of friendships in adolescents with and without a history of Specific Language Impairment. *Child Development*, *78*, 1441–1457.

Filippi, R., & Karmiloff-Smith, A. (2013). What can developmental disorders teach us about typical development? In C. R. Marshall (Ed.), *Current issues in developmental disorders* (pp. 193–209). London: Psychology Press.

Fodor, J. A. (1983). *Modularity of mind: An essay on faculty psychology*. Cambridge, MA: MIT Press.

Fonteneau, E., & van der Lely, H. K. J. (2008). Electrical brain responses in language-impaired children reveal grammar-specific deficits. *PLoS ONE*, *3*(3): e1832.

Friedmann, N., & Novogrodsky, R. (2008). Subtypes of SLI: SySLI, PhoSLI, LeSLI, and PraSLI. In A. Gavarró, & M. João Freitas (Eds.), *Language acquisition and development* (pp. 205–217). Newcastle-upon-Tyne: Cambridge Scholars Press.

Gallon, N., Harris. J. & van der Lely, H. K. J. (2007). Non-word repetition: An investigation of phonological complexity in children with Grammatical SLI. *Clinical Linguistics and Phonetics*, *21*, 435–455.

Gathercole, S. E., & Baddeley, A. D. (1990). The role of phonological memory in vocabulary acquisition: A study of young children learning new names. *British Journal of Psychology*, *81*(4), 439–454.

Gopnik, M. & Crago, M. B. (1991). Familial aggregation of a developmental language disorder. *Cognition*, *39*, 1–50.

Gopnik, M. (1990). Genetic basis of grammar defect. *Nature*, *347* (6288): 26–27.

Grant, J., Valian, V., & Karmiloff-Smith, A. (2002). A study of relative clauses in Williams syndrome. *Journal of Child Language*, *29*, 403–416.

Hasson, N., Dodd, B., & Botting, N. (2012). Dynamic assessment of sentence structure (DASS): Design and evaluation of a novel procedure for the assessment of syntax in children with language impairments. *International Journal of Language and Communication Disorders*, *47*, 285–299.

Henry, L. A., Messer, D. J. & Nash, G. (2012). Executive functioning in children with specific language impairment. *Journal of Child Psychology and Psychiatry*, *53*, 37–45.

Hick, R., Botting N., & Conti-Ramsden, G. M. (2005). Short-term memory and vocabulary development in children with Down syndrome and children with specific language impairment. *Developmental Medicine and Child Neurology* (+ Supp), *47*, 532–538.

Joanisse, M.F., Seidenberg, M.S. (2003). Phonology and syntax in Specific Language Impairments: Evidence from a connectionist model. *Brain and Language*, *86*, 40–56.

Karmiloff-Smith, A. (1992). *Beyond modularity: A developmental approach to cognitive science*. Cambridge, MA: MIT Press.

Karmiloff-Smith, A. (1998). Development itself is the key to understanding developmental disorders. *Trends in Cognitive Sciences*, *2*, 389–398.

Karmiloff-Smith, A. (2009). Nativism versus neuroconstructivism: Rethinking the study of developmental disorders. *Developmental Psychology*, *45*, 56–63.

Karmiloff-Smith, A., Grant, J., Berthoud, I., Davies, M., Howlin, P., & Udwin, O. (1997). Language and Williams syndrome: How intact is "intact"? *Child Development*, *68*, 246–262.

Lai, C. S. L., Fisher, S. E., Hurst, J. A., Vargha-Khadem, F., & Monaco, A. P. (2001). A fork-head-domain gene is mutated in a severe speech and language disorder. *Nature*, *413*, 519–523.

Lai, C. S. L., Gerrelli, D., Monaco, A. P., Fisher, S. E., & Copp, A. J. (2003). *FOXP2* expression during brain development coincides with adult sites of pathology in a severe speech and language disorder. *Brain*, *126*, 2455–2462.

Leonard, L. B. 1998. *Children with Specific Language Impairment.* Cambridge, MA: MIT Press.

Leonard, L., & Dromi, E. (1994). The use of Hebrew verb morphology by children with specific language impairment and children developing language normally. *First Language*, *14*, 283–304.

Levy, Y. & Kave, G. 1999. Language breakdown and linguistic theory: A tutorial overview. *Lingua 107*, 95–143.

Lidstone, J., Meins, E., & Fernyhough, C. (2012). Verbal mediation of cognition in children with Specific Language Impairment. *Development and Psychopathology*, *24*, 651–660.

Lindgren, K. A., Folstein, S. E., Tomblin, J. B. & Tager-Flusberg, H. (2009), Language and reading abilities of children with autism spectrum disorders and specific language impairment and their first-degree relatives. *Autism Research*, *2*, 22–38

Lorch, M. & Hellal, P. (2012). The "idioglossia" cases of the 1890s and the clinical investigation and treatment of developmental language impairment. *Cortex*, *48*, 1052–1060.

Lukács, Á., Leonard, L., Kas, B., & Pléh, C. (2009). The use of tense and agreement by Hungarian-speaking children with language impairment. *Journal of Speech, Language, and Hearing Research*, *52*, 98–117.

Lum, J. A. G., Conti-Ramsden, G., Page, D. & Ullman, M. T. (2012). Working, declarative and procedural memory in specific language impairment. *Cortex*, *48*, 1138–1154.

Marshall, C. R. & van der Lely, H. K. J. (2006). A challenge to current models of past tense inflection: the impact of phonotactics. *Cognition*, *100*, 302–320.

Marshall, C. R. & van der Lely, H. K. J. (2007). Derivational morphology in children with Grammatical-SLI. *Clinical Linguistics and Phonetics*, *42*, 71–91.

Marshall, C. R. & van der Lely, H. K. J. (2009). Effects of word position and stress on onset cluster production: Evidence from typical development, SLI and dyslexia. *Language*, *85*, 39–57.

Mason, K., Rowley, K., Marshall, C. R., Atkinson, J. R., Herman, R., Woll, B. & Morgan, G. (2010). Identifying SLI in Deaf children acquiring British Sign Language: Implications for theory and practice. *British Journal of Developmental Psychology*, *28*, 33–49.

Melby-Lervåg, M., Lervåg, A., Halaas-Lyster, S-A., Klem, M., Hagtvet, B. & Hulme, C. (2012). Nonword-repetition ability does not appear to be a causal influence on children's vocabulary development. *Psychological Science*, *23*, 1092–1098.

Mervis, C. B., & Becerra, A. M. (2007). Language and communicative development in Williams syndrome. *Mental Retardation and Developmental Disabilities Research Reviews*, *13*, 3–15.

Mervis, C. B., & Robinson, B. F. (2000). Expressive vocabulary of toddlers with Williams syndrome or Down syndrome: A comparison. *Developmental Neuropsychology*, *17*, 111–126.

Munson, B., Kurtz, B.A., & Windsor, J. (2005). The influence of vocabulary size, phonotactic probability, and wordlikeness on nonword repetitions of children with and without language impairments. *Journal of Speech, Language, and Hearing Research*, *48*, 1033–1047.

Newbury, D. F., Fisher, S. E., & Monaco, A. P. (2010). Recent advances in the genetics of language impairment. *Genome Medicine*, *2*, 1053–1076.

Niemi, J. (1999). Production of grammatical number in specific language impairment: An elicitation experiment on Finnish. *Brain and Language*, *68*, 262–267.

Paradis, J. & Crago, M. (2001). The morphosyntax of specific language impairment in French: Evidence for an extended optional default account. *Language Acquisition*, *9*, 269–300.

Paterson, S. J., Brown, J. H., Gsödl, Johnson, M. H., & Karmiloff-Smith, A. (1999). Cognitive modularity and genetic disorders. *Science*, *286*, 2355–2358.

Paul, R. & Cohen, D. J. (1982). Communication development and its disorders: a psycholinguistic perspective. *Schizophrenia Bulletin*, *8*, 279–293.

Peets, E., & Bialystock, E. (2011). An integrated approach to the study of specific language impairment and bilingualism. *Applied Psycholinguistics*, *31*, 315–319.

Pecini, C., Casalini, C., Brizzolara, D., Cipriani, P., Pfanner, L. & Chilosi, A. (2005). Hemispheric specialization for language in children with different types of specific language impairment. *Cortex*, *41*, 157–167.

Pinker, S. (1994). *The language instinct*. London: Penguin.

Pinker, S. (1999). *Words and rules*. London: Weidenfeld & Nicolson.

Price, C. J. (2012). A review and synthesis of the first 20 years of PET and fMRI studies of heard speech, spoken language and reading. *Neuroimage*, *62*, 816–847.

Quinto-Pozos, D., Singleton, J. L., & Hauser, P. C. (2017). A case of specific language impairment in a deaf signer of American Sign Language. *Journal of Deaf Studies and Deaf Education*, *22*, 204–218.

Reilly, S., Tomblin, B., Law, J., McKean, C., Mensah, F. K., Morgan, A., … & Wake, M. (2014). Specific language impairment: a convenient label for whom?. *International Journal of Language & Communication Disorders*, *49*(4), 416–451.

Rice, M., & Wexler, K. (1996). Toward tense as a clinical marker of Specific Language Impairment in English-speaking children. *Journal of Speech and Hearing Research*, *39*, 1239–1257.

Rice, M. L. (1993). "Don't talk to him; he's weird": A social consequences account of language and social interactions. In A. P. Kaiser & David B. Gray (Eds.), *Enhancing children's communication: Research foundations for intervention. Communication and language intervention series*, Vol. *2*, (pp. 139–158). Baltimore, MD: Paul H. Brookes Publishing.

Ring, M., & Clahsen, H. (2005). Distinct patterns of language impairment in Down's syndrome and Williams syndrome: The case of syntactic chains. *Journal of Neurolinguistics*, *18*, 479–501.

Rumelhart, D. E., McClelland, J. L., & the PDP Research Group (1986). *Parallel distributed processing: Explorations in the microstructure of cognition*. Cambridge, MA: MIT Press.

Siegler, R. S., & Chen, Z. (1998). Developmental differences in rule learning: A microgenetic analysis. *Cognitive Psychology*, *36*, 273–310.

Snowling, M. J., & Hulme, C. (2012). Annual research review: The nature and classification of reading disorders – a commentary on proposals for DSM-5. *Journal of Child Psychology and Psychiatry*, *53*, 593–607.

Stavrakaki, S. (2001). Comprehension of reversible relative clauses in Specifically Language Impaired and normally developing Greek children. *Brain and Language*, *77*, 419–431.

Stromswold, K. (1998). Genetics of spoken language disorders. *Human Biology*, *70*, 293–320.

Thomas, M.S.C., Annaz, D., Ansari, D., Serif, G., Jarrold, C. and Karmiloff-Smith, A. (2009). Using developmental trajectories to understand developmental disorders. *Journal of Speech, Language, and Hearing Research*, *52*, 336–358

Tomasello, M. (2003). *Constructing a language: A usage-based theory of language acquisition*. Cambridge, MA: Harvard University Press.

Tomblin, J. B., Freese, P. R., & Records, N. L. (1992). Diagnosing Specific Language Impairment in adults for the purpose of pedigree analysis. *Journal of Speech and Hearing Research*, *35*, 832–843.

Tomblin, J. B., Records, N. L., Buckwater, P. Zhang, X., Smith, E., & O'Brien, M., (1997). Prevalence of Specific Language Impairment in kindergarten children. *Journal of Speech, Language and Hearing Research*, *40*, 1245–1260.

Ullman, M. T. & Pierpont, E. I. (2005). Specific Language Impairment is not specific to language: The Procedural Deficit Hypothesis. *Cortex*, *41*, 399–433.

Valian, V. (2009). Innateness and learnability. In E. Bavin (Ed), *The Cambridge handbook of child language* (pp. 15–34). Cambridge: Cambridge University Press.

van der Lely, H. K. J. (1996). Specifically language impaired and normally developing children: Verbal passive vs adjectival passive sentence interpretation. *Lingua*, *98*, 243–272.

van der Lely, H. K. J., (1997). Narrative discourse in grammatical-Specific Language Impaired children: A modular language deficit? *Journal of Child Language*, *24*, 221–256.

van der Lely, H. K. J. & Battell, J. (2003). Wh-movement in children with grammatical SLI: a test of the RDDR Hypothesis. *Language*, *79*, 153–181.

van der Lely, H. K. J., & Stollwerck, L. (1997). Binding theory and Specifically Language Impaired children. *Cognition*, *62*, 245–290.

van der Lely, H. K. J., & Ullman, M. (2001). Past tense morphology in specifically language impaired children and normally developing children. *Language and Cognitive Processes*, *16*, 177–217.

Vargha-Khadem, F., Watkins, K., Alcock, K. J., Fletcher, P., & Passingham, R. (1995). Praxic and nonverbal cognitive deficits in a large family with a genetically transmitted speech and language disorder. *Proceedings of the National Academy of Sciences*, *92*, 930–933.

Wadman, R., Botting, N., Durkin, K., & Conti-Ramsden, G. (2011). Changes in emotional health symptoms in adolescents with specific language impairment. *International Journal of Language & Communication Disorders*, *46*(6), 641–656.

Wong, A. M.-Y., Leonard, L., Fletcher, P., & Stokes, S. (2004). Questions without movement: A study of Cantonese-speaking children with and without specific language impairment. *Journal of Speech, Language, and Hearing Research*, *47*, 1440–1453.

# 7

# Empathy Problems in Youth with Disruptive Behavior Disorders, with and without Callous Unemotional Traits

Jarla Pijper, Minet de Wied, Stephanie van Goozen, and Wim H. J. Meeus

Empathy, generally defined as the ability to understand and share in another's emotional state, is important for moral understanding, motivating prosocial behavior (Eisenberg & Miller, 1987; Hoffman, 2008), and inhibiting unwanted behaviors such as delinquency and aggression (Miller & Eisenberg, 1988). Empathy problems are often associated with oppositional defiant disorder (ODD), and conduct disorder (CD), also referred to as disruptive behavior disorders (DBD) (American Psychiatric Association, 2000). Children and adolescents with DBD may have empathy problems that are most striking in those with psychopathic tendencies or callous unemotional (CU) traits. CU traits are a precursor of the interpersonal–affective dimension of adult psychopathy, and central to the construct of psychopathic tendencies in youth (Frick & Hare, 2001; Lynam & Gudonis, 2005). In the fifth edition of the *Diagnostic Statistical Manual of Mental Disorders* (DSM-5) a specifier *with limited prosocial emotions* has been added to the classification of CD. This specifier applies to those who meet the criteria of CD, and also show a callous and unemotional interpersonal style, that is, lack of empathy, lack of guilt, and shallow affect (American Psychiatric Association, 2013). Given the clinical importance of CU traits, it is important to examine whether lack of empathy can contribute to a differentiation between CD subtypes.

A growing body of research suggests that CU traits and psychopathic tendencies in children and adolescents are associated with significant impairments in empathy, especially emotional empathy (Blair, 2008, 2013; Blair, Leibenluft, & Pine, 2014). Yet, relatively few studies have directly compared youth with a CD diagnosis with and without CU traits on empathic responsiveness. In addition, although CU traits are tied to CD in the DSM-5 taxonomy of externalizing spectrum disorders, CU traits also co-occur with ODD and attention deficit hyperactivity disorder (ADHD) (e.g., Herpers, Rommelse, Bons, Buitelaar, & Scheepers, 2012). ODD and CD are

*The Wiley Handbook of Developmental Psychopathology*, First Edition. Edited by Luna C. Centifanti and David M. Williams.

frequently comorbid with ADHD (American Psychiatric Association, 2013), and ADHD, in turn, has been linked to reduced empathy (e.g., Barkley, 2006; Braaten & Rosén, 2000; Marton, Wiener, Rogers, Moore, & Tannock, 2009), raising the question as to whether the empathy problems associated with CU traits are similar for those with pure DBD as for those with ADHD comorbidity.

Furthermore, empathy is a rather complex multidimensional construct (Davis, 2006), including affective and cognitive components, trait empathy (the tendency of an individual to respond empathically across different situations), state empathy (empathic reactions evoked within empathy-inducing situations), empathy-related processes and behavior. Previous reviews on empathy dysfunction in psychopathic youth (Blair, 2013; De Wied, Gispen-De Wied, & Van Boxtel, 2010; Frick, Ray, Thornton, & Kahn, 2013) have solely focused on aspects of affective versus cognitive empathy, but have made no distinction between trait and state empathy. This distinction is important, however, for at least two reasons: First, reviews on empathy in relation to pathological aggression (Lovett & Sheffield, 2007) and normative levels of externalizing behavior (Miller & Eisenberg, 1988) demonstrate stronger inverse relationships between empathy and antisocial behaviors for questionnaire measures of trait empathy than for indexes of state empathy. Second, and more important, based on the hypothesis that CU traits may have a strong underlying genetic component (see Viding & McCrory, 2012 for a review), affecting neural circuits including the amygdala (Blair, 2013), there is reason to suggest that youth with CU traits will show particular deficits in both state and trait empathy. This chapter will take full account of the multidimensional construct of empathy, and discuss results obtained with measures of affective versus cognitive state and trait empathy separately.

A first aim of this chapter is to examine the nature of empathy problems in clinically referred DBD youth with CU traits. A second aim is to examine whether a lack of empathy contributes to a differentiation between DBD subtypes. A third aim is to explore whether the empathy problems associated with CU traits are similar for those with pure DBD as for those with ADHD comorbidity. We start by considering the various components of empathy, using Davis' organizational model (1996, 2006), which emphasizes the connections between all components. Next, we reflect on the DSM-5 (American Psychiatric Association, 2013) classifications of ODD and CD, summarize studies conducted with undifferentiated samples (not accounting for CU or psychopathic traits) of DBD youth, followed by studies examining empathy problems in DBD children and adolescents with high versus low CU traits. We close the chapter with clinical implications and suggestions for future research.

## Empathy-Related Components

Davis' (1996, 2006) *organizational model of empathy-related constructs* treats empathy as a multidimensional phenomenon, involving traits (empathic tendencies), states (intrapersonal outcomes), affective and cognitive components. Affective empathy is a vicarious affective response more in line with another's situation than one's own (Hoffmann, 2000). A distinction is often made between empathy, sympathy, and personal distress (Batson, 2009; Eisenberg, Shea, Carlo, & Knight, 1991). Empathy concerns an affect match between an observer and someone else's affective state, that is, feeling *with* another person. Sympathy, also labeled empathic concern, is an

**Table 7.1** Key terms in Chapter 7.

| | |
|---|---|
| **Trait empathy** | The tendency of an individual to respond empathically across different situations. |
| **State empathy** | Empathic reactions evoked during empathy-inducing situations. |
| **Motor empathy** | Spontaneous and automatic mimicry processes, which may lead to the automatic transmission of emotions. |
| **Affective empathy** | A vicarious affective response more in line with another person's situation than one's own. Affect matches, sympathy and/or personal distress are all considered aspects of affective empathy. |
| **Cognitive empathy** | The ability to understand and represent another person's emotional state, thoughts and beliefs. Perspective taking, ToM, and empathic accuracy may all be considered aspects of cognitive empathy. |

emotion oriented towards the other, that is, feeling *for* the other person. Personal distress is an aversive, self-focused, reaction which may consist of feelings of discomfort or anxiety when perceiving someone else's affective state, thus feeling *by* another person (Batson, 2009). Cognitive empathy is the ability to understand someone else's affective state without necessarily being in an affective condition oneself (Walter, 2012). Perspective taking, Theory of Mind (ToM; the ability of an individual to infer what another person is feeling or thinking, and what he or she may do based on those inferences), and empathic accuracy may all be considered aspects of cognitive empathy (see Table 7.1).

The tendency to share affective responses (affective trait empathy), and to engage in empathy-related cognitive processes such as role taking (cognitive trait empathy) may affect both empathy-related processes and intrapersonal outcomes (i.e., affective and/or cognitive state empathy). Empathy-related processes, in turn, may differ in terms of cognitive control, ranging from primitive processes such as motor mimicry to the most advanced cognitive processes such as perspective taking. Motor mimicry, sometimes referred to as motor empathy (Blair, 2007), is thought to be an early component in the process of empathy. Motor mimicry may lead to the automatic transmission of emotions, and contribute to emotional contagion (Hatfield, Rapson, & Le, 2009). Evidence suggests that both humans (Molenberghs, Cunnington, & Mattingley, 2012) and other primate species (Iacoboni, 2005; Rizzolatti, 2005) possess a mirror neuron system underlying automatic mimicry, suggesting an evolutionary history for the capacity of empathy. Motor mimicry plays an important role in the development of empathy, especially in the preverbal years (Hoffman, 2000). As the cognitive system develops, higher order cognitive processes come to play a more important role, producing more sophisticated affective and cognitive empathic responses. Table 7.1 provides an overview of the key terms discussed in this chapter.

Brain-imaging studies suggest that distinct but interacting brain structures are involved in affective and cognitive empathy (see Shamay-Tsoory, 2009; Singer, 2006; Völlm et al., 2006). The insula and limbic structures are involved in affective empathy, while prefrontal brain areas are involved in perspective-taking processes and ToM. The cognitive and affective empathy networks may also include the mirror neuron system in premotor areas (Carr, Iacoboni, Dubeau, Mazziotta, & Lenzi, 2003). As such, it is possible that motor, affective and cognitive components of empathy become selectively, or jointly impaired with consequential differences in conduct problems and treatment options.

## Measuring Empathy

Different empathy indexes have been developed to assess motor mimicry and aspects of either the affective or cognitive components (or both) of state and trait empathy (e.g., Eisenberg & Fabes, 1990; Zhou, Valiente, & Eisenberg, 2003). Motor mimicry is usually studied within a laboratory setting where individuals are exposed to static or dynamic emotional facial expressions. Facial mimicry can be assessed using visual coding techniques (e.g., Marsh, Beauchaine, & Williams, 2008a), or facial electromyographic (EMG) procedures (e.g., De Wied, Van Boxtel, Zaalberg, Goudena, & Matthys, 2006). Facial EMG is a more sensitive measure, which may capture both automatic facial mimicry and facial expressions of vicarious emotional experiences (e.g., Dimberg, 1990; Dimberg, Thunberg, & Elmehed, 2000).

State empathy is routinely assessed within laboratory or field settings. Empathic responses are often elicited by more complex, empathy inducing stimuli, such as video-vignettes portraying other persons experiencing negative or positive emotions (e.g., Cohen & Strayer, 1996; De Wied, Van Boxtel, Matthys, & Meeus, 2012). Affective and cognitive outcomes can be measured at different levels of empathic functioning. Self-report, facial and autonomic indexes of empathy have all been used to assess empathy-related responses in children and adolescents with DBD (e.g., Cohen & Strayer, 1996; De Wied et al., 2012; Marsh et al., 2008a). In addition, brain event-related potential (ERP) technique (e.g., Cheng, Hung, & Decety, 2012) and functional Magnetic Resonance Imaging (fMRI) (e.g., Decety, Michalska, Akitsuki, & Lahey, 2009) have been employed to assess brain activity while respondents witness another person experiencing pain.

There are advantages and disadvantages associated with each type of index (e.g., Zhou et al., 2003). Self-report indexes are easy to administer, but appear to be affected by demand characteristics, such as the sex of the experimenter, and social desirability. Social desirability bias may influence facial indexes of empathy, although facial EMG responses suffer less from such biases than observational measures since it captures – in part – automatic mimicry processes (Dimberg, Thunberg, & Grunedal, 2002). Autonomic indexes of empathy, such as heart rate (HR), are relatively free from social desirability bias, but may be difficult to interpret. Some researchers consider HR acceleration to reflect empathy (e.g., Anastassiou-Hadjicharalambous & Warden, 2008b), others suggest that HR acceleration reflects self-focused personal distress reactions, and HR deceleration empathic concern (e.g., Eisenberg et al., 1988a, 1988b).

Over the years, various questionnaire measures have been developed to assess the dispositional tendency to engage in empathy-related processes (trait empathy) such as perspective taking or vicarious affective responding. Frequently used self-report questionnaire measures of empathy are the Empathy Index for Children and Adolescents (IECA, Bryant, 1982) and the Interpersonal Reactivity Index (IRI, Davis, 1983). The IECA is a 22-item self-report questionnaire, developed to assess affective empathy in children from the age of six years and older. The IRI is a 28-item self-report questionnaire, developed to assess both affective and cognitive empathy in adolescents and adults.

## DBD: A Heterogeneous Disorder

### Diagnostic Criteria for ODD and CD

In the DSM-5 (American Psychiatric Association, 2013) ODD and CD are categorized as the disruptive, impulsive-control, and conduct disorders. ODD is characterized by a frequent and persistent pattern of angry/irritable mood, argumentative/defiant behavior or vindictiveness. ODD may be a developmental precursor of CD, especially for those with the childhood-onset type. The essential feature of CD is a repetitive and persistent pattern of behavior in which the basic rights of others or major age-appropriate societal norms or rules are violated. The behaviors fall into four main groupings: aggression towards people and animals, destruction of property, deceitfulness or theft, and serious violations of rules. A distinction is made between individuals who show at least one symptom of CD prior to 10 years of age (childhood-onset type), and those who show no symptom characteristics before 10 years of age (adolescent-onset type). Moreover, a specifier *with limited prosocial emotions* has been added to the DSM-5 classification of CD, which applies to those who meet the criteria for CD, and also show a callous and unemotional interpersonal style. Characteristics of the specifier are lack of guilt, lack of empathy, no concern about performance and shallow affect. Those who qualify for the specifier are most likely to have the childhood-onset type of CD, and to have conduct disorder that persists into adulthood.

### Multiple Pathways to Conduct Disorder

The subtyping of CD is based on research suggesting that antisocial individuals with CU traits not only differ in the severity and stability of antisocial behavior (Lynam & Gudonis, 2005), but also exhibit distinct emotional and cognitive characteristics (Frick et al., 2013), discrete pathophysiology (Blair, 2013; Blair et al., 2014), and different responses to treatment (Waller, Gardner, & Hyde, 2013), suggesting an etiologically distinct subgroup of antisocial youth. In their developmental model of antisocial behavior, Frick and Viding (2009) have outlined three pathways to conduct problems: one adolescent-onset pathway and two childhood-onset pathways. Youth with adolescent-onset conduct problems are proposed to show an exaggeration of normal adolescent rebellion. Youth with childhood-onset conduct problems may show distinct pathways depending on the presence or absence of CU traits. Youth with CU traits show a temperamental style characterized by low emotional arousal and insensitivity to punishment cues that interferes with the normal development of empathy, guilt and other aspects of conscience. Youth without CU traits may show high levels of emotional arousal, cognitive deficits, such as low verbal intelligence, and problems related to ineffective parenting, which may lead to emotion regulation problems (Frick & Viding, 2009, see also Frick et al., 2013 for a comprehensive review).

### Empathy Problems in DBD Subtypes

Blair (2007, 2013) suggests that DBD youth with CU traits are likely to encounter *affective* empathy problems because of a genetic predisposition to show reduced amygdala responsiveness to distress cues. The amygdala contributes to aversive conditioning and the processing of distress cues, especially fear-related information (Olsson & Phelps, 2007). Abnormalities in this circuit may critically hamper socialization, and structurally affect empathy development. Indeed, brain imaging studies show reduced amygdala activation while processing fearful facial expressions in DBD youth with CU traits (Marsh et al., 2008b) and in boys with conduct problems and CU traits (Jones, Laurens, Herba, Barker, & Viding, 2009), relative to controls. Significant differences between DBD subtypes have more recently been demonstrated by Viding and colleagues (2012): DBD boys with high-CU traits show less amygdala reactivity to pre-attentively presented fearful faces than those with low CU traits. Amygdala dysfunction in individuals with psychopathic traits may also affect the attention network (White et al., 2012), possibly leading to fear-recognition deficits (e.g., Dadds, El Masry, Wimalaweera, & Guestella, 2008a). Reduced amygdala responsiveness to distress cues can structurally affect empathy development in youth with high CU traits. This may become apparent in dispositional characteristics (trait empathy), but also in primitive processes (such as mimicry) and more sophisticated empathic responses (state empathy).

DBD youth without CU traits may also show empathy problems (e.g., De Wied et al., 2012). However, their ability to empathize with others may be affected by different sources, such as negative sentiments, hostile attributions, or poor regulatory skills. The tendency to misperceive others intentions as more threatening or hostile than is the case, is listed as an associated feature of CD in the DSM-5 (American Psychiatric Association, 2013). Negative sentiments and hostility may reduce empathic responding, as demonstrated in studies with healthy students (e.g., Lanzetta & Englis, 1989; Singer, 2006). Alternatively, it is possible that poor regulatory skills are related to empathy problems in DBD youth without CU traits. Eisenberg and colleagues (1994) argue that people who are sensitive to others' distress, but poor in emotion regulation, may be prone to personal distress. This could be true for DBD individuals without CU traits because they may have a highly sensitive *basic threat circuit* (amygdala, hypothalamus, periquaductal grey (PAG)) due to early trauma, violence or neglect (Blair, 2013), and poor regulatory skills (e.g., Beauchaine, Gatzke-Kopp, & Mead, 2007). To summarize, both DBD subtypes are likely to have empathy problems. However, youth with DBD and high CU traits may have empathy problems because of under-responsiveness to distress cues, whereas those without CU traits may have empathy problems because of over-responsiveness to distress cues, poor regulatory skills, and/or hostility bias (De Wied et al., 2010).

## Empirical Evidence for Empathy Problems in DBD Youth

An increasing number of studies suggest that antisocial youth with CU or psychopathic traits are poor empathizers (e.g., Blair, 2013; Blair et al., 2014; Frick et al., 2013). Still, only a minority of studies have investigated empathy dysfunction in *clinical* samples of youth with DBD. This chapter focuses on empathy dysfunction in clinical samples of children and adolescents with DBD. We will start reviewing studies conducted with undifferentiated samples of DBD youth, followed by studies that accounted for CU or psychopathic traits. We included studies that investigated a) clinical samples of ODD or CD youth (8-18 years) diagnosed according the DSM-IV

(American Psychiatric Association, 2000) criteria by clinicians, or with a well-validated and reliable diagnostic instrument, and b) state and/or trait empathy. Accordingly, we did not include studies conducted with community samples using screening instruments to assess conduct problems (ODD/CD) (e.g., Lockwood et al., 2013; Sebastian et al., 2012), or studies with children from special schools without clinical assessments of ODD/CD (Blair, 1999). However, we did include one study with children attending special schools scoring in the clinical range of CD problems as assessed with a screening instrument following DSM-IV criteria (Jones, Happé, Gilbert, Burnett, & Viding, 2010).

## Studies with Undifferentiated Groups of DBD Youth

*Motor Empathy.* De Wied and colleagues (2006) investigated facial EMG responses to dynamic facial expressions in DBD boys and controls. DBD boys showed subnormal facial EMG reactivity to angry faces, but not to happy faces. Using the same sample, De Wied and colleagues also examined facial EMG responses to more complex empathy-inducing film clips (De Wied, Van Boxtel, Posthumus, Goudena, & Matthys, 2009). Because EMG responses to empathy-inducing film clips may reflect facial expressions of empathic experiences in addition to spontaneous mimicry responses, findings from this study will be discussed below with other studies on *affective state empathy*.

*Affective State Empathy.* A total of five studies investigated affective empathy, three with DBD boys (De Wied, Goudena, & Matthys, 2005; De Wied et al., 2009; Marsh et al., 2008a) and two with CD adolescents (Cohen & Strayer, 1996; Decety et al., 2009). De Wied and colleagues examined verbal, facial and autonomic responses to empathy-inducing film clips portraying negative (sadness and anger) and positive (happiness) emotions. Relative to controls, DBD boys reported less empathy (De Wied et al., 2005), and showed less facial EMG and HR reactivity in response to negative (not positive) emotions (De Wied et al., 2009). Consistent with the one study on motor empathy (discussed above), the results of De Wied and colleagues (2005, 2009) suggest that DBD boys are selectively impaired in dysphoric (not euphoric) empathy. Marsh and colleagues (2008a), however, found no indications of affective empathy impairments in DBD boys on various autonomic measures and an observational measure of facial mimicry to a sadness-inducing film clip. As for studies with adolescents, Cohen and Strayer (1996) were the first to show that CD adolescents reported less affective empathy in relation to various empathy-inducing film clips than controls. Decety and colleagues (2009) demonstrated that DBD boys, relative to controls, show increased brain reactivity in parts of the limbic system (involved in affective empathy) to pictures of others in pain accidentally inflicted by someone else. In sum, these studies support that DBD boys have impaired affective empathy, especially when witnessing other persons in distress.

*Cognitive state empathy.* To our knowledge, three studies have investigated cognitive empathy in DBD youth, two with children (Downs & Smith, 2004; Happé & Frith, 1996) and one with adolescents (Cohen & Strayer, 1996). Downs and Smith (2004) demonstrated that ODD boys obtained lower scores than controls on emotion recognition and false belief tasks. Similarly, Cohen and Strayer (1996) demonstrated that CD adolescents showed impaired cognitive attributions to empathy-inducing film clips. In contrast, Happé and Frith (1996), found no differences between CD children and controls on a false belief task. However, the CD children scored lower than controls on items that required ToM according to the Vineland Adaptive Behavior Scales (VABS; Sparrow, Balla, & Cicchetti, 1984) interview (Happé & Frith, 1996). Given the distinct methods, samples, and the limited number of studies, it is still too soon to draw conclusions about possible cognitive empathy impairments in DBD youth.

*Affective and Cognitive Trait Empathy.* One study with DBD boys (De Wied et al., 2005) and two with CD adolescents (Cohen & Strayer, 1996; Sterzer, Stadler, Poustka, & Kleinschmidt, 2007), showed that both DBD boys and CD adolescents obtained lower scores on questionnaire measures of affective empathy. Cohen and Strayer (1996) also demonstrated that CD adolescents are impaired in their perspective-taking abilities, assessed with Davis' IRI (1983).

In sum, most studies with undifferentiated samples of DBD youth suggest a systematic impairment in affective trait and state empathy. Impairments in cognitive empathy have also been demonstrated, though studies are few, and results are inconsistent. Initial evidence suggests that DBD boys may have impaired motor empathy, but these findings need replication before we can draw conclusions.

## Empirical Studies with DBD Subtypes

*Affective State Empathy.* In total six studies examined affective state empathy, two with children (Anastassiou-Hadjicharalambous & Warden, 2008b; Schwenck et al., 2012) and four with adolescents (Cheng et al., 2012; De Wied et al., 2012; Marsh et al., 2011; Marsh et al., 2013). The majority of these studies reveal affective empathy problems in both DBD subtypes. Anastassiou-Hadjicharalambous and Warden (2008b) assessed self-report and autonomic responses of CD children (24% had comorbid ADHD) and controls to an empathy-inducing film clip portraying fear. Both CD children with and without CU traits reported less empathy than controls; no significant differences were found between subtypes. Interestingly, CD children with high CU traits showed lower HR activity and lower HR change from baseline than CD children with low CU traits and controls, suggesting less empathic concern. Those with low CU traits did not differ from controls on HR indexes of empathy. Schwenck and colleagues (2012) used self-report indexes to examine empathy in CD children (34% comorbid ADHD) and controls to empathy-inducing film clips (specific emotions were not reported). CD children with high CU traits reported less affective empathy than controls. No differences occurred between the CD subtypes, nor did the low CU children report less affective empathy than controls. Findings remained the same after excluding children with ADHD.

As for studies with adolescents, Marsh and colleagues (2011) asked DBD adolescents (62% had ADHD comorbidity) with psychopathic traits and controls to recall emotional events, and to report their experienced physiological arousal during those events. Relative to controls, DBD adolescents with psychopathic traits reported less physiological arousal during fearful experiences. De Wied and colleagues (2012) examined empathy in DBD male adolescents (68% had ADHD comorbidity) with high and low CU traits and controls, using facial EMG, self-report and autonomic indexes of empathy. All respondents were exposed to film clips involving negative (sadness, anger) and positive (happiness) emotions. Compared to controls, both subtypes showed less facial responsiveness (less frowning muscle activity) to sadness, and reported less empathic happiness. Moreover, high CU adolescents reported less empathic sadness, and showed less HR deceleration to sadness than controls. Importantly, significant differences in HR change from baseline were found between DBD subtypes: DBD adolescents with high CU traits showed less HR change from baseline during sadness than those with low CU traits, indicating less empathic concern. Low-CU adolescents did not differ from controls in HR change from baseline during sadness. Because the majority of the adolescents also had ADHD, the authors were unable to determine whether the results were exemplary for pure DBD or DBD with ADHD comorbidity (De Wied et al., 2012).

In an ERP study, Cheng and colleagues (2012) studied the cortical reactivity of CD adolescent offenders with high or low psychopathic traits (ADHD comorbidity not reported) and controls. Researchers measured cortical reactivity from brain regions associated with early affective arousal and late cognitive processing, during exposure to pictures of individuals in painful or non-painful situations. In response to painful situations (relative to non-painful situations), CD adolescents with high psychopathic traits showed early affective arousal and late cognitive-processing deficits, whereas those with low psychopathic traits only showed late cognitive-processing deficits. The psychopathic subtype, however, demonstrated intact late cognitive-processing reactivity in response to pictures in which someone was intentionally harmed. In other words, findings suggest an impaired early affective arousal to empathy-eliciting stimuli for CD adolescents with high (not low) psychopathic traits, but an intact capacity to understand social situations in which someone is intentionally harmed.

In one fMRI study, Marsh and colleagues (2013) compared DBD adolescents (57% had ADHD comorbidity) and psychopathic traits with a control group. All adolescents were exposed to pictures of hands and feet in a painful or non-painful situation, and asked to imagine that the situation was either happening to themselves or to someone else. Relative to controls, DBD adolescents with psychopathic traits showed reduced reactivity in the anterior cingulate cortex (ACC) and ventral striatum, cortical areas associated with pain. In response to pictures of others in pain, they also showed reduced reactivity in the left amygdala/uncus, left superior frontal gyrus, and insula than controls. Results remained unchanged when those with ADHD were excluded from the analyses, suggesting that ADHD did not affect the results. In short, studies with DBD children and adolescents quite consistently reveal that both DBD subtypes are impaired in affective empathy as assessed by self-report, facial and autonomic measures of empathy. Differences between DBD subtypes have only been found on autonomic indexes of affective empathy.

*Cognitive State Empathy.* Three studies examined ToM in children with CD (Anastassiou-Hadjicharalambous & Warden, 2008a; Schwenck et al., 2012) and children with clinical levels of CD problems (Jones et al., 2010), with inconsistent results. Anastassiou-Hadjicharalambous and Warden (2008a) examined affective and cognitive perspective taking (aspects of cognitive empathy) in CD children (31% had ADHD comorbidity) with high versus low CU traits and controls. Relative to controls, the CD children with low CU traits showed impaired affective and cognitive perspective taking. The CD children with high CU traits only showed impaired affective perspective taking compared to controls. Interestingly, the high-CU children still outperformed the low CU children on affective perspective taking. The authors suggested that the weak cognitive perspective-taking skills of those with low CU traits may negatively affect their affective perspective-taking skills. A second study conducted by Jones and colleagues (2010) revealed no differences in ToM abilities between children with CD problems and high or low CU traits (ADHD comorbidity not reported), both subtypes also did not differ relative to controls. Likewise, clinically diagnosed CD children (34% had ADHD comorbidity) with high and low CU traits showed no differences in ToM, and both groups also showed no differences relative to controls. Omitting children with ADHD from the analyses did not change the results (Schwenck et al., 2012).

*Affective and Cognitive Trait Empathy.* Three studies with children (Anastassiou-Hadjicharalambous & Warden, 2008b; Jones et al., 2010; Pasalich, Dadds, & Hawes, 2014), and one with adolescent offenders (Cheng et al., 2012) reveal inconsistent results. Using an affective empathy self-report questionnaire (IECA, Bryant, 1982), Anastassiou-Hadjicharalambous and Warden (2008b) demonstrated that CD children with both high and low CU traits report less affective empathy than controls, with no significant differences between CD subtypes. Jones and colleagues (2010) demonstrated that boys with CD problems (comorbid symptoms not reported) and high-CU traits care less about being punished for their actions, care less about their victim's feelings, and place greater value on being the boss than controls. No significant differences emerged between those with high and low CU traits, nor between those with low CU traits and controls (Jones et al., 2010). A more recent correlational study (Pasalich et al., 2014), revealed an inverse relationship between CU traits and parent-reported affective and cognitive empathy in DBD children (24% ADHD), as assessed by the Griffith Empathy Measure (GEM: Dadds et al., 2008b). Researchers also found some evidence for an interaction effect between CU traits and ASD symptoms in relation to affective empathy. That is, higher CU traits were associated with lower affective empathy for moderate to high ASD symptoms. In addition, ASD symptoms were negatively related to cognitive empathy. Results did not change when researchers accounted for ADHD comorbidity. In the Cheng and colleagues (2012) study, CD adolescent offenders (ADHD comorbidity not reported) with high or low psychopathic traits and controls completed a self-report questionnaire measuring both affective and cognitive trait empathy (IRI, Davis, 1996). Surprisingly, both subtypes reported less cognitive rather than affective trait empathy compared with controls. No differences emerged between CD subtypes. In sum, results suggest that CD children with high CU traits have impaired affective trait empathy, but CD subtypes do not seem to differ in this respect. Interestingly, preliminary evidence suggests that CU traits might also be related to impaired cognitive trait empathy.

## Discussion

This chapter reviewed empirical studies on empathy problems in clinically referred DBD youth with and without CU traits. A first aim was to examine the nature of empathy dysfunction in those with CU traits. The relatively few studies show consistent evidence for impaired affective empathy in DBD children and adolescents with CU traits on indexes of both state (Anastassiou-Hadjicharalambous & Warden, 2008b; Cheng et al., 2012; De Wied et al., 2012; Marsh et al., 2011; Marsh et al., 2013; Schwenck et al., 2012) and trait empathy (Anastassiou-Hadjicharalambous & Warden, 2008b; Jones et al., 2010; Pasalich et al., 2014). Studies with undifferentiated groups of DBD youth also show consistent evidence for affective empathy impairment on indexes of both state and trait empathy (e.g., Cohen & Strayer, 1996;

Decetey et al., 2009; De Wied et al., 2005, 2006, 2009; Sterzer et al., 2007), suggesting that impaired affective empathy is common across the broader range of disruptive behavior disorders.

As for cognitive empathy, the overall pattern of results is less consistent in samples of both undifferentiated and differentiated DBD youth. At least three studies suggest that CU traits may be associated with impaired cognitive empathy (Anastassiou-Hadjicharalambous & Warden, 2008a; Cheng et al., 2012; Pasalich et al., 2014). Interestingly, two studies used measures of cognitive empathy that might also involve affective components, that is, affective perspective taking (Anastassiou-Hadjicharalambous & Warden, 2008a), and cognitive trait empathy assessed with questionnaire items that might tap into affective components (Pasalich et al., 2014). Accordingly, the above-mentioned impairments in cognitive empathy could be due to the involvement of affective components in the assessment tools. Negative associations between CU traits and aspects of cognitive empathy have previously been found when affective components were involved. For example, adult offenders with significant levels of psychopathic traits showed impaired affective (not cognitive) ToM abilities, relative to controls (Shamay-Tsoory, Harari, Aharon-Peretz, & Levkovitz, 2010). High-CU individuals may have an affective-specific impairment, which becomes apparent in their weak affective empathy, but also in their cognitive empathy abilities when it taps into emotional components.

A second aim was to investigate whether a lack of empathy contributes to a differentiation between DBD subtypes. As of yet, no between-group differences have been reported with indexes of cognitive state empathy, or with self-report and facial indexes of affective state empathy. However, significant differences have been demonstrated with autonomic indexes of affective state empathy. DBD subtypes differ in heart rate reactivity while observing others in distress, that is, high CU individuals show less heart rate change from baseline than low CU individuals. Interestingly, this pattern is seen in children with CD (Anastassiou-Hadjicharalambous & Warden, 2008b) and adolescents with DBD (De Wied et al., 2012). Similar results have also been found in an earlier study with emotionally disturbed children (DSM classifications of ODD and/or CD were not reported) conducted by Blair (1999). Blair obtained children's skin conductance responses to distressing (e.g., crying face), threatening (e.g., angry face), and neutral pictures (e.g., hairdryer). Children with high levels of psychopathic traits showed less skin conductance responses to distressed pictures than those with low levels of psychopathic traits and controls. Thus, high- and low-CU individuals from different samples, show distinct patterns of autonomic reactivity to distress cues, which possibly stem from genetically influenced abnormalities in the limbic system including the amygdala (Blair, 2013).

Abnormalities in the amygdala are proposed to affect the processing of distress cues (Olsson & Phelps, 2007), which may hamper socialization. Distortions in the amygdala are also thought to affect aversive stimulus-reinforcement associations. Accordingly, children with lesions in this area may learn to use (instrumental) aggression to achieve their goals because they do not acquire an uncomfortable feeling (i.e., aversive arousal) of others' distress. In others words, they do not feel aversely aroused or "punished" for their aggressive acts (Blair, Peschardt, Budhani, Mitchell, & Pine, 2006).

So far, no studies have demonstrated significant differences between the DBD subtypes on self-report indexes of affective (or cognitive) trait empathy. Based on the assumption that CU traits delineate a distinct causal pathway to conduct problems

(Frick et al., 2013), we may expect particular deficits in both state and trait empathy for high CU individuals. It is quite possible that self-report questionnaires of empathy are not sensitive enough to capture differences in trait empathy between the DBD subtypes. Even so, amygdala dysfunction, early trauma, and/or neglect may all hamper empathy development, leading to reduced empathic experiences across different situations for both DBD subtypes.

It is suggested that the mechanisms underlying empathy problems may be different for DBD subtypes. High-CU individuals may show little empathy due to reduced sensitivity to distress cues (Blair, 2013), or impaired attention to the eyes (Dadds et al., 2006; Dadds et al., 2008a; Dadds, Jambrak, Pasalich, Hawes, & Brennan, 2011) because of a hyposensitive amygdala. Low-CU individuals may show little empathy for a variety of reasons (De Wied et al., 2012), such as hostility bias (Dodge, Price, Bachorowski, & Newman, 1990; Orobio de Castro, Veerman, Koops, Bosch, & Monshouwer, 2002), and/or enhanced sensitivity to distress cues combined with poor regulatory skills (Eisenberg et al., 1994). It is thought that individuals with low CU traits may have a hypersensitive basic threat circuit (Blair, 2013), as seen in their increased amygdala reactivity to fearful faces (Viding et al., 2012). To date, empirical studies on empathy dysfunction in DBD subtypes are scarce, and most studies demonstrate deficits without providing evidence for the mechanisms involved. Understanding the underlying mechanisms is essential, however, to improve prevention and intervention programs.

A third aim of the chapter was to explore whether the empathy problems associated with CU traits are similar for those with pure DBD as for those with comorbid ADHD. Upon examination of the samples, we can observe that five studies were conducted with CD youth and four with DBD youth. Seven out of nine studies reported on ADHD comorbidity, but only three tested whether the results remained the same after controlling for ADHD (Marsh et al., 2013; Pasalich et al., 2014; Schwenck et al., 2012). Although strong conclusions cannot be drawn, initial evidence seems to suggest that empathy problems in youth with DBD are not related to ADHD comorbidity. Because ADHD has also been related to empathy problems (Barkley, 2006) accounting for ADHD is important to gain more insight into the nature of empathy problems in DBD. Future studies should aim to control for ADHD or recruit samples with pure DBD individuals, and compare empathy-related responding to samples with pure ADHD individuals.

## Clinical Implications

A clear understanding of the nature and cause of empathy problems associated with DBD and DBD subtypes is crucial to improve differential diagnostic procedures and treatment options. Currently, limited empirical evidence suggests that self-report measures of affective empathy (state and trait) are not able to make a distinction between the DBD subtypes. This stresses the need to develop new empathy indexes for diagnostic purposes in clinical practice.

The hypothesis that empathy inhibits aggression implies that enhancing empathic skills may reduce aggressive behavior. It is therefore not surprising that empathy training is generally included in broader interventions to reduce aggressive behavior in antisocial youth. Yet, it seems that these interventions mainly focus on enhancing aspects of cognitive empathy, that is, perspective-taking skills. For example, the EQUIP program – an intervention to reduce antisocial behavior in juvenile delinquents – focuses on improving moral development by enhancing perspective-taking skills (Gibbs, Potter, & Goldstein, 1995). Strengthening perspective-taking skills is perhaps the best option so far, given the current lack of programs to improve affective empathy. However, based on the assumption that the two empathy components interact (see Shamay-Tsoory, 2009; Singer, 2006; Völlm et al., 2006), it could be possible that promoting aspects of cognitive empathy may also enhance affective empathy.

In addition, it is suggested that the empathy problems in DBD subtypes are related to impairments in distinct underlying mechanisms. This may call for different treatment approaches to improve empathy-related responding in both subtypes. For those with CU traits, for example, improving emotion recognition (because of the possibility of impaired attention to the eyes) may enhance empathy-related responding. Indeed, initial findings suggest that emotion recognition training significantly improves affective trait empathy and conduct problems in children with significant levels of CU traits (Dadds, Cauchi, Wimalaweera, Hawes, & Brennan, 2012). For those without CU traits, however, one could speculate that improving self-regulation skills might be more effective to stimulate empathy.

## Conclusion

It is proposed that distinct underlying mechanisms may be involved in the empathy problems associated with DBD subtypes. Relatively few studies have investigated empathy in clinically referred DBD youth, and those that have reveal deficits without providing evidence for the mechanisms involved. Both DBD subtypes show more consistent impairments in aspects of affective than cognitive empathy. Evidence for significant differences between subtypes is scarce, and is only demonstrated in studies that used autonomic measures of affective state empathy. Given the limited number of studies, considerably more research with multi-measure approaches is needed to examine the nature and causes of not only state but also trait empathy in DBD youth with and without CU traits.

## Acknowledgements

The research was funded by the Netherlands Organisation for Scientific Research (Brain & Cognition, 056-21-010).

## References

American Psychiatric Association. (2000). *Diagnostic and statistical manual of mental disorders* (4th ed., text rev.). Washington, DC: American Psychiatric Association.

American Psychiatric Association. (2013). *Diagnostic and statistical manual of mental disorders* (5th ed.). Arlington, VA: American Psychiatric Association.

Anastassiou-Hadjicharalambous, X., & Warden, D. (2008a). Cognitive and affective perspective-taking in conduct-disordered children high and low on callous- unemotional traits. *Child and Adolescent Psychiatry and Mental Health*, *2*(16). doi: 10.1186/1753-2000-2-16

Anastassiou-Hadjicharalambous, X., & Warden, D. (2008b). Physiologically-indexed and self-perceived affective empathy in conduct-disordered children high and low on callous-unemotional traits. *Child Psychiatry and Human Development, 39*, 503–517. doi:10.1007/s10578-008-0104-y

Barkley, R. A. (2006). *Attention-deficit hyperactivity disorder: A handbook for diagnosis and treatment* (3rd ed.). New York: Guilford Press.

Batson, C. D. (2009). These things called empathy: Eight related but distinct phenomena. In J. Decety & W. Ickes (Eds.), *The social neuroscience of empathy* (pp. 3–15). Cambridge, MA: MIT Press.

Beauchaine, T. P., Gatzke-Kopp, L., & Mead, H. K. (2007). Polyvagal theory and developmental psychopathology: Emotion dysregulation and conduct problems from preschool to adolescence. *Biological Psychology, 74*, 174–184. doi: 10.1016/j.biopsycho.2005.08.008

Blair, R. J. R. (1999). Responsiveness to distress cues in the child with psychopathic tendencies. *Personality and Individual Differences, 27*, 135–145. Retrieved from http://www.sciencedirect.com/science/article/pii/S0191886998002311#

Blair, R. J. R. (2007). Empathic dysfunction in psychopathic individuals. In T.F.D. Farrow & P.W.R. Woodruff (Eds.), *Empathy in mental illness* (pp. 3–16). New York: Cambridge University Press.

Blair, R. J. R. (2008). Fine cuts of empathy and the amygdala: Dissociable deficits in psychopathy and autism. *The Quarterly Journal of Experimental Psychology, 61*, 157–170. doi:10.1080/17470210701508855

Blair, R. J. R. (2013). The neurobiology of psychopathic traits in youths. *Nature Reviews Neuroscience, 14*, 786–799. doi:10.1038/nrn3577

Blair, R. J. R., Leibenluft, E., & Pine, D. S. (2014). Conduct disorder and callous-unemotional traits in youth. *The New England Journal of Medicine, 371*, 2207–2216. doi: 10.1056/NEJMra1315612

Blair, R. J. R., Peschardt, K. S., Budhani, S., Mitchell, D. G. V., & Pine, D. S. (2006). The development of psychopathy. *Journal of Child Psychology and Psychiatry, 47*, 262–275. doi: 10.1111/j.1469-7610.2006.01596.x

Braaten, E. B., & Rosén, L. A. (2000). Self-regulation of affect in Attention Deficit-Hyperactivity Disorder (ADHD) and non-ADHD boys: Differences in empathic responding. *Journal of Consulting and Clinical Psychology, 68*, 313–321. doi: 10.1037//0022-006X.68.2.313

Bryant, B. K. (1982). An index of empathy for children and adolescents. *Child Development, 53*, 413–425.

Carr, L., Iacoboni, M., Dubeau, M-C., Mazziotta, J. C., & Lenzi, G. L. (2003). Neural mechanisms of empathy in humans: A relay from neural systems for imitation to limbic areas. *PNAS, 100*, 5497–5502. doi:10.1073.pnas.0935845100

Cheng, Y., Hung, A.-Y., & Decety, J. (2012). Dissociation between affective sharing and emotion understanding in juvenile psychopaths. *Developmental and Psychopathology, 24*, 623–636. 10.1017/S095457941200020X

Cohen, D., & Strayer, J. (1996). Empathy in conduct-disordered and comparison youth. *Developmental Psychology, 32*, 988–998. doi:10.1037//0012-1649.32.6.988

Dadds, M. R., Cauchi, A. J., Wimalaweera, S., Hawes, D. J., & Brennan, J. (2012). Outcomes, moderators, and mediators of empathic-emotion recognition training for complex conduct problems in childhood. *Psychiatry Research, 199*, 201–207. Retrieved from http://dx.doi.org/10.1016/j.psychres.2012.04.033

Dadds, M. R., El Masry, Y., Wimalaweera, S., & Guastella, A. J. (2008a). Reduced eye gaze explains "fear blindness" in childhood psychopathic traits. *Journal of the American Academy of Child and Adolescent Psychiatry, 47*, 455–463. doi: 10.1097/CHI.0b013e31816407f1

Dadds, M. R., Hunter, K., Hawes, D. J., Frost, A. D. J., Vassallo, S., Bunn, P., … El Masry, Y. (2008b). A measure of cognitive and affective empathy in children using parent ratings. *Child Psychiatry and Human Development, 39*, 111–122. doi:10.1007/s10578-007-0075-4

Dadds, M. R., Jambrak, J., Pasalich, D., Hawes, D. J., & Brennan, J. (2011). Impaired attention to the eyes of attachment figures and the developmental origins of psychopathy. *Journal of Child Psychology and Psychiatry, 52*, 238–245. doi: 10.1111/j.1469-7610.2010.02323.x

Dadds, M. R., Perry, Y., Hawes, D. J., Merz, S., Riddel, A. C., Haines, D. J., ... Abeygunawardane, A. I. (2006). Attention to the eyes and fear-recognition deficits in child psychopathy. *British Journal of Psychiatry, 189*, 280–281. doi: 10.1192/bjp.bp.105.018150

Davis, M. H. (1983). Measuring individual differences in empathy: Evidence for a multidimensional approach. *Journal of Personality and Social Psychology, 44*, 113–126.

Davis, M. H. (1996). *Empathy: A social psychological approach*. Boulder, CO: Westview Press.

Davis, M. H. (2006). Empathy. In J. E. Stets & J. H. Turner (Eds.), *Handbook of the sociology of emotions* (pp. 443–466). New York: Springer.

Decety, J., Michalska, K. J., Akitsuki, Y., & Lahey, B. B. (2009). Atypical empathic responses in adolescents with aggressive conduct disorder: A functional MRI investigation. *Biological Psychology, 80*, 203–211. doi: 10.1016/j.biopsycho.2008.09.004

De Wied, M., Gispen-De Wied, C., & Van Boxtel, A. (2010). Empathy dysfunction in children and adolescents with disruptive behavior disorders. *European Journal of Pharmacology, 626*, 97–103. doi:10.1016/j.ejphar.2009.10.016

De Wied, M., Goudena, P. P., & Matthys, W. (2005). Empathy in boys with disruptive behavior disorders. *Journal of Child Psychology and Psychiatry, 46*, 867–880. doi: 10.1111/j.1469-7610.2004.00389.x

De Wied, M., Van Boxtel, A., Matthys, W., & Meeus, W. (2012). Verbal, facial and autonomic responses to empathy-eliciting film clips by disruptive male adolescents with high versus low callous-unemotional traits. *Journal of Abnormal Child Psychology, 40*, 211–223. doi:10.1007/s10802-011-9557-8

De Wied, M., Van Boxtel, A., Posthumus, J. A., Goudena, P. P., & Matthys, W. (2009). Facial EMG and heart rate responses to emotion-inducing film clips in boys with disruptive behavior disorders. *Psychophysiology, 46*, 996–1004. doi:10.1111/j.1469-8986.2009.00851.x

De Wied, M., Van Boxtel, A., Zaalberg, R., Goudena, P. P., & Matthys, W. (2006). Facial EMG responses to dynamic emotional facial expressions in boys with disruptive behavior disorders. *Journal of Psychiatric Research, 40*, 112–121. doi: 10.1016/j.jpsychires.2005.08.003

Dimberg, U. (1990). Facial electromyography and emotional-reactions. *Psychophysiology, 27*, 481–494.

Dimberg, U., Thunberg, M., & Elmehed, K. (2000). Unconscious facial reactions to emotional facial expressions. *Pyschological Science, 11*, 86–89. doi:10.1111/1467-9280.00221

Dimberg, U., Thunberg, M., & Grunedal, S. (2002). Facial reactions to emotional stimuli: automatically controlled emotional responses. *Cognition and Emotion, 16*, 449–471. doi:10.1080/02699930143000356

Dodge, K. A., Price, J. M., Bachorowski, J.-A., & Newman, J. P. (1990). Hostile attributional biases in severely aggressive adolescents. *Journal of Abnormal Psychology, 99*, 385–392. Retrieved from http://psych.wisc.edu/newman/SecurePDF/dodge1990.pdf

Downs, A., & Smith, T. (2004). Emotional understanding, cooperation, and social behavior in high-functioning children with autism. *Journal of Autism and Developmental Disorders, 34*, 625–635.

Eisenberg, N., & Fabes, R. A. (1990). Empathy: Conceptualization, measurement, and relation to prosocial behavior. *Motivation and Emotion, 14*, 131–149.

Eisenberg, N., Fabes, R. A., Bustamante, D., Mathy, R. M., Miller, P. A., & Lindholm, E. (1988a). Differentiation of vicariously induced emotional reactions in children. *Developmental Psychology, 24*, 237–246.

Eisenberg, N., Fabes, R. A., Murphy, B., Karbon, M., Maszk, P., Smith, M., ... Suh, K. (1994). The relations of emotionality and regulation to dispositional and situational empathy-related responding. *Journal of Personality and Social Psychology, 66*, 776–797. doi:10.1037/0022-3514.66.4.776

Eisenberg, N., & Miller, P. A. (1987). The relation of empathy to prosocial and related behaviors. *Psychological Bulletin*, *101*, 91–119. doi:10.1037//0033-2909.101.1.91

Eisenberg, N., Schaller, M., Fabes, R. A., Bustamante, D., Mathy, R. M., Shell, R., & Rhodes, K. (1988b). Differentiation of personal distress and sympathy in children and adults. *Developmental Psychology*, *24*, 766–775. doi:10.1037//0012-1649.24.6.766

Eisenberg, N., Shea, C. L., Carlo, G., & Knight, G. P. (1991). Empathy-related responding and cognition: A "chicken and egg" dilemma. In W. M. Kurtines (Ed.), *Handbook of moral behavior and development: Vol. 2. Research* (pp. 63–88). Hillsdale, NJ: Erlbaum.

Frick, P. J., & Hare, R. D. (2001). *Antisocial process screening device (APSD).* Toronto: Multi-Health Systems.

Frick, P. J., Ray, J. V., Thornton, L. C., & Kahn, R. E. (2013). Can callous-unemotional traits enhance the understanding, diagnosis, and treatment of serious conduct problems in children and adolescents? A comprehensive review. *Psychological Bulletin*, *140*, 1–57. doi:10.1037/a0033076

Frick, P. J., & Viding, E. (2009). Antisocial behavior from a developmental psychopathology perspective. *Development and Psychopathology*, *21*, 1111–1131. doi: 10.1017/S0954579409990071

Gibbs, J. C., Potter, G. B., & Goldstein, A. P. (1995). *The EQUIP program: Teaching youth how to think and act responsibly through a peer-helping approach.* Champaign, IL: Research Press.

Happé, F., & Frith, U. (1996). Theory of mind and social impairment in children with conduct disorder. *British Journal of Development Psychology*, *14*, 385–398. Retrieved from http://onlinelibrary.wiley.com/doi/10.1111/j.2044-835X.1996.tb00713.x/pdf

Hatfield, E., Rapson, R. L., & Le, Y. L. (2009). Emotional contagion and empathy. In: J. Decety & W. Ickes (Eds.), *The social neuroscience of empathy* (pp. 19–30). Cambridge, MA: MIT Press.

Herpers, P. C. M., Rommelse, N. N. J., Bons, D. M. A., Buitelaar, J. K., & Scheepers, F. E. (2012). Callous-unemotional traits as a cross-disorders construct. *Social Psychiatry and Psychiatric Epidemiology*, *47*, 2045–2064. doi:10.1007/s00127-012-0513-x

Hoffman, M. L. (2000). *Empathy and moral development: Implications for caring and justice.* Cambridge, UK: Cambridge University Press.

Hoffman, M.L. (2008). Empathy and prosocial behavior. In M. Lewis, J.M. Haviland-Jones, & L. F. Barrett (Eds.), *Handbook of Emotions*, third edition (pp. 440–455). New York: The Guilford Press.

Iacoboni, M. (2005). Understanding others: Imitation, language, and empathy. In S. Hurley & N. Chater (Eds.), *Perspectives on imitations: From neuroscience to social science – Volume 1: Mechanisms of imitation and imitation in animals* (pp. 77–101). Cambridge, MA: MIT Press.

Jones, A. P., Happé, F. G. E., Gilbert, F., Burnett, S., & Viding, E. (2010). Feeling, caring, knowing: Different types of empathy deficit in boys with psychopathic tendencies and autism spectrum disorder. *Journal of Child Psychology and Psychiatry*, *51*, 1188–1197. doi:10.1111/j.1469-7610.2010.02280.x

Jones, A. P., Laurens, K. R., Herba, C. M., Barker, G. J., & Viding, E. (2009). Amygdala hypoactivity to fearful faces in boys with conduct problems and callous-unemotional traits. *American Journal of Psychiatry*, *166*, 95–102.

Lanzetta, J. T., & Englis, B. G. (1989). Expectations of cooperation and competition and their effects on observers' vicarious emotional responses. *Journal of Personality and Social Psychology*, *56*, 543–554.

Lockwood, P. L., Sebastian, C. L., McCrory, E. J., Hyde, Z. H., Gu, X., De Brito, S. A., & Viding, E. (2013). Association of callous traits with reduced neural response to others' pain in children with conduct problems. *Current Biology*, *23*, 901–905. Retrieved from http://dx.doi.org/10.1016/j.cub.2013.04.018

Lovett, B. J., & Sheffield, R. A. (2007). Affective empathy deficits in aggressive children and adolescents: A critical review. *Clinical Psychology Review*, *27*, 1–13. doi:10.1016/j.cpr.2006.03.003

Lynam, D. R., & Gudonis, L. (2005). The development of psychopathy. *Annual Review of Clinical Psychology*, *1*, 381–407. doi:10.1146/annurev.clinpsy.1.102803.144019

Marsh, P., Beauchaine, T. P., & Williams, B. (2008a). Dissociation of sad facial expressions and autonomic nervous system responding in boys with disruptive behavior disorders. *Psychophysiology*, *45*, 100–110. doi:10.1111/j.1469-8986.2007.00603.x

Marsh, A. A., Finger, E. C., Fowler, K. A., Adalio, C. J., Jurkowitz, I. T. N., Schechter, J. C., … Blair, R. J. R. (2013). Empathic responsiveness in amygdala and anterior cingulate cortex in youths with psychopathic traits. *Journal of Child Psychology and Psychiatry*, *54*, 900–910. doi:10.1111/jcpp.12063

Marsh, A. A., Finger, E. C., Mitchell, D. G. V., Reid, M. E., Sims, C., Kosson, D. S., … Blair, R. J. R. (2008b). Reduced amygdala response to fearful expressions in children and adolescents with callous-unemotional traits and disruptive behavior disorders. *American Journal of Psychiatry*, *165*, 712–720.

Marsh, A. A., Finger, E. C., Schechter, J. C., Jurkowitz, I. T. N., Reid, M. E., & Blair, R. J. R. (2011). Adolescents with psychopathic traits report reductions in physiological responses to fear. *Journal of Child Psychology and Psychiatry*, *52*, 834–841. doi: 10.1111/j.1469-7610.2010.02353.x

Marton, I., Wiener, J., Rogers, M., Moore, C., & Tannock, R. (2009). Empathy and social perspective taking in children with Attention-Deficit/Hyperactivity Disorder. *Journal of Abnormal Child Psychology*, *37*, 107–118. doi:10.1007/s10802-008-9262-4

Miller, P. A., & Eisenberg, N. (1988). The relation of empathy to aggressive and externalizing/antisocial behavior. *Psychological Bulletin*, *103*, 324–344. doi:10.1037/0033-2909.103.3.324

Molenberghs, P., Cunnington, R., & Mattingley, J. B. (2012). Brain regions with mirror properties: A meta-analysis of 125 human fMRI studies. *Neuroscience and Biobehavioral Reviews*, *36*, 341–349. doi:10.1016/j.neubiorev.2011.07.004

Olsson, A., & Phelps, E. A. (2007). Social learning of fear. *Nature Neuroscience*, *10*, 1095–1102. doi:10.1038/nn1968

Orobio de Castro, B., Veerman, J. W., Koops, W., Bosch, J. D., & Monshouwer, H. J. (2002). Hostile attribution of intent and aggressive behavior: A meta-analysis. *Child Development*, *73*, 916–934. doi:0009-3920/2002/7303-0017

Pasalich, D. S., Dadds, M. R., & Hawes, D. J. (2014). Cognitive and affective empathy in children with conduct problems: Additive and interactive effects of callous-unemotional traits and autism spectrum disorders symptoms. *Psychiatry Research*, *219*, 625–630. doi: http://dx.doi.org/10.1016/j.psychres.2014.06.025

Rizzolatti, G. (2005). The mirror neuron system and imitation. In S. Hurley & N. Chater (Eds.), *Perspectives on imitation: From neuroscience to social science – Volume 1: Mechanisms of imitation and imitation in animals* (pp. 55–76). Cambridge, MA: MIT Press.

Schwenck, C., Mergenthaler, J., Keller, K., Zech, J., Salehi, S., Taurines, R., … Freitag, C. M. (2012). Empathy in children with autism and conduct disorder: group-specific profiles and developmental aspects. *Journal of Child Psychology and Psychiatry*, *53*, 651–659. doi:10.1111/j.1469-7610.2011.02499.x

Sebastian, C. L., McCrory, E. J. P., Cecil, C. A. M., Lockwood, P. L., De Brito, S. A., Fontaine, N. M. G., & Viding, E. (2012). Neural responses to affective and cognitive theory of mind in children with conduct problems and varying levels of callous-unemotional traits. *Archives of General Psychiatry*, *69*, 814–822.

Shamay-Tsoory, S. G. (2009). Empathic processing: Its cognitive and affective dimensions and neuroanatomical basis. In J. Decety & W. Ickes (Eds.), *The social neuroscience of empathy* (pp. 215–232). Cambridge, MA: MIT Press.

Shamay-Tsoory, S. G., Harari, H., Aharon-Peretz, J., & Levkovitz, Y. (2010). The role of orbitofrontal cortex in affective theory of mind deficits in criminal offenders with psychopathic tendencies. *Cortex*, *46*, 668–677. doi: 10.1016/j.cortex.2009.04.008

Singer, T. (2006). The neuronal basis and ontogeny of empathy and mind reading: Review of literature and implications for future research. *Neuroscience and Biobehavioral Reviews*, *30*, 855–863. doi:10.1016/j.neubiorev.2006.06.011

Sparrow, S., Balla, D., & Cicchetti, D. (1984). *Vineland Adaptive Behavior Scales: Survey Form Manual.* Circle Pines, MN: American Guidance Service.

Sterzer, P., Stadler, C., Poustka, F., & Kleinschmidt, A. (2007). A structural neural deficit in adolescents with conduct disorder and its association with lack of empathy. *NeuroImage*, *37*, 335–342. doi:10.1016/j.neuroimage.2007.04.043

Viding, E., & McCrory, E. J. (2012). Genetic and neurocognitive contributions to the development of psychopathy. *Development and Psychopathology*, *24*, 969–983. doi: 10.1017/S095457941200048X

Viding, E., Sebastian, C. L., Dadds, M. R., Lockwood, P. L., Cecil, C. A. M., De Brito, S. A., & McCrory, E. J. (2012). Amygdala response to preattentive masked fear in children with conduct problems: The role of callous-unemotional traits. *American Journal of Psychiatry*, *169*, 1109–1116.

Völlm, B. A., Taylor, A. N. W., Richardson, P., Corcoran, R., Stirling, J., McKie, S., ... Elliott, R. (2006). Neuronal correlates of theory of mind and empathy: A functional magnetic resonance imaging study in a nonverbal task. *NeuroImage*, *29*, 90–98. doi: 10.1016/j.neuroimage.2005.07.022

Waller, R., Gardner, F., & Hyde, L. W. (2013). What are the associations between parenting, callous-unemotional traits, and antisocial behavior in youth? A systematic review of evidence. *Clinical Psychology Review*, *33*, 593–608. doi:10.1016/j.cpr.2013.03.001

Walter, H. (2012). Social cognitive neuroscience of empathy: concepts, circuits, and genes. *Emotion Review*, *4*, 9–17. doi:10.1177/1754073911421379

White, S. F., Williams, W. C., Brislin, S. J., Sinclair, S., Blair, K. S., Fowler, K. A., ... Blair, R. J. (2012). Reduced activity within the dorsal endogenous orienting of attention network to fearful expressions in youth with disruptive behavior disorders and psychopathic traits. *Development and Psychopathology*, *24*, 1105–1116. doi: 10.1017/S0954579412000569

Zhou, Q., Valiente, C., & Eisenberg, N. (2003). Empathy and its measurement. In S. J. Lopez & C. R. Snyder (Eds.), *Positive psychological assessment: A handbook of models and measures* (pp. 269–284). Washington, DC: American Psychological Association.

# Part 2
# Developmental Neurobiology

# 8

# Developmental Cognitive Neuroscience

Stefanie Hoehl

## Developmental Cognitive Neuroscience

Developmental cognitive neuroscience is concerned with how infants and children structure and process the sensory input they encounter, how they allocate their limited attentional resources toward relevant stimuli in the environment and how they learn. The neural bases of motor, perceptual, and cognitive development are subject to lifelong processes of change and plasticity starting well before birth and extending beyond the years of childhood. However, because brain plasticity is highest during infancy and childhood, the early years of development bear both great opportunities and risks for the developing mind and brain. On the one hand, adverse environments have the most detrimental effects on cognitive development very early in childhood (Fox, Almas, Degnan, Nelson, & Zeanah, 2011). On the other hand, treatments and trainings may take advantage of the increased brain plasticity in early years and enable prevention of developmental disorders in infants and children at risk before the full syndrome is manifested (Dawson, 2008).

In recent years, researchers have increasingly employed neuroscience techniques to investigate brain development and to relate brain activity to behavioral outcomes. One of the advantages of using cognitive neuroscience techniques is that brain responses can be recorded without registration of a motor or verbal response. This enables the investigation of cognitive processes even in very young individuals and in children with severe cognitive and communicative impairments. These studies have deepened our understanding of typical and atypical social, cognitive, and emotional development. A comprehensive review of the cognitive neuroscience research on developmental psychopathology is beyond the scope of this chapter. Therefore, following a brief introduction of the most widely used methods, recent work in two fields of research is reviewed, featuring studies on autism spectrum disorders and childhood anxiety. It will conclude with a discussion of the advantages and limitations of neuroscience approaches for research on developmental psychopathology.

*The Wiley Handbook of Developmental Psychopathology*, First Edition. Edited by Luna C. Centifanti and David M. Williams.

## Methods of Developmental Cognitive Neuroscience

A range of neuroscience methods is now available for use with infants and children. These methods differ from each other regarding their feasibility for application with developing populations in general and children with developmental and psychological disorders in particular. Furthermore, some methods are more commonly used than others because of their relatively low costs.

One of the currently most widely used neuroscience techniques is electroencephalography (EEG). EEG provides a measure of electrical brain activity. It is a non-invasive technique that can be applied with infants and children at all ages, although measuring EEG in developing populations poses some practical challenges (Hoehl & Wahl, 2012). For instance, EEG requires participants not to move excessively in order to obtain acceptable data quality. Artefacts caused by eye and body movements pose a serious problem when working with infants and children, and attrition rates with these groups are often high (Stets, Stahl, & Reid, 2012). Still, among the available neuroscience techniques, EEG is one of the most commonly used, which is in part due to its relatively low cost and the availability of hardware and software suitable for use with infants and young children.

Different measures can be derived from the EEG, all providing potentially interesting information with regard to developmental psychopathology. For instance, evoked and spontaneous brain oscillations in different frequency bands have been associated with cognitive processes and attention (Saby & Marshall, 2012). EEG coherence measures provide information on the coupling and functional association between brain regions and are able to reveal individual differences between individuals as well as brain-behavior associations across development (e.g., Bell & Fox, 1992). Hemispheric asymmetry in resting brain activity is often measured in studies on affective processes and emotional development (Davidson & Fox, 1982, 1989).

**Table 8.1** Advantages and disadvantages of different neuroscience techniques most commonly used in developmental studies.

| *Method* | *Advantages* | *Disadvantages* |
|---|---|---|
| EEG | High temporal resolution<br>Applicable with infants and severely impaired participants<br>Relatively inexpensive | Low spatial resolution<br>Does not capture subcortical activity<br>Prone to movement artefacts |
| MEG | High temporal resolution | Expensive; requires sophisticated equipment |
| fNIRS | Localization of brain activity<br>Applicable with infants and severely impaired participants<br>Relatively inexpensive | Low temporal resolution<br>Does not capture subcortical activity |
| fMRI | Localization of brain activity with high spatial resolution<br>Captures subcortical activity | Low temporal resolution<br>Expensive; requires sophisticated equipment<br>Requires participants to lie still in a scanner<br>Noisy<br>Not readily applicable with very young or severely impaired participants |

In addition, event-related potentials (ERPs) provide information on the timing and sequence of cognitive processes (Hoehl & Wahl, 2012).

In order to analyze ERPs, segments of the EEG signal in response to auditory, visual, or somatosensory stimuli are averaged such that random noise and non-stimulus-related brain activity are removed and systematic responses to certain kinds of stimulation can be revealed. The resulting ERP is composed of positive and negative deflections which are commonly referred to as components. Despite the relatively low spatial resolution of EEG measures, high-density recording systems now allow for the analysis of cortical sources of activation based on infant head models that have recently been made available for research purposes (Reynolds & Richards, 2009). However, EEG measures primarily capture postsynaptic potentials from pyramidal cells of the cortex and do not provide information on activity stemming from subcortical nuclei and the brain stem (Davidson, Jackson, & Larson, 2000).

Magnetoencephalography (MEG) measures small magnetic field that are caused by the electrical activity of nerve cells. It can be applied with children (Oram Cardy, Flagg, Roberts, & Roberts, 2008), infants (Cheour et al., 2004), and even fetuses within their mothers' wombs (Draganova et al., 2005). However, in comparison to EEG, MEG is much more costly and requires extensive technical equipment, limiting its use in developmental cognitive neuroscience.

A further, more novel method for investigating brain activity in infancy and early childhood is functional near-infrared imaging (fNIRS). In contrast to recording electrical brain activity, this technique measures the hemodynamic response to neuronal activation through optical imaging, and thus enables the localization of cortical regions of activation (Lloyd-Fox, Blasi, & Elwell, 2010). The advantage of this technique when compared with other imaging methods measuring cerebral blood flow and the hemodynamic response is evident: Whereas positron emission tomography (PET) and functional magnetic resonance imaging (fMRI) require participants to lie still in large scanner systems, fNIRS light sources and detectors are mounted on the participant's head and the technique is relatively tolerant to infants' movements. Functional NIRS is non-invasive and relatively inexpensive.

Functional MRI, on the other hand, is much more feasible in older children and adolescents than in young children and infants. This method tolerates very little movement by participants and, because of the noise level within the scanner, it is important to protect participants' ears. Similar to fNIRS, fMRI provides a measure of the hemodynamic response by registering activity-related changes in blood oxygenation. In comparison to the methods mentioned above, fMRI provides excellent spatial resolution, though its temporal resolution is limited by the latency of the hemodynamic response. fMRI is a non-invasive technique and has the advantage that, in contrast to fNIRS, it also captures the activity of subcortical structures.

The implementation of new technologies such as fNIRS and the adaptation of neuroscience techniques such as EEG and fMRI for developing populations have recently stimulated a tremendous growth and advancement of the field of developmental cognitive science. It is now possible to address a single research question from different perspectives using multiple methods. For instance, separate studies have investigated biological motion processing in infants by applying EEG (Reid, Hoehl, Landt, & Striano, 2008) and fNIRS (Lloyd-Fox, Blasi, Everdell, Elwell, & Johnson, 2011). It can be expected that multiple methods will increasingly be used simultaneously in the future, thus combining the advantages of several methods. For instance, linking

EEG with fNIRS or fMRI provides excellent temporal resolution (EEG) together with spatial localization of brain activity (fNIRS, fMRI). The combined use of several techniques poses severe challenges, however. Apart from technical aspects of co-registration from multiple data sources, it requires the development of novel paradigms and experimental designs suitable for all of the respective measures. Therefore, the majority of studies still rely on one technique for registering brain activity.

In the following sections I will review recent work on autism spectrum disorders and childhood anxiety in order to illustrate how a cognitive neuroscience approach can contribute to a better understanding of developmental psychopathology.

## Developmental Cognitive Neuroscience of Autism Spectrum Disorders

Autism spectrum disorders (ASD) are characterized by qualitative impairments in social interaction, impaired communication and the occurrence of restricted and repetitive behaviors. Early indicators of abnormal social behavior can already be observed in affected children during the first and second year or life (Wetherby et al., 2004). For instance, home video observations of children later diagnosed with ASD demonstrate reduced interest in faces by the time of their first birthday (Osterling & Dawson, 1994). An increasing amount of aberrant social behaviors is observed during the second year of life, such as eye contact avoidance and the absence of emotional expressions (Adrien et al., 1993). Consequently, ASD can currently be diagnosed in children by two years of age (Lord et al., 2006). Below I will review two cognitive neuroscience accounts on the development and neural basis of ASD. Importantly, these accounts are not mutually exclusive and may, in fact, focus on different factors contributing jointly to this complex multifactorial disorder.

Dawson and colleagues suggested that early face-processing deficits may lie at the root of ASD (Dawson, Webb, & McPartland, 2005). They noted that many of the earliest social impairments in ASD are related to a failure in responding to information from faces, e.g. the avoidance of eye contact, reduced engagement in joint attention interactions and aberrant responding to others' emotional expressions. On the behavioral level there is evidence that children and adults with ASD have impaired face-recognition abilities (Weigelt, Koldewyn, & Kanwisher, 2012). However, it is currently a matter for debate whether these impairments are indeed specific for the discrimination of and memory for faces as opposed to more general perceptual and cognitive difficulties (Ewing, Pellicano, & Rhodes, 2013).

Looking at face processing in the brain may provide clues regarding the specificity of the abnormalities observed on the behavioral level. In particular, a region of the fusiform gyrus is thought to be specifically involved in processing faces as compared to other visual object categories (Kanwisher, McDermott, & Chun, 1997). The fusiform gyrus seems to represent invariant aspects of faces that allow for face identity recognition, whereas other brain structures such as the superior temporal sulcus (STS) and the amygdala process dynamic and variable aspects of faces, i.e. eye gaze and emotional expressions (Haxby, Hoffman, & Gobbini, 2000). fMRI studies with adults have shown that individuals with ASD do engage the fusiform gyrus when viewing faces if a fixation point prompts participants to keep their gaze fixated on the eye region of the stimuli (Hadjikhani et al., 2004). When viewing video recordings of natural scenes, individuals with ASD display reduced fixation of the eye region compared to healthy controls, suggesting that reduced attention to the eyes may be one of the factors accounting for abnormal face processing in autism (Klin, Jones, Schultz, Volkmar, & Cohen, 2002). However, even when fixation on the eye region is ensured, hypoactivation in many structures of the so-called "social brain" network are detected in adults with ASD when viewing faces, including the amygdala and STS (Hadjikhani, Joseph, Snyder, & Tager-Flusberg, 2007).

Neuroimaging studies using fMRI with children with autism are still quite rare. One study reported amygdala and fusiform gyrus activation in an 11-year-old boy with ASD during a discrimination task involving cartoon characters in which the boy had a special interest but not during perceptual discrimination of familiar and unfamiliar faces (Grelotti et al., 2005). In another study children diagnosed with ASD aged 6–12 showed normal fusiform gyrus activity when viewing the face of their mother or of other children, but not when viewing unfamiliar adult faces (Pierce & Redcay, 2008). Both findings suggest that involvement of the fusiform gyrus when viewing faces depends on the level of interest in or personal engagement with the depicted individual in children with autism. As in adults with ASD, reduced activation in response to faces in subcortical structures, especially the amygdala, has been reported in children with autism (Bookheimer, Wang, Scott, Sigman, & Dapretto, 2008; Kleinhans et al., 2011).

Altered neural responses to faces, indicating less-specialized processing, were also found using electrophysiological methods (Dawson et al., 2005). In particular, by three years of age children with autism show abnormalities both at the level of the N170 component, reflecting structural encoding of faces, and of the later-occurring and more frontally distributed Nc (negative central component), reflecting processes of face recognition and attention. How may these abnormalities in the neural processing of faces come about in ASD?

Typically, developing infants show a very early emerging interest in faces. Newborns prefer to look at faces when compared to other similarly complex visual stimuli (Johnson, Dziurawiec, Ellis, & Morton, 1991) and also prefer to look at their mother's face compared to a stranger's face soon after birth (Bushnell, Sai, & Mullin, 1989). Johnson (2005) suggested that infants' early interest in faces, and especially the eyes (Gliga & Csibra, 2007), is driven by subcortical structures, including the amygdala, which mature early. According to his view, this early subcortically driven attention bias for faces ensures that infants gain ample experience in processing these stimuli. Frequent viewing of faces then leads to the "interactive specialization" of the social brain network, including the fusiform gyrus and STS, and, on the behavioral level, to specific expertise in the discrimination and identification of faces (Johnson et al., 2005).

According to Johnson et al. (2005) this input-dependent interactive specialization is impaired in individuals with ASD, leading to less fine-tuned and less prioritized processing of faces than in typically developing children and adults (Grice et al., 2005; Johnson et al., 2005). Similarly, Dawson et al. (2005) suggested that early impairments in social motivation and a failure to represent social interactions as rewarding in individuals with autism may lead to a lack of attention to faces and social stimuli in general from early on in development. Consequently, children with ASD may fail to develop expertise in face processing and in using information from faces like eye gaze and emotional expressions. Later in development these early, fundamental impairments in social information processing result in difficulties in more sophisticated social cognitive tasks, e.g. theory of mind and perspective-taking, that are well-documented in ASD (Baron-Cohen, 1995).

Another cognitive neuroscience account on autism is based on the observation that children and adults with ASD have difficulties in imitation tasks (Williams, Whiten, Suddendorf, & Perrett, 2001). This has been attributed to a dysfunctional mirror neuron system ("broken mirror", Ramachandran & Oberman, 2006). Mirror neurons have first been observed in the premotor cortex of the macaque monkey and are activated both when the monkey performs an action and when the monkey observes the same action performed by someone else (di Pellegrino, Fadiga, Fogassi, Gallese, & Rizzolatti, 1992). In humans the prefrontal and parietal mirror neuron system is particularly active during imitation, i.e. during simultaneous action observation and performance (Iacoboni et al., 1999).

When observing the initial steps of a known action sequence typically developing children already show activation of muscles that are needed later on in the action sequence. For instance, muscles around the mouth are already activated when the child grabs a snack. This is also the case when the child observes someone else grabbing a snack (Cattaneo et al., 2007). This "predictive mirroring" may support action prediction and imitation and is absent in children with ASD (Cattaneo et al., 2007). This might explain why individuals with autism are particularly impaired when trying to imitate complex action sequences as opposed to more simple actions (Williams et al., 2001). Neuroimaging studies have also demonstrated reduced mirror neuron activation in children and adults with ASD compared to healthy controls when performing imitation tasks (Dapretto et al., 2006; Williams et al., 2006). Possibly, individuals with autism have difficulties in matching their own actions with those of other people from very early on in development. This might impair imitation and also imitative learning of novel actions.

It has furthermore been suggested that "direct matching" of observed actions to one's own motor system may be fundamental to the development of perspective-taking and relating one's own mental states to those of others in early childhood (Meltzoff & Decety, 2003). Newborn infants are able to imitate simple facial gestures (Meltzoff & Moore, 1977; but see Oostenbroek et al., 2016) suggesting that motor mirroring mechanisms are in place shortly after birth. According to Meltzoff and Decety infants then successively learn to relate their own motor actions to their own mental states, e.g. desires and intentions. When perceiving others' actions, infants match these actions to their own motor system and increasingly become able to draw inferences about others' mental states by referring to their own experiences. Thus, early impairments in direct matching or "simulation" may have accumulating detrimental effects on theory of mind and perspective-taking later on in development in autism.

Here I have briefly reviewed two cognitive neuroscience accounts on the development of ASD. Both are based on the observation of behavioral impairments, one focusing on difficulties in face recognition and the other on imitation, and they relate those behavioral impairments to abnormal brain activations in areas of the so-called social brain network. Common to both accounts is also that the roots of the disorder are traced back to early infancy and related to abilities that are already present in healthy newborns. Again, it should be mentioned that both accounts are not mutually exclusive and that a lack of social motivation as postulated by Dawson et al. (2005) may cause both a disinterest in faces and in other people's actions. However, due to a lack of neuroimaging studies with newborns it can only be speculated which neural systems are involved in early face detection and imitation. It is currently unclear whether newborns who later develop ASD are actually impaired in these early abilities or whether impairments kick in only later when typically developing children use and build upon these supposedly innate mechanisms. Prospective studies with large samples of infants at risk for developing ASD (e.g. siblings of affected children) are needed to determine the very early indicators and possible causes of the disorder.

## Temperamental Fearfulness, Anxiety and Attention Biases in Children

According to epidemiological studies on lifetime prevalence, anxiety disorders are the most frequently occurring class of mental disorders (Kessler, Ruscio, Shear, & Wittchen, 2010). These disorders often affect children and adolescents and usually have a chronic-recurrent course (Kessler et al., 2010; LeBeau et al., 2010). Notably, early-onset anxiety disorders are associated with later mental health problems and substance use, making early interventions particularly important (Kessler et al., 2010). Taking a look at developmental psychopathology is thus especially informative, and a number of cognitive neuroscience studies have provided useful insights into the brain correlates of anxiety in childhood.

One particularly relevant brain structure related to fear and anxiety is the amygdala. The amygdala is thought to support the detection of biologically relevant stimuli from early on in development (Johnson, 2005) and it triggers fight or flight reactions to threats in the environment (LeDoux, 1996). This subcortical structure, located within the medial temporal lobe, is involved in fear conditioning as well as social fear learning (Olsson & Phelps, 2007) and responds to facial expressions of fear in adults even if these are presented subliminally (Whalen et al., 1998).

Increased amygdala volume, but no differences in other brain structures, has been reported in children and adolescents with generalized anxiety disorder (De Bellis et al., 2000). In an fMRI study, children with generalized anxiety or panic disorder showed elevated amygdala responses to fearful vs. neutral faces when compared to a healthy control group (Thomas et al., 2001). The magnitude of this activity difference for fearful vs. neutral faces in anxious children was positively correlated with self-reported severity of anxiety symptoms. Another fMRI study found elevated amygdala responses to angry faces presented for only 17 ms in children and adolescents with generalized anxiety disorders (Monk et al., 2008). Thus, children with generalized anxiety disorder show both structural and functional abnormalities regarding the amygdala. In particular, the amygdala of patients with anxiety seems to be hyperresponsive to threat stimuli, which fits well with findings from behavioral experiments demonstrating biased attention orienting towards threatening stimuli in anxious individuals from early on in development (Shechner et al., 2012).

These studies leave open, however, whether abnormal amygdala structure and function make children vulnerable for developing an anxiety disorder or whether anxiety disorders lead to abnormal amygdala development. Prospective studies on this topic are still lacking and – as mentioned above – neuroimaging methods that are able to capture subcortical structures (e.g. fMRI) are not readily applicable with very young participants. Nevertheless, cognitive neuroscience approaches have been developed to investigate the early roots of anxiety and increased orienting towards threat in some individuals.

Two factors can help identify children at risk for developing an anxiety disorder. First, children of parents with an anxiety disorder are more likely to develop an anxiety disorder themselves (Ginsburg, 2009). Observational learning from their caregivers' behavior together with genetic dispositions seem to contribute to the development of anxiety and phobias especially in children with affected parents (Ginsburg, 2009; Kendler, Karkowski, & Prescott, 1999). For instance, mothers' reported expression of fear in front of their children correlates with child-reported fears (Muris, Steerneman, Merckelbach, & Meesters, 1996). Second, temperamental fearfulness and behavioral inhibition in early childhood are associated with the emergence of anxiety disorders in adolescence (Perez-Edgar & Fox, 2005). Behavioral inhibition is characterized by distress in response to novelty, which can be observed from very early on in development and which seems to be a moderately stable trait across childhood and adolescence (Perez-Edgar & Fox, 2005). Both temperament and parental factors should not be considered separately from each other because the effects of parents' behavior may interact with children's temperament. For instance, inhibited children are more likely to develop social anxiety disorder when compared with children without behavioral inhibition, especially if their parents are also diagnosed with an anxiety disorder (Biederman et al., 2001).

As mentioned above, there are tools to measure temperament very early in development, such as the Infant Behavior Questionnaire (Gartstein & Rothbart, 2003). This allows for testing whether temperament is related to elevated attention to threat and emotional expressions of fear even in infancy. For instance, de Haan, Belsky, Reid, Volein, and Johnson (2004) looked at associations of infants' ERPs to fearful and happy faces with maternal personality and infant temperament in 7-month-olds. In general, infants at this age respond with an increased amplitude of the fronto-central Nc component to fearful as compared to happy faces, which is often interpreted in terms of elevated attention toward potential threat (Peltola, Leppänen, Maki, & Hietanen, 2009). In the study by de Haan and colleagues highly fearful infants showed an increased Nc response for fearful compared with happy faces on the right hemisphere, whereas infants scoring low on temperamental fearfulness did not (de Haan et al., 2004). In addition, maternal affect interacted with infant temperament in that highly positive infants (i.e. infants smiling and laughing a lot) with highly positive mothers showed a larger Nc for fearful than happy faces on both hemispheres, whereas no significant difference was found for the other groups (de Haan et al., 2004). The authors conclude that both high familiarity with positive affect (and thus decreased sensitivity to this expression) and temperamental fearfulness (and thus increased reactions to novelty and/or the threat-related signal value of fearful faces) may contribute to the observed attention bias with partly different neuronal signatures for both factors.

More recently, Grossmann and colleagues looked at gene polymorphisms related to dopamine and serotonin activity in the brain and their effects on 7-month-olds' attention bias to fearful as compared with happy faces (Grossmann et al., 2011). Both dopamine and serotonin have been implicated in anxiety in adults (Durant, Christmas, & Nutt, 2010). They found that variants of the *COMT* gene that affect dopamine concentration in prefrontal cortex are related to infants' neuronal responses to fearful faces. Variants of the *5-HTTLPR* that are associated with the serotonin system, in contrast, were related to infants' processing of positive facial expressions. Both genetic variants also correlated with infant temperament. *COMT* variation was associated with infants' recovery from distress as reported by their parents, while *5-HTTLPR* was linked with reported smiling and laughter and duration of orienting.

Leppänen and colleagues have examined individual differences in infants' ability to disengage attention from emotionally salient stimuli in order to shift gaze to a peripheral target (Leppänen et al., 2011). Overall, 7-month-olds in this study had the greatest difficulties in disengaging attention from a centrally presented fearful face as compared to a happy or neutral face or a matched visual noise stimulus. In addition, the authors report a significantly greater number of missed saccades (i.e. infants kept fixating on the central stimulus) for carriers of the T-allele compared to G/G homozygotes of the *TPH2* gene which has been related to serotonin concentrations in the brain (Leppänen et al., 2011). This effect was particularly strong in trials with emotionally significant faces (happy and fearful) as central stimuli. Furthermore, through its influence on attention disengagement as a means of emotion regulation, the *TPH2* was linked with infants' temperamental soothability as reported by their parents: Infants who had greater difficulty in disengaging from an emotional stimulus were reported to be less easily soothed by their parents (Leppänen et al., 2011).

In sum, by 7 months of age infants preferentially attend to fearful more than happy faces, especially infants scoring high on temperamental fearfulness. Furthermore, infants at this age have greater difficulties in disengaging attention away from a centrally presented fearful face compared with other stimuli to shift gaze towards a peripheral target. This ability is related to temperamental soothability. The functional significance and developmental mechanisms of these biases are not yet fully understood. Nevertheless, it is remarkable that fearfulness and soothability as temperamental traits measurable in infants seem to be associated with a key feature of anxiety disorders, namely attention biases toward emotional and threatening stimuli. Relating individual differences in these early attention biases to gene polymorphisms and other factors, such as parental behavior, may prove informative regarding their functional meaning and later consequences in terms of vulnerabilities for anxiety disorders.

## Advantages and Limitations of Cognitive Neuroscience Approaches in the Context of Developmental Psychopathology

As illustrated in the sections above, cognitive neuroscience approaches are used to study the development of psychopathology, for instance, in research on autism and anxiety disorders. There are several advantages of examining brain processes and neural development in this context. Whereas behavioral responses reflect the end results of underlying neurocognitive processes, neuroscience methods can help to elucidate these processes dynamically while they are happening in the brain and they can help identify the involved brain structures.

ERPs, for instance, provide insights on cognitive processes taking place within milliseconds after a certain sensory or cognitive event. EEG measures, in general, have the advantage that they can be applied even with very young infants and with severely impaired children and adults, because they do not require behavioral or verbal responses and little to no verbal instruction is necessary. Unfortunately, EEG measures

**Table 8.2** Advantages and limitations of cognitive neuroscience approaches to the study of developmental psychopathology.

| *Advantages* | *Limitations* |
|---|---|
| Enable investigation of the dynamics of cognitive processes in addition to the behavioral outcomes. | Limited sensitivity for identifying individuals with or at risk for developing a psychological disorder. |
| Often do not require behavioral or verbal responses or instructions; suitable for studying infants and children with severe impairments. | Difficulties regarding the interpretation of differences on the neural level both in the absence and in the presence of behavioral differences between groups. |
| Can provide useful information on brain functions affected by intervention (e.g., training, behavioral therapy, medication) in longitudinal studies. | |

do not capture activation of subcortical structures, such as the amygdala, which is a highly relevant structure in the context of several types of disorders. fMRI, which can be used to examine amygdala activity, on the other hand, is very rarely used with children under the age of six to seven years, because it requires participants to lie still in a large MRI scanner and to tolerate noise as well as the possibly rather frightening laboratory environment. Thus, whereas there are plausible theoretical assumptions relating early attention biases in infants to functions of the amygdala, and impairments in amygdala function to altered brain and behavioral development in psychopathology, these assumptions are very difficult to test empirically. Thus, it is often unclear what comes first: abnormalities in brain function and structure or behavioral impairments.

Furthermore, it should be noted that the utility of measures of brain activity for diagnosis is very limited at the moment. Even though clear differences in brain activity may be observed at the group level between control groups and those with a diagnosis, it is often not possible to decide which group any given individual belongs to based on brain data alone due to the huge inter-individual variance within groups (Picton & Taylor, 2007). This is true especially when working with developing populations, whose data are often more contaminated by artifacts and noise and consequently provide a poorer signal-to-noise ratio than adult data. Thus, the sensitivity of measures of brain activity for identifying individuals with or at risk for developing a psychological disorder is most often not sufficient.

Further, when looking at brain activity and concomitant behavioral differences in the same task, problems can occur. If a clinical group and a control group differ on a relevant behavioral measure, the concomitant brain data are hard to interpret because differences in brain activity may reflect different task difficulties or strategies across groups. For instance, in an fMRI study on facial imitation in children with and without autism great care was taken to ensure that children of both groups did not differ in their behavioral performance (Dapretto et al., 2006). Any behavioral difference between groups would likely have involved differential engagement of the neural motor system, thus leading to distinctive brain responses simply because children did not perform the task equally.

If, on the other hand, two groups of individuals do not show differences in task performance on the behavioral level but only on the neural level there is often debate over what these alterations in brain activity actually reflect. For instance, several neuroimaging studies reported differences in activation of the mirror neuron system during imitation in groups with and without ASD in the absence of differences in behavioral performance (Dapretto et al., 2006; Williams et al., 2006). This apparent dissociation between behavioral imitation and mirror neuron system activation led Southgate, Gergely, and Csibra (2008) to question whether activity in areas of the mirror neuron system is actually crucial for eliciting imitative behavior and to what extent individuals with autism are really impaired in voluntary imitation. Thus, both differences on the behavioral level and the absence of differences in behavior can be problematic in neuroimaging studies comparing groups of participants with and without a diagnosis.

Despite these caveats, it is important to note that neuroscience approaches offer a useful additional level of analysis when combined with conventional methods of diagnosis. Based on knowledge on normal brain processes related to imitation and face processing it was possible to develop hypotheses regarding the early development of ASD. Similarly, knowledge on the implication of the amygdala in threat orienting and social fear learning has inspired research on the role of this structure in the development of anxiety in children (see sections above for a review of these lines of research).

Furthermore, neuroimaging techniques are used successfully in longitudinal research on treatment effects. To mention just two examples, Dawson et al. (2012) investigated the effects of a two-year behavioral intervention designed by the authors, the Early Start Denver Model, on brain responses to pictures of faces and objects in children aged 4–6 who were diagnosed with ASD. They compared brain activations in these children to an age-matched typically developing control group and a group of children with ASD who received a commonly available community intervention. A randomized controlled trial was conducted, i.e. children with ASD were randomly assigned to the Early Start Denver Model or the common intervention at the beginning of the study. Following intervention, both the ASD group taking part in the Early Start Denver Model and the typically developing control group responded to faces relative to objects with shorter Nc latency and greater cortical activation in a passive viewing task. Thus, normal brain responses to faces were observed in children with ASD who had received the intervention developed by the authors. Children with ASD who had received the commonly available community intervention, in contrast, showed the opposite pattern of brain responses, i.e., shorter Nc latency and greater activation in response to objects relative to faces. Furthermore, EEG measures were correlated with improvements in children's social behavior as assessed by the PDD Behavior Inventory (Cohen, Schmidt-Lackner, Romanczyk, & Sudhalter, 2003). Thus, brain activations and behavioral measures provided complementary information in this study. In line with the authors' hypotheses, the findings suggest that very basic mechanisms of face processing as assessed using EEG are related to more complex processes guiding children's social behavior in ASD.

As a second example, a longitudinal fMRI study on threat orienting in adolescents with generalized anxiety disorder reported treatment-related changes in brain activity following cognitive behavioral therapy or medication with serotonin reuptake inhibitors (Maslowsky et al., 2010). Across measurements patients in both treatment groups achieved comparable improvements in anxiety symptoms as assessed using the Pediatric Anxiety Rating Scale ("The Pediatric Anxiety Rating Scale (PARS): development and psychometric properties," 2002). Both groups also displayed similar changes in brain activation in response to angry faces vs. baseline across both time points (before/after intervention). On the behavioral level, however, neither of the treatment groups showed altered threat orienting in the experimental task administered during fMRI, suggesting that brain measures may sometimes be more sensitive than behavioral measures in tracking changes following intervention. However, in the case of this study, the behavioral implications of the reported changes in brain activation remain unclear, as they could not be related to reductions in anxiety symptoms.

## Conclusion

In the present chapter I have provided an overview of neuroscience methods used in the study of developmental psychopathology. By describing some cognitive neuroscience approaches on ASD and anxiety I have illustrated how these methods are applied to gain insights on the early development and brain bases of psychological and developmental disorders. Even though many neuroscience techniques are applicable with infants and children, there are limitations in the use of certain techniques at very young ages (e.g., fMRI). Nevertheless, cognitive neuroscience approaches allow for the development and testing of hypotheses regarding dynamic neurocognitive processes underlying psychopathology and thus provide useful information on the early roots of many common disorders.

## Acknowledgments

The writing of this chapter was supported by the Deutsche Forschungsgemeinschaft (DFG) [grant number HO 4342/2-3].

## References

Adrien, J. L., Lenoir, P., Martineau, J., Perrot, A., Hameury, L., Larmande, C., & Sauvage, D. (1993). Blind ratings of early symptoms of autism based upon family home movies. *Journal of the American Academy of Child and Adolescent Psychiatry*, *32*(3), 617–626.

Baron-Cohen, S. (1995). *Mindblindness: An essay on autism and theory of mind*. Cambridge, MA: Bradford/MIT Press.

Bell, M. A., & Fox, N. A. (1992). The relations between frontal brain electrical activity and cognitive development during infancy. *Child Development*, *63*(5), 1142–1163.

Biederman, J., Hirshfeld-Becker, D. R., Rosenbaum, J. F., Herot, C., Friedman, D., Snidman, N.,… Faraone, S. V. (2001). Further evidence of association between behavioral inhibition and social anxiety in children. *American Journal of Psychiatry*, *158*(10), 1673–1679.

Bookheimer, S. Y., Wang, A. T., Scott, A., Sigman, M., & Dapretto, M. (2008). Frontal contributions to face processing differences in autism: evidence from fMRI of inverted face processing. *J Int Neuropsychol Soc*, *14*(6), 922–932. doi: 10.1017/S135561770808140X

Bushnell, I. W. R., Sai, F., & Mullin, J. T. (1989). Neonatal recognition of the mother's face. *British Journal of Developmental Psychology*, *7*, 3–15.

Cattaneo, L., Fabbri-Destro, M., Boria, S., Pieraccini, C., Monti, A., Cossu, G., & Rizzolatti, G. (2007). Impairment of actions chains in autism and its possible role in intention understanding. *Proceedings of the National Academy of Science U S A*, *104*(45), 17825–17830. doi: 0706273104 [pii] 10.1073/pnas.0706273104

Cheour, M., Imada, T., Taulu, S., Ahonen, A., Salonen, J., & Kuhl, P. (2004). Magnetoencephalography is feasible for infant assessment of auditory discrimination. *Experimental Neurology, 190* Suppl 1, S44–51. doi: S0014-4886(04)00270-5 [pii] 10.1016/j.expneurol.2004.06.030

Cohen, I. L., Schmidt-Lackner, S., Romanczyk, R., & Sudhalter, V. (2003). The PDD Behavior Inventory: a rating scale for assessing response to intervention in children with pervasive developmental disorder. *Journal of Autism and Developmental Disorders, 33*(1), 31–45.

Dapretto, M., Davies, M. S., Pfeifer, J. H., Scott, A. A., Sigman, M., Bookheimer, S. Y., & Iacoboni, M. (2006). Understanding emotions in others: mirror neuron dysfunction in children with autism spectrum disorders. *Nature Neuroscience, 9*(1), 28–30. doi: nn1611 [pii] 10.1038/nn1611

Davidson, R. J., & Fox, N. A. (1982). Asymmetrical brain activity discriminates between positive and negative affective stimuli in human infants. *Science, 218*(4578), 1235–1237.

Davidson, R. J., & Fox, N. A. (1989). Frontal brain asymmetry predicts infants' response to maternal separation. *Journal of Abnormal Psychology, 98*(2), 127–131.

Davidson, R. J., Jackson, D., & Larson, C. (2000). Human Electroencephalography. In J. T. Caccioppo, L. G. Tassinary & G. Berntson (Eds.), *Principles of Psychophysiology* (2nd Edition ed.). Cambridge: Cambridge University Press.

Dawson, G. (2008). Early behavioral intervention, brain plasticity, and the prevention of autism spectrum disorder. *Developmental Psychopathology, 20*(3), 775–803. doi: 10.1017/S0954579408000370

Dawson, G., Jones, E. J., Merkle, K., Venema, K., Lowy, R., Faja, S.,...Webb, S. J. (2012). Early behavioral intervention is associated with normalized brain activity in young children with autism. *J Am Acad Child Adolesc Psychiatry, 51*(11), 1150–1159. doi: 10.1016/j.jaac.2012.08.018

Dawson, G., Webb, S. J., & McPartland, J. (2005). Understanding the nature of face processing impairment in autism: insights from behavioral and electrophysiological studies. *Developmental Neuropsychology, 27*(3), 403–424. doi: 10.1207/s15326942dn2703_6

De Bellis, M. D., Casey, B. J., Dahl, R. E., Birmaher, B., Williamson, D. E., Thomas, K. M.,...Ryan, N. D. (2000). A pilot study of amygdala volumes in pediatric generalized anxiety disorder. *Biological Psychiatry, 48*(1), 51–57.

de Haan, M., Belsky, J., Reid, V., Volein, A., & Johnson, M. H. (2004). Maternal personality and infants' neural and visual responsivity to facial expressions of emotion. *Journal of Child Psychology and Psychiatry, 45*(7), 1209–1218. doi: 10.1111/j.1469-7610.2004.00320.x [pii] JCPP320

di Pellegrino, G., Fadiga, L., Fogassi, L., Gallese, V., & Rizzolatti, G. (1992). Understanding motor events: a neurophysiological study. *Experimental Brain Research, 91*(1), 176–180.

Draganova, R., Eswaran, H., Murphy, P., Huotilainen, M., Lowery, C., & Preissl, H. (2005). Sound frequency change detection in fetuses and newborns, a magnetoencephalographic study. *Neuroimage, 28*(2), 354–361. doi: S1053-8119(05)00412-X [pii] 10.1016/j.neuroimage.2005.06.011

Durant, C., Christmas, D., & Nutt, D. (2010). The pharmacology of anxiety. *Current Topics in Behavioral Neurosciences, 2*, 303–330.

Ewing, L., Pellicano, E., & Rhodes, G. (2013). Reevaluating the selectivity of face-processing difficulties in children and adolescents with autism. *Journal of Experimental Child Psychology, 115*(2), 342–355. doi: 10.1016/j.jecp.2013.01.009

Fox, N. A., Almas, A. N., Degnan, K. A., Nelson, C. A., & Zeanah, C. H. (2011). The effects of severe psychosocial deprivation and foster care intervention on cognitive development at 8 years of age: findings from the Bucharest Early Intervention Project. *Journal of Child Psychology and Psychiatry, 52*(9), 919–928. doi: 10.1111/j.1469-7610.2010.02355.x

Gartstein, M. A., & Rothbart, M. K. (2003). Studying infant temperament via the Revised Infant Bevahior Questionnaire. *Infant Behavior and Development, 26*(1), 64–86.

Ginsburg, G. S. (2009). The Child Anxiety Prevention Study: intervention model and primary outcomes. *Journal of Consulting and Clinical Psychology*, *77*(3), 580–587. doi: 2009-08093-018 [pii] 10.1037/a0014486

Gliga, T., & Csibra, G. (2007). Seeing the face through the eyes: a developmental perspective on face expertise. *Progress in Brain Research*, *164*, 323–339. doi: S0079-6123(07)64018-7 [pii] 10.1016/S0079-6123(07)64018-7

Grelotti, D. J., Klin, A. J., Gauthier, I., Skudlarski, P., Cohen, D. J., Gore, J. C.,...Schultz, R. T. (2005). fMRI activation of the fusiform gyrus and amygdala to cartoon characters but not to faces in a boy with autism. *Neuropsychologia*, *43*(3), 373–385. doi: 10.1016/j.neuropsychologia.2004.06.015

Grice, S. J., Halit, H., Farroni, T., Baron-Cohen, S., Bolton, P., & Johnson, M. H. (2005). Neural correlates of eye-gaze detection in young children with autism. *Cortex*, *41*(3), 342–353.

Grossmann, T., Johnson, M. H., Vaish, A., Hughes, D. A., Quinque, D., Stoneking, M., & Friederici, A. D. (2011). Genetic and neural dissociation of individual responses to emotional expressions in human infants. *Developmental Cognitive Neuroscience*, *1*(1), 57–66. doi: S1878-9293(10)00002-2 [pii] 10.1016/j.dcn.2010.07.001

Hadjikhani, N., Joseph, R. M., Snyder, J., Chabris, C. F., Clark, J., Steele, S.,...Tager-Flusberg, H. (2004). Activation of the fusiform gyrus when individuals with autism spectrum disorder view faces. *Neuroimage*, *22*(3), 1141–1150. doi: 10.1016/j.neuroimage.2004.03.025 [pii] S1053811904001636

Hadjikhani, N., Joseph, R. M., Snyder, J., & Tager-Flusberg, H. (2007). Abnormal activation of the social brain during face perception in autism. *Human Brain Mapping*, *28*(5), 441–449. doi: 10.1002/hbm.20283

Haxby, J. V., Hoffman, E. A., & Gobbini, M. I. (2000). The distributed human neural system for face perception. *Trends in Cognitive Sciences*, *4*(6), 223–233. doi: S1364-6613(00)01482-0

Hoehl, S., & Wahl, S. (2012). Recording infant ERP data for cognitive research. *Developmental Neuropsychology*, *37*(3), 187–209. doi: 10.1080/87565641.2011.627958

Iacoboni, M., Woods, R. P., Brass, M., Bekkering, H., Mazziotta, J. C., & Rizzolatti, G. (1999). Cortical mechanisms of human imitation. *Science*, *286*(5449), 2526–2528. doi: 8142

Johnson, M. H. (2005). Subcortical face processing. *Nature Reviews Neuroscience*, *6*(10), 766–774. doi: nrn1766 [pii] 10.1038/nrn1766

Johnson, M. H., Dziurawiec, S., Ellis, H., & Morton, J. (1991). Newborns' preferential tracking of face-like stimuli and its subsequent decline. *Cognition*, *40*(1–2), 1–19. doi: 0010-0277(91)90045-6

Johnson, M. H., Griffin, R., Csibra, G., Halit, H., Farroni, T., de Haan, M.,...Richards, J. (2005). The emergence of the social brain network: evidence from typical and atypical development. *Developmental Psychopathology*, *17*(3), 599–619. doi: S0954579405050297 [pii] 10.1017/S0954579405050297

Kanwisher, N., McDermott, J., & Chun, M. M. (1997). The fusiform face area: a module in human extrastriate cortex specialized for face perception. *Journal of Neuroscience*, *17*(11), 4302–4311.

Kendler, K. S., Karkowski, L. M., & Prescott, C. A. (1999). Fears and phobias: reliability and heritability. [Research Support, U.S. Gov't, P.H.S.]. *Psychological Medicine*, *29*(3), 539–553.

Kessler, R. C., Ruscio, A. M., Shear, K., & Wittchen, H. U. (2010). Epidemiology of anxiety disorders. *Current Topics in Behavioral Neurosciences*, *2*, 21–35.

Kleinhans, N. M., Richards, T., Johnson, L. C., Weaver, K. E., Greenson, J., Dawson, G., & Aylward, E. (2011). fMRI evidence of neural abnormalities in the subcortical face processing system in ASD. *Neuroimage*, *54*(1), 697–704. doi: 10.1016/j.neuroimage.2010.07.037

Klin, A., Jones, W., Schultz, R., Volkmar, F., & Cohen, D. (2002). Visual fixation patterns during viewing of naturalistic social situations as predictors of social competence in individuals with autism. *Archives of General Psychiatry, 59*(9), 809–816. doi: yoa10221

LeBeau, R. T., Glenn, D., Liao, B., Wittchen, H. U., Beesdo-Baum, K., Ollendick, T., & Craske, M. G. (2010). Specific phobia: a review of DSM-IV specific phobia and preliminary recommendations for DSM-V. [Review]. *Depression and Anxiety, 27*(2), 148–167. doi: 10.1002/da.20655

LeDoux, J. E. (1996). *The Emotional Brain*. New York: Simon and Schuster.

Leppänen, J. M., Peltola, M. J., Puura, K., Mantymaa, M., Mononen, N., & Lehtimaki, T. (2011). Serotonin and early cognitive development: variation in the tryptophan hydroxylase 2 gene is associated with visual attention in 7-month-old infants. *Journal of Child Psychology and Psychiatry, 52*(11),1144–1152. doi: 10.1111/j.1469-7610.2011.02391.x

Lloyd-Fox, S., Blasi, A., & Elwell, C. E. (2010). Illuminating the developing brain: the past, present and future of functional near infrared spectroscopy. *Neuroscience and Biobehavioral Reviews, 34*(3), 269–284. doi: S0149-7634(09)00104-3 [pii] 10.1016/j.neubiorev.2009.07.008

Lloyd-Fox, S., Blasi, A., Everdell, N., Elwell, C. E., & Johnson, M. H. (2011). Selective cortical mapping of biological motion processing in young infants. *Journal of Cognitive Neuroscience, 23*(9), 2521–2532. doi: 10.1162/jocn.2010.21598

Lord, C., Risi, S., DiLavore, P. S., Shulman, C., Thurm, A., & Pickles, A. (2006). Autism from 2 to 9 years of age. *Archives of General Psychiatry, 63*(6), 694–701. doi: 10.1001/archpsyc.63.6.694

Maslowsky, J., Mogg, K., Bradley, B. P., McClure-Tone, E., Ernst, M., Pine, D. S., & Monk, C. S. (2010). A preliminary investigation of neural correlates of treatment in adolescents with generalized anxiety disorder. *Journal of Child and Adolescent Psychopharmacology, 20*(2), 105–111. doi: 10.1089/cap.2009.0049

Meltzoff, A. N., & Decety, J. (2003). What imitation tells us about social cognition: a rapprochement between developmental psychology and cognitive neuroscience. *Philosophical Transactions of the Royal Society of London: B Biological Sciences, 358*(1431), 491–500. doi: 10.1098/rstb.2002.1261

Meltzoff, A. N., & Moore, M. K. (1977). Imitation of facial and manual gestures by human neonates. *Science, 198*(4312), 75–78. doi: 198/4312/75 [pii] 10.1126/science.198.4312.75

Monk, C. S., Telzer, E. H., Mogg, K., Bradley, B. P., Mai, X., Louro, H. M.,...Pine, D. S. (2008). Amygdala and ventrolateral prefrontal cortex activation to masked angry faces in children and adolescents with generalized anxiety disorder. *Archives of General Psychiatry, 65*(5), 568–576. doi: 10.1001/archpsyc.65.5.568

Muris, P., Steerneman, P., Merckelbach, H., & Meesters, C. (1996). The role of parental fearfulness and modeling in children's fear. *Behavior Research and Therapy, 34*(3), 265–268.

Olsson, A., & Phelps, E. A. (2007). Social learning of fear. *Nature Neuroscience, 10*(9), 1095–1102. doi: nn1968 [pii]10.1038/nn1968

Oostenbroek, J., Suddendorf, T., Nielsen, M., Redshaw, J., Kennedy-Costantini, S., Davis, J., ... (2016). Comprehensive Longitudinal Study Challenges the Existence of Neonatal Imitation in Humans. *Curr Biol, 26*(10), 1334–1338.

Oram Cardy, J. E., Flagg, E. J., Roberts, W., & Roberts, T. P. (2008). Auditory evoked fields predict language ability and impairment in children. *International Journal of Psychophysiology, 68*(2), 170–175. doi: S0167-8760(08)00036-6 [pii] 10.1016/j.ijpsycho.2007.10.015

Osterling, J., & Dawson, G. (1994). Early recognition of children with autism: a study of first birthday home videotapes. *Journal of Autism and Developmental Disorders, 24*(3), 247–257.

The Pediatric Anxiety Rating Scale (PARS): development and psychometric properties. (2002). *Journal of the American Academy of Child and Adolescent Psychiatry, 41*(9), 1061–1069.

Peltola, M. J., Leppänen, J. M., Maki, S., & Hietanen, J. K. (2009). Emergence of enhanced attention to fearful faces between 5 and 7 months of age. *Social Cognitive and Affective Neuroscience, 4*, 134–142. doi: nsn046 [pii] 10.1093/scan/nsn046

Perez-Edgar, K., & Fox, N. A. (2005). Temperament and anxiety disorders. [Review]. *Child and Adolescent Psychiatric Clinics of North America 14*(4), 681–706, viii. doi: 10.1016/j.chc.2005.05.008

Picton, T. W., & Taylor, M. J. (2007). Electrophysiological evaluation of human brain development. *Developmental Neuropsychology, 31*(3), 249–278. doi: 10.1080/87565640701228732

Pierce, K., & Redcay, E. (2008). Fusiform function in children with an autism spectrum disorder is a matter of "who". *Biological Psychiatry, 64*(7), 552–560. doi: 10.1016/j.biopsych.2008.05.013

Ramachandran, V. S., & Oberman, L. M. (2006). Broken mirrors: a theory of autism. *Scientific American, 295*(5), 62–69.

Reid, V. M., Hoehl, S., Landt, J., & Striano, T. (2008). Human infants dissociate structural and dynamic information in biological motion: evidence from neural systems. *Social Cognitive and Affective Neuroscience, 3*(2), 161–167. doi: nsn008 [pii] 10.1093/scan/nsn008

Reynolds, G. D., & Richards, J. E. (2009). Cortical source localization of infant cognition. *Developmental Neuropsychology, 34*(3), 312–329. doi: 910996962 [pii] 10.1080/87565640902801890

Saby, J. N., & Marshall, P. J. (2012). The utility of EEG band power analysis in the study of infancy and early childhood. *Developmental Neuropsychology, 37*(3), 253–273. doi: 10.1080/87565641.2011.614663

Shechner, T., Britton, J. C., Perez-Edgar, K., Bar-Haim, Y., Ernst, M., Fox, N. A.,...Pine, D. S. (2012). Attention biases, anxiety, and development: toward or away from threats or rewards? *Depression and Anxiety, 29*(4), 282–294. doi: 10.1002/da.20914

Southgate, V., Gergely, G., & Csibra, G. (2008). Does the mirror neuron system and its impairment explain human imitation and autism?.In J. A. Pineda (Ed.), *The Role of Mirroring Processes in Social Cognition*: Humana Press.

Stets, M., Stahl, D., & Reid, V. M. (2012). A meta-analysis investigating factors underlying attrition rates in infant ERP studies. *Developmental Neuropsychology, 37*(3), 226–252. doi: 10.1080/87565641.2012.654867

Thomas, K. M., Drevets, W. C., Dahl, R. E., Ryan, N. D., Birmaher, B., Eccard, C. H.,... Casey, B. J. (2001). Amygdala response to fearful faces in anxious and depressed children. *Archives of General Psychiatry, 58*(11), 1057–1063. doi: yoa01058

Weigelt, S., Koldewyn, K., & Kanwisher, N. (2012). Face identity recognition in autism spectrum disorders: a review of behavioral studies. *Neuroscience and Biobehavioral Reviews, 36*(3), 1060–1084. doi: 10.1016/j.neubiorev.2011.12.008

Wetherby, A. M., Woods, J., Allen, L., Cleary, J., Dickinson, H., & Lord, C. (2004). Early indicators of autism spectrum disorders in the second year of life. *Journal of Autism and Developmental Disorders, 34*(5), 473–493.

Whalen, P. J., Rauch, S. L., Etcoff, N. L., McInerney, S. C., Lee, M. B., & Jenike, M. A. (1998). Masked presentations of emotional facial expressions modulate amygdala activity without explicit knowledge. *Journal of Neuroscience, 18*(1), 411–418.

Williams, J. H., Waiter, G. D., Gilchrist, A., Perrett, D. I., Murray, A. D., & Whiten, A. (2006). Neural mechanisms of imitation and 'mirror neuron' functioning in autistic spectrum disorder. *Neuropsychologia, 44*(4), 610–621. doi: S0028-3932(05)00245-9 [pii] 10.1016/j.neuropsychologia.2005.06.010

Williams, J. H., Whiten, A., Suddendorf, T., & Perrett, D. I. (2001). Imitation, mirror neurons and autism. *Neuroscience and Biobehavioral Reviews, 25*(4), 287–295. doi: S0149-7634(01)00014-8

9

# Early Neurocognitive Markers of Developmental Psychopathology

Emily J.H. Jones and Mark H. Johnson

## Introduction

The behavioral symptoms that lead to a diagnosis of developmental psychopathology likely emerge from a complex interaction between pre-existing vulnerabilities and the child's environment. Initial genetic and environmental risk factors alter brain structure and function, compromising the child's ability to adapt to their environment. Early emerging behavioral symptoms alter the child's self-directed patterns of attention, changing their experience of the environment and further restricting social learning opportunities. Compensatory skills and pre-existing protective factors also contribute to the emergence of the full clinical phenotype. Understanding early markers of developmental psychopathology is thus critical to mapping the developmental mechanisms that underlie symptom emergence.

In this chapter, we review *neurocognitive* markers of developmental psychopathology that have been identified in the first three years of life. Recent developments in technology have significantly advanced our ability to study neurocognitive development in infants and toddlers, with techniques such as electroencephalography (EEG), Near Infrared Spectroscopy (NIRS) and eye tracking becoming increasingly widespread. Moving beyond behavior to study neurocognitive markers of later psychopathology is important for three reasons. First, atypicalities in neurocognitive systems underlie and may be apparent before the emergence of behavioral symptoms. Studying neurocognitive markers is thus critical to understanding causal paths to symptom emergence, and may facilitate earlier detection of children at risk. Second, neurocognitive markers can be more easily linked to genetic variation than behavioral symptoms, because they are situated at an early step in the causal path between gene and the behavioral phenotype that characterizes the disorder. Neurocognitive measures may thus form "endophenotypes" that facilitate the discovery of new genes associated with psychopathology. Third, neurocognitive markers are more easily studied across species than observable behaviors, which may have very different surface features. This facilitates the use of animal models to characterize the

*The Wiley Handbook of Developmental Psychopathology*, First Edition. Edited by Luna C. Centifanti and David M. Williams.

neurobiology of psychopathology, and the development and testing of potential pharmacological treatment approaches.

Studying neurocognitive markers of later developmental psychopathology requires longitudinal prospective studies of infants who later develop symptoms. However, the population prevalence of developmental psychopathologies, whilst significant from a clinical perspective, nonetheless poses a challenge to prospective work. Large cohort studies such as the Avon Longitudinal Study of Parents and Children (ALSPAC) and the Millenium Cohort Study in the UK provide one route to identifying sufficient numbers of infants with later symptoms of psychopathology. This approach has many strengths, such as studying risk for multiple disorders in a single cohort; having the statistical power to answer more complex questions about the relations between different markers; and allowing conclusions that are generalizable to the general population. However, the scale and cost of these studies mean that relatively few neurocognitive measures can be included. An alternative strategy is to examine groups of infants with elevated genetic or environmental risk for psychopathology. This allows more intensive study of smaller cohorts, whilst maintaining sufficient power to detect predictors of later psychopathology.

## Studying Groups with Elevated Risk for Psychopathology

### Premature Infants

Infants born very prematurely have a significantly increased risk of later psychopathology. Prevalence typically ranges from 20 to 30 % (e.g. Johnson, Hollis, Kochhar, & Hennessy, 2010), representing a three- to four-fold increased risk relative to the general population. Thus, identifying predictors of the development of psychopathology is both feasible and of clinical utility within populations of premature infants. However, the generalizability of neurocognitive markers observed in preterm infants may be limited by evidence that developmental psychopathology has different patterns of cause and consequence in this population. For example, symptoms of psychopathology are more strongly associated with poor cognitive skills in preterm infants than in the general population, suggesting that examining whether early markers are related to cognitive skill is critical (Johnson et al., 2010). Common patterns of gender predominance (like enrichment of ADHD in males or anxiety disorders in females) may also be less apparent (e.g. Johnson et al., 2010). Further, patterns of comorbidity may differ; for example, premature children with ADHD are less likely to have comorbid conduct disorders than full term children with ADHD (Johnson et al., 2010). Thus, there are likely different mechanisms contributing to risk for psychiatric disorders in premature versus full term infants.

### Infants at Familial Risk

An alternate research strategy is to study infants at high familial risk for a disorder because they have an older sibling or parent with the condition of interest. This strategy is effective where disorders are highly heritable, and where symptoms emerge early enough in development to make prospective studies feasible. The field of autism research has recently embraced this strategy, since recurrence rates in younger siblings approach 20 % (Ozonoff et al., 2011) compared to a population prevalence of ~1 % (Baird, Simonoff, Pickles, Chandler, & Loucas, 2006). Prospective studies of infants who later develop Autism Spectrum Disorders (ASD) are thus feasible within a familial high-risk design. This strategy has been used for other disorders with high heritability such as language impairment (Benasich, Gou, Choudhury, & Harris, 2008), Attention Deficit Hyperactivity Disorder (ADHD; Auerbach, Faroy, & Ebstein, 2001) and schizophrenia (Gilmore, 2010). A low-risk control group, composed of children with no family history of the disorder in question, is typically followed in parallel. This design allows researchers to examine whether infant measures predict later development of the disorder of interest. However, the degree to which mechanisms generalize beyond those at familial risk to *de novo* cases is currently unclear.

## Environmental Stress

Early institutionalization presents a significant risk factor for the development of psychopathology. For example, the Bucharest Early Intervention Project (BEIP) is a randomized controlled trial of foster placement and institutionalization in abandoned infants and toddlers in Romania (Zeanah et al., 2009). In this cohort, 53 % of children who had experienced any institutional rearing met DSM criteria for a psychiatric diagnosis at age 4 to 5 years, compared to 22 % of children from the community. A less extreme but more common form of environmental challenge is low socioeconomic status, which also raises risk for psychopathology (Johnson, Cohen, Dohrenwend, Link, & Brook, 1999). This is likely influenced by a range of factors such as exposure to neurotoxins, poor nutrition, prenatal drug, alcohol or smoking exposure, and elevated stress during pregnancy (Evans & Kantrowitz, 2002). Studying children from low-SES families thus presents a further opportunity to examine risk factors for a range of outcomes. However, the mixed etiology of impairments may make identification of clear neurocognitive markers difficult. Further, families under significant economic stress can find it difficult to participate in longitudinal research studies, increasing the potential for attrition.

## Genetic Polymorphisms

A further strategy to identify children at risk for particular developmental psychopathologies is to examine infants who have common genetic polymorphisms that are enriched in particular developmental psychopathologies. Polymorphisms that have been studied in populations of infants include dopamine receptor genes like *DRD4* (e.g. Holmboe et al., 2010); and the serotonin transporter promoter (HTTLPR; e.g. Auerbach et al., 2001), both of which have been linked to ADHD (Gizer, Ficks, & Waldman, 2009). Looking at neurocognitive development in infants with particular forms of these genes can provide insight into the potential mechanisms through which neuropsychopathologies emerge. However, there are few longitudinal studies of such populations, and the small proportion of the variance accounted for by each polymorphism in relation to psychopathology means that either large samples and/or analyses of combinations of polymorphisms will be required to detect robust effects.

## Studying Specific Domains of Neurocognition

In this section, we review key findings from the literature on early neurocognitive markers of later developmental psychopathology. In addition to reviewing studies that examine prediction of later categorical outcome, we include studies that take a dimensional approach to later symptomatology. This approach reflects the ongoing debate within this field as to the categorical vs. dimensional nature of psychopathology (Coghill & Sonuga-Barke, 2012). We organize the review by broad neurocognitive systems known to play a critical role in early learning, including attention, memory, social processing, and communication and language. These domains are consistent with the Research Domain Criteria laid out by the US National Institutes of Mental Health, a new framework that provides a heuristic for the incorporation of behavioral neuroscience in the study of psychopathology (Sanislow, Pine, & Quinn, 2010). This framework provides a structure within which to examine early risk factors for later psychopathology that cuts across DSM-defined disorders. The substantial comorbidity within developmental psychopathology provides one pressing reason for such an approach: in a recent study of 3024 children from the United States aged 8 to 14, 14 % of the 1 in 8 children with at least one of six DSM diagnoses had at least one additional diagnosis (Merikangas, He, Brody, & Fisher, 2010). Examining how particular markers relate to continuous variation in symptomatology in different domains is critical to better mapping the underlying etiologies of developmental psychopathology. The ultimate goal of such an approach is to provide etiological and trajectory-based information that could help the field to reformulate current categorization systems for developmental psychopathology.

### Attention

Attention can be broadly divided into three components (Posner & Petersen, 1989): alerting and arousal, orienting and attention-shifting, and sustained attention. Atypicalities in all three components during the first three years have been associated with later psychopathology. First, orienting and arousal regulation difficulties have been noted early in the development of children with ASD or ADHD. For example, general regulation of sleep–wake cycles at 3 months is related to later ADHD diagnosis (Gurevitz, Geva, Varon, & Leitner, 2014), and severe sleep disturbance in infancy and longer sleep latency predicts diagnosis of ADHD at age 5 (Thunström, 2002). Parent concern about sleep at 12 months also relates to later ASD diagnosis (Kincade et al., 2013), and infants who spent time in neonatal intensive care and who later develop ASD show a preference for atypically high-frequency stimulation at 4 months (Karmel, Gardner, Meade, & Cohen, 2010), which may also reflect atypical arousal modulation. Dysregulation of arousal may thus be a common factor in the early development of ASD and ADHD, though further work is required to determine whether this represents a common risk pathway.

Second, difficulties with the shifting of visual attention (disengagement) in the first year of life are one of the most replicated findings in infants at high familial risk who develop ASD (Elsabbagh et al., 2013; Zwaigenbaum et al., 2005). Interestingly, Elsabbagh and colleagues (2011) found that high-risk infants who were less distracted by peripheral stimuli when fixating a repetitive stimulus (but not a variable stimulus) showed greater impairment in social interaction at 36 months. Thus, increased difficulty in disengaging from repetitive stimuli may be one route to impairment. However, faster disengagement is not always "better". In a group of typically developing infants, greater disengagement from a variable stimulus was related to common polymorphisms associated with increased risk of ADHD (Holmboe et al., 2010). Further, a greater difference in distractibility between repetitive and variable stimuli at 9 months was related to better spatial conflict resolution but *worse* effortful control at age 2 years (Holmboe, Pasco Fearon, Csibra, Tucker, & Johnson, 2008). This raises the intriguing possibility that ASD and ADHD may be associated with different profiles of disengagement in early infancy, a prediction that will be important to test in future work.

Such work should also consider the broader literature showing that shorter looks and more gaze shifting during visual attention tasks are associated with generally better cognitive and language development. For example, Rose and colleagues have shown that faster shifting and shorter looks during presentation of paired stimuli (when combined with other measures of processing speed and memory) predict better language skills and cognitive skills at age 3 (Rose, Feldman, & Jankowski, 2009), and better executive functioning skills (Rose, Feldman, & Jankowski, 2012) at age 11 years. Further, infant or toddler performance in these domains mediates the effect of prematurity on later cognitive development (Rose, Feldman, & Jankowski, 2005).

The third aspect of attention, sustained attention, appears to relate to symptoms of psychopathology in later development, with greater sustained attention associating with reduced risk. For example, Kochanska & colleagues (2000) found that more focused attention at 9 months was related to better effortful control, more regulated anger and joy and stronger restraint at 22 and 33 months. Qualitative ratings of attention on a 1 to 3 scale (very attentive, moderately attentive, very inattentive) at 1 and 2 years together predict observed attention and inattention, cognitive performance and maternal ratings of hyperactivity and behavioral problems at 3.5 years (Lawson & Ruff, 2004a). Outcomes were particularly bad for low-attentive children who also had higher negativity. Further, less focused attention (manipulation with an interested expression) in very low birth weight infants at 7 months predicts more hyperactivity and inattention at 4 to 5 years, and poorer cognitive skills (Lawson & Ruff, 2004b). This range of evidence suggests that lack of focused attention during toy play in infancy is related to ADHD-type symptoms in the preschool years. Examining the relation between such markers and later diagnosis of ADHD and other related conditions is an important next step.

## Social Cognition

Early atypicalities in social cognition have been most extensively studied in the emergence of ASD, because social atypicalities are the hallmark of this group of conditions. Broadly, social behavior appears relatively typical in the first year of life for infants at high familial risk who later develop ASD. For example, 6-month-olds later diagnosed with ASD show typical patterns of engagement and affect in response to initiation and termination of maternal interaction (Rozga, Hutman, Young, & Rogers, 2011). At the same age, infants later diagnosed with ASD show preferential attention to a face in a complex display (Elsabbagh, Gliga, Pickles, & Hudry, 2012a); and gaze to faces, social smiling, directed vocalizations and social engagement to an unfamiliar adult appears typical at 6 months in infants later diagnosed with ASD (Ozonoff et al., 2010). However, neural responses to dynamic gaze shifts are atypical in 6- to 10-month-old infants who later developed ASD (Elsabbagh et al., 2012b), suggesting that neurocognitive atypicalities are present from early development. Interestingly, in the ALSPAC longitudinal study, children later diagnosed with ASD were more likely to have deficits in social, communication and fine motor skills from 6 months (Bolton, Golding, Emond, & Steer, 2012). Possibly, this study had greater power to detect effects at 6 months than previous work with infants at familial risk; alternatively, infants who develop ASD within families at familial risk may not be representative of infants who develop ASD in the population as a whole.

Behavioral atypicalities in a range of social skills become clearer in the second year of life for children later diagnosed with ASD. For example, by 12 to 14 months infants later diagnosed with ASD are less likely to show or point than other infants (Rozga et al., 2011) and produce fewer gestures when interacting with familiar or unfamiliar adults (Talbott, Nelson, & Tager-Flusberg, 2013). Clear deficits in social attention also become apparent around the end of the first year of life. By 12 months, Ozonoff and colleagues (2010) found that infants with a later diagnosis of ASD were less likely to look at faces or make directed vocalizations during a cognitive assessment than infants with a typical outcome, and by 18 months they showed a reduced level of social smiling. Further, deficits in responding to own name (a skill that is emerging by 4 to 6 months in typically developing infants) also appear to emerge by age 9 to 12 months, but are unclear at earlier time-points (Nadig, Ozonoff, Young, & Rozga, 2007). By 13 months, infants are less likely to attend longer to a referred-to object (Bedford et al., 2012), and imitation appears poorer (Macari et al., 2012), though this may be shared with children with other developmental delays (Young, Rogers, Hutman, & Rozga, 2011).

The specificity of such social delays to later ASD is unclear, because there are few studies that have examined early social processing in relation to symptoms in other domains. However, a recent study suggests that this will be an important step. For example, Slopen and colleagues (2012) measured visual event-related potential responses to faces at 22 months in the context of the Bucharest Early Intervention Project. Peak amplitudes of early neural responses to faces were blunted in the intervention group, and aspects of this response mediated the association between institutionalization and ADHD symptoms (but not ODD, depression or anxiety) at 4 to 5 years. Thus, early social processing may be disrupted in other disorders. However, since no non-social comparison stimulus was included in this study, the specificity of these results to the social domain remains unclear.

## Memory and Learning

The majority of studies of early memory and learning in in infants with later psychopathology have used visual recognition memory paradigms. Here, infants are presented with a stimulus for a fixed or infant-controlled period; the infant's subsequent visual preference for a novel stimulus relative to this familiarized stimulus is used as an index of visual recognition memory. Early work with such tasks suggested that failure to show novelty preferences on a battery of visual recognition tasks between 3 and 7 months could predict later developmental delay (Fagan, Singer, Montie, & Shepherd,

1986). This test, marketed as the "Fagan Test of Infant Intelligence" has been widely used in a variety of at-risk populations. Broadly, infant scores on this task predict language and memory in toddlerhood for both at-risk and typical populations (Guzzetta, Mazzotti, Tinelli, & Bancale, 2006; Thompson, Fagan, & Fulker, 1991). In a series of studies, Rose and colleagues have shown that performance on visual recognition memory tasks in infancy relates to language skills at age 3 (Rose et al., 2009), and executive functioning skills (Rose et al., 2012) at age 11 years. Further, infant performance mediates the effect of prematurity on later cognitive development (Rose et al., 2005). Thus, it appears that compromised visual recognition memory may be a general early sign of vulnerability, and relate to poorer development across a range of domains.

## Language and Communication

A wide range of evidence indicates that early language-processing skills are predictive of variation in later language development in both normal and at-risk infant populations. Early neural responses to non-speech stimuli in infants with a family history of language impairment correlate with linguistic skills at 2 years (Benasich, Choudhury, & Friedman, 2006), and threshold for rapid auditory processing at 6 to 9 months is predictive of language outcome at age 3 years in the same population (Benasich, Thomas, & Choudhury, 2002), suggesting that general auditory processing in infancy is an important baseline skill for language development. Syllable processing is also predictive: neural responses to consonant–vowel combinations at birth predict whether vocabulary will be in the normal range for healthy newborns with 80 % accuracy (Molfese, 2000), and predict language skills at 2.5 years and verbal memory at age 5 in infants at familial risk for dyslexia (Guttorm, Leppänen, Poikkeus, & Eklund, 2005). Measures of neural tuning to the language environment suggest that delayed specialization in the first year of life predicts lower language skills at age 2 years (Kuhl, Conboy, & Padden, 2005). As children grow older, difficulties with more complex tasks become the most predictive of later skill. For example, late onset of babbling assessed at 10 months predicts poorer expressive language in the second and third years (Oller, Eilers, Neal, & Schwartz, 1999), and ability to segment speech from a continuous stream before 12 months predicts language ability at 4 to 6 years (Newman, Ratner, & Jusczyk, 2006). Thus, poorer performance in emerging language processing skills in infancy predict later variation in language skill in childhood.

The majority of studies examining early language processing have used continuous measures of language skills as an outcome measure, and most variation is within the normal range. However, a recent prospective study of "late talkers" indicates that early impairments in receptive language are a significant risk factor for later clinically significant speech and language impairment. Thal and colleagues examined a large group of 1100 children tested longitudinally from 10 to 28 months. In a follow-up of 577 children at school age, 3.7 % of late producers (children with delays in expressive language but intact receptive language at 16 m) and 8.6 % of the late comprehenders (delays in both receptive and expressive language at 16 m) had a clinical diagnosis of Specific Language Impairment (Ellis & Thal, 2008), relative to 1.5 % of the typically developing infants. Thus, early delays in comprehension are associated with later language delay.

Delays in word learning and vocabulary growth are also widely reported in infants who later develop ASD. Several studies have identified delays in understanding gesture by 12 months relative to children with typical development (Mitchell et al., 2006; Zwaigenbaum et al., 2005). By 18 months, decreased comprehension of single words is added to these earlier emerging difficulties (Mitchell et al., 2006). Parents also report that infants with later ASD produce fewer words by 18 months relative to typically developing infants (Mitchell et al., 2006; Zwaigenbaum et al., 2005). Further, Paul and colleagues (2010) found subtle delays in emerging vocal behaviors (types of consonant) were associated with later diagnosis of social developmental problems. However, findings from infants at familial risk for autism broadly suggest that early language atypicalities are not specific to autism outcome, but are rather associated with later language skills. First, delays observed in infants who later develop ASD can be of similar magnitude as those in infants with other social communication delays for at least the first two years (Landa & Garrett-Mayer, 2006; Paul et al., 2010). Second, in cohorts of infants with ASD who did not show significant language impairments at time of diagnosis, earlier delays were not apparent (Hudry et al., 2014; Talbott et al., 2013). Further work should examine whether there is any evidence of a discontinuity in the relation between infant and childhood language skills across the ASD vs. no ASD clinical boundary. This will provide crucial evidence as to whether early language delay is a marker for ASD per se, or a predictor of variation in later language skills within children in general.

Atypicalities in early language have also been noted in relation to other psychopathologies. In a large population cohort, increased rate of child vocalizations at 12 months was related to later diagnosis of disruptive behavior disorder (Allely, Purves, McConnachie, & Marwick, 2013), though this may be less related to language skill and more to early externalizing behaviors. Delays in speech and language development at age 9 and 18 months have also been noted in children later diagnosed with ADHD (Gurevitz et al., 2014). Examination of the range of more specific language processing skills identified in typical development (e.g. speech segmentation, syllable processing, native language specialization) in infants who develop later psychopathology is critical to determining whether behavioral differences in language acquisition have distinct neurocognitive roots.

## Motor Skills

Delayed achievement of motor milestones is observed across multiple types of psychopathology, and thus likely reflects a general indicator of a compromised nervous system. For example, delayed attainment of motor milestones increases the risk of later development of schizophrenia in a dose-dependent manner (Clarke, Tanskanen, & Huttunen, 2011). Delayed attainment of motor milestones is also seen in infants of mothers with schizophrenia (Henriksson & McNeil, 2004). Delays in gross and fine motor skills have been observed in children diagnosed with ASD at 24 months (Landa & Garrett-Mayer, 2006). Children with ADHD also show significant delays in gross motor development at age 3 months that persist but diminish in magnitude through 9 and 18 months (Gurevitz et al., 2014). However, it is interesting to note that children later diagnosed with ADHD seemed to perform at the extremes, with either particularly early or particularly late achievement of motor milestones. This intriguing observation of early attainment of milestones appears relatively unique to the ADHD literature, and warrants further investigation.

Several studies have examined more specific features of early motor development. Differences in muscular tone have also been observed in the first few months in infants later diagnosed with ADHD (Gurevitz et al., 2014) and ASD (Karmel et al., 2010). This is consistent with the Minnesota High Risk Study (Jacobvitaz & Sroufe, 1987), who found that low motor maturity at birth differentiated hyperactive from non-hyperactive young children. Further, activity level is lower at 6 months in infants with later ASD (Zwaigenbaum et al., 2005). Intriguingly, 7-month-old infants at familial risk for ADHD and 12-month-olds with the *L-DRD4* ADHD risk allele show *higher* activity levels than comparison infants (Auerbach et al., 2004). The degree to which activity levels relate to attainment of motor milestones across different disorders is an important direction for future work in this area.

## Conclusion

Recent work has made significant progress towards identifying early neurocognitive markers of later psychopathology, particularly in the case of Autism Spectrum Disorders. Progress in this field has been driven predominantly by studies of infants at high familial risk for ASD, and has identified many candidate early markers of later diagnosis. Less is known about other predictors of clinical diagnosis of other disorders; however, there is a range of early markers for later variation in cognitive, language, and externalizing behaviors in typical and at-risk infants. This body of work provides important clues to key mechanisms of symptom emergence. However, we are still a long way from understanding the causal paths that lead to symptom emergence in developmental psychopathology. In conclusion, we highlight several key future directions for the field.

### Markers Should be Studied in Relation to More Than One Clinical "Outcome"

The vast majority of early-risk-marker studies have included one clinical outcome group or symptom domain. Whilst these studies provide critical information about early paths to symptoms, the *specificity* of relations can only be determined when a range of outcomes are studied. The importance of a comparative approach is highlighted by the fact that where markers have been studied in multiple cohorts, very few examples of specificity are seen. For example, late attainment of motor milestones is related to later diagnosis of schizophrenia (Sørensen, Mortensen, & Schiffman, 2010), ASD (Landa & Garrett-Mayer, 2006), and ADHD (Gurevitz et al., 2014) in addition to general psychopathology (Sørensen et al., 2010). Of course, there may be multiple distinct neurocognitive mechanisms that underlie delays in motor milestones, and paths in each disorder may thus be distinct. However, more detailed investigation of the nature of motor delays in each disorder is required to resolve this question. Further, there is a range of evidence that there is an *increased* rate of growth of head circumference in the first year of life in early autism (e.g. Hazlett et al., 2012; Webb et al., 2007). However, Rommelse, Peters, & Oosterling (2011) compared early head circumference, height and weight over nine time-points between birth and 18 months in 129 children with ASD and 59 children with non-ASD psychiatric disorders. No significant differences between groups were observed, casting doubt on the specificity of changes in head circumference to ASD.

Broadening investigations to studies of more than one outcome group also implies a shift away from studying earlier behavioral manifestations of the core symptoms of a particular condition. For example, many studies of early autism have focused on the early emergence of social and communication behaviors. Knowing when early clinical symptoms emerge is important, because it can help with early identification of children at risk. However, to identify causal paths to symptomatology we need to move beyond behaviors with face validity to clinical diagnoses. For example, processing speed, attention, and visual recognition memory all contribute to cognitive and language development (e.g. Rose et al., 2009). Investigating such core learning mechanisms in relation to a range of outcome diagnoses may provide key information about the mechanisms that lead to the emergence of behavioral symptoms.

Investigations that solely focus on earlier manifestations of *behavioral* symptoms of a disorder are unlikely to provide information that helps us reformulate diagnostic categories. Rather than starting with the clinical disorder and moving back in development to find early markers, an important alternative strategy is to start with neurocognitive domains defined by patterns of gene expression, networks of brain regions and factor analyses of performance on a range of tasks in infancy. The integrity of these neurocognitive domains can then be examined in relation to dimensional assessments of a broad range of different outcomes. Such an approach will also allow empirical testing of how predictors of dimensional variation relate to predictors of clinical diagnosis of associated disorders. This may vary by disorder; Coghill & Sonuga-Barke (2012) recently discussed a range of evidence that ADHD appears to mark the extreme end of typical variation in attention skills, whilst ASD appears to reflect a qualitatively different category. One may thus predict that a particular marker should relate to both quantitative variation in attention skills and to ADHD diagnosis; that this would not necessarily be the case for quantitative variation in social-communication skills and ASD diagnosis. Testing how causal paths map on to both dimensional measures of symptoms and our current diagnostic categories is a key empirical question, and such data could ultimately be key to reformulating our conceptualization of diagnostic categories in psychopathology.

## Markers Should be Studied in More Than One Risk Group

Comparing the relation between early neurocognitive markers and later psychopathology across different risk groups will provide important information about models of symptom emergence. For example, Elsabbagh & Johnson (2010) describe several ways in which early markers could contribute to later emergence of autism symptoms in high-risk infants (see Figure 9.1). There could be a one-to-one relation between risk markers and later psychopathology, such that the presence of any one of a number of risk factors leads to the disorder (a); conversely, development of psychopathology may require the presence of multiple risk factors that interact additively (b); or multiple early risk factors could compound each other over developmental time to produce the clinical phenotype (c). Examining multiple risk groups can provide information to help evaluate such models. If a risk factor has a one to one relation with a disorder,

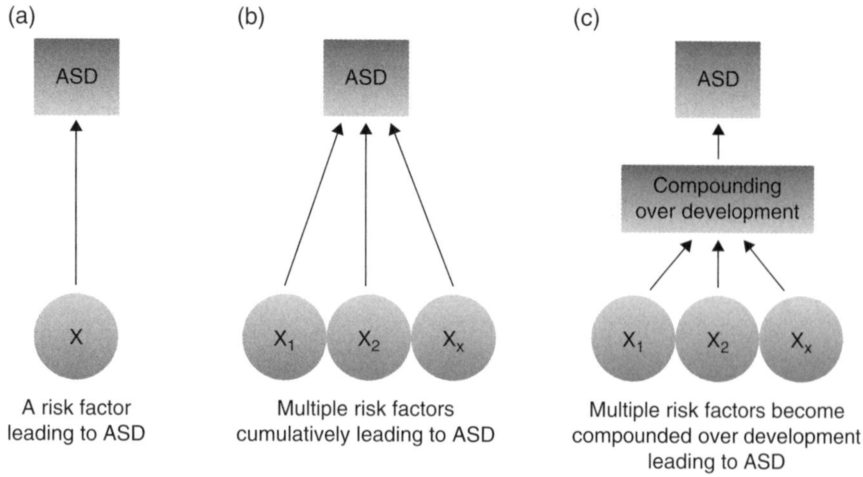


**Figure 9.1** Different models for how single or multiple genetic and/or environmental risk factors in infancy lead to ASD behavioral outcomes in childhood. In model (c), risk factors predict outcomes through dynamic changes over the course of development. Alternatively, the developmental process might buffer initial vulnerability, canalizing the impact of risk. © Elsabbagh & Johnson (2010).

the presence of that risk factor should always be associated with diagnosis across risk groups. However, if it is necessary for a particular set of risk factors to be present together, single risk factors may or may not associate with psychopathology in different populations based on the likelihood that other necessary risk factors are present (Rommelse et al., 2010).

## Implications for Screening Should be Carefully Considered

Identifying neurocognitive markers of developmental psychopathology has the potential to help us identify children at risk earlier in development, such that earlier treatment can be provided. This latter goal requires markers that are relatively sensitive and specific to later psychopathology, and this poses a significant challenge to the field. Many markers that are present at a population level do not appear to be strongly predictive of current diagnostic categories in individual cases. For example, groups of infants later diagnosed with schizophrenia show later attainment of motor milestones than infants with later neurotypical outcomes (Sørensen et al., 2010). However, on an individual level only 21 % of the schizophrenia outcome group showed significant developmental delays in motor milestones (more than 1 SD), and significant delays were present in 18 % of adults with other psychiatric diagnoses and 14% of the adults who did not develop psychopathology. In the case of ASD, failure to respond to own name is one of the most consistently documented early signs and thus is a good candidate for a screening marker. Nadig and colleagues examined the sensitivity and specificity of this marker at 12 months in a group of infants at high familial risk for ASD (Nadig et al., 2007). Specificity was 0.89 for any ASD, and 0.94 for any developmental delay, suggesting that infants who failed to respond at 12 months were likely to have developmental difficulties. However, sensitivity was only 0.5 for ASD and

0.39 for any development delay, indicating that many children with later difficulties did not show deficits in this domain. Composite measures that examine performance across multiple markers perform better; for example, a broad behavioral assessment that included measures of play, requesting, directing attention and motor imitation in 12 to 23-month-old infants with older siblings with autism showed sensitivity of 0.95 and a specificity of 0.73 (Stone, McMahon, & Henderson, 2008).

One challenge of evaluating the utility of markers for screening is that if our diagnostic categories based on behavioral symptoms represent groupings of heterogeneous causal mechanisms, we would not expect early markers to map on well to later outcomes. Further, infant treatments may be better targeted to those causal mechanisms than to the behavioral profile associated with the clinically defined disorder. Studying particular neurocognitive systems may reveal markers that can be used to design treatments targeted to particular causal paths. For example, joint attention skills are associated with later language development (e.g. Sigman et al., 1999), and joint attention is an early-emerging symptom for some children with autism (e.g. Charman et al., 2003). Based on this literature, Kasari and colleagues thus devised an intervention approach that targeted joint attention skills for children with ASD; this intervention had positive effects on long-term language development (Kasari, Paparella, & Freeman, 2008). Identifying developmental precursors to variation in core cognitive and behavioral domains in later childhood is critical to devising better intervention programs, and identifying children who may benefit from that intervention.

## Taking Development Seriously

The majority of early neurocognitive markers have been studied at a single age, or analyzed with a cross-sectional approach. However, it may be the *change* in neurocognitive skill that is particularly associated with developmental psychopathology. For example, Elsabbagh and colleagues (2013) found that infants who later developed autism did not show the typical decrease in the cost of attention disengagement between 6 and 12 months; rather, infants who developed ASD showed an *increase* in disengagement difficulty. Further, Landa and colleagues (2012)used latent class analysis to show that a slowing of social communication growth over the first two years is particularly characteristic of high-risk infants with an autism outcome. Understanding developmental patterns of neurocognitive atypicality is critical to establishing the mechanisms that underlie symptom emergence. For example, atypicalities that emerge over developmental time and that affect visual areas before frontal areas of the brain may suggest disruptions to the typical progression of synaptic pruning (Thomas, Knowland, & Karmiloff-Smith, 2011). Further, children who show early expression of risk factors but later develop typically may allow the identification of protective factors that contribute to canalization of brain development down a typical path (Elsabbagh & Johnson, 2010; see Figure 9.2). In addition, examining the additive versus multiplicative nature of early risk markers (see Figure 9.1, (b) vs. (c)) requires longitudinal data. Testing such models requires a greater focus on studying neurocognitive markers at multiple time-points, and using more complex statistical approaches to understand how patterns of change relate to later diagnosis of psychopathology (e.g. Bedford et al., in press).

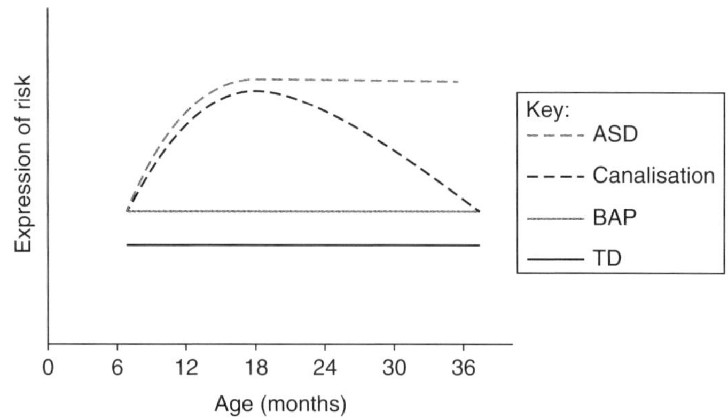


**Figure 9.2** Hypothetical trajectories for expression of risk in infant siblings at both neural and behavioral levels. The ASD trajectory is characterized by a high-dose of mediating risk factors, the impact of which becomes compounded and amplified over time. The BAP characterizes infants with a low-dose of risk factors leading to subclinical expression of the condition. Canalization involves similar initial expression of risk but eventual restoration of the typical developmental trajectory. © Elsabbagh & Johnson (2010).

## Risk Factors, Protective Factors and Differential Susceptibility

A statistical association between an infant behavior and later psychopathology does not distinguish between protective factors, risk factors and markers of differential susceptibility. Protective factors are those that enable relatively typical development in the context of other risk factors for psychopathology. For example, Johnson (2012)suggests that executive functioning may represent a protective factor for disorders such as ASD and ADHD, because the prefrontal cortex may have a critical role in compensatory reorganization of other compromised brain regions. It can be difficult to distinguish risk factors from protective factors in traditional single-diagnosis designs, because both manifest as poorer performance on a measure in the clinical group. One important step is to test infants at risk for a range of clinical disorders, since risk factors may be more likely to differ by disorder than protective factors. A second strategy is to examine performance in infants with risk factors for psychopathology but who have an outcome of typical development. Better performance on a marker in these infants relative to those with no risk factors would be consistent with a protective factor. To the extent that there are common protective factors across different developmental disorders, it may be that generic interventions designed to boost these natural mechanisms of adaptation will be an effective route for designing early treatment.

Some neurocognitive markers that are associated with later diagnosis may function as risk factors or protective factors, depending on the child's wider environment. These markers likely reflect differential sensitivity to environmental perturbation (Belsky & Pluess, 2009; Boyce & Ellis, 2005). Children with such markers may do very well in highly supportive environments, but particularly badly in more challenging environments. Negativity is one early characteristic that has been characterized in this fashion. For example, Poehlmann and colleagues (2011)showed that 9-month-old preterm infants with high negativity had more externalizing problems at age 3 years than lower-negative infants if they experienced more critical parenting, but *fewer* externalizing problems than lower-negative infants if they experienced positive parenting. High (but not low) distress in infancy was also associated with parenting-related variation in cognitive skills at age 3. Identifying markers of differential susceptibility requires studying the interaction between the marker and environmental variation, and observing the characteristic U-shaped curve between environment and outcome in children with the marker. Identifying markers of differential susceptibility also has clinical relevance, because these markers may indicate which children will likely benefit most from environmentally-focused interventions.

## Summary

Prospective studies of infants at risk for developmental psychopathology has revealed a range of potential risk factors emerging in the first years of life. The current review has identified several key themes for future work. First, potential markers should be examined in relation to more than one aspect of later psychopathology within the same cohort. Using multiple methods and measures to assess the integrity of neurocognitive systems that could form developmental pathways to a range of psychopathologies is an important strategy. Second, potential markers should be studied in more than one risk group, in order to determine the generality of particular causal paths to symptom emergence. Third, since one important goal is clinical utility, carefully considering potential for screening is important. Fourth, determining whether particular markers can be characterized as risk factors, protective factors, or markers of differential susceptibility is critical from both theoretical and clinical perspectives.

## Acknowledgements

This work was supported by MRC Programme Grant Nr. G0701484; the BASIS funding consortium led by Autistica, and by the Innovative Medicines Initiative Joint Undertaking under grant agreement no. 115300, resources of which are composed of financial contribution from the European Union's Seventh Framework Programme (FP7/2007–2013) and EFPIA companies' in-kind contribution.

## References

Allely, C. S., Purves, D., McConnachie, A., & Marwick, H. (2013). Parent–infant vocalisations at 12 months predict psychopathology at 7 years. *Research in Developmental Disabilities*, *33*, 2292–2300.

Auerbach, J. G., Atzaba-Poria, N., Berger, A., & Landau, R. (2004). Emerging developmental pathways to ADHD: Possible path markers in early infancy. *Neural plasticity*, *11*, 29–42.

Auerbach, J. G., Faroy, M., & Ebstein, R. (2001). The Association of the dopamine D4 receptor gene (DRD4) and the serotonin transporter promoter gene (5-HTTLPR) with temperament in 12-month-old infants. *Journal of Child Psychology and Psychiatry*, *42*, 777–783.

Baird, G., Simonoff, E., Pickles, A., Chandler, S., & Loucas, T. (2006). Prevalence of disorders of the autism spectrum in a population cohort of children in South Thames: The Special Needs and Autism Project (SNAP). *The Lancet*, *368*, 210–215.

Bedford, R., Elsabbagh, M., Gliga, T., Pickles, A., Senju, A., Charman, T., et al. (2012). Precursors to social and communication difficulties in infants at-risk for autism: Gaze following and attentional engagement. *Journal of Autism and Developmental Disorders*, *42*, 2208–2218.

Belsky, J., & Pluess, M. (2009). Beyond diathesis stress: Differential susceptibility to environmental influences. *Psychological Bulletin*, *135*, 885–908.

Benasich, A. A., Choudhury, N., & Friedman, J. T. (2006). The infant as a prelinguistic model for language learning impairments: Predicting from event-related potentials to behavior. *Neuropsychologia*, *44*, 396–411.

Benasich, A. A., Gou, Z., Choudhury, N., & Harris, K. D. (2008). Early cognitive and language skills are linked to resting frontal gamma power across the first 3 years. *Behavioural Brain Research*, *195*, 215–222.

Benasich, A. A., Thomas, J. J., & Choudhury, N. (2002). The importance of rapid auditory processing abilities to early language development: Evidence from converging methodologies. *Developmental Psychobiology*, *40*, 278–292.

Bolton, P. F., Golding, J., Emond, A., & Steer, C. D. (2012). Autism Spectrum Disorder and autistic traits in the Avon Longitudinal Study of Parents and Children: Precursors and early signs. *Journal of the American Academy of Child & Adolescent Psychiatry*, *51*(3), 249–260.e25.

Boyce, W. T., & Ellis, B. J. (2005). Biological sensitivity to context: I. An evolutionary–developmental theory of the origins and functions of stress reactivity. *Development and Psychopathology*, *44*, 293–300.

Charman, T., Baron-Cohen, S., Swettenham, J., Baird, G., Drew, A., & Cox, A. (2003). Predicting language outcome in infants with autism and pervasive developmental disorder. *International Journal of Language & Communication Disorders*, *38*(3), 265–285.

Clarke, M. C., Tanskanen, A., & Huttunen, M. (2011). Increased risk of schizophrenia from additive interaction between infant motor developmental delay and obstetric complications: evidence from a population-based longitudinal study. *American Journal of Psychiatry*, *168*, 1295–1302.

Coghill, D., & Barke, E. S. (2012). Annual Research Review: Categories versus dimensions in the classification and conceptualisation of child and adolescent mental disorders–implications of recent empirical study. *Journal of Child Psychology and Psychiatry*. doi: 10.1111/j.1469-7610.2011.02511.x

Ellis, E. M., & Thal, D. J. (2008). Early language delay and risk for language impairment. *Perspectives on Language Learning and Education*, *15*, 93–100.

Elsabbagh, M., & Johnson, M. H. (2010). Getting answers from babies about autism. *Trends in Cognitive Sciences*, 81–87.

Elsabbagh, M., Fernandes, J., Webb, S. J., Dawson, G., Charman, T., Johnson, M. H., & British Autism Study of Infant Siblings Team. (2013). Disengagement of visual attention in infancy is associated with emerging autism in toddlerhood. *Biological Psychiatry*, *74*(3), 189–194.

Elsabbagh, M., Gliga, T., Pickles, A., & Hudry, K. (2012a). The development of face orienting mechanisms in infants at-risk for autism. *Behavioural Brain Research*, *251*, 147–154.

Elsabbagh, M., Holmboe, K., Gliga, T., Mercure, E., Hudry, K., Charman, T., et al. (2011). Chapter 11: Social and attention factors during infancy and the later emergence of autism characteristics. In O. Braddick, J. Atkinson, J., & G. M. Innocenti (Eds.), *Gene expression to neurobiology and behavior: Human Brain development and developmental disorders* (Vol. *189*, pp. 195–207). Amsterdam: Elsevier BV.

Elsabbagh, M., Mercure, E., Hudry, K., Chandler, S., Pasco, … & Basis Team (2012b). Infant neural sensitivity to dynamic eye gaze is associated with later emerging autism. *Current Biology*, 1–5.

Evans, G. W., & Kantrowitz, E. (2002). Socioeconomic status and health: the potential role of environmental risk exposure. *Annual Review of Public Health*, *23*, 303–331.

Fagan, J. F., Singer, L. T., Montie, J. E., & Shepherd, P. A. (1986). Selective screening device for the early detection of normal or delayed cognitive development in infants at risk for later mental retardation. *Pediatrics, 78*, 1021–1026.

Gilmore, J. H. (2010). Understanding what causes schizophrenia: a developmental perspective. *American Journal of Psychiatry, 167*, 8–10.

Gizer, I. R., Ficks, C., & Waldman, I. D. (2009). Candidate gene studies of ADHD: a meta-analytic review. *Human genetics, 128*, 51–90.

Gurevitz, M., Geva, R., Varon, M., & Leitner, Y. (2014). Early markers in infants and toddlers for development of ADHD. *Journal of Attention Disorders, 18*(1), 14–22. doi: 10.1177/1087054712447858

Guttorm, T. K., Leppänen, P., Poikkeus, A. M., & Eklund, K. M. (2005). Brain event-related potentials (ERPs) measured at birth predict later language development in children with and without familial risk for dyslexia. *Cortex, 41*, 291–303.

Guzzetta, A., Mazzotti, S., Tinelli, F., & Bancale, A. (2006). Early assessment of visual information processing and neurological outcome in preterm infants. *Neuropediatrics, 37*, 278–285.

Hazlett, H. C., Gu, H., McKinstry, R. C., Shaw, D. W. W., Botteron, K. N., Dager, S. R., et al. (2012). Brain Volume Findings in 6-month-old infants at high familial risk for autism. *American Journal of Psychiatry, 169*(6), 601–608.

Henriksson, K. M., & McNeil, T. F. (2004). Health and development in the first 4 years of life in offspring of women with schizophrenia and affective psychoses: Well-Baby Clinic information. *Schizophrenia Research, 70*, 39–48.

Holmboe, K., Nemoda, Z., Fearon, R. M. P., Csibra, G., Sasvari-Szekely, M., & Johnson, M. H. (2010). Polymorphisms in dopamine system genes are associated with individual differences in attention in infancy. *Developmental Psychology, 46*(2), 404–416.

Holmboe, K., Pasco Fearon, R. M., Csibra, G., Tucker, L. A., & Johnson, M. H. (2008). Freeze-Frame: A new infant inhibition task and its relation to frontal cortex tasks during infancy and early childhood. *Journal of Experimental Child Psychology, 100*(2), 89–114.

Hudry, K., Chandler, S., Bedford, R., Pasco, G., Gliga, T. ... & Charman, T. (2014). Early language profiles in infants at high-risk for Autism Spectrum Disorders. *Journal of Autism and Developmental Disorders, 44*(1), 154–167.

Johnson, J. G., Cohen, P., Dohrenwend, B. P., Link, B. G., & Brook, J. S. (1999). A longitudinal investigation of social causation and social selection processes involved in the association between socioeconomic status and psychiatric disorders. *Journal of Abnormal Psychology, 108*(3), 490–499.

Johnson, M. H. (2012). Executive function and developmental disorders: the flip side of the coin. *Trends in Cognitive Sciences, 16*(9), 454–457.

Johnson, S., Hollis, C., Kochhar, P., & Hennessy, E. (2010). Psychiatric disorders in extremely preterm children: longitudinal finding at age 11 years in the EPICure study. *Journal of the American Academy of Child and Adolescent Psychiatry, 49*, 453–463.

Karmel, B. Z., Gardner, J. M., Meade, L. S., & Cohen, I. L. (2010). Early medical and behavioral characteristics of NICU infants later classified with ASD. *Pediatrics, 126*, 454–467.

Kasari, C., Paparella, T., & Freeman, S. (2008). Language outcome in autism: randomized comparison of joint attention and play interventions. *Journal of Consulting and Clinical Psychology, 73*,125–137.

Kochanska, G., Murray, K. T., & Harlan, E. T. (2000). Effortful control in early childhood: continuity and change, antecedents, and implications for social development. *Developmental Psychology, 36*, 220–223.

Kuhl, P. K., Conboy, B. T., & Padden, D. (2005). Early speech perception and later language development: Implications for the" Critical Period." *Language Learning and Development, 1*, 237–264.

Landa, R. J., & Holman, K. C. (2007). Social and communication development in toddlers with early and later diagnosis of autism spectrum disorders. *Archives of general Psychiatry*, *64*, 853–864.

Landa, R., & Garrett-Mayer, E. (2006). Development in infants with autism spectrum disorders: a prospective study. *Journal of Child Psychology and Psychiatry*, *47*(6), 629–638.

Landa, R. J., Gross, A. L., & Stuart, E. A. (2012). Latent class analysis of early developmental trajectory in baby siblings of children with autism. *Journal of Child Psychology and Psychiatry*, *53*, 986–996.

Lawson, K. R., & Ruff, H. A. (2004a). Early attention and negative emotionality predict later cognitive and behavioural function. *International Journal of Behavioral Development*, *28*, 157–165.

Lawson, K. R., & Ruff, H. A. (2004b). Early focused attention predicts outcome for children born prematurely. *Journal of Developmental & Behavioral Pediatrics*, *25*, 399.

Macari, S. L., Campbell, D., Gengoux, G. W., Saulnier, C. A., Klin, A. J., & Chawarska, K. (2012). Predicting Developmental status from 12 to 24 months in infants at risk for Autism Spectrum Disorder: A Preliminary report. *Journal of Autism and Developmental Disorders*, *42*(12), 2636–2647.

Merikangas, K. R., He, J. P., Brody, D., & Fisher, P. W. (2010). Prevalence and treatment of mental disorders among US children in the 2001–2004 NHANES. *Pediatrics*, *125*, 75–81.

Mitchell, S., Brian, J., Zwaigenbaum, L., Roberts, W., Szatmari, P., Smith, I., & Bryson, S. (2006). Early language and communication development of infants later diagnosed with autism spectrum disorder. *Journal of Developmental & Behavioral Pediatrics*, *27*(2), S69–S78.

Molfese, D. L. (2000). Predicting dyslexia at 8 years of age using neonatal brain responses. *Brain and Language*, *72*, 238–245.

Nadig, A. S., Ozonoff, S., Young, G. S., & Rozga, A. (2007). A prospective study of response to name in infants at risk for autism. *JAMA Pediatrics*, *161*, 378–383.

Newman, R., Ratner, N. B., & Jusczyk, A. M. (2006). Infants' early ability to segment the conversational speech signal predicts later language development: A retrospective analysis. *Developmental Psychology*, *42*, 643–655.

Oller, D. K., Eilers, R. E., Neal, A. R., & Schwartz, H. K. (1999). Precursors to speech in infancy: The prediction of speech and language disorders. *Journal of Communication Disorders*, *32*, 223–225.

Ozonoff, S., Iosif, A. M., Baguio, F., Cook, I. C., Hill, … & Young, G. S. (2010). A Prospective study of the emergence of early behavioral signs of autism. *Journal of the American Academy of Child & Adolescent Psychiatry*, *49*(3), 256–266.

Ozonoff, S., Young, G. S., Carter, A., Messinger, D., Yirmiya, N., Zwaigenbaum, L., et al. (2011). Recurrence risk for Autism Spectrum Disorders: A Baby Siblings Research Consortium Study. *Pediatrics*, *128*, 488–495.

Paul, R., Fuerst, Y., Ramsay, G., Chawarska, K., & Klin, A. (2010). Out of the mouths of babes: Vocal production in infant siblings of children with ASD. *Journal of Child Psychology and Psychiatry*, *52*(5), 588–598.

Poehlmann, J., Schwichtenberg, A. J. M., Shlafer, R. J., Hahn, E., Bianchi, J.-P., & Warner, R. (2011). Emerging self-regulation in toddlers born preterm or low birth weight: Differential susceptibility to parenting? *Development and Psychopathology*, *23*(1), 177–193.

Posner, M. I., & Petersen, S. E. (1989). The attention system of the human brain. *Annual Review of Neuroscience*, *13*, 25–42.

Rommelse, N., Franke, B., Geurts, H. M., Hartman, C. A., & Buitelaar, J. K. (2010) Shared heritability of attention-deficit/hyperactivity disorder and autism spectrum disorder. *European Child and Adolescent Psychiatry*, *19*, 281–295.

Rommelse, N., Peters, C., & Oosterling, I. J. (2011). A pilot study of abnormal growth in autism spectrum disorders and other childhood psychiatric disorders. *Journal of Autism and Developmental Disorders*, *41*, 44–54.

Rose, S. A., Feldman, J. F., & Jankowski, J. J. (2005). Pathways from prematurity and infant abilities to later cognition. *Child Development, 76*, 1172–1184.

Rose, S. A., Feldman, J. F., & Jankowski, J. J. (2009). A cognitive approach to the development of early language. *Child Development, 80*, 134–150.

Rose, S. A., Feldman, J. F., & Jankowski, J. J. (2012). Implications of infant cognition for executive functions at age 11. *Psychological Science, 23*, 1345–1355.

Rozga, A., Hutman, T., Young, G. S., & Rogers, S. J. (2011). Behavioral profiles of affected and unaffected siblings of children with autism: Contribution of measures of mother–infant interaction and nonverbal communication. *Journal of Autism and Developmental Disorders, 41*, 287–301.

Sanislow, C. A., Pine, D. S., & Quinn, K. J. (2010). Developing constructs for psychopathology research: research domain criteria. *Journal of Abnormal Psychology, 119*, 631–639.

Sigman, M., Ruskin, E., Arbelle, S., Corona, R., Dissanayake, C., Espinosa, M., et al. (1999). Continuity and Change in the social competence of children with autism, Down syndrome, and developmental delays. *Monographs of the Society for Research in Child Development, 64*(1).

Slopen, N., McLaughlin, K. A., & Fox, N. A. (2012). Alterations in Neural processing and psychopathology in children raised in institutions. *JAMA Psychiatry, 69*, 1022–1030.

Stone, W. L., McMahon, C. R., & Henderson, L. M. (2008). Use of the Screening tool for autism in two-year-olds (STAT) for children under 24 months An exploratory study. *Autism, 12*, 557–573.

Sørensen, H. J., Mortensen, E. L., & Schiffman, J. (2010). Early developmental milestones and risk of schizophrenia: a 45-year follow-up of the Copenhagen Perinatal Cohort. *Schizophrenia Research, 118*, 1–3.

Talbott, M. R., Nelson, C. A., & Tager-Flusberg, H. (2013). Maternal gesture use and language development in infant siblings of children with Autism Spectrum Disorder. *Journal of Autism and Developmental Disorders.*

Thomas, M. S. C., Knowland, V. C. P., & Karmiloff-Smith, A. (2011). Mechanisms of developmental regression in autism and the broader phenotype: A neural network modeling approach. *Psychological Review, 118*(4), 637–654.

Thompson, L. A., Fagan, J. F., & Fulker, D. W. (1991). Longitudinal prediction of specific cognitive abilities from infant novelty preference. *Child Development, 62*, 530–538.

Thunström, M. (2002). Severe sleep problems in infancy associated with subsequent development of attention-deficit/hyperactivity disorder at 5.5 years of age. *Acta Paediatrica, 91*, 584–592.

Webb, S. J., Nalty, T., Munson, J., Brock, C., Abbott, R., & Dawson, G. (2007). Rate of Head circumference growth as a function of autism diagnosis and history of autistic regression. *Journal of Child Neurology, 22*(10), 1182–1190.

Young, G. S., Rogers, S. J., Hutman, T., & Rozga, A. (2011). Imitation from 12 to 24 months in autism and typical development: A longitudinal Rasch analysis. *Developmental Psychology, 47*, 1565–1578.

Zeanah, C., Egger, H., & Smyke, A. (2009). Institutional rearing and psychiatric disorders in Romanian preschool children. *American Journal of Psychiatry, 166*, 777–785.

Zwaigenbaum, L., Bryson, S., Rogers, T., Roberts, W., Brian, J., & Szatmari, P. (2005). Behavioral manifestations of autism in the first year of life. *International Journal of Developmental Neuroscience, 23*(2–3), 143–152.

Zwaigenbaum, L., Thurm, A., Stone, W., & Baranek, G. (2007). Studying the emergence of autism spectrum disorders in high-risk infants: methodological and practical issues. *Journal of Autism and Developmental Disorders, 37*, 466–480.

# 10

# Sleep and Anxiety

Alice Jones Bartoli and Alice M. Gregory

Sleep comprises a significant and important proportion of a child's life, and has been associated with many physical and mental health outcomes (e.g. Gregory & Sadeh, 2016), as well as school-based outcomes (Kronholm et al., 2015). Sleep disturbances are relatively common during infancy, childhood and adolescence (e.g. Leahy & Gradisar, 2012; Meltzer & Mindell, 2006; Simola et al., 2010) and it has been argued that a good understanding of sleep and associated difficulties is essential when considering a child presenting with emotional difficulties; up to 90% of young people referred to mental health services have at least one sleep-related problem (Alfano, Zakem, Costa, Taylor, & Weems, 2009). This chapter aims to consider the literature pertaining to sleep-related problems, and in particular considers the well-established link between sleep problems and anxiety.

## Definitions and Assessment—Some Considerations

Sleep disturbances can be conceptualized in a number of ways, and using different classification systems such as the DSM-5 (American Psychiatric Association, 2013) and the third edition of the International Classification of Sleep Disorders (American Academy of Sleep Medicine, 2014). In the ICSD-3, sleep disorders are classified into six main categories: insomnia; sleep-related breathing disorders; central disorders of hypersomnolence; circadian rhythm sleep–wake disorders; parasomnias; and sleep-related movement disorders. Different studies use quite different conceptualizations of sleep disturbances and much of the pediatric research in this field considers sleep-related problems broadly rather than looking at specific disorders.

Similarly to the variation in the definition of sleep problems, there is considerable heterogeneity in the way that anxiety is defined and described. Anxiety may be considered as part of an "internalizing" symptom list, where is it is considered in tandem with depression symptoms, or it may be considered in terms of state or trait symptoms (Seligman, Ollendick, Langley, & Baldacci, 2004). Other studies examining sleep and anxiety have used clinical definitions of anxiety, basing diagnoses on DSM criteria (American Psychiatric Association, 2013). Indeed, in the DSM-5, anxiety subtypes include, amongst others, Generalized Anxiety Disorder (GAD); Separation Anxiety

*The Wiley Handbook of Developmental Psychopathology*, First Edition. Edited by Luna C. Centifanti and David M. Williams.

Disorder (SAD); and Specific Phobias. Other studies have also considered related constructs such as anxiety sensitivity (Weiner, Elkins, Pincus, & Comer, 2015). This chapter will give an overview of anxiety symptoms in general and clinical populations, using a full range of the definitions and assessments of anxiety.

## Measurement

In addition to the myriad ways that sleep quality or sleep-related problems are defined, there are also many measurement tools that have been developed. This section aims to provide a brief overview of these assessment methods, but a more in-depth review is available elsewhere (e.g. for a discussion of pediatric sleep questionnaires, see Spruyt & Gozal, 2011). Most commonly used are self- or informant-report questionnaires. Subjective instruments include the parent-report Children's Sleep Habit Questionnaire (CSHQ; Owens, Spirito, & McGuinn, 2000); the child-report Sleep Self Report measure (Owens, Spirito, & McGuinn, 2000) and the Child Report of Sleep Patterns (Meltzer et al., 2013). These questionnaires were originally designed for use with children under 12, but an adolescent Sleep Habit Survey has also been validated (Wolfson et al., 2003). Other studies have used the sleep items from the Child Behavior Checklist (CBCL; Achenbach, 1991). Although these items are inadequate for a thorough assessment of sleep-related problems, they are likely to be useful in indicating disordered sleep in clinical cases where sleep-related problems are not being specifically examined (for a comparison of the CBCL sleep items with data from sleep diaries, actigraphy and polysomnography, see Gregory et al., 2011; see also Becker, Ramsey, & Byars, 2015). Some studies have used just two items "Do you have trouble sleeping?" and "Do you have trouble waking up in the morning?" (Alfano, Pina, Zerr, & Villalta, 2010) or a single-item method, "Does your child have sleep problems?" (Touchette et al., 2012). These methods are useful for large research samples, or for collecting information cheaply and quickly. However, it is important to consider bias that might be introduced by the respondent. Some studies report that parents underestimate child sleep problems, while some work with clinical samples report to the contrary, that parents report a greater amount of sleep-related problems than the child (Owens, Spirito, McGuinn, & Nobile, 2000; Storch et al., 2008). Sleep diaries such as 'The Consensus Sleep Diary' (Carney et al., 2012) are considered particularly useful. Sleep diaries typically ask responders to report on their sleep timings, wakings and sleep quality. This method of reporting has been demonstrated to have good concurrent validity, and has some associations with objective measures of sleep, including actigraphy (Werner, Molinari, Guyer, & Jenni, 2008). Objective methods of assessing sleep include actigraphy (a small computerized device, usually worn as a watch, that records body movement in order to track sleep latency, duration and wakings). Other objective methods include polysomnography which includes electroencephalography (EEG) to measure brain activity; electrooculography (to measure eye movements); electromyography (a measure of muscle activity) and electrocardiography (ECG; to track heart rhythm). Assessment using these tools can be costly and time-consuming and, some argue, lack ecological validity when conducted in the laboratory as individuals must attempt to sleep in unfamiliar surroundings, for example. It is possible to use polysomnography in the home, but this is done less frequently. Recently, the Children's Sleep Habit Questionnaire has been validated against other methods of assessment and the researchers found little relationship between the CSHQ and measures of polysomnography and actigraphy. These results suggest that while the CSHQ may be useful as a broad screening tool, it is important to consider that while actigraphy and self-report measures both have utility as clinical and research tools, they measure slightly different sleep-related outcomes, and so using multiple sources of information may be a gold standard to aim for (Markovich, Gendron, & Corkum, 2014).

### Normative Sleep

There is great variability in sleep patterns across childhood and adolescence. Total sleep duration declines during childhood. For example, one paper suggested that on average children might sleep for 13 hours at six months (with the range comprising 9.5 to almost 17 hours sleep) to around nine hours at 11 years (Blair et al., 2012), with most children of that age getting between 8.5 and 11 hours sleep per night. One of the key variables predicting shorter sleeping duration is the time that children go to bed (Nixon et al., 2008). During later childhood, most children attend school, so their wake-up hours are, to a large extent, dictated by school hours. There are campaigns to change school start times to allow students to get more sleep, including the "Zzz's to A's" Act proposed by US Representative Zoe Lofgren, of California (2014). In Blair and colleagues' large population study in the UK, 95% of 11-year-olds had a regular bedtime between approximately 8 p.m. and 11:30 p.m. Sleep duration has also been reported to be declining as a whole across childhood and adolescence (Matricciani, Olds, & Petkov, 2012). One potential factor in later bedtimes may be "screen time," that is, use of television, computers, tablets, mobile phones, and consoles. Hale and Guan (2015) report that use of technology is robustly associated with shorter sleep duration and later bedtimes, but note that it is not currently possible to ascertain a causal relationship between screen time and sleep quality, or the mechanisms by which this association occurs.

### Prevalence

Sleep disturbances are fairly common— although the exact prevalence depends on the precise phenotype under investigation, the age of the child and the method of assessment. Generally, it has been proposed that during the first three years of life, 10–40% of parents report sleep problems, including night-waking, difficulty falling asleep, nightmares and restless sleep (Byars, Yolton, Rausch, Lanphear, & Beebe, 2012; Mindell et al., 2006). During childhood, up to 25–45% of children and adolescents are reported to experience problems with sleep for at least brief periods (Leahy & Gradisar, 2012; Meltzer & Mindell, 2006; Simola et al., 2010). In adolescence, one study found that 54% of Swiss teenagers endorsed a wish for "more sleep" than they were currently getting (Strauch & Meier, 1988).

## Importance of Healthy Sleep

Given that we spend a significant proportion of our lives sleeping, it appears that it serves an important functional purpose. Sleep has been hypothesized to be restorative for brain metabolism (Xie et al., 2013) and to play a role in memory consolidation and learning (Ashworth, Hill, Karmiloff-Smith, & Dimitriou, 2014; Molfese et al., 2013). It is also hypothesized that sleep plays an important role in brain maturation, particularly during childhood (Marks, Shaffery, Oksenberg, Speciale, & Roffwarg, 1995). Animal work has served to demonstrate the importance of sleep on neuronal plasticity (Abel, Havekes, Saletin, & Walker, 2013; Frank, Jha, & Coleman, 2006), and neuropsychological studies have demonstrated a link between sleep and academic and cognitive functioning in children and adolescents (Astill, Van der Heijden, Van IJzendoorn, & Van Someren, 2012; Beebe, 2011; Kronholm et al., 2015; O'Brien, 2009; Wolfson & Carskadon, 1998). Restriction of sleep by just one hour in children was reported to be associated with different brain activity during three different neurocognitive tasks performed during ERP (Molfese et al., 2013). The marked decrease in brain processing was suggested to be related to the sleep restriction and was particularly noticeable on tasks with high processing demands. Good-quality infant sleep has also been associated with more favorable language learning outcomes (Dionne et al., 2011). Sleep quality is also associated with emotional and behavioral outcomes (see Gregory & Sadeh, 2016). Nap-deprived toddlers showed poorer and less mature self-regulation skills in the face of a challenging task (Miller, Seifer, Crossin, & Lebourgeois, 2015), poorer emotion regulation and increased negative mood was also reported amongst adolescents who were sleep-deprived under experimental conditions during one week (Baum et al., 2014). These studies utilizing short durations of sleep deprivation demonstrate the importance of healthy sleep for optimal emotional functioning. Poor sleep has also been associated with poorer behavioral outcomes, both concurrently and longitudinally (Gregory, Van der Ende, Willis, & Verhulst, 2008; Shanahan, Copeland, Angold, Bondy, & Costello, 2014; Smedje, Broman, & Hetta, 2001).

Sleep disturbances not only impact the child, but also have the potential to affect the well-being of the family (Eckerberg, 2004; Lam, Hiscock, & Wake, 2003). Prolonged disrupted sleep for parents has not been studied widely in the general population, but has in groups where disrupted sleep is more common (e.g. children with neurodevelopmental difficulties and physical health conditions, Goldman, Bichell, Surdyka, & Malow, 2012; Meltzer & Montgomery-Downs, 2011; Meltzer & Moore, 2007). Sleep disturbances in children, adolescents, and young adults with severe psychomotor impairments has been reported to correlate strongly with parental sleep disturbances, parental impairment of physical and mental functioning, parental social functioning, and parental working ability (Tietze, Zernikow, Michel, & Blankenburg, 2014). Some treatment options for sleep problems in children with neurodevelopmental disorders have been reported to yield important effects for the parents, but others, including use of weighted blankets and melatonin appear to have had more mixed sleep-related outcomes, and, in the case of melatonin, come with some warnings about use (Gringras et al., 2012, 2014; Johnson et al., 2013; Kennaway, 2015; Tilford et al., 2015).

## Sleep and Anxiety

Links between sleep and emotional difficulties have been well established (e.g. for a recent review of the association between sleep and anxiety, see Willis and Gregory, 2015). Until relatively recently, research had most often combined depression and anxiety when considering the link between emotional difficulties and sleep, and yielded clear associations. For example, poor sleep quality and anxiety and depression symptoms have been reported to be related at 6 and 11 years, as well as in a second study sampling children aged 4–15 (Gregory & O'Connor, 2002; Johnson, Chilcoat, & Breslau, 2000). Emotional difficulties have also been associated with nightmares (Mindell & Barrett, 2002; Schredl, Fricke-Oerkermann, Mitschke, Wiater, & Lehmkuhl, 2009). In adolescents, sleep problems have also been associated with self-harm, with a dose response relationship between the severity of sleep problems and self-harm behaviors. Only some of this association was explained by depression symptoms, suggesting that it is of clinical importance to consider sleep-related problems when working with youth presenting with clinically significant internalizing behaviors (Hysing, Sivertsen, Stormark, & O'Connor, 2015).

More recent studies have sought to investigate the link between sleep and anxiety as a concept distinct from depression. Gregory and colleagues (2006) examined anxiety and eight separate parent-reported sleep-related problems for children aged eight, and reported that anxiety was only associated with bedtime resistance. However, the same group also examined self-reports of sleep and anxiety in 8–11-year-olds and reported associations between anxiety symptoms and bedtime resistance, being afraid of sleeping alone, and the dark and nightmares (Gregory & Eley, 2005; Gregory, Rijsdijk, & Eley, 2006). Alfano and colleagues (2009) examined the association between sleep and anxiety in a sample of 6–17-year-olds, and reported that anxiety was a significant predictor of sleep problems in under-12s, even after controlling for demographics and depression symptoms. For the adolescent group (13–17 years), depression symptoms accounted for the largest proportion of the variance contributing towards sleep problems. This interesting developmental shift may be explained rather simply, by a typical reduction with age in night-time (and other) fears (Muris, Merckelbach, Gadet, & Moulaert, 2000). It is sometimes considered that depression is more commonly noted to have its onset during adolescence or adulthood, while most anxiety disorders typically have a younger age of onset (Gregory et al., 2007; Kessler et al., 2005). However, there are also data to suggest that Major Depressive Disorder may precede Generalized Anxiety Disorder as much as vice versa (see Moffitt et al., 2007).

Associations between anxiety disorders and sleep-related problems have also been reported in clinic-recruited samples of children and adolescents. Chase and Pincus (2011) report on a sample of children and adolescents with a primary diagnosis of generalized anxiety disorder, separation anxiety disorder, social phobia, or obsessive-compulsive disorder, presenting for assessment at an anxiety specialty clinic. Of the 175 children sampled, 90% demonstrated at least one sleep-related problem, and 82% reported two or more. However, type of sleep problems varied by diagnostic category, where children with separation anxiety disorder reported a greater number of sleep-related problems than those without. These children were more likely to want to sleep with a light on, want to sleep with someone else at night, experience nightmares, and walk or talk in their sleep. Findings also revealed strong associations between sleep-related problems and a range of child anxiety measures, as well as a predictive relationship whereby number of anxiety disorders predicted number of sleep problems. Sleep quality has also been examined in a sample of children and adolescents with anxiety disorders by Alfano, Ginsburg, & Kingery (2007). In their sample, 88% experienced at least one sleep-related problem, and over half experienced three or more. The total number of sleep-related problems was positively associated with anxiety severity and interference in family functioning. Sleep disturbances have also been assessed using polysomnography. Forbes and colleagues (2008) examined sleep quality in a sample of children and adolescents with anxiety disorder, major depressive disorder and healthy comparison children over two consecutive nights in a sleep lab. According to objective sleep measurements, the group of children with diagnosed anxiety exhibited more wakings than the group with depression, and greater sleep latency than the group with depression or the comparison group. On subjective measures, young people with anxiety reported greater sleep latency both nights of the trial (as compared to controls and the group with major depressive disorder).

One other study exists focusing on children with diagnosed Generalized Anxiety Disorder (Alfano, Reynolds, Scott, Dahl, & Mellman, 2013). Compared to typically developing controls, children with GAD showed significantly increased sleep onset latency and reduced latency to rapid eye movement (REM) sleep compared to controls. Small differences were also reported in sleep efficiency and increased total REM sleep in children with GAD compared to controls. The precise function of REM sleep is still debated, but it appears to be important for consolidation and learning; disrupted REM sleep has been associated with impaired memory and learning for new skills (Marshall, Acheson, Risbrough, Straus, & Drummond, 2014; Varga et al., 2014).

Sleep-related problems have also been reported in a sample of children and adolescents receiving clinic treatment for Obsessive Compulsive Disorder (OCD; Storch et al., 2008)—which was classified as an anxiety disorder in DSM IV (American Psychiatric Association, 2008). Of their sample, 92% reported experiencing at least one sleep-related problem and over a quarter reported five or more. Consistent with the Alfano et al. (2007) study described above, the most common sleep-related problems included experiencing nightmares, being overtired, needing to sleep next to someone in family, and parent and child reports of having trouble sleeping.

## Longitudinal Studies of Sleep and Anxiety

Most of the studies discussed so far have used cross-sectional designs, and so little can be said about the directionality of associations between sleep and anxiety. However, the few longitudinal studies that have been carried out have reported somewhat conflicting outcomes. Gregory and O'Connor (2002) were amongst the first to report that child sleep problems (at four years of age) predicted internalizing symptoms in adolescence (13–15 years). Such an association was also found for child sleep problems and their prediction of anxiety (but not depression) disorders in adults (Gregory et al., 2005). In a different sample, similar findings were reported, with parent ratings of child sleep problems (including "sleeps less than others," "has trouble sleeping," and "is overtired") predicted self-reported internalizing symptoms in adulthood (Gregory et al., 2008). One further study reported a non-significant association between sleep problems at age 6 and internalizing symptoms at 11 years of age (Johnson et al., 2000). However, Johnson and colleagues have also reported converse directional findings, where anxiety symptoms were reported to precede sleep-related problems. One study examining insomnia, depression, and anxiety in a group of children and adolescents, reported that prior anxiety predicted current insomnia, but prior insomnia was not associated with current anxiety disorders

(Johnson, Roth, & Breslau, 2006). One further study also demonstrated that childhood sleep problems predict later Generalized Anxiety Disorder and higher rates of internalizing symptoms. It was also the case that anxiety symptoms predicted sleep-related problems (Shanahan et al., 2014). A review of the literature to date (which included studies focusing on childhood and adulthood and depression as well as anxiety) suggested a bidirectional association between sleep disturbance, anxiety and depression (Alvaro, Roberts, & Harris, 2013). It was also pointed out that certain childhood studies indicate that sleep disturbances predict anxiety/depression but not vice versa.

## Mechanisms Underpinning Sleep and Anxiety Associations

Although it is clear that further research is needed to better understand the associations between sleep and anxiety, it is worth considering some potential mechanisms that might help to explain the reported links. These mechanisms are unlikely to be independent, and are more likely to interact, but the ways in which these interactions might occur are a topic for future investigation.

### Genetic Contributions

Twin studies have been instrumental in our understanding of sleep as being influenced by genetic and environmental factors in infancy, childhood, and adolescence (for a review, see Barclay & Gregory, 2013).

Sleep problems in children appear to have a genetic component. For example, in a sample of 3-year-old twins, genetic influences accounted for 61% of variance in sleep problems, with the remaining variance due to the non-shared environment (van den Oord, Verhulst, & Boomsma, 1996). In older children (eight years old), the majority of the variance relating to generally defined dyssomnias and parasomnias was also explained by genetic influences (Gregory, 2008). In adolescence, genetic influences accounted for only almost a third of the variance related to sleep problems (Moore, Slane, Mindell, Burt, & Klump, 2011). Similarly, childhood anxiety of different types has been shown to be heritable, with estimates of a genetic contribution of around 50% reported across different anxiety diagnoses and samples (Chen, Yu, Li, & Zhang, 2015; Eley, Rijsdijk, Perrin, O'Connor, & Bolton, 2008; Gregory & Eley, 2007).

Developmental changes in the genetic and environmental contributions to sleep and anxiety comorbidity may also occur. For example, Van den Oord and colleagues (2000) report that the associations between sleep problems and emotional difficulties in a sample of 3-year-old twins was largely explained by shared environmental factors, but studies looking at samples of young adults note a substantial overlap between the genes influencing sleep problems and anxiety, with 74% of the covariance between these two difficulties being explained by genetic influences (Gregory et al., 2011). There are many explanations for differences in heritability estimates in these studies. For example, it is important to note that these studies use different measures and focus on slightly different phenotypes. Furthermore, heritability is a population statistic, and it is possible that genes become more important in explaining individual differences in older as compared to younger participants (as found with other phenotypes such as general intelligence, Bergen, Gardener & Kendler, 2007). One possible reason for this is that certain genes may be "switched on" during certain points of development.

Twin studies do not typically shed light on the precise genes involved in both sleep-related problems and anxiety, but given the associations with both sleep and anxiety, it seems sensible to postulate that genes associated with serotonin pathways may be possible candidates for further investigation (Monti, 2011; Ursin, 2002; Willis & Gregory, 2015). For further information about specific genes involved in sleep disorders see elsewhere (Parsons, 2015).

## Environmental Influences

Given that both shared and non-shared environment may also be important in the overlap between sleep-related problems and anxiety at certain stages of development, it seems sensible to consider some of the potential environment factors that might be influencing these difficulties in young people. Studies have examined family and home environment, as well as voluntary behaviors that influence sleep. Parents are likely to play a large role in the environmental contributions to sleep quality in young children, and sleep schedule has been robustly associated with sleep latency and duration. For example, in one group of 5-year-olds, those who took longer to fall asleep had a lower sleep quality, a later bedtime, a later sleep onset time, a shorter nocturnal sleep period and a longer daytime nap (Iwata, Iwata, Iemura, Iwasaki, & Matsuishi, 2012). Some studies have examined sleep hygiene which refers to practices that encourage good quality sleep and associated daytime functioning. Indeed, bedtime practices have been studied in UK preschoolers (Jones & Ball, 2014). In this study, bedtime behaviors (e.g. regular bedtime, reading at bedtime, falling asleep in bed) were associated both with each other, and with longer night-time sleep. Those children whose parents did not implement regular bedtime practices compensated for their night-time sleep deficit during the day instead. Regular bedtime practices were reported to be more common in those with high socioeconomic status compared to those with low socioeconomic status, and reasons for not practicing good bedtime practices included difficulty, inability, or inconvenience. Studies have also sought to examine the contribution of co-sleeping to sleep quality. In a study carried out in the United States, bed-sharing was one factor associated with poor sleep (Chung et al., 2014). Among 120 preschoolers, 52% shared a bed and 53% shared a room at least once per week. Poor sleep quality was correlated with the frequency of sharing a room with parents, falling asleep with the TV on, sleeping in a place that was too bright, and inversely related to sleeping alone in one's own bed. However, in a culture where bed-sharing is more typical, a study carried out with 5-year-olds in Japan reporting that co-sleeping per se was not associated with child sleep duration or quality, but rather the latency between child and parent bedtimes (Iwata, Iwata, & Matsuishi, 2013). Good sleep hygiene practices have been associated with good sleep outcomes across childhood and adolescence. A large-scale study noted that across childhood, a late bedtime was associated with longer sleep onset latency and shorter total sleep time. Children over three years of age who did not have a consistent bedtime routine also were reported to obtain less sleep. Furthermore, a television in the bedroom and regular caffeine consumption were associated with shorter total sleep time (Mindell, Meltzer, Carskadon, & Chervin, 2009).

In adolescence, environmental factors are of clear importance. During adolescence, there is a marked shift toward later bedtimes, but no potential for later waking due to constraints placed by school starting times (Carskadon, Wolfson, Acebo, Tzischinsky, & Seifer, 1998). Such constraints affect not only night-time sleep duration but also increase reports of daytime sleepiness. Adolescents' use of technology is also associated with bedtime and sleep latency, although further research is required to ascertain the directionality of these behaviors (Arora, Broglia, Thomas, & Taheri, 2014; Hale & Guan, 2015). A meta-analysis of sleep practices amongst 12–18-year-olds reported that good sleep hygiene and greater amounts of physical activity were associated with earlier bedtimes (Bartel, Gradisar, & Williamson, 2015). Potential risk factors for poor sleep in adolescents included use of tobacco, evening use of technology, light evenings, and a negative home environment.

Stress and trauma have also been demonstrated to have an adverse effect on sleep and anxiety (Charuvastra & Cloitre, 2009). A study following children and adolescence who experienced Hurricane Katrina in 2005 reported clear links between sleep disturbances, fear of sleeping alone, and post-traumatic stress symptoms (Brown, Mellman, Alfano, & Weems, 2011). In this group, sleep-related problems two years post Katrina also predicted post-traumatic stress symptoms 30 months post-event.

### Cognitive Processes

It is perhaps unsurprising that cognition might be associated with both sleep and anxiety, and may prove to be a useful pathway by which to address difficulties in both areas. The cognitive model of insomnia illustrates how cognitions regarding disturbed sleep may feed into a loop of further sleep disruption (Harvey, 2002). Work focusing on individuals with insomnia proposes that genetic and personality dimensions (e.g. serotonin genes and neuroticism) lead to disrupted sleep via increased stress-reactivity, which results in learning negative associations around sleep, further exacerbating the problem (Harvey, Gehrman, & Espie, 2014). In young people, evidence for this has been provided by Alfano et al (2009) who report that sleep problems were associated with negative cognitions including an internal locus of control for negative events, and selective attention to negative aspects of events. Sleep quality has also been associated with catastrophizing, another negative cognitive style and this link has been demonstrated in children and adolescents (Gregory, Noone, Eley, Harvey, & the STEPS team, 2010; Noone et al., 2014). Such cognitive styles are also implicated in the development of anxiety and depression (Noël, Francis, Williams-Outerbridge, & Fung, 2012), and it may be helpful to focus on these aspects of cognitive style in treatment for sleep disturbances.

## Treatment

It is clear that sleep-related problems in childhood are associated with a range of poor health, emotional, behavioral, and cognitive outcomes both concurrently and longitudinally. Prevention is considered best—and research suggests that even providing parents of infants aged 3 months with a booklet about the importance of routines and methods that can be used to settle an infant can prove effective in preventing problems (Kerr, Jowett, & Smith, 1996).

Once problems have developed, treatment programmes have had some success in ameliorating sleep-related difficulties (such as short sleep latency and duration); and some of these will be discussed here. Firstly, trials of parental education programmes have yielded promising results. One such trial carried out with preschoolers attending Head Start programs in the United States combined one session for parents with around 3 hours of learning about sleep spread over eight sessions delivered in two weeks for the preschoolers (Wilson, Miller, Bonuck, Lumeng, & Chervin, 2014). At immediate follow-up, the treatment group reported a 30-minute increase in sleep duration as well as improvements in parents' knowledge and attitudes about sleep, but these improvements were not maintained at one-month follow-up. It may be that more intensive education programmes, including reinforcement sessions for parents, may yield more consistent results. Another intervention focusing on preschoolers was carried out online (Schlarb & Brandhorst, 2012). The Mini-KISS assessment was designed to obtain information about demographic and diagnostic information (e.g. amount/duration of night waking, sleep onset latency), sleep hygiene factors (e.g. does the child watch TV in bed?), as well as parental behavior regarding sleep situation (e.g. what the parent does if a child refuses to sleep). The intervention consisted of weekly treatment sessions for the parents, which included different facets of psychoeducation and cognitive behavioral and relaxation techniques to use, as well as information about how to manage difficult situations arising at bedtime. Post-intervention follow-up suggested improvements in all areas of sleep according to both questionnaires and sleep diaries completed. Parents also reported good engagement with this intervention, and stated they would recommend it to others.

For children whose sleep-related problems are primarily related to physical issues, such as for some of those with sleep apnea, surgery may be an effective method of treatment. Surgery such as adenotonsillectomy has been shown not only to improve sleep apnea—but interestingly to additionally ameliorate depressive symptoms and problem behaviors and improve neurocognitive functioning (Kohler, 2010; Yilmaz, Sedky, & Bennett, 2013). It may be the case that this physiology-based apnea has related outcomes such as ADHD-type symptoms, which may improve after surgery (Aksu, Günel, Özgür, Toka & Başak, 2015).

For children suffering with anxiety, there is emerging evidence to suggest that treatments for anxiety also have a positive effect on sleep. One small-scale study of targeted behavioral therapy for anxiety demonstrated improvements in worry and sleep (Clementi & Alfano, 2014), while another suggested that massage increased nighttime sleep and reduced anxiety in a sample of psychiatric inpatient adolescents (Field et al., 1992). While pharmacological-based treatments have yielded positive effects on anxiety symptoms (Strawn, Welge, Wehry, Keeshin, & Rynn, 2015), most studies examining the effect of anti-anxiolytics do not also consider the pharmacological effects of medication on sleep.

In adolescents and young adults, online-based CBT programmes to address anxiety and insomnia was tested in university students (Morris et al., 2015). The anxiety-focused programme yielded both reductions in anxiety and increases in sleep quality, while the insomnia-focused programme yielded improvements in sleep quality only. Another CBT-based intervention for adolescents focused on OCD symptoms and yielded improvements for most sleep outcomes (including parasomnias, nightmares, sleep latency and too little sleep). However sleep problems also interfered with treatment outcomes, with more severe sleep difficulties related to poorer treatment outcome (Ivarsson & Skarphedinsson, 2015). It is clear that cognitive behavioral treatments for anxiety have the potential to also ameliorate sleep-related problems, but more research is needed in terms of maintenance of these improvements and how far these improvements are also shown following other types of intervention, particularly for pharmacological treatments.

Just as treatment for anxiety appears to have the potential to positively influence sleep the converse may also be true. For example, in adults, treating the symptoms of insomnia and nightmares has been associated with improved symptoms related to PTSD (Krakow et al., 2001), and improving sleep in adolescents has also been reported to have a positive outcome for symptoms of depression (Dewald-Kaufmann, Oort, & Meijer, 2014). Although these findings do not relate directly to childhood anxiety and sleep-related problems, future research should explore this possibility.

## Conclusions

It is clear from the literature that sleep disturbances and anxiety in childhood and adolescence are related. Additionally, sleep disturbances may represent a "red flag"—indicating that anxiety (as well as other difficulties) could develop over time. What is less clear is the mechanisms underlying these associations. Recently there has been a surge of interest in this area, with researchers with rich and diverse expertise converging to tackle the issue. Indeed, we are beginning to understand more about the social, genetic, cognitive, and neuropsychological (amongst others) mechanisms underlying associations. Clinically, an understanding of the links between sleep and anxiety has multiple advantages. Indeed, sleep disturbances can be a less sensitive issue to address as compared to anxiety—and dealing with the former at initial consultations can help a clinician to build a rapport with a family. There is also promise that tackling sleep problems may have pervasive effects beyond simply improving sleep and may reduce levels of anxiety. Future well-designed studies need to carefully examine this exciting possibility.

## References

Abel, T., Havekes, R., Saletin, J. M., & Walker, M. P. (2013). Sleep, plasticity and memory from molecules to whole-brain networks. *Current Biology*, *23*(17), R774–R788. doi: 10.1016/j.cub.2013.07.025

Achenbach, T. M. (1991). *Manual for the Child Behavior Checklist/4 –18 and 1991 Profile.* Burlington, Vt: University of Vermont, Department of Psychiatry.

Aksu, H., Günel, C., Özgür, B.G., Toka, A., & Başak, S. (2015). Effects of adenoidectomy/adenotonsillectomy on ADHD symptoms and behavioral problems in children. *International Journal of Pediatric Otorhinolaryngology*, *79*, 1030–1033.

Alfano, C. A., Ginsburg, G. S., & Kingery, J. N. (2007). Sleep-related problems among children and adolescents with anxiety disorders. *Journal of the American Academy of Child and Adolescent Psychiatry*, *46*(2), 224–232. doi: 10.1097/01.chi.0000242233.06011.8e

Alfano, C. A., Pina, A. A., Zerr, A. A., & Villalta, I. K. (2010). Pre-sleep arousal and sleep problems of anxiety-disordered youth. *Child Psychiatry & Human Development*, *41*(2), 156–167. doi: 10.1007/s10578-009-0158-5

Alfano, C. A., Reynolds, K., Scott, N., Dahl, R. E., & Mellman, T. A. (2013). Polysomnographic sleep patterns of non-depressed, non-medicated children with generalized anxiety disorder. *Journal of Affective Disorders*, *147*(1–3), 379–384. doi: 10.1016/j.jad.2012.08.015

Alfano, C. A., Zakem, A. H., Costa, N. M., Taylor, L. K., & Weems, C. F. (2009). Sleep problems and their relation to cognitive factors, anxiety, and depressive symptoms in children and adolescents. *Depression and Anxiety*, *26*(6), 503–512. doi: 10.1002/da.20443

Alvaro, P. K., Roberts, R. M., & Harris, J. K. (2013). A systematic review assessing bidirectionality between sleep disturbances, anxiety, and depression. *Sleep*, *36*(7), 1059–1068. doi: 10.5665/sleep.2810

American Academy of Sleep Medicine. (2014). *International classification of sleep disorders*. Darien, IL: American Academy of Sleep Medicine.

American Psychiatric Association. (2013). *Diagnostic and statistical manual of mental disorders (*5th ed.*)* (DSM-V). Arlington, VA: American Psychiatric Publishing.

Arora, T., Broglia, E., Thomas, G. N., & Taheri, S. (2014). Associations between specific technologies and adolescent sleep quantity, sleep quality, and parasomnias. *Sleep Medicine*, *15*(2), 240–247. doi: 10.1016/j.sleep.2013.08.799

Ashworth, A., Hill, C. M., Karmiloff-Smith, A., & Dimitriou, D. (2014). Sleep enhances memory consolidation in children. *Journal of Sleep Research*, *23*(3), 304–310. doi: 10.1111/jsr.12119

Astill, R. G., Van der Heijden, K. B., Van IJzendoorn, M. H., & Van Someren, E. J. W. (2012). Sleep, cognition, and behavioral problems in school-age children: A century of research meta-analyzed. *Psychological Bulletin*, *138*(6), 1109–1138. doi: 10.1037/a0028204

Barclay, N. L., & Gregory, A. M. (2013). Quantitative genetic research on sleep: a review of normal sleep, sleep disturbances and associated emotional, behavioural, and health-related difficulties. *Sleep Medicine Reviews*, *17*(1), 29–40. doi: 10.1016/j.smrv.2012.01.008

Bartel, K. A., Gradisar, M., & Williamson, P. (2015). Protective and risk factors for adolescent sleep: A meta-analytic review. *Sleep Medicine Reviews*, *21*, 72–85. doi: 10.1016/j.smrv.2014.08.002

Baum, K. T., Desai, A., Field, J., Miller, L. E., Rausch, J., & Beebe, D. W. (2014). Sleep restriction worsens mood and emotion regulation in adolescents. *Journal of Child Psychology and Psychiatry, and Allied Disciplines*, *55*(2), 180–190. doi: 10.1111/jcpp.12125

Becker, S. P., Ramsey, R. R., & Byars, K. C. (2015). Convergent validity of the Child Behavior Checklist sleep items with validated sleep measures and sleep disorder diagnoses in children and adolescents referred to a sleep disorders center. *Sleep Medicine*, *16*(1), 79–86. doi: 10.1016/j.sleep.2014.09.008

Beebe, D. W. (2011). Cognitive, Behavioral, and Functional Consequences of Inadequate Sleep in Children and Adolescents. *Pediatric Clinics of North America*, *58*(3), 649–665. doi: 10.1016/j.pcl.2011.03.002

Bergen, S.E., Gardner, C.O. & Kendler, K.S. (2007). Age-related changes in heritability of behavioral phenotypes over adolescence and young adulthood: A meta-analysis. *Twin Research and Human Genetics*, *10*, 423–433. doi:10.1375/twin.10.3.423.

Blair, P. S., Humphreys, J. S., Gringras, P., Taheri, S., Scott, N., Emond, A., … Fleming, P. J. (2012). Childhood Sleep duration and associated demographic characteristics in an English cohort. *SLEEP*. doi: 10.5665/sleep.1694

Brown, T. H., Mellman, T. A., Alfano, C. A., & Weems, C. F. (2011). Sleep fears, sleep disturbance, and PTSD symptoms in minority youth exposed to Hurricane Katrina. *Journal of Traumatic Stress*, *24*(5), 575–580. doi: 10.1002/jts.20680

Byars, K. C., Yolton, K., Rausch, J., Lanphear, B., & Beebe, D. W. (2012). Prevalence, patterns, and persistence of sleep problems in the first 3 years of life. *PEDIATRICS*, *129*(2), e276–e284. doi: 10.1542/peds.2011-0372

Carney, C. E., Buysse, D. J., Ancoli-Israel, S., Edinger, J. D., Krystal, A. D., Lichstein, K. L., & Morin, C. M. (2012). The Consensus Sleep Diary: Standardizing prospective sleep self-monitoring. *SLEEP*. doi: 10.5665/sleep.1642

Carskadon, M. A., Wolfson, A. R., Acebo, C., Tzischinsky, O., & Seifer, R. (1998). Adolescent sleep patterns, circadian timing, and sleepiness at a transition to early school days. *Sleep*, *21*(8), 871–881.

Charuvastra, A., & Cloitre, M. (2009). Safe enough to sleep: Sleep disruptions associated with trauma, posttraumatic stress, and anxiety in children and adolescents. *Child and Adolescent Psychiatric Clinics of North America*, *18*(4), 877–891. doi: 10.1016/j.chc.2009.04.002

Chase, R. M., & Pincus, D. B. (2011). Sleep-related problems in children and adolescents with anxiety disorders. *Behavioral Sleep Medicine*, *9*(4), 224–236. doi: 10.1080/15402002.2011.606768

Chen, J., Yu, J., Li, X., & Zhang, J. (2015). Genetic and environmental contributions to anxiety among Chinese children and adolescents—a multi-informant twin study. *Journal of Child Psychology and Psychiatry, and Allied Disciplines*, *56*(5), 586–594. doi: 10.1111/jcpp.12310

Chung, S., Wilson, K. E., Miller, A. L., Johnson, D., Lumeng, J. C., & Chervin, R. D. (2014). Home Sleeping conditions and sleep quality in low-income preschool children. *Sleep Medicine Research*, *5*(1), 29–32.

Clementi, M. A., & Alfano, C. A. (2014). Targeted behavioral therapy for childhood generalized anxiety disorder: A time-series analysis of changes in anxiety and sleep. *Journal of Anxiety Disorders*, *28*(2), 215–222. doi: 10.1016/j.janxdis.2013.10.006

Dewald-Kaufmann, J. F., Oort, F. J., & Meijer, A. M. (2014). The effects of sleep extension and sleep hygiene advice on sleep and depressive symptoms in adolescents: a randomized controlled trial. *Journal of Child Psychology and Psychiatry, and Allied Disciplines*, *55*(3), 273–283. doi: 10.1111/jcpp.12157

Dionne, G., Touchette, E., Forget-Dubois, N., Petit, D., Tremblay, R. E., Montplaisir, J. Y., & Boivin, M. (2011). Associations between sleep–wake consolidation and language development in early childhood: A longitudinal twin study. *SLEEP*. doi: 10.5665/sleep.1148

Eckerberg, B. (2004). Treatment of sleep problems in families with young children: effects of treatment on family well-being. *Acta Paediatrica*, *93*(1), 126–134. doi: 10.1080/08035250310007754

Eley, T. C., Rijsdijk, F. V., Perrin, S., O'Connor, T. G., & Bolton, D. (2008). A multivariate genetic analysis of specific phobia, separation anxiety and social phobia in early childhood. *Journal of Abnormal Child Psychology*, *36*(6), 839–848. doi: 10.1007/s10802-008-9216-x

Field, T., Morrow, C., Valdeon, C., Larson, S., Kuhn, C., & Schanberg, S. (1992). Massage reduces anxiety in child and adolescent psychiatric patients. *Journal of the American Academy of Child & Adolescent Psychiatry*, *31*(1), 125–131. doi: 10.1097/00004583-199201000-00019

Forbes, E. E., Bertocci, M. A., Gregory, A. M., Ryan, N. D., Axelson, D. A., Birmaher, B., & Dahl, R. E. (2008). Objective sleep in pediatric anxiety disorders and major depressive disorder. *Journal of the American Academy of Child & Adolescent Psychiatry*, *47*(2), 148–155. doi: 10.1097/chi.0b013e31815cd9bc

Frank, M. G., Jha, S. K., & Coleman, T. (2006). Blockade of postsynaptic activity in sleep inhibits developmental plasticity in visual cortex: *NeuroReport*, *17*(13), 1459–1463. doi: 10.1097/01.wnr.0000233100.05408.e4

Goldman, S. E., Bichell, T. J., Surdyka, K., & Malow, B. A. (2012). Sleep in children and adolescents with Angelman syndrome: association with parent sleep and stress. *Journal of Intellectual Disability Research*, *56*(6), 600–608. doi: 10.1111/j.1365-2788.2011.01499.x

Gregory, A. M. (2008). A Genetic decomposition of the association between parasomnias and dyssomnias in 8-year-old twins. *Archives of Pediatrics & Adolescent Medicine*, *162*(4), 299. doi: 10.1001/archpedi.162.4.299

Gregory, A. M., Buysse, D. J., Willis, T. A., Rijsdijk, F. V., Maughan, B., Rowe, R., … Eley, T. C. (2011). Associations between sleep quality and anxiety and depression symptoms in a sample of young adult twins and siblings. *Journal of Psychosomatic Research*, *71*(4), 250–255. doi: 10.1016/j.jpsychores.2011.03.011

Gregory, A. M., Caspi, A., Eley, T. C., Moffitt, T. E., O'Connor, T. G., & Poulton, R. (2005). Prospective longitudinal associations between persistent sleep problems in childhood and anxiety and depression disorders in adulthood. *Journal of Abnormal Child Psychology*, *33*(2), 157–163. doi: 10.1007/s10802-005-1824-0

Gregory, A. M., Caspi, A., Moffitt, T. E., Koenen, K., Eley, T. C., & Poulton, R. (2007). Juvenile mental health histories of adults with anxiety disorders. *The American Journal of Psychiatry*, *164*(2), 301–308. doi: 10.1176/appi.ajp.164.2.301

Gregory, A. M., & Eley, T. C. (2005). Sleep problems, anxiety and cognitive style in school-aged children. *Infant and Child Development*, *14*(5), 435–444. doi: 10.1002/icd.409

Gregory, A. M., & Eley, T. C. (2007). Genetic influences on anxiety in children: what we've learned and where we're heading. *Clinical Child and Family Psychology Review*, *10*(3), 199–212. doi: 10.1007/s10567-007-0022-8

Gregory, A. M., Noone, D. M., Eley, T. C., Harvey, A. G., & THE STEPS TEAM. (2010). Catastrophizing and symptoms of sleep disturbances in children. *Journal of Sleep Research*, *19*(1p2), 175–182. doi: 10.1111/j.1365-2869.2009.00794.x

Gregory, A. M., & O'Connor, T. G. (2002). Sleep problems in childhood: A longitudinal study of developmental change and association with behavioral problems. *Journal of the American Academy of Child & Adolescent Psychiatry*, *41*(8), 964–971. doi: 10.1097/00004583-200208000-00015

Gregory, A. M., Rijsdijk, F. V., & Eley, T. C. (2006). A twin-study of sleep difficulties in school-aged children. *Child Development*, *77*(6), 1668–1679. doi: 10.1111/j.1467-8624.2006.00966.x

Gregory, A.M. & Sadeh, A. (2016). Annual Research Review: Sleep problems in childhood psychiatric disorders – a review of the latest science. *Journal of Child Psychology and Psychiatry*, *57*(3), 296–317 . doi: 10.1111/jcpp.12469.

Gregory, A. M., Van der Ende, J., Willis, T. A., & Verhulst, F. C. (2008). Parent-reported sleep problems during development and self-reported anxiety/depression, attention problems, and aggressive behavior later in life. *Archives of Pediatrics & Adolescent Medicine*, *162*(4), 330. doi: 10.1001/archpedi.162.4.330

Gringras, P., Gamble, C., Jones, A. P., Wiggs, L., Williamson, P. R., Sutcliffe, A., ... on behalf of the MENDS Study Group. (2012). Melatonin for sleep problems in children with neurodevelopmental disorders: Randomised double masked placebo controlled trial. *BMJ*, *345*(nov05 1), e6664–e6664. doi: 10.1136/bmj.e6664

Gringras, P., Green, D., Wright, B., Rush, C., Sparrowhawk, M., Pratt, K., ... Wiggs, L. (2014). Weighted Blankets and sleep in autistic children--a randomized controlled trial. *PEDIATRICS*, *134*(2), 298–306. doi: 10.1542/peds.2013-4285

Hale, L., & Guan, S. (2015). Screen time and sleep among school-aged children and adolescents: A systematic literature review. *Sleep Medicine Reviews*, *21*, 50–58. doi: 10.1016/j.smrv.2014.07.007

Harvey, A. G. (2002). A cognitive model of insomnia. *Behaviour Research and Therapy*, *40*(8), 869–893.

Harvey, C.-J., Gehrman, P., & Espie, C. A. (2014). Who is predisposed to insomnia: A review of familial aggregation, stress-reactivity, personality and coping style. *Sleep Medicine Reviews*, *18*(3), 237–247. doi: 10.1016/j.smrv.2013.11.004

Hysing, M., Sivertsen, B., Stormark, K. M., & O'Connor, R. C. (2015). Sleep problems and self-harm in adolescence. *The British Journal of Psychiatry: The Journal of Mental Science*. doi: 10.1192/bjp.bp.114.146514

Ivarsson, T., & Skarphedinsson, G. (2015). Sleep problems and cognitive behavior therapy in pediatric obsessive-compulsive disorder have bidirectional effects. *Journal of Anxiety Disorders*, *30*, 28–33. doi: 10.1016/j.janxdis.2014.12.009

Iwata, S., Iwata, O., Iemura, A., Iwasaki, M., & Matsuishi, T. (2012). Sleep architecture in healthy 5-year-old preschool children: Associations between sleep schedule and quality variables. *Acta Paediatrica*, *101*(3), e110–e114. doi: 10.1111/j.1651-2227.2011.02515.x

Iwata, S., Iwata, O., & Matsuishi, T. (2013). Sleep patterns of Japanese preschool children and their parents: Implications for co-sleeping. *Acta Paediatrica*, *102*(6), e257–e262. doi: 10.1111/apa.12203

Johnson, C. R., Turner, K. S., Foldes, E., Brooks, M. M., Kronk, R., & Wiggs, L. (2013). Behavioral parent training to address sleep disturbances in young children with autism spectrum disorder: A pilot trial. *Sleep Medicine*, *14*(10), 995–1004. doi: 10.1016/j.sleep.2013.05.013

Johnson, E. O., Chilcoat, H. D., & Breslau, N. (2000). Trouble sleeping and anxiety/depression in childhood. *Psychiatry Research*, *94*(2), 93–102. doi: 10.1016/S0165-1781(00)00145-1

Johnson, E. O., Roth, T., & Breslau, N. (2006). The association of insomnia with anxiety disorders and depression: Exploration of the direction of risk. *Journal of Psychiatric Research*, *40*(8), 700–708. doi: 10.1016/j.jpsychires.2006.07.008

Jones, C. H. D., & Ball, H. (2014). Exploring socioeconomic differences in bedtime behaviours and sleep duration in English preschool children. *Infant and Child Development*, *23*(5), 518–531. doi: 10.1002/icd.1848

Kennaway, D.J. (2015). Paediatric use of melatonin. *European Journal of Paediatric Neurology*, *19*, 489–490. doi: 10.1016/j.ejpn.2015.02.004

Kerr, S. M., Jowett, S. A., & Smith, L. N. (1996). Preventing sleep problems in infants: A randomized controlled trial. *Journal of Advanced Nursing*, *24*(5), 938–942.

Kessler, R. C., Berglund, P., Demler, O., Jin, R., Merikangas, K. R., & Walters, E. E. (2005). Lifetime prevalence and age-of-onset distributions of DSM-IV disorders in the national comorbidity survey replication. *Archives of General Psychiatry*, *62*(6), 593. doi: 10.1001/archpsyc.62.6.593

Kohler, M. (2010). Neurocognitive performance and behavior before and after treatment for sleep-disordered breathing in children. *Nature and Science of Sleep*, *159*. doi: 10.2147/NSS.S6934

Krakow, B., Johnston, L., Melendrez, D., Hollifield, M., Warner, T. D., Chavez-Kennedy, D., & Herlan, M. J. (2001). An open-label trial of evidence-based cognitive behavior therapy for nightmares and insomnia in crime victims with PTSD. *The American Journal of Psychiatry*, *158*(12), 2043–2047.

Kronholm, E., Puusniekka, R., Jokela, J., Villberg, J., Urrila, A. S., Paunio, T., ... Tynjälä, J. (2015). Trends in self-reported sleep problems, tiredness and related school performance among Finnish adolescents from 1984 to 2011. *Journal of Sleep Research*, *24*(1), 3–10. doi: 10.1111/jsr.12258

Lam, P., Hiscock, H., & Wake, M. (2003). Outcomes of Infant sleep problems: A longitudinal study of sleep, behavior, and maternal well-being. *PEDIATRICS*, *111*(3), e203–e207. doi: 10.1542/peds.111.3.e203

Leahy, E., & Gradisar, M. (2012). Dismantling the bidirectional relationship between paediatric sleep and anxiety: Paediatric sleep and anxiety. *Clinical Psychologist*, *16*(1), 44–56. doi: 10.1111/j.1742-9552.2012.00039.x

Lofgren, Z. (2014). Zzz's to A's Act. Available at: http://media.cmgdigital.com/shared/news/documents/2014/09/22/Sleep_Bill.pdf

Markovich, A. N., Gendron, M. A., & Corkum, P. V. (2014). Validating the Children's Sleep Habits Questionnaire against polysomnography and actigraphy in school-aged children. *Frontiers in Psychiatry*, *5*, 188. doi: 10.3389/fpsyt.2014.00188

Marks, G. A., Shaffery, J. P., Oksenberg, A., Speciale, S. G., & Roffwarg, H. P. (1995). A functional role for REM sleep in brain maturation. *Behavioural Brain Research*, *69*(1–2), 1–11. doi: 10.1016/0166-4328(95)00018-O

Marshall, A. J., Acheson, D. T., Risbrough, V. B., Straus, L. D., & Drummond, S. P. A. (2014). Fear conditioning, safety learning, and sleep in humans. *The Journal of Neuroscience: The Official Journal of the Society for Neuroscience*, *34*(35), 11754–11760. doi: 10.1523/JNEUROSCI.0478-14.2014

Matricciani, L., Olds, T., & Petkov, J. (2012). In search of lost sleep: Secular trends in the sleep time of school-aged children and adolescents. *Sleep Medicine Reviews*, *16*(3), 203–211. doi: 10.1016/j.smrv.2011.03.005

Meltzer, L. J., Avis, K. T., Biggs, S., Reynolds, A. C., Crabtree, V. M., & Bevans, K. B. (2013). The Children's Report of Sleep Patterns (CRSP): A self-report measure of sleep for school-aged children. *Journal of Clinical Sleep Medicine*, *9*(3), 235–245. doi: 10.5664/jcsm.2486

Meltzer, L. J., & Mindell, J. A. (2006). Sleep and sleep disorders in children and adolescents. *The Psychiatric Clinics of North America*, *29*(4), 1059–1076; abstract x. doi: 10.1016/j.psc.2006.08.004

Meltzer, L. J., & Montgomery-Downs, H. E. (2011). Sleep in the family. *Pediatric Clinics of North America*, *58*(3), 765–774. doi: 10.1016/j.pcl.2011.03.010

Meltzer, L. J., & Moore, M. (2007). Sleep disruptions in parents of children and adolescents with chronic illnesses: Prevalence, causes, and consequences. *Journal of Pediatric Psychology*, *33*(3), 279–291. doi: 10.1093/jpepsy/jsm118

Miller, A. L., Seifer, R., Crossin, R., & Lebourgeois, M. K. (2015). Toddler's self-regulation strategies in a challenge context are nap-dependent. *Journal of Sleep Research*, *24*(3), 279–287. doi: 10.1111/jsr.12260

Mindell, J. A., & Barrett, K. M. (2002). Nightmares and anxiety in elementary-aged children: is there a relationship? *Child: Care, Health and Development*, *28*(4), 317–322. doi: 10.1046/j.1365-2214.2002.00274.x

Mindell, J. A., Kuhn, B., Lewin, D. S., Meltzer, L. J., Sadeh, A., & American Academy of Sleep Medicine. (2006). Behavioral treatment of bedtime problems and night wakings in infants and young children. *Sleep*, *29*(10), 1263–1276.

Mindell, J. A., Meltzer, L. J., Carskadon, M. A., & Chervin, R. D. (2009). Developmental aspects of sleep hygiene: Findings from the 2004 National Sleep Foundation Sleep in America Poll. *Sleep Medicine*, *10*(7), 771–779. doi: 10.1016/j.sleep.2008.07.016

Moffitt, T. E., Harrington, H.L., Caspi, A., Kim-Cohen, J., Goldberg, D., Gregory, A. M., Poulton, R. (2007). Depression and generalized anxiety disorder: cumulative and sequential comorbidity in a birth cohort followed prospectively to age 32. *Archives of General Psychiatry*, *64*, 651–660.

Molfese, D. L., Ivanenko, A., Key, A. F., Roman, A., Molfese, V. J., O'Brien, L. M., … Hudac, C. M. (2013). A one-hour sleep restriction impacts brain processing in young children across tasks: Evidence from event-related potentials. *Developmental Neuropsychology*, *38*(5), 317–336. doi: 10.1080/87565641.2013.799169

Monti, J. M. (2011). Serotonin control of sleep–wake behavior. *Sleep Medicine Reviews*, *15*(4), 269–281. doi: 10.1016/j.smrv.2010.11.003

Moore, M., Slane, J., Mindell, J. A., Burt, S. A., & Klump, K. L. (2011). Genetic and environmental influences on sleep problems: a study of preadolescent and adolescent twins. *Child: Care, Health and Development*, *37*(5), 638–641. doi: 10.1111/j.1365-2214.2011.01230.x

Morris, J., Firkins, A., Millings, A., Mohr, C., Redford, P., & Rowe, A. (2015). Internet-delivered cognitive behavior therapy for anxiety and insomnia in a higher education context. *Anxiety, Stress, & Coping*, 1–17. doi: 10.1080/10615806.2015.1058924

Muris, P., Merckelbach, H., Gadet, B., & Moulaert, V. (2000). Fears, worries, and scary dreams in 4- to 12-year-old children: Their content, developmental pattern, and origins. *Journal of Clinical Child Psychology*, *29*(1), 43–52. doi: 10.1207/S15374424jccp2901_5

Nixon, G. M., Thompson, J. M. D., Han, D. Y., Becroft, D. M., Clark, P. M., Robinson, E., … Mitchell, E. A. (2008). Short sleep duration in middle childhood: risk factors and consequences. *Sleep*, *31*(1), 71–78.

Noël, V. A., Francis, S. E., Williams-Outerbridge, K., & Fung, S. L. (2012). Catastrophizing as a predictor of depressive and anxious symptoms in children. *Cognitive Therapy and Research*, *36*(4), 311–320. doi: 10.1007/s10608-011-9370-2

Noone, D. M., Willis, T. A., Cox, J., Harkness, F., Ogilvie, J., Forbes, E., ... Gregory, A. M. (2014). Catastrophizing and poor sleep quality in early adolescent females. *Behavioral Sleep Medicine*, *12*(1), 41–52. doi: 10.1080/15402002.2013.764528

O'Brien, L. M. (2009). The neurocognitive effects of sleep disruption in children and adolescents. *Child and Adolescent Psychiatric Clinics of North America*, *18*(4), 813–823. doi: 10.1016/j.chc.2009.04.008

Owens, J. A., Spirito, A., & McGuinn, M. (2000). The Children's Sleep Habits Questionnaire (CSHQ): Psychometric properties of a survey instrument for school-aged children. *Sleep*, *23*(8), 1043–1051.

Owens, J. A., Spirito, A., McGuinn, M., & Nobile, C. (2000). Sleep habits and sleep disturbance in elementary school-aged children. *Journal of Developmental and Behavioral Pediatrics: JDBP*, *21*(1), 27–36.

Parsons, M.J. (2015). On the genetics of sleep disorders: GWAS and beyond. *Advances in Genetics and Genomics*, *5*, 293–303.

Schlarb, A., & Brandhorst. (2012). Mini-KiSS Online: an Internet-based intervention program for parents of young children with sleep problems – influence on parental behavior and children's sleep. *Nature and Science of Sleep*, 41. doi: 10.2147/NSS.S28337

Schredl, M., Fricke-Oerkermann, L., Mitschke, A., Wiater, A., & Lehmkuhl, G. (2009). Longitudinal study of nightmares in children: Stability and effect of emotional symptoms. *Child Psychiatry and Human Development*, *40*(3), 439–449. doi: 10.1007/s10578-009-0136-y

Seligman, L. D., Ollendick, T. H., Langley, A. K., & Baldacci, H. B. (2004). The utility of measures of child and adolescent anxiety: A meta-analytic review of the Revised Children's Manifest Anxiety Scale, the State–Trait Anxiety Inventory for Children, and the Child Behavior Checklist. *Journal of Clinical Child & Adolescent Psychology*, *33*(3), 557–565. doi: 10.1207/s15374424jccp3303_13

Shanahan, L., Copeland, W. E., Angold, A., Bondy, C. L., & Costello, E. J. (2014). Sleep problems predict and are predicted by Generalized Anxiety/Depression and Oppositional Defiant Disorder. *Journal of the American Academy of Child & Adolescent Psychiatry*, *53*(5), 550–558. doi: 10.1016/j.jaac.2013.12.029

Simola, P., Niskakangas, M., Liukkonen, K., Virkkula, P., Pitkäranta, A., Kirjavainen, T., & Aronen, E. T. (2010). Sleep problems and daytime tiredness in Finnish preschool-aged children – A community survey. *Child Care, Health and Development*, *36*(6), 805–811. doi: 10.1111/j.1365-2214.2010.01112.x

Smedje, H., Broman, J.-E., & Hetta, J. (2001). Associations between disturbed sleep and behavioural difficulties in 635 children aged six to eight years: A study based on parents' perceptions. *European Child & Adolescent Psychiatry*, *10*(1), 1–9. doi: 10.1007/s007870170041

Spruyt, K., & Gozal, D. (2011). Pediatric sleep questionnaires as diagnostic or epidemiological tools: A review of currently available instruments. *Sleep Medicine Reviews*, *15*(1), 19–32. doi: 10.1016/j.smrv.2010.07.005

Storch, E. A., Murphy, T. K., Lack, C. W., Geffken, G. R., Jacob, M. L., & Goodman, W. K. (2008). Sleep-related problems in pediatric obsessive-compulsive disorder. *Journal of Anxiety Disorders*, *22*(5), 877–885. doi: 10.1016/j.janxdis.2007.09.003

Strauch, I., & Meier, B. (1988). Sleep need in adolescents: A longitudinal approach. *Sleep*, *11*(4), 378–386.

Strawn, J. R., Welge, J. A., Wehry, A. M., Keeshin, B., & Rynn, M. A. (2015). Efficacy and tolerability of antidepressants in pediatric anxiety disorders: A systematic review and meta-analysis. *Depression and Anxiety*, *32*(3), 149–157. doi: 10.1002/da.22329

Tietze, A. L., Zernikow, B., Michel, E., & Blankenburg, M. (2014). Sleep disturbances in children, adolescents, and young adults with severe psychomotor impairment: impact on parental quality of life and sleep. *Developmental Medicine & Child Neurology*, *56*(12), 1187–1193. doi: 10.1111/dmcn.12530

Tilford, J. M., Payakachat, N., Kuhlthau, K. A., Pyne, J. M., Kovacs, E., Bellando, J., … Frye, R. E. (2015). Treatment for sleep problems in children with autism and caregiver spillover effects. *Journal of Autism and Developmental Disorders*. doi: 10.1007/s10803-015-2507-5

Touchette, E., Chollet, A., Galéra, C., Fombonne, E., Falissard, B., Boivin, M., & Melchior, M. (2012). Prior sleep problems predict internalising problems later in life. *Journal of Affective Disorders*, *143*(1–3), 166–171. doi: 10.1016/j.jad.2012.05.049

Ursin, R. (2002). Serotonin and sleep. *Sleep Medicine Reviews*, *6*(1), 55–67. doi: 10.1053/smrv.2001.0174

Van den Oord, E. J., Boomsma, D. I., & Verhulst, F. C. (2000). A study of genetic and environmental effects on the co-occurrence of problem behaviors in three-year-old twins. *Journal of Abnormal Psychology*, *109*(3), 360–372.

van den Oord, E. J., Verhulst, F. C., & Boomsma, D. I. (1996). A genetic study of maternal and paternal ratings of problem behaviors in 3-year-old twins. *Journal of Abnormal Psychology*, *105*(3), 349–357.

Varga, A. W., Kishi, A., Mantua, J., Lim, J., Koushyk, V., Leibert, D. P., … Ayappa, I. (2014). Apnea-induced rapid eye movement sleep disruption impairs human spatial navigational memory. *The Journal of Neuroscience*, *34*(44), 14571–14577. doi: 10.1523/JNEUROSCI.3220-14.2014

Weiner, C. L., Elkins, R., Pincus, D., & Comer, J. (2015). Anxiety sensitivity and sleep-related problems in anxious youth. *Journal of Anxiety Disorders*, *32*, 66–72. doi: 10.1016/j.janxdis.2015.03.009

Werner, H., Molinari, L., Guyer, C., & Jenni, O. G. (2008). Agreement rates between actigraphy, diary, and questionnaire for children's sleep patterns. *Archives of Pediatrics & Adolescent Medicine*, *162*(4), 350. doi: 10.1001/archpedi.162.4.350

Willis, T. A., & Gregory, A. M. (2015). Anxiety Disorders and sleep in children and adolescents. *Sleep Medicine Clinics*, *10*(2), 125–131. doi: 10.1016/j.jsmc.2015.02.002

Wilson, K. E., Miller, A. L., Bonuck, K., Lumeng, J. C., & Chervin, R. D. (2014). Evaluation of a sleep education program for low-income preschool children and their families. *SLEEP*. doi: 10.5665/sleep.3774

Wolfson, A. R., & Carskadon, M. A. (1998). Sleep schedules and daytime functioning in adolescents. *Child Development*, *69*(4), 875–887.

Wolfson, A. R., Carskadon, M. A., Acebo, C., Seifer, R., Fallone, G., Labyak, S. E., & Martin, J. L. (2003). Evidence for the validity of a sleep habits survey for adolescents. *Sleep*, *26*(2), 213–216.

Xie, L., Kang, H., Xu, Q., Chen, M. J., Liao, Y., Thiyagarajan, M., … Nedergaard, M. (2013). Sleep drives metabolite clearance from the adult brain. *Science*, *342*(6156), 373–377. doi: 10.1126/science.1241224

Yilmaz, E., Sedky, K., & Bennett, D. S. (2013). The relationship between depressive symptoms and obstructive sleep apnea in pediatric populations: A meta-analysis. *Journal of Clinical Sleep Medicine*. doi: 10.5664/jcsm.3178

# Part 3
# Genetics

# 11

# The Genetic Basis of Psychological Traits in Infancy

## *Implications for Understanding the Causes of Developmental Psychopathology*

Kostas A. Papageorgiou and Angelica Ronald

## Overview

This chapter reviews studies that have aimed to identify genes influencing psychological traits in infancy (from birth to age 12 months), and considers how this research informs us about the causes of developmental psychopathology. Specifically, this chapter systematically reviews findings from studies that associated common genetic variants with individual variation in infants' attention, temperament and behavior, and attachment disorganization. DRD4 and 5-HTTLPR genes were the most frequently studied candidate genes. Possibly the most coherent set of results relates to the L-DRD4 genotype, which is significantly associated with infant attention, temperament, and attachment style. Research in infant genetics has been strengthened by a careful focus on uniform age ranges within studies, by several longitudinal studies, and by exploration of gene–environment interactions between genes and maternal characteristics. However there is also considerable inconsistency in results in this field and possible reasons for this are discussed. The chapter outlines the main genetic methods that have been used and reviews what new genetic approaches such as polygenic risk scores could offer infant genetics. Recent findings suggest that some traits during infancy predict individual differences in developmental psychopathology in childhood. It is argued that infant genetic research has considerable potential for the identification of populations at risk for psychopathology in later life, and this remains an area open for future research.

## Introduction

Genetic research in infancy has the potential to inform us about the causes of developmental psychopathology. For example, it is possible to test whether genetic variants associated with psychopathology in later development are also associated with infant

*The Wiley Handbook of Developmental Psychopathology*, First Edition. Edited by Luna C. Centifanti and David M. Williams.

traits that may relate to later psychopathology. A recent study reported that newborns' average dwell time (average looking time at visual stimuli) was negatively associated with childhood surgency and behavioral difficulties, such as hyperactivity-inattention and peer problems in later childhood (Papageorgiou, Farroni, Johnson, Smith & Ronald, 2015). These findings show that part of the variance in behavioral problems is explained by factors already present on the first few days of life. As such, the origins of individual differences in developmental psychopathology are not likely to be wholly due to the postnatal environment; this concurs with much evidence from other research designs, such as twin studies (Plomin, DeFries, Knopic, & Neiderhiser, 2013). These early causal factors could be genetic or stem from the prenatal environment. As such, future research could investigate genetic variation that contributes to both individual differences in infant psychological phenotypes at birth and to individual differences in developmental psychopathology in childhood. The identification of genes that influence individual differences in infancy would provide clues about the mechanisms involved in early brain development (Johnson, 2011). Furthermore, knowledge about genetic risk that can be applied to infant samples has considerable potential for the identification of populations at risk of developmental psychopathology, based on genetic propensity, and thus for informing the development of early prevention and intervention approaches (Papageorgiou & Ronald, 2013).

## Methods That Have Been Used in Genetic Research in Infancy

### The Candidate Gene Association Design

Candidate gene association studies seek to identify associations between genetic markers and phenotypes using linear regression analysis. This assumes a relationship between mean value of the trait and genotype (Balding, 2006). The standard choice in genetic association studies involves exploring main effects of individual alleles on a trait of interest. Candidate gene studies are based on variants, where there is some knowledge of the functional role of the genetic variant and the variant is hypothesized to contribute to the phenotype's causal pathway (Ronald, 2011).

For psychological traits, examples of such candidate gene variants influence the neurotransmitters dopamine and serotonin. The dopamine receptor D4 (DRD4) gene has been selected as a dopamine system gene that might affect frontal cortex functioning in infancy, since it is expressed in the retina and the prefrontal cortex; its polymorphisms have been associated with several phenotypes, including an increased risk of attention deficit hyperactivity disorder (ADHD), impulsivity, lower levels of response inhibition, and sensation seeking in toddlers, when combined with poor parenting (parenting quality was assessed using a videotaped free-play procedure; the raters observed the child–parent interaction and assessed on a seven-point Likert scale, parents': (a) supportive presence (showing positive regard and emotional support); (b) respect for autonomy (unintrusive in interactions with child); (c) stimulation of cognitive development (shows directed instruction, teaching); (d) hostility (shows anger, rejection, negative regard); and (e) confidence (shows confidence in interactions with child; Holmboe et al., 2010; Sheese Voelker, Rothbart & Posner, 2007). The main focus of the majority of the studies reviewed in this chapter is the investigation of the association between dopamine-related genes and attention, temperament, attachment, and behavior.

### Genome-Wide Association Studies (GWAS)

A characteristic of candidate gene studies has been a degree of failure to replicate associations across studies (Plomin, 2013). Genome-wide association studies (GWAS) test common genetic variation across the entire human genome for association with a trait or disorder of interest (Manolio & Collins 2009). GWAS are more systematic than candidate gene studies because instead of focusing on just one genetic variant, they capture most of the common variation in the genome (both inside and outside of coding regions). The advantage of GWAS is that it is not necessary to have a priori hypotheses about which specific genetic variants are involved, which allows novel genetic variants to be identified (Plomin, 2013).

## Method

PubMed (http://www.ncbi.nlm.nih.gov/pubmed/), Google Scholar (http://scholar.google.co.uk/schhp?hl=en&tab=ws) and PsychINFO (http://www.apa.org/pubs/databases/psycinfo/index.aspx) databases were employed to conduct a systematic search on genetic studies in infancy. The last literature search was performed in July 2015. The following inclusion criteria to select studies have been used:

1 the participants' age did not exceed 12 months;
2 longitudinal studies that have aimed to identify genes that influence psychological trait phenotypes in older ages are also reviewed if they included data on infants;
3 studies had to include psychological phenotypes. Biological or physical phenotypes were not the subject of this review;
4 the review excluded research on known genetic syndromes (e.g., Williams syndrome) because these represent a different genetic model where the genes associated with the phenotype have been identified. The review focused on complex traits with largely unknown genetic etiology.

The following three sections systematically review findings from studies that associated common genetic variants with individual variation in infants' attention (seven studies), temperament and behavior (fifteen studies), and attachment disorganization (ten studies), respectively. Table 11.1 provides a quick look summary of the 32 studies. It includes the phenotypes and the genetic markers and it outlines, for each study, whether the association between the genetic marker and the phenotype was significant or non-significant based on the authors' criteria.

## Associations between Common Genetic Variants and Visual Attention

Because the dopaminergic pathways are a core factor in many aspects of attention (Sheese Voelker, Posner, & Rothbart, 2009), genes related to dopamine (e.g. DRD4) have been hypothesized to be associated with attention in infancy. In this section, the findings from seven studies that have linked attentional parameters with candidate genes in infancy are presented.

**Table 11.1** Quick Look summary of the 32 genetic studies on psychological phenotypes in infancy (presented chronologically within phenotype domain).

| *Study* | *Sample (n & age)* | *Phenotype* | *Genes* | *Association (Yes ✓ No ✗)* |
|---|---|---|---|---|
| Auerbach, J. et al., 2001a | 64 12-month-olds | Attention | DRD4 | ✓ |
| | | | 5-HTTLPR | ✗ |
| Laucht, M. et al., 2006 | 232 3-month-olds (A longitudinal study that followed participants from birth to adolescence) | Attention | DRD4 | ✓ |
| Sheese, B.E. et al., 2009 | Longitudinal study of infants at age 6–7 months (50 participants) and 18–20 months (37 participants) | Attention | COMT | ✗ |
| | | | SNAP25 | ✗ |
| | | | CHRNA4 | ✓ |
| Holmboe, K. et al., 2010 | 102 9-month-olds | Attention | DRD4 | ✗ |
| | | | DRD2 | ✗ |
| | | | DAT1 | ✓ |
| | | | COMT | ✓ |
| Leppanen, J. K. et al., 2011 | 66 7-month-olds | Attention | TPH2 | ✓ |
| Forssman, L. et al., 2013 | 139 5-and-7-month-olds | Attention | TPH2 | ✗ |
| | | | HTR1A | ✗ |
| Markant, J. et al., 2014 | 88 7-month-olds | Attention | COMT | ✓ |
| | | | CHRNA4 | ✗ |
| | | | DAT1 | ✗ |
| Ebstein, R. P. et al., 1998 | 81 2-week-old infants | Temperament | DRD4 | ✓ |
| | | | 5-HTTLPR | ✗ |
| Auerbach, J. et al., 1999 | 76 2-month-olds | Temperament | DRD4 | ✓ |
| | | | 5-HTTLPR | ✓ |
| Jorm, A. F. et al., 2000 | 660 participants, assessed for temperament from 4–8 months to 15–16 years, and for behavior problems from 3–4 years to 15–16 years | Temperament | 5-HTTLPR | ✗<br>13–14 years of age ✓ |
| Jorm, A. F. et al., 2001 | See Jorm, A. F. et al., 2000 | Temperament | DAT1 | ✗ |
| De Luca, A. et al., 2001 | 122 1 and 5-month-olds | Temperament | DRD4 | 1 month of age ✓<br>5 months of age ✗ |

| | | | | |
|---|---|---|---|---|
| Auerbach, J. G. et al., 2001 | 61 12-month-olds | Temperament | DRD4<br>5-HTTLPR | ✔<br>✔ |
| Lakatos, K. et al., 2003 | 90 12-month-olds | Temperament | DRD4<br>5-HTTLPR | ✔<br>✔ |
| Sheese, B. E. et al., 2009 | Longitudinal study of infants at age 6–7 months ($n$ = 50) and 18–20 months ($n$ = 37) | Temperament | COMT<br>SNAP25<br>CHRNA4 | ✔<br>✔<br>✔ |
| Becker, K. et al., 2010 | Longitudinal study of 384 participants at 3 months and 2, 4.5, 8, 11, and 15 years | Temperament | DRD4 | ✔ |
| Holmboe, K. et al., 2011 | 90 4- and 9-month-olds | Temperament | DRD4<br>5-HTTLPR | ✔<br>✔ |
| Pluess, M. et al., 2011 | 1136 6-month-olds | Temperament | 5-HTTLPR | ✗ |
| Zhang, M. et al., 2011 | 331 6-month-olds and their mothers | Temperament | MAOA | ✔ |
| Hill, J. et al., 2013 | 209 5-week-olds and their mothers | Temperament | MAOA | ✔ |
| Pickles, A. et al., 2013 | 193 14-month-olds and their mothers | Temperament | MAOA | ✗ |
| Markant, J. et al., 2014 | 97 7-month-olds | Temperament | COMT | ✔ |
| Lakatos, K. et al., 2000 | 90 12–13-month-olds | Attachment Disorganization | DRD4 | ✔ |
| Lakatos, K. et al., 2002 | 95 12-month-olds | Attachment Disorganization | DRD4 | ✔ |
| Lakatos, K. et al., 2003 | 90 12-month-olds | Attachment Disorganization | DRD4<br>5-HTTLPR | ✔<br>✗ |
| Bakermans-Kranenburg, M. J. & Van Ijzendoorn, M. H., 2004 | 76 same-sex 12-month-old twin pairs | Attachment Disorganization | DRD4 | ✗ |
| Gervai, J. et al., 2005 | 95 12-month-olds and their mothers (same sample as Lakatos et al., 2000, 2002, 2003) | Attachment Disorganization | DRD4 | ✔ |

(*Continued*)

**Table 11.1** (Continued)

| *Study* | *Sample (n & age)* | *Phenotype* | *Genes* | *Association (Yes ✓ No ✗)* |
|---|---|---|---|---|
| Van Ijzendoorn, M. H., & Bakermans-Kranenburg M. J., 2006 | 85 mother-infant dyads (infants were 8–11 and 15 months old when the mothers completed the questionnaire; mothers were videotaped when the infants were 10–11 months of age and interviewed when the infants were 12-months old) | Attachment Disorganization | DRD4 | ✓ |
| Gervai, J. et al., 2007 | 138 mother-infant dyads from a Hungarian sample (infants were 12 months old) and 42 mother-infant dyads from a US sample (infants were 18 months old) | Attachment Disorganization | DRD4 | ✓ |
| Spangler, G. et al., 2009 | 106 12-month-olds | Attachment Disorganization | DRD4<br>5-HTTLPR | ✗<br>✓ |
| Raby, K. L. et al., 2012 | Longitudinal study of 154 infants at age 12 and 18 months old and their mothers | Attachment | 5-HTTLPR | ✓ |
| Pappa, I. et al., 2015 (The first GWAS study in infancy.) | 657 14-month-olds (on average) | Attachment Disorganization | Genome-wide association analysis | ✗<br>No genome-wide significant associations between single SNPs and attachment disorganization were reported.<br>✓<br>Gene-based analysis provided evidence of three genes – the Histone Deacetylase 1 (HDAC1), Zinc Finger Protein 675 (ZNF675) and BSD Domain Containing 1(BSDC1) genes – to be associated with attachment disorganization |

Note. Reported significant or nonsignificant association based on authors' criteria.

## DRD4 & 5-HTTLPR and Infant Attention

A study genotyped 12-month-old infants on the dopamine receptor D4 (DRD4) and the serotonin-transporter-linked polymorphic region (5-HTTLPR) gene variants and assessed their sustained attention and information processing (Auerbach, Benjamin, Faroy, Geller, & Ebstein, 2001a). Sustained attention was measured using the laboratory observation of temperament (Goldsmith & Rothbart, 1996a, b). Information processing was measured using the Fagan test of infant intelligence that assesses infants' novelty preference (Fagan & Shepherd, 1991). A basic measure of infant information processing in infancy is the tendency of the infant to look longer at a new target (called novelty preference) than at one previously seen (Fagan, 1970); Studies of the infant's preference for novelty have shown that such processes of knowledge acquisition underlie performance on intelligence tests later in life (Fagan & Montie, 1988). The results revealed that infants with the L-DRD4 variant exhibited significantly shorter duration of looking and significantly shorter latencies to the first look away in comparison to infants without this variant. The findings suggest that having the L-DRD4 variant in infancy is indicative of less sustained attention. In addition, infants with the L-DRD4 and the s/s 5-HTTLPR variant exhibited the shortest duration of looking. Finally, infants with the L-DRD4 variant exhibited poorer information processing than infants without this variant on the Fagan test (Auerbach et al., 2001a).

A second study did not find an association between the L-DRD4 variant and proportion of looks to the distractors, as well as 9-month-old infants' ability to inhibit looks to visual distractors (assessed in the Freeze Frame task; Holmboe Fearon, Csibra, Tucker, & Johnson, 2008)—an ability that is linked to frontal cortex functioning and executive attention (Holmboe et al., 2010). As such, this second study contradicts the first study (Auerbach et al., 2001a) by not finding an association between the L-DRD4 variant and attention.

## Other Candidate Genes and Infant Attention

This section will present findings from four studies that have linked attentional parameters with other candidate genes in infancy.

Holmboe et al., (2010) tested for associations between the catechol-O-methyltransferase gene (COMT), the dopamine D2 receptor gene (DRD2) and the dopamine transporter gene (DAT1), with performance of 9-month-old infants on the Freeze-Frame task (Holmboe et al., 2010). They found that infants carrying the Met/Met genotype exhibited lower distractibility levels in comparison to infants with the Val/Val genotype, a finding that provided evidence for the association of variation in COMT gene and frontal cortex functioning. In addition, they found that the effect was present only in those participants who did not carry two copies of the DAT1 10-repeat variant. This suggests that epistasis (gene × gene interaction; e.g. where the expression of one gene is dependent on the presence of another gene) is occurring; as such, epistasis could partially account for the unreplicated findings in candidate gene studies. Finally, DRD2 TaqIA (a polymorphism of the DRD2 that is also known with the SNP name *rs1800497*) did not associate with performance on the Freeze-Frame task at 9 months of age (Holmboe et al., 2010).

A study examined the association of the tryptophan hydroxylase 2 gene (TPH2) with attention (assessed using a paradigm which measures disengagement and shifting of attention while infants were seeing a human face with three different expressions: neutral, happy and fearful facial expression) and temperament (measured by asking the mother to complete the Infant Behavior Questionnaire) in 7-month-old infants (Leppänen et al., 2011). The authors reported that infants with the T-carrier genotype displayed significantly increased missing attention shifts, in comparison to infants with the G/G TPH2 genotype. According to the authors, disengaging attention away from an aversive stimulus (such as a face with a fearful facial expression) is a key factor on infant's attempt to regulate their negative emotionality. They claimed that, because the increased missing attention shifts were associated with less effective regulation of negative affect (soothability), the TPH2 gene can regulate indirectly the infants' soothability via its direct effect on attention disengagement. As such, the results suggest a possible relationship between common genetic factors, attention and temperament in infancy (Leppänen et al., 2011).

Recently, another study assessed the main effect of the TPH2 and the 5-Hydroxytryptamine (Serotonin) Receptor 1A, G Protein-Coupled (HTR1A) genes—as well as the interactive effect of those genes with early life stress—in contributing to variation in attention to social signals of fear in 5- and-7-month-old infants (Forssman et al., 2013). The authors assessed infants' attention and temperament using the same protocol as Leppänen and colleagues (2011), described above. In addition, they assessed maternal stress and depressive symptoms using the recent life events questionnaire (based on Brugha, Babington, Tennant & Hurry, 1985) and the 10-item Edinburgh Postnatal Depression Scale (Cox, Holden, & Sagovsky, 1987). The results showed that the increase in missing attention shifts for happy expressions in TPH2 T-carriers—that was reported by Leppänen and colleagues, 2011—did not replicate in this independent sample. Despite that, there was a significant difference between the TPH2 T-carriers and carriers of the G/G genotype in the number of missing saccades for fearful facial expression with the former showing more missing saccades than the latter. There was no main effect of the HTR1A genotype on attention disengagement. Finally, TPH2 T-carriers with mothers who scored higher on postnatal depression exhibited the highest levels of missing attention shifts for fearful facial expression (Forssman et al., 2013).

The most recent study to date that explored the association between genetic markers and attention in infancy examined the relationship between the Cholinergic Receptor, Nicotinic, Alpha 4 (CHRNA4), DAT1 and COMT genes and orienting attention assessed on a spatial cueing task in 88 infants aged 7 months (Markant, Cicchetti, Hetzel & Thomas, 2014). Specifically, in this task, attention is engaged at a central location while a peripheral cue appears, a brief delay is imposed, and a target is subsequently presented in either the cued or non-cued location. The timing of the cue-to-target delay (or stimulus–onset asynchrony [SOA]) is critical, as varying this delay can elicit different orienting responses. Individuals typically respond faster to targets in the cued location (Markant et al., 2014). The experimenter monitored the infant's eye movements and indicated when the infant looked at the center, left, right, or away from the screen, while the computer calculated the cumulative duration of looking during each trial. The results showed that DAT1 and CHRNA4 genotypes did not associate with orienting attention in infancy. Carriers of the COMT-Val genotype showed faster overall response times to cued locations in comparison to COMT-Met carriers, suggesting higher scores on orienting attention (Markant et al., 2014).

## Longitudinal Studies of Infant Attention

This section will present findings from two longitudinal studies that aimed to identify candidate genes that contribute to variation in attentional parameters in infancy and in psychological trait phenotypes in childhood and adolescence.

A longitudinal study examined the association of DRD4 with visual exploratory behavior in 3-month-old infants and novelty seeking (NS) in adolescence. While male infants who were habituating faster showed higher scores of NS as adolescents, females did not show a significant correlation between infant habituation measures and NS in adolescence. Male infants carrying the L-DRD4 variant habituated faster in a habituation–dishabituation paradigm than males without L-DRD4 variant. These same individuals with L-DRD4 showed higher scores of NS (measured using the Junior Temperament and Character Inventory) in adolescence. In females, L-DRD4 did not show a significant association with either attention or adolescent NS (Laucht, Becker & Schmidt, 2006).

Finally, a longitudinal study found that the T/T genotype of the Cholinergic receptor nicotinic alpha 4 (CHRNA4) was associated with a higher percentage of looks that were considered correct anticipations in 6–7-month-old infants (Sheese et al., 2009). Recent work suggests that in infancy, self-regulation depends upon orienting attention (Petersen & Posner, 2012). At 18-months of age participants homozygous for the T allele were found to have less effortful control, in comparison to infants who were either heterozygous or homozygous for the C allele (Sheese et al., 2009). Since being homozygous for the T allele of the CHRNA4 was associated with higher percentage of looks that were correct anticipations in 6- to 7-month-old infants, one could expect that being homozygous for the T allele of the CHRNA4 will be associated with better effortful control at 18 months of age (since effortful control, anticipatory looking, and orienting attention are linked). This puzzling finding could be explained by findings that suggest that, while in infancy self-regulation depends primarily upon a brain network involved in orienting to sensory events, self-regulation in childhood and adulthood depends on the executive attention system (Petersen & Posner, 2012; Posner, Rothbart, Sheese, & Voelker, 2012). It is therefore possible that the advantage of being homozygous for the T allele of the CHRNA4 in infancy on anticipatory looking (hence self-regulation) did not hold later in development because the control of self-regulation is passed from the orienting attention system to the executive attention system (Voelker, Sheese, Rothbart, & Posner, 2009).

To summarize infant genetic studies on attention, L-DRD4 was the most studied genetic variant and it was found to be associated with less sustained attention and poorer information processing ability in infancy (Auerbach, et al., 2001a); but also with faster habituation rates in infancy and higher novelty seeking in adolescence in males (Laucht et al., 2006). Whilst the current findings are inconclusive, future research with larger sample sizes and more reliable measures of infant attention (such as those derived from eye tracking) could investigate further the role of the L-DRD4 variant—-as well as other genetic variants on infants' visual attention and on those traits with which attention is linked, in infancy and later in development. Given that early visual attention has been shown to associate with behavioral problems later in childhood (see Papageorgiou et al., 2014, 2015); exploring genetic variation that may contribute to both individual differences in visual attention in infancy and to traits of psychopathology in childhood and adolescence has significant implications for understanding the mechanisms involved in early brain development and for identifying populations at risk of attentional problems in later life.

## Associations between Common Genetic Variants and Temperament and Behavior

In this section we will present findings from the seven candidate gene studies that have associated variants in the DRD4 and 5-HTTLPR genes with infant temperament and behavior; the two studies that have associated variants in other genes (other than the DRD4 and 5-HTTLPR) with infant temperament and behavior; the two longitudinal studies that associated variants in the DRD4 and 5-HTTLPR genes with infant temperament and childhood/adolescent behavior; and the four longitudinal studies that associated variants in other genes (other than the DRD4 and 5-HTTLPR genes) with infant temperament and childhood/adolescent behavior.

### DRD4 & 5-HTTLPR and Infant Temperament and Behavior

*Birth to 4 Months of Age* It was found that 2-week-old infants with the L-DRD4 variant had higher scores on the scales of orientation, motor organization, range, and regulation of state of the Neonatal Brazelton Assessment Scale (NBAS; Brazelton & Nugent, 1995), in comparison to infants with the short DRD4 variant (S-DRD4; Ebstein et al., 1998). The orientation scale measures the infant's ability to attend to animate and inanimate auditory and visual stimuli. The motor organization score is an index of the infant's quality of L-DRD4 movement and tone. Range of state is a measure of the infant's arousal; regulation of state assesses the infant's ability to regulate his state during increasing levels of stimulation (Ebstein et al., 1998). Moreover, they found that infants homozygous for the short variant (s/s) of the 5-HTTLPR gene exhibited significantly lower performance on the orientation scale. No direct effect of the 5-HTTLPR was found on any of the temperamental clusters (Ebstein et al., 1998).

The same infants were followed up at 2 months of age, and carriers of the L-DRD4 variant were reported by their mothers on the Rothbart's Infant Behavior questionnaire (Rothbart, 1981) to exhibit better response to frustration (questionnaire scale of distress to limitations) and to display less negative emotionality in comparison to those with the S-DRD4 variant. Infants who were carrying the s/s 5-HTTLPR variant exhibited the highest scores on distress to limitations and negative emotionality in comparison to both l/s and l/l variants. Interestingly, infants with the s/s 5-HTTLPR genotype, who were also lacking the L-DRD4, were reported to display higher negative emotionality and to exhibit poorer responses to frustration (Auerbach et al., 1999).

The effect of the L-DRD4 on infants' temperament has been replicated by another separate longitudinal study, which found that 1-month-olds with the L-DRD4 variant showed significantly lower scores on the adaptability scale of the Italian version of the Early Infancy Temperament Questionnaire (Medoff-Cooper, Carey, & McDevitt, 1993) in comparison to infants lacking the L-DRD4 variant. According to the authors, the lower adaptability scores were indicative of the reduced difficulty with which the child adapts himself to changes, and therefore of better responses to novel situations. This study failed to replicate the results in the same sample at 5 months of age (De Luca et al., 2001). The findings of this study are in line with the findings of Auerbach and colleagues (1999) and Ebstein and colleagues (1998) in that L-DRD4 carriers score higher than S-RDRD4 carriers on several "positive" temperament traits, such as adaptability.

*4 to 9 Months of Age* A longitudinal study that employed parental reports of the Revised Infant Behavior Questionnaire (IBQ-R; Gartstein & Rothbart, 2003) found that L-DRD4 variant was consistently associated with higher levels of negative affect in 4- and-9-month-old infants (Holmboe, Nemoda, Fearon, Savari-Szekely & Johnson, 2011). In addition, participants carrying both the L-DRD4 variant and the highest expressing l/l 5-HTTLPR genotype displayed the highest level of negative affect (Holmboe et al., 2011).

Another study that used the Infant Behavior Questionnaire-Revised (Gartstein & Rothbart, 2003) and the Brief Symptom Inventory (Derogatis & Melisaratos, 1983) found that 6-month-old infants with the s/s 5-HTTLPR genotype had higher negative emotionality scores (in comparison to those carrying the l/l 5-HTTLPR), but only under the condition that their mothers had reported high anxiety levels during pregnancy (Pluess et al., 2011).

*12 Months of Age* A third follow-up of the infant sample described above (Auerbach et al., 1999; Ebstein et al., 1998), reported that infants with the L-DRD4 variant showed less negative emotionality and higher activity level scores at 12 months of age (Auerbach, Faroy, Ebstein, Kahana & Levine, 2001b). Infants with the s/s 5-HTTLPR genotype showed lower scores on the fearful distress composite and significantly longer latency to the first fear expression, but they scored lower on a positive emotionality composite (Auerbach et al., 2001b). The 12-month-old participants were assessed using the Laboratory Temperament Assessment Battery (Lab-TAB-Locomotor version; Goldsmith & Rothbart, 1996a, b).

Finally an independent study that used the Rothbart's Infant Behavior Questionnaire (Rothbart, 1981) and the Ainsworth's Strange Situation procedure (Ainsworth, Blehar, Waters & Walls, 1978) tested the effect of the DRD4 and 5-HTTLPR on infants' temperament. They found that 12-month-old infants who carried the L-DRD4 variant and the s/s 5-HTTLPR genotype exhibited higher anxiety and were uninterested in interacting with a stranger. Participants who carried the L-DRD4 variant and the l/l 5-HTTLPR genotype were calmer and interacted smoothly with an unfamiliar person (Lakatos et al., 2003), suggesting gene–gene interaction effects.

## Other Candidate Genes and Infant Temperament and Behavior

A novel study tested for an association between the Monoamine oxidase-A gene (MAOA) and 6-month-old infants' self-regulatory behavior. In order to measure the self-regulatory behavior, the researchers showed the infants a large toy chimpanzee (aversive event) and measured how long the infants looked away from the chimpanzee. The toy chimpanzee was used as a novel threatening stimuli that caused infants to exhibit vocal and facial expressions indicating clear distress, such as crying or whining (Zhang et al., 2011).The authors reported that a common functional MAOA variable number tandem repeat (MAOA-uVNTR), was associated with the self-regulatory behavior of the female infants. More specifically, the more active 4/4 genotype was associated with better regulatory behavior, but this effect was present only in girls (Zhang, et al., 2011).

Associations between COMT gene and 7-month-old infants' cognitive stability and flexibility have also been tested (Markant et al., 2014). Cognitive stability and flexibility was assessed using a motor approach task, which measures the infants' latencies to grasp a toy that was presented to them for the first time, as well as a habituation–dishabituation task that assesses the total cumulative look duration and looking times at stimuli, and the revised version of the Infant Behavioral Questionnaire, which measures infant temperament domains of surgency, negative affect and orientation/regulation. The results indicated that COMT-Val carriers were faster to reach for novel toys during the motor approach task and received higher scores on the temperament trait of approach to novelty; COMT-Met carriers showed enhanced dishabituation to the novel stimulus during the habituation task and received higher scores on the temperament measures of sustained attention and behavioral regulation. The authors concluded that the COMT-Met and COMT-Val genotypes are associated with increased cognitive stability and flexibility, respectively (Markant et al., 2014).

## Longitudinal Studies of Infant Temperament and Childhood/Adolescent Behavior

*DRD4 & 5-HTTLPR* A sample was assessed longitudinally from 4–8 months to 15–16 years on the temperamental parameter of approach-withdrawal, from 3–4 to 15–16 years on anxiety and from 11–12 years to 15–16 years on depression. Associations with the 5-HTTLPR genotype were tested. No significant associations at all ages were reported between the 5-HTTLPR and all of the temperamental domains measured in that study; however at 13–14 years and 15–16 years the l/l variant of the 5-HTTLPR were associated with higher anxiety (Jorm et al., 2000).

Another longitudinal study, which assessed temperamental characteristics and regulatory problems based on observations of infants' behavior and structured parent interview data at age 3 months found that individuals with the L-DRD4 variant and classified as having regulatory problems at 3 months of age had higher risk of developing ADHD symptoms in childhood. Individuals with either the L-DRD4 variant or with a history of regulatory problems in infancy were not at elevated risk for ADHD (Becker et al., 2010).

*Other Candidate Genes* Apart from DRD4 and the 5-HTTLPR genes, two studies examined longitudinally the relationship between other dopamine-related genes and infants' temperament. The first study tested for an association between the dopamine transporter gene (DAT1) and temperamental traits (from 4–8 months to 15–16 years) as well as behavior problems (from 3–4 years to 15–16 years), but failed to report any significant association at any age (Jorm et al., 2001).

The second study measured temperament longitudinally on the same sample of infants at 6–7 months and 18 months and tested for association with the COMT, the CHRNA4 and the Synaptosomal-associated protein, 25KDa (SNAP25). They found that infants with the G/A COMT genotype exhibited higher positive affect at 6–7-months old, in comparison to infants with the G/G or A/A COMT genotype. No equivalent associations were found at age 18 months. Finally 6-month-old infants with one or two copies of the SNAP25 C allele exhibited lower negative affect, as compared to those that were homozygous for the T allele; the same effect was also present at age 18 months (Sheese et al., 2009).

A longitudinal gene by environment (G × E) interaction study examined whether genetic variation in the MAOA gene interacts with environmental factors during pregnancy to predict negative emotionality in a sample of 209 5-week-old infants (Hill et al., 2013). Infants' negative emotionality was assessed with the Brazelton Neonatal Behavioral Assessment scale (NBAS; Brazelton & Nugent, 1995); mothers completed the Life History Calendar (LHC; Caspi et al., 1996) at 32 weeks gestation, which assessed the total number of life events during pregnancy. LHC was developed in the context of longitudinal research to record central events that can occur in a respondent's life, such as birthdays or deaths (Caspi et al., 1996). The results revealed that MAOA-Linked Polymorphic Region (LPR; that is a MAOA polymorphism with a 30 base pair repeat in the promoter region) low-activity variant showed an interaction with total number of life events leading to significantly higher levels of negative emotionality in 5-week-old infants. Specifically, there was a three-times increase in the likelihood of infants to react with fussing or crying, if they were carrying the low-activity MAOA-LPR and if their mothers were reporting four or more life events during pregnancy. On the contrary, infants with the MAOA-LPR high activity variant and with mothers who were reporting four or more life events during pregnancy were either unaffected or they were exhibiting less negative emotionality (Hill et al., 2013).

Another longitudinal G × E interaction study explored the main effect of MAOA genotype and interactions with maternal sensitivity on infant temperament (Pickles et al., 2013). The authors assessed infant temperament at 29 weeks and 14 months of age using the Infant Behavioral Questionnaire – Revised (Gartstein & Rothbart, 2003); and maternal sensitivity at 29 weeks postnatal with a 15-min laboratory-based procedure (NICHD Early Child Care Research Network, 1999). The mothers' sensitivity was rated from video recordings on a global five-point scale reflecting mothers' appropriate, supportive, warm responding to infant communications, playful bids or distress (Pickles et al., 2013). There were no significant associations between MAOA status and infant temperament at 29 weeks or at 14 months of age. There was a significant interaction between MAOA status and maternal sensitivity at 29 weeks of age; Participants carrying the low-expression genotype (MAOA-L carriers versus MAOA-H carriers) and with mothers who were exhibiting low sensitivity showed the highest scores on proneness to anger at 14 months of age (Pickles et al., 2013).

To summarize, L-DRD4 was the most studied genetic variant in relation to infant temperament and it was found to be associated with several infant temperament traits such as reduced difficulty with which the child adapts to changes at 1 month of age (De Luca et al., 2001), higher activity levels at 12 months of age (Auerbach et al., 2001b) and less negative emotionality at 2 and 12 months of age (Auerbach et al., 1999; 2001b). L-DRD4 was also found to be associated with higher levels of negative affect at 4 and 9 months of age (Holmboe et al., 2011); while other studies found no significant main effect of the L-DRD4 on several infant temperament traits such as smiling, soothability and surgency (for example, Lakatos et al., 2003). It should be noted that genetic research on infant temperament involved the most diverse studies in terms of age in comparison to the reviewed studies on infant attention and attachment.

In regards to predicting risk for later psychopathology, longitudinal genetic research in infancy has returned promising results. For example a study has shown that individuals with the L-DRD4 variant and classified as having regulatory problems at 3 months of age had higher risk of developing ADHD symptoms in childhood (Becker et al., 2010). More longitudinal research with larger samples is necessary in order to establish the degree to which the L-DRD4—as well as other genetic variation, such as the 5-HTTLPR—influences temperament traits in infancy and predicts psychopathology later in development.

## Attachment Disorganization

The attachment theory refers to the long-term relationship between infants and their caregivers and suggests that infants can learn to cope with stressful events and to regulate their negative emotionality in an organized manner (Van Ijzendoorn, Schuengel & Bakermans-Kranenburg, 1999). Based on the ways that infants cope with the stressful event of two short separations from the caregiver in the Ainsworth's Strange Situation and the behavior that they display after reunion, they are categorized as secure, insecure-resistant and insecure-avoidant infants (Ainsworth et al., 1978; Lakatos et al., 2000). Given that 15% and 80% of non-clinical low- and high-risk infants, respectively, could not be categorized in one of the three attachment dimensions, a new scalable dimension has been defined by Main and Solomon (1990) as disorganized attachment status (D); this reflects infants' inability to resolve anxiety and to regulate their negative emotionality during the stressful event of separation from their caregiver (Lakatos et al., 2000). Disorganization of early attachment is pertinent to developmental psychopathology. For example, it has been found to be a risk factor for behavioral problems (e.g. aggressive behavior) in childhood (Lyons-Ruth, 1996).

In this section we will present findings of the six candidate gene studies that associated genes with attachment in infancy; the three longitudinal studies that associated variants in the 5-HTTLPR gene with infant and childhood attachment; and the findings of the first GWAS study in infancy.

### DRD4 and 5-HTTLPR Gene and Infant Attachment Disorganization (D)

The first genetic association study of infants' attachment style videotaped 12–13-month-old infants and their mothers in the Ainsworth Strange Situation (Ainsworth et al., 1978) and found that infants who were carrying the L-DRD4 variant were at a fourfold risk of being classified as disorganized in comparison to those without an L-DRD4 variant (Lakatos et al., 2000). In a later study, the interaction between the L-DRD4 variant and the -521 C/T genotype, that is a genetic variant in the upstream regulatory region of the DRD4, were studied in the same sample of infants (as per Lakatos et al., 2000) (Bakermans-Kranenburg & Van Ijzendoorn, 2004). Neither genetic variant had a main effect on infants' D but the -521 C/T genotype interacted with the L-DRD4 variant and as a result the presence of both variants increased tenfold the risk for D in infancy (Lakatos et al., 2002). A year later Lakatos and colleagues (2003) tested in the same sample of infants (as per Lakatos et al., 2000, 2002) the main and interactive effect of the L-DRD4 and 5-HTTLPR genes. While they found that the L-DRD4 variant was present in higher frequency in infants classified as disorganized, they reported neither a main effect of the 5-HTTLPR gene nor an interaction of the L-DRD4 and 5-HTTLPR in infant's D (Lakatos et al., 2003). Bakermans-Kranenburg and Van Ijzendoorn (2004) used the Ainsworth's Strange Situation (1978) in 12-month-olds but they failed to replicate the findings provided by Lakatos and colleagues (2000; 2002) that infants with the L-DRD4 variant are more likely to have disorganized attachment (Bakermans-Kranenburg & Van Ijzendoorn, 2004).

Gervai and colleagues (2005) used the same sample of infants (that were used in Lakatos et al., 2000, 2002, 2003) and parental genetic data to investigate whether heterozygous parents transmitted the L-DRD4 variant more often to infants displaying D. The results showed a significant preferential transmission of the L-DRD4 variant to disorganized infants and a significant non-transmission of the same allele to securely attached infants. This suggests that not carrying the long haplotype of the DRD4 gene may act as a resilience factor in the optimal development of early attachment (Gervai et al., 2005).

A few studies investigated G × E: whether it is not the presence of a particular polymorphism alone, but the interaction of this polymorphism with certain environmental factors that could put individuals at risk for D status. A G × E study examined the hypothesis that maternal unresolved loss or trauma or the threatening behavior that the parent might display towards the child, might interact with the L-DRD4 (or with the combination of the L-DRD4 and -521 C/T genotype) to form a group of infants that will be susceptible to D status (Van Ijzendoorn & Bakermans-Kranenburg, 2006). They reported that 12-month-old infants with the L-DRD4 who had traumatized mothers scored significantly higher on the D scale compared to participants without these two risk factors. The -521 C/T genotype alone did not have an effect (main or interactive with the maternal frightening behavior) in the infants' D classification (Van Ijzendoorn & Bakermans-Kranenburg, 2006).

A second G × E study reported that the disruption of communication between mothers and infants had an effect on the infants' D, but this relationship held only for infants that did not carry the L-DRD4. This study failed to report an association of the L-DRD4 with increased D in infancy (12-months of age), which contradicts the findings of the previous studies that all used the same sample of infants (Gervai et al., 2005; Lakatos et al., 2000, 2002, 2003). Instead, they reported that the L-DRD4 had a protective role for those infants whose communication with their mothers was disrupted (Gervai et al., 2007).

Another G × E study examined the main effects of the DRD4, -521 C/T and 5-HTTLPR variants on infants' D and a potential interaction of these genes with low parental responsiveness. Surprisingly, they found no significant association between the L-DRD4 or the -521 C/T variants on 12-month-old infants' D. In addition, the two variants did not interact with low parental responsiveness to contribute to individual variation in D. Instead, they found that the 5-HTTLPR variant interacted with low parental responsiveness to increase infants' risk developing D (Spangler, Johann, Ronai, & Zimmermann, 2009).

## Longitudinal Studies of Infant Attachment

A longitudinal G × E study examined the genetic and caregiving-based contributions to individual differences in infant attachment classifications in 154 mother–infant pairs (Raby et al., 2012). The mother's responsiveness to their 6-month-old infants was evaluated on the Ainsworth's global scales of maternal sensitivity and cooperation (Ainsworth et al., 1978) during two 30-minute feeding situations and one 20-minute play situation on two different days in their homes. The infants' attachment was assessed twice in the Ainsworth Strange Situation procedure (Ainsworth et al., 1978), when the infants were 12 and 18 months. The infants were classified as securely attached, insecure-avoidant, or insecure-resistant. In addition, infants were categorized in a high- or low-distress group based on the level of emotional distress that they exhibited in response to the Strange Situation procedure (the attachment disorganization classification was not included in this study). The results revealed that greater maternal responsiveness at 6 months of age was associated with a greater likelihood of secure attachment at 12 months of age, but not at 18 months of age. Maternal responsiveness did not show a main effect or an interaction with the short variant of the 5-HTTLPR in predicting infants' level of emotional distress at 12 months and 18 months of age. The 5-HTTLPR showed neither a main effect nor an interaction with maternal responsiveness in predicting attachment security at 12 months and 18 months of age (Raby et al., 2012).

## GWAS on Infant Attachment

Recently the first genome-wide association study (GWAS) in infancy was conducted (Pappa et al., 2015). The study, included a sample of 657 infants (mean age in months = 14) with both observed attachment and genome-wide data. The authors conducted a GWAS to identify single nucleotide polymorphisms (SNPs) associated with disorganized attachment status (D; continuous variable); subsequently, they annotated the SNPs into genes and functional pathways (Pappa et al., 2015). Similarly to the previous studies on infant attachment, mother–infant dyads were observed in the Strange Situation Procedure. No genome-wide significant associations between single SNPs and D were found. However, gene-based analysis provided evidence of three genes—the Histone Deacetylase 1 (HDAC1), Zinc Finger Protein 675 (ZNF675) and BSD Domain Containing 1(BSDC1) genes—to be associated with D (Pappa et al., 2015). The pathway analysis indicated two biological processes (synaptic transmission and cation transport) overrepresented in the associations with D. The results point to pathways involved in neuronal function and synaptic plasticity (Pappa et al., 2015). The authors concluded that—similarly to other complex psychological traits—D is influenced by multiple genes with very small effects; as such, larger samples and replication of the findings in independent samples is necessary in order to shed light on the genetic architecture of infant attachment (Pappa et al., 2015).

To summarize genetic research on infants' attachment, this field has mainly explored the role of the L-DRD4 variant in relation to D. Research has shown that L-DRD4 increases the risk for developing D in infancy (Lakatos et al., 2000) and that participants with the L-DRD4 who were exposed to traumatized mothers score significantly higher on the D scale compared to participants without these two risk factors (Van Ijzendoorn & Bakermans-Kranenburg, 2006). However the findings have not been replicated in independent samples and one study has even shown that L-DRD4 might have a protective effect against developing D in infancy (Gervai et al., 2007). It is promising that the first GWA study on infants' D—and indeed the first GWAS in infancy—has been conducted. Whilst the study was underpowered to detect associations between genetic variants and infants' D, pathway analysis returned promising results indicating biological processes that could underlie the development of D in infancy (Pappa et al., 2015).

Finally, it is noteworthy that longitudinal genetic research that aimed to explore the association between genes and D in infancy, and the degree to which infants' D interacts with genetic variation to predict later psychopathology is currently limited (one study; Raby et al., 2012). Disorganization of early attachment has been found to be an important risk factor for behavioral problems (e.g. aggressive behavior) in childhood (Lyons-Ruth, 1996). As such, further exploration of the association between a priori (such as the L-DRD4) and novel genetic variants (such as those discovered in GWAS) in relation to infants' D is pertinent for understanding the early origins of later psychopathology.

## Summary

This chapter reviewed the literature on genetic studies of psychological phenotypes in human infancy. This section will summarize the main findings and discuss possible next steps in genetic research in infancy with relevance to understanding the causes of developmental psychopathology. This discussion will also highlight how genetic approaches, such as polygenic risk scoring, can advance the field.

All but one genetic study in infancy employed the candidate gene association design. The psychological phenotypes could be broadly split into attention, temperament and behavior, and attachment. None of the significant associations have consistently replicated across studies. DRD4 and 5-HTTLPR genes were the most frequently used candidate genes. Possibly the most coherent set of results were on the L-DRD4 variant. This variant was significantly associated with several "positive" infant psychological phenotypes, namely orientation, motor organization, range of state, and regulation of state (*range of state* is a measure of the infant's arousal, and *regulation of state* assesses the infant's ability to regulate his state during increasing levels of stimulation; Ebstein et al., 1998) at 2 weeks of age, better responses to novel situation at 1 month of age, less negative emotionality and less distress to limitations at 2 and 12 months of age, higher activity levels at 12 months of age and more rapid habituation at 3 months of age. L-DRD4 was also associated with higher levels of negative affect at 4 and 9 months of age, enhanced risk of developing D, shorter looking duration, shorter latencies to the first look away, less sustained attention, and lower information processing ability at 12 months of age. Finally, other studies found no significant main effect of the L-DRD4 on infants' activity, smiling, distress to novel stimuli, soothability, positive emotionality at 2 months of age; surgency, extraversion and orientation at 4 and 9 months of age; adaptability at 5 months of age; infants' performance in the Freeze-Frame task at 9 months of age; infants' risk of developing D at 12 months of age. For the field of developmental psychopathology, it is of value to see how genetic variants thought to be associated with problems such as ADHD and depression in later childhood and adulthood may also influence individual differences in traits such as attention and temperament at an earlier stage in life.

The first GWAS study in infancy has recently been conducted. Although the study was underpowered to detect genome-wide significant associations between SNPs and disorganized attachment in infancy, the gene pathway analysis indicated that pathways involved in neuronal function and synaptic plasticity may play a role on D in infancy. It noteworthy that the first GWAS in infancy has been conducted more than ten years after the first successful utilization of the GWA methodology in adult sample and for a medical disorder (Klein et al., 2005). As such, to follow the example of genetic research in other domains such as psychiatric genetics research, a constructive move forward for research in developmental psychopathology would be to establish consortia across infant research labs in order to share data and achieve the sample sizes required to identify reliable genetic associations with infant psychological traits.

## How Can the Mixed Evidence be Interpreted and What Could Be the Next Steps in Genetic Research of Infancy?

The inconsistent findings across different infant ages may reflect "true" changes in the genetic architecture on a particular domain across infant development. Alternatively, lack of replication across ages could be due to other more prosaic reasons such as measurement issues, lack of power, or other problems with a study design.

In terms of the measurement explanation, infant genetic research on psychological phenotypes has the demanding task of developing age-appropriate measures that pick up on reliable individual differences. Distinct domains within a trait might involve different measures. If longitudinal studies on infancy are conducted then researchers need to be sure their measures are tapping the same underlying constructs at different ages.

The power of each study reviewed here has not been explicitly discussed; several reviews exist which outline the power issues present in candidate gene studies and genetic research on complex traits (e.g. Eichler et al., 2010; Hirschhorn, Lohmueller, Byrne, & Hirschhorn, 2002). Several authors have claimed that one of the limitations of candidate gene studies is that researchers did not correctly adjust the significance level in light of the numbers of tests that they performed. Not reducing the significance level to below 5% in the presence of multiple related statistical tests can lead to false positive results (Van Gestel & Van Broekhoven, 2003).

Recent theoretical ideas can provide other viewpoints to explain some of the less consistent findings. For example, Belsky's differential susceptibility hypothesis proposes that subgroups of the population are more susceptible to environmental factors they are exposed to than others (Belsky & Pluess, 2009). Experimental evidence from studies on older children supports this theory, for example, while children with the L-DRD4 variant and unresponsive mothers showed more externalizing behavior problems in comparison to children without the L-DRD4 variant, children with the L-DRD4 variant and responsive mothers showed the lowest levels of externalizing problems (Bakermans-Kranenburg & van Ijzendoorn, 2007, 2011). It has been reported above, for example, in several studies (Lakatos et al., 2000, 2002, 2003) that used the same sample of infants, that the L-DRD4 variant was associated with an increased risk for infants to develop D. In addition, a G × E interaction study reported that infants with the L-DRD4, who were exposed to traumatized mothers, scored higher on the D scale compared to participants without these two risk factors (Van Ijzendoorn & Bakermans-Kranenburg, 2006). Despite these findings, a second G × E interaction study reported that the L-DRD4 had a protective role on those infants whose communication with their mothers was disrupted (Gervai et al., 2007). These inconclusive findings might come about because of different environmental modifiers between studies or differences across studies in the ratios of infants who are more susceptible and less susceptible to environmental effects (Belsky & Pluess, 2009).

Another theory-based perspective for considering why the same trait might show mixed findings in terms of genetic associations across infant development and later ages is to question whether there are different underlying mechanisms involved on the same trait domains at different ages. For example, being homozygous for the T allele of the CHRNA4 might be advantageous for orienting attention only in infancy and not later in development (Sheese et al., 2009). In terms of the development of different systems of attention, the control of self-regulation is passed from the orienting attention system to the executive attention system with age (Petersen & Posner, 2012). As such, it is possible that the advantage of being homozygous for the T allele of the CHRNA4 in infancy for orienting attention might not hold later in development, if other genetic variants are associated with influencing the later-developing executive attention system.

Another proposed explanation for the lack of replicable findings in candidate genes studies, though not specific to this age group, is a weak a priori hypothesis. Plomin (2013) suggests that: "One problem with the candidate gene approach is that we often do not have strong hypotheses as to which genes are candidate genes. Indeed, the general rule of pleiotropy (each gene has many effects) suggests that most of the thousands of genes expressed in the brain could be considered as candidates." (Plomin, 2013, p. 107).

In sum, several challenges face infant genetics, including the potential role of environmental modifiers and reliable assessment of domains across age. Lack of power also likely plays a major role in lack of replication in candidate gene association studies of psychological traits in infancy.

## Other Genetic Approaches for Identifying Genes Associated with Psychological Traits in Infancy and Implications for Developmental Psychopathology

*Polygenic Risk Score Analytic Approach* An analytic approach that is informative in predicting risk in developmental psychopathology is polygenic risk score (PRS) analysis (e.g., Sieradzka et al., 2014). For behavioral traits, the largest effect sizes are very small (e.g., Benyamin et al., 2014). Although individually significant genetic markers in GWAS account for a small proportion of the heritability of complex traits, a moderate proportion of variation in complex traits can be accounted by the ensemble of common genetic markers not achieving significance individually due to the study's sample size (Dudbridge, 2013). PRS analysis has the potential to provide a predictor with better discrimination properties in comparison to one based on individual genetic markers and to maximize the study's statistical power to detect an association (Wray, Goddard, & Visscher, 2007; Wray et al., 2014). Given that the main target of the PRS analytic protocol is to predict risk of disorder or individual's trait values, polygenic risk score analysis will be particularly informative when used in samples at the earliest stage of development (e.g. infancy).

*Sequencing* Whole-genome sequencing involves identifying the entire sequence of DNA code in an individual's genome. Recent developments in genetic technology have dramatically reduced the time and cost of DNA sequencing enabling researchers to conduct studies that involve many millions of sequencing reads (Shendure & Aiden, 2012). In general, GWAS remain more affordable per participant than sequencing but sequencing is particularly valuable for identifying rare inherited genetic variants and de novo genetic variants associated with traits and disease.

New genetic methodologies can address some of the limitations of the infant genetics literature but will also bring new challenges. Succeeding in this task will help to better understand human development and, specifically, the common and rare genetic variation that influence the development of infant traits from the very earliest stages of life; as well as how those traits associate with later symptoms of psychopathology. It is hoped that a better understanding of the genes that influence those traits in infancy will be informative for *predicting* risk, instead of diagnosing disorder only once symptoms/features have appeared. In turn, this might allow developmental psychopathologists to focus on the prevention of disorder, instead of curing the symptoms, difficulties, and challenges that have already manifested once a disorder has been diagnosed.

## References


Ainsworth, M., Blehar, M., Waters, E., & Wall, S. (1978). *Patterns of attachment: A psychological study of the strange situation.* Hillsdale, NJ: Lawrence Erlbaum Associates.

Auerbach, J., Geller, V., Lezer, S., Shinwell, E., Belmaker, R. H., Levine, J. & Ebstein, R. (1999). Dopamine D4 receptor (D4DR) and serotonin transporter promoter (5-HTTLPR) polymorphisms in the determination of temperament in 2-month-old infants. *Molecular Psychiatry, 4*(4), 369–373.

Auerbach, J. G., Faroy, M., Ebstein, R., Kahana, M. & Levine, J. (2001b). The association of the dopamine D4 receptor gene (DRD4) and the serotonin transporter promoter gene (5-HTTLPR) with temperament in 12-month-old infants. *Journal of Child Psychology and Psychiatry, 42*(6), 777–783.

Auerbach, J. G., Benjamin, J., Faroy, M., Geller, V. & Ebstein, R. (2001a). DRD4 related to infant attention and information processing: a developmental link to ADHD? *Psychiatric Genetics, 11*(1), 31–35.

Bakermans-Kranenburg, M. J. & Van Ijzendoorn, M. H. (2004). No association of the dopamine D4 receptor (DRD4) and -521 C/T promoter polymorphisms with infant attachment disorganization. *Attachment and Human Development, 6*(3), 211–218. doi: 10.1080/14616730412331281584

Bakermans-Kranenburg, M. J., & van Ijzendoorn, M. H. (2007). Genetic vulnerability or differential susceptibility in child development: The case of attachment. *Journal of Child Psychology and Psychiatry, 48*, 1160–1173. doi: 10.1111/j.1469-7610.2007.01801.x

Bakermans-Kranenburg, M. J., & van Ijzendoorn, M. H. (2011). Differential susceptibility to rearing environment depending on dopamine-related genes: New evidence and a meta-analysis. *Development and Psychopathology 23*, 39–52. doi:10.1017/S0954579410000635

Balding, D. (2006). A tutorial on statistical methods for population association studies. *Nature Reviews Genetics, 7*, 781–791. doi:10.1038/nrg1916

Becker, K., Blomeyer, D., El-Faddach, M., Esser, G., Schmidt, M. H., Banaschewski, T. & Laucht, M. (2010). From regulatory problems in infancy to attention-deficit/hyperactivity disorder in childhood: a moderating role for the dopamine D4 receptor gene? *Journal of Pediatrics, 156*(5), 798–803.

Belsky, J., & Pluess, M. (2009). Beyond diathesis stress: Differential susceptibility to environmental influences. *Psychological Bulletin, 135*(6), 885–908. doi: 10.1037/a0017376

Benyamin, B., Pourcain, B., Davis, O. S., Davies, G., Hansell, N. K., Brion, M. J.,... & Visscher, P. M. (2014). Childhood intelligence is heritable, highly polygenic and associated with FNBP1L. *Molecular Psychiatry*, *19*(2), 253–258.

Brazelton, T. B., & Nugent, J. K. (1995). *Neonatal Behavior Assessment Scale*, 3rd edition. London: MacKeith Press

Brugha, T., Babington, P., Tennant, C., & Hurry, J. (1985). The list of threatening experiences: A subset of 12 life event categories with considerable long-term contextual threat. *Psychological Medicine*, *15*(1), 189–194.

Butcher, L. M., Davis, O. S., Craig, I. W., &Plomin, R. (2008). Genome-wide quantitative trait locus association scan of general cognitive ability using pooled DNA and 500K single nucleotide polymorphism microarrays. *Genes Brain and Behavior 7*, 435–446. doi: 10.1111/j.1601-183x.2007.00368.x

Caspi, A., Moffitt, T. E., Thornton, A., Freedman, D., Amell, J. W., Harrington, H. L., Smeijers, J. & Silva, P. A. (1996) The life history calendar: A research and clinical assessment method for collecting retrospective event-history data. *International Journal of Methods in Psychiatric Research*, *6*(2), 101–114. doi: 10.1002/(SICI)1234-988X(199607)6:2<101::AID-MPR156>3.3.CO;2-E

Cox, J. L., Holden, J. M. & Sagovsky, R. (1987). Detection of postnatal depression. Development of the 10-item Edinburgh Postnatal Depression Scale. *British Journal of Psychiatry,150*, 782–786. doi:10.1192/bjp.150.6.782

De Luca, A., Rizzardi, M., Torrente, I., Alessandroni, R., Salvioli, G. P., Filograsso, N., ... Novelli, G. (2001). Dopamine D4 receptor (DRD4) polymorphism and adaptability trait during infancy: A longitudinal study in 1- to 5-month-old neonates. *Neurogenetics*, *3*, 79–82. doi: 10.1007/s100480100106

Derogatis, L. R., & Melisaratos, N. (1983). The Brief Symptom Inventory: An introductory report. *Psychological Medicine 13*(3), 595–605.

Docherty, S. J., Davis, O. S., Kovas, Y., Meaburn, E. L., Dale, P. S., Petrill, S. A., ... Plomin, R. (2010). A genome-wide association study identifies multiple loci associated with mathematics ability and disability. *Genes Brain and Behavior 9*, 234–47. doi: 10.1111/j.1601-183x.2009.00553.x

Dudbridge, F. (2013). Power and predictive accuracy of polygenic risk scores. *PLoS Genetics*, *9*. e1003348

Ebstein, R. P., Levine, J., Geller, V., Auerbach, J., Gritsenko, I. & Belmaker, R. H. (1998). Dopamine D4 receptor and serotonin transporter promoter in the determination of neonatal temperament. *Molecular Psychiatry*, *3*(3), 238–246.

Eichler, E. E., Flint, J., Gibson, G., Kong, A., Leal S. M., Moore, J. H. & Nadeau, H., (2010). Missing heritability and strategies for finding the underlying causes of complex disease. *Nature Reviews Genetics*, *11*, 446–450. doi:10.1038/nrg2809

Fagan, J.F. (1970). Memory in the infant. *Journal of Experimental Child Psychology*, *9*, 217–226.

Fagan J. F., &Shepherd P (1991). *Manual: The Fagan Test of Infant Intelligence*. Cleveland, OH: Infantest Corp.

Fagan, J. F., & Montie, J. E. (1988). The behavioral assessment of cognitive well-being in the infant. In J. Kavanagh (Ed.), *Understanding mental retardation: Research accomplishments and new frontiers* (pp. 207–222). Baltimore, MD: Paul H. Brooke.

Forssman, L., Peltola, M., Yrttiaho, S., Puura, K., Mononen, N., Lehtimäki, T., & Leppänen, J. (2014). Regulatory variant of the TPH2 gene and early life stress are associated with heightened attention to social signals of fear in infants. *Journal of Child Psychology & Psychiatry*, *55*, 793–801. doi: 10.1111/jcpp.12181

Gartstein, M. A. & Rothbart, M. K. (2003). Studying infant temperament via the Revised Infant Behavior Questionnaire. *Infant Behavior & Development*, *26*(1), 64–86.

Gervai, J., Nemoda, Z., Lakatos, K., Ronai, Z., Toth, I., Ney, K. & Sasvari-Szekely, M. (2005). Transmission disequilibrium tests confirm the link between DRD4 gene polymorphism and infant attachment. *American Journal of Medical Genetics Part B: Neuropsychiatric Genetics, 132B*(1), 126–130.

Gervai, J., Novak, A., Lakatos, K., Toth, I., Danis, I., Ronai, Z., …Lyons-Ruth, K. (2007). Infant genotype may moderate sensitivity to maternal affective communications: Attachment disorganization, quality of care, and the DRD4 polymorphism. *Social Neuroscience, 2*, 307–319. doi: 10.1002/ajmg.b.30102

Goldsmith, H. H. & Rothbart, M. K. (1996a). *Prelocomotor and locomotor Laboratory Temperament Assessment Battery (Lab-TAB; version 3.0, Technical Manual)*. Madison, WI: University of Wisconsin, Department of Psychology.

Goldsmith, H. H., & Rothbart, M. (1996b). *The Laboratory Temperament Assessment Battery (Locomotor version)*. Madison, WI: Department of Psychology, University of Wisconsin.

Hill, J., Breen G., Quinn, J., Tibu, F., Sharp, H., & Pickles, A. (2013). Evidence for interplay between genes and maternal stress in utero: Monoamine oxidase A polymorphism moderates effects of life events during pregnancy on infant negative emotionality at 5 weeks. *Genes Brain and Behavior*. doi: 10.1111/gbb.12033

Hirschhorn J., Lohmueller K., Byrne, E., & Hirschhorn, K. (2002). A comprehensive review of genetic association studies. *Genetics in Medicine, 4*, 45–61. doi:10.1097/00125817-200203000-00002

Holmboe, K., Fearon, R. M. P., Csibra, G., Tucker, L. A., & Johnson, M. H. (2008). Freeze-Frame: A new infant inhibition task and its relation to frontal cortex tasks during infancy and early childhood. *Journal of Experimental Child Psychology, 100*(2), 89–114.

Holmboe, K., Nemoda, Z., Fearon, R. M., Csibra, G., Sasvari-Szekely, M. & Johnson, M. H. (2010). Polymorphisms in dopamine system genes are associated with individual differences in attention in infancy. *Developmental Psychology, 46*, 404–416. doi: 10.1037/a0018180

Holmboe, K., Nemoda, Z., Fearon, R. M., Sasvari-Szekely, M. & Johnson, M. H. (2011). Dopamine D4 receptor and serotonin transporter gene effects on the longitudinal development of infant temperament. *Genes Brain and Behavior, 10*, 513–522. doi: 10.1111/j.1601-183X.2010.00669.x

Johnson, M. H. (2011). *Developmental cognitive neuroscience*. (3rd edition). New York: John Wiley & Sons.

Jorm, A. F., Prior, M., Sanson, A., Smart, D., Zhang, Y., & Easteal, S. (2000). Association of a functional polymorphism of the serotonin transporter gene with anxiety-related temperament and behavior problems in children: a longitudinal study from infancy to the mid-teens. *Molecular Psychiatry, 5*(5), 542–547.

Jorm, A. F., Prior, M., Sanson, A., Smart, D., Zhang, Y. & Easteal, S. (2001), Association of a polymorphism of the dopamine transporter gene with externalizing behavior problems and associated temperament traits: A longitudinal study from infancy to the mid-teens. *American Journal of Medical Genetics, 105*, 346–350. doi: 10.1002/ajmg.1355

Klein, R. J., Zeiss, C., Chew, E. Y., Tsai, J. Y., Sackler, R. S., Haynes, C.,… & Hoh, J. (2005). Complement factor H polymorphism in age-related macular degeneration. *Science, 308*(5720), 385–389.

Lakatos, K., Nemoda, Z., Birkas, E., Ronai, Z., Kovacs, E., Ney, K., … & Gervai, J. (2003). Association of D4 dopamine receptor gene and serotonin transporter promoter polymorphisms with infants' response to novelty. *Molecular Psychiatry, 8*(1), 90–97.

Lakatos, K., Nemoda, Z., Toth, I., Ronai, Z., Ney, K., Sasvari-Szekely, M. & Gervai, J. (2002). Further evidence for the role of the dopamine D4 receptor (DRD4) gene in attachment disorganization: Interaction of the exon III 48-bp repeat and the -521 C/T promoter polymorphisms. *Molecular Psychiatry, 7*(1), 27–31.

Lakatos, K., Toth, I., Nemoda, Z., Ney, K., Sasvari-Szekely, M. & Gervai, J. (2000). Dopamine D4 receptor (DRD4) gene polymorphism is associated with attachment disorganization in infants. *Molecular Psychiatry, 5*(6), 633–637.

Laucht, M., Becker, K. & Schmidt, M. H. (2006). Visual exploratory behaviour in infancy and novelty seeking in adolescence: Two developmentally specific phenotypes of DRD4? *Journal of Child Psychology and Psychiatry, 47*, 1143–1151. doi:10.1111/j.1469-7610.2006.01627.x

Leppanen, J. M., Peltola, M. J., Puura, K., Mantymaa, M., Mononen, N., & Lehtimaki, T. (2011). Serotonin and early cognitive development: variation in the tryptophan hydroxylase 2 gene is associated with visual attention in 7-month-old infants. *Journal of Child Psychology and Psychiatry, 52*, 1144–1152. doi:10.1111/j.1469-7610.2011.02391.x

Lyons-Ruth, K. (1996). Attachment relationships among children with aggressive behavior problems: The role of disorganized early attachment patterns. *Journal of Consulting and Clinical Psychology, 64*(1), 64–73.

Main, M & Solomon, J (1990). Procedures for identifying infants during the disorganized/disoriented Ainsworth Strange Situation. In M. Greenberg, D. Cicchetti & E. Cummings (Eds), *Attachment in the preschool years: Theory, research and intervention* (pp. 121–160). Chicago: University of Chigago Press.

Manolio, T. A. & Collins, F. S. (2009). The HapMap and genome-wide association studies in diagnosis and therapy. *Annual Review of Medicine, 60*, 443–456. doi: 10.1146/annurev.med.60.061907.093117.

Markant, J., Cicchetti, D., Hetzel, S., & Thomas, K. M. (2014). Relating dopaminergic and cholinergic polymorphisms to spatial attention during infancy. *Developmental Psychology, 50* (2), 360–369. doi: 10.1037/a0033172

Meaburn, E.L., Harlaar, N., Craig, I.W., Schalkwyk, L.C., & Plomin, R. (2008). Quantitative trait locus association scan of early reading disability and ability using pooled DNA and 100K SNP microarrays in a sample of 5760 children. *Molecular Psychiatry, 13*, 729–740.

Medoff-Cooper, B., Carey, W. B., & McDevitt, S. C. (1993). The Early Infancy Temperament Questionnaire. *Journal of Development and Behavioral Pediatrics, 14*(4), 230–235.

Pappa, I., Szekely, E., Mileva-Seitz, V. R., Luijk, M. P., Bakermans-Kranenburg, M. J., van IJzendoorn, M. H., & Tiemeier, H. (2015). Beyond the usual suspects: A multidimensional genetic exploration of infant attachment disorganization and security. *Attachment & Human Development, 17*(3), 288–301.

Papageorgiou, K. A., Farroni, T., Johnson, M. H., Smith, T. J., Ronald, A. (2015). Individual differences in newborn visual attention associate with temperament and behavioral difficulties in later childhood. *Scientific Reports 11264.* doi:10.1038/srep11264

Papageorgiou, K. A., Smith, T. J., Wu, R., Johnson, M. H., Kirkham, N. Z., & Ronald, A. (2014). Individual differences in infant fixation duration relate to attention and behavioral control in childhood. *Psychological Science,* 0956797614531295.

Papageorgiou, K. A. & Ronald, A. (2013). "He who sees things grow from the beginning will have the finest view of them." A systematic review of genetic studies on psychological traits in infancy. *Neuroscience and Biobehavioral Reviews, 37.*

Petersen, S. E., & Posner, M. I., (2012). The attention system of the human brain: 20 years after. *Annual Review of Neuroscience, 35*, 73–89. doi: 10.1146/annurev-neuro-062111-150525

Pickles, A., Hill, J., Breen, G., Quinn, J., Abbott, K., Jones, H., & Sharp, H. (2013). Evidence for interplay between genes and parenting on infant temperament in the first year of life: monoamine oxidase A polymorphism moderates effects of maternal sensitivity on infant anger proneness. *Journal of Child Psychology and Psychiatry, 54*(12), 1308–1317.

Plomin, R. (2013). Child development and molecular genetics: 14 years later. *Child Development, 84*(1), 104–120. doi: 10.1111/j.1467-8624.2012.01757.x.

Plomin, R., DeFries, J. C., Knopic, V. S., & Neiderhiser, J. M. (2013). *Behavior genetics* 6th edition. New York, Worth Publishers.

Pluess, M., Velders, F. P., Belsky, J., Van, I. M. H., Bakermans-Kranenburg, M. J., Jaddoe, V. W., … & Tiemeier, H. (2011). Serotonin transporter polymorphism moderates effects of prenatal maternal anxiety on infant negative emotionality. *Biological Psychiatry, 69*, 520–525. doi:10.1016/j.biopsych.2010.10.006

Posner, M. I., Rothbart M. K., Sheese B. E., & Voelker, P. (2012). Control networks and neuromodulators of early development. *Developmental Psychology*, *48*(3), 827–835. doi: 10.1037/a0025530

Raby, K. L., Cicchetti, D., Carlson, E. A., Cutulli, J. J., Englund, M. M. & Egeland, B. (2012). Genetic and caregiving-based contributions to infant attachment: Unique associations with distress reactivity and attachment security. *Psychological Science*, *23*(9), 1016–1023. doi: 10.1177/0956797612438265

Ronald, A. (2011). Is the child 'father of the man'? Evaluating the stability of genetic influences across development. *Developmental Science*, *14*(6), 1471–1478. doi: 10.1111/j.1467-7687.2011.01114.x

Rothbart, M. K. (1981). Measurement of temperament in infancy. *Child Development*, *52*, 569–578.

Sheese, B. E., Voelker, P., Posner, M. I., & Rothbart, M. K. (2009). Genetic variation influences on the early development of reactive emotions and their regulation by attention. *Cognitive Neuropsychiatry*, *14*(4–5), 332–355. doi: 10.1080/13546800902844064

Sheese, B. E., Voelker, P. M., Rothbart, M. K., & Posner, M. I. (2007). Parenting quality interacts with genetic variation in dopamine receptor D4 to influence temperament in early childhood. *Development and psychopathology*, *19*(4), 1039–1046.

Shendure, J. & Aiden, E. L. (2012). The expanding scope of DNA sequencing. *Nature Biotechnology*, *30*(11), 1084–1094. doi: 10.1038/nbt.2421

Sieradzka, D., Power, R. A., Freeman, D., Cardno, A. G., McGuire, P., Plomin, R.,... & Ronald, A. (2014). Are genetic risk factors for psychosis also associated with dimension-specific psychotic experiences in adolescence? *PloS one*, *9*(4), e94398.

Spangler, G., Johann, M., Ronai, Z. & Zimmermann, P. (2009). Genetic and environmental influence on attachment disorganization. *Journal of Child Psychology and Psychiatry*, *50*(8), 952–961. doi:10.1111/j.1469-7610.2008.02054.x

Van Gestel, S. & Van Broeckhoven, C. (2003). Genetics of personality: Are we making progress? *Molecular Psychiatry*, *8* (10), 840–852.

Van Ijzendoorn, M. H. & Bakermans-Kranenburg, M. J. (2006). DRD4 7-repeat polymorphism moderates the association between maternal unresolved loss or trauma and infant disorganization. *Attachment and Human Development*, *8*(4), 291–307. doi: 10.1080/14616730601048159

Van Ijzendoorn, M. H., Schuengel, C. & Bakermans-Kranenburg, M. J. (1999). Disorganized attachment in early childhood: meta-analysis of precursors, concomitants, and sequelae. *Developmental Psychopathology*, *11*(2), 225–249.

Voelker, P., Sheese B. E., Rothbart M. K., & Posner, M. I. (2009). Variations in COMT Gene interact with parenting to influence attention in early development. *Neuroscience*, *164*(1), 121–130. doi: 10.1016/j.neuroscience.2009.05.059

Wray, N.R., Goddard, M.E., & Visscher, P.M. (2007). Prediction of individual genetic risk to disease from genome-wide association studies. *Genome Research*, *17*, 1520–1528.

Wray, N. R., Lee, S. H., Mehta, D., Vinkhuyzen, A. A. E., Dudbridge, F. & Middeldorp, C. M. (2014). Research review: Polygenic methods and their application to psychiatric traits. *Journal of Child Psychology and Psychiatry*. doi: 10.1111/jcpp.12295

Zhang, M., Chen, X., Way, N., Yoshikawa, H., Deng, H., Ke, X., Ye, W., Chen, P., He, C., Chi, X. & Lu, Z. (2011). The association between infants' self-regulatory behavior and MAOA gene polymorphism. *Developmental Science*, *14*, 1059–1065. doi: 10.1111/j.1467-7687.2011.01047.x

# 12

# Generalist Genes and Developmental Psychopathology

Yulia Kovas and Maria Grazia Tosto

Developmental psychopathology has been defined as "… normal development gone awry" (Wenar, 1994, p. 23). Deviations from normal development include learning disabilities (LDs)—difficulties experienced by children in learning. These can have significant effects on educational progress and other important life outcomes, including social adjustment (e.g., Butterworth & Kovas, 2013). LDs often co-occur with each other, and with other developmental disorders, such as autism spectrum disorder (ASD) and attention deficit hyperactivity disorder (ADHD). Behavioral genetic methodology can be used to evaluate the relative contribution of genetic and environmental factors to LDs and to comorbidity among different LDs. Recent research has shown that much of the genetic contribution to LDs is general: the same set of genes affects different LDs to a large extent. However, some genetic factors seem to be specific to each LD. Behavioral genetic research has also contributed to the understanding of a central issue in the study of psychopathology: the distinction between normal and abnormal behavior. Research has suggested that the same genetic factors are involved in LDs as those affecting normal variation in ability. This chapter provides examples of results from behavioral genetic studies, with particular focus on the etiology of co-occurrence among mathematical and reading disabilities.

Many learners experience a variety of difficulties in acquiring information and knowledge. Some experience problems with specific areas of learning, such as language, reading or mathematics. These relatively specific problems—specific learning disabilities (SLDs)—are often accompanied by intelligence scores in the normal range (e.g., Siegler, 1989). To date, no agreement has been achieved on the best way of measuring and diagnosing SLDs, with some arguing for low ability cut-offs (Fuchs, Fuchs, & Prentice, 2004) and others for taking into account discrepancy with IQ (see Vaughn & Fuchs, 2003, for a discussion). Irrespective of precise ways of classifying and measuring SLDs, they are common, with an average estimated frequency in the population of 4%–10% (e.g., Landerl, Fussenegger, Moll, & Willburger, 2009; Butterworth & Kovas, 2013). SLDs can be contrasted with other syndromes, such as Down syndrome and Prader-Willi syndrome that are characterized by multiple physical and cognitive problems, with specific patterns of strengths and difficulties, as

*The Wiley Handbook of Developmental Psychopathology*, First Edition. Edited by Luna C. Centifanti and David M. Williams.

well as low scores on tests of general intelligence (e.g., Karmiloff-Smith, 2009). These conditions have low incidence in the general population. For example, the prevalence of Down syndrome is 1.72 per 1000 (Irving, Basu, Richmond, Burn, & Wren, 2008), and the prevalence of Prader-Willi is 1 in 10,000 to 30,000 (Cassidy, Schwartz, Miller, & Driscoll, 2012).

Dyscalculia and dyslexia are among the most common SLDs. Individuals with developmental dyscalculia fail to reach adequate mathematical school achievement and have problems with understanding symbolic (numerals) and non-symbolic (numerosity) magnitudes, enumerating small sets of objects, counting and doing arithmetic calculations. The prevalence of dyscalculia in the population is estimated to be 3%–7% (Butterworth, 2005; Butterworth & Kovas, 2013). Individuals with developmental dyslexia experience problems with comprehension of written and oral language, reading and writing. The prevalence of dyslexia in the population is estimated to be 4%–8% (Butterworth, 2005; Butterworth & Kovas, 2013). Dyslexia and dyscalculia may occur in the presence of normal cognitive functions, such as normal working memory and normal IQ (e.g., Gabrieli, 2009; Landerl, Bevan, & Butterworth, 2004; Siegel, 1989). The two syndromes are often comorbid, with the prevalence of their co-occurrence higher than expected given their single prevalence (Butterworth & Kovas, 2013).

SLDs may stem from impairments in specific mechanisms, such as phonological processing or numerosity processing—sometimes referred to as *core cognitive deficits* (e.g., Landerl et al., 2009). Although, it is hypothesized that such "core deficits" are domain-specific (e.g., phonological processing deficits underlying dyslexia), it is possible that such deficits are more general, underlying more than one impairment. Moreover, the core deficits themselves may stem from disruption in more general (e.g., visual or attentional) processes—the so called *domain-general deficits* that may also explain much of the observed comorbidity across SLDs (see Butterworth & Kovas, 2013, for a discussion). It remains unclear whether the mechanisms underlying SLDs (dyslexia for example) are different from those underlying similar reading problems when they co-occur with other difficulties (mathematical disability or low intelligence). It is likely that the etiology of SLDs is highly heterogeneous, with each learner's characteristics driven by a unique combination of genetic and environmental factors, reflected in different brain and cognitive profiles (Butterworth & Kovas, 2013; Kovas & Plomin, 2012).

Recent quantitative genetic research has contributed to the conceptualization of SLDs by providing insights into the etiology of variation and comorbidity. The next section summarizes the results of the relevant behavioral genetic research into the etiology of developmental dyscalculia and dyslexia, as well as their co-occurrence with each other and with other developmental problems, such as ASD and ADHD (e.g., Dworzynski et al., 2007; Haworth & Plomin, 2010; Willcutt et al., 2010).

## The Etiology of Learning Disabilities

Twin studies (see Box 12.1 for details of the Twin Method) have provided a wealth of information on the relative contributions of multiple genetic and environmental factors to different learning abilities and disabilities. These studies show that reading and mathematical abilities are moderately to highly heritable; the environment, both shared and non-shared, has also been found to contribute to variation in these traits (e.g., Kovas, Haworth, Dale, & Plomin, 2007a; Stromswold, 2001).

## Box 12.1 Twin Method

Twin method is the most commonly used research design that enables us to estimate the relative contribution of genetic and environmental factors to individual differences in a population in a particular trait. The method is based on the comparison in resemblance (correlation or concordance) between monozygotic (MZ) twins, who are genetically identical, and dizygotic (DZ) twins who share on average 50% of segregating (variable) DNA.

*Heritability* indexes the proportion of the phenotypic (observed) variance in a trait that can be attributed to genetic differences among individuals. Heritability is computed as twice the difference between MZ and DZ twin correlations.

*Non-shared (individual specific) environments* index the extent to which MZ twins are not identical (MZ correlation on a trait is not 100%). Non-shared environmental factors may include injury or illness not shared by the co-twins, but also include measurement error.

*Shared (common) environments* contribute to twin similarity in a trait and are computed as the difference between the MZ twin correlation and the heritability. Shared home environment, school, or teachers may contribute to similarity among family members (although they may also contribute to differences, see Kovas et al. (2015) for discussion).

All three components of the variance represent population-based statistics. For example, heritability indexes the proportion of variation in a trait in a specific population (e.g., the UK), of particular age (e.g., elementary school children), at a particular time (e.g., in current educational setting that includes a unified National Curriculum). Therefore, heritability can vary as a function of changes in the environment (see Plomin, DeFries, Knopik, & Neiderhiser, 2013 for details).

Apart from examining the etiology of variation in individual traits, the twin method can be used to estimate the extent to which genetic and environmental factors contribute to the covariation among traits. Applying twin design to longitudinal data allows for estimation of the extent to which the same genetic and environmental factors contribute to continuity and change of traits over time.

Behavioral genetic investigations can be used to address a question of whether SLDs have different etiology from that of normal variation in ability. Using DF extremes analysis (see Box 12.2 for details), twin studies demonstrated that, rather than being qualitatively different, SLDs represent extreme performance on ability dimensions with continuous underlying etiology (e.g., Plomin, Haworth, & Davis, 2009).

For example, a study that used a sample of 8- to 20-year-old US twins estimated heritability of low mathematical ability at .38 from probandwise concordances of .73 and .56 for MZ and DZ twins respectively (Alarcón, DeFries, Light, & Pennington, 1997). In a sample of 7-year-olds from a UK representative sample, Twins Early Development Study (TEDS), the low-ability group heritability was .65 (Oliver et al., 2004). The discrepancies in the heritability estimates between the two studies need to be considered in relation to the age, environmental conditions and size of the samples (see notes in Box 12.1 regarding heritability). In TEDS, the heritability of the low-ability group was very similar to that of the unselected twin sample (.66 vs .65) suggesting the

## Box 12.2 DeFries–Fulker Extremes Analysis

In dealing with disabilities and disorders, one of the issues is whether they are etiologically different from the normal dimensions. The DeFries–Fulker (DF) extremes analysis (DeFries & Fulker, 1985) examines probandwise concordances—the probability of a twin displaying a low/high score (proband) having a co-twin who scores in the same low/high range. The comparison of MZ and DZ twin concordances on a trait allows to estimate the group heritability.

*Group heritability* indexes the extent to which the observed mean differences between the proband and the unselected sample (the normal population) are explained by genetic differences; the higher the group heritability the stronger the genetic links between the normal and low-ability groups. If there were no genetic links between normal and low performance, the group heritability would be zero. The DF extremes analysis also estimates the extent to which the links between normal and low/high performance can be due to shared and non-shared environmental factors (see Plomin et al., 2013 for more details on the method).

Research using DF extremes analysis suggests very similar etiologies for low ability and the normal range of performance. In other words, a disability arises as a result of an accumulation of genetic risk factors (ability-decreasing alleles) that push an individual below a "diagnosis" threshold. The same alleles discriminate between better and worse performance in the normal range. Therefore "abnormal" can be considered as etiologically "normal," as low and high abilities represent the extremes of the same etiological continuum.

same etiology for low and normal mathematical performance. When the twins in TEDS were 10 years of age, they were assessed on different aspects of mathematical ability, according to the UK National Curriculum: Understanding Number, Non-Numerical Processes, Computation and Knowledge. The results showed very similar heritability estimates across the different aspects of mathematics and in both low-ability (average .43) and unselected-ability (average .40) groups (Kovas, Haworth, Dale, Petrill, & Plomin, 2007b). When TEDS twins were 12, heritability of low mathematical and normal performance was .56 and .49 respectively (Haworth et al., 2009).

Genetic factors have also been shown to contribute to the development of communication disorders such as expressive language, mixed receptive and expressive language disorder, phonological disorder, and stuttering (as identified by the previous edition of the *Diagnostic and Statistical Manual of Mental Disorders, DSM-IV*; American Psychiatric Association, 1994). For example, an early adoption study showed that the biological parents' history of speech and language problems was the best predictor of offspring being affected, suggesting that these disorders "run in families" (Felsenfeld, & Plomin, 1997). The heritability of problems in expressive language and articulation was estimated .54 and .97 respectively by comparing MZ and DZ probandwise concordances in a sample of 6-year-old US twins (DeThorne et al., 2006). In the TEDS sample at the age of 4, language impairments showed a strong genetic etiology (heritability of .96, Bishop & Hayiou-Thomas, 2008). Similar estimates were reported in the same sample when the children were older and were assessed on a range of language and reading abilities: at the age of 7, 9 and 10 the heritability of literacy problems, as assessed by teacher ratings of the children's school achievement based on the UK National Curriculum, was .75, .83 and .84 respectively (Kovas et al., 2007a). The same study reported heritability estimates of .65 for reading fluency problems at age 7 and of .43 for reading comprehension problems at age 10. These examples suggest that genetic factors are the main source of individual differences in a range of language and communication problems across development. Moreover, the results suggest that the same factors are involved in reading and language LDs and in normal variation in these traits (e.g., Kovas et al., 2007a; Haworth et al., 2009).

The few existing longitudinal studies also suggest that persistence of LDs is largely explained by genetic factors that operate across development. For example, one study found that 61% of the relationship between low reading fluency at the age of 7 and low reading comprehension at age of 10 was explained by common genetic factors (Kovas et al., 2007a).

Overall, the research shows that genetic effects on mathematics, reading and language abilities fit the Quantitative Trait Loci (QTL) model (see Box 12.3). According to the QTL model, disabilities are not aetiologically different from abilities, as the genetic influences contributing to individual differences are the same for the whole range of performance.

### **Box 12.3** Quantitative Trait Loci (QTL) Model

Establishing that a trait is heritable to a degree means that variation in DNA is to some extent related to the individual differences in this trait. Most of the DNA sequence is invariant (the same for all individuals). However, every 100 to 1000 letter (*locus*) of the DNA code differs across individuals. The different variants (*alleles*) found at these loci are referred to as *single nucleotide polymorphisms (SNPs)*. Other types of DNA variability include differences in the number of repeats of particular stretches of DNA—*copy number variants* (*CNVs*), deletions, insertions, and substitutions in the DNA sequence.

Behavioral genetic research provides evidence that individual differences in cognitive and learning abilities, learning disabilities, and developmental disorders are under the influence of many DNA variants of very small effects (for a discussion see Plomin, Haworth, & Davis, 2009; Plomin et al., 2013). Such traits are called *polygenic*. Polygenic traits' variance is the result of a combination of multiple genetic factors, as well as multiple environments. Most of the genetic effects seem to be additive in nature, whereby the influence of many independent alleles is summed up. However, some genetic factors act in an *epistatic* way, whereby the effect of one genetic factor depends on, or moderates the effect of another factor.

This polygenic nature of *complex* or *quantitative traits* has been captured by the *quantitative trait locus* (QTL) model. According to the QTL model, individual differences in complex traits, such as reading ability, stem from influences of many genetic variants (DNA loci). In other words, an ability-decreasing allele (risk allele) of a particular genetic variant can decrease ability at both the high and the low end of the performance continuum. On the contrary, in the case of monogenic disorders, one gene is necessary and sufficient to cause the disorder in an "all or nothing" fashion: possessing an ability decreasing allele of such genetic variant necessarily pushes an individual towards low ability functions.

## Etiology of Comorbidity

Behavioral genetic research suggests that comorbidity among domains largely stems from overlapping genetic effects (e.g., Hart et al., 2010; Kovas et al., 2007a) described as Generalist Genes (see Box 12.4). For example, in a sample of over 1500 17–18 year-old twins, the genetic correlation between reading and mathematical problems was estimated to be ~.60, suggesting that 60% of the genetic factors involved in mathematical disability were also involved in reading disability. The study also showed that 95% of the observed comorbidity between reading and mathematical disability was explained by these common genetic factors (Markowitz, Willemsen,

### **Box 12.4** Mechanisms of Generalist Genes Effects on Learning Disabilities

Multivariate genetic research shows moderate to high genetic overlap among traits and syndromes. These shared genetic influences—Generalist Genes—seem to be largely responsible for the observed covariation across traits (Kovas & Plomin, 2006).

A large body of evidence that shows strong *genetic correlations* (or genetic overlap which indexes the extent to which the same genetic factors affect different traits) across learning abilities suggests that genetic effects are largely generalist, rather than trait-specific (e.g., Haworth et al., 2009).

The effects of generalist genes may be explained by *pleiotropy*—a biological mechanism through which one gene affects multiple traits. Pleiotropic effects may work in three different ways: (1) a gene may influence one brain area, which in turn influences various cognitive functions; (2) a gene may influence different brain areas, which in turn influence different cognitive process; and (3) multiple genes influence several areas of the brain, which affect many cognitive processes (see Kovas & Plomin, 2006, for details). Learning disabilities therefore may stem from common genetic, brain and cognitive processes that are responsible for the normal variation.

Similar to the QTLs (see Box 12.3), the *quantitative trait neural processes* (QTN) model has been proposed to describe the general neural processes of small effect that mediate the effects of QTLs and underlie variation and covariation in complex traits (see Kovas & Plomin, 2006, for details).

In addition to pleiotropy, genetic overlaps may also result from *causality*: if trait A causes trait B, the genetic factors influencing trait A will exert their influences on trait B via expression of trait A.

The co-twin control design (Kendler et al., 1993) allows to test which of the mechanisms (pleiotropy vs. causality) is more plausible for a particular comorbidity. In this design, monozygotic twin pairs discordant for the first trait (for example when one twin is affected with reading disability and the other is not) are compared in terms of their risk for mathematics disability. Under a causal model, only the twins affected for reading disability will be at increased risk for mathematics disability. Under genetic pleiotropy, this risk will be increased in both twins, because they share the same genes (for more details see Ligthart & Boomsma, 2012).

Trumbetta, van Beijsterveldt, & Boomsma, 2005). In another study, 55% of the observed comorbidity between reading and mathematical problems in school age twins was explained by genetic factors (Light & DeFries, 1995). A similar genetic correlation (.53) was observed between reading disability and mathematical disability in a sample with a wider age range (8–20 years; Knopik, Alarcón, & DeFries, 1997). The co-occurrence of reading and mathematical problems with other learning disabilities also seems to be strongly influenced by genetic factors; an average genetic correlation of .67 was found among low-reading, low-mathematics, low-language and low-IQ groups (Haworth et al., 2009).

Strong genetic overlap between LDs suggests similar general genetic effects as those found for the normal range of learning abilities. For instance, in the TEDS sample at age 12, an average genetic correlation of .85 was shown between reading, language, mathematics, as well as *g*—general cognitive ability—assessed by a number of verbal and non-verbal intelligence tests (Davis, Haworth, & Plomin, 2009).

Low-mathematical, low-reading and low-communication problems often co-occur with other syndromes, most notably with attention deficit hyperactivity disorder (ADHD) (e.g., Hart et al., 2010; Trzesniewski, Moffitt, Caspi, Taylor, & Maughan, 2006). Twin studies have consistently shown ADHD to be one of the most heritable psychiatric disorders, with an average heritability of .75 (Faraone et al., 2005). The inattentive and hyperactivity-impulsivity symptoms have been found to be partially genetically correlated (.55) with partially distinct genetic etiology (Greven, Rijsdijk, & Plomin, 2011). Given that ADHD, reading disability, and mathematical disability are highly heritable individually, it is not surprising that genetic factors have been implicated in their overlap (Hart et al., 2010; Polderman et al., 2011; Willcutt et al., 2010). In fact, twin studies have shown that shared genes (rather than shared environments) are primarily responsible for the comorbidity among these disorders (Trzesniewski et al., 2006; Willcutt, Pennington, & DeFries, 2000; Willcutt, Pennington, Olson, & DeFries, 2007).

Interestingly, the two ADHD dimensions relate differentially to reading and mathematical disabilities, with a stronger phenotypic association with inattentiveness than hyperactivity–impulsivity (Antonini et al., 2013; Massetti et al., 2008; Willcutt & Pennington, 2000). One recent investigation found a genetic correlation of –.31 between reading and inattentiveness; and of –.16 between reading and hyperactivity-impulsivity (Greven, Harlaar, Dale, & Plomin, 2011). Highly similar genetic correlations were found in TEDS between mathematics and inattentiveness (–.41) and mathematics and hyperactivity–impulsivity (–.22). The genetic correlation between inattentiveness and mathematics was largely independent of genetic influences that inattentiveness and mathematics share with hyperactivity–impulsivity, and could moderately be accounted for only by genetic influences shared also with reading and IQ (Greven, Kovas, Willcutt, Petrill, & Plomin, 2013).

Autism spectrum disorder (ASD) is another neurodevelopmental disorder that shows overlap with LDs. According to the latest version of the Diagnostic and Statistical Manual of Mental Disorders (*DSM 5*; American Psychiatric Association, 2013) classification system, ASD is characterized by a dyad of impairments: (1) social-communication problems and (2) repetitive and stereotyped interests and behaviors (American Psychiatric Association, 2013). It remains unresolved, whether autism should be viewed as fractionable into largely independent sets of clinical features or whether the principal features of this disorder are developmentally related to each other (see Hobson, 2014).

ASD is highly heritable, with twins' heritability estimates between .64 and .81 (Ronald et al., 2006). Problems in the social-communication and repetitive-stereotyped ASD domains have been shown to have largely different genetic etiology (Dworzynski, Happé, Bolton, & Ronald, 2009; Ronald et al., 2006; Ronald, Happé, & Plomin, 2005). Similar to the etiology of LDs, ASD appears to be an etiologically continuously distributed trait (Piven, Palmer, Jacobi, Childress, & Arndt, 1997; Robinson et al., 2011). High genetic influences on ASD suggest that its comorbidity with LDs largely stems from genetic factors. One study has shown that genetic influences almost entirely mediated the relationship between ASD and early language problems in 2 and 4 year-old children (Dworzynski et al., 2007). However, early language was significantly associated only with the social and communication subtypes of ASD but not with the restrictive and repetitive behaviors and interests. It is important to note that the overlap (comorbidity) between SLD and ASD is only modest (e.g., ~.20 in Dworzynski et al., 2007), leaving potentially a high degree of behavioral, neurobiological, and etiological specificity (see Williams, Botting, & Boucher, 2008).

Very few studies have looked at the aetiology of comorbidity between ADHD and ASD symptomatology. The limited research available suggests that the phenotypic overlap between them is largely explained by genetic factors (Ronald et al., 2008; Taylor et al., 2012).

The effects of the generalist genes can be explained by pleiotropic or causal processes (see Box 12.4 for further details). However, not all of the observed associations among developmental problems can be explained by overlapping genetic effects. For example, the association between poor reading and antisocial behavior has been found to be largely mediated by common environmental factors (Trzesniewski et al., 2006). More research is needed to gain further insights into the etiology of comorbidity among LDs, as well as into the mechanisms involved in generalist genetic and environmental effects.

## Finding the Genes

Molecular genetic research has begun to identify specific genetic variants involved in learning disabilities. These studies have provided evidence for generalist genetic effects across LDs and across ability and disability. For example, several polymorphisms were found to be associated with mathematics at the age of 7, 9, 10 and 12 and with reading and cognitive ability/disability (Docherty et al., 2010a; Docherty, Kovas, Perill, & Plomin, 2010b; Meaburn, Harlaar, Craig, Schalkwyk, & Plomin, 2008). Common genetic factors have also been identified between poor reading and ADHD (Fisher et al., 1999; Gayán et al., 1999; Gayán et al., 2005; Grigorenko, Wood, Meyer, & Pauls, 2000; Willcutt et al., 2002). The etiological continuity across the ability range is supported by several polymorphisms found to be associated to mathematics across the whole distribution of abilities (Docherty et al., 2010a). Similarly, the *KIAA0319* gene, previously associated with developmental dyslexia, was also found to be associated with reading ability in the general population (Paracchini et al., 2008).

Despite the fast progresses in molecular genetic methods and technology, identifying specific genetic factors involved in LDs and comorbidity among them has been relatively slow. As many variants of low penetrance (having a very small effect on the trait) are likely to be involved, the associations between genetic polymorphisms and

LDs are difficult to detect. The gap between strong genetic effects on variation and co-variation between traits and the weak effects of the actual polymorphisms identified to date has been referred to as "Missing Heritability" (Maher, 2008; Manolio et al., 2009; Thapar & Harold, 2014). This gap is likely to narrow in the next few years, particularly with rapidly reducing costs of genome-wide sequencing which allows to study rare and common genetic variants (see Plomin, 2013 for a discussion; Trzaskowski, Dale, & Plomin, 2013). Once the genetic factors involved in developmental psychopathology have been identified, we can begin to understand the biological paths from each specific DNA polymorphism to associated brain processing to behavioral expression—facilitating further research into the relevant gene–environment processes (see Plomin, 2014). Identifying the relevant DNA variants will also provide definitive evidence for the existence of "generalist and specialist genes," helping to clarify issues of the overlap and specificity among different SLDs.

## Conclusion

Quantitative genetic investigations show a large degree of genetic overlap across a wide range of abilities and disabilities. Recent molecular genetic investigations provide further support for the genetic overlap at the level of specific genetic variants. These studies also suggest an etiological link between abilities and disabilities. Both quantitative and molecular studies suggest that contribution of any specific genetic polymorphism to any complex trait is very small. Both common and rare genetic variants may contribute to variability in complex traits. New molecular genetic strategies will provide further insights into the specific genetic factors involved in learning disabilities. Identifying specific genetic factors involved in generalist and specialist effects on learning disabilities will contribute to their conceptualization and classification. Moreover understanding specific genetic pathways and mechanisms underlying genetic effects can help with developing successful prediction, prevention and intervention strategies for specific and comorbid disabilities.

## References


Alarcón, M., DeFries, J. C., Light, J. G., & Pennington, B. F. (1997). A twin study of mathematics disability. *Journal of Learning Disabilities, 30*, 617–623.

American Psychiatric Association (1994). *Diagnostic and Statistical Manual of Mental Disorders (DSM-IV)*. Washington, DC: American Psychiatric Association.

American Psychiatric Association (2013). *Diagnostic and Statistical Manual of Mental Disorders (DSM-5)*. Washington, DC: American Psychiatric Association.

Antonini, T. N., Kingery, K. M., Narad, M. E., Langberg, J. M., Tamm, L., & Epstein, J. N. (2016). Neurocognitive and behavioral predictors of math performance in children with and without ADHD. *Journal of Attention Disorders, 20*(2), 108–118. doi: 10.1177/1087054713504620

Bishop, D. V. M., & Hayiou-Thomas, M. E. (2008). Heritability of specific language impairment depends on diagnostic criteria. *Genes Brain and Behavior, 7*(3), 365–372.

Butterworth, B. (2005) Developmental dyscalculia. In J. I. D. Campbell (Ed.), *Handbook of mathematical cognition* (pp. 455–467) Abingdon: Psychology Press.

Butterworth, B., & Kovas, Y. (2013). Understanding neurocognitive developmental disorders can improve education for all. *Science, 340*(6130), 300–305.

Cassidy, S. B., Schwartz, S., Miller, J. L., & Driscoll, D. J. (2012). Prader-Willi syndrome. *Genetics in Medicine*, *14*(1), 10–26.

Davis, O. S., Haworth, C. M., & Plomin, R. (2009). Learning abilities and disabilities: generalist genes in early adolescence. *Cognitive Neuropsychiatry*, *14*(4–5), 312–331.

DeFries, J. C., & Fulker, D. W. (1985). Multiple regression analysis of twin data. *Behavior Genetics*, *15*, 467–473. doi: 10.1007/BF01066239

DeThorne, L. S., Hart, S. A., Petrill, S. A., Deater-Deckard, K., Thompson, L. A., Schatschneider, C., & Davison, M. D. (2006). Children's history of speech-language difficulties: Genetic influences and associations with reading-related measures. *Journal of Speech, Language and Hearing Research*, *49*(6), 1280–1293.

Docherty, S. J., Davis, O. S. P., Kovas, Y., Meaburn, E. L., Dale, P. S., Petrill, S. A., ... & Plomin, R. (2010a). A genome-wide association study identifies multiple loci associated with mathematics ability and disability. *Genes Brain and Behavior*, *9*(2), 234–247.

Docherty, S. J., Kovas, Y., Petrill, S. A., & Plomin, R. (2010b). Generalist genes analysis of DNA markers associated with mathematical ability and disability reveals shared influence across ages and abilities. *BMC Genetics*, *11*(1), 61.

Dworzynski, K., Happé, F., Bolton, P., & Ronald, A. (2009). Relationship between symptom domains in autism spectrum disorders: A population-based twin study. *Journal of Autism and Developmental Disorders*, *39*(8), 1197–1210.

Dworzynski, K., Ronald, A., Hayiou-Thomas, M., Rijsdijk, F., Happé, F., Bolton, P. F., & Plomin, R. (2007). Aetiological relationship between language performance and autistic-like traits in childhood: a twin study. *International Journal of Language & Communication Disorders*, *42*(3), 273–292.

Faraone, S. V., Perlis, R. H., Doyle, A. E., Smoller, J. W., Goralnick, J. J., Holmgren, M. A., & Sklar, P. (2005). Molecular genetics of attention-deficit/hyperactivity disorder. *Biological Psychiatry*, *57*(11), 1313–1323.

Felsenfeld, S., & Plomin, R. (1997). Epidemiological and offspring analyses of developmental speech disorders using data from the Colorado Adoption Project. *Journal of Speech, Language and Hearing Research*, *40*(4), 778–791.

Fisher, S.E., Marlow, A.J., Lamb, J., Maestrini, E., Williams, D.F., Richardson, A.J., Weeks, D.E., Stein, J.F., & Monaco, A.P. (1999). A quantitative trait locus on chromosome 6p influences different aspects of developmental dyslexia. *American Journal of Human Genetics*, *64*, 146–156.

Fuchs, L. S., Fuchs, D., & Prentice, K. (2004). Responsiveness to mathematical problem-solving instruction comparing students at risk of mathematics disability with and without risk of reading disability. *Journal of Learning Disabilities*, *37*(4), 293–306.

Gabrieli, J. D. (2009). Dyslexia: A new synergy between education and cognitive neuroscience. *Science*, *325*(5938), 280–283.

Gayán, J., Willcutt, E. G., Fisher, S. E., Francks, C., Cardon, L. R., Olson, R. K., ... & DeFries, J. C. (2005). Bivariate linkage scan for reading disability and attention-deficit/hyperactivity disorder localizes pleiotropic loci. *Journal of Child Psychology and Psychiatry*, *46*(10), 1045–1056.

Gayán, J., Smith, S.D., Cherny, S.S., Cardon, L.R., Fulker, D.W., Brower, ... & DeFries, J.C. (1999). Quantitative trait locus for specific language and reading deficits on chromosome 6p. *American Journal of Human Genetics*, *64*, 157–164.

Greven, C.U., Harlaar, N., Dale, P.S., & Plomin, R. (2011). Genetic overlap between ADHD symptoms and reading is largely driven by inattentiveness rather than hyperactivity-impulsivity. *Journal of the Canadian Academy of Child and Adolescent Psychiatry*, *20*, 6–14.

Greven, C. U., Kovas, Y., Willcutt, E. G., Petrill, S. A., & Plomin, R. (2013). Evidence for shared genetic risk between ADHD symptoms and reduced mathematics ability: A twin study. *Journal of Child Psychology and Psychiatry*, *55*(1), 39–48.

Greven, C. U., Rijsdijk, F. V., & Plomin, R. (2011). A twin study of ADHD symptoms in early adolescence: hyperactivity-impulsivity and inattentiveness show substantial genetic overlap but also genetic specificity. *Journal of Abnormal Child Psychology, 39*(2), 265–275.

Grigorenko, E. L., Wood, F. B., Meyer, M. S., & Pauls, D. L. (2000). Chromosome 6p influences on different dyslexia-related cognitive processes: Further confirmation. *American Journal of Human Genetics, 66*, 715–723.

Hart, S. A., Petrill, S. A., Willcutt, E., Thompson, L. A., Schatschneider, C., Deater-Deckard, K., & Cutting, L. E. (2010). Exploring how symptoms of Attention-Deficit/Hyperactivity Disorder are related to reading and mathematics performance general genes, general environments. *Psychological Science, 21*(11), 1708–1715.

Haworth, C., Kovas, Y., Harlaar, N., Hayiou-Thomas, M. E., Petrill, S. A., Dale, P. S., & Plomin, R. (2009). Generalist genes and learning disabilities: a multivariate genetic analysis of low performance in reading, mathematics, language and general cognitive ability in a sample of 8000 12-year-old twins. *Journal of Child Psychology and Psychiatry, 50*(10), 1318–1325.

Haworth, C., & Plomin, R. (2010). Quantitative genetics in the era of molecular genetics: Learning abilities and disabilities as an example. *Journal of the American Academy of Child & Adolescent Psychiatry, 49*(8), 783–793.

Hobson, R. P. (2014). The coherence of autism. *Autism, 18*(1), 6–16.

Irving, C., Basu, A., Richmond, S., Burn, J., & Wren, C. (2008). Twenty-year trends in prevalence and survival of Down syndrome. *European Journal of Human Genetics, 16*(11), 1336–1340.

Karmiloff-Smith, A. (2009). Nativism versus neuroconstructivism: Rethinking the study of developmental disorders. *Developmental Psychology, 45*(1), 56–63.

Kendler, K. S., Neale, M. C., MacLean, C. J., Heath, A. C., Eaves, L. J., & Kessler, R. C. (1993). Smoking and major depression: a causal analysis. *Archives of General Psychiatry, 50*(1), 36–43.

Knopik, V. S., Alarcón, M., & DeFries, J. C. (1997). Comorbidity of mathematics and reading deficits: Evidence for a genetic etiology. *Behavior Genetics, 27*(5), 447–453.

Kovas, Y., Garon-Carrier, G., Boivin, M., Petrill, S. A., Plomin, R. … & Vitaro, F. (2015). Why children differ in motivation to learn: insights from over 13,000 twins from 6 countries. *Personality and Individual Differences, 80*, 51–63. doi: 10.1016/j.paid.2015.02.006

Kovas, Y., Haworth, C. M. A., Dale, P. S., Petrill, S. A., & Plomin, R. (2007b). Mathematical ability of 10-year-old boys and girls: genetic and environmental etiology of typical and low performance. *Journal of Learning Disabilities, 40*(6), 554–567.

Kovas, Y., Haworth, C. M. A., Dale, P. S., & Plomin, R. (2007a). *The genetic and environmental origins of learning abilities and disabilities in the early school years.* Monographs of the Society for Research in Child Development, *72*(3), vii, 1–160.

Kovas, Y., & Plomin, R. (2006). Generalist genes: implications for the cognitive sciences. *Trends in Cognitive Sciences, 10*(5), 198–203.

Kovas, Y., & Plomin, R. (2012). Genetics and genomics: good, bad and ugly. In S. Della Sala, & M. Anderson, M. (Eds.), *Neuroscience in education: The good, the bad and the ugly* (pp.155–173). Oxford: Oxford University Press.

Landerl, K., Bevan, A., & Butterworth, B. (2004). Developmental dyscalculia and basic numerical capacities: A study of 8–9-year-old students. *Cognition, 93*(2), 99–125.

Landerl, K., Fussenegger, B., Moll, K., & Willburger, E. (2009). Dyslexia and dyscalculia: Two learning disorders with different cognitive profiles. *Journal of Experimental Child Psychology, 103*(3), 309–324.

Light, J. G., & DeFries, J. C. (1995). Comorbidity of reading and mathematics disabilities genetic and environmental etiologies. *Journal of Learning Disabilities, 28*(2), 96–106.

Ligthart, L., & Boomsma, D. I. (2012). Causes of comorbidity: pleiotropy or causality? Shared genetic and environmental influences on migraine and neuroticism. *Twin Research and Human Genetics, 15*(2), 158–165.

Maher, B. (2008). The case of the missing heritability. *Nature, 456*(7218), 18–21.

Manolio, T. A., Collins, F. S., Cox, N. J., Goldstein, D. B., Hindorff, L. A., Hunter, D. J., … & Visscher, P. M. (2009). Finding the missing heritability of complex diseases. *Nature, 461*(7265), 747–753.

Markowitz, E. M., Willemsen, G., Trumbetta, S. L., van Beijsterveldt, T. C. E. M., & Boomsma, D. I. (2005). The etiology of mathematical and reading (dis)ability covariation in a sample of Dutch twins. *Twin Research and Human Genetics, 8*, 585–593.

Massetti, G. M., Lahey, B. B., Pelham, W. E., Loney, J., Ehrhardt, A., Lee, S. S., & Kipp, H. (2008). Academic achievement over 8 years among children who met modified criteria for attention-deficit/hyperactivity disorder at 4–6 years of age. *Journal of Abnormal Child Psychology, 36*(3), 399–410.

Meaburn E.L., Harlaar N., Craig I.W., Schalkwyk L.C., & Plomin R. (2008). Quantitative trait locus association scan of early reading disability and ability using pooled DNA and 100K SNP microarrays in a sample of 5760 children. *Molecular Psychiatry. 13*(7), 729–740.

Oliver, B., Harlaar, N., Hayiou Thomas, M. E., Kovas, Y., Walker, S. O., Petrill, S. A., … & Plomin, R. (2004). A twin study of teacher-reported mathematics performance and low performance in 7-year-olds. *Journal of Educational Psychology, 96*(3), 504–517.

Paracchini, S., Steer, C., Buckingham, L. L., Morris, A., Ring, S., Scerri, T., … & Monaco, A. (2008). Association of the KIAA0319 dyslexia susceptibility gene with reading skills in the general population. *American Journal of Psychiatry, 165*(12), 1576–1584.

Plomin, R. (2013). Child development and molecular genetics: 14 years later. *Child Development, 84*(1), 104–120.

Plomin, R. (2014). Genotype–environment correlation in the era of DNA. *Behavior Genetics. 44*(6), 629–638. doi: 10.1007/s10519-014-9673-7

Plomin, R., DeFries, J. C., Knopik, V. S., & Neiderhiser, J. M. (2013). *Behavioral genetics*, 6th edition. New York: Worth Publishers.

Plomin, R., Haworth, C. M. A., & Davis, O. S. P. (2009). Common disorders are quantitative traits. *Nature Reviews Genetics, 10*, 872–878.

Piven, J., Palmer, P., Jacobi, D., Childress, D., & Arndt, S. (1997). Broader autism phenotype: evidence from a family history study of multiple-incidence autism families. *American Journal of Psychiatry, 154*(2), 185–190.

Polderman, T. J., Huizink, A. C., Verhulst, F. C., van Beijsterveldt, C. E., Boomsma, D. I., & Bartels, M. (2011). A genetic study on attention problems and academic skills: Results of a longitudinal study in twins. *Journal of the Canadian Academy of Child and Adolescent Psychiatry, 20*(1), 22–34.

Siegel, L. S. (1989). IQ is irrelevant to the definition of learning disabilities. *Journal of Learning Disabilities, 22*(8), 469–478.

Robinson, E. B., Koenen, K. C., McCormick, M. C., Munir, K., Hallett, V., Happé, F., … & Ronald, A. (2011). Evidence that autistic traits show the same etiology in the general population and at the quantitative extremes (5%, 2.5%, and 1%). *Archives of General Psychiatry, 68*(11), 1113–1121.

Ronald, A., Happe, F., Bolton, P., Butcher, L. M., Price, T. S., Wheelwright, S., … & Plomin, R. (2006). Genetic heterogeneity between the three components of the autism spectrum: A twin study. *Journal of the American Academy of Child & Adolescent Psychiatry, 45*(6), 691–699.

Ronald, A., Happé, F., & Plomin, R. (2005). The genetic relationship between individual differences in social and nonsocial behaviors characteristic of autism. *Developmental Science, 8*, 444–458.

Ronald, A., Simonoff, E., Kuntsi, J., Asherson, P., & Plomin, R. (2008). Evidence for overlapping genetic influences on autistic and ADHD behaviors in a community twin sample. *Journal of Child Psychology and Psychiatry, 49*(5), 535–542.

Stromswold, K. (2001). The heritability of language: A review and metaanalysis of twin, adoption and linkage studies. *Language, 77*, 647–723.

Taylor, M. J., Charman, T., Robinson, E. B., Plomin, R., Happé, F., Asherson, P., & Ronald, A. (2012). Developmental associations between traits of autism spectrum disorder and attention deficit hyperactivity disorder: A genetically informative, longitudinal twin study. *Psychological Medicine, 1*(1), 1–12.

Thapar, A., & Harold, G. (2014). Editorial perspective: Why is there such a mismatch between traditional heritability estimates and molecular genetic findings for behavioral traits?. *Journal of Child Psychology and Psychiatry, 55*(10), 1088–1091.

Trzaskowski, M., Dale, P. S., & Plomin, R. (2013). No genetic influence for childhood behavior problems from DNA analysis. *Journal of the American Academy of Child & Adolescent Psychiatry, 52*(10), 1048–1056.

Trzesniewski, K. H., Moffitt, T. E., Caspi, A., Taylor, A., & Maughan, B. (2006). Revisiting the association between reading achievement and antisocial behavior: New evidence of an environmental explanation from a twin study. *Child Development, 77*(1), 72–88.

Vaughn, S., & Fuchs, L. S. (2003). Redefining learning disabilities as inadequate response to instruction: The promise and potential problems. *Learning Disabilities Research & Practice, 18*(3), 137–146.

Wenar C. (1994). *Developmental psychopathology: From infancy through adolescence*. New York: McGraw-Hill.

Willcutt, E. G., & Pennington, B. F. (2000). Comorbidity of reading disability and attention-deficit/hyperactivity disorder Differences by gender and subtype. *Journal of Learning Disabilities, 33*(2), 179–191.

Willcutt, E. G., Pennington, B. F., & DeFries, J. C. (2000). Twin study of the etiology of comorbidity between reading disability and attention-deficit/hyperactivity disorder. *American Journal of Medical Genetics, 96*(3), 293–301.

Willcutt, E. G., Pennington, B. F., Duncan, L., Smith, S. D., Keenan, J. M., Wadsworth, S., … & Olson, R. K. (2010). Understanding the complex etiologies of developmental disorders: behavioral and molecular genetic approaches. *Journal of Developmental and Behavioral Pediatrics, 31*(7), 533–544.

Willcutt, E. G., Pennington, B. F., Olson, R. K., & DeFries, J. C. (2007). Understanding comorbidity: A twin study of reading disability and attention-deficit/hyperactivity disorder. *American Journal of Medical Genetics Part B: Neuropsychiatric Genetics, 144*(6), 709–714.

Willcutt, E. G., Pennington, B. F., Smith, S. D., Cardon, L. R., Gayán, J., Knopik, V. S., … & DeFries, J. C. (2002). Quantitative trait locus for reading disability on chromosome 6p is pleiotropic for attention-deficit/hyperactivity disorder. *American Journal of Medical Genetics, 114*(3), 260–268.

Williams, D., Botting, N., & Boucher, J. (2008). Language in autism and specific language impairment: Where are the links? *Psychological Bulletin, 134*(6), 944–963.

# 13

# Comorbidity

David M. Williams

It is striking that the majority of developmental disorders do not have a known (molecular) genetic cause, despite robust evidence that most forms of developmental psychopathology are highly heritable. In recent years, the field has begun to identify specific gene variants ("polymorphisms") that are reliably associated with disorder (see Kovas & Tosto, Chapter 12 of this volume). However, it is arguable that unreliability is more common than reliability in molecular genetic studies; that is, failure to replicate promising findings is common in this field (see Papageorgiou and Ronald, Chapter 11 of this volume). Moreover, even when replicable findings are established, the amount of variance in behavior/feature severity explained is typically small. Thus, we are left with a problem of "dark heritability" or "missing heritability"—we have very good evidence from behavioural genetic studies that most disorders have a substantial genetic basis, but molecular genetic studies frequently fail to identify the genetic cause that we suspect (e.g., Maher, 2008). There are, of course, a number of potential explanations for this struggle. In all likelihood, one major reason is that developmental disorders are heterogeneous at the genetic level. It is unlikely that a single set of genes is a necessary and sufficient cause of all cases of most disorders. Rather, it is more likely that a number of different genotypes (or environmental conditions) are capable of producing the same set of behavioral features that are diagnostic of any given disorder. Moreover—and even more important—the causal chain between genes and behavior is long and complex. This makes the search the search for the etiology of developmental disorders a long and complicated one. Part of the complication comes from the need to understand comorbidity *between* developmental disorders. The aim of this chapter is to provide an overview of the issue of comorbidity, and its importance for both research and clinical practice, as well as to consider possible strategies for teasing apart explanations for this phenomenon. Key discussion points will be about a) whether the genetic level of explanation is the right one to explain comorbidity, as many researchers tend to implicitly assume, and; b) how psychology and genetics can be mutually informative when it comes to understanding the nature and basis of developmental disorder and comorbidity between disorders.

---

*The Wiley Handbook of Developmental Psychopathology*, First Edition. Edited by Luna C. Centifanti and David M. Williams.

## Comorbidity in Developmental Psychopathology

In developmental psychopathology research, comorbidity is said to occur when one or more disorders (disorders *B* and *C* etc.) co-occur with a primary disorder (disorder *A*) at rates significantly above chance/the population rate. For example, around 70% of individuals with a primary diagnosis of autism spectrum disorder (ASD) also have diagnoses (or, at least, clinically significant features of) at least one other disorder (Simonoff, Pickles, Charman, Chandler, Loucas, T. & Baird 2008). More than half of individuals with ASD have clinically significant signs/features of social anxiety disorder and almost one-third have the features of attention deficit hyperactivity disorder (ADHD). In this case, social anxiety disorder, or ADHD (or whatever disorder; i.e., disorder *B*) is said to be comorbid with ASD (disorder *A*).

It is probably safe to say that comorbidity between developmental disorders is the rule, rather than the exception. "Pure" forms of developmental psychopathology are relatively rare. Even in individuals who have a single diagnosis of one and only one disorder, "subclinical" traits of another disorder are often present. For example, a person with a pure ASD diagnosis might appear somewhat "spaced out" and have difficulty following instructions, much like someone with a diagnosis of attention deficit hyperactivity disorder (ADHD), albeit to a lesser extent than someone with a formal ADHD diagnosis. There is a tendency in the field to interpret comorbidity between disorders as indicating a genuine overlap between the disorders (Simonoff et al., 2008). That is—implicitly, at least—the tendency is to assume that when the behavioral features diagnostic of one disorder (e.g., ADHD) are present in a person with a different primary diagnosis (e.g., ASD), the co-occurrence of behavior reflects a shared underlying cause. As Simonoff et al. argue, "Until exclusionary rules are based on evidence demonstrating that additional symptom constellations are best conceptualized as a clinical variant of the underlying disorder, we advocate for research purposes the identification of multiple disorders" (p. 927). In other words, if a person with a diagnosis of ASD (for example) has (or reports having) the behavioral features of ADHD, then we should assume the person has *both* ASD and ADHD until it can be proven that the ADHD features resulted directly from the ASD itself, rather than comorbid ADHD.

This approach appears sensible from a clinical perspective. It is not difficult to imagine a clinician being faced with a person with ASD who reports a significant number of ADHD (or "ADHD-like") symptoms that appear to contribute to his/her difficulties in attaining qualifications, independent living, and personal goals. The clinician diagnoses additional/comorbid ADHD in this person and then recommends the kinds of treatment that have proven to be effective in ameliorating the features of "pure" ADHD. However, behavior is multifaceted and any instance of behavior can have a large variety of distinct underlying causes. Just because a person with ASD has behavioral features that resemble the behavioral features of ADHD does not mean necessarily that they have the very *same* ADHD that a person with a diagnosis of ADHD has. That is, ADHD features in a person with ASD may have a different underlying (cognitive, neurobiological, genetic, and/or environmental) basis to the ADHD features in a person with "pure" ADHD. This argument applies to comorbidity between any two disorders. Just because behaviorally defined disorders *A* and *B* co-occur in a person does not mean that the underlying causes of those disorders are the same as the causes of *A* or *B* in isolation (see Caron & Rutter, 1991). An alternative possibility is that *when A* and *B* co-occur, the features of one disorder (disorder *A*) cause (or predispose) a person to developing the other disorder (disorder *B*). In that case, a comorbid case of disorder *B* would represent a "phenocopy" or a "phenomimic" of pure forms of disorder *B* (see Bishop, 2006). An intuitive example of such phenomimicry might be when social anxiety disorder is diagnosed in people with ASD (as it is in around 70% of people with ASD). ASD is a developmental disorder diagnosed on the basis of profound difficulties with social-communication. The disorder is associated with significant difficulties with social cognition, especially understanding other minds. As such, it seems a plausible (and testable) hypothesis to suggest that social anxiety among people with ASD results from the underlying social cognitive difficulties that are diagnostic of ASD. After all, if one has profound difficulties with social-communication and understanding other people, the social anxiety should be an expected. If true, this would mean that social anxiety in people with ASD represents a "phenocopy" or "phenomimic" of social anxiety disorder, rather than representing comorbidity between ASD and social anxiety disorder.

The problem in trying to decide if one disorder is comorbid with another disorder, or whether it is merely a phenomimic, is that there is no absolute diagnostic test for most developmental disorders. Judgments are made on the basis of expert clinical opinion about *behavioral* presentations. Yet, as highlighted above, behavior has multiple possible underlying causes and making judgments on the basis of behavior provides little basis for deciding between the comorbidity vs. phenomimic explanations. We do not believe that the common cold and influenza are comorbid, despite the fact that they frequently share several overlapping symptoms (stuffy nose, sneezing, cough etc.), because we have valid and reliable biological tests to identify the distinct viruses that cause these (overlapping) symptoms. Given the reliance on behavioral diagnoses of developmental disorders, it is questionable whether the notion of comorbidity makes sense/should be invoked. However, the clinical and research reality is that patients present with a variety of behavioral features that move beyond the diagnostic criteria for disorder. Given that this is the rule, rather than the exception, we need to understand it. This goal can only be achieved by investigating the *causal chain* between genes and behavior, via (complex interactions with) neurobiology, cognition, and the environment. A promising avenue of investigation also concerns the search for so-called "endophenotypes" or "cognitive markers". These represent intermediate levels between genes and behavior that can be tapped using psychological (or biological) measures. In essence, the aim is to identify genetic liability to disorder via performance on a valid and reliable measure of some or other cognitive task, or particular biological function. To qualify as a cognitive marker (see Gottesman & Gould, 2003), task performance must be:

1 heritable;
2 associated with the disorder in question (overall level, or patterns, of performance should reliably distinguish those with the disorder from those who do not have the disorder).

   Moreover, such performance should be:

3 Present at all stages of the disorder, even if the behavioral features/manifestations of the disorder have resolved/are no longer apparent/measurable, and;
4 apparent in non-affected family members of a person with the disorder (i.e., in family members who do not themselves have any disorder) at levels greater than chance.

If cognitive marker tasks could be found for developmental disorders, then would help greatly to identify genetically stable/homogenous groups of individuals. Moreover, it would help to resolve the debate about whether overlapping behavioral features across disorders reflects comorbidity or phenomimicry. If the behavioral features of one disorder (disorder *B*) are present in a person who is diagnosed with a separate disorder (disorder *A*) represent comorbidity, then cognitive marker task performance in people with *A* plus *B* should follow the same patterns of heritability, association with the features of disorder *B*, and family co-segregation as in people with disorder *B* only.

To illustrate how a consideration of the causal chain between genes and behavior, including consideration of cognitive marker task performance, can help distinguish comorbidity from phenomimicry, this chapter discusses a debate about the overlap between two developmental disorders that are currently considered mutually exclusive in diagnostic classification manuals.

## Autism Spectrum Disorder and Language Disorder

### Behavioral Similarities

In *DSM-V* (American Psychiatric Association, 2013), ASD is diagnosed on the basis of severe impairments in social communication, and a restricted, repetitive repertoire of behavior and interests. An additional specifier is used to denote whether or not a person with ASD has significant impairments language. On current estimates, approximately 50% of people with ASD have a clinically significant impairment in structural language (semantics, grammar, and/or phonology). Henceforth, language-impaired individuals with ASD will be referred to as "autism language-impaired" (ALI), whereas individuals with ASD who have unimpaired structural language will be referred to as "autism language-normal" (ALN). Language impairments are common to a number of developmental disorders, including those of known genetic origin (e.g., Down syndrome). What is potentially important about ASD, however, is that only some people with the disorder have language impairments. The fact that some people with ASD do not have language difficulties despite having all the core features of ASD (autism language-normal; ALN) suggests that ASD cannot itself be a direct cause of structural language difficulties.[1]Based on this logic, some have suggested that language impairment in ASD represents a comorbid language disorder (or "specific language impairment"; SLI). Specifically, some have suggested that people with ALI have had a "double genetic hit", inheriting both ASD and SLI.

Language impairment is diagnosed on the basis of significant difficulties with the comprehension and/or expression of structural language (semantics, grammar, and or phonology) that are not in keeping with general intelligence and are not explained by sensory or neurological impairments, or any other medical condition. If language impairment in people with ASD represents a comorbid language disorder (or SLI), then this is very important and would provide direction for intervention efforts, as well as the search for the genes that underpin language disorder. Why, though, have researchers suggested that SLI (rather than any other disorder that involves language deficits) is comorbid with ASD? In part, this is likely to be because the early profile of language impairment in ALI resembles the profile of language difficulties seen in children with SLI. Around half of children with SLI manifest difficulties with comprehension and expression of all areas of structural language (phonology, grammar–syntax and morphology—and semantics), but especially phonology and grammar (Conti-Ramsden, Botting, & Faragher, 2001). This profile also characterizes a significant proportion of *pre*school children with ALI (see Rapin, 1996). Strikingly, however, the profile of difficulties changes over time among children with ALI to a much greater extent than among children with SLI (among whom the pattern remains fairly consistent over time). By school age, the majority of children with ALI do not have clinically significant difficulties with phonology, and grammar problems appear less severe than problems with semantics (Conti-Ramsden & Botting, 1999). Thus, the extent to which language difficulties in ALI resemble those in SLI depend on the age at which individuals are assessed. The different developmental trajectories of language in ALI and SLI represents an important issue to consider, but it does not decide whether language impairment in ALI is comorbid SLI. For that, we need to dig below the surface of behavior.

## Cognitive Underpinnings of Language Impairment in SLI and ALI

It is well-established that nonsense word repetition, sentence repetition, and tests of grammatical tense marking are all sensitive tests of SLI. Non-word repetition involves hearing a series of nonsense words (e.g., "blonterstaping") and repeating each item immediately after presentation. Sentence repetition involves hearing a series of sentences of increasing length/complexity and repeating each sentence immediately after presentation. Tense-marking tasks involve presenting participants with stories and then asking them to produce versions of those stories that include grammatical morphemes (e.g., past tense "-ed", or plural "s"). An example of past tense elicitation probe/story would be "Every day, John rakes leaves. Yesterday was just like every other day and John ...... the leaves," which is designed to elicit the past tense form of "rake", namely "rak*ed*". At the group level, a large number of studies have indicated that children with SLI perform significantly less well on these tasks than either age-matched or language-matched comparison children (e.g., Gathercole & Baddeley, 1990). Thus, children with SLI show an impairment on these tasks that is worse than would be expected on the basis of their level of language; they show "deviant," rather than merely delayed, performance. Indeed, performance on each of these types of task has high accuracy in distinguishing children with SLI from neurotypical children. Setting a criterion of performing > -1.25 SD below the mean on these tasks has a sensitivity of over 70% (i.e., over 70% of individuals perform more than 1.25 SDs below the mean) and a specificity of over 90% (i.e., less than 10% of neurotypical individuals perform more than 1.25 SDs below the mean), which provides an overall accuracy rate of over 80%.

The *patterns* of performance on these tasks in SLI also gives clues about the neurocognitive impairment that directly underpins the behavioral features of this disorder. For example, many consider non-word repetition to be a highly sensitive measure of verbal short-term memory (the ability to store verbal information in mind for short periods of time—allowing the information to be transferred to long-term memory). Several studies have found that children with SLI show poorer non-word repetition performance than neurotypical individuals only when stimuli contain more than two syllables (e.g., Coady & Evans, 2008). In other words, repetition of short items that do not tax short-term memory capacity is unproblematic for children with SLI, suggesting that the root of the non-word repetition problem in this disorder is with a limited capacity verbal/phonological store (Gathercole & Baddeley, 1990). Although there are alternative (and persuasive) accounts of the non-word repetition problem in SLI (see e.g., Marshall & van der Lely, 2009), the "non-word length effect" is a robust finding in SLI and is accompanied by a parallel difficulty with repeating sequences of even simple digits (i.e., digit span is reduced in SLI; e.g., Botting & Conti-Ramsden, 2001). This suggests that limited short-term memory makes at least some contribution to the non-word repetition impairments (and behavioral language features, more generally) in SLI. So, how do children with ALI perform on non-word repetition tests, and is short-term memory implicated in the language phenotype of this disorder? If language impairment in people with ALI represents comorbid SLI, then one might expect to see similar levels and patterns of performance on non-word repetition (and other such sensitive) tasks in ALI and SLI.

Several studies have now explored non-word repetition ability in ASD with a view to addressing the potential comorbidity with SLI. Across these studies, there is considerable consensus that individuals with ALI, but *not* individuals with ALN, perform significantly less well than age-matched neurotypical comparison participants (Hill, van Santen, Gorman, Langhorst, & Fombonne, 2015; Riches, Loucas, Baird, Charman, & Simonoff, 2010; Whitehouse, Barry, & Bishop, 2008; Williams, Payne, & Marshall, 2013). This should come as no great surprise; comparing any group of children with structural language impairment (and thus a verbal mental age that is *substantially below* chronological age) on a language-based task with a group of age-matched neurotypical children is bound to produce a between-group difference on that task. Most important, do children with ALI show poorer non-word repetition performance than would be expected on the basis of their language level (as children with SLI do)? The only study to address this issue found almost identical levels of performance in children with ALI and a language-matched group of (younger) neurotypical children (Williams et al., 2013). As such, non-word repetition performance appears merely delayed, rather than deviant, in ALI (unlike in SLI). Moreover, all studies that have included matched groups of SLI and ALI children report significantly poorer non-word repetition performance in SLI than ALI, indicating a more severe deficit in SLI than in ALI. Most important, all studies that have explored *patterns of* non-word repetition task performance in ALI report important differences in this disorder from the pattern that is seen in children with SLI. For example, children with ALI do not show the same (degree of) non-word length effect as children with SLI (Riches et al., 2010; Whitehouse et al., 2008) and neither are they affected in the same ways as children with SLI by the phonological complexity of non-words (Williams et al., 2013). These findings point to a distinct underlying cognitive cause of non-word repetition problems in ALI than in SLI. In particular, a limited capacity verbal short term memory store does not seem to be implicated in language (or non-word repetition) difficulties among people with ASD. This conclusion is indicated not only by analysis of patterns of non-word repetition performance in ALI, but also by the fact that the vast majority of studies that have explored digit span among children with ALI report no significant impairment (Boucher and Warrington, 1976; Farrant, Boucher, & Blades, 1999; Fein et al., 1996; Frith, 1970; Fyffe & Prior, 1978; Siegel, Minshew, & Goldstein, 1996; Williams et al., 2013). Verbal short-term memory capacity and processes appear to be relatively unimpaired among people with ALI

(Russell, Jarrold, & Henry, 1996; Williams, Happe, & Jarrold, 2008; Williams & Jarrold, 2010). Thus, a verbal short-term memory deficit is not likely to be a major cause of language or non-word repetition impairments in ALI. At the neurocognitive level, this difference between ALI and SLI is striking and implies that comorbidity of behavioral features is only superficial and does not reflect the same underlying neurocognitive impairment. At the genetic/endophenotypic levels, greater evidence of genuine overlap between these two disorders might be apparent, however.

## Genetics and Endophenotypes: Linking Genes to Behavior

SLI is a highly heritable disorder that confers significant familial risk (e.g., Tomblin & Buckwalter, 1994)). Approximately one-quarter to one-third of relatives (parents/siblings) of children with SLI show clinically significant levels of language impairment (Conti-Ramsden, Simkin, & Pickles, 2006; Tomblin & Buckwalter, 1994), and monozygotic twins show significantly greater concordance for the disorder than do monozygotic co-twins (which indicates a substantial genetic contribution to the disorder; e.g., Bishop, 1995). Genome-wide molecular genetic studies have indicated reliable linkage to regions/gene(s) on the long arms of chromosomes 16 and 19. Moreover, variation in eight regions of the contactin-associated protein-like 2 (CNTNAP2) gene on the long arm of chromosome 7 have also been implicated in SLI. CNTNAP2 encodes for proteins involved in cell adhesion/binding of synapses. Importantly, expression of CNTNAP2 is enriched in language-related regions of the brain (Abrahams et al., 2007), and appears to be implicated in the production of long-range connections between frontal lobes and subcortical structures, including the striatum (Scott-Van Zeeland et al., 2010). Moreover, variation in CNTNAP2 is associated with normal language development (Whitehouse, Bishop, Ang, Pennell, & Fisher, 2011) and is regulated by another gene on chromosome 7, forkhead box protein P2 (FOXP2), a mutation to which was found in a family with a severe speech sound disorder (e.g., Gopnik & Crago, 1991). Perhaps of greatest importance, these genes have been linked to performance on those specific cognitive tasks that are highly sensitive to SLI (non-word repetition, sentence repetition, and tense marking). Several findings point to the possibility that these tasks represent cognitive markers/endophenotypes for SLI. For example, non-word repetition meets all of the criteria for an endophenotype outlined above. It is:

1 heritable in SLI (e.g., Bishop, North, & Donlan, 1996; Bishop et al., 1999); associated with SLI (see above).
2 Moreover, poor performance is:
3 Present at all stages of the disorder, even if the behavioral features/manifestations of the disorder have resolved and children no longer meet diagnostic criteria for SLI (e.g., Conti-Ramsden et al., 2001), and;
4 apparent in non-affected family members of a person with the disorder (i.e., in family members who do not themselves have any disorder) at levels greater than chance (e.g., Barry, Yasin, & Bishop, 2006).

At the molecular genetic level, all variation in all eight regions of the CNTNAP2 gene on chromosome 7 that have been implicated in SLI are specifically associated with non-word repetition ability in this disorder (for a summary, see Table 1 of Peñagarikano & Geschwind, 2012). Genes on chromosomes 16 (CMIP and ATP2C2) and 19 have also been implicated directly in the non-word repetition deficits in SLI (e.g., Newbury et al., 2009). This discussion of SLI serves to illustrate that we know a good deal about the pattern of, and mechanisms underpinning, inheritance of language impairments in this disorder. The fact that cognitive marker tasks can identify a "genetically stable" group of children with heritable SLI is of high importance. If language impairment in people with ALI is comorbid SLI (i.e., ASD plus SLI), then we might well expect to see, across disorders, similar inheritance patterns/familial co-segregation of a) the language phenotype, and b) performance on cognitive marker tasks, such as non-word repetition. In fact, however, the reality is rather different.

Although the core diagnostic features of ASD (impaired social-communication, and restricted behavior and interests) are both familial and heritable (see Colvert et al., 2014, for example), family and twin studies reveal almost no evidence that structural language deficits run in families (see Lindgren, Folstein, Tomblin, & Tager-Flusberg, 2009; for review, see Williams, Botting & Boucher, 2008) or are heritable (Dworzynski et al., 2008). Most important, there is almost no evidence of familial aggregation of impairments on cognitive marker tests of SLI. Whitehouse, Barry, & Bishop (2007) explored non-word repetition ability in the parents of children with ALI, children with ALN, and SLI. Crucially, significant deficits were found in the parents of children with SLI, but not among parents of either children with ALI or ALN. Likewise, Lindgren et al. (2009) found non-word repetition impairments in the siblings of children with SLI, but not the siblings of either children with ALI or children with ALN. Strikingly, the relatives of children with ALI may have *superior* non-word repetition ability relative to the parents of neurotypical children (Bishop et al., 2004). In sum, language impairment in people with ALI does not show the same familial aggregation as it does in people with SLI. Most important, impairments on cognitive marker tasks clearly aggregate (and are heritable) in the families of people with SLI, yet they do not in the families of people with ALI. The evidence from studies of neurocognition and endophenotypes, as well as family studies, provides positive (but not conclusive, as we will see below) evidence that language impairments in people with ALI represent phenomimics of SLI, rather than evidence of genuine comorbidity between the two disorders. The study of molecular genetics in ALI, however, may call this conclusion into question.

In recent years, there has been a significant advance in our understanding of the genetics of ASD, with genes on multiple chromosomes linked to the disorder (see e.g., International Molecular Genetic Study of Autism Consortium, 2005). However, there is only limited evidence to date of an overlap between the genes associated with SLI and the genes associated with ALI. The CMIP gene on chromosome 16 has been implicated in one girl with ASD who has severe developmental delay and other "non-core" impairments (Van der Aa et al., 2012), but no large-scale genetic studies have yet found evidence of linkage to the region of chromosome 16 that CMIP is located on. The only gene that has reliably been implicated in both ALI and SLI is CNTNAP2 on chromosome 7. Two early studies found evidence for a role of CNTNAP2 in ALN and, most clearly, in ALI (Alarcón et al., 2008; Arking et al., 2008). The Alarcón et al. study reported a specific association between variation in region rs2710102 of CNTNAP2 and age of first words among males with ASD. Although age at first word (i.e., late talking) should not be considered a reliable indicator of language disorder (because many late talkers do not develop language impairment; e.g., Desmarais, Sylvestre, Meyer, Bairati, & Rouleau, 2008), the finding that variation in CNTNAP2 might be related to the language phenotype in ASD (as it is in SLI) is potentially important. Although there is understandable interest in, and excitement about, the association between CNTNAP2 and autism (e.g., Peñagarikano & Geschwind, 2012), there is reason for some caution alongside optimism. The evidence for the role of CNTNAP2 is not yet definitive (e.g., Bakkaloglu et al. 2008), and, in general, genome-wide association studies of ASD have been underpowered to conclude with absolute confidence that common gene variants are *reliably* implicated in ASD (see Devlin, Melhem, & Roeder 2011; also Murdoch & State, 2013).

In relation to the potential overlap between ALI and SLI, the finding that CNTNAP2 is implicated in both disorders is, of course, of potential importance. Here again, however, some caution is warranted. First, the regions of CNTNAP2 that show variation associated with ASD do not overlap with the regions implicated in the language phenotype and cognitive endophenotype of SLI (apart from the one finding by Alarcón et al., 2008), although they are adjacent to those regions (see Peñagarikano & Geschwind, 2012). Second, and much more important, variation in CNTNAP2 is implicated in multiple developmental disorders, including these that do not involve language impairments (see e.g., Rodenas-Cuadrado, Ho, & Vernes, 2014). If these findings are reliable, then it seems safe to assume that CNTNAP2 counts as a pleiotropic gene that is expressed in several different phenotypes. Indeed, the finding that it is associated with levels of normal language development suggest that it is the kind of "generalist gene" that is increasingly implicated in developmental disorders (see Kovas & Tosto, Chapter 12 of this volume). This would be an important finding and would point to a link between seemingly diverse developmental disorders, including between ALI and SLI. However, we are left with a puzzle in that case. How is it that familial aggregation and heritability of language impairment in SLI so strikingly different from that seen in ALI, despite some apparent overlap in genetic cause? As discussed above, there is overwhelming evidence that language impairments are familial and heritable in SLI, whereas there is almost no evidence that language impairments are familial and heritable in ALI.

Computational modelling evidence from Bishop (2010) suggests a possible explanation for how SLI and ALI could have overlapping genetic causes, despite the fact that language impairment aggregates in families of people with SLI only. A model in which one gene variant that contributes to SLI also contributes to ALI, but has its deleterious effects on language magnified when inherited alongside a *particular* combination of ASD risk genes (and only that combination), fitted the real-world data on familial transmission relatively closely. In other words, each parent (or sibling) of individuals with ALI might not themselves manifest structural language impairments even though they carry the risk (shared) SLI gene variant, because they do not *also* carry the combination of ASD risk genes that interact with the SLI risk gene and increase its negative effect on language ability. However, their children inherit both the SLI risk gene and the specific combination of ASD risk genes that result in ALI.

Bishop's (2010) explanation is plausible and, if true, would represent an important advance on our understanding of the risk factors for SLI and ASD, as well as their comorbidity. The discovery of the actual shared risk variant might allow early identification/prediction of language problems in children showing early signs of ASD. Moreover, it might allow interventions to be targeted toward structural language in these children. It may also assist future studies—particularly molecular genetic studies—by reducing heterogeneity as a result of accurate identification of genetically homogenous subgroups. However, even if this explanation is correct (and, as things stand, it is only a computational model of the real world, rather than real-world data itself), it highlights the difficulties with classifying developmental disorders and understanding comorbidity between them. In this language impairment in ASD and SLI have partially overlapping genetic causes. Much (or most) of the variation in language ability in each disorder has a unique (i.e., non-shared) genetic basis. Moreover, what genetic risk factors are shared between the two disorders do not appear to produce the same neurobiological, cognitive, or (largely) even behavioral effects in each disorder (see Williams et al., 2008). This is problematic, because currently interventions are aimed solely at the behavioral and cognitive levels of description/explanation. There is likely little to be gained from targeting treatments at (for example) enhancing verbal short-term memory in both ALI and SLI, because only the latter involves impairments in this cognitive ability. In addition, the differences between ALI and SLI in terms of language profile and other behavioral features, means that different interventions would likely be needed. Thus, the finding of shared genetic risk factors is not particularly helpful in this case, because the chain of explanation from genes to behavior is not the same in each disorder and because the differences between the disorders are far greater than the similarities between them (see Williams & Lind, 2010). Of course, this is pure speculation, because there are no treatment studies directly comparing the two disorders. This would be useful, both for informing clinical practice, but also as a further means of understanding the links and differences between the disorders.

The central issue that comes out of this discussion concerns the extent to which the genetic level is always the best level of explanation when considering comorbidity. In the case of ALI and SLI, there are good reasons to think it is not. The fact that ALI and SLI might share one of many genetic risk factors tells us almost nothing about the ways that language impairments develop, or about what the more proximal (neurocognitive) basis of language impairment is in each disorder. Only once the entire causal chain from genes through to behavior (including the developmental process itself) is considered should we draw firm conclusions about the nature of comorbidity.

## Note

1 This is not strictly true. It may be that people with ALN have the same liability to language impairment as people with ALI, but that people with ALN possess some protective factor(s) or other that prevent that liability from ever manifesting itself.

## References

Abrahams, B. S., Tentler, D., Perederiy, J. V., Oldham, M. C., Coppola, G., & Geschwind, D. H. (2007). Genome-wide analyses of human perisylvian cerebral cortical patterning. *Proceedings of the National Academy of Sciences, 104*(45), 17849–17854.

Alarcón, M., Abrahams, B. S., Stone, J.L., Duvall, J.A., Perederiy, J.V., … & Geschwind, D.H. (2008). Linkage, association, and gene-expression analyses identify CNTNAP2 as an autism-susceptibility gene. *American Journal of Human Genetics, 82*, 150–159.

American Psychiatric Association. (2013). *Diagnostic and statistical manual of mental disorders* (5th edition) *DSM-V*. Washington, DC: American Psychiatric Association.

Arking, D. E., Cutler, D. J., Brune, C. W., Teslovich, T. M., West, K., ... & Chakravarti, A. (2008). A common genetic variant in the neurexin superfamily member CNTNAP2 increases familial risk of autism. *American Journal of Human Genetics*, *82*, 160–164.

Bakkaloglu, B., O'Roak, B. J., Louvi, A., Gupta, A. R., Abelson, J. F., Morgan, T. M., ... & Tanriover, G. (2008). Molecular cytogenetic analysis and resequencing of contactin associated protein-like 2 in autism spectrum disorders. *American Journal of Human Genetics*, *82*, 165–173.

Barry, J. G., Yasin, I., & Bishop, D. V. M. (2006). Heritable risk factors associated with language impairments. *Genes Brain and Behavior*, *6*(1), 66–76.

Bishop, D. V. M. (2006). Developmental cognitive genetics: How psychology can inform genetics. *Quarterly Journal of Experimental Psychology*, *59*(7), 1153–1168.

Bishop, D. V. M. (2010). Overlaps between autism and language impairment: phenomimicry or shared etiology? *Behavior Genetics*, *40*, 618–629.

Bishop, D. V. M., Maybery, M., Wong, D., Maley, A., Hill, W., & Hallmayer, J. (2004). Are phonological processing deficits part of the broad autism phenotype? *American Journal of Medical Genetics: Neuropsychiatric Genetics*, *128*(B), 54–60.

Bishop, D. V. M., Bishop, S. J., Bright, P., James, C., Delaney, T., & Tallal, P. (1999). Different origin of auditory and phonological processing problems in children with language impairment: Evidence from a twin study. *Journal of Speech, Language, and Hearing Research*, *42*, 155–168.

Bishop, D. V. M., North, T., & Donlan, C. (1996). Nonword repetition as a behavioral marker for inherited language impairment: Evidence from a twin study. *Journal of Child Psychology and Psychiatry*, *37*(4), 391–403.

Botting, N., & Conti-Ramsden, G. (2001). Non-word repetition and language development in children with specific language impairment (SLI). *International Journal of Language and Communication*, *36*(4), 421–434.

Boucher, J., & Warrington, E. K. (1976). Memory deficits in early infantile autism: Some similarities to the amnesic syndrome. *British Journal of Psychology*, *67*, 73–87.

Caron, C., & Rutter, M. (1991). Comorbidity in child psychopathology: Concepts, issues and research strategies. *Journal of Child Psychology and Psychiatry*, *32(7)*, 1063–1080.

Coady, J., & Evans, J. (2008). The uses and interpretations of nonword repetition tasks in children with and without specific language impairments. *International Journal of Language & Communication Disorders*, *43*(1), 1–40.

Colvert, E., Tick, B., McEwen, F., Stewart, C., Curran, S. R. ... & Bolton, P. (2014). Heritability of autism spectrum disorder in a UK population-based twin sample. *JAMA Psychiatry*, *72*(5), 415–423.

Conti-Ramsden, G. and N. Botting (1999). Classification of children with specific language impairment: Longitudinal considerations. *Journal of Speech Language and Hearing Research*, *42*, 1195–1204.

Conti-Ramsden, G., Botting, N., & Faragher, B. (2001). Psycholinguistic markers for specific language impairment (SLI). *Journal of Child Psychology and Psychiatry*, *42*(6), 741–748.

Conti-Ramsden, G., Simkin, Z., & Pickles, A. (2006). Estimating familial loading in SLI: A comparison of direct assessment versus parental interview. *Journal of Speech, Language, and Hearing Research*, *49*(1), 88–101.

Desmarais, C., Sylvestre, A., Meyer, F., Bairati, I., & Rouleau, N. (2008). Systematic review of the literature on characteristics of late-talking toddlers. *International Journal of Language & Communication Disorders*, *43*(4), 361–389.

Devlin, B., Melhem, N., & Roeder, K. (2011). Do common variants play a role in risk for autism? Evidence and theoretical musings. *Brain Research*, *1380*, 78–84.

Dworzynski, K., Ronald, A., Hayiou-Thomas, M., McEwen, F., Happé, F., Bolton, P., & Plomin, R. (2008). Developmental path between language and autistic-like impairments: A twin study. *Infant and Child Development*, *17*(2), 121–136.

Farrant, A., Boucher, J., & Blades, M. (1999). Metamemory in children with autism. *Child Development*, *70*(1), 107–131.

Fein, D., Dunn, M. A., Allen, D. M., Aram, R., Hall, N., Morris, R., & Wilson, B. C. (1996). Neuropsychological and language findings. In I. Rapin (Ed.), *Preschool children with inadequate communication: Developmental language disorder, autism, low IQ* (pp. 123–154). London: MacKeith Press.

Frith, U. (1970). Studies in pattern detection in normal and autistic children: I. Immediate recall of auditory sequences. *Journal of Abnormal Psychology*, *76*, 413–420.

Fyffe, C., & Prior, M. (1978). Evidence for language recoding in autistic, retarded, and normal children: A re-examination. *British Journal of Psychology*, *69*, 393–402

Gathercole, S. E., & Baddeley, A. D. (1990). Phonological memory deficits in language disordered children: Is there a causal connection? *Journal of Memory and Language*, *29*, 336–360.

Gopnik, M., & Crago, M. B. (1991). Familial aggregation of a developmental language disorder. *Cognition*, *39*(1), 1–50.

Gottesman, I. I., & Gould, T. D. (2003). The endophenotype concept in psychiatry: Etymology and strategic intentions. *American Journal of Psychiatry*, *160*(4), 636–645.

Hill, A. P., van Santen, J., Gorman, K., Langhorst, B. H., & Fombonne, E. (2015). Memory in language-impaired children with and without autism. *Journal of Neurodevelopmental Disorders*, *7*(1), 19.

International Molecular Genetic Study of Autism Consortium (2005). Analysis of IMGSAC autism susceptibility loci: Evidence for sex-limited and parent-origin-specific effects. *Journal of Medical Genetics*, *42*, 132–137.

Lindgren, K. A., Folstein, S. E., Tomblin, J. B., & Tager-Flusberg, H. (2009). Language and reading abilities of children with autism spectrum disorders and specific language impairment and their first-degree relatives. *Autism Research*, *2*, 22–38.

Maher, B. (2008). The case of the missing heritability. *Nature*, *456*(7218), 18–21.

Marshall, C. R., & van der Lely, H. K. J. (2009). Effects of word position and stress on onset cluster production: Evidence from typical development, specific language impairment, and dyslexia. *Language*, *85*, 39–57.

Murdoch, J. D., & State, M. W. (2013). Recent developments in the genetics of autism spectrum disorders. *Current Opinion in Genetics & Development*, *23*(3), 310–315.

Newbury D.F., Winchester, L., Addis, L., Paracchini, S., Buckingham, L.L., Clark, A., Cohen, W., et al. (2009). CMIP and ATP2C2 modulate phonological short-term memory in language impairment. *American Journal of Human Genetics*, *85*(2), 64–72. doi: 10.1016/j.ajhg.2009.07.004.

Peñagarikano, O., & Geschwind, D. H. (2012). What does CNTNAP2 reveal about autism spectrum disorder? *Trends in Molecular Medicine*, *18*(3), 156–163.

Rapin, I. (1996). *Preschool children with inadequate communication*. London: MacKeith Press.

Riches, N. G., Loucas, T., Baird, G., Charman, T., & Simonoff, E. (2010). Non-word repetition in adolescents with specific language impairment and autism plus language impairments: A qualitative analysis. *Journal of Communication Disorders*, *44*, 23–36.

Riches, N. G., Loucas, T., Baird, G., Charman, T., & Simonoff, E. Non-word repetition in adolescents with specific language impairment and autism plus language impairments: A qualitative analysis. *Journal of Communication Disorders*, *44*(1), 23–36.

Rodenas-Cuadrado, P., Ho, J., & Vernes, S. C. (2014). Shining a light on CNTNAP2: complex functions to complex disorders. *European Journal of Human Genetics*, *22*(2), 171–178.

Russell, J., Jarrold, C., & Henry, L. (1996). Working memory in children with autism and with moderate learning difficulties. *Journal of Child Psychology and Psychiatry*, *37*, 673– 686.

Scott-Van Zeeland, A. A., Abrahams, B. S., Alvarez-Retuerto, A. I., Sonnenblick, L. I., Rudie, J. D., Ghahremani, D., ... & Bookheimer, S. Y. (2010). Altered functional connectivity in frontal lobe circuits is associated with variation in the autism risk gene CNTNAP2. *Science Translational Medicine*, *2*(56), 56ra80–56ra80.

Siegel, D., Minshew, N., & Goldstein, G. (1996). Wechsler IQ profiles in diagnosis of high-functioning autism. *Journal of Autism and Developmental Disorders*, *26*, 389–406.

Simonoff, E., Pickles, A., Charman, T., Chandler, S., Loucas, T. & Baird, G. (2008). Psychiatric disorders in children with autism spectrum disorders: prevalence, comorbidity, and associated factors in a population-derived sample. *Journal of the American Academy of Child and Adolescent Psychiatry*, *47*, 921–929.

Tomblin, J. B., & Buckwalter, P. R. (1994). Heritability of poor language achievement among twins. *Journal of Speech, Language, and Hearing Research*, *41*, 188–189.

Van der Aa, N., Vandeweyer, G., Reyniers, E., Kenis, S., Dom, L., Mortier, G., Rooms, L., & Kooy, R.F. (2012). Haploinsufficiency of CMIP in a girl with autism spectrum disorder and developmental delay due to a de novo deletion on chromosome 16q23.2. *Autism Research*, *5*(4), 277–281.

Whitehouse, A. J. O., Barry, J. G., & Bishop, D. V. M. (2007). The broader language phenotype of autism: A comparison with specific language impairment. *Journal of Child Psychology and Psychiatry*, *48*(8), 822–830.

Whitehouse, A. J. O., Barry, J. G., & Bishop, D. V. M. (2008). Further defining the language impairment of autism: Is there a specific language impairment subtype? *Journal of Communication Disorders*, *41*, 319–336.

Whitehouse, A. J. O., Bishop, D. V., Ang, Q. W., Pennell, C. E., & Fisher, S. E. (2011). CNTNAP2 variants affect early language development in the general population. *Genes, Brain and Behavior*, *10*(4), 451–456.

Williams, D., & Jarrold, C. (2010). Predicting inner speech use in autism spectrum disorder: The roles of verbal ability and cognitive profile. *Journal of Autism and Developmental Disorders*, *40*, 907–913.

Williams, D., & Lind, S. (2012). Comorbidity and diagnosis of developmental disorders. In C. Marshall (Ed.), *Current Issues in Developmental Psychology* (pp.19–45). Hove: Psychology Press.

Williams, D., Botting, N., & Boucher, J. (2008). Language in autism and specific language impairment: Where are the links? *Psychological Bulletin*, *134*, 944–963.

Williams, D., Happé, F., & Jarrold, C. (2008). Intact inner speech in children with autism spectrum disorders: Evidence from a short-term memory task. *Journal of Child Psychology and Psychiatry*, *48*, 51–58.

Williams, D., Payne, H., & Marshall, C. (2013). Non-word repetition impairment in autism and specific language impairment: Evidence for distinct underlying neuro-cognitive causes. *Journal of Autism and Developmental Disorders*, *43*, 404–417.

# Section III
# Environmental Influences

# Part 1
# Family/Peer Issues

# 14

# Parenting Influences on Development and Psychopathology

David J. Hawes

## Introduction

Questions concerning the influences of parenting on child outcomes have driven some of the most noteworthy shifts in models of psychopathology seen in recent decades. At the same time, these advances have informed changing conceptualizations of the very processes by which parenting may be best understood. There is no question that the scientific study of parenting has evolved considerably during this time and has added much to the evidence base that can now be brought to bear on the core tenets of developmental psychopathology. However, as outlined in this chapter, efforts to formulate the role of parenting within increasingly sophisticated models of psychopathology have often served to highlight the very limits of this evidence base, and the significant challenges that researchers face.

Guided by ethological accounts of the parent–infant relationship, developmental researchers have long sought to understand how relational patterns experienced early in life are "internalized" to become part of the developing child's mind, body, and behavior (Bowlby, 1969; Lorenz, 1950; Rutter & Sroufe, 2000). The processes through which stable child competencies are shaped by the parent–child relationship for better or worse have likewise been framed in terms of "entrained self-regulation" (Dishion & Patterson, 2006). Entrainment refers to the role of environments in structuring neural pathways implicated in automatic, overlearned behavior patterns (Lewis, 2000). This conceptualization is based on an ecological perspective on child psychopathology, wherein the development of self-regulatory capacities is understood to be highly embedded in the multiple contexts or ecologies (e.g., family, school, peers) that are nested within a child's broader environment. Critically, the parent–child relationship is the primary context in which development unfolds, and in which the earliest foundations for risk and resilience emerge.

*The Wiley Handbook of Developmental Psychopathology*, First Edition. Edited by Luna C. Centifanti and David M. Williams.

## Parenting Risk Factors

The specific variables that have been invoked to describe and define quality of parenting and the parent–child relationship have varied considerably, as have theoretical perspectives on the processes through which they have been proposed to operate. A primary distinction can be made between research concerned with parenting behaviors versus social-cognitive processes (e.g., social information processing; parental reflective functioning). As discussed shortly, social-cognitive processes appear to play an important role in determining the behaviors through which parents relate to their children. However, it is the repeatedly executed sets of behaviors in which parents engage—varying in rhythms, intensities, frequencies, and durations—that are understood to be most proximal to child development, and to impact most profoundly early in life (see Feldman, 2012). Research concerned with parenting behaviors can be further divided into that focused on parenting typologies/styles versus specific dimensions/components of parenting; levels/rates of parenting behaviors versus patterns/sequences of parent–child interactions; and properties of the parent–child relationship versus characteristics thought to be distinguishable to the individual parent or child (O'Connor, 2002).

Interestingly, despite the heterogeneity that has characterized this research, there has been surprising consensus in approaches to measuring and categorizing parenting behavior with respect to healthy and maladaptive practices. The parenting variables that have been most consistently associated with individual differences in child adjustment can be grouped along two broad dimensions (O'Connor, 2002; Sroufe, Duggal, Weinfield, & Carlson, 2000). The first concerns parental control behaviors, including the method and degree of monitoring and limit-setting on children's behavior (e.g., coercive, inductive). The second concerns the parental behaviors that convey affect toward the child, and spans the negative features of harsh discipline (hostility, criticism, rejection) through to warmth/support and sensitivity/responsiveness. Constructs derived from attachment theory, including emotional availability (Beeghly, 2012) and mutually responsive orientation (Aksan, Kochanska, & Ortmann, 2006), are among the variables researched in this second domain. Additionally, there is growing evidence that a somewhat distinct set of emotion-related parenting practices concerning the socialization of emotion are important to consider alongside those traditionally emphasized in this second dimension (Eizenberg, et al., 1998). These include attempts to directly teach children about emotion regulation and expression, and the role of emotion in social contexts—often referred to as emotion coaching (Gottman et al., 1997).

Although these dimensions have often been researched in isolation from one another, there is considerable evidence that risk process may often implicate joint contributions from both. The most influential conceptualization of parenting based on clusters or typologies is Baumrind's (1971) tripartite classification of parenting styles. Research based on this model, much of which has focused on the period of adolescence, has found that the promotion of healthy child adjustment is most likely to occur through authoritative parenting, conceptualized as a balanced synthesis of two orthogonal dimensions—demandingness and responsiveness. Accordingly, such a parent is responsive to a child's needs but not indulgent, and is firm but not rigid in setting limits on behavior. In contrast, risk for adverse outcomes has been associated with parenting styles that are authoritarian (i.e., high demandingness with low responsiveness), and permissive (i.e., low demandingness with high responsiveness). Maccoby and Martin

(1983) subsequently proposed the addition of a disengaged or neglectful parenting style, wherein parents are uninvolved and emotionally detached from their children. Recent innovations based on such typologies include research into the joint contributions of maternal warmth and directiveness to child conduct problems using twin designs. Burt, Klahr, Neale, and Klump (2013), recently reported the first biometric evidence of such contributions to conduct problems in middle-childhood, finding that shared environmental influences were accentuated by colder, less directive or less engaged mothering, whereas genetic influences were strongest when the child was experiencing warmer, more directive or more authoritative parenting.

Recent research into parenting typologies has also made use of latent profile analysis to derive classes of parenting behaviors. Borden et al. (2014), for example, found that parents of young children ($n = 514$) with externalizing problems could be grouped into four classes (Positive Only, Negative Only, Positive/Negative, and Neither Positive/Negative) that comprised a quarter of the sample each, and were characterized by distinct child and family correlates. Measurement research with adolescent samples has likewise emphasized how interrelated various parenting constructs may be. Using structural equation modelling with data from high-risk youth (aged 11–14 years), Dishion, Burraston, and Li (2003) performed a multitrait, multimethod analysis of five parenting dimensions: limit setting, monitoring, problem solving, positive reinforcement, and relationship quality. Of key interest was the extent to which various parenting practices loaded onto distinct dimensions, as well as the extent to which measurement method (i.e., reporting agent—parent, child, independent coder) accounts for covariation among such data. Method of measurement accounted for around 50 % of the variation, thereby highlighting the need for careful consideration of the perspectives of multiple informants when assessing parenting. Although support was found for the construct validity of the various parenting dimensions, they were also found to be so highly intercorrelated as to suggest the existence of a parenting "*g*-factor". Particularly high correlations were also apparent between particular sets of these constructs. The correlation between limit setting and monitoring was so high as to suggest that at this age these practices are difficult to reliably differentiate, while positive reinforcement and relationship quality were also very highly correlated.

Such research suggests that the parenting variables emphasized as risk factors for psychopathology may often be overlapping, embedded within one other, or operate synergistically. However, it is widely recognized that global parenting constructs are limited in the extent to which they may inform perspectives on the distinct psychological processes that are thought to govern distinct domains of socialization in the family (Grusec & Davidov, 2010; Turiel, 2010). The models of child psychopathology that have emerged in recent decades owe much to research concerned with "unpacking" the various components or dimensions that comprise broader parenting typologies. Indeed, the most empirically-supported process models, and those that have been most widely translated into evidence-based interventions, are based not on typologies, but on sequential patterns within the parent–child relationship (Dishion & Stormshak, 2007).

Some of the most important advances in this literature have arisen from the direct observation of parent–child interactions, and the analysis of the functional relationships between problematic child behavior and the family interactions in which it occurs (see Hawes, Dadds & Pasalich, 2013). Microsocial (or molecular) coding systems have been widely used to code the stream of parent–child interaction in terms of fine-grained behavioral units (e.g., eye contact, criticism) assigned to parents and children respectively. In doing so, such coding can capture the relationship processes that underlie dysfunction and adjustment at both individual and systemic levels, specifying excesses/deficits in specific parent behaviors, as well as rates of parental contingency based on the analysis of patterns or sequences of parent and child behaviors. Contingencies of this kind are now understood to be particularly proximal to children's adjustment, with observational research showing that contingencies supplied by family members may account for 40% to 60% of variance in child conduct problems (Snyder and Patterson, 1995, Snyder et al., 1997). Likewise, parents' use of strategies that are timed to preempt parent–child conflict have been found to predict immediate and long-term child compliance (Gardner, Sonuga-Barke, & Sayal, 1999). Microsocial coding was integral to the classic observational studies conducted by Patterson and colleagues at the Oregon Social Learning Center beginning in the 1960s and 1970s (see Patterson, Reid, & Dishion, 1992). These influential studies examined the moment-to-moment parent–child interactions within families of aggressive and oppositional children, and the functional dynamics between these interactions and children's antisocial behavior.

In addition to the study of variables derived from parent and child behavior respectively, variables assumed to reflect properties of the underlying parent–child relationship have also been researched extensively using observational paradigms. These often involve global or molar coding systems based on behavioral categories that are more inclusive than those of microsocial systems, and thereby able to take the broad context of behavior into account. Aksan, Kochanska, and Ortmann's (2006) system for coding mutually responsive orientation (MRO) in the parent–child relationship is one such example. This system was developed to measure attachment-related dynamics in parent–child interactions, with the aim of characterizing such dynamics based on both parent and child data. MRO is coded using global ratings that emphasize the joint-aspect of parent–child interaction (e.g., "Interaction flows smoothly, is harmonious; communication flows effortlessly and has a connected back-and-forth quality"). The authors contrast this method with traditional attachment paradigms (e.g., Strange Situation; Ainsworth et al., 1978) in which both parent and child are typically involved, yet only the behavior of the child is coded (Aksan et al., 2006).

In recent years, innovations in observational paradigms have been key to expanding the range of parenting variables that have contributed to models in the field of developmental psychopathology, particularly those related to emotional dynamics. A particularly noteworthy example is the state space grid (SSG), based on dynamic systems (DS) theory—a mathematical language used to describe the internal feedback processes of a system in adapting to new conditions. Developed by Lewis, Lamey, and Douglas (1999), the SSG is a graphical and quantitative tool used to plot a topographical map of the behavioral repertoire of a system (e.g., parent–child dyad). In doing so, it allows researchers to investigate risk processes associated with the structure, or the relative flexibility versus rigidity, that characterizes exchanges within the parent–child relationship. As discussed shortly, there has been growing interest in integrating principles from DS theory into more established (e.g., social learning theory) accounts of child psychopathology. Although the application of such theory remains in its infancy, various researchers have emphasized the potential for methods such as SSGs to provide new perspectives on longstanding questions in the parenting literature. For example, given the capacity for DS methods to capture the structure of parent–child dyads, it is thought that they may be well suited to the investigation of attachment dynamics. Specifically, SSGs could potentially represent secure family dynamics in terms of flexible, nonreactive, and synchronous interactive patterns that are "organized" as coordinated and mutual action–reaction patterns (Dishion & Snyder, 2004; Lunkenheimer et al., 2011).

## Social-cognitive Influences on Parenting

The parenting variables noted here have been found to capture vast individual differences in quality of parenting within populations of typically developing children as well as those referred to clinical services. Efforts to explain these individual differences have implicated contextual stressors such as marital discord, along with parent characteristics including psychopathology, personality, substance abuse, and biological factors (e.g., Sturge-Apple et al., 2012). There is also much evidence that social-cognitive processes in which parents engage are particularly proximal to the quality of their parenting. Accounts of these processes in the developmental literature have focused largely on the periods of infancy and early childhood, and the qualities of the attachment relationship that are thought to arise from parental reflective functioning (i.e., a parent's capacity to understand a child's behavior in terms of underlying mental states and intentions) (Sleed & Fonagy, 2013). In much the same way, clinical researchers have focused on biases in parental attributions around child behavior, and have shown that parents who engage in harsh and inconsistent discipline often holding explanations for child difficulties that emphasize the child's hostile intent, negative characteristics of the parent, or historical experiences in the family (see review by Johnston & Ohan, 2005). Other research has emphasized the role of social information processing biases concerning parents' attention to (i.e., encoding) and interpretation (i.e., appraisal) of child cues (e.g., Lorber, O'Leary, & Kendziora, 2003).

Recent developments in this area include emerging perspectives on parenting problems and emotional flooding—a social-cognitive process previously described in distressed couples (see Gottman (1993). Emotional flooding occurs when one partner increasingly perceives the other's negative affect as unpredictable and overwhelming. This is assumed to lead to emotional (escape) conditioning, involving a state of hypervigilance to the cues conditioned to the flooding. The flooded individual then begins to distort ambiguous cues in the biased direction of seeing them as threatening or frustrating, which in turn makes the individual more prone to arousal. A defining characteristic of emotional flooding is that it disrupts higher-order cognitive processes such as those required for problem-solving, thereby compromising the individual's capacity to respond adaptively in conflict situations. Snyder et al. (1994) proposed that emotional flooding may represent a mechanism through which child anger compromises parents' capacity to effectively problem-solve discipline scenarios, resulting in a reliance on over-learned strategies. This is consistent with research showing that maternal anger organizes and directs behavior toward coercion and away from strategies that soothe and reduce child arousal (Dix, 1991). Mence et al. (2013) recently reported the first investigation of emotional flooding in a sample of clinic-referred families, in which it was found to predict levels of hostile discipline among parents of children with conduct problems. Also consistent with theoretical assumptions, this association was strongest among parents who also exhibited negative biases in the appraisal of their child's emotional cues, as indexed using a novel observational paradigm.

## From Risk Factors to Risk Mechanisms

The number of parenting variables supported as risk factors for child psychopathology extends well beyond those noted already, all of which show significant, albeit often modest correlations with a broad range of childhood symptoms. However, compared to what is known about the parenting variables that predict child outcomes, considerably less is known about the mechanisms through which risk is conferred. It is here that marked divergence can be seen among researchers who may otherwise be interested in remarkably similar aspects of parenting. These mechanisms represent the processes through which parenting variables contribute to the emergence, amplification, and transformation of child dysfunction across development, or protect against deviations from a healthy trajectory. They in turn specify the targets that are most likely to translate into child behavior change in clinical interventions that aim to modify the family environment.

In contrast to the notion that parenting risk factors are specific to distinct disorders, research has emphasized considerable overlap among the parenting processes that are common to trajectories of both externalizing and internalizing dysfunction (Levy, Hawes, & Johns, 2015; O'Connor, 2002). Nonetheless, it is in the area of child-conduct problems that the most comprehensive and established accounts of parenting mechanisms can presently be found. Randomized controlled trials (RCTs) have served not only to establish parenting interventions as evidence-based treatments for child conduct problems, but have been employed as a tool for building theories of parenting through experimental manipulation. Such tests have been critical in allowing researchers to move beyond the correlational research that has dominated the literature, and upon which theories of parental influence have often relied.

The programs of research that best exemplify these experimental tests have been those guided by conceptualizations of family risk mechanisms based in social learning (operant) theory (see Patterson & Fisher, 2002). These conceptualizations attribute the maintenance and amplification of child conduct problems to escalating cycles of parent–child coercion that function as interlocking "reinforcement traps." These coercive cycles are maintained by escape-avoidance mechanisms through which aversive control tactics (e.g., whining, nagging, shouting, hitting) are rewarded, and positive/warm family interactions extinguished (Dishion & Patterson, 2006). The contingencies supplied by parents in terms of relative rates of reinforcement for socially competent versus deviant behavior are seen to represent the most proximal influences on child outcomes. Likewise, the same reinforcement mechanisms that operate on child behavior are assumed to encompass the alteration and shaping of parenting behavior. Observational data indicate that in the families of children with conduct problems, coercive reactions from parents are often successful in terminating a child's coercive behavior, and the prediction that the contingencies supplied by children function to (negatively) reinforce these very reactions (Snyder & Patterson, 1995). Based on the bidirectional dynamics emphasized in this model, the child with conduct problems has been described as both victim and architect of a coercive family system (Patterson, 1976).

In addition to specifying the processes through which parent–child contingencies play out on a moment-to-moment time scale, coercion theory also emphasizes the longer-term, developmental time scale across which cascading risk processes are set in train. Often first initiated by age 2, the longer that coercive cycles persist over time, the more rapidly they are likely to escalate, and the higher they are likely to push the upper amplitudes of family aggression. As children become increasingly skilled in their use of coercion, discipline becomes increasingly challenging. Deficits in social competencies expand to other domains of development, and soon generalize to contexts outside of the home (Dishion & Patterson, 2006).

Coercion theory forms the basis for the parent training programs that are recognized as the most effective treatment for conduct problems currently available (Eyberg, Nelson, & Boggs, 2008; Hawes & Allen, 2016). Indeed, some of the most convincing support for this model has been seen in RCT evidence from large preventive interventions in high risk populations including children in foster-care (e.g., Chamberlain et., 2008) and families characterized by social adversity (e.g., Dishion et al 2013). Impressive data have likewise been reported on the long-term social outcomes (e.g., increased standing of living) that can be attributed to the cascading effects of parent training in clinical populations up to nine years post-intervention (Patterson et al., 2010). These parent-training programs typically commence with skills training to increase positive reinforcement of desirable child behavior, followed by discipline-focused components in which parents are trained to use consistent, non-forceful consequences (e.g., time-out) to set limits on negative behavior. Research examining the mechanisms through which such interventions operate has found child outcomes to be accounted for both by reductions in harsh/inconsistent parenting, and increases in positive parenting practices (e.g., Beauchaine, Webster-Stratton, & Reid, 2005; Brotman et 2009; Hawes & Dadds, 2006). The most effective interventions for conduct problems in late childhood and adolescence are those that combine parent training components with child-focused skills training targeting social-cognitive deficits related to emotion regulation and social problem-solving (e.g., multisystemic therapy). The effects of such interventions are likewise mediated in part by changes in parenting practices (e.g., Dekovic et al., 2012), thereby emphasizing the importance of parenting mechanisms to child adjustment across both childhood and adolescence.

Among the competing theories of parenting that have been proposed to explain child conduct problems, coercion theory can be considered particularly compelling given the wealth of experimental evidence now available. From a theoretical perspective, a further strength of this model is also apparent on the grounds of parsimony. That is, the components of coercion theory are more amenable to observation and measurement than those of competing theories, and able to account for causal influence in fewer mechanisms. For example, accounts of child adjustment based on social learning theory and attachment theory both agree on the centrality of caregiver contingencies (or responsiveness) in bringing about self-regulated behavior. However, in predicting how it changes child behavior, attachment theory relies on constructs that refer to internal states and representations that are not easily operationalized without the use of proxy measures (Patterson & Fisher, 2002).

Literature on coercion theory exemplifies the move toward theoretical integration that has marked developmental psychopathology in recent years, spurred by growing recognition that multiple theoretical perspectives are needed to account for the synergistic processes that shape child outcomes within the family. One approach to such integration has focused on the interplay between operant and attachment mechanisms. The unique dynamics that characterize the attachment system help to explain some child behavior that operant principles cannot, such as why some children seem driven to elicit potentially harmful attention from parents, and why parent attention is so powerful a reinforcer at particular ages (Greenberg, Speltz, & Deklyen, 1993). This perspective has informed parent-training programs for child-conduct problems such as that manualized by Dadds and Hawes (2006), which aims not to improve attachment security, but to act on operant mechanisms in the family using strategies that are compatible with concurrent attachment dynamics. This includes maximizing parents' use of contingent reinforcement strategies that emphasize caregiver proximity, and training them to implement limit-setting strategies (e.g., time-out) in ways that do not inadvertently threaten attachment security. Although attachment constructs have often been researched in isolation from those emphasized in coercion theory, support for such integration has been provided by longitudinal studies involving both. For example, Kochanska et al. (2009) found that parental coercion (power-assertive discipline) in early childhood directly predicted prospective levels of conduct problems, while children's attachment status did not. However, attachment insecurity was found to interact with coercive parenting to enhance risk for later conduct problems. Other approaches to extending coercion theory beyond operant conditioning include the integration of dynamic systems principles. From this perspective, children at risk for early-onset conduct problems are characterized by an overall rigidity in their parent–child interactions regardless of the content of those interactions (see Granic & Patterson, 2006). Support for this view has been provided by longitudinal evidence regarding the joint contributions of parent–child affect and dyadic flexibility to children's behavioral adjustment (e.g., Lunkenheimer et al., 2011).

Although family-based risk factors are likewise emphasized in current models of internalizing problems, the mechanisms through which this risk is conferred have received considerably less attention than those implicated in externalizing problems. The critical/rejecting parenting associated with coercion in the families of children with conduct problems has also been associated with risk for internalizing problems—in particular child and adolescent depression (McLeod, Weisz & Wood, 2007). Alternatively, risk for anxiety disorders has been associated most strongly with overprotective/overcontrolling parenting, wherein parents excessively restrict children's engagement with situations or behaviors based on anticipation of potential threat (Rapee, Schniering, & Hudson, 2009). This may extend to psychological control expressed through intrusive or passive–aggressive parenting behaviors that inhibit autonomy granting. Such parents may withdraw affection or induce guilt as means of discipline, creating a family environment in which acceptance is contingent on a child's behavior (Barber, 1996). These parenting behaviors have been proposed to confer risk through a number of mechanisms, potentially functioning to (a) model anxious responding to innocuous events, (b) enhance children's threat interpretations, (c) prevent the habituation of anxious arousal by limiting children's exposure to fear-provoking events, and (d) interfere with the adaptive development of children's emotion-regulation skills (Ollendick, Costa, & Benoit, 2010).

Guided by the conceptualization of transactional parent–child dynamics emphasized in models of conduct problems, research has likewise supported the occurrence of transactional parent–child dynamics in accounts of internalizing problems (LaFreniere & Dumas, 1992). In line with this, Dadds and Roth (2001) proposed an "anxious–coercive cycle", in which fearful children solicit attention, comfort, and protection from their parents during novel situations, which in turn functions to reinforce children's avoidance and dependence on parents. There has since been considerable support for the notion that child anxiety is maintained by parenting responses that are in part a product of maladaptive child behavior. For example, intensive observational research has found that the controlling behavior of anxious children predicted aversive parent responses likely to enhance child distress (Williams et al., 2012). Such evidence suggests that interventions for anxiety that ignore parent–child interactions may place children at risk of reinstating relationship dynamics that contribute to the amplification of anxiety in the family. At present, evidence-based treatments for internalizing problems place considerably less emphasis on parenting targets than those for externalizing problems; however, RCT research has provided growing experimental support for the role of parenting mechanisms in child anxiety. Such research has emphasized the therapeutic value of training parents in behavior management skills that emphasize calm and consistent responding, and teaching parents to manage children's anxiety using cognitive-behavioral strategies such as graded exposure, problem solving, and behavioral experiments (Cartwright-Hatton et al., 2011; Hawes & Allen, 2016).

## Interplay Between Parenting and Child Factors

In recent years, some of the most noteworthy developments to have informed perspectives on parenting mechanisms in child psychopathology relate to the interplay between family environment and child characteristics that are biologically based. Two areas in which such evidence has grown considerably pertain to transactional or bidirectional parent–child dynamics, namely, (1) the influences of parenting on child temperament, regulatory capacities (including executive function), and related biological systems, and in turn, (2) the influences of these child factors on the parent–child relationship. A third area of noteworthy progress concerns (3) the role that child factors play in moderating parenting influences, with evidence of such interactive effects informing developmental models of distinct risk pathways to various child outcomes. As outlined below, the novel findings that have emerged in these areas in recent years indicate key directions for future research.

### Parenting Influences on Child Temperament and Biology

Definitions of child temperament have traditionally emphasized individual differences rooted in biological systems, as have conceptualizations of executive functions (Goldsmith et al., 1987). Although it has long been assumed that such characteristics are not determined by biological causes exclusively, it is only very recently that researchers have begun to systematically investigate the influences of parenting on these domains. The same is true of developmental disorders such as ADHD that are thought to arise largely from genetic factors. There is now considerable support for the view that parenting processes contribute to some child outcomes and protect against others by amplifying or dampening child characteristics of this kind. It has been proposed that characteristics including response perseveration, behavioral inhibition, hyperactivity, and irritability, are potentiated through thousands of interactions and routines within the family and broader social contexts across development. It has accordingly been argued that such characteristics might be most accurately conceptualized as entrained biosocial traits (Dishion & Stormshak, 2007).

Longitudinal studies of parenting in community samples have provided evidence consistent with this perspective. Taylor et al. (2013), for example, found that across early childhood, intrusive parenting was indirectly associated with later ego resiliency through its effects on children's effortful control. Likewise, in a large community cohort of children aged 4–10 years ($n = 976$), Hawes et al. (2013a) reported that parental involvement and inconsistent discipline were associated with prospective (12 month) levels of hyperactivity/inattention, controlling for baseline levels and comorbid features of ODD and CD. Furthermore, experimental evidence of parenting effects on child temperament is also now available from RCT research. Somech and Elizur (2012) found that a 14-session social learning based parent-training program delivered to families of children (aged 2–5 years) with clinically significant conduct problems produced lasting improvements in child callous–unemotional (CU) traits, as well as effortful control. This change in CU traits following modification of parenting replicates results reported by McDonald, Dodson, Rosenfield, and Jouriles (2011), who further showed that such change was mediated by change in parents' psychological aggression.

Additionally, growing evidence of such parenting effects can be seen among studies incorporating biological indices, particularly those pertaining to the HPA-axis. Blair et al. (2011) found that concentrations of cortisol-mediated associations between positive parental support and prospective EF across the infant and toddler years. Similarly, it has been found that among children of depressed mothers, those exposed to hostile parenting exhibit greater cortisol reactivity (Dougherty, Tolep, Smith, & Rose, 2013). Some experimental evidence is also available with regard to the plasticity of the HPA-axis in response to parenting. Brotman et al. (2007), for example, found that a family-based prevention program including parent training normalized cortisol reactivity to a social challenge in children at risk for developing conduct problems (aged 33–63 months).

Interestingly, there is also growing evidence that quality of parenting is associated with structural indices of brain development during adolescence. Whittle et al. (2009) found that the extent to which mothers exhibited punishing responses to their adolescents' affective expressions, as observed during problem-solving interactions, was associated with orbitofrontal cortex and anterior cingulate cortex volumes in these adolescents (Whittle et al. 2009). Whittle et al. (2014) subsequently found that such parenting predicted brain changes in males including attenuated volumetric growth in the amygdala, and accelerated cortical thinning in the anterior cingulate.

## Child-driven Influences on Parenting

It has long been recognized that parent–child relationships are reciprocal systems in which both parent and child initiate and respond to changes in one another (Bell, 1968). However, despite widespread recognition of such bidirectional dynamics, the predominant focus of parenting research has been on parent-to-child influences, with child-to-parent influences often ignored. Questions related to parenting as a product of child-driven effects have nonetheless been the focus of a number of highly influential studies, which can also be considered among the most innovative examples of parenting research in recent decades. These include experimental studies of parents interacting with unfamiliar children, such as that conducted by Anderson, Lytton, and Romney (1986), who found that mothers of typically developing boys became significantly more aversive when interacting with boys diagnosed with conduct disorder. Likewise, Barkley, Karlsson, Pollard, and Murphy (1985) demonstrated that administering stimulant drugs to hyperactive children was followed by a decrease in maternal aversive behavior that corresponded to medication dose. It has since been shown that such bidirectional influences are by no means specific to the socialization processes involved in children's behavioral and emotional adjustment, but extend across other developmental domains including language (Bornstein, Tamis-LeMonda, & Haynes, 1999). Moreover, a growing number of studies have concluded that child-driven effects on parenting are as strong (if not stronger) than parent-to-child effects on symptoms of psychopathology (Pardini, 2008).

Longitudinal data indicate that the features of externalizing problems explain change in both harsh parenting and sensitivity beginning in early childhood (Bradley & Corwyn, 2013). Interestingly, as evidence has grown regarding the various factors that characterize putative subgroups of antisocial children, it has become apparent that individual differences related to temperament are implicated in child-driven influences on parenting, independent of those produced by conduct problems themselves. Most notably, CU traits have been found to explain increased levels of negative (harsh and inconsistent) parenting and reduced levels of positive (warm) parenting over time (Hawes, Dadds, Frost, & Hasking, 2011; Salihovic, Kerr, Ozdemir, & Pakalniskiene, 2012). Both of these studies found that associations between CU traits and prospective parenting were independent of child conduct problems, and in both cases, the influences of CU traits on parenting appeared to be more potent than parent-driven influences on CU traits. Likewise, other research has found that conduct problems are most likely to elicit escalating levels of parental distress when accompanied by CU traits (Fanti & Munoz-Centifanti, 2014).

Children with CU traits have now been shown to demonstrate consistent impairments in eye contact toward their parents in a number of observational studies (e.g., Dadds et al., 2011). These studies indicate that this lack of eye contact is primarily child-driven. It does not appear to be a function of reduced eye contact from mothers; however, it does appear that fathers of high-CU boys may show a similar deficit. Given the importance of eye contact for emotional communication in the parent–child relationship, it is easy to imagine that this child behavior may in part contribute to the deterioration in parental warmth that has been associated with CU traits (Hawes et al., 2011). At the same time, this lack of eye contact with attachment figures early in life may prevent them from participating in the critical parent–child exchanges that establish the foundations for emotion understanding, conscience, and empathy, and set in train a developmental cascade involving ongoing failures of adaptation across these domains (Dadds et al., 2011).

There has been much interest in the use of genetically informed designs to disentangle environmental influences within the parent–child relationship from those that reflect genetic endowments that may be shared by both children and their parents (e.g., passive gene–environment interactions) (see Chapter # in this book). In a particularly noteworthy study involving multiple levels of analysis, Hayden et al. (2013) reported findings implicating a specific child polymorphism (DAT1 gene) in eliciting negative parenting, via its contributions to child negative affect. Such evidence is beginning to inform conceptualizations of the mechanisms through which transactional parent–child dynamics shape risk in trajectories of internalizing problems.

## Interactions between Parenting and Child Factors

Few questions have dominated the field of developmental psychopathology over the past decade like the question of why children exposed to the same parenting risk factors often show very different outcomes. Research into questions of this kind have focused increasingly on the notion that biologically based child characteristics moderate the influences of family environment on child outcomes, as seen in gene × environment interactions. A growing body of evidence has implicated such interactions in the trajectories of both internalizing and externalizing problems (Fujisawa et al. 2012; Natsuaki et al. 2013). Although interpretations of such interactions have traditionally followed a diathesis–stress model (i.e., the prediction that vulnerable individuals are most affected by negative parenting), there is growing evidence that they may often reflect differential susceptibility to socialization (Belsky & Pluess, 2013). This differential susceptibility view proposes that biologically based characteristics may increase children's responsiveness to parenting, both positive and negative. For example, children with a specific form of temperament may be more likely to both flounder in response to negative parenting and flourish in response to positive parenting, compared to children without such a temperament. Recent examples of differential susceptibility to parenting have been reported for child genotype, in relation to parenting influences on moral internalization (Kochanska et al., 2011) and noncompliance in early childhood (Sulik et al., 2012).

Among the various lines of clinical research that have been concerned with moderators of parenting influences in recent years, some of the most noteworthy progress has been made in relation to CU traits and antisocial behavior. There is now considerable evidence that the conduct problems of children with high versus low levels of CU traits develop through somewhat distinct causal pathways that implicate distinct neurobiological and parenting processes (Frick, Ray, Thornton, & Kahn, 2014). Compared to the conduct problems of children who are free from these traits, those of high-CU children appear to be less proximally associated with negative parenting practices such as harsh/inconsistent discipline (e.g., Wootton, Frick, Shelton, & Silverthorn, 1997). For high-CU children, it is a lack of parental warmth/involvement, rather than exposure to negative parenting, that appears to be most proximal to the development and maintenance of their conduct problems. Interestingly, there is evidence to suggest that parental warmth may be more robustly associated with the conduct problems of children with CU traits than those without (e.g., Pasalich, Dadds, Hawes, & Brennan, 2011). Such findings are consistent with analogous early childhood research into interactions between child temperament (e.g., fearlessness) and parenting in predicting conscience development (e.g., Fowles & Kochanska, 2000).

There is growing evidence from RCTs to indicate that CU traits both predict and moderate the effects of treatments for conduct problems that involve the modification of parenting (e.g., Dadds, Cauchi, Wimalaweera, Hawes, & Brennan, 2012; Hawes & Dadds, 2005; Hawes, Dadds, Brennan, Rhodes, & Cauchi, 2013; Manders, Deković, Asscher, van der Laan, & Prins, 2013). Although the evidence regarding CU traits and parenting has at times been mixed (see Hawes, Price, & Dadds, 2014; Waller et al., 2013), the findings generally converge with those of research into related child characteristics. For example, the emotionally dysregulated temperament that is thought to characterize low-CU children with conduct problems has been associated with increased responsiveness to parent training (Scott & O'Connor, 2012).

## Conclusions

The neurosciences have had a sweeping impact on clinical psychology and psychiatry in recent years, with the focus of much research shifting from the environments that shape dysfunction to the biological systems that underpin it. However, the more that such research has illuminated the role of biology in risk processes, the more it has in turn highlighted the very importance of environmental inputs. Nowhere has this been more apparent than in research investigating the parent–child relationship. It is now well recognized that child outcomes are shaped by transactional parent–child dynamics that feedback into quality of parenting as they play out over time. Moreover, it has become increasingly apparent that these dynamics may serve to potentiate the expression of biological vulnerabilities, and in doing so enhance risk that is carried forward across the lifespan. In addition, there is now much evidence that the same parenting behaviors do not influence the outcomes of all children uniformly, just as the same biological vulnerabilities do not. Rather, the contributions of one may often be determined by the other, as indicated by the gene × environment interactions that have now been reported across a range of outcomes. Models of these processes promise to become increasingly precise as parenting research continues to incorporate multiple levels of analysis and experimental tests of theory.

## References


Ainsworth, M. D. S., Blehar, M. C., Waters, E., & Wall, S. (1978). *Patterns of attachment: A psychological study of the strange situation.* Hillsdale, NJ: Erlbaum.

Aksan, N., Kochanska, G., & Ortmann, M. R. (2006). Mutually responsive orientation between parents and their children: Towards methodological advances in the science of relationships. *Developmental Psychology, 42*, 833–848. doi:10.1037/00121649.42.5.833

Alexandra Burt, S., Klahr, A. M., Neale, M. C., & Klump, K. L. (2013). Maternal warmth and directiveness jointly moderate the etiology of childhood conduct problems. *Journal of Child Psychology and Psychiatry, 54*, 1030–1037. doi:10.1111/jcpp.12095

Anderson, K. E., Lytton, H., & Romney, D. M. (1986). Mothers' interactions with normal and conduct-disordered boys: Who affects whom? *Developmental Psychology, 22*, 604–609.

Barber, B. K. (1996). Parental psychological control: Revisiting a neglected construct. *Child Development, 67*, 3296–3319. doi:10.1111/j.1467-8624.1996.tb01915.x

Barkley, R. A., Karlsson, J., Pollard, S., & Murphy, J. V. (1985). Developmental changes in the mother–child interactions of hyperactive boys: Effects of two dose levels of Ritalin. *Journal of Child Psychology and Psychiatry, 26*, 705–715.

Baumrind, D. (1971). Current patterns of parental authority. *Developmental Psychology Monograph, 4*, 1–103. doi:10.1037/h0030372

Beauchaine, T. P., Webster-Stratton, C., & Reid, M. J. (2005). Mediators, moderators, and predictors of 1-year outcomes among children treated for early-onset conduct problems: A latent growth curve analysis. *Journal of Consulting and Clinical Psychology, 73*, 371–388. doi:10.1037/0022-006X.73.3.371

Beeghly, M. (2012). A developmental psychopathology perspective on emotional availability research: Current trends and challenges. *Development and Psychopathology, 24*, 107–111. doi:10.1017/S0954579411000691

Bell, R. Q. (1968). A reinterpretation of the direction of effects in studies of socialization. *Psychological Review, 75*, 81–95. doi:10.1037/h0025583

Belsky J., & Pluess, M. (2013a). Beyond risk, resilience, and dysregulation: Phenotypic plasticity and human development. *Development and Psychopathology*, *25*, 1243–1261. doi:10.1017/S095457941300059X

Belsky, J., & Pluess, M. (2013b). Genetic moderation of early child-care effects on social functioning across childhood: A developmental analysis. *Child Development*, *84*, 1209–1225. doi:10.1111/cdev.12058

Blair, C., Granger, D. A., Willoughby, M., Mills-Koonce, R., Cox, M., Greenberg, M. T., et al. (2011). Salivary cortisol mediates effects of poverty and parenting on executive functions in early childhood. *Child Development*, *82*, 1970–1984. doi:10.1111/j.14678624.2011.01643.x

Borden, L. A., Herman, K. C., Stormont, M., Goel, N., Darney, D., Reinke, W. M., et al. (2014). Latent profile analysis of observed parenting behaviors in a clinical sample. *Journal of Abnormal Child Psychology*, *42*, 731–742. doi:10.1007/s10802-013-9815-z

Bornstein, M. H., Tamis-LeMonda, & Haynes, M. O. (1999). First words in the second year: Continuity, stability, and models of concurrent and predictive correspondence in vocabulary and verbal responsiveness across age and context. *Infant Behavior and Development*, *22*, 65–85. doi:10.1016/S0163-6383(99)80006-X

Bowlby, J. (1969). *Attachment and loss: Vol. 1. Attachment.* New York: Basic Books.

Bradley, R. H., & Corwyn, R. (2013). From parent to child to parent…: Paths in and out of problem behavior. *Journal of Abnormal Child Psychology*, *41*, 515–529. doi:10.1007/s10802-012-9692-x

Brotman, L. M., Gouley, K. K., Huang, K.-Y., Kamboukos, D., Fratto, C., & Pine, D. S. (2007). Effects of a psychosocial family-based preventive intervention on cortisol response to a social challenge in preschoolers at high risk for antisocial behavior. *Archives of General Psychiatry*, *64*, 1172–1179. doi:10.1001/archpsyc.64.10.1172

Brotman, L. M., O'Neal, C. R., Huang, K. Y., Gouley, K. K., Rosenfelt, A., & Shrout, P. E. (2009). An experimental test of parenting practices as a mediator of early childhood physical aggression. *Journal of Child Psychology and Psychiatry*, *50*, 235–245. doi:10.1111/j.1469-7610.2008.01929.x

Cartwright-Hatton, S., McNally, D., Field, A. P., Rust, S., Laskey, B., Dixon, C., et al. (2011). A new parenting-based group intervention for young anxious children: Results of a randomized controlled trial. *Journal of the American Academy of Child and Adolescent Psychiatry*, *50*, 242–251. doi:10.1016/j.jaac.2010.12.015

Chamberlain, P., Price, J., Leve, L. D., Laurent, H., Landsverk, J. A., & Reid, J. B. (2008). Prevention of behavior problems for children in foster care: Outcomes and mediation effects. *Prevention Science*, *9*, 17–27. doi:10.1007/s11121-007-0080-7

Dadds, M. R., Cauchi, A. J., Wimalaweera, S., Hawes, D. J., & Brennan, J. (2012). Outcomes, moderators, and mediators of empathic-emotion recognition training for complex conduct problems in childhood. *Psychiatry Research*, *199*, 201–207. doi:10.1016/j.psychres.2012.04.033

Dadds, M. R., & Hawes, D. (2006). *Integrated family intervention for child conduct problems: A behaviour-attachment-systems intervention for parents.* Brisbane: Australian Academic Press.

Dadds, M. R., Jambrak, J., Pasalich, D., Hawes, D. J., & Brennan, J. (2011). Impaired attention to the eyes of attachment figures and the developmental origins of psychopathy. *Journal of Child Psychology and Psychiatry*, *52*, 238–245. doi:10.1111/j.1469-7610.2010.02323.x

Dadds, M. R., & Roth, J. H. (2001). Family processes in the development of anxiety problems. In M. W. Vasey & M. R. Dadds (Eds.), *The developmental psychopathology of anxiety* (pp. 75–81). London: Oxford University Press.

Dekovic, M., Asscher, J. J., Manders, W. A., Prins, P. J. M., & van der Laan, P. (2012). Within intervention change: Mediators of intervention effects during multisystemic therapy. *Journal of Consulting and Clinical Psychology*, *80*, 574–587. doi:10.1037/a0028482

Dishion, T. J., Brennan, L. M., Shaw, D. S., McEachern, A. D., Wilson, M. N., & Jo, B. (2014). Prevention of problem behavior through annual family check-ups in early childhood: Intervention effects from the home to the second grade of elementary school. *Journal of Abnormal Child Psychology*, *42*, 343–354. doi:10.1007/s10802-013-9768-2

Dishion, T. J., Burraston, B., & Li, F. (2003). Family management practices: Research design and measurement issues. In Z. Sloboda & W. Bukowski (Eds.), *Handbook for drug abuse prevention: Theory, science, and practice* (pp. 587–607). New York: Kluwer.

Dishion, T. J., & Patterson, G. R. (2006). The development and ecology of antisocial behavior. In D. Cicchetti & D. J. Cohen (Eds.), *Developmental psychopathology*. Vol. *3*: Risk, disorder, and adaptation. New York: Wiley.

Dishion, T. J., & Stormshak, E. (2007). *Intervening in children's lives: An ecological, family centered approach to mental health care*. Washington, DC: APA Books.

Dishion, T. J., & Snyder, J. (2004). An introduction to the special issue on advances in process and dynamic system analysis of social interaction and the development of antisocial behavior. *Journal of Abnormal Child Psychology*, *32*, 575–578. doi:10.1023/B:JACP.0000047317.96104.ca

Dix, T. (1991). The affective organization of parenting: Adaptive and maladaptive processes. *Psychological Bulletin*, *110*, 3–25. doi:10.1037/0033-2909.110.1.3

Dougherty, L. R., Tolep, M. R., Smith, V. C., & Rose, S. (2013). Early exposure to parental depression and parenting: Associations with young offspring's stress physiology and oppositional behavior. *Journal of Abnormal Child Psychology*, *41*, 1299–1310. doi:10.1007/s10802-013-9763-7

Eisenberg, N., Cumberland, A., & Spinrad, T. L. (1998). Parental socialization of emotion. *Psychological Inquiry*, *9*, 241–273. doi:10.1207/s15327965pli0904_1

Eyberg, S. M., Nelson, M. M., & Boggs, S. R. (2008). Evidence-based treatments for child and adolescent disruptive behavior disorders. *Journal of Clinical Child and Adolescent Psychology*, *37*, 213–235. doi:10.1080/15374410701820117

Feldman, R. (2012). Parenting behavior as the environment where children grow. In L. C. Mayes and M. Lewis (Eds.). *The Cambridge handbook of environment in human development* (pp. 535–567). New York: Cambridge University Press.

Fanti, K. A., & Muñoz Centifanti, L. C. (2014). Childhood callous-unemotional traits moderate the relation between parenting distress and conduct problems over time. *Child Psychiatry and Human Development*, *45*, 173–184. doi:10.1007/s10578-013-0389-3

Fowles, D. C., & Kochanska, G. (2000). Temperament as a moderator of pathways to conscience in children: The contribution of electrodermal activity. *Psychophysiology*, *37*, 788–795. doi:10.1017/S0048577200981848

Frick, P. J., Ray, J. V., Thornton, L. C., & Kahn, R. E. (2014). Can callous-unemotional traits enhance the understanding, diagnosis, and treatment of serious conduct problems in children and adolescents? A comprehensive review. *Psychological Bulletin*, *140*, 1–57. doi:10.1037/a0033076

Fujisawa, K. K., Yamagata, S., Ozaki, K., & Ando, J. (2012). Hyperactivity/inattention problems moderate environmental but not genetic mediation between negative parenting and conduct problems. *Journal of Abnormal Child Psychology*, *40*, 189–200. doi:10.1007/s10802-011-9559-6

Gardner, F. E., Sonuga-Barke, E. J., & Sayal, K. (1999). Parents anticipating misbehaviour: An observational study of strategies parents use to prevent conflict with behaviour problem children. *Journal of Child Psychology and Psychiatry*, *40*, 1185–1196.

Goldsmith, H. H., Buss, A. H., Plomin, R., Rothbart, M. K., Thomas, A., Chess, S., et al. (1987). Roundtable: What is temperament? Four approaches. *Child Development*, *58*, 505–529. doi:10.2307/1130527

Gottman, J. M. (1993). A theory of marital dissolution and stability. *Journal of Family Psychology*, *7*, 57–75. doi:10.1037/0893-3200.7.1.57

Gottman, J. M., Katz, L. F., & Hooven, C. (Eds.). (1997). *Meta-emotion: How families communicate emotionally*. Hillsdale, NJ: Erlbaum.

Granic, I., & Patterson, G. R. (2006). Toward a comprehensive model of antisocial development: A systems dynamic systems approach. *Psychological Review*, *113*, 101–131. doi:10.1037/0033-295X.113.1.101

Greenberg, M. T., Speltz, M. L. & DeKlyen, M. (1993). The role of attachment in the early development of disruptive behavior problems. *Development and Psychopathology*, *5*, 191–213.

Grusec, J. E., & Davidov, M. (2010). Integrating different perspectives on socialization theory and research: A domain-specific approach. *Child Development*, *81*, 687–709. doi:10.1111/j.1467-8624.2010.01426.x

Hawes, D.J., & Allen, J. (2016). Evidence-based parenting interventions: Current perspectives and clinical strategies. In M. Hodes & S. Gau (Eds.) *Positive Mental Health, Fighting Stigma, and Promoting Resiliency for Children and Adolescent* (Chap 10) Academic Press, Elsevier.

Hawes, D. J., & Dadds, M. R. (2005). The treatment of conduct problems in children with callous-unemotional traits. *Journal of Consulting and Clinical Psychology*, *73*(4), 737–741. doi:10.1037/0022-006X.73.4.737

Hawes, D. J., & Dadds, M. R. (2006). Assessing parenting practices through parent-report and direct observation during parent-training. *Journal of Child and Family Studies*, *15*, 554–567. doi:10.1007/s10826-006-9029-x

Hawes, D. J., & Dadds, M. R. (2013). Parent and family assessment strategies. In B. D. McLeod, A. Jensen-Doss, & T. Ollendick (Eds.), *Diagnostic and behavioral assessment in children and adolescents* (pp. 316–347). New York: Guilford Press.

Hawes, D. J., Dadds, M. R., Frost, A. D. J., & Hasking, P. A. (2011). Do childhood callous-unemotional traits drive change in parenting practices? *Journal of Clinical Child & Adolescent Psychology*, *40*, 507–518. doi:10.1080/15374416.2011.581624

Hawes, D. J., Dadds, M. R., Brennan, J., Rhodes, T., & Cauchi, A. (2013). Re-visiting the treatment of conduct problems in children with callous-unemotional traits. *Australian and New Zealand Journal of Psychiatry*, *47*(7), 646–653. doi:10.1177/0004867413484092

Hawes, D. J., Dadds, M. R., Frost, A. D. J., & Russell, A. (2013). Parenting practices and prospective levels of hyperactivity/inattention across early- and middle-childhood. *Journal of Psychopathology and Behavioral Assessment*, *35*, 273–282. doi:10.1007/s10862-013-9341-x

Hawes, D. J., Dadds, M. R., & Pasalich, D. (2013). Observational coding strategies. In J. Comer & P. Kendall (Eds.), *The Oxford handbook of research strategies for clinical psychology* (pp. 120–141). New York: Oxford University Press.

Hawes, D. J., Price, M. J., & Dadds, M. R. (2014). Callous-unemotional traits and the treatment of conduct problems in childhood and adolescence: A comprehensive review. *Clinical Child and Family Psychology Review*, *17*, 248–267. doi:10.1007/s10567-014-0167-1

Hayden, E. P., Hanna, B., Sheikh, H. I., Laptook, R. S., Kim, J., Singh, S. M., et al. (2013). Child dopamine active transporter 1 genotype and parenting: Evidence for evocative gene-environment correlations. *Development and Psychopathology*, *25*, 163–173. doi:10.1017/S0954579412000971

Johnston, C., & Ohan, J. L. (2005). The importance of parental attributions in families of children with attention-deficit/hyperactivity and disruptive behaviour disorders. *Clinical Child and Family Psychology Review*, *8*, 167–182. doi:10.1007/s105670056663-6

Kochanska, G., Barry, R. A., Stellern, S. A., & O'Bleness, J. J. (2009). Early attachment organization moderates the parent-child mutually coercive pathway to children's antisocial conduct. *Child Development*, *80*, 1288–1300. doi:10.1111/j.1467-8624.2009.01332.x

Kochanska, G., Kim, S., Barry, R. A., & Philibert, R. A. (2011). Children's genotypes interact with maternal responsive care in predicting children's competence: Diathesis stress or differential susceptibility? *Development and Psychopathology, 23*, 605–616. doi:10.1017/S0954579411000071

LaFrenière, P. J., & Dumas, J. E. (1992). A transactional analysis of early childhood anxiety and social withdrawal. *Development and Psychopathology, 4*, 385–402. doi:10.1017/S0954579400000857

Levy, F., Hawes, D. J., & Johns, A. (2015). Externalizing and internalizing comorbidity. In T. P. Beauchaine & S. P. Hinshaw (Eds.), *The Oxford Handbook of Externalizing Spectrum Disorders* (pp. 443–460). New York: Oxford: University Press.

Lewis, M. D. (2000). The promise of dynamic systems approaches for an iated account of human development. *Child Development, 71*(1), 36–43.

Lewis, M. D., Lamey, A. V., Douglas, L. (1999). A new dynamic systems method for the analysis of early socioemotional development. *Developmental Science, 2*, 457–475. doi:10.1111/1467-7687.00090

Lorber, M. F., O'Leary, S. G., & Kendziora, K. T. (2003). Mothers' overreactive discipline and their encoding and appraisals of toddler behavior. *Journal of Abnormal Child Psychology, 31*, 485–494. doi:10.1023/A:1025496914522

Lorenz, K. Z. (1950). The comparative method in studying innate behaviour patterns. *Symposia of the Society for Experimental Biology, 4*, 221–268.

Lunkenheimer, E. S., Olson, S. L., Hollenstein, T., Sameroff, A. J., & Winter, C. (2011). Dyadic flexibility and positive affect in parent-child coregulation and the development of child behavior problems. *Development and Psychopathology, 23*, 577–591. doi:10.1017/S095457941100006X

Maccoby, E. E., & Martin, J. A. (1983). Socialization in the context of the family: Parent–child interaction. In P. H. Mussen & E. M. Hetherington (Eds.), *Handbook of child psychology.* Vol. *4*, Socialization, personality, and social development (4th ed.). New York: Wiley.

Manders, W. A., Deković, M., Asscher, J. J., van der Laan, P. H., & Prins, P. J. (2013). Psychopathy as predictor and moderator of multisystemic therapy outcomes among adolescents treated for antisocial behavior. *Journal of Abnormal Child Psychology, 41*, 1–12. doi:10.1007/s10802-013-9749-5

McDonald, R., Dodson, M. C., Rosenfield, D., & Jouriles, E. N. (2011). Effects of a parenting intervention on features of psychopathy in children. *Journal of Abnormal Child Psychology, 39*, 1013–1023. doi:10.1007/s10802-011-9512-8

McLeod, B. D., Weisz, J. R., & Wood, J. J. (2007). Examining the association between parenting and childhood depression: A meta-analysis. *Clinical Psychology Review, 27*, 986–1003. doi:10.1016/j.cpr.2007.03.001

Mence, M., Hawes, D. J., Wedgwood, L., Morgan, S., Barnett, B., Kohlhoff, J., et al. (2014). Emotional flooding and hostile discipline in the families of toddlers with disruptive behavior problems. *Journal of Family Psychology, 28*, 12–21. doi:10.1037/a0035352

Natsuaki, M. N., Leve, L. D., Neiderhiser, J. M., Shaw, D. S., Scaramella, L. V., Ge, X. et al. (2013). Intergenerational transmission of risk for social inhibition: The interplay between parental responsiveness and genetic influences. *Development and Psychopathology, 25*, 261–274. doi:10.1017/S0954579412001010

O'Connor, T. G. (2002). Annotation: the "effects" of parenting reconsidered: Findings, challenges, and applications. *Journal of Child Psychology and Psychiatry, 43*, 555–572. doi:10.1111/1469-7610.00046

Ollendick, T. H., Costa, N. M., & Benoit, K. E. (2010). Interpersonal processes and the anxiety disorders of childhood. In G. Beck (Ed.), *Interpersonal processes in the anxiety disorders: Implications for understanding psychopathology and treatment* (pp. 71–95). Washington, DC: APA Books.

Pardini, D. A. (2008). Novel Insights into longstanding theories of bidirectional parent–child influences: Introduction to the special section. *Journal of Abnormal Child Psychology, 36*, 627–631.

Pasalich, D. S., Dadds, M. R., Hawes, D. J., & Brennan, J. (2011). Do callous-unemotional traits moderate the relative importance of parental coercion versus warmth in child conduct problems? An observational study. *Journal of Child Psychology and Psychiatry, and Allied Disciplines*, *52*, 1308–1315. doi:10.1111/j.1469-7610.2011.02435.x

Patterson, G. R. (1976). The aggressive child: Victim and architect of a coercive system. In E. J. Mash, L. A. Hamerlynck, & L. C. Handy (Eds.), *Behavior modification and families*. Vol. *1*. Theory and research (pp. 267–316). New York: Brunner/Mazel.

Patterson, G. R., & Fisher, P. A. (2002). Recent developments in our understanding of parenting: Birdirectional effects, causal models, and the search for parsimony. In M. H. Bornstein (Ed.), *Handbook of parenting*. Vol. *5*. Practical issues in parenting (pp. 59–88). Mahwah, NJ: Erlbaum.

Patterson, G. R., Forgatch, M. S., & Degarmo, D. S. (2010). Cascading effects following intervention. *Development and Psychopathology*, *22*, 949–970. doi:10.1017/S0954579410000568

Patterson, G. R., Reid, J. B., & Dishion, T. J. (1992). *Antisocial boys. A social interactional approach*. Vol. *4*. Eugene, OR: Castalia.

Rapee, R. M., Schniering, C. A., & Hudson, J. L. (2009). Anxiety disorders during childhood and adolescence: Origins and treatment. *Annual Review of Clinical Psychology*, *5*, 335–365. doi:10.1146/annurev.clinpsy.032408.153628

Rutter, M., & Sroufe, L. A. (2000). Developmental psychopathology: Concepts and challenges. *Development and Psychopathology*, *12*, 265–296. doi:10.1017/S0954579400003023

Salihovic, S., Kerr, M., Ozdemir, M., & Pakalniskiene, V. (2012). Directions of effects between adolescent psychopathic traits and parental behavior. *Journal of Abnormal Child Psychology*, *40*, 957–969. doi:10.1007/s10802-012-09623-x

Scott, S., & O'Connor, T. G. (2012). An experimental test of differential susceptibility to parenting among emotionally-dysregulated children in a randomized controlled trial for oppositional behavior. *Journal of Child Psychology and Psychiatry*, *53*, 1184–1193. doi:10.1111/j.1469-7610.2012.02586.x

Sleed, M., & Fonagy, P. (2012). Parental care and attachment. In L. Mayes & M. Lewis (Eds.), *The Cambridge handbook of environment in human development* (pp. 191–221). Cambridge: Cambridge University Press.

Snyder, J., Edwards, P., McGraw, K., Kilgore, K., & Holton, A. (1994). Escalation and reinforcement in mother-child conflict: Social processes associated with the development of physical aggression. *Development and Psychopathology*, *6*, 305–321. doi:10.1017/S0954579400004600

Snyder, J., Horsch, E., & Childs, J. (1997). Peer relationships of young children: Affiliative choices and the shaping of aggressive behavior. *Journal of Clinical Child Psychology*, *26*, 145–156. doi:10.1207/s15374424jccp2602_3

Snyder, J., & Patterson, G. (1995). Individual differences in social aggression: A test of a reinforcement model of socialization in the natural environment. *Behavior Therapy*, *26*, 371–391. doi:10.1016/S0005-7894(05)80111-X

Somech, L. Y., & Elizur, Y. (2012). Promoting self-regulation and cooperation in pre-kindergarten children with conduct problems: A randomized controlled trial. *Journal of the American Academy of Child and Adolescent Psychiatry*, *51*, 412–422.

Sroufe, L. A., Duggal, S., Weinfield, N., & Carlson, E. (2000). Relationships, development, and psychopathology. In A. J. Sameroff, M. Lewis, & S. M. Miller (Eds.), *Handbook of developmental psychopathology*, 2nd ed. New York: Kluwer Academic.

Sturge-Apple, M. L., Cicchetti, D., Davies, P. T., & Suor, J. H. (2012). Differential susceptibility in spillover between interparental conflict and maternal parenting: Evidence for OXTR and 5-HTT genes. *Journal of Family Psychology*, *26*, 431–442.

Sulik, M. J., Eisenberg, N., Lemery-Chalfant, K., Spinrad, T. L., Silva, K. M., Eggum, N. D., et al. (2012). Interactions between serotonin transporter gene haplotypes and quality of mothers' parenting predict the development of children's noncompliance. *Developmental Psychology*, *48*, 740–754. doi:10.1037/a0025938

Taylor, Z. E., Eisenberg, N., Spinrad, T. L., & Widaman, K. F. (2013). Longitudinal relations of intrusive parenting and effortful control to ego-resiliency during early childhood. *Child Development, 84*, 1145–1151. doi:10.1111/cdev.12054

Turiel, E. (2010). Domain specificity in social interactions, social thought, and social development. *Child Development, 81*, 720–726. doi:10.1111/j.14678624.2010.01429.x

Waller, R., Gardner, F., & Hyde, L. W. (2013). What are the associations between parenting, callous-unemotional traits, and antisocial behavior in youth? A systematic review of evidence. *Clinical Psychology Review, 33*(4), 593–608. DOI: 10.1016/j.cpr.2013.03.001

Whittle, S., Simmons, J. G., Dennison, M., Vijayakumar, N., Schwartz, O., Yap, M. B., et al. (2014). Positive parenting predicts the development of adolescent brain structure: A longitudinal study. *Developmental Cognitive Neuroscience, 8*, 7–17. doi:10.1016/j.dcn.2013.10.006

Whittle, S., Yap, M. B. H., Yücel, M., Sheeber, L., Simmons, J. G., Pantelis, C., et al. (2009). Maternal responses to adolescent positive affect are associated with adolescents' reward neuroanatomy. *Social Cognitive and Affective Neuroscience, 4*, 247–256. doi:10.1093/scan/nsp012

Williams, S. R., Kertz, S. J., Schrock, M. D., & Woodruff-Borden, J. (2012). A sequential analysis of parent–child interactions in anxious and nonanxious families. *Journal of Clinical Child and Adolescent Psychology, 41*(1), 64–74.

Wootton, J. M., Frick, P. J., Shelton, K. K., & Silverthorn, P. (1997). Ineffective parenting and childhood conduct problems: The moderating role of callous-unemotional traits. *Journal of Consulting and Clinical Psychology, 65*, 301–308. doi:10.1037/0022-006X.65.2.292.b

# 15

# Peer Processes and Child Psychopathology

## *A Focus on Externalizing Behaviors*

Luna C. Muñoz Centifanti, Scott Risser, and Bethany Little

Many children and youths who show extreme behavior or emotional problems do so in the presence of other people, and some of these problems are defined by how well children are able to engage with others. Youths develop enormously by negotiating their friendships and their friends shape their development further. Thus, models of the development of psychopathology must consider friendships and peer interactions. These interactions are shaped by previous interactions, social competence, self-regulation, antisocial traits, and non-peer relations, such as parental involvement.

In this chapter, we outline research, theory, and diagnoses related to externalizing behaviors and peer relations. Because understanding these phenomena require examining other aspects of adjustment, we also included selected discussions of internalizing problems, especially depression. In discussing these problems it is important to notice that peers not only influence maladaptive behavior, but they can also serve as strong reinforcement for continuance of those behaviors. Additionally, these transactional relationships are evidenced by research showing that maladaptive behavior influences social status and friendships, both of which relate to current and later adjustment. Lastly, we argue that future research should consider the antisocial traits that some youth bring to these interactions; these callous–unemotional traits may prove the inciting factor for maladjustment in many peer systems.

## Friends and Friendlessness

To understand peer interactions and their effects, many have turned to the phenomenon of friendship. Much of the research concerning friendships has used reciprocated nominations of friendships, and indeed beginning in late preschool, children within mutually nominated friendship dyads spend more time together (Vaughn, 2001), quarrel more (Laursen & Hartup, 1989), and resolve conflicts differently (Hartup, Laursen, Stewart, & Eastenson, 1988) than non-friends. As they age, children describe their own friendships as increasing in trust, loyalty, and especially intimacy (Berndt, 2002;

*The Wiley Handbook of Developmental Psychopathology*, First Edition. Edited by Luna C. Centifanti and David M. Williams.

Buhrmester, & Furman, 1987), creating fertile ground for socialization of values and behaviors (for review see Brechwalk & Prinstein, 2011), and frequent interdependencies that present risk for negative emotionality (Berscheid, 1983; Laursen, 1993). Indeed, even absence or loss of friendships have been investigated in relation to adjustment.

The processes that lead to friendlessness are tied to psychopathology. For instance, research by Blachman and Hinshaw (2002) demonstrated that not only do youth diagnosed with ADHD have fewer friendships compared to other youth, but the friendships they do have are less stable and are of a lower reported friendship quality. Adults perceive youths that are friendless as less socially competent and as exhibiting more behavior problems, and their peers see them as shy, timid, and easily angered (e.g. Parker & Seal, 1996). Indeed, depressed youths may have difficulty maintaining friendships and report friendships of lower quality because of their interpersonal problems (Hammen & Rudolph, 2003). These friendship difficulties may only be perceived by the youths themselves or they may be real, yet changes in friendships may signal symptoms of psychopathology.

Disruptions or termination of peer relationships are linked with feelings of loneliness, depression, and anger, as well as physiological dysregulation and increased risk of victimization (Laursen, Hartup, & Koplas, 1996; Parker & Seal, 1996). Additionally, acute or chronic friendlessness is associated with feelings of loneliness, internalizing problems, and risk of peer victimization (Brendgen, Vitaro, & Bukowski, 2000; Kochenderfer & Ladd, 1997; Ladd & Troop-Gordon, 2003). Lacking a close friend not only puts children at risk for peer victimization, but may also augment the risk of that victimization as shown by moderation effects of friendship on the association between peer victimization and externalizing and internalizing problems (Hodges, Boivin, Vitaro, & Bukowski, 1999).

## Reciprocated Relationships, Homophily, and Social Contagion

When considering youth dyadic relationships and associations, high-quality and reciprocated friendships are often considered a protective factor against psychopathology. Indeed, having a supportive friendship acts as moderator of the association between genetic, personality, familial, and situational risk factors and maladjustment (Brendgen et al., 2013; Laursen, Bukowski, Aunola, & Nurmi, 2007; Muñoz, Kerr, & Besic, 2008; Wasserstein & La Greca, 1996). However, several processes within friendships are risk factors, correlates, and outcomes of internalizing or externalizing problems.

Some of the influence peers have may be explicitly transferred to youths. Friends may directly embolden youth and reinforce antisocial behaviors (Capaldi, Dishion, Stoolmiller, & Yoerger, 2001; Dishion & Tipsord, 2011). Of interest specifically to understanding externalizing behaviors in females, research has found hanging out with antisocial peers designated a group of females who engaged in antisocial behavior throughout childhood and adolescence (Odgers et al., 2008). However, peers also may implicitly exert influence on adolescent behavior by a process of social contagion. That is, they may influence behavior through competition, status-enhancing norms, and other social-cognitive mechanisms (Centifanti, Modecki, MacLellan, & Gowling, 2014; Cohen & Prinstein, 2006; Rebellon & Modecki, 2014). For example, higher peer status and popularity have been shown to be related to girls' use of relational aggression—to hurt others via gossiping, spreading rumors, or freezing people from friendship groups (Goldweber, Cauffman, & Cillessen, 2014). Thus, it may be that female peers are accepting and possibly attracted to highly relationally aggressive girls who perpetrate aggression to gain status or desired objects (i.e., proactive aggression)—behaviors that may be seen as acceptable for girls to exhibit. Although these girls may not be well-liked, they may still attract high peer status (Goldweber et al., 2014). In addition to peer socialization processes explaining youths' association with deviant peers, youth may select peers who mirror their own normative beliefs about risk and problem behavior (Monahan, Steinberg, & Cauffman, 2009).

Youths who engage in antisocial behavior tend to have similarly antisocial peers, showing homophily—friendship based on shared activities or characteristics. Physically aggressive girls have been shown to be rejected by their female peers due to their deviation from the gender norm, and they gravitate more towards male-dominated peer groups who may be more similar in the use of physical force (Pepler & Craig, 2005). Related homophilic processes within friendships may explain peers' influence on youth alcohol use (Bosari & Carey, 2001), violent criminal behaviors (Dishion, Eddy, Haas, Li, & Spracklen, 1997), and smoking (Kobus, 2003). Selection of like-minded friends may also play a role in socialization of problematic behavior. Selection factors accounted for friendships with peers who drank greater amounts of alcohol for youths who were more socially popular (Mathys, Burk, & Cillessen, 2013). Delinquency also shows selection and influence factors (Knecht, Snijders, Baerveldt, Steglich, & Raub, 2010; Baerveldt, Völker, & Van Rossem, 2008), although influence factors may be moderated by antisocial personality traits (Kerr, Van Zalk, & Stattin, 2012). Additionally, selection factors that are based on *perceptions* of finding like-minded individuals may explain the initiation of a friendship, but then socialization may maintain the friendship and make youths more similar over time (Molano, Jones, Brown, & Aber, 2013). Thus, the transactions over time may differ such that influence and selection work intermittently.

Both research and theory concerning depression and interpersonal difficulties illustrate a transactional relationship, such that interpersonal stressors predict youth depression (Carter & Garber, 2011; Hankin, Mermelstein, & Roesch, 2007), and depressed individuals may experience relationship processes that maintain or promote depression over time (Joiner & Timmons, 2009). Some of these processes may be related to interpersonal deficits and involve behaviors such as social withdrawal, negative-feedback-seeking, and excessive reassurance-seeking (Agoston & Rudolph, 2011). Many of these behaviors have concurrent associations with positive friendship quality, but at extremes, may also have longitudinal associations with internalizing symptoms.

In some cases, depression spreads through peer groups or friendships, especially for girls, similar to peer or sibling contagion of antisocial behaviors (Conway, Rancourst, Adelman, Burk, & Prinstein, 2011; van Zalk, Kerr, Branje, Stattin, & Meeus, 2010). The processes of this contagion are somewhat unclear. However, one possibility is that friendship dyadic partners excessively discuss their personal (or interpersonal) problems, a behavior termed co-rumination (Rose, 2002). To further muddy the waters, the association between internalizing symptoms and co-rumination varies by gender. In one longitudinal study, co-rumination in preadolescent girls predicted increases in depression and anxiety, which in turn, along with increases in friendship quality, predicted increased co-rumination. Thus, girls may perceive co-rumination as supportive behavior from their friends but this reinforces their thoughts. For boys, high friendship qualities and anxiety predicted co-rumination, which in turn increased positive friendship qualities (Rose, Carlson, & Waller, 2007), suggesting co-rumination may be interpreted as a signal of a close friendship. Another study, however, using a developmental cascade model, found transactional longitudinal associations between interpersonal stressors, co-rumination, and internalizing symptoms (Hankin, Stone, & Wright, 2010).

Other maladaptive behaviors related to body image and eating disorders may also be socialized within friendship dyads and larger friendship groups. Recent work has shown that preadolescent boys' body image concerns and body change behaviors were predicted by their friend groups' dieting behaviors (Rancourt, Conway, Burk, & Prinstein, 2013). The process behind this socialization may involve a similar form of "fat talk" (Nichter & Vuckovic, 1994), a term for conversations and comments, both negative and positive, concerning appearance, dieting techniques, and desire for weight loss that may play a role in relationship maintenance for adolescent girls (Nichter, 2002). Unfortunately, evidence suggests that exposure to fat talk significantly increases body dissatisfaction in adolescent and young adult females (Stice, Maxfield, & Wells, 2003), which may in turn put individuals at risk for eating disorders or other internalizing problems. This is akin to the "deviant talk" that antisocial friendship dyads engage in (Dishion, Patterson, & Griesler, 1994). Deviant talk among antisocial peer groups may provide reinforcement for aggressive behavior, but also may provide cues as to the type of behavior that will be reinforced in the future. Thus, youths learn rapidly what is encouraged within the peer group and may exacerbate their maladaptive behavior in response.

As adolescents mature they are better able to resist the influence of peers; this seems to relate to increases in cognitive maturity (Steinberg & Monahan, 2007). Further, Steinberg and Monahan (2007) argue for the particular change in resistance to peer influence observed from the ages of 14 to 18 years to likely reflect individuation from parents at the same time as seeking greater involvement from peers. As a result of this change, and given that adolescent risk taking almost always occurs in groups, some scholars speculate that the presence of peers stimulates adolescent antisocial behavior by increasing the salience of potential short-term rewards (Chein, Albert, O'Brien, Uckert, & Steinberg, 2011). For example, Steinberg's biobehavioral model suggests that having peers in the vicinity automatically triggers the activation of reward-processing centers of the brain, and incites adolescents toward greater risk (Chein et al., 2011; O'Brien, Albert, Chein, & Steinberg, 2011). As youths age and enter adulthood, the rewarding aspects of peer influence become dampened by inhibitory and executive processes in the brain which manage and modulate emotions.

## Peer Rejection and Enmity

One of the most robust and consistent predictors of antisocial behaviors is that of peer-rejected status (Dodge, Coie, & Lynam, 2006). This association has been found across development in school-age children (Lansford, Malone, Dodge, Pettit, & Bates, 2010; Prinstein & Cillessen, 2003), and research demonstrates that rejected status is prospectively associated with illegal, oppositional, physically aggressive, and delinquent behaviors (Prinstein, Rancourt, Guerry, & Browne, 2009) as well as indirect and relational aggression (Prinstein & Cillessen, 2003). Additionally, in a study with rejected and non-rejected fourth-grade boys, upon entering a new peer group for six weekly play sessions, rejected boys were already rejected by their new peers by week three (Coie & Kupersmidt, 1983). Similar findings occur when unacquainted boys are brought together, such that rejected status occurs quickly and is often associated with verbal hostility and initiating fights for both instrumental purposes and angry retaliation (Dodge, 1983; Dodge, Coie, Pettit, & Price, 1990). Rejected status, which may reflect a child's socially aversive behaviors and disposition, contributes to increased antisocial behavior in school-aged children, such that studies that examine aggression and status at early time points, find increased aggressive behavior even when previous aggression was statistically controlled (Dodge et al., 2003; Haselager, Cillessen, Van Lieshout, Riksen-Walraven & Hartup, 2002; Kupersmidt & Coie, 1990). Thus, it is especially problematic that rejected status occurs quickly and appears stable across peer contexts, even with novel peers.

The process for identifying children as rejected by their peers involves using sociometric methods. Sociometric statuses can be determined by peer nominations, peer ratings, and paired comparisons, which often involve questions that fall into either emotional criteria ("who do you like most/least" or "who is your best friend") or reputational criteria ("who starts fights" or "who is popular," Moreno, 1934). Each method yields five status types: popular (few "dislikes," many "likes"), rejected (many "dislikes," few "likes"), neglected (few "likes" and "dislikes"), controversial (both "likes" and "dislikes"), and average (youth with acceptance and rejection rates around the mean). Typically though, peer nomination methods are often used because they take less time than both ratings and paired comparisons, while retaining their validity (Cillessen, 2009). It is also important to note that sociometric assessments for rejection provide unique information when compared to other reporters. When comparing sociometric assessments to teacher reports, Cillessen Terry, Coie, and Lochman (1992) found agreement between teacher and peer reports of aggressive behavior, but low agreement for social status, such that teachers rated rejected children as controversial and average students as popular. Further, classification of rejected youth has shown that the greatest risk for future externalizing problems is within a group of youth who are rejected and aggressive when compared to other, non-aggressive, rejected youth and non-rejected, aggressive youth (Prinstein & La Greca, 2004).

Several theoretical processes may explain the association between rejection and maladjustment. Sociometric status may be a measure of social competence, such that children who are more socially competent attract greater peer acceptance ratings, whereas social rejection may be an indicator of social incompetence (Ladd, 2005). Because adequate relationships with peers during development are necessary for cognitive and social growth, rejected children's poor relationships with peers put them at risk (Hartup, 1983; Sullivan, 1953). For example, early negative peer experiences associated with rejected status may lead to cognitive biases in rejected youth. That is, normally neutral social behaviors and their related cues may start to be interpreted as originating from hostile intent. Indeed, research has shown that rejected youth demonstrate high levels of hostile attribution biases—interpreting ambiguous events as the product of other people's hostile intentions (Dodge & Coie, 1987). These biases may prevent rejected youth from encoding and interpreting social cues accurately and from generating appropriate social responses that align with future social goals (Crick & Dodge, 1994; Dodge, Bates, & Pettit, 1990). Furthermore, children's poor interactions with peers have an impact on future competence/incompetence and adjustment/maladjustment, creating reciprocal relationships between adjustment, competence, and peer relationships. This may involve a two-stage process where behavior drives status, then later, status drives behavior (Coie, 1990). In the emergence stage of peer status, youths may make their decisions about status based on children's aggressive and aversive behaviors and poor competence. Later, in the maintenance stage, youths base their judgments of their peers on existing reputations rather than actual behaviors, denying opportunities for change in acceptance.

In understanding how peer interactions, especially aggressive and antisocial acts, may set up youth for rejection, it is important to consider that aggressive behavior may be perceived differentially within peer groups. Also, different peer groups have varying norms for the acceptability for aggression. For example, when aggression is used in a self-defensive way or in response to direct provocation, it is evaluated positively among peers. Other factors, such as gender, may determine if peer groups reject aggressive children. Again, the association between rejection and overt aggression is much stronger for girls than for boys (Lancelotta & Vaughn, 1989), probably stemming from a cultural norm of more acceptance of male aggression (Dodge et al., 2006). In some samples, traits such as leadership and social competence protected aggressive youth from a rejected status (Kupersmidt & Dodge, 2004), and poor social competence (argumentative and less socially attentive) separated youth who were aggressive and rejected from those rated as aggressive but not rejected (Bierman, Smoot, & Aumiller, 1993).

It may be that peers' perception of the acceptable use of aggression may underlie maladaptive trajectories; that is, the aggression exhibited by rejected status youths may be associated with later problems due to negative perceptions from conventional or prosocial peers. Indeed, in addition to aggressive behaviors, rejected youth are at risk for other maladaptive problems. Peer rejection is associated with later problematic alcohol, cigarette, and marijuana use (Dishion, Capaldi, Spracklen, & Li, 1995; Zettergren, Bergman, & Wångby, 2006). Additionally, rejected status has been associated with internalizing symptoms, most robustly with loneliness (Hymel, Rubin, Rowden, & LeMare, 1990; Lochman & Wayland, 1994).

Another peer relationship process worthy of mention is youth antipathy, which involves relationship problems with a specific peer rather than with a peer group. These types of relationships are especially worrisome because of their ongoing, negative, and adversarial nature (Pope, 2003). Some members of these dyads might experience internalizing problems as a result of avoiding interactions with their enemy. Other youth with aggressive tendencies or emotional dysregulation may experience an exacerbation in antisocial behavior because of repeated negative interactions with their enemy. Equally likely, youth with social problems, whether antisocial or impaired, may be at a greater risk for having these relationships because of early rejection by their peers (Pope & Beirman, 1999).

Researchers examining the concept of "enemies," especially when looking at children in middle childhood, have often operationalized enemies as the existence of a mutual dislike among peers. This operationalization is done via sociometric ratings such as "Someone I do not like," hence the term mutual antipathy (Abecassis, Hartup, Haselager, Scholte, & van Lieshout, 2002). Developmentally, evidence suggests that mutual animosities are rare among pre-school-age children (Hayes, Gershman, & Bolin, 1980), but are relatively common in school-age youth (Hartup, 2003; Abecassis et al., 2002). Whereas boys are likely to be involved in mutual antipathies overall, both genders were involved in mixed-sex antipathies at comparable rates. Same-sex antipathies in both middle childhood and adolescence are related to increases in antisocial behaviors and social withdrawal, as well as social emotionality and nervousness in adolescence (Abecassis et al., 2002; Parker & Gamm, 2003). Mixed-sex antipathies were related to physical aggression for boys, and social withdrawal and depression for girls. In middle childhood, because interactions often children of the same sex (Maccoby, 1988), it is likely that the same-sex antipathies have more opportunities to interact and engage in aggressive acts than mixed-sex antipathies (Pope, 2003). These same-sexed animosities may therefore have a greater impact on maladjustment.

Unlike singular aggressive interactions, animosity relationships exist over time and each member of these dyads likely experience personalized and intense rejection from the other. Continued membership in mutual antipathetic relationships might lead to augmented anxiety, social stress, and negative self-attitudes (Abecassis et al., 2002). Socially, members of these dyads would have a ready trigger for aggressive behaviors—both physical and relational—and this prolonged engagement in antisocial acts leads to an escalation of negative behaviors over time as well as the potential to develop additional antipathies in the peer group. Murray-Close and Crick (2006) examined longitudinal associations of aggression and dyadic antipathy, finding that for boys, increases in the number of antipathies led to a growth in both physical aggression and victimization. However, for girls, increases in antipathy relationships were related to increased relational aggression over time.

How and why do these relationships develop? Some of these relationships may begin as rivalries or terminated friendships (Abecassis et al., 2002); however, the process is unclear. Members of these relationships perceive the other's behavior as more hostile and they use more hostile social strategies with their enemy than they do with other peers (Peets, Kikas, Hodges, & Salmivalli, 2007). It is possible that these attributions lead to actual mutually antisocial behavior or equally likely that these repeated behaviors lead to these attributions or strategies. Another possibility is that youths with behavior problems or emotional dysregulation are more likely to interact with other aggressive youths (Cairns & Cairns, 1994) and in turn fall into "reinforcement traps" (Patterson, Reid, & Dishion, 1992) that produce continued or increased aggression within the dyad or with other peers.

When examining friendship development, researchers often focus on similarity, and in turn when investigating relationships of animosity, research has examined dissimilarity. Indeed, dissimilarity itself can lead to dislike (Rosenbaum, 1986). Güroğlu Haselager, van Lieshout, and Scholte (2009) clustered preadolescents and adolescents by their social behaviors (antisocial, prosocial, victimized, etc.) and found that two-thirds of the sample's antipathy dyads had dissimilar behavioral profiles. Specifically, in their analysis, 40% of these relationships involved one withdrawn and one antisocial member. This suggests that some of these relationships may include bully–victim relationships, whereas in others, the antisocial member's greater dominance and approach-related behaviors are a mismatch with the withdrawn member's social incompetence and possibly temperamental inhibition.

In light of these findings, it is important to consider that friends often spend more time interacting with one another than enemies do, and may in turn have a much greater impact upon adjustment/maladjustment (Hartup et al., 1988). Additional research is necessary on the social processes involved in the formation of mutual antipathies and their psychosocial adjustment outcomes. Also, these social processes do not always happen without parents knowing about these transactions with peers. Parents may seek to gain knowledge through asking their children about their friends and attempting to monitor friendships by talking to the friends' parents (Stattin & Kerr, 2000), and parental actions may moderate the effects of problematic friendships.

## The Role of Parenting

If rejection by conventional peers is accompanied by poor parental monitoring, rejected children may start to associate with deviant peers, and these associations in turn may preclude adequate monitoring, since antisocial behavior often occurs outside of the purview of adults. Association with a deviant peer group also weakens the child's attachment to conventional social bonds (e.g., parents, authorities, and school; Thornberry, 1987). Weaker bonds to conventional others facilitates a child's unchecked engagement in antisocial behavior—deriving desirable goods using antisocial means (see Moffitt, 1999). During adolescence, parenting becomes less important to the maintenance and possibly the exacerbation of antisocial behavior once it is established (Campbell, Pierce, Moore, Marakovitz, & Newby, 1996; Dodge & Pettit, 2003). In contrast, peer influences become increasingly important in maintaining and possibly aggravating aggressive and antisocial behavior (Campbell et al., 1996).

Some adolescents may seek to individuate themselves from their parents due to the desire to be independent and to seek to be free of their parents' control (Tilton-Weaver et al., 2010). Adolescence is a time of independence-seeking and the normative increase in antisocial behavior could make antisocial peer group members more versatile in their antisocial behavior. According to self-determination theory (Ryan & Deci, 2000), for example, basic needs include psychological autonomy and relatedness. Adolescents may perceive parents' actions as hindering the fulfillment of autonomy, potentially negatively affecting their relationships with peers. If adolescents perceive their parents as exerting excessive control, they may feel their autonomy-seeking is being blocked (see Tilton-Weaver et al., 2010). In response, they might seek out activities where adults are absent and where their activities with peers go unsupervised. The pursuit of unstructured activities with peers where adult supervision is lacking may thus lead to antisocial behaviors (Persson, Kerr, & Stattin, 2007) and aggression. In addition, when youths feel their individuation strategies are not being reciprocated by parents such that parents continue to attempt to control them, they may feel overcontrolled and resort to engaging in antisocial behavior in secrecy (Tilton-Weaver et al., 2010). This may differ by gender. For example, Henggeler, Edwards, and Borduin (1987) found girls who had an early start to their antisocial behavior more often reported having problems with their parents. However, in at least one study, parental control was not as predictive of adolescent antisocial behavior as was peer delinquency (Haynie, 2003; Weerman & Hoeve, 2012).

Deviant peers may actually impede effective parenting. Association with deviant peers shows reciprocal indirect relationships with parenting. Parental negativity fosters children's association with antisocial peers, particularly when children show aggression for instrumental means (Kim, Hetherington, & Reiss, 1999). Children's avoidance of negative parenting experiences may reinforce further interactions with deviant peers, who usually share antisocial attitudes and history (homophily; Dishion et al., 1994). Indeed, peers, even antisocial ones, provide positive affective and interpersonal interactions (Dishion et al., 1994). Thus, effective parental monitoring may become more difficult when antisocial children avoid interactions with their parents and associate more with antisocial peers (Dodge & Pettit, 2003). Parents may also strive to reduce monitoring efforts, because monitoring and subsequent knowledge of bad behavior cause conflict and further aversive experiences with their aggressive children (Muñoz, Pakalniskiene, & Frick, 2011; Dodge & Pettit, 2003). However, parents can indirectly affect peer influence by offering advice, and monitoring and managing children's peer relations. Children may be protected from engaging in problem behavior with deviant peers if we assume that peer-management strategies work to veer children away from the negative influence of peers (Soenens, Vansteenkiste, Luyckx, & Goossens, 2006).

## Externalizing Behavior Problems: Violence and Aggression

The developmental factors leading to the expression of externalizing behavior problems are grouped into those originating from processes thought to be constitutionally-based—child-driven effects such as personality—and those resulting from transactions with the social environment. Here, we focus on the social influences, specifically peers, which might cause or indeed result from childhood behavior problems. Thornberry (1987) expounded on a social interactional perspective on the causes of delinquency. A social interactional perspective emphasizes a reciprocal exchange with one's environment (e.g., Thornberry, 1987). Violent behavior, like all behavior, is assumed to be complex and the result of many factors influencing each other. A child's biological predisposition first makes the child behave in ways that might evoke a particular response from others, either parents or peers. Peers' responses then feed back to the child, influencing later behavior. For a child with behavior problems, this interchange makes problem behavior more likely and is likely to be repeated with peers during childhood and into adolescence. A child who shows antisocial and aggressive behaviors might experience difficulties in maintaining satisfying relationships with others, leading peers to ultimately refrain from keeping the relationship.

Children show individual differences in how and when they choose to hurt their peers. When children aim to be mean, they use physical aggression, verbal attacks, or property damage (Coie & Dodge, 1998). Indeed, peer-directed aggression has been observed at the end of the first year of life (Caplan, Vespo, Pedersen, & Hay, 1991), and aggression and conflict are particularly frequent, intense, and normative during the second year, occurring in as many as 70% of participants in community samples (National Institute of Child Health and Human Development Early Child Care Research Network [NICHD ECCRN], 2004; Trivers, 1974). Beginning in the preschool years however, differences begin to emerge, such that children's expressive vocabulary is negatively related to engaging in physical aggression (Dionne, Boivin, Tremblay, Laplante, & Perusse, 2003). These differences persist into young adult samples, such that low verbal intelligence is related to a continuance of Conduct Disorder symptoms in longitudinal studies (Lahey et al., 1995). Relatedly, beginning in preschool interactions, boys engage in physical aggression more often than boys (Crick, Casas, & Mosher, 1997; Underwood, 2003). By elementary-school years, the decline in physically aggressive behaviors continues to as low as 12% in some samples

(NICHD ECCRN, 2004). This marked drop may reflect increases in effortful control (Eisenberg et al., 2004; Posner & Rothbart, 1998) and delayed gratification (Mischel, 1974), or may be the result of peer socialization processes where peers begin providing negative feedback on aggressive acts that diminishes engagement (Dodge et al., 2006).

The aggressive behavior of some elementary-aged youth does not decline over this period. For instance, aversive behaviors like temper tantrums, tirades, and fight-starting may be somewhat normative for preschool-age youth, but become clinically significant by third grade (Loeber, Lahey, & Thomas, 1991). During this age, covert antisocial activities, such as cheating, stealing, and lying, occur with increasing frequency, along with a greater diversity of overt delinquency such as setting fires, weapon use, and vandalism (Loeber, Farrington, Stothamer,-Loeber, & van Kammen, 1998). Developmental researchers have labeled these chronically persistent aggressive youth as early starters (Moffitt, 1993) and have shown that a great proportion (75%) of juvenile offenders was reconvicted during young adulthood (Farrington, 1995).

Among the diagnoses within the fifth edition of the Diagnostic and Statistical Manual of Mental Disorders (DSM-5) that include overtly aggressive behaviors, three disorders within the disruptive, impulse-control, and conduct disorders bear mentioning. Oppositional defiant disorder (ODD) includes criteria for loss of temper, anger, non-compliance to authority, and spiteful/vindictive behavior. ODD can be diagnosed in children as young as six, and evidence supports that symptom criteria for both ODD and conduct disorder are as valid for preschoolers as they are for older youth (Keenan & Wakschlag, 2004). Clinical levels of anger and vindictiveness for ODD are based on frequency and intensity of behavior. Intermittent explosive disorder includes criteria for verbal aggression, property damage, and outbursts of anger. Clinical levels of maladaptive externalizing for intermittent explosive disorder are marked by impairment of functioning and inability to control anger and aggression. Again, this diagnosis can be made with children as young as 6 years. Conduct disorder (CD) includes criteria for physical fights, weapon use, property destruction, dishonesty, forced sexual contact, and cruelty. Whereas no specific age floor is indicated, specifiers for age-of-onset set a threshold of ten as demarcating childhood from adolescent onset. Additionally, one diagnostic criteria for antisocial personality disorder is evidence of conduct disorder onset prior to the age of fifteen (American Psychiatric Association, 2013). When examining differential diagnoses, conduct disorder often involves non-aggressive behaviors that intermittent explosive disorder does not, along with a focus on more premeditated aggression. In differentiating conduct disorder from oppositional defiant disorder, the behaviors, including aggression, are markedly more severe for a diagnosis of conduct disorder and also include aggression towards animals, property damage, and deceit.

Among the common comorbid disorders with conduct disorder, attention deficit hyperactivity disorder (ADHD) shares the same potential association for future antisocial behavior (Weiss & Hechtman, 1993). Indeed, half of children who share CD and ADHD diagnoses may later develop antisocial personality disorder (Hofvander, Ossowski, Lundström, & Anckarsäter, 2009). One possible explanation is that youths with conduct disorder alone, or comorbid with ADHD, seem to have lower levels of autonomic arousal in response to neutral and aversive stimuli (Fowles, Kochanska, & Murray, 2000; Herpertz et al., 2005; Raine, 2002), a trait shared those with the shallow emotions of youth with psychopathic affective traits (Frick & White, 2008; Muñoz, Frick, Kimonis, & Aucoin, 2008), or callous–unemotional traits discussed later in this review. Additionally, a diagnosis of ADHD is strongly related to both an earlier onset and more severe course of conduct disorder (Klahr & Burt, 2014). However, ADHD symptoms alone may not be as highly predictive of later delinquency as when those problems combine with other peer problems or chemical use. In a prospective study examining the later criminality of 207 boys diagnosed with ADHD, a developmental cascade model was supported, such that youth with non-comorbid ADHD developed adult criminal behaviors only when they developed either antisocial or substance use disorders in adolescence (Mannuzza, Klein, & Moulton, 2008).

Youths, especially boys, who show earlier symptoms of CD tend to show a more frequent and severe course (Frick & Dickens, 2006). These boys show more aggressive behaviors in childhood and adolescence and are more likely to continue antisocial and criminal acts into adulthood (Frick & Loney, 1999). Additionally, early-onset CD boys have differing personality and environmental correlates than adolescent-onset boys. Early-onset boys tend to have increased impulsivity and more familial dysfunction (Moffitt, 2003). As an explanation of these two groups and their differential prognoses, Moffitt (2003) contends that adolescent-onset youth are expressing an exaggerated, yet relatively normative, adolescent rebelliousness and adult-status seeking behavior. However, they differ from non CD youth in that they are engaging in these behaviors within an already antisocial peer group that, in turn, encourages continued antisocial behavior through further socialization and encouragement. Childhood-onset boys, on the other hand, may have dispositional risk factors, such as impulsivity and low expressive vocabularies, along with environmental deficits, such as poor parental monitoring and school settings. These risk factors lead to further developmental deficits across multiple domains.

Unlike boys' trajectories, childhood-onset overt aggression and conduct problems are rare in girls. More common is adolescent-onset aggressive and antisocial behavior. Whereas adolescent-onset CD in boys, which is considered milder and typically desists in early adulthood, adolescent-onset CD in girls has a much poorer prognosis with more severe antisocial symptoms, increased chance of adult criminal convictions, increased risk of substance abuse, and substantial economic problems (Fontaine, Carbonneau, Vitaro, Barker, & Tremblay, 2009). Interestingly, this adolescent-onset or "delayed-onset pathway" to antisocial behavior for girls may share many of the same correlates as childhood-onset CD for boys, such as impulsivity and familial dysfunction, in addition to higher levels of callous–unemotional traits (Frick & Dickens, 2006; Frick & Viding, 2009). Another possibility however, is that it is more normative starting in early childhood for girls to manifest more circuitous and covert forms of aggressive behavior, rather than physical and overt aggression.

## Externalizing Behavior Problems: Social and Relational Aggression

Children may use other more subtle behavior, such as social aggression, to harm or manipulate their peers' friendships or social status (Cairns, Cairns, Neckerman, Ferguson, & Gariépy, 1989; Galen & Underwood, 1997). Social aggression may take different forms and may become more sophisticated with development; a preschooler may use the "silent treatment" to exclude a newcomer, a third grader may tell a peer that the other will not be invited to his birthday party unless he complies with a request, two middle school children may roll their eyes in an attempt to discredit a third peer's comments, a teenager may spread a false rumor about a rival (Crick et al., 1997; Underwood, 2003). This form of aggression, which can be reliably identified as early as age three (Crick et al., 1997), has often been categorized as "female aggression," however empirical evidence is mixed on gender differences throughout development (see Underwood, Galen, & Paquette, 2001 for a discussion). On the one hand, when peer-reports are utilized for assessing relational aggression, gender differences increase with age, such that girls exhibit more aggressive behavior into adolescence (Archer, 2004). On the other hand, when additional reporters (observer-, self-, parent-, peer-, and teach-reports) are considered, only a "trivial" gender difference emerged (favoring girls) for social aggression, and no developmental differences emerged (Card, Stucky, Sawalani, & Little, 2008). Furthermore, because gender differences also covary with peer acceptance and overt aggression (Smith, Rose, & Schwartz-Mette, 2009), a straightforward, mean-level gender difference may be beyond reach. An additional complication is that this core set of manipulative and covert antisocial behaviors, that have more in common than not, has been researched under three different names: indirect, social, and relational aggression (Archer & Coyne, 2005).

For some time, research concerning the long-term effects of aggressive behavior in children focused upon physical aggression, especially perpetrated by boys (Coie & Dodge, 1998). More recently however, studies have suggested that socially aggressive behaviors are also troubling. Children rate physical, verbal, and exclusionary behaviors as hurtful (Crick & Grotpeter, 1995; Galen & Underwood, 1997) and rate those children who behave aggressively as less likable (Foster, DeLawyer, & Guevremont, 1986). Yet, being the victim of social aggression is related to anxiety, loneliness, depression, and other forms of low self-concept (Craig, 1998; Crick & Grotpeter, 1996; Paquette & Underwood, 1999).

In addition, engaging in social aggression leads to children being rejected by peers (Rys & Bear, 1997; Tomada & Schneider, 1997). In a preschool sample, both boys and girls who engaged in this type of behavior were rated as disliked by their peers (Crick et al., 1997). Grade school children who were rated as relationally aggressive reported more loneliness, depression and isolation than their peers (Crick & Grotpeter, 1995) and performed more poorly academically (Risser, 2013). Additionally, the association between anxiety disorder symptoms and relational aggression persists even after controlling for the effects of overt forms of aggression (Marsee, Weems, & Taylor, 2008). Engaging in social aggression may also put older children, especially girls, at risk for later difficulties, including depression and eating disorders (Crick et al., 1997; Underwood, 2003).

Marsee et al. (2014) examined the forms and functions of aggression in their study of community, detained, and residential youths (ages 11–20 years). Findings revealed that some girls exhibited elevated relational aggression without showing elevated physical aggression; these relationally aggressive girls also showed high rates of delinquency and high levels of callous–unemotional (CU) traits, which serve as a specifier for conduct disorder in the DSM-5 but are renamed as limited prosocial emotions (American Psychiatric Association, 2013). People with CU traits perpetrate aggression for their own personal gain but also react with aggression when provoked (Fanti, Frick, & Georgiou, 2009; Marsee et al., 2014; Muñoz, Frick et al., 2008). Interpersonal traits, such as lacking in caring and lacking in prosocial emotions have consistently been related to delinquency and aggression in both boys and girls. These CU traits designate a subgroup of antisocial youth who show risky decision making, such as a stable and violent pattern of delinquent and aggressive behavior (Frick & White, 2008; Muñoz & Frick, 2012). Indeed, the highest levels of CU traits were shown in the group of girls with a combination of high reactive and proactive *relational* aggression (Marsee et al., 2014). This has also been shown in a detained sample of girls, where the combined reactive/proactive *relational* group of girls was highest on CU traits (Stickle, Marini, & Thomas, 2012). Relational aggression in girls, therefore, may be a marker for "extreme overall level of disturbance" (Stickle et al., 2012, p. 523).

## Reactive and Proactive Aggression

When considering the function of aggressive behaviors, two types of aggression have been identified in the literature: reactive and proactive (Dodge & Coie, 1987). Reactive aggression is characterized by impulsive defensive responses to a perceived provocation or threat, whereas proactive or instrumental aggression is predatory and is characterized by the manipulation of others (Dodge & Coie, 1987; Eisenberg & Fabes, 1992). Additionally, the proactive subtype is associated with a relatively unemotional display of aggression that involves a focus on goals (Eisenberg & Fabes, 1992). These two functional types of aggression can be reliably distinguished by middle childhood by observers, teachers, and clinicians (Coie et al., 1999; Dodge, Lockman, Harnish, Bates, & Pettit, 1997), and are differentially associated with anxiety and delinquency (Vitaro, Brendgen, & Tremblay, 2002). Those who use proactive aggression tend to show higher levels of aggression and show blunted emotion or emotion that is inconsistent with their behavioral displays (Bobadilla, Wampler, & Taylor, 2012; Hubbard et al., 2002; Muñoz, Frick, et al., 2008). On the other hand, reactive aggression has been related to interpersonal problems in other areas of their lives (e.g., dating violence; Brendgen, Vitaro, Tremblay, & Lavoie, 2001). The link between reactive and proactive aggression and delinquency has a robust history in the research literature (Fite, Colder, Lochman, & Wells, 2008; Fite, Raine, Stouthamer-Loeber, Loeber, & Pardini, 2009; Vitaro et al., 2002). Fite and colleagues (2008) find prospective associations over time, such that proactive aggression predicts delinquency one year later. Of note, an early onset of proactive aggressive behavior predisposes children to a lifelong pattern of damaged social relationships, ultimately ending in crime, unemployment, or health problems (see Dodge & Pettit, 2003; Pulkkinen, 1996; Vitaro, Gendreau, Tremblay, & Oligny, 1998).

Proactive aggressive children are less often rejected than reactive aggressive children are by their peers (Poulin & Boivin, 2000). Proactive aggressive children engage in "niche picking," whereby those with similar proactive aggressive tendencies seek each other for friendship. Children who became friends at a later time-point had been previously more similar in proactive aggression than were those children who ceased to be friends with proactive aggressive children (Poulin & Boivin, 2000). Poulin and Boivin (2000) assessed changes in similarity solely in fourth- through sixth-grade proactive aggressive friends. Proactive aggressive friends did not become more similar after the year they were first surveyed (Poulin & Boivin, 2000). Thus, proactive aggression may develop outside of peer influence. In addition, the coercive transactions that were previously reinforced with parents, as we discussed above, may become reinforced and reciprocated through interactions with deviant peers, which then undermines associations with conventional peers (see Poulin & Boivin, 2000). One study that examined peer delinquency and subtypes of aggression over time found bidirectional positive effects only between reactive aggression and peer delinquency (Fite & Colder, 2007).

It may be that peer delinquency has the greatest effect on children's proactive aggressive behavior within particular contexts. Proactive aggression has been found to develop in the context of neighborhood disadvantage (Fite, Wynn, Lochman, & Wells, 2009) and within unsafe neighborhoods (Fite et al., 2010). Unsafe or disorganized neighborhoods provide a rich context for social modeling, which may underlie the expression of proactive aggression (Dodge, 1991). The additional negative modeling of delinquent peers may further solidify the negative social models present within unsafe communities (Fite et al., 2010). Poulin and Boivin (2000) propose that friendships among proactive aggressive children may help to maintain stability in proactive aggression and may lead to other cascading maladaptive outcomes. Antisocial peers' difficulty in school has been found to reinforce proactive aggressive children's low school motivation, for example (see Chen, Chang, & He, 2003). The transaction among proactive aggressive friends may reinforce each other's aggressive tendencies and negative attitudes toward conventional activities, which may happen more easily within unsafe neighborhoods where antisocial behavior may be more normative.

Adolescents do not tend to show exclusively one type of aggression, however; in fact, reactive and proactive aggression show high correlations, leading recent research to study clusters or groups based on covariations between the two subtypes. Many studies (Marsee et al., 2014; Muñoz, Frick, et al., 2008; Stickle et al., 2012) find a group of aggressive adolescents that display high levels of both types of aggression and a group that display a high level of reactive aggression with not as high a level of proactive aggression. Some further argue that high CU traits designate this group of youths who are high on both forms of aggression (e.g., Muñoz & Frick, 2012). Because youth with CU traits tend to have antisocial peers (Kimonis, Frick, & Barry, 2004) and CU traits are related to combined types of aggression, it is unsurprising that peer delinquency is associated with combined reactive and proactive aggression (Centifanti, Fanti, Thomson, Demetriou, & Anastassiou-Hadjicharalambous, 2015). As would be predicted, youths who use aggression to retaliate for some perceived provocation *in addition* to attempting to gain favors over others display CU traits (Marsee et al., 2014; Stickle et al., 2012). Thus, a small but significant sample of youths may be identified who show a combined form of aggression and can be differentiated by levels of CU traits. Both youths who show high levels of CU traits and those who show high levels of proactive aggression (possibly combined aggression) may be relatively immune to the influence of peers, based on their lack of emotional lability.

## Conclusions

The transactions one has with one's peers may trigger or exacerbate psychopathology. We concentrated more of our discussion on externalizing behavior, but we also considered internalizing disorders like depression. From our discussion, it is clear that peer socialization factors have an effect on childhood psychopathology: Peers may act as models of behavior, they may implicitly reinforce behavior by demonstrating their approval or failing to register disapproval, or they may explicitly incite youths to engage in behaviors related to psychopathological functioning. Furthermore, reciprocal effects have been documented, with peers responding to the presence of psychopathology. Peers may reject youths based on the presence of psychopathology, for instance. Indeed, although having negative friendships may be problematic, not having any friends at all can be bad too, given that exclusion from peer groups and prosocial peer groups in particular is associated with psychopathology. To add insult to injury, adults may recognize a "rejected" child and might find it difficult to avoid similarly shunning such a difficult-to-manage child. The reasons for rejection by peers may be apparent to other people. Thus, the behaviors related to the child's psychopathology may similarly frustrate or annoy teachers or other adults. These experiences therefore limit the positive social interactions that are available to children with psychopathology.

We reviewed research, however, that showed some forms of psychopathology appear to be less dependent on peer influences and may be related to having good peer relationships. That is, youths with CU traits engage in aggression and antisocial behavior, and their motivation for engaging in this behavior may stem from factors outside of peer influence; their motivation may stem from exercising instrumental means of obtaining things that they desire. Further, it may be that they incite others to engage in aggression or antisocial behavior due to their early-onset conduct problem behavior. Some suggest that those children with lifelong problem behaviors may serve as models of rebelliousness and antisocial behavior for youths testing out antisocial behavior during adolescence (Moffitt, 1999). Yet, there may be protective factors, such that youths with CU traits may be held back from escalating their antisocial behavior when they maintain friendships with prosocial peers (Muñoz, Kerr et al., 2008). Future research is needed, then, to inform how peers might be risky or promotive, when in development they may have the most effect, and when they may act as a signal that a child requires intervention such that they have no meaningful social affiliations or only enemies.

## References

Abecassis, M., Hartup, W., Haselager, G., Scholte, R. & van Lieshout, C., (2002). Mutual antipathies and their significance in middle childhood and adolescence. *Child Development*, *73*(5), 1543–1556.

Agoston, A. M., & Rudolph, K. D. (2011). Transactional associations between youths' responses to peer stress and depression: The moderating roles of sex and stress exposure. *Journal of Abnormal Child Psychology*, *39*(2), 159–171.

American Psychiatric Association (2013). *Diagnostic and statistical manual of mental disorders* (5th ed.). Arlington, VA: American Psychiatric Association.

Archer, J. (2004). Sex differences in aggression in real-world settings: A meta-analytic review. *Review of General Psychology*, *8*(4), 291–322.

Archer, J., & Coyne, S. (2005). An integrated review of indirect, relational, and social aggression. *Personality and Social Psychology Review*, *9*(3), 212–230.

Baerveldt, C., Völker, B., & Van Rossem, R. (2008). Revisiting selection and influence: An inquiry into the friendship networks of high school students and their association with delinquency. *Canadian Journal of Criminology and Criminal Justice*, *50*(5), 559–587.

Berndt. T. (2002). Friendship quality and social development. *Current Directions in Psychological Science*, *11*(1), 7–10.

Berscheid, E. (1983). Emotion. In H. Kelley, E. Berscheid, A. Christensen, J. Harvey, T. Huston, G. Levinger, et al. (Eds.), *Close relationships*. New York: Freeman.

Bierman, K. L., Smoot, D. L., & Aumiller, K. (1993). Characteristics of aggressive-rejected, aggressive (nonrejected), and rejected (nonaggressive) boys. *Child Development*, *64*(1), 139–151.

Blachman, D., & Hinshaw, S. (2002). Patterns of friendship among girls with and without attention-deficit/hyperactivity disorder. *Journal of Abnormal Child Psychology*, *30*(6), 625–640.

Bobadilla, L., Wampler, M., & Taylor, J. (2012). Proactive and reactive aggression are associated with different physiological and personality profiles. *Journal of Social and Clinical Psychology*, *31*(5), 458–487.

Borsari, B., & Carey, K. B. (2001). Peer influences on college drinking: A review of the research. *Journal of Substance Abuse*, *13*(4), 391–424.

Brechwald, W., & Prinstein, M. (2011). Beyond homophily: A decade of advances in understanding peer influence processes. *Journal of Research on Adolescence*, *21*(1), 166–176.

Brendgen, M., Vitaro, F., & M. Bukowski, W. (2000). Deviant friends and early adolescents' emotional and behavioral adjustment. *Journal of Research on Adolescence*, *10*(2), 173–189.

Brendgen, M., Vitaro, F., Bukowski, W., Dionne, G., Tremblay, R., & Boivin, B. (2013). Can friends protect genetically vulnerable children from depression? *Development and Psychopathy*, *25*(2), 277–289.

Brendgen, M., Vitaro, F., Tremblay, R. E., & Lavoie, F. (2001). Reactive and proactive aggression: Predictions to physical violence in different contexts and moderating effects of parental monitoring and caregiving behavior. *Journal of Abnormal Child Psychology*, *29*(4), 293–304.

Buhrmester, D., & Furman, W. (1987). The development of companionship and intimacy. *Child Development*, *58*, 1101–1103.

Cairns, R., & Cairns, B. (1994). *Lifelines and risks*. Cambridge: Cambridge University Press.

Cairns, R., Cairns, B., Neckerman, H., Ferguson, L., & Gariépy, J. (1989). Growth and aggression: I. Childhood to early adolescence. *Developmental Psychology*, *25*(2), 320–330. doi:10.1037/0012-1649.25.2.320

Campbell, S. B., Pierce, E. W., Moore, G., Marakovitz, S., & Newby, K. (1996). Boys' externalizing problems at elementary school age: Pathways from early behavior problems, maternal control, and family stress. *Development and Psychopathology*, *8*(4), 701–719.

Capaldi, D. M., Dishion, T. J., Stoolmiller, M., & Yoerger, K. (2001). Aggression toward female partners by at-risk young men: The contribution of male adolescent friendships. *Developmental Psychology*, *37*(1), 61–73.

Caplan, M., Vespo, J., Pedersen, J., & Hay, D. (1991). Conflict over resources in small groups of 1- and 2-year-olds. *Child Development*, *62*(6), 1513–1524.

Card, N., Stucky, B., Sawalani, G., & Little, T. (2008). Direct and indirect aggression during childhood and adolescence: a meta-analytic review of gender differences, intercorrelations, and relations to maladjustment. *Child Development*, *79*(5), 1185–1229. doi:10.1111/j.1467-8624.2008.01184.x

Carter, J., & Garber, J. (2011). Predictors of the first onset of a major depressive episode and changes in depressive symptoms across adolescence: Stress and negative cognitions. *Journal of Abnormal Psychology*, *120*(4), 779–796.

Centifanti, L., Fanti, K. A., Thomson, N. D., Demetriou, V., & Anastassiou-Hadjicharalambous, X. (2015). Types of relational aggression in girls are differentiated by callous-unemotional traits, peers and parental overcontrol. *Behavioral Sciences*, *5*(4), 518–536.

Centifanti, L. C. M., Modecki, K. L., MacLellan, S., & Gowling, H. (2014). Driving under the influence of risky peers: An experimental study of adolescent risk taking. *Journal of Research on Adolescence*, *6*(1), 207–222.

Chein, J., Albert, D., O'Brien, L., Uckert, K., & Steinberg, L. (2011). Peers increase adolescent risk taking by enhancing activity in the brain's reward circuitry. *Developmental Science, 14*(2), F1–F10.

Chen, X., Chang, L., & He, Y. (2003). The peer group as a context: Mediating and moderating effects on relations between academic achievement and social functioning in Chinese children. *Child Development, 74*(3), 710–727.

Cillessen, A. H. N. (2009). Sociometric methods. In K. Rubin, W. Bukowski, & B. Laursen (Eds.), *Handbook of peer interactions, relationships, and groups* (pp. 82–99). New York: Guilford Press.

Cillessen, A. H. N., Terry, R., Coie, J., & Lochman, J. E. (1992, April). *Accuracy of teacher-identification of children's sociometric status positions.* Paper presented at the biennial Conference on Human Development, Atlanta, GA.

Cohen, G. L., & Prinstein, M. J. (2006). Peer contagion of aggression and health risk behavior among adolescent males: An experimental investigation of effects on public conduct and private attitudes. *Child Development, 77*(4), 967–983.

Coie, J. (1990). Toward a theory of peer rejection. In S. R. Asher & J. D. Coie (Eds.), *Peer rejection in childhood* (pp. 365–401). New York: Cambridge University Press.

Coie, J. D., Cillessen, A. H., Dodge, K. A., Hubbard, J. A., Schwartz, D., Lemerise, E. A., et al. (1999). It takes two to fight: A test of relational factors and a method for assessing aggressive dyads. *Developmental Psychology, 35*(5), 1179–1185.

Coie, J. D., & Dodge, K. A. (1998). Aggression and antisocial behavior. In N. Eisenberg (Vol. Ed.) & D. William & R. M. Lerner (Eds.), *Handbook of child psychology*. Vol. *3*. Social, emotional, and personality development (pp. 779–862). Hoboken, NJ: John Wiley & Sons.

Coie, J., & Kupersmidt, J. (1983). A behavioral analysis of emerging social status in boys' groups. *Child Development, 54*, 1400–1416.

Conway, C., Rancourt, D., Adelman, C., Burk, W., & Prinstein M. (2011). Depression socialization with friendship groups at the transition to adolescence: The roles of gender and group centrality as moderators of peer influence. *Journal of Abnormal Psychology, 120*(4), 857–867.

Craig, W. M. (1998). The relationship among bullying, victimization, depression, anxiety, and aggression in elementary school children. *Personality and Individual Differences, 24*(1), 123–130.

Crick, N., Casas, J., & Mosher, M. (1997). Relational and overt aggression in preschool. *Developmental Psychology, 33*(4), 589–600.

Crick, N., & Dodge, K. (1994). A review and reformulation of social information processing mechanisms in children's social adjustment. *Psychological Bulletin, 115*(1), 74–101.

Crick, N. R., & Grotpeter, J. K. (1995). Relational aggression, gender, and social-psychological adjustment. *Child Development, 66*(3), 710–722.

Crick, N. R., & Grotpeter, J. K. (1996). Children's treatment by peers: Victims of relational and overt aggression. *Development and Psychopathology, 8*(2), 367–380.

Dionne, G., Boivin, M., Tremblay, R., Laplante, D., & Perusse, D. (2003). Physical aggression and expressive vocabulary in 19-month-old twins. *Developmental Psychology, 39*(2), 261–273.

Dishion, T., Capaldi, D., Spracklen, K., & Li, F. (1995). Peer ecology of male adolescent drug use. *Development and Psychopathology, 7*(4), 803–824.

Dishion, T., Eddy, M., Haas, E., Li, F., & Spracklen, K. (1997). Friendships and violent behavior during adolescence. *Social Development, 6*(2), 207–223.

Dishion, T. J., Patterson, G. R., & Griesler, P. C. (1994). Peer adaptations in the development of antisocial behavior. In L. R. Huesmann (Ed.), *Aggressive behavior: Current perspectives* (pp. 61–95). New York: Plenum Press.

Dishion, T. J., & Tipsord, J. M. (2011). Peer contagion in child and adolescent social and emotional development. *Annual Review of Psychology, 62*, 189–214.

Dodge, K. (1983). Behavioral antecedents of peer social status. *Child Development, 54*, 1386–1399.

Dodge, K. (1991). *The structure and function of reactive and proactive aggression*. In Earlscourt Symposium on Childhood Aggression, June, 1988. Toronto, ON. Lawrence Erlbaum.

Dodge, K., Bates, J., & Pettit, G. (1990). Mechanisms in the cycle of violence. *Science, 250*(4988), 1678–1683.

Dodge, K., & Coie, J. (1987). Social-information-processing factors in reactive and proactive aggression in children's peer groups. *Journal of Personality and Social Psychology, 53*(6), 1146–1158.

Dodge, K., Coie, J., & Lynam, D. (2006). Aggression and antisocial behavior in youth. In N. Eisenberg (Vol. Ed.) & D. William & R. M. Lerner (Eds.), *Handbook of child psychology*. Vol. *3*. Social, emotional, and personality development (6th ed., pp. 719–788). Hoboken, NJ: Wiley.

Dodge, K., Coie, J., Pettit, G., & Price, J. (1990). Peer status and aggression in boys' groups: Developmental and contextual analyses. *Child Development, 61*(5), 1289–1309.

Dodge, K. A., Lansford, J. E., Burks, V. S., Bates, J. E., Pettit, G. S., Fontaine, R., et al. (2003). Peer rejection and social information-processing factors in the development of aggressive behavior problems in children. *Child Development, 74*(2), 374–393.

Dodge, K., Lockman, J., Harnish, J., Bates, J., & Pettit, G. (1997). Reactive and proactive aggression in school children and psychiatrically impaired chronically assaultive youth. *Journal of Abnormal Psychology, 106*(1), 37–51.

Dodge, K. A., & Pettit, G. S. (2003). A biopsychosocial model of the development of chronic conduct problems in adolescence. *Developmental Psychology, 39*(2), 349–371.

Eisenberg, N., & Fabes, R. A. (1992). Emotion, regulation, and the development of social competence. In M. S. Clark (Ed.), *Emotion and social behavior. Review of personality and social psychology*, Vol. *14* (pp. 119–150). Thousand Oaks, CA: Sage.

Eisenberg, N., Spinrad, T., Fabes, R., Reiser, M., Cumberland, A., Shepard, S., et al. (2004). The relations of effortful control and impulsivity to children's resiliency and adjustment. *Child Development, 75*(1), 25–46.

Fanti, K. A., Frick, P. J., & Georgiou, S. (2009). Linking callous-unemotional traits to instrumental and non-instrumental forms of aggression. *Journal of Psychopathology and Behavioral Assessment, 31*(4), 285–298.

Farrington, D. (1995). The development of offending and antisocial behavior from childhood: Key findings from the Cambridge study in delinquent development. *Journal of Child Psychology and Psychiatry, 6*(36), 929–964.

Fite, P. J., & Colder, C. R. (2007). Proactive and reactive aggression and peer delinquency implications for prevention and intervention. *The Journal of Early Adolescence, 27*(2), 223–240.

Fite, P. J., Colder, C. R., Lochman, J. E., & Wells, K. C. (2008). Developmental trajectories of proactive and reactive aggression from fifth to ninth grade. *Journal of Clinical Child & Adolescent Psychology, 37*(2), 412–421.

Fite, P. J., Raine, A., Stouthamer-Loeber, M., Loeber, R., & Pardini, D. A. (2009). Reactive and proactive aggression in adolescent males: Examining differential outcomes 10 years later in early adulthood. *Criminal Justice and Behavior, 37*(2), 141–157.

Fite, P. J., Vitulano, M., Wynn, P., Wimsatt, A., Gaertner, A., & Rathert, J. (2010). Influence of perceived neighborhood safety on proactive and reactive aggression. *Journal of Community Psychology, 38*(6), 757–768.

Fite, P. J., Wynn, P., Lochman, J. E., & Wells, K. C. (2009). The effect of neighborhood disadvantage on proactive and reactive aggression. *Journal of Community Psychology, 37*(4), 542–546.

Fontaine, N., Carbonneau, R., Vitaro, F., Barker, E. D., & Tremblay, R. E. (2009). Research review: A critical review of studies on the developmental trajectories of antisocial behavior in females. *Journal of Child Psychology and Psychiatry, 50*(4), 363–385.

Foster, S. L., DeLawyer, D. D., & Guevremont, D. C. (1986). A critical incidents analysis of liked and disliked peer behaviors and their situational parameters in childhood and adolescence. *Behavioral Assessment*, *8*(2), 115–133.

Fowles, D., Kochanska, G., & Murray, K. (2000). Electrodermal activity and temperament in preschool children. *Psychophysiology*, *37*(6), 777–787.

Frick, P., & Dickens, C. (2006). Current perspectives on conduct disorder. *Current Psychiatry Reports*, *8*(1), 59–72.

Frick, P., & Loney, B. (1999). Outcomes of children and adolescents with conduct disorder and oppositional defiant disorder. In H. Quay & A. Hogan (Eds.), *Handbook of disruptive behavior disorders* (pp. 507–524). New York: Plenum Press.

Frick, P., & Viding, E. (2009). Antisocial behavior from a developmental psychopathology perspective. *Developmental Psychopathology*, *21*(4), 1111–1131.

Frick, P., & White, S. (2008). Research review: The importance of callous-unemotional traits for developmental models of aggressive and antisocial behavior. *Journal of Child Psychology and Psychiatry*, *49*(4), 359–375. doi:10.1111/j.1469-7610.2007.01862.x

Galen, B. R., & Underwood, M. K. (1997). A developmental investigation of social aggression among children. *Developmental Psychology*, *33*(4), 589–600.

Goldweber, A., Cauffman, E., & Cillessen, A. H. (2014). Peer status among incarcerated female offenders: Associations with social behavior and adjustment. *Journal of Research on Adolescence*, *24*(4), 720–733.

Güroğlu, B., Haselager, G., van Lieshout, C., & Scholte, R. (2009). Antagonists in mutual antipathies: A person-oriented approach. *Journal of Research on Adolescence*, *19*(1), 35–46.

Hammen, C., & Rudolph, K. D. (2003). Childhood mood disorders. *Child Psychopathology*, *2*, 233–278.

Hankin, B., Mermelstein, R., & Roesch., L. (2007). Sex differences in adolescent depression: Stress exposure and reactivity models in interpersonal and achievement contextual domains. *Child Development*, *78*(1), 279–295.

Hankin, B., Stone, L., & Wright, P. (2010). Corumination, interpersonal stress generation, and internalizing symptoms: Accumulating effects and transactional influence in a multiwave study of adolescents. *Development and Psychopathology*, *22*(1), 217–235. doi:10.1017/S0954579409990368

Hartup, W. (1983). Peer relations. In E. M. Hetherington (Vol. Ed.) & P. H. Mussen (Series Ed.), *Handbook of child psychology*. Vol. *4*. Socialization, personality, and social development (pp. 103–196). New York: Wiley.

Hartup, W. (2003). Toward understanding mutual antipathies in childhood and adolescence. In E. V. E. Hodges & N. A. Card (Eds.), *Enemies and the darker side of peer relations. New directions for child and adolescent development*, No. 102 (pp. 111–123). San Francisco: Jossey-Bass.

Hartup, W., Laursen, B., Stewart, M., & Eastenson, A. (1988). Conflict and the friendship relations of young children. *Child Development*, *59*, 1590–1600.

Haselager, G. J., Cillessen, A. H., Van Lieshout, C. F., Riksen-Walraven, J. M. A., & Hartup, W. W. (2002). Heterogeneity among peer-rejected boys across middle childhood: Developmental pathways of social behavior. *Developmental Psychology*, *38*(3), 446–456.

Hayes, D., Gershman, E., & Bolin, L. (1980). Friends and enemies: Cognitive bases for preschool children's unilateral and reciprocal relationships. *Child Development*, *51*, 1276–1279.

Haynie, D. L. (2003). Contexts of risk? Explaining the link between girls' pubertal development and their delinquency involvement. *Social Forces*, *82*(1), 355–397.

Henggeler, S. W., Edwards, J., & Borduin, C. M. (1987). The family relations of female juvenile delinquents. *Journal of Abnormal Child Psychology*, *15*(2), 199–209.

Herpertz, S., Mueller, B., Qunaibi, M., Lichterfeld, C., Konrad, K., & Herpertz-Dahlmann, B. (2005). Responses to emotional stimuli in boys with conduct disorder. *The American Journal of Psychiatry*, *162*, 1100–1107.

Hodges, E. V., Boivin, M., Vitaro, F., & Bukowski, W. M. (1999). The power of friendship: protection against an escalating cycle of peer victimization. *Developmental Psychology*, *35*(1), 94–101.

Hofvander, B., Ossowski, D., Lundström, S., & Anckarsäter, H. (2009). Continuity of aggressive anti-social behavior from childhood to adulthood: The question of phenotype definition. *International Journal of Law and Psychiatry*, *32*(4), 224–234.

Hubbard, J. A., Smithmyer, C. M., Ramsden, S. R., Parker, E. H., Flanagan, K. D., Dearing, K. F., et al. (2002). Observational, physiological, and self–report measures of children's anger: Relations to reactive versus proactive aggression. *Child Development*, *73*(4), 1101–1118.

Hymel, S., Rubin, K. H., Rowden, L., & LeMare, L. (1990). Children's peer relationships: Longitudinal prediction of internalizing and externalizing problems from middle to late childhood. *Child Development*, *61*(6), 2004–2021.

Joiner, T., & Timmons, K. (2009). Depression and its interpersonal context. In I. H. Gotlib & C. L. Hammen (Eds.), *Handbook of depression* (2nd ed., pp. 322–339). New York: Guilford Press.

Keenan, K., & Wakschlag, L. (2004). Are oppositional defiant and conduct disorder symptoms normative behaviors in preschool? A comparison of referred and nonreferred children. *American Journal of Psychiatry*, *161*, 356–358.

Kerr, M., Van Zalk, M., & Stattin, H. (2012). Psychopathic traits moderate peer influence on adolescent delinquency. *Journal of Child Psychology and Psychiatry*, *53*(8), 826–835.

Kim, J. E., Hetherington, E. M., & Reiss, D. (1999). Associations among family relationships, antisocial peers, and adolescents' externalizing behaviors: Gender and family type differences. *Child Development*, *70*(5), 1209–1230.

Kimonis, E. R., Frick, P. J., & Barry, C. T. (2004). Callous-unemotional traits and delinquent peer affiliation. *Journal of Consulting and Clinical Psychology*, *72*(6), 956–966.

Klahr, A., & Burt, S. (2014). Evaluations of the known behavioral heterogeneity in conduct disorder to improve its assessment and treatment. *Journal of Child Psychology and Psychiatry*, *55*, 1300–1310.

Knecht, A., Snijders, T. A., Baerveldt, C., Steglich, C. E., & Raub, W. (2010). Friendship and delinquency: Selection and influence processes in early adolescence. *Social Development*, *19*(3), 494–514.

Kobus, K. (2003). Peers and adolescent smoking. *Addiction*, *98*(s1), 37–55.

Kochenderfer, B. J., & Ladd, G. W. (1997). Victimized children's responses to peers' aggression: Behaviors associated with reduced versus continued victimization. *Development and Psychopathology*, *9*(1), 59–73.

Kupersmidt, J. B., & Coie, J. D. (1990). Preadolescent peer status, aggression, and school adjustment as predictors of externalizing problems in adolescence. *Child Development*, *61*(5), 1350–1362.

Kupersmidt, J., & Dodge, K. (Eds.). (2004). *Children's peer relations: From development to intervention to policy: A festschrift to honor John D. Coie*. Washington, DC: American Psychological Association.

Ladd, G. W. (2005). *Children's peer relations and social competence. A century of progress*. New Haven, CT: Yale University Press.

Ladd, G. W., & Troop-Gordon, W. (2003). The role of chronic peer difficulties in the development of children's psychological adjustment problems. *Child Development*, *74*(5), 1344–1367.

Lahey, B. B., Loeber, R., Hart, E. L., Frick, P. J., Applegate, B., Zhang, Q., et al. (1995). Four-year longitudinal study of conduct disorder in boys: Patterns and predictors of persistence. *Journal of Abnormal Psychology*, *104*(1), 83–93.

Lancelotta, G., & Vaughn, S. (1989). Relation between types of aggression and sociometric status: Peer and teacher perceptions. *Journal of Educational Psychology*, *81*(1), 86–90.

Lansford, J. E., Malone, P. S., Dodge, K. A., Pettit, G. S., & Bates, J. E. (2010). Developmental cascades of peer rejection, social information processing biases, and aggression during middle childhood. *Development and Psychopathology, 22*(3), 593–602.

Laursen, B. (1993). The perceived impact of conflict on adolescent relationships. *Merrill-Palmer Quarterly, 39*, 535–550.

Laursen, B., Bukowski, W. M., Aunola, K., & Nurmi, J. E. (2007). Friendship moderates prospective associations between social isolation and adjustment problems in young children. *Child Development, 78*(4), 1395–1404.

Laursen, B., & Hartup, W. (1989). The dynamics of preschool children's conflicts. *Merrill-Palmer Quarterly, 35*, 281–297.

Laursen, B., Hartup, W. W., & Koplas, A. L. (1996). Towards understanding peer conflict. *Merrill-Palmer Quarterly, 42*(1), 76–102. Retrieved January 10, 2017 from http://www.jstor.org/stable/23090521

Lochman, J. E., & Wayland, K. K. (1994). Aggression, social acceptance, and race as predictors of negative adolescent outcomes. *Journal of the American Academy of Child & Adolescent Psychiatry, 33*(7), 1026–1035.

Loeber, R., Farrington, D., Stothamer-Loeber, M., & van Kammen, W. (1998). *Antisocial behavior and mental health problems: Explanatory factors in childhood and adolescence.* Mahwah, NJ: Erlbaum.

Loeber, R., Lahey, B., & Thomas, C. (1991). Diagnostic conundrum of oppositional defiant disorder and conduct disorder. *Journal of Abnormal Psychology, 100*(3), 379–390.

Maccoby, E. (1988). Gender as a social category. *Developmental Psychology, 24*(6), 744–765.

Mannuzza, S., Klein, R. G., & Moulton, J. L. (2008). Lifetime criminality among boys with attention deficit hyperactivity disorder: A prospective follow-up study into adulthood using official arrest records. *Psychiatry Research, 160*(3), 237–246.

Marsee, M. A., Frick, P. J., Barry, C. T., Kimonis, E. R., Centifanti, L. C. M., & Aucoin, K. J. (2014). Profiles of the forms and functions of self-reported aggression in three adolescent samples. *Development and Psychopathology, 26*(3), 705–720.

Marsee, M., Weems, C., & Taylor, L. (2008). Exploring the association between aggression and anxiety in youth: A look at aggressive subtypes, gender, and social cognition. *Journal of Family Studies, 17*(1), 154–168.

Mathys, C., Burk, W. J., & Cillessen, A. H. (2013). Popularity as a moderator of peer selection and socialization of adolescent alcohol, marijuana, and tobacco use. *Journal of Research on Adolescence, 23*(3), 513–523.

Mischel, W. (1974). Processes in delay of gratification. In L. Berkowitz (Ed.), *Advances in experimental social psychology* (Vol. *7*, pp. 249–392). New York: Academic Press.

Moffitt, T. (1993). Adolescence-limited and life-course-persistent antisocial behavior: A developmental taxonomy. *Psychological Review, 100*(4), 674–701.

Moffitt, T. E. (1999). Adolescent-limited and life-course persistent antisocial behavior: A developmental taxonomy. In F. R. Scarpitti & A. L. Nielson (Eds.), *Crime and criminals: Contemporary and classic readings.* Los Angeles: Roxbury.

Moffitt, T. (2003). Life-course persistent and adolescence-limited antisocial behavior: A 10-year research review and research agenda. In B. Lahey, T. Moffitt, & A. Caspi (Eds.), *Causes of conduct disorder and juvenile delinquency* (pp. 49–75). New York: Guilford Press.

Molano, A., Jones, S. M., Brown, J. L., & Aber, J. L. (2013). Selection and socialization of aggressive and prosocial behavior: The moderating role of social-cognitive processes. *Journal of Research on Adolescence, 23*(3), 424–436.

Monahan, K. C., Steinberg, L., & Cauffman, E. (2009). Affiliation with antisocial peers, susceptibility to peer influence, and antisocial behavior during the transition to adulthood. *Developmental Psychology, 45*(6), 1520–1530.

Moreno, J. (1934). *Who shall survive?: A new approach to the problem of human interrelations.* Washington, DC: Nervous and Mental Disease Publishing.

Muñoz, L. C., & Frick, P. J. (2012). Callous-unemotional traits and their implication for understanding and treating aggressive and violent youths. *Criminal Justice and Behavior, 39*(6), 794–813.

Muñoz, L. C., Frick, P. J., Kimonis, E. R., & Aucoin, K. J. (2008). Types of aggression, responsiveness to provocation, and callous-unemotional traits in detained adolescents. *Journal of Abnormal Child Psychology, 36*(1), 15–28.

Muñoz, L. C., Kerr, M., & Besic, N. (2008). The peer relationships of youths with psychopathic personality traits a matter of perspective. *Criminal Justice and Behavior, 35*(2), 212–227.

Muñoz, L. C., Pakalniskiene, V., & Frick, P. J. (2011). Parental monitoring and youth behavior problems: Moderation by callous-unemotional traits over time. *European Child & Adolescent Psychiatry, 20*(5), 261–269.

Murray-Close, D., & Crick, N. R. (2006). Mutual antipathy involvement: Gender and associations with aggression and victimization. *School Psychology Review, 35*(3), 472–492.

National Institute of Child Health and Human Development Early Child Care Research Network. (2004). Trajectories of physical aggression from toddlerhood to middle childhood. *Monographs of the Society for Research in Child Development, 69*(4), 1–144.

Nichter, M. (2002). *Fat talk.* Cambridge, MA: Harvard University Press.

Nichter, M., & Vuckovic, N. (1994). Fat talk: Body image among adolescent girls. In N. Sault (Ed.), *Many mirrors: Body image and social relations* (pp. 109–131). New Brunswick, NJ: Rutgers University Press.

O'Brien, L., Albert, D., Chein, J., & Steinberg, L. (2011). Adolescents prefer more immediate rewards when in the presence of their peers. *Journal of Research on Adolescence, 21*(4), 747–753.

Odgers, C. L., Moffitt, T. E., Broadbent, J. M., Dickson, N., Hancox, R. J., Harrington, H., et al. (2008). Female and male antisocial trajectories: From childhood origins to adult outcomes. *Development and Psychopathology, 20*(02), 673–716.

Paquette, J. A., & Underwood, M. K. (1999). Gender differences in young adolescents' experiences of peer victimization: Social and physical aggression. *Merrill-Palmer Quarterly, 45*, 242–266.

Parker, J., & Gamm, B. (2003). Describing the dark side of preadolescents' peer experiences: Four questions (and data) on preadolescents' enemies. *New Directions for Child and Adolescent Development, 102*, 55–72.

Parker, J. G., & Seal, J. (1996). Forming, losing, renewing, and replacing friendships: Applying temporal parameters to the assessment of children's friendship experiences. *Child Development, 67*(5), 2248–2268. doi:10.1111/1467-8624.ep9706060165

Patterson, G., Reid, J., & Dishion, T. (1992). *Antisocial boys.* Eugene, OR: Castalia.

Peets, K., Kikas, E., Hodges, E., & Salmivalli, C. (2007). Hostile attributions and behavioral strategies in children: Does relationship type matter? *Developmental Psychology, 43*, 889–900.

Pepler, D. J., & Craig, W. M. (2005). Aggressive girls on troubled trajectories: A developmental perspective. In D. Pepler, K. Madsen, K. Levene, & C. Webster (Eds.), *The development and treatment of girlhood aggression* (pp. 3–28). Hillsdale, NJ: Ellbaum.

Persson, A., Kerr, M., & Stattin, H. (2007). Staying in or moving away from structured activities: Explanations involving parents and peers. *Developmental Psychology, 43*(1), 197–207.

Pope, A. (2003). Developmental risk associated with mutual dislike in elementary school. *New Directions for Child and Adolescent Development, 102*, 89–101.

Pope, A. W., & Bierman, K. L. (1999). Predicting adolescent peer problems and antisocial activities: The relative roles of aggression and dysregulation. *Developmental Psychology, 35*(2), 335–346.

Posner, M., & Rothbart, M. (1998). Attention, self-regulation, and consciousness. *Transactions of the Philosophical Society of London, B, 353*, 1915–1927.

Poulin, F., & Boivin, M. (2000). The role of proactive and reactive aggression in the formation and development of boys' friendships. *Developmental Psychology, 36*(2), 233–240.

Prinstein, M., & Cillessen, A. (2003). Forms and functions of adolescent peer aggression associated with high levels of peer status. *Merrill-Palmer Quarterly, 49*, 310–342.

Prinstein, M., & La Greca, A. (2004). Childhood peer rejection and aggression as predictors of adolescent girls' externalizing and health risk behaviors: A 6-year longitudinal study. *Journal of Consulting and Clinical Psychology, 72*(1), 103–112.

Prinstein, M., Rancourt, D., Guerry, J., & Browne, C. (2009). Peer reputations and psychological adjustment. In K. Rubin, W. Bukowski, & B. Laursen (Eds.), *Handbook of peer interactions, relationships, and groups* (pp. 548–567). New York: Guilford Press.

Pulkkinen, L. (1996). Proactive and reactive aggression in early adolescence as precursors to anti- and prosocial behavior in young adults. *Aggressive Behavior, 22*(4), 241–257.

Raine, A. (2002). The role of prefrontal deficits, low autonomic arousal, and early health factors in the development of antisocial and aggressive children. *Journal of Child Psychology and Psychiatry, 43*(4), 417–434.

Rancourt, D., Conway, C., Burk, W., & Prinstein, M. (2013). Gender composition of preadolescents' friendship groups moderates peer socialization of body change behaviors. *Health Psychology, 32*(3), 283–292.

Rebellon, C. J., & Modecki, K. L. (2014). Accounting for projection bias in models of delinquent peer influence: The utility and limits of latent variable approaches. *Journal of Quantitative Criminology, 30*(2), 163–186.

Risser, S. (2013). Relational aggression and academic performance in elementary school. *Psychology in Schools, 50*(1), 13–26.

Rose, A. J. (2002). Co-rumination in the friendships of girls and boys. *Child Development, 73*(6), 1830–1843.

Rose, A. J., Carlson, W., & Waller, E. M. (2007). Prospective associations of co-rumination with friendship and emotional adjustment: Considering the socioemotional trade-offs of co-rumination. *Developmental Psychology, 43*(4), 1019–1031. doi:10.1037/0012-1649.43.4.1019

Rosenbaum, M. (1986). The repulsion hypothesis: On the nondevelopment of relationships. *Journal of Personality and Social Psychology, 51*(6), 1156–1166.

Ryan, R. M., & Deci, E. L. (2000). Self-determination theory and the facilitation of intrinsic motivation, social development, and well-being. *American Psychologist, 55*(1), 68–78.

Rys, G. S., & Bear, G. G. (1997). Relational aggression and peer relations: Gender and developmental issues. *Merrill-Palmer Quarterly, 43*, 87–106.

Smith, R., Rose, A., & Schwartz-Mette, R. (2009). Relational and overt aggression in childhood and adolescence: Clarifying mean-level gender differences and associations with peer acceptance. *Social Development, 19*(2), 243–269. doi:10.1111/j.1467-9507.2009.00541.x

Soenens, B., Vansteenkiste, M., Luyckx, K., & Goossens, L. (2006). Parenting and adolescent problem behavior: An integrated model with adolescent self-disclosure and perceived parental knowledge as intervening variables. *Developmental Psychology, 42*(2), 305–318.

Stattin, H., & Kerr, M. (2000). Parental monitoring: A reinterpretation. *Child Development, 71*(4), 1072–1085.

Steinberg, L., & Monahan, K. C. (2007). Age differences in resistance to peer influence. *Developmental Psychology, 43*(6), 1531–1543.

Stice, E., Maxfield, J., & Wells, T. (2003). Adverse effects of social pressure to be thin on young women: An experimental investigation of the effects of fat talk. *International Journal of Eating Disorders, 34*(4), 108–117.

Stickle, T. R., Marini, V. A., & Thomas, J. N. (2012). Gender differences in psychopathic traits, types, and correlates of aggression among adjudicated youth. *Journal of Abnormal Child Psychology, 40*(4), 513–525.

Sullivan, H. S. (1953). *The interpersonal theory of psychiatry.* New York: Norton.

Thornberry, T. P. (1987). Toward an interactional theory of delinquency. *Criminology*, *25*(4), 863–892.

Tilton-Weaver, L., Kerr, M., Pakalniskeine, V., Tokic, A., Salihovic, S., & Stattin, H. (2010). Open up or close down: How do parental reactions affect youth information management? *Journal of Adolescence*, *33*(2), 333–346.

Tomada, G., & Schneider, B. H. (1997). Relational aggression, gender, and peer acceptance: Invariance across culture, stability over time, and concordance among informants. *Developmental Psychology*, *33*(4), 601–609.

Trivers, R. (1974). Parental-offspring conflict. *American Zoologist*, *46*, 35–57.

Underwood, M. (2003). *Social aggression among girls*. New York: Guilford Press.

Underwood, M. K., Galen, B. R., & Paquette, J. A. (2001). Top ten challenges for understanding gender and aggression in children: Why can't we all just get along? *Social Development*, *10*(2), 248–266.

Van Zalk, M., Kerr, M., Branje, S., Stattin, H., & Meeus, W. (2010). It takes three: Selection, influence, and de-selection processes of depression in adolescent friendship networks. *Developmental Psychology*, *46*(4), 927–938. doi:10.1037/a0019661

Vaughn, B. (2001). Dyadic analyses of friendship in a sample of preschool children attending Head Start: Correspondence between measures. *Child Development*, *72*(3), 862–878.

Vitaro, F., Brendgen, M., & Tremblay, R. (2002). Reactively and proactively aggressive children: Antecedent and subsequent characteristics. *Journal of Child Psychology and Psychiatry*, *43*(4), 495–505.

Vitaro, F., Gendreau, P. L., Tremblay, R. E., & Oligny, P. (1998). Reactive and proactive aggression differentially predict later conduct problems. *Journal of Child Psychology and Psychiatry*, *39*(03), 377–385.

Wasserstein, B., & La Greca, A. (1996). Can peer support buffer against behavioral consequences of parental discord? *Journal of Clinical Child Psychology*, *25*(2), 177–182.

Weerman, F. M., & Hoeve, M. (2012). Peers and delinquency among girls and boys: Are sex differences in delinquency explained by peer factors? *European Journal of Criminology*, *9*(3), 228–244.

Weiss, G., & Hechtman, T. (1993). *Hyperactive children grown up: ADHD in children, adolescents, and adults*. New York: Guilford Press.

Zettergren, P., Bergman, L., & Wångby, M. (2006). Girls' stable peer status and their adulthood adjustment: A longitudinal study from age 10 to age 43. *International Journal of Behavioral Development*, *30*(4), 315–325.

# 16

# Environmental Influences

## *The Special Case of Gender*

Hedwig Eisenbarth

## Introduction

Gender differences in prevalence of different psychopathologies are crucial for both the understanding of developmental pathways and for treatment interventions. Understanding why more girls than boys develop depression in adolescence (Nolen-Hoeksema, 1990) and why more boys than girls develop attention deficit hyperactivity disorder (ADHD; Gaub & Carlson, 1997) can inform theories of developmental pathways of psychopathology. For example, while early-onset disorders such as conduct disorder, autism or ADHD are more prevalent in boys, late-onset disorders such as depressive, anxiety, and eating disorders show a higher prevalence in girls, which points to different developmental pathways (see Zahn-Waxler, Shirtcliff, & Marceau, 2008). There are a variety of environmental factors that have been found repeatedly to have an impact on the development of psychopathology, such as poverty, violent neighborhoods, harsh parenting, rejection, parental mental illness, marital problems and maltreatment. However, it seems like the impact of those factors is moderated by gender. While factors such as early-life stress have a relevant impact on the development of both internalizing and externalizing psychopathology (Andersen & Teicher, 2009; Barnow & Freyberger, 2003; Heim & Binder, 2012; Nurius, Green, Logan-Greene, & Borja, 2015), girls might show a different response to those events compared to boys. At the same time, there might be risk factors that are specific for each gender just by their nature, such as schooling. This chapter reviews existing findings on gender-specific environmental risk factors for psychopathology, covering the most frequently found risk-factor categories: parenting, early life events, exposure to substances/violence, and an area that might have gender-specific impact: school environment.

## Gender-specific Parenting Variables

Parenting variables have repeatedly shown to have a strong impact on the development of psychopathology on the one hand, but can also serve as a buffer for other risk factors on the other hand. Positive parenting in infancy for example has a diminishing

*The Wiley Handbook of Developmental Psychopathology*, First Edition. Edited by Luna C. Centifanti and David M. Williams.

influence on externalizing behavior: toddlers and children who receive positive maternal parenting show less externalizing behaviors as adolescents, but even controlling for higher levels of externalizing behavior and less positive parenting towards boys compared to girls, the protective character of positive maternal parenting for externalizing was shown to be stronger for girls (Boeldt et al., 2012). However, when comparing effects of parenting on externalizing versus internalizing symptoms, the impact on externalizing seems to be stronger than the impact on internalizing. For example Feinberg Button, Neiderhiser, Reiss, and Hetherington (2007) found that parental warmth and negativity moderates the genetic influence on antisocial behavior, such that with an increase in parental negativity the genetically induced variance in antisocial behavior increases as well. But in this study, the authors did not find any significant predictive validity of parental warmth or negativity for depression symptoms (Feinberg et al., 2007). They were not able to investigate gender differences in this sample due to small power, but suggest that especially the non-significant model for depression could be due to interaction effects with gender. In fact, when comparing the association between adverse types of parenting, such as aberrant, discordant, or hazardous parenting and depressive symptoms across adolescence, it diminishes for boys over time, while it remains static and significant for girls (St Clair et al., 2015). This could be an indication for neurodevelopmental gender differences of coping with adverse environment. Indications for that can be found for inhibitory control and stress reactivity: these variables moderate the stability of internalizing problems only in girls while in boys negative parenting seems to have a stronger impact on development of internalizing problems (Hastings et al., 2015). Similarly, attachment disorders related behaviors are associated with harsh parenting, but there is a stronger genetic influence for those behaviors in boys compared to girls (Minnis et al., 2007): In a twin study that investigated the impact of parenting on attachment problems, conduct problems, emotional problems and hyperactivity, the authors (Minnis et al., 2007) found that harsh parenting was highly predictive of attachment problems. However, analyses of genetic vs. environmental influences differed between girls and boys: while in boys the attachment problems were predominantly explained by additive genetic effects, in girls especially inhibited attachment problems were predominantly explained by environmental effects. Emotional disorders have also been linked to parenting variables: parental consistency and positive interaction were linked to such childhood disorders, but mainly in boys (Browne, Odueyungbo, Thabane, Byrne, & Smart, 2010). Thus, harsh parenting seems to have a negative impact on boys, while positive parenting has a more protective effect in girls. Based on findings in animal models, these differences might be related to the activity of the stress system (e.g., Veenema & Neumann, 2009; Wigger & Neumann, 1999).

## Gender-specific Early-life Events

Early-life adversity, especially parental neglect or abuse, increases the risk for psychopathology (e.g., Amado, Arce, & Herraiz, 2015; Gibb, Chelminski, & Zimmerman, 2007; Norman et al., 2012), presumably by an impact on emotion development. The stress acceleration hypothesis states that early-life adversity changes structural and functional development of fear- and emotion-related brain circuitries, including the amygdala and the hippocampus (Callaghan & Tottenham, 2016). Findings on gender differences in the development of psychopathological symptoms after early-life events have been mixed so far. For example, in a population based sample in New Zealand, no gender difference in the impact that childhood sexual abuse had on mental health and psychological wellbeing variables has been found (Fergusson, McLeod, & Horwood, 2013), while meta-analyses confirm inconsistency of gender differences in the impact of childhood sexual abuse (Hillberg, Hamilton-Giachritsis, & Dixon, 2011).

However, taking into account another form of early life events, such as physical abuse, both, the family environment and the form of abuse seem to have differential effects on girls versus boys: in male adolescents, depressive symptoms and levels of general distress could be predicted by self-reported physical abuse and by family cohesion and conflict, while in female adolescents, depressive symptoms and levels of general distress were predicted by child sexual abuse and family conflict only (Meyerson, Long, Miranda Jr., & Marx, 2002). Thus, there seem to be less gender differences in development of internalizing psychopathologies after childhood sexual abuse, but there are indications for differential impact of other adverse childhood events, such as physical abuse.

Regarding externalizing behavior as a consequence of early adversity, a series of studies have been implicating a strong link between adverse events and adult violent behavior (Loeber et al., 2005; Stouthamer-Loeber, Loeber, Homish, & Wei, 2001). However, a Swedish twin study did not find a strong link between early-life stress and later violent behavior, when also controlling for gender effects, but a rather strong effect of family environment (Forsman, Lichtenstein, Andershed, & Larsson, 2008). Therefore, also gender differences regarding the development of externalizing behavior need further investigation, especially using twin studies.

## Gender Specifics in Exposure to Substances and Parental Crime

A strong environmental risk factors in addition to the ones listed above is parental substance abuse. For example, it has been found that a family history of substance dependence and early exposure to substances are highly predictive (Area under the Curve = 0.79) for adult substance abuse and dependency in addition to the environmental risk factors such as low socioeconomic status, childhood conduct disorder, childhood depression and an early start of substance problems (Meier et al., 2015). Male gender adds significantly to predicting persistent substance abuse in adulthood (Area under the Curve = 0.78), which points to a moderating effect of gender in the prediction of substance abuse.

In juvenile offenders, who could be defined as a group showing externalizing symptoms, gender differences have been documented in terms of higher rates of early adversity (physical, emotional, and sexual abuse as well as physical neglect) and of higher rates of family history of mental illness compared to male offenders (McCabe, Lansing, Garland, & Hough, 2002). Interestingly, parental history of antisocial behavior, thus an antisocial learning environment was present in both male and female adolescents to the same extent (McCabe et al., 2002). In male juveniles it has indeed been shown that parental imprisonment predicts antisocial–delinquent behavior above and beyond separation from parents caused by death, hospital stays, family disharmony, or other reasons (Murray & Farrington, 2005). Even after controlling for parental convictions and other childhood risk factors such as IQ, family socioeconomic status, or parental attitudes, parental imprisonment was found to be most predictive of antisocial behavior in those boys. However, this has not been replicated in a Swedish sample, where controlling for parental convictions did eliminate the effect of parental imprisonment on juvenile antisocial behavior (Murray, Janson, & Farrington, 2007). A review by those authors on the effects of parental imprisonment (Murray & Farrington, 2008) comes to the conclusion that parental imprisonment as a proxy for parental antisocial behavior does predict antisocial behavior and violent behavior with a higher odds ratio compared to drug use, school failure, or unemployment. Furthermore, they report that parental imprisonment seems to affect girls and boys similarly, referring to a prospective longitudinal study in New Zealand (Moffitt, Caspi, Rutter & Silva, 2001).

## Gender-specific Schooling Effects

A factor that seems to be less intensively studied regarding being a risk factor for internalizing or externalizing behavior are schooling variables. Large-cohort studies focused rather on school problems or attendance. But, if children and juveniles attend school, they do spend a significant amount of time in that environment. For example, some investigations found high levels of self-criticism increase the risk for internalizing and externalizing symptoms (Leadbeater, Kuperminc, Blatt, & Hertzog, 1999). However, a positive perceived school climate can reduce the impact of self-criticism for both male and female adolescents (Kuperminc, Leadbeater, & Blatt, 2001).

Interestingly, single-sex schools seem to have a positive impact on perceived stress levels of adolescent girls only, after controlling for socioeconomic status, parental support, academic performance, and quality of teacher–pupil relationships (Brutsaert & Van Houtte, 2004). This effect seems to be due to an increased sense of belonging, a factor that might specifically relevant for girls and depends on school characteristics. This effect of school environment on externalizing behavior could be transmitted by the support of relational aggression. A study in a primarily urban minority school sample found that both, individual beliefs about aggression as well as individual perceptions of the school environment rather than school norms on aggression and other school-level variables of environment were predictive for relational aggressive behavior (Elsaesser, Gorman-Smith, & Henry, 2012). In this case, the predictive validity of individual perception of school environment was higher for girls than for boys and the authors suggest that this might be due to a higher prevalence of specifically relational aggression in girls. However, parental variables still seem to have an impact on the relationship between school environment and mental health. Parental involvement in school questions, such as communication between school and parents and frequency of parent–teacher meetings seems to have the strongest predictive validity for mental health. In addition, the perception of peer interpersonal relations, sharing of school resources, and even the physical appearance of the school building predict both, externalizing and internalizing symptoms (Suldo, McMahan, Chappel, & Loker, 2012), equally for boys and girls. However, for girls only, teacher–pupil relations were related to wellbeing reports.

Referring to school failure as a problematic outcome variable, defined by the transfer from age-appropriate regular class, or disruptive behavior in kindergarten, family adversity and gender are predictive for both girls and boys (Masse & Tremblay, 1999).

However, girls seem to be affected later than boys, as to experiencing no-transfers at a later age.

Thus, school environmental variables do seem to have somewhat gender-specific impact on the development of internalizing as well as externalizing symptoms and should be included in future investigations of environmental factors in population-based studies.

## Summary

This chapter reviewed a series of relevant environmental variables for the development of externalizing and internalizing psychopathology. While for some variables there is some evidence for clear gender differences in terms of the impact of the environmental factors, for other variables there seem to be mixed findings or no clear evidence for gender differences. Regarding parenting, the protective role of positive parenting for externalizing and internalizing symptoms is stronger for girls than for boys, and a negative influence of aberrant parenting regarding internalizing symptoms has a long-standing effect in girls, while in boys negative or harsh parenting has a stronger impact on the development of internalizing, although that influence diminishes over time. Thus, it seems that boys react more strongly to negative parenting, while girls profit more from positive parenting. This seems highly relevant in terms of prevention strategies, which should target those specific effects, e.g. regarding reduction of negative and reinforcement of positive parenting behavior.

The second most prominent environmental factor for the development of externalizing or internalizing symptomatology are life events. These seem to have a consistent negative effect on both genders, especially when it comes to childhood sexual abuse. Only when including other types of early-life adversity, such as physical abuse, depressive symptoms, and levels of general distress are predicted by family cohesion and conflict in boys. For girls, depressive symptoms and levels of general distress are predicted by family conflict only in the context of childhood sexual abuse. The prediction of externalizing symptoms by early life events does not differ between boys and girls: these symptoms develop similarly across gender.

Some risk factors have a specific impact for specific outcomes, e.g. substance abuse can be predicted be by a family history of substance abuse, though only for boys. Another very specific factor, parental antisocial behavior and imprisonment affects both girls and boys similarly.

An interesting environmental variable that usually does not appear in large prospective studies but that has been investigated in terms of effects on the development of psychopathological symptoms is schooling. These studies found that perceived school climate can reduce externalizing and internalizing symptoms in both boys and girls, but reduces relational aggressive behavior mainly in girls. In addition, single-sex schooling seems to reduce perceived stress only in girls, and they profit more from a good teacher–pupil relationship, while parental involvement is relevant for both boys and girls. Thus, individually perceived school climate and parental involvement in schooling can have a positive impact on both boys and girls, but girls specifically profit from a positive relationship with their teacher.

Even though there is a body of research covering gender differences in environmental influences on the development of psychopathology, many studies do not include these aspects and either focus on boys only, especially, when it comes to externalizing symptoms, such as antisocial behavior, or do not include all potential environmental factors, such as schooling. Still, taken together, the group of variables that needs most gender-specific development could be parenting, based on the reported study base.

## References

Amado, B. G., Arce, R., & Herraiz, A. (2015). Psychological injury in victims of child sexual abuse: A meta-analytic review. *Psychosocial Intervention*, *24*(1), 49–62. doi:10.1016/j.psi.2015.03.002

Andersen, S. L., & Teicher, M. H. (2009). Desperately driven and no brakes: Developmental stress exposure and subsequent risk for substance abuse. *Neuroscience and Biobehavioral Reviews*, *33*(4), 516–524. doi:10.1016/j.neubiorev.2008.09.009

Barnow, S., & Freyberger, H. J. (2003). The family environment in early life and aggressive behavior in adolescents and young adults. In M. Mattson (Ed.), *Neurobiology of aggression: Understanding and preventing violence* (pp. 213–229). Totowa, NJ: Humana Press.

Boeldt, D. L., Rhee, S. H., Dilalla, L. F., Mullineaux, P. Y., Schulz-Heik, R. J., Corley, R. P., et al. (2012). The association between positive parenting and externalizing behavior. *Infant and Child Development*, *21*(1), 85–106. doi:10.1002/icd.764

Browne, D. T., Odueyungbo, A., Thabane, L., Byrne, C., & Smart, L. A. (2010). Parenting-by-gender interactions in child psychopathology: Attempting to address inconsistencies with a Canadian national database. *Child and Adolescent Psychiatry and Mental Health*, *4*(1), 1–13. doi:10.1186/1753-2000-4-5

Brutsaert, H., & Van Houtte, M. (2004). Gender context of schooling and levels of stress among early adolescent pupils. *Education and Urban Society*, *37*(1), 58–73. doi:10.1177/0013124504268070

Callaghan, B. L., & Tottenham, N. (2016). The Stress Acceleration Hypothesis: Effects of early-life adversity on emotion circuits and behavior. *Current Opinion in Behavioral Sciences*, *7*, 76–81. doi:10.1016/j.cobeha.2015.11.018

Elsaesser, C., Gorman-Smith, D., & Henry, D. (2012). The role of the school environment in relational aggression and victimization. *Journal of Youth and Adolescence*, *42*(2), 235–249. doi:10.1007/s10964-012-9839-7

Feinberg, M. E., Button, T. M. M., Neiderhiser, J. M., Reiss, D., & Hetherington, E. M. (2007). Parenting and adolescent antisocial behavior and depression: Evidence of genotype x parenting environment interaction. *Archives of General Psychiatry*, *64*(4), 457–465. doi:10.1001/archpsyc.64.4.457

Fergusson, D. M., McLeod, G. F., & Horwood, L. J. (2013). Childhood sexual abuse and adult developmental outcomes: Findings from a 30-year longitudinal study in New Zealand. *Child Abuse and Neglect*, *37*(9), 664–674. doi:10.1016/j.chiabu.2013.03.013

Forsman, M., Lichtenstein, P., Andershed, H., & Larsson, H. (2008). Genetic effects explain the stability of psychopathic personality from mid- to late adolescence. *Journal of Abnormal Psychology*, *117*(3), 606–617.

Gaub, M., & Carlson, C. L. (1997). Gender differences in ADHD: A meta-analysis and critical review. *Journal of the American Academy of Child & Adolescent Psychiatry*, *36*(8), 1036–1045. doi:10.1097/00004583-199708000-00011

Gibb, B. E., Chelminski, I., & Zimmerman, M. (2007). Childhood emotional, physical, and sexual abuse, and diagnoses of depressive and anxiety disorders in adult psychiatric outpatients. *Depression and Anxiety*, *24*(4), 256–263. doi:10.1002/da.20238

Hastings, P., Helm, J., Mills, R. L., Serbin, L., Stack, D., & Schwartzman, A. (2015). Dispositional and environmental predictors of the development of internalizing problems in childhood: Testing a multilevel model. *Journal of Abnormal Child Psychology*, *43*(5), 831–845. doi:10.1007/s10802-014-9951-0

Heim, C., & Binder, E. B. (2012). Current research trends in early life stress and depression: Review of human studies on sensitive periods, gene–environment interactions, and epigenetics. *Experimental Neurology*, *233*(1), 102–111. doi:10.1016/j.expneurol.2011.10.032

Hillberg, T., Hamilton-Giachritsis, C., & Dixon, L. (2011). Review of meta-analyses on the association between child sexual abuse and adult mental health difficulties: A systematic approach. *Trauma Violence Abuse*, *12*(1), 38–49. doi:10.1177/1524838010386812

Kuperminc, G. P., Leadbeater, B. J., & Blatt, S. J. (2001). School social climate and individual differences in vulnerability to psychopathology among middle school students. *Journal of School Psychology*, *39*(2), 141–159. doi:10.1016/S0022-4405(01)00059-0

Leadbeater, B. J., Kuperminc, G. P., Blatt, S. J., & Hertzog, C. (1999). A multivariate model of gender differences in adolescents' internalizing and externalizing problems. *Developmental Psychology*, *35*(5), 1268–1282. doi:10.1037/0012-1649.35.5.1268

Loeber, R., Pardini, D., Homish, D. L., Wei, E. H., Crawford, A. M., Farrington, D. P., et al. (2005). The prediction of violence and homicide in young men. *Journal of Consulting and Clinical Psychology*, *73*(6), 1074–1088. doi:10.1037/0022-006X.73.6.1074

Masse, L. C., & Tremblay, R. E. (1999). Kindergarten disruptive behaviour, family adversity, gender, and elementary school failure. *International Journal of Behavioral Development*, *23*(1), 225–240. doi:10.1080/016502599384080

McCabe, K. M., Lansing, A. E., Garland, A. N. N., & Hough, R. (2002). Gender differences in psychopathology, functional impairment, and familial risk factors among adjudicated delinquents. *Journal of the American Academy of Child & Adolescent Psychiatry*, *41*(7), 860–867. doi:10.1097/00004583-200207000-00020

Meier, M. H., Hall, W., Caspi, A., Belsky, D. W., Cerdá, M., Harrington, H. L., et al. (2015). Which adolescents develop persistent substance dependence in adulthood? Using population-representative longitudinal data to inform universal risk assessment. *Psychological Medicine, FirstView*, 1–13. doi:10.1017/S0033291715002482

Meyerson, L. A., Long, P. J., Miranda Jr, R., & Marx, B. P. (2002). The influence of childhood sexual abuse, physical abuse, family environment, and gender on the psychological adjustment of adolescents. *Child Abuse & Neglect*, *26*(4), 387–405. doi:10.1016/S0145-2134(02)00315-0

Minnis, H., Reekie, J., Young, D., O'Connor, T., Ronald, A., Gray, A., et al. (2007). Genetic, environmental and gender influences on attachment disorder behaviours. *British Journal of Psychiatry*, *190*(6), 490–495. doi:10.1192/bjp.bp.105.019745

Moffitt, T. E., Caspi, A., Rutter, M., & Silva, P. A. (2001). *Sex differences in antisocial behaviour: Conduct disorder, delinquency, and violence in the Dunedin Longitudinal Study.* Cambridge: Cambridge University Press.

Murray, J., & Farrington, D. P. (2005). Parental imprisonment: Effects on boys' antisocial behaviour and delinquency through the life-course. *Journal of Child Psychology and Psychiatry*, *46*(12), 1269–1278. doi:10.1111/j.1469-7610.2005.01433.x

Murray, J., & Farrington, D. P. (2008). The effects of parental imprisonment on children. In M. Tonry (Ed.), *Crime and justice: A review of research* (Vol. *37*, pp. 133–206). Chicago, IL: University of Chicago Press.

Murray, J., Janson, C.-G., & Farrington, D. P. (2007). Crime in adult offspring of prisoners: A cross-national comparison of two longitudinal samples. *Criminal Justice and Behavior*, *34*(1), 133–149. doi:10.1177/0093854806289549

Nolen-Hoeksema, S. (1990). *Sex differences in depression.* Stanford, CA: Stanford University Press.

Norman, R. E., Byambaa, M., De, R., Butchart, A., Scott, J., & Vos, T. (2012). The long-term health consequences of child physical abuse, emotional abuse, and neglect: A systematic review and meta-analysis. *PLoS Med*, *9*(11), e1001349. doi:10.1371/journal.pmed.1001349

Nurius, P. S., Green, S., Logan-Greene, P., & Borja, S. (2015). Life course pathways of adverse childhood experiences toward adult psychological well-being: A stress process analysis. *Child Abuse & Neglect*, *45*, 143–153. doi:10.1016/j.chiabu.2015.03.008

St Clair, M. C., Croudace, T., Dunn, V. J., Jones, P. B., Herbert, J., & Goodyer, I. M. (2015). Childhood adversity subtypes and depressive symptoms in early and late adolescence. *Development and Psychopathology*, *27*(3), 885–899. doi:10.1017/S0954579414000625

Stouthamer-Loeber, M., Loeber, R., Homish, D. L., & Wei, E. (2001). Maltreatment of boys and the development of disruptive and delinquent behavior. *Development and Psychopathology*, *13*(4), 941–955.

Suldo, S. M., McMahan, M. M., Chappel, A. M., & Loker, T. (2012). Relationships between perceived school climate and adolescent mental health across genders. *School Mental Health*, *4*(2), 69–80. doi:10.1007/s12310-012-9073-1

Veenema, A. H., & Neumann, I. D. (2009). Maternal separation enhances offensive play-fighting, basal corticosterone and hypothalamic vasopressin mRNA expression in juvenile male rats. *Psychoneuroendocrinology*, *34*(3), 463–467.

Wigger, A., & Neumann, I. D. (1999). Periodic maternal deprivation induces dender-dependent alterations in behavioral and neuroendocrine responses to emotional stress in adult rats. *Physiology & Behavior*, *66*(2), 293–302. doi:10.1016/S0031-9384(98)00300-X

Zahn-Waxler, C., Shirtcliff, E. A., & Marceau, K. (2008). Disorders of childhood and adolescence: Gender and psychopathology. *Annual Review of Clinical Psychology*, *4*(1), 275–303. doi:10.1146/annurev.clinpsy.3.022806.091358

# Part 2
# Adverse Circumstances – Upbringing

# 17

# Development under Adverse Circumstances as a Risk for Psychopathology

## *An Intergenerational Study of Children from Disadvantaged High-Risk Backgrounds*

Dale M. Stack, Lisa A. Serbin, Célia Matte-Gagné, Danielle Kingdon, Kelly Doiron, and Alex E. Schwartzman

Experiencing adversity as a child has the potential to alter and disrupt normative development (Noltemeyer & Bush, 2013), and places children at high risk for psychopathology (Cicchetti, 2013) and other difficulties that can persist across the lifespan. However, because the concept of risk is inherently probabilistic, it follows that some individuals from moderate- to high-risk backgrounds are likely to develop well, despite their apparently poor prospects in infancy or early childhood. Hence, within a high-risk population, there will likely be a range of outcomes, in terms of adaptation and competence across the lifespan. It is, therefore, essential to determine both positive and negative factors that can buffer or increase the effect of disadvantage, in order to break the cycle of poverty and family distress and optimize the development of society's most vulnerable children (Rutter, 2013). In so doing, we need to understand the processes by which disadvantage interacts with other individual, family, and contextual factors, and their complex interplay in the intergenerational continuity of risk and psychopathology.

In the present chapter we review the findings of an ongoing intergenerational study of psychosocially at-risk children. In so doing, our goal is to understand the processes by which poverty and disadvantage work with other factors to create an environment that can lead to risk for mental health and psychiatric problems, and the transmission of risk and psychopathology across generations. Intergenerational studies are unique and important because they focus on comparisons between generations at similar points in development, attempting to identify the processes that predict outcomes across generations. An innovative feature of these intergenerational designs is that they typically allow the researcher to predict behavior across the transition into

*The Wiley Handbook of Developmental Psychopathology*, First Edition. Edited by Luna C. Centifanti and David M. Williams.

parenthood in order to understand the mechanisms of intergenerational transmission. The numerous studies that will be reviewed in this chapter have taken place over time and across generations, and are framed by both a developmental psychopathology framework (Cicchetti & Toth, 2009) and the transactional model, whereby developmental outcomes occur as a result of the complex interplay between a child and his or her environment (Sameroff, 2009).

## Overview

In the current chapter we describe the growth and development of children from the Concordia Longitudinal Risk Project (henceforth referred to as the Concordia Project) who were raised under adverse circumstances and followed from childhood into adulthood. As these children reached adulthood some became parents and were followed into parenthood; subsequently their children were assessed and followed. The Concordia Project began over 35 years ago in Montreal, Quebec, Canada with the screening of 4109 francophone schoolchildren in regular grade 1 (years of birth: 1969–1971), grade 4 (years of birth: 1966–1968), and grade 7 (years of birth: 1963–1966) classes. These children were rated by peers on dimensions of aggression and social withdrawal, and subsequently assessed at various stages of development, during childhood, adolescence, and adulthood (for a more extensive description of the original methodology and characteristics of the sample, see Schwartzman, Ledingham, & Serbin, 1985; Serbin et al., 1998). This Concordia Project sample (recruited 1976–78) was composed of children attending inner-city schools from economically disadvantaged neighborhoods in Montreal (Ledingham, Schwartzman, & Serbin, 1984). The parents of the children who were recruited are the first generation, the G1 in the present chapter. The second generation, referred to as G2, were in elementary school (age 6–12) when they were recruited, and are now themselves parents of the third generation, the G3. The G3 currently range in age from late adolescence to adulthood.

Few research programs have the opportunity to examine disadvantage and its relation to maladaptive behavioral patterns, such as aggression and social withdrawal, across time and generations. Aggression and social withdrawal are two major dimensions of childhood behavioral disturbance that have been demonstrated to be linked to a myriad of negative outcomes over the life course (see Table 17.1 for an overview of findings from the Concordia Project). Aggression refers to externalizing behavior problems that can include hyperactivity-impulsivity, aggression, and disruptive and oppositional behaviors. Social withdrawal refers to internalizing behavior problems that can include emotional problems such as depression and anxiety (Achenbach, 1991; Serbin, Moskowitz, Schwartzman, & Ledingham, 1991). Early externalizing and internalizing problems, such as aggression and social withdrawal, have been found to precede adult psychopathology (Fanti & Henrich, 2010). As we illustrate in the chapter, these maladaptive behaviors of aggression and withdrawal can interact with adverse circumstances to set children on a difficult trajectory that persists across adulthood and can impair their capacity to respond to their own children's needs. Subsequently as parents, they place their children at risk for mental health problems and in doing so, perpetuate the transmission of psychopathology across generations.

**Table 17.1** Concordia Project studies showing the relation between parent-related risk factors and child outcomes.

| *Study* | *Parenting Predictor* | *Child Outcome* |
|---|---|---|
| Ben-Dat Fisher et al., 2007 | Unsupportive maternal parenting, second-hand smoke, maternal history of childhood social withdrawal | Dysregulated cortisol response |
| Campisi et al., 2009 | Greater maternal language complexity | Increased expressive language |
| | Maternal history of childhood aggression and social withdrawal | Increased expressive language and improved early elementary language and math academic abilities |
| De Genna et al., 2007 | Parental history of childhood aggression and social withdrawal | Greater number of health problems, including headaches/migraines, more prescribed medication for respiratory problems and the prescription of Ritalin |
| | Maternal smoking during pregnancy | Increased body mass index (BMI) |
| | Single parenthood | Greater number of health problems |
| Granger et al., 1998 | Higher levels of family conflict, parenting stress, mother's current psychosocial problems, maternal history of childhood social withdrawal | Dysregulated cortisol response |
| Grunzeweig et al., 2009 | Maternal history of childhood aggression and social withdrawal, intrusive requests | Non-compliance |
| Hastings et al., 2011 | Maternal punishment | Higher cortisol levels and boys' increased levels of externalizing problems |
| Martin et al., 2012 | Maternal childhood histories of aggression and social withdrawal | Poorly sophisticated problem solving |
| Mills et al., 2012 | Less positive and more critical parenting, maternal negative emotionality, family socioeconomic disadvantage | Increased levels of internalizing problems |
| Pougnet et al., 2011 | Fathers' presence | Girls' decreased levels of internalizing problems |
| | Greater paternal positive parental control | Higher cognitive functioning and fewer internalizing problems |
| Saltaris et al., 2004 | Lowered parenting stress, maternal scaffolding, higher quality of the home environment | Improved cognitive functioning (IQ) |
| Serbin & Bukowski, 2009 | Greater maternal education, maternal involvement in early schooling, and supportive parenting style | Improved school readiness skills |

(*Continued*)

**Table 17.1** (Continued)

| *Study* | *Parenting Predictor* | *Child Outcome* |
|---|---|---|
| Serbin, Stack, & Kingdon, 2013 | Greater maternal education, family income, and supportive parenting | Improved academic performance |
| Serbin, Stack & Schwartzman, 2000 | Maternal history of childhood aggression and social withdrawal, maternal smoking, lower levels of parental education, low SES, poor quality of home environment, high parental stress, less supportive parenting | Pediatric illness, perinatal health problems, developmental, cognitive, language, and behavioural problems/delays |
| Serbin, Peters, et al., 1991 | Poor quality of the home environment, young age at first pregnancy, maternal childhood history of aggression | Developmental delay |
| Serbin et al., 1998 | Maternal childhood histories of aggression and lower levels of childhood social withdrawal, lowered levels of maternal education | Aggression |
| Serbin et al., 1996 | Maternal childhood histories of aggression and social withdrawal | Elevated rates of infections and injuries, higher rates of emergency room visits and hospitalizations |
| Serbin et al., 2002 | Maternal childhood histories of aggression and social withdrawal, lowered levels of maternal education, teen parenthood, less responsive parenting | Perinatal problems, elevated rates of infections and injuries, higher rates of emergency room visits, aggression, restlessness, language difficulties, cognitive delays, developmental delays, and behavioral problems |
| Stack et al., 2012 | Maternal history of childhood social withdrawal | Less responsiveness and involvement during parent–child interactions |
| | Greater maternal structuring | Greater responsiveness |
| | Greater maternal sensitivity and structuring | Greater involvement |
| | More maternal social support, better home environment, lower parental stress | Better mother–child relationship quality |

## Growing Up in Poverty and Disadvantage (from G1 to G2)

By studying a high-risk population in a prospective, longitudinal design across generations, the Concordia Project provides a unique opportunity to examine the disadvantaged contexts that shape some children's upbringing and the impact of disadvantage across time. Consistent with recent research underscoring the impact of poverty and low SES (usually including family income, parental education, and occupational status) over time (Bradley & Corwyn, 2002; Hertzman & Boyce, 2010; Reiss, 2013), studies from the Concordia Project have shown that growing up in a disadvantaged environment characterized by multiple risk factors places children at risk for various problems that may carry into adulthood and lead to mental health problems. Poverty creates an environment that fails to foster academic achievement and limits levels of social support, leading to a dearth of opportunities and, consequently, contributes to the recursive nature of family poverty across time and generation (Duncan, Yeung, Brooks-Gunn, & Smith, 1998). Consistent with this environment, high rates of school drop-out, low educational and occupational attainment (Serbin, Stack, Kingdon, Mantis, & Enns, 2011), and high levels of child aggression and social withdrawal (Ledingham & Schwartzman, 1984) were found in the Concordia Project families that have more serious financial pressures or lower SES backgrounds. Although both men and women with high-risk childhoods, in our sample, had lower academic achievement, men were more likely to drop out of school. However, when women dropped out of school, they were at greatest risk for living in poverty and experiencing limited career and income opportunities.

Consistent with the fact that sustained exposure to environmental adversity and stress contribute to the development of various types of psychopathology (van Praag, de Kloet, & van Os, 2004), results from the Concordia Project have also shown that poverty and other related risk factors put children at further risk for psychiatric symptoms such as substance abuse, anxiety and depression (Lee-Genest, 2010; Martin-Storey, Serbin, Stack, Ledingham, & Schwartzman, 2011; Martin-Storey et al., 2013; Schwartzman, Serbin, Stack, Hodgins, & Ledingham, 2009; Schwartzman, Verlaan, Peters, & Serbin, 1995; Serbin, Stack, Kingdon, et al., 2011). However, similar risk histories lead to the development of different disorders based on gender and the level of stress experienced. For both men and women, living in a low-income and low educational attainment neighborhood was found to be associated with an increased risk of alcohol abuse. Although childhood histories of aggression predicted substance abuse during adulthood only for men, women who were rated as being highly aggressive during childhood were also at an increased risk for alcohol, cigarette smoking, and illegal substance use during adolescence, and women were at increased risk for depression during adulthood. Furthermore, participants with low SES and high levels of stress who were highly aggressive and/or socially withdrawn in childhood were found to be at an increased risk for psychiatric symptoms. These findings suggest that while poverty is a major area of disadvantage, there are other related-risks that can make development challenging and that can make for a difficult environment, including stress and maladaptive behavioral patterns such as aggression and social withdrawal. Difficult environments are both by-products and predictors of poverty that intertwine to create the environments within which children will grow (Serbin, Stack, Kingdon, et al., 2011), and which can affect individuals throughout the lifespan and lead to negative outcomes such as low educational attainment and psychopathology. When negative outcomes follow individuals into adulthood, the environment in which subsequent generations are raised can be impaired. Abundant research supports the notion of a cycle of economic disadvantage, whereby, when children are raised in poverty, they will likely continue to live in poverty throughout their adult lives (e.g., Musick & Mare, 2006; Serbin, Stack, Kingdon, et al., 2011). Supporting the intergenerational cycle of risk and poverty, a direct link was found between the SES of G1 and G2 during adulthood in the Concordia Project sample (Serbin et al., 2010). Children raised in poverty were found to be more likely to live in poverty during adulthood and to raise their own children in poverty (Serbin et al., 2010).

Fortunately, there are protective factors that can buffer against adverse circumstances such as higher education and intellectual functioning, and the extent of social support and positive relationships. Higher education can broaden career opportunities and increase the level of income (Serbin, Stack, Kingdon, et al., 2011); these factors allow for greater financial opportunities and social supports that have inverse relationships with stress and subsequent psychopathology (Serbin, Stack, Kingdon, et al., 2011). For example, men with more positive resources such as high academic achievement, academic attainment, and occupational prestige, were found to have decreased stress loads and, consequently, less psychiatric vulnerability (Schwartzman et al., 2009). Such protective factors can help to raise people from poverty and disrupt the continuity of risk across time and generation (Serbin, Stack, Kingdon, et al., 2011), as well as disrupt the intergenerational transmission of psychopathology observed in other studies.

## The Intergenerational Transmission of Psychopathology from G2 to G3

According to the developmental psychopathology framework, a multifaceted approach is therefore important in understanding processes and intergenerational transmission, and psychiatric problems can be transmitted from one generation to the next. A growing body of research indicates that children whose parents have histories of psychiatric disorder are themselves at risk for psychopathology (e.g., Enlow, Egeland, Carlson, Blood, & Wright, 2014; Harold et al., 2011; Kim-Cohen et al., 2009). Supporting the contention that psychopathology can be transferred across generations, parents' symptoms of anxiety and depression in the Concordia Project were found to be related to negative outcomes in children such as cognitive delays, behavioral and emotional problems, and stress response (Granger et al., 1998; Karp, Serbin, Stack, & Schwartzman, 2004; Serbin, Stack, & Schwartzman, 2000; Serbin et al., 1998). While many mental health disorders are heritable to some degree, genetic accounts do not fully explain the considerable continuity of psychopathology across generations (Belsky & Jafee, 2006). According to the developmental psychopathology framework, there are multiple processes acting additively, exponentially or co-synergistically in the transmission of psychopathology (Cicchetti & Toth, 2009). Parenting is one suggested mechanism that may interact with genetic risk in the transmission of mental disorder from one generation to the next (Enlow et al., 2014; Goodman & Gotlib, 1999).

### Parenting as a Contributor to the Development and Transmission of Risk and Psychopathology

According to the developmental psychopathology literature, disadvantaged contexts indirectly affect child maladjustment through the quality of parenting and exposure to stressful life experiences (Grant et al., 2003; Rutter, 1987). A substantial array of empirical work has established links between a (mal)adaptive parenting environment and several child outcomes throughout various stages of child development (Belsky & Jaffee, 2006; Cicchetti & Toth, 2005). Consequently, it is important to examine parenting behaviors in disadvantaged families and communities in order to understand the specific components of the disadvantaged environment that are associated with subsequent (mal)adaptive outcomes.

In the Concordia Project, we have demonstrated that growing up in a disadvantaged environment places children (G2) at risk for various problems that can carry over into adolescence and adulthood and manifest themselves in various ways. When negative outcomes follow individuals into adulthood, the transition to parenthood can also be fraught with difficulties, thus impacting the environment in which subsequent generations are raised and increasing risk for distress and psychiatric vulnerability (Conger & Donnellan, 2007). Studies from the Concordia Project have shown for example that aggressive and socially withdrawn girls from high-risk backgrounds have an increased risk for unprotected sexual activity, teenage pregnancy, and birth complications (Serbin et al., 2010; Serbin, Peters, McAffer, & Schwartzman, 1991; Serbin et al., 1998; Serbin, Stack, Kingdon, et al., 2011). Giving birth during adolescence sets parents and children on a difficult path, which may include difficulties completing high school and complications with delivery that can put both maternal and child health in jeopardy (Serbin, Stack, Hubert, Schwartzman, & Ledingham, 2011; Serbin, Stack, Kingdon, et al., 2011). In our studies, parents with childhood histories of disadvantage, aggression, and social withdrawal have also been shown to be more likely than their low-risk counterparts to raise their children in single parent households (Serbin & Karp, 2004; Serbin et al., 2010). Generally, women are more likely than men to raise their children alone (Serbin et al., 2010), which is especially true for those that grew up in single parent households themselves (Pougnet, Serbin, Stack, Ledingham, & Schwartzman, 2012). From an economic standpoint, this puts the family at an increased risk for living in poverty, as income is limited to one person (Serbin, Stack, Kingdon, et al., 2011).

Through lack of social support, financial burden, and poor health (Serbin & Karp, 2004), single parenthood also increases levels of stress and psychiatric problems, particularly anxiety and depression (Serbin, Stack, Kingdon, et al., 2011). When parents experience stress and psychiatric symptoms or disorders, their ability to meet the needs of their children can be limited (Stack, Serbin, Schwartzman, & Ledingham, 2005). According to studies from the Concordia Project, parenting difficulties often occur in women and men from disadvantaged, high-risk backgrounds (Serbin et al., 2002). When mothers have childhood histories of risk (i.e. aggression and social withdrawal) they tend to be more hostile toward their children (Stack et al., 2012), they are also more likely to repeat requests of their children (Grunzeweig, Stack, Serbin, Ledingham, & Schwartzman, 2009) and, they report more violence between spouses, but also towards offspring (Temcheff et al., 2008). Thus, growing up in a disadvantaged environment characterized by multiple risk factors can influence the manner in which parents raise their own children and ultimately may create conflictual and unsafe environments for children to be raised (Temcheff et al., 2008).

While favorable environmental experiences, especially those embedded within early care-giving relationships, have often been shown to have a positive impact on child development, a disadvantaged family environment is frequently cited as a major risk factor in the development of the child (Teti & Cole, 2011). Thus, the disadvantaged parenting environment created in part by poverty and other related risk factors also places the next generation (G3) at risk for multiple physical, psychological and developmental problems that can lead to psychopathology. Results from the Concordia Project have demonstrated that a number of parenting behaviors, such as critical parenting, and hostility and punishment, are risk factors for children. These parenting behaviors, combined with other parent-related risk factors such as father absence, lack of parental resources, and low social support, have been demonstrated to be associated with several adverse developmental outcomes for children such as poor physical health, social and cognitive development and intellectual functioning (for a more detailed review of the findings, see Table 17.1). Parents' childhood histories of aggression or social withdrawal have also been found to predict negative outcomes for offspring in cognitive, behavioral, and health domains, both directly through the continuity of these childhood behavioral patterns into mother–child interactions 20+ years later, and indirectly through intervening negative life experiences such as school drop-out, substance abuse or poor physical health. While not causal links, our findings indicate that children growing up in disadvantaged and at-risk family environments and being raised by parents who have a lack of resources and poor parenting skills are at-risk of developing social, developmental, behavioral, and health problems that lead to more difficulty later in life. By demonstrating the associations between (mal)adaptive parenting behaviors and child (mal)adaptive outcomes in a high-risk disadvantaged community sample, the results from the Concordia Project support the developmental psychopathology framework by highlighting the importance of parenting and its relation to risk and resilience. While parental psychopathology has been demonstrated to be an important risk factor for child psychopathology, other risk factors such as parenting and disadvantaged family conditions can also place children at risk, as well as interact with genetic risk, for developing mental health problems. These factors may serve as mechanisms for the intergenerational transmission of psychopathology from one generation to the next and consequently facilitate the development of more comprehensive explanatory models to understand and "unpack" these effects over time and generation.

## Psychopathology in At-risk Children (G3) from the Concordia Project

In the previous sections, our review underscored that individuals living with adversity and coming from high-risk backgrounds face a variety of threats to their own development that can persist across their life span and impair their capacity to respond to their children's needs. Subsequently as parents, they place their children at risk for mental health problems and in so doing perpetuate the transmission of psychopathology across generations. Consistent with the fact that children from socioeconomically disadvantaged backgrounds are over-identified in rates of emotional and behavioral problems in the literature (e.g., McLoyd, 1998), our results have indicated that G3 children are at increased risk for developing psychopathology. More specifically, internalizing and externalizing problems (Kingdon, Serbin, & Stack, 2014), as well as clinical levels of anxiety and depressive disorders (Ma et al., 2012) were found to be approximately one and a half to two times above population base rates in G3 children. Understanding the processes through which environmental disadvantage place children at risk for psychopathology across age and time is a major goal of the Concordia Project. Our results have highlighted the dynamic, transactional nature of the processes through which environmental disadvantage interacts with characteristics of the child and parent to increase risk for the development of internalizing problems.

In a study utilizing data from the Concordia Project and two additional independent samples at risk for the development of early emerging internalizing problems (Mills et al., 2012), we found that family socioeconomic disadvantage, child inhibition, less positive and more critical parenting, and maternal negative emotionality were directly associated with increased levels of internalizing problems. In addition, there was evidence that family disadvantage, including both socioeconomic disadvantage (e.g., low income and low level of education) and challenging structural characteristics (e.g., single-parent family, fewer biological parents in the home, large family size), and mothers' negative emotionality had indirect relations to children's internalizing problems through less positive and critical parenting. These findings provide evidence that well-established family risk factors in children's development (Conger & Dogan, 2007) may exert their effects on children's psychological adjustment through multiple processes that posit a chain of reciprocating influences from environmental disadvantage to parental stress, parenting quality, and children's psychological adjustment (Bronfenbrenner & Ceci, 1994). Moreover, our results highlight that parenting is an important intergenerational mechanism that is one explanation for the transmission of psychopathology (and other behaviors) from one generation to the next.

## Parenting, the Stress Response and Psychopathology

Incorporation of a biological perspective to the study of environmental disadvantage and developmental psychopathology has been critical to elucidating the mechanisms through which family disadvantage "gets under the skin" to increase children's risk of psychological maladjustment. One proposed mechanism is that exposure to adverse early environments can alter biological stress response systems such as the hypothalamic–pituitary–adrenal (HPA) axis (Taylor, Lerner, Sage, Lehman, & Seeman, 2004). When stress-response systems are impaired, children may have difficulty regulating emotions and coping with stressful situations, placing the child at an increased risk of engaging in maladaptive behaviors and developing psychopathology (Shirtcliff, Granger, Booth, & Johnson, 2005). Incorporating a multiple-levels-of-analysis approach, studies from the Concordia Project have shown that exposure to non-optimal early environments including poverty, unsupportive parenting, lack of stimulation, and maternal punishment may diminish the child's ability to cope with stress, as indexed by dysregulated activity of the HPA axis, measured through cortisol secretion (Ben-Dat Fisher et al., 2007; Granger et al., 1998; Hastings et al., 2011). Other research, integrating samples from the Concordia Project and two other data sets, has shown that maternal care is associated with regulated HPA functioning and psychological adjustment (Hastings et al., 2011). In Granger et al.'s (1998) study, children's blunted cortisol response was also predicted by mothers' histories of aggression, as well as current maternal functioning and parenting style, suggesting that children living in high-conflict family environments may become habituated to conflict and as a result show blunted physiological reactivity in response to stress. Together, these findings indicate that appropriate care through parent-child relationships serves to modulate infants' and young children's stress physiology and, eventually, confer capacities for emotion self-regulation. Conversely, exposure to the chronic stress of being raised in a negative home environment may lower young children's ability to cope with stress and increase their risk for poor adjustment. Supporting this hypothesis, HPA axis functioning (indexed by cortisol secretion) during adolescence was related to prior and current levels of internalizing and externalizing behavior problems (Ruttle et al., 2011). These findings suggest that the experience of a mental health issue, in and of itself, may be operating as a stressor that increases future risk for psychopathology.

## Developmental Changes in Emotional and Behavior Problems Over Time

Not only can family adversity contribute to the development of mental health problems through both direct and indirect pathways, the experience of a mental health problem early in life can increase the risk for continuation of problems in childhood, adolescence, and adulthood. Given the merits in the burgeoning use of trajectory approaches in developmental psychopathology work, in a recent study (Kingdon et al., 2014) we employed latent growth curve analysis to examine the nature, shape and rate of change of children's internalizing and externalizing problems and their trajectories from school entry to early adolescence. Consistent with prior research documenting the clustering of behavior problems in at-risk children, both boys and girls experienced a high degree of co-occurring internalizing and externalizing problems across time. Trajectory analyses revealed that externalizing behaviors in early school age did not predict a problematic developmental course for boys (i.e., increasing internalizing or externalizing problems over time), however for girls, early externalizing problems predicted increases in externalizing problems in later childhood and adolescence. In addition, boys and girls who experienced internalizing problems in early childhood demonstrated increasing trajectories of internalizing problems over the course of childhood and early adolescence. These findings parallel earlier results from the Concordia project, which highlighted the continuity of difficulties experienced by G2 individuals with childhood histories of aggression or social withdrawal (Serbin, Moskowitz, et al., 1991; Serbin, Peters, et al., 1991; Serbin et al., 2004). In addition, we find consistent evidence that externalizing or aggressive behavior problems experienced by girls are problematic and predict increasing trajectories of externalizing problems and a range of negative sequelae for themselves and their offspring (Serbin, Moskowitz, et al., 1991; Serbin, Peters, et al., 1991; Serbin et al., 1998; Stack et al., 2005).

As alluded to previously, although some forms of child behavior problems are normal and transient developmental phenomena, a substantial proportion of child behavior problems reach clinically significant problems over time. Of the children who were rated low on internalizing problems at preschool age, the majority did not go on to develop an internalizing disorder in pre-adolescence (Ma et al., 2012). However, for the children rated high on internalizing symptoms at preschool age, half received a diagnosis for anxiety, depression, or both at preadolescence. These results underscore the enduring effects of early emotional and behavior problems across the lifespan and signal the importance of early preventive intervention approaches. Together, these findings highlight the fact that the experience of emotional and behavioral problems in childhood among at-risk populations is associated with continued problems in adolescence (and beyond). Paralleling findings in earlier stages of the project, G3 children in our disadvantaged sample, like their parents, face continuing negative trajectories. The "life cycle" of psychopathology (Caspi & Elder, 1988) and the processes through which psychological problems seem to recur in the same families are also underscored by our findings.

### Transactional Processes between Parents and Children

Although the literature discussed previously focused on the influence of parents on the development of their children, children also influence the parenting they receive and the environments they are exposed to (Belsky & Jaffee, 2006). In the Concordia Project, examination of temperament, parenting, and children's early behavior problems provide evidence of the dynamic, bidirectional, transactional processes through which psychopathology develops (Sameroff, 2009). Consistent with previous findings in the literature, maternal perceptions of children's temperament profiles in the Concordia Project were found to predict their level of behavior problems (Serbin & Karp, 2004). However, bidirectional relations between child and mother functioning were found such that difficult child temperament (rated by mothers and independent observers) predicted increases in mothers' parenting stress. Not only may difficult children elicit negative reactions from parents, and consequently increase parenting stress, but also mothers who experience more parenting stress may become upset and frustrated when interacting with their children, which may increase the severity of their child's difficult temperament and behavior problems.

In another study, we (Serbin, Kingdon, Ruttle, & Stack, 2015) examined change in bidirectional relations between child and parent behavior across three successive developmental periods, spanning early childhood to adolescence. Different types of reciprocal relations between specific aspects of child and parent behavior were illustrated: internalizing problems predicted an increase in positive parenting (characterized by higher levels of structure and support) over time, which subsequently led to a reduction in internalizing problems over time. In contrast externalizing problems predicted reduced levels of positive parenting, in a reciprocal sequence that extended across two successive intervals and predicted increased levels of externalizing problems over time. The quality of parenting is thought to be critical to the understanding of why some children persist in their problem behavior, while others develop normally. Our results illustrate this differentiation by showing that parents who are able to respond adaptively to their children's internalizing problems with increased support and structure may reduce the severity and chronicity of their child's symptoms. In contrast, parents who respond to children's externalizing problems with poorer parenting (e.g., lowered support and structure, higher levels of harsh punishment) may exacerbate the child's externalizing difficulties, putting them on a trajectory for persisting problems. These results are consistent with an increasing body of studies showing that children's temperament and behaviors impact their parents' behaviors toward them (e.g., Ciciolla, Crnic, & West, 2013; Lengua & Kovacs, 2005). Through transactional processes, maladaptive parent–child interactions can develop that place children at increased risk for trajectories conducive to developing further psychopathology and other negative developmental outcomes.

## Conclusions

Dynamic, developmental processes are complex to study and challenging to "unpack". Multiple influences, both acute and chronic, can affect these processes over time and across generations. Identifying the processes through which disadvantage and other related risk factors such as maladaptive behaviors and psychopathology place families at risk, and how these may be conferred to the next generation, is crucial. In this way, at-risk families and children can be identified early, and appropriate and comprehensive intervention can be provided. In the policy arena, a major goal is to disrupt the intergenerational cycles that may help to create and sustain a disadvantaged underclass. However, in order to achieve prevention-oriented goals, interventions must be supported by research to successfully ensure that they are both effective and cost efficient. Targets for preventive intervention that have been identified and are covered in our chapter include poverty, maladaptive behavior, parenting, stress, and mental health.

In addition, "unpacking" some of these well-established risk factors, such as school dropout, early parenthood, parental absence, and family poverty, will be an important step in designing preventive interventions (Serbin, Stack, Kingdon, et al., 2011). We need to know the specific sequence and mechanisms that underlie intergenerational patterns of risk to health and development. A number of risk factors for psychopathology were identified and highlighted in each of the three sections of the chapter. Related to disadvantage, these include poverty, low SES, single parenthood, and parental absence. Related to parenting processes, these include harsh and inconsistent parenting/discipline, low warmth and responsivity, family conflict, and lack of stimulation. Related to child outcomes, these include the stress response system, children's cognitive and language development, and early internalizing and externalizing problems. Taken together, we have shown that disadvantage and maladaptive behavioral styles (e.g., childhood histories of aggression and social withdrawal) place children at increased risk for developing further psychopathology and other negative developmental outcomes. These childhood risk histories follow individuals into adolescence and parenthood, affecting their own parenting practices and the environments wherein the next generation will be raised.

Results from the Concordia Project provide solid grounds for the inference that the mechanisms through which disadvantage and mental health problems are transferred across generations is through a transactional approach, whereby the environment, parent and child characteristics influence each other and make reciprocal contributions to developmental outcomes (Sameroff, 2009). These findings are in line with literature indicating that the processes of poverty and low SES render a "cycle of deprivation and mental health problems" (Reiss, 2013). Understanding transactional processes is necessary to more effectively intervene in the intergenerational cycle of both poverty and psychopathology.

While there are mechanisms through which risk is transferred, such as maladaptive parenting behaviors, stress, low educational attainment, early pregnancy, parental absence, and childhood psychopathology and behavior problems, as well as genetic mechanisms, there are also buffering factors (notably social and economic support, coping ability, positive parenting, relationship quality, and educational achievement) that have been identified within the Concordia Project. These factors may protect individuals from negative outcomes, even under disadvantaged conditions, and have been shown in the Concordia Project to be contextual modulators of the long-term outcomes. Risk and protective factors combine to influence the direction and sequence of future events and the trajectory of the child's development over the life span (Rutter, 1987). Recent statistical advances in the modeling of longitudinal data have allowed us to address more complex questions about the nature, shape, and rate of change in the development of psychopathology in the Concordia Project studies. These trajectories highlight the continuity in early problems across development, underscoring the need for early intervention; and early intervention is recommended to decrease socioeconomic inequalities (Reiss, 2013). The increasing frequency of trajectory approaches in developmental psychopathology work will enable us to examine interactions between risk and protective factors over time and how the developmental trajectories linked to maladjustment and psychopathology may change over time in light of these factors. In this way we will be better positioned to "unpack" developmental processes leading to psychopathology and intergenerational transmission of risk and psychopathology.

While risk is probabilistic, it is clear that there are individuals within disadvantaged populations, such as the inner-city Concordia sample, who are at especially high-risk for long-term psychosocial difficulties and psychopathology. These problems are cumulative, and extend beyond the individual to the functioning of the individual's family and future offspring. If we are to optimize the development of the most vulnerable children in society, it is incumbent upon us to identify the predictors of risk and resilience within high-risk populations and the experiences and characteristics that may protect or buffer children who come from disadvantaged backgrounds (Rutter, 2013). Because risk is cumulative in these families and risk factors can be identified at various points in the course of development, there are likely multiple opportunities for preventive intervention. Addressing the complex risk profiles of the most vulnerable individuals will require early and targeted preventative intervention in order to improve the long-term course of their development.

## Summary

In the first part of our chapter we illustrated how disadvantage in childhood (G1) works with other factors to create a disadvantaged context in adulthood that can lead to psychiatric problems. In Part II of the chapter, it was the children (G2) from the Concordia Project that became parents that were followed into parenthood in order to understand: a) how the disadvantaged parenting environment created in part by poverty and other related risk factors places the next generation (G3) at risk for multiple negative outcomes that can lead to psychopathology; and b) how maladaptive behaviors and developmental and psychosocial problems are transferred from one generation to the next in part through the parent-child relationship and parenting behaviors. Part III of the chapter focused on understanding how psychopathology develops among at-risk groups and within disadvantaged contexts by examining mental health outcomes and psychopathology in G3 (the offspring of G2), as well as some of the transactional and interactive processes.

In conclusion, the content of our chapter called attention to a number of important themes. Among these are that poverty is multifaceted: it is not just income that matters but the cluster of associated risk and problems that are related that increase the risk for psychopathology. That is, poverty works with other related factors to explain the later development of psychopathology. The interplay between individual, environmental and contextual factors (positive and negative) is important in order to understand processes through which disadvantage may lead to psychopathology and mental health problems. In addition, poverty makes parenting more difficult. It is parenting, its relation to risk and resilience in children, and the transactional processes between parent and child that present important considerations and challenges, and a potential mechanism for intergenerational transfer. As we noted, at-risk children have higher rates of psychopathology, highlighting that disadvantage operates as both a direct and indirect risk factor for psychopathology. Furthermore, some gender differences in trajectories of both poverty and psychopathology were underlined. Finally, the continuity of problems across time and generations was accentuated in our studies. Intergenerational studies are unique and important because they focus on comparisons between generations at similar points in development, attempting to identify the processes that predict outcomes across generations. The Concordia Project has important implications for public (educational, social, and health) policies designed to give children born into a legacy of risk and growing up in adverse circumstances an opportunity to break the cycle.

## Acknowledgments

This research was conducted by authors at the Department of Psychology and the Centre for Research in Human Development (CRDH), Concordia University over the years. The research described in this chapter was partially supported by grants from Fonds de Recherche Québécois sur la Société et la Culture (FRQ-SC), and the Social Sciences and Humanities Research Council of Canada (SSHRC) awarded to Dale M. Stack and Lisa A. Serbin, and Canadian Institutes of Health Research, Child & Youth Mental Health and Well-Being (Health Canada), and Human Resources Development Canada, as well as support from Concordia University and CRDH awarded to Serbin, Stack and Schwartzman. The Concordia Project originated in 1976 under the direction of Jane Ledingham and Alex E. Schwartzman. The intergenerational project is currently directed by Lisa A. Serbin, Dale M. Stack, and Alex E. Schwartzman. We extend our gratitude to Catherine Delisle, Joelle Belisle-Cuillerier, Kimberly Burnside, and Samantha Bouchard for help with the final preparation of the chapter. We also wish to thank Claude Senneville, Nadine Girouard and the Concordia Project team over the years for their assistance in data collection and analysis. Finally, we are most indebted to the participants in the study.

E-mail correspondence concerning this chapter may be sent to dale.stack@concordia.ca or lisa.serbin@concordia.ca.

## References

Achenbach, T. M. (1991). The derivation of taxonomic constructs: A necessary stage in the development of developmental psychopathology. In D. Cicchetti & S. L. Toth (Eds.), *Rochester Symposium on Developmental Psychopathology: Models and integrations* (Vol. *3*, pp. 43–74). Rochester, NY: University of Rochester Press.

Belsky, J., & Jaffee, S. R. (2006). The multiple determinants of parenting. In D. Cicchetti & D. J. Cohen (Eds.), *Developmental psychopathology: Risk, disorder, and adaptation* (2nd ed., Vol. *3*, pp. 38–85). Hoboken, NJ: John Wiley & Sons.

Ben-Dat Fisher, D., Serbin, L. A., Stack, D. M., Ruttle, P. L., Ledingham, J. E., & Schwartzman, A. E. (2007). Intergenerational predictors of diurnal cortisol secretion in early childhood. *Infant and Child Development*, *16*(2), 151–170. doi:10.1002/icd.474

Bradley, R. H., & Corwyn, R. F. (2002). Socioeconomic status and child development. *Annual Review of Psychology*, *53*(1), 371–399. doi:10.1146/annurev.psych.53.100901.135233

Bronfenbrenner, U., & Ceci, S. J. (1994). Nature–nurture reconceptualized in developmental perspective: A bioecological model. *Psychological Review, 101*(4), 568–586. doi:10.1037/0033-295X.101.4.568

Campisi, L., Serbin, L., Stack, D. M., Ledingham, J. E., & Schwartzman, A. E. (2009). Precursors of language ability and academic performance: An intergenerational longitudinal study of at-risk children. *Infant and Child Development, 18*(5), 377–403. doi:10.1002/icd.628

Caspi, A., & Elder, G. (1988). Childhood precursors of the life course: Early personality and life disorganization. In E. M. Hetherington & R. M. Lerner (Eds.), *Child development in life-span perspective* (pp. 115–142). Hillsdale, NJ: Erlbaum.

Cicchetti, D. (2013). Annual research review: Resilient functioning in maltreated children – Past, present, and future perspectives. *Journal of Child Psychology and Psychiatry, 54*(4), 402–422. doi:10.1111/j.1469-7610.2012.02608.x

Cicchetti, D., & Toth, S.L. (2005). Child maltreatment. *Annual Review of Clinical Psychology, 1*(1), 409–438. doi:10.1146/annurev.clinpsy.1.102803.144029

Cicchetti, D., & Toth, S. L. (2009). The past achievements and future promises of developmental psychopathology: The coming age of a discipline. *Journal of Child Psychology and Psychiatry, 50*(1–2), 16–25. doi:10.1111/j.1469-7610.2008.01979.x

Ciciolla, L., Crnic, K. A., & West, S. G. (2013). Determinants of change in maternal sensitivity: Contributions of context, temperament, and developmental risk. *Parenting: Science And Practice, 13*(3), 178–195. doi:10.1080/15295192.2013.756354

Conger, R. D., & Dogan, S. J. (2007). Social class and socialization in families. In J. E. Grusec & P. D. Hastings (Eds.), *Handbook of socialization: Theory and research* (pp. 433–460). New York: Guilford Press.

Conger, R. D., & Donnellan, M. (2007). An interactionist perspective on the socioeconomic context of human development. *Annual Review of Psychology, 58*, 175–199. doi:10.1146/annurev.psych.58.110405.085551

De Genna, N., Stack, D. M., Ledingham, J. E., & Schwartzman, A. E. (2007). Maternal and child health problems: The inter-generational consequences of early maternal aggression and withdrawal. *Social Science and Medicine, 64*(12), 2417–2426. doi:10.1016/j.socscimed.2007.03.001

Duncan, G. J., Yeung, W., Brooks-Gunn, J., & Smith, J. R. (1998). How much does childhood poverty affect the life chances of children? *American Sociological Review, 63*(3), 406–423. doi:10.2307/2657556

Enlow, M. B., Egeland, B., Carlson, E., Blood, E., & Wright, R. J. (2014). Mother–infant attachment and the intergenerational transmission of posttraumatic stress disorder. *Development and Psychopathology, 26*(1), 41–65. doi:10.1017/S0954579413000515

Fanti, K. A., & Henrich, C. C. (2010). Trajectories of pure and co-occurring internalizing and externalizing problems from age 2 to age 12: Findings from the National Institute of Child Health and Human Development Study of Early Child Care. *Developmental Psychology, 46*(5), 1159–1175. doi:10.1037/a0020659

Goodman, S. H., & Gotlib, I. H. (1999). Risk for psychopathology in the children of depressed mothers: A developmental model for understanding mechanisms of transmission. *Psychological Review, 106*(3), 458–490. doi:10.1037/0033-295X.106.3.458

Granger, D. A., Serbin, L. A., Schwartzman, A., Lehoux, P., Cooperman, J., & Ikeda, S. (1998). Children's salivary cortisol, internalizing behaviour problems, and family environment: Results from the Concordia longitudinal risk project. *International Journal of Behavioral Development, 22*(4), 707–728. doi:10.1080/016502598384135

Grant, K. E., Compas, B. E., Stuhlmacher, A. F., Thurm, A. E., McMahon, S. D., & Halpert, J. A. (2003). Stressors and child and adolescent psychopathology: Moving from markers to mechanisms of risk. *Psychological Bulletin, 129*(3), 447–466. doi:10.1037/0033-2909.129.3.447

Grunzeweig, N., Stack, D. M., Serbin, L. A., Ledingham, J. E., & Schwartzman, A. E. (2009). Maternal request strategies and child compliance and noncompliance: Effects of age, context, and risk. *Journal of Applied Developmental Psychology*, *30*(6), 724–737. doi:10.1016/j.appdev.2009.02.001

Harold, G. T., Rice, F., Hay, D. F., Boivin, J., van den Bree, M., & Thaper, A. (2011). Familial transmission of depression and antisocial behavior symptoms: Disentangling the contribution of inherited and environmental factors and testing the mediating role of parenting. *Psychological Medicine*, *41*(6), 1175–1185. doi:10.1017/S0033291710001753

Hastings, P. D., Ruttle, P., Serbin, L. A., Mills, R. S. L., Stack, D. M., & Schwartzman, A. E. (2011). Adrenocortical responses to strangers in preschoolers: Relations with parenting, temperament, and psychopathology. *Developmental Psychobiology*, *53*(7), 694–710. doi: 10.1002/dev.20545

Hertzman, C., & Boyce, T. (2010). How experience gets under the skin to create gradients in developmental health. *Annual Review of Public Health*, *31*, 329–347.

Karp, J., Serbin, L. A., Stack, D. M., & Schwartzman, A. E. (2004). An observational measure of children's behavioral style: Evidence supporting a multi-method approach to studying temperament. *Infant and Child Development*, *13*(2), 135–158. doi:10.1002/icd.346

Kim-Cohen, J., Arseneault, L., Newcombe, R., Adams, F., Bolton, H., Cant, L., … Moffitt, T. (2009). Five-year predictive validity of DSM-IV conduct disorder research diagnosis in 4½–5-year-old children. *European Child and Adolescent Psychiatry*, *18*(5), 284–291. doi:10.1007/s00787-008-0729-1

Kingdon, D., Serbin, L. A., & Stack, D. M. (2014, July). *Sex differences in the co-development of children's internalizing and externalizing problem behaviors.* Poster presented at the International Society for the Study of Behavioural Development 2014 Biennial Meeting, Shanghai, China.

Ledingham, J. E., & Schwartzman, A. E. (1984). A 3-year follow-up of aggressive and withdrawn behaviour in childhood: Preliminary findings. *Journal of Abnormal Child Psychology*, *12*(1), 157–168. doi:10.1007/BF00913467

Ledingham, J. E., Schwartzman, A. E., & Serbin, L. A. (1984). Current adjustment and family functioning of children behaviorally at risk for adult schizophrenia. In A. Doyle, D. Gold, & D. S. Moskowitz (Eds.), *Children in families under stress: New directions for child development* (No. 24, pp. 99–112). San Francisco: Jossey-Bass.

Lee-Genest, K. (2010). *Gender and stress-related propensities to depression and substance use disorder from childhood to maturity: A prospective study.* Unpublished doctoral dissertation. Concordia University, Montréal, Canada.

Lengua, L. J., & Kovacs, E. A. (2005). Bidirectional associations between temperament and parenting and the prediction of adjustment problems in middle childhood. *Journal of Applied Developmental Psychology*, *26*(1), 21–38. doi:10.1016/j.appdev.2004.10.001

Ma, D., Kingdon, D., Serbin, L. A., Stack, D. M., Hastings, P. D., & Mills, R. S. L. (2012, July). *From internalizing problems in early childhood to clinical disorders in adolescence: A novel approach to studying risk for anxiety disorders and depression.* Symposium presented at the International Society for the Study of Behavioural Development 2012 Biennial Meeting, Edmonton, Alberta.

Martin, J., Stack, D. M., Serbin, L. A., Ledingham, J. E., & Schwartzman, A. E. (2012). Social problem solving in high-risk mother–child dyads: An intergenerational study. *Social Development*, *21*(1), 47–67. doi:10.1111/j.1467-9507.2011.00600.x

Martin-Storey, A., Ruttle, P. L., Temcheff, C. E., Serbin, L. A., Stack, D. M., Ledingham, J. E., … Schwartzman, A. E. (2013). Longitudinal and concurrent pathways to alcoholism: The importance of perception of neighborhood disorder. *Journal of Community Psychology*, *41*(2), 156–174. doi:10.1002/jcop.21520

Martin-Storey, A., Serbin, L. A., Stack, D. M., Ledingham, J. E., & Schwartzman, A. E. (2011). Self and peer perceptions of childhood aggression, social withdrawal and likeability predict adult substance abuse and dependence in men and women: A 30-year prospective longitudinal study. *Addictive Behaviors*, *36*(12), 1267–1274. doi:10.1016/j.addbeh.2011.07.043

McLoyd, V. C. (1998). Socioeconomic disadvantage and child development. *American Psychologist*, *53*(2), 185–204. doi:10.1037-0003-066X.53.2.185

Mills, R. S. L., Hastings, P. D., Serbin, L. A., Etezadi, J., Stack, D. M., Schwartzman, A. E., Li, H. H. ... Helm, J. (2012). Temperamental, parental and contextual contributors to early-emerging internalizing problems: A new integrative analysis approach. *Social Development*, *21*(2), 229–253. doi:10.1111/j.1467-9507.2011.00629.x

Musick, K., & Mare, R. D. (2006). Recent trends in the inheritance of poverty and family structure. *Social Science Research*, *35*(2), 471–499. doi:10.1016/j.ssresearch.2004.11.006

Noltemeyer, A. L., & Bush, K. R. (2013). Adversity and resilience: A synthesis of international research. *School Psychology International*, *34*(5), 474–487. doi:10.1177/0143034312472758

Pougnet, E., Serbin, L. A., Stack, D. M., & Schwartzman, A. E. (2011). Fathers and their children's cognitive and behavioural development in a disadvantaged Canadian sample. *Canadian Journal of Behavioural Science*, *43*(3), 173–182. doi:10.1037/a0023948

Pougnet, E., Serbin, L. A., Stack, D. M., Ledingham, J. E., & Schwartzman, A. E. (2012). The intergenerational continuity of fathers' absence in a socio-economically disadvantaged sample. *Journal of Marriage and Family*, *74*(3), 540–555. doi:10.1111/j.1741-3737.2012.00962.x

Reiss, F. (2013). Socioeconomic inequalities and mental health problems in children and adolescents: A systematic review. *Social Science & Medicine*, *90*, 24–31. doi:10.1016/j.socscimed.2013.04.026

Rutter, M. (1987). Psychosocial resilience and protective mechanisms. *American Journal of Orthopsychiatry*, *57*(3), 316–331. doi:10.1111/j.1939-0025.1987.tb03541.x

Rutter, M. (2013). Annual research review: Resilience – clinical implications. *The Journal of Child Psychology and Psychiatry*, *54*(4), 474–487. doi:10.1111/j.1469-7610.2012.02615.x.

Ruttle, P. L., Shirtcliff, E. A., Serbin, L. A., Ben-Dat Fisher, D., Stack, D. M., & Schwartzman, A. E. (2011). Disentangling psychobiological mechanisms underlying internalizing and externalizing behaviors in youth: Longitudinal and concurrent associations with cortisol. *Hormones and Behavior*, *59*(1), 123–132. doi:10.1016/j.yhbeh.2010.10.015

Saltaris, C., Serbin, L. A., Stack, D. M., Karp, J. A., Schwartzman, A. E., & Ledingham, J. E. (2004). Nurturing cognitive competence in preschoolers: A longitudinal study of intergenerational continuity and risk. *International Journal of Behavioral Development*, *28*(5–6), 105–115. doi:10.1080/01650250344000316

Sameroff, A. (2009). The transactional model. In A. Sameroff (Ed.), *The transactional model of development: How children and contexts shape each other* (pp. 3–21). Washington, DC,: American Psychological Association. doi:10.1037/11877-001

Schwartzman, A. E., Ledingham, J. E., & Serbin, L. A. (1985). Identification of children at risk for adult schizophrenia: A longitudinal study. *International Review of Applied Psychology*, *34*(3), 363–380. doi:10.1111j.1464-0597.1985.tb01333.x

Schwartzman, A. E., Serbin, L., Stack, D., Hodgins, S., & Ledingham, J. E. (2009). Likeability, aggression, and social withdrawal in childhood, psychiatric status in maturity: A prospective study. *European Journal of Developmental Science*, *3*(1), 51–63. doi: 10.3233/DEV-2009-3107

Schwartzman, A. E., Verlaan, P., Peters, P., & Serbin, L. A. (1995). Sex Roles as coercion. In J. McCord (Ed.), *Coercion and punishment in long-term perspective* (pp. 362–375). Cambridge: Cambridge University Press. doi:10.1017/CBO9780511527906.021

Serbin, L. A., & Bukowski, W. M. (2009). *The transition from primary to secondary schooling: Strategies for success in vulnerable populations.* Final report for Actions concertée portent sur la Persévérance et la réussite scolaire, *Fonds de recherche sur la société et la culture (FQRSC)*, Gouvernement du Québec [Grant#: 2005-PS-103501].

Serbin, L. A., Cooperman, J. M., Peters, P. L., Lehoux, P. M., Stack, D. M., & Schwartzman, A. E. (1998). Intergenerational transfer of psychosocial risk in woman with childhood histories of aggression, withdrawal, or aggression and withdrawal. *Developmental Psychology, 34*(6), 1246–1262. doi:10.1037/0012-1649.34.6.1246

Serbin, L. A., & Karp, J. (2004). The intergenerational transfer of psychosocial risk: Mediators of vulnerability and resilience. Invited chapter, *Annual Review of Psychology, 55*(1), 333–363. doi:10.1146/annurev.psych.54.101601.145228

Serbin, L. A., Kingdon, D., Ruttle, P. L., & Stack, D. M. (2015). The impact of children's internalizing and externalizing problems on parenting: Transactional processes and reciprocal change over time. *Development and Psychopathology, 27*(4), 969–986. doi:10.1017/S0954579415000632

Serbin, L. A., Moskowitz, D. S., Schwartzman, A. E., & Ledingham, J. E. (1991). Aggressive, withdrawn, and aggressive/withdrawn children in adolescence: Into the next generation. In D. J. Pepler & K. H. Rubin (Eds.), *The development and treatment of childhood aggression* (pp. 55–70). Hillsdale, NJ: Lawrence Erlbaum.

Serbin, L. A., Peters, P. L., McAffer, V. J., & Schwartzman, A. E. (1991). Childhood aggression and withdrawal as predictors of adolescent pregnancy, early parenthood and environmental risk for the next generation. *Canadian Journal of Behavioral Science, 23*(3), 318–331. doi: 10.1037/h0079014

Serbin, L. A., Peters, P. L., & Schwartzman, A. E. (1996). Longitudinal study of early childhood injuries and acute illnesses in the offspring of adolescent mothers who were aggressive, withdrawn, or aggressive-withdrawn in childhood. *Journal of Abnormal Psychology, 105*(4), 500–507. doi: 10.1037/0021-843X.105.4.500

Serbin, L. A., Stack, D. M., De Genna, N., Grunzeweig, N., Temcheff, C. E., Schwartzman, A. E., … Ledingham, J. (2004). When aggressive girls become mothers: Problems in parenting, health, and development across two generations. In M. Putallaz & K. L. Bierman (Eds.), *Aggression, antisocial behavior, and violence among girls: A developmental perspective* (pp. 262–285). New York: Guilford Press.

Serbin, L. A., Stack, D. M., Hubert, M., Schwartzman, A. E., & Ledingham, J. (2011). The transfer of developmental and health risk from women with histories of aggressive behavior to their children: Recent results from the Concordia Longitudinal Project. In M. Kerr, H. Stattin, R. E. Engels, G. Overbeek, & A.-K. Andershed (Eds.), *Understanding girls' problem behavior: How girls' delinquency develops in the context of maturity and health, co-occurring problems, and relationships* (pp. 207–230). London: Wiley-Blackwell. doi:10.1002/9780470977453.ch9

Serbin, L. A., Stack, D. M., & Kingdon, D. (2013). Academic success across the transition from primary to secondary schooling among lower-income adolescents: Understanding the effects of family resources and gender. *Journal of Youth Adolescence, 42*(9), 1331–1347. doi:10.1007/s10964-013-9987-4

Serbin, L. A., Stack, D. M., Kingdon, D., Mantis, I., & Enns, L. N. (2011). Unpacking the effects of childhood poverty: A psychosocial approach to intergenerational risk. In G. Frechet, D. Gauvreau, & J. Poirier (Eds.), *Social exclusion, poverty and social statistics: Perspectives from Quebec, Canada and abroad* (pp. 113–122). Montreal, QC: Presses de l'Université de Montréal.

Serbin, L. A., Stack, D. M., & Schwartzman, A. E. (2000). *Identification and prediction of risk and resiliency in high-risk preschoolers: An intergenerational study.* Final Report (#6070-10-5/9515); Child, Youth and Family Unit, Child and Youth Division, Health Canada.

Serbin, L. A., Stack, D. M., Schwartzman, A. E., Cooperman, J. M., Bentley, V., Saltaris, C., … Ledingham, J. E. (2002). A longitudinal study of aggressive and withdrawn children into adulthood: Patterns of parenting and risk to offspring. In R. Peters & R. McMahon (Eds.), *The effects of parental dysfunction on children* (pp. 43–69). New York: Kluwer Academic.

Serbin, L. A., Temcheff, C. E., Cooperman, J. M., Stack, D. M., Ledingham, J. E., & Schwartzman, A. E. (2010). Predicting family poverty and other threats to parenting from childhood aggression and social withdrawal: A 30-year longitudinal study. *International Journal of Behavioral Development*, *35*(2), 97–106. doi:10.1177/0165025410372008

Shirtcliff, E. A., Granger, D. A., Booth, A., & Johnson, D. (2005). Low salivary cortisol levels and externalizing behavior problems in youth. *Development and Psychopathology*, *17*(1), 167–184. doi:10.1017/S0954579405050091

Stack, D. M., Serbin, L. A., Girouard, N., Enns, L., Bentley, V., Ledingham, J. E., ... Schwartzman, A. E. (2012). The quality of the mother–child relationship in high-risk dyads: An intergenerational, longitudinal study. *Development and Psychopathology*, *24*(1), 93–105. doi:10.1017/S095457941100068X

Stack, D. M., Serbin, L. A., Schwartzman, A. E., & Ledingham, J. (2005). Girls' aggression across the life course: Long-term outcomes and inter-generational risk. In D. Pepler, K. Madsen, C. Webster, & K. Levene (Eds.), *Development and the treatment of girlhood aggression* (pp. 253–283). Hillsdale, NJ: Erlbaum.

Taylor, S. E., Lerner, J. S., Sage, R. M., Lehman, B. J., & Seeman, T. E. (2004). Early environment, emotions, responses to stress, and health. *Journal of Personality*, *72*(6), 1365–1393. doi:10.1111/j.1467-6494.2004.00300.x

Temcheff, C. E., Serbin, L., Martin-Storey, A., Stack, D., Hodgins, S., Ledingham, J. E., ... Schwartzman, A. E. (2008). Continuity and pathways from aggression in childhood to family violence in adulthood: A 30-year longitudinal study. *Journal of Family Violence*, *23*(4), 231–242. doi:10.1007/s10896-007-9147-2

Teti, D. M., & Cole, P. M. (2011). Parenting at risk: New perspectives, new approaches. *Journal of Family Psychology*, *25*(5), 625–634. doi:10.1037/a0025287

van Praag, H. M., de Kloet, R., & van Os, J. (2004). *Stress, the brain, and depression*. Cambridge: Cambridge University Press.

# 18

# Family Context and Psychopathology

## *The Mediating Role of Children's Emotion Regulation*

Amanda Sheffield Morris, Benjamin J. Houltberg, Michael M. Criss, and Cara D. Bosler

A plethora of research and clinical anecdote point to characteristics of the family as a leading *cause* of psychopathology in childhood and adolescence. Whether it is harsh parenting, a rejecting mother, partner violence, or a genetic link, the family has been implicated in most developmental theories of psychopathology. Nevertheless, little is known regarding the specific mechanisms through which families impact the development of psychopathology, despite strong links between family factors and child and adolescent adjustment. We posit that one important way the family influences children's adjustment is through its impact on children's ability to regulate emotions, or emotion regulation. Emotion regulation can be defined as the ability to manage the expression of emotions, both positive and negative, in socially appropriate and adaptive ways (Eisenberg & Morris, 2002). Difficulties in emotion regulation have been associated with the development of antisocial and aggressive behavior, as well as anxiety and depression (Eisenberg, Spinrad, & Eggum, 2010; Silk, Steinberg, & Morris, 2003). Moreover, a growing body of research indicates that aspects of the family, particularly parenting, impact children's emotion-regulation abilities (e.g., Eisenberg, Losoya, Fabes, et al., 2001; Fabes, Leonard, Kupanoff, & Martin, 2001; Morris et al., 2011). This chapter builds on the tripartite model of Morris, Silk, Steinberg, Myers, & Robinson (2007) of the impact of the family on children's emotion regulation and adjustment by reviewing recent literature and including a detailed discussion of the influences of the family on emotion regulation throughout the first two decades of life. Specifically, we focus on how the family, with a focus on parenting, affects the development of emotion regulation and adjustment in infancy and early childhood, middle childhood, adolescence, and emerging adulthood. We end our chapter with a discussion of gaps in the literature and potential future directions.

In Morris et al.'s (2007) model, they argued that the family impacts emotion regulation in three primary ways: through modeling/observation; the socialization of emotion regulation/parenting practices focused on emotion regulation; and the

*The Wiley Handbook of Developmental Psychopathology*, First Edition. Edited by Luna C. Centifanti and David M. Williams.

emotional climate of the family (i.e., attachment, parenting style, marital and sibling relations, and emotion expressivity). In this chapter, we will briefly review literature on each of these potential influences.

The observation/modeling pathway suggests that children may learn about emotions and emotion regulation by observing parents, siblings, peers, and other adults' emotional displays and interactions. Theory and research regarding modeling, emotion contagion, and social referencing provide evidence for the observational learning of emotion regulation processes (Eisenberg & Morris, 2002). Parental socialization of emotion, or parenting practices focused on emotion regulation, reflect attempts to directly teach children about emotion regulation and emotion expression, and the role of emotions in social situations. Specific parenting practices related to emotion regulation (e.g., labeling emotions, aiding children in responding to emotions) have a strong impact on the development of emotion management abilities and related outcomes, because such practices allow parents to teach children regulatory skills and strategies (Gottman, Katz, & Hooven, 1997). A parent can be supportive of emotions and help children to manage emotions on their own, what Gottman et al. (1997) call "emotion coaching." Alternatively, parents can dismiss an emotion or derogate a child for expressing an emotion. As children grow older, parents become less actively involved in children's emotion-regulation strategies, with parental attempts to regulate their children's emotions gradually giving way to children's self-regulation (Eisenberg & Morris, 2002). Nevertheless, parents remain an important influence in adolescent and emerging adults' emotion regulation by providing emotional support and general guidance.

Research indicates that the emotional climate of the family (Darling & Steinberg, 1993) shapes children's emotion regulation and expression by providing the emotional foundation of the parent–child relationship. Children residing in a family that is warm and supportive and has clear rules and limits (parents are authoritative) are typically emotionally secure, know what to expect with regard to emotions displayed in the home, and have parents who respond appropriately and consistently to their emotional displays (Chan, Bowes, & Wyver, 2009; Snyder et al., 2013). In contrast, children residing in families where parents are overly controlling, harsh, and/or permissive may experience life as unpredictable and adults as hostile. In such situations, children are at risk for becoming highly emotionally reactive or emotionally blunted (see Morris et al., 2007; Morris, Cui, & Steinberg, 2013).

In applying a developmental focus to the study of the influence of family on emotion regulation and psychopathology, it is important to have a foundational understanding of development and to know key developmental processes at different ages. Thus, we begin each section of our chapter with a discussion of key developmental tasks in relation to emotion regulation and mental health. Then, we discuss studies that have examined both positive and negative aspects of the family in relation to emotion regulation and adjustment. It should be noted that despite our strong focus on parenting as an influence on children's development within the family, we also emphasize the whole family system in this chapter for several reasons. First, family systems develop qualities that characterize regular patterns of interaction within the family system as a whole (Whitchurch & Constantine, 1993), and such interaction patterns likely affect the development of emotion regulation (Henry, Morris, & Harrist, 2015; Houltberg, Henry, & Morris, 2012). Second, family systems are composed of subsystems, including the couple, parent–child dyads and siblings that operate distinctly but are connected to and combine to produce the whole. These subsystems are important in the development of emotion regulation and psychopathology as well (Henry et al., 2015), and repeated interactions within the family system and subsystems can create an emotional climate that significantly impacts child and adolescent development (Barber & Beuhler, 1996; Cox & Paley, 2003; Parke, 2004).

## Infancy and Early Childhood (Birth–4 Years)

It is beyond the scope of this chapter to review the significant amount of development that occurs between birth to four years of age. Thus, we focus on the most salient developmental factors that influence the development of emotion regulation during the first years of life. In general, as infants and children grow older, they begin to rely more on cognitive strategies for emotion regulation (Eisenberg & Morris, 2002; Walden & Smith, 1997). Their understanding of emotions and attentional development aid children in regulating emotions as they develop. Indeed, children's ability to shift their attention away from emotion arousing events is an important emotion regulation strategy, and the attentional processes present early in life develop as a result of increases in visual, auditory, and memory abilities (Wilson & Gottman, 1996). In the first three months of life, children's emotion regulation consists of simple behaviors and reflexes. Infants regulate emotions by sucking to self-soothe or turning their head away from a distracting stimulus. As infants develop, they become more aware of different arousal states and realize that their emotions can be influenced by their own actions and the actions of others. Around age one, infants are more capable of distracting themselves and shifting attention away from distressful stimuli, and are better able to effectively communicate their emotional needs to care-givers (Eisenberg & Morris, 2002; Kopp, 1989).

Emotion regulation among toddlers and preschoolers becomes progressively more advanced with age, as cognitive ability increases significantly. For example, representational and recall memory improve, and children begin to understand the causes of emotional distress. Children's development of self-awareness allows them to understand that they not only feel distress but can minimize it through their own initiative (Kopp, 1989). In addition, children begin to use more complex emotion-regulation strategies. They regulate sensory intake (e.g., cover eyes or ears), seek nurturance, use reassuring self-talk, remove themselves from or avoid distressing situations, and alter their goals to avoid distress (e.g., playing by oneself rather than with an angry peer; Bretherton, McNew, & Beeghly-Smith, 1981; Thompson, 1990). Another important development in early childhood relevant to the development of emotion regulation involves language comprehension and production as there is an increase in language regarding emotion between 18 and 30 months. For example, children learn how to use emotion labels to comment on their own feelings and communicate with others about emotion during this developmental period (Bretherton, Fritz, Zahn-Waxler, & Ridgeway, 1986).

### Modeling

Throughout early development, various factors in the family influence emotion regulation, including modeling. The modeling hypothesis suggests that parents' own emotional profiles and interactions implicitly teach children which emotions are acceptable and expected in the family environment, and how to manage the experience of those emotions. Children learn that certain situations provoke emotions, and they observe the reactions of others to know how they "should" react in similar situations (Denham, Mitchell-Copeland, Strandberg, Auerbach, & Blair, 1997). The overall amount of emotion in the family, particularly negative emotionality, may actually induce negative emotions in children. Studies suggest that emotional contagion, or the "catching" of an emotion, occurs in early infancy and beyond. Emotion contagion is said to occur when a facial, vocal, or emotional gesture generates a similar response in another person (Saarni, Mumme, & Campos, 1998). For example, 2-day-old infants cry in response to the cry of another infant, especially if the cry is genuine, rather than in response to a computer-generated cry or their own tape-recorded cry (Martin & Clark, 1982). Infants also respond to and imitate parents' emotional responses, and researchers suggest that mothers' emotional expressions directly induce affect in their infants (Termine & Izard, 1988). Infants are capable of matching others' facial expressions, and long-term exposure to specific affective displays impacts emotional development. For example, in a face-to-face interaction study (Malatesta & Haviland, 1982), mother–infant pairs showed similarities in their facial expression of emotions and in the frequency of specific emotions expressed, with similarities increasing from 3 to 6 months. In other words, compared to younger infants, older infants were more adept at duplicating the facial expression of their mothers. Another study found that high rates of maternal modeling of joy at 2½ months were related to increased amounts of joy when infants were 7½ months (Malatesta, Grigoryev, Lamb, Albin, & Culver, 1986). In a sample of preschool children, Denham et al. (1997) found that children displayed more positive affect during peer interactions if their parents were more affectionate and warm at home.

Research on children of depressed and anxious mothers also points to emotional contagion and modeling processes. Zahn-Waxler and Kochanska (1990) found that children of depressed mothers were more likely than children of non-depressed mothers to experience guilt and have emotion-regulation problems. Similarly, Lundy, Field, and Pickens (1996) found that infants of depressed mothers showed less modeling of facial expressions than infants of non-depressed mothers. In a literature review focusing on the responsivity of depressed mothers' infants, Field, Diego, and Hernandez-Reif (2009) compiled evidence that infants of depressed mothers displayed poorer emotional responsiveness (e.g., fewer happy expressions, lower attentiveness, less empathetic responses) than infants of non-depressed mothers. Apart from the obvious genetic linkages, one reason for these findings may be that children internalize the strategies and emotions of their care-givers (e.g., Parke, 1994; Thayer & Meyers, 1998). Parents who experience high levels of daily stress and/or have different forms of psychopathology may have problems with emotion regulation themselves, but they also may promote dysregulation in their children through modeling and similar processes (Cole, Michel, & Teti, 1994).

Another way that children and infants learn about emotions and emotion regulation is through social referencing. Social referencing is the process of looking to another person for information about how to respond, think, or feel about an environmental event or stimuli (Saarni et al., 1998). For example, using the visual cliff paradigm (a procedure using an apparatus designed to test infants' depth perception), researchers found that (1) when parents displayed a fearful facial expression infants did not cross, (2) when parents displayed an angry face few infants crossed, and

(3) when parents displayed a happy face most infants crossed (Sorce, Emde, Campos, & Klinnert, 1985). Another study found that when a stranger entered the room a child smiled more at the stranger if the mother spoke to the infant in a positive tone (Feinman & Lewis, 1983).

## Emotion Socialization

The socialization of emotion regulation starts in toddlerhood, when parents first begin to talk with children about emotions and how to manage them (Eisenberg & Morris, 2002). As children age, parents begin to teach them about emotions by labeling them, helping them to manage emotions, and by responding to emotions in specific ways (Morris et al., 2011). Such behaviors set the foundation for children's emotion-regulation abilities and emotional expression. For example, Denham (1993) found that parents' calm/neutral reactions to toddlers' anger was associated with lower levels of expressed anger and fearfulness in other contexts. In another study, results indicated that maternal emotion socialization, including discussion of emotions as well as reactions to the child's emotions, predicted better emotional understanding in preschoolers (Denham, Zoller, & Couchoud, 1994). Similarly, Garner and Estep (2010) found that preschoolers whose parents responded angrily to their negative emotions were more likely to respond with non-constructive anger in other situations.

## Emotional Climate

Parent–child attachment can be thought of as a reflection of the emotional climate between parent and child in that it sets the foundation for social and emotional development, and subsequent beliefs about the self in relation to others. In the first few years of a child's life, the parent is responsible for much of a child's emotion regulation. As such, parents must respond to children's emotional needs in a consistent, nurturing manner that facilitates the development of a secure emotional attachment to the care-giver. As is widely known, a secure attachment is thought to reflect a responsive, sensitive parenting style, whereas an insecure attachment reflects inconsistent and unresponsive parenting (Bowlby, 1988). Research regarding specific attachment classifications assessed via the Strange Situation indicates that infants who are insecurely attached at the end of the first year of life display distinctive patterns of emotional arousal during separation and reunion with care-givers, and exhibit less optimal regulation strategies than securely attached infants. Insecure-resistant infants exhibit more separation distress, take longer to recover from distress, and display fewer self-regulatory behaviors as compared to securely attached infants. Insecure-avoidant infants typically display less intense separation distress, use more self-comforting strategies, focus more on toys and less on the mother during reunions, and show little social referencing, when compared to securely attached infants. The insecure-avoidant pattern of emotionality and regulation suggests that these infants have found alternate methods of emotion regulation (methods not related to the care-giver), or that these infants are masking negative affect (Cassidy, 1994; Malatesta, 1990).

Research supports such a premise. For example, Gaensbauer, Connell, and Schultz (1983) observed infants between 12 and 18 months in a laboratory paradigm assessing attachment behaviors and infant's discrete emotional expressions. The authors reported that infant emotionality and attachment/affiliative behaviors were closely related. In particular, infants' distress, fear, anger, and sadness were associated with insecure maternal attachment and affiliative behaviors in several laboratory situations (e.g., stranger approach, maternal separation), whereas infants' pleasure and interest were related to secure attachment and affiliative behaviors. In another study focused on preschoolers' emotional competence and behavior problems, preschoolers categorized as insecurely attached (especially those who utilized highly coercive attachment strategies), as measured by the Strange Situation, scored lower on emotional understanding and emotion regulation than their securely attached counterparts (Kidwell et al., 2010). Belsky, Fish, and Isabella (1991) examined the stability of infant emotionality assessed observationally at 3, 9, and 12 months. Their results demonstrated that continuity and discontinuity in both positive and negative aspects of the family context interacted to predict attachment security and children's emotionality. Specifically, infants' display of less negative and more positive affect at 12 months was linked to mental health in mothers and fathers, adaptive marital relations, harmonious mother/care-giver–infant interactions, and high levels of parental engagement. In contrast, infants' display of high negative and low positive affect was associated with less optimal parent personality, negative marital relations, negative parent–child interactions, and insecure parent–child attachment. These results indicate that changes and stability in children's attachment, emotionality, and emotion regulation are associated with the emotional climate of the family.

### Linking Emotion Regulation to Behavior

A strong link between emotion regulation in infancy and early childhood and behavior problems has been established in the literature. For instance, in a longitudinal study investigating the impact of emotion-regulation strategies on behavior, results indicated that negative emotionality at age 18 months was significantly correlated with externalizing behavior at 18 and 42 months (Supplee, Skuban, Shaw, & Prout, 2009). In a similar study, Halligan et al. (2013) assessed children's emotion regulation and behavior problems at 12–18 months and again at 5 years. Results indicated that better emotion regulation at 12–18 months was significantly associated fewer externalizing behaviors concurrently and at age 5. Another investigation focusing on predictors of internalizing behavior found that negative emotionality in infancy was linked to later internalizing problems (Shaw, Keenan, Vondra, Delliquadri, & Giovannelli, 1997). In a recent study evaluating emotion regulation in Head Start children, results indicated that children with poor regulation skills were more likely to have internalizing problems (Morgan, Izard, & Hyde, 2014). This research demonstrates that emotion regulation is an important predictor of behavior problems in young children, and points to potential mechanisms that underlie the link between family factors and child adjustment.

## Middle Childhood (Ages 5–9 Years)

The cognitive advances that occur in middle childhood increase the ability for more self-monitoring, problem-solving skills and consideration of other people's perspectives (Berk, 2012). The interaction between increases in brain development and environmental expectations associated with school-aged children also may contribute to increases in self-control and behavior regulation. These changes require an increased level of autonomy, emotion regulation abilities and more advanced problem solving strategies that utilize internal and external resources in an effort to adapt to new environments and situations (Davies & Cummings, 2006; Stroufe, Egeland, Carlson, & Collins,2005). Difficulties in these domains during middle childhood may reflect previous maladaptation in infancy and toddlerhood but also may emerge from the inability to adjust to new developmental tasks that are required during this period of development (Masten & Cicchetti, 2010).

Children at this age also begin to develop meta-emotion capabilities and learn to employ strategies for redirecting emotional responses such as the use of distraction and cognitive reinterpretations (Eisenberg & Morris, 2002). Eisenberg and Morris (2002) highlight the increased reliance on intraorganismic regulation, advances in internal cognitive coping strategies and increased ability to select strategies to deal with stressors as among the important changes that enhance emotion regulation abilities in middle childhood. Although children advance in the ability to regulate their own emotions, parents continue to play an active role in socializing emotion regulation during this age period (Eisenberg, Cumberland, & Spinrad, 1998). For example, parents often provide the scaffolding for moving from mainly "other regulation" that is required in infancy and toddlerhood to more self-regulation in middle childhood (Saarni, 1999; Sameroff, 2010). These changes require that parents continue to adapt parenting techniques to meet the developmental and temperamental needs of the child (Rothbart, Ahadi, Hershey, & Fisher, 2001).

## Emotion Socialization

Interactions with parents in middle childhood become the foundation for developing emotion-regulation abilities that translate to expanding interpersonal relationships (e.g., peers, teachers) that occur with school-aged children (Morris et al., 2007). When parents are supportive and responsive to children's emotional expressions and provide guidance in how to manage emotions, children at this age learn how to regulate emotions in socially adaptive ways (Davidov & Grusec 2006; Eisenberg, Cumberland, Spinrad, et al., 2001; Fabes et al., 2001; Repetti, Taylor, & Seeman, 2002). Parents who view children's negative affect as developmentally normal and as opportunities for teaching (e.g. emotion coaching) tend to have children who show greater capacity for emotion regulation in middle childhood (Gottman, Katz, & Hooven, 1996; Katz & Gottman, 1997). Conversely, parents that dismiss negative affective states of children or attempt to protect children from negative emotions (e.g. emotion-dismissing) may inhibit children from learning how to effectively manage emotions on their own (Cassano & Zeman, 2010) and serve as a risk factor for poor emotion regulation and behavioral problems (Lunkenheimer, Shields, & Cortina, 2007).

## Emotional Climate

In addition to specific parenting practices, the overall emotional climate of the family has been shown to be important in the socialization of emotion regulation (Morris et al., 2007). The quality of relationships in the family (e.g. parent–child attachment, parenting style) and the day-to-day expression of positive and negative emotions between family members relate to emotional security that can impact feelings of safety in expressing and regulating emotions during middle childhood (Blair, 2010; Cummings & Davies, 1996; Darling & Steinberg, 1993; Eisenberg, et al., 1998). Alternatively, chaotic and disruptive home environments may negatively impact parent–child attachment and a sense of safety, security, and predictability (see Morris et al., 2013 for a review) which can compromise a child's ability to employ strategies for regulating emotions (Blair, 2010; Kerns & Brumariu, 2014; Valiente et al., 2006).

Although much of the research on the socialization of emotions in middle childhood has focused on the parent–child subsystem, inter-parental conflict and sibling relationships also can contribute to the emotional climate of the family and thus impact children's emotion regulation. For example, children exposed to intimate partner violence in middle childhood (ages 6–8) demonstrated higher levels of observed emotion dysregulation (Zarling et al., 2013). This finding is consistent with research that showed that exposure to high levels of parental conflict negatively influences children's ability to manage their own emotions (Davies & Cummings, 1994). Children also spend increasing amounts of time alone with siblings in middle childhood (McHale, Updegraff, & Whiteman, 2012) and engage in emotionally charged interactions (Kramer & Kowal, 2005). Thus, the quality of the relationship and nature of interactions with siblings may be formative in children's emotion-regulation abilities (Padilla-Walker, Harper, & Jensen, 2010). However, there is a need for further research to examine overall family characteristics and interactions in subsystems that shape children's emotion regulation (Fosco & Grych, 2013).

## Linking Emotion Regulation to Behavior

Emotion-regulation difficulties in middle childhood have been linked to both externalizing and internalizing problem behavior (Eisenberg, Cumberland, Spinrad, et al., 2001; Rydell, Berlin, & Bohlin, 2003) and to social competence and prosocial outcomes (Spinrad et al., 2006). Further, there is evidence that decreased emotion regulation in middle childhood is predictive of later adolescent internalizing and externalizing behavior (Caspi, Henry, McGee, Moffitt, & Silva, 1995). Several longitudinal studies have established the link between emotion dysregulation and externalizing behaviors in middle childhood (see Röll, Koglin, & Petermann, 2012 for review). These findings have been established in normative and non-normative samples and identify emotion dysregulation as placing children at significant risk for later externalizing and aggressive problem behavior (Eisenberg, Carlo, Murphy, & Van Court, 1995; Eisenberg et al., 1997; Kim & Cicchetti, 2010). Additionally, Kim-Spoon, Cicchetti, and Rogosch (2013) found high levels of emotion regulation and low levels of emotion reactivity at age 7 predicted low levels of internalizing symptoms at age 10. This finding is consistent with studies that have found concurrent negative associations between emotion regulation and internalizing problems (Silk et al., 2003). Thus, the development of emotion-regulation strategies in middle childhood is critical to adjustment, and the inability to manage emotions can lead to both internalizing and externalizing problems (Morris et al., 2011).

In middle childhood, there is an increasing amount of empirical support for emotion-regulation processes as an underlying mechanism for how the family and parenting are related to child adjustment. For example, emotion coaching has been shown to be indirectly related to child outcomes through its direct effect on emotion regulation in both concurrent (Ramsden & Hubbard, 2002) and longitudinal studies (Cunningham, Kliewer, & Garner, 2009; Gottman et al., 1996). Further, Dunsmore, Booker, and Ollendick (2013) found an indirect link (via emotion regulation) between maternal emotional coaching and internalizing problem behavior in a sample of children and early adolescents diagnosed with oppositional defiant disorder. Moreover, emotion regulation has been shown to mediate the relationship between secure attachment in early childhood and less anxiety in late childhood (Bosquet & Egeland, 2006; Brumariu & Kerns, 2013). Additionally, aspects of negative parenting (e.g., chaotic homes, negative affect, psychological control) have been linked to emotion regulation problems, which in turn, are related to children's externalizing and internalizing symptoms (Chang, Shelleby, Cheong, & Shaw, 2012; Eisenberg, Cumberland, Spinrad, et al., 2001; Valiente et al., 2006). Further, inter-parental violence has been associated with internalizing and externalizing symptoms of children a year later through its association with emotion regulation in a sample of children ranging from 6 to 8 at initial data collection (Zarling et al., 2013).

## Adolescence (Ages 10–17 Years)

Although early research may have overstated the amount of storm and stress that occurs during adolescence, this developmental period, nevertheless, is a critical transitional period characterized by a number of developmental transformations within the youth and within the parent–child relationship that are pertinent to this chapter (Steinberg, 1990; Steinberg & Morris, 2001). For instance, there are advances in cognitive and social cognitive abilities as adolescents display more advanced perspective taking (Selman, 1980) and abstract thinking abilities compared to childhood (Smetana, 1989; Steinberg, 2011). In addition, transformations in physical appearance associated with puberty often lead to changes in how the adolescent views him or herself but also how others inside (e.g., parents, siblings) and outside (e.g., teachers, peers) the family view the adolescent (Mezulis, Hyde, Simonson, & Charbonneau, 2011; Paikoff & Brooks-Gunn, 1991). The socially mediated effects of hormonal changes and associated changes in physical appearance place the adolescent in new situations, contexts, and quasi-adult roles (e.g., employee, romantic partner) that are potentially both emotionally exhilarating and potentially overwhelming, posing new challenges for the adolescent's emotion-regulation capabilities (Steinberg et al., 2006). In addition to puberty, adolescence is characterized by maturation in brain regions and systems tied to self-regulation (behavior and emotion) and the evaluation of risk and rewards, many of which play a role in the development of behavior problems (Paus, 2009; Steinberg et al., 2006). For instance, research has shown greater activation of subcortical limbic regions tied to emotionality, such as the amygdala, among adolescents compared to adults (Ernst et al., 2005; Hare et al., 2008), suggesting that adolescents may be more susceptible to emotional interference (Hare et al., 2008).

In addition to the developmental changes within the adolescent, there are also changes in the relationships between adolescents and their parents. Specifically, while parent–child relationships during early and middle childhood tend to be more vertical and imbalanced with the parent often unilaterally making decisions (Collins, Madsen,

& Susman-Stillman, 2002), parent–child relationships during adolescence become more horizontal, balanced, and peer-like (Paikoff & Brooks-Gunn, 1991; Steinberg, 1990). Moreover, adolescents' perceptions of parental authority changes as youth begin to see their parents as having less jurisdiction over certain topics (e.g., clothing and music; Smetana, 2000). In addition, evidence from the literature has indicated that adolescents spend less time with families (and more with peers) compared to early to middle childhood (Larson, Richards, Moneta, Holmbeck, & Duckett, 1996). Despite these developmental transformations, the existing evidence has clearly indicated that families continue to be important contexts for socialization during adolescence (Collins, Maccoby, Steinberg, Hetherington, & Bornstein, 2000).

## Emotion Socialization

Consistent with the theoretical model proposed by Morris and colleagues (2007), evidence from the literature has demonstrated significant links between emotion-related parenting practices and adolescent's emotion regulatory abilities (Buckholdt, Parra, & Jobe-Shields, 2014; Cunningham et al., 2009; Hersh & Hussong, 2009; Roth, Assor, Niemiec, Ryan, & Deci, 2009). Overall, the findings indicate that emotion socialization efforts marked by high level of emotion coaching, acceptance, and parental awareness of emotions and low levels of emotion dismissing/rejection have been found to be associated with high levels of effective emotion regulation during adolescence. For example, using a sample of 9–13-year-old African American youth, Cunningham et al. (2009) reported that high levels of positive emotion socialization (measured by a meta-emotion philosophy interview) were significantly related to better adolescent emotion regulation (i.e., negative reactivity, emotion regulation, control of emotions). In addition, Hersh and Hussong (2009) found that high levels of observed parent emotion coaching were significantly related to low levels of adolescent daily negative mood (assessed via experience sampling method). These findings are consistent with a study by Buckholdt et al. (2014) who found that high levels of parental invalidation of emotions were related to high levels of youth emotion regulation difficulties in a sample of 12–18 year olds. In addition, the results from Roth and colleagues (2009) indicated that high levels of maternal and paternal conditional regard (i.e., negative emotion socialization) were significantly related to high levels of anger and fear dysregulation.

Whereas parental dismissing attitudes/behaviors in reaction to emotions have been linked to poor emotion regulation, other social scientists have shown that similar parental responses to autonomy-related issues also are related to adolescent emotion dysregulation (Cui, Morris, Criss, Houltberg, & Silk, 2014; Liew, Kwok, Chang, Chang, & Yeh, 2014; Luebbe, Bump, Fussner, & Rulon, 2014; Walton & Flouri, 2010). Using a sample of Chinese American adolescents, Liew et al. (2014) found that high levels of parental autonomy support were significantly related to high levels of adolescent emotional self-control, executive functioning, and anger control and low levels of negative emotionality. In addition, Luebbe et al. (2014) reported that maternal (but not paternal) psychological control was significantly and positively related to emotional (anger, sadness, and worry combined) dysregulation in sample of sixth- and seventh-graders. These results are consistent with Cui et al. (2014) who found that high levels of parental psychological control were significantly related to low levels of anger (but not sadness) regulation in a sample of adolescents (ages 10–18 years).

In a pair of studies using a sample of 11–18 year old youth in London, Walton and Flouri (2010) demonstrated that high levels of parent psychological control were significantly related to high levels of emotional difficulties.

## Modeling

In addition to parenting practices and styles, parents may shape their adolescent's emotion regulatory skills through their own expression and regulation of emotions (Buckholdt et al., 2014; Fosco & Grych, 2013; Jaser et al., 2008). Labeled "observation" in the model proposed by Morris et al. (2007), this component is based on the supposition that the development of adolescent emotion regulation is shaped, in part, through various processes such has modeling, social referencing, and emotion contagion. The evidence in the existing literature supports this hypothesis. For example, using a sample of fourth- and fifth-graders, Fosco and Grych (2013) reported the high levels of maternal and paternal emotion regulation were significantly related to high levels of youth emotion regulation. Moreover, Jaser et al. (2008) found that high levels of maternal sadness and depression were significantly related to high levels of adolescent affective problems. Similarly, Buckholdt et al. (2014) documented that high levels of parent emotion-regulation difficulties were related to high levels of poor youth emotion regulation.

## Emotional Climate

Research also has investigated whether adolescent emotion regulation is shaped by the emotional climate of the family. Collectively, this body of literature has demonstrated that effective emotion-regulatory skills are best facilitated in the context of parent–child relationships marked by a secure attachment, high levels of positive relationship quality (e.g., warmth, acceptance, emotional support), and low levels of conflict and resentment (Fosco & Grych, 2013; Roth et al., 2009; Walton & Flouri, 2010). In contrast, high levels of inter-parental conflict have been linked to the development of negative emotionality and emotion dysregulation (Fosco & Grych, 2013; Schwarz, Stutz, & Ledermann, 2012; Siffert & Schwarz, 2011). Other researchers, focusing on family-level variables, have demonstrated that adolescents are better able to regulate their negative emotions when living in families characterized by high levels of family positivity/expressiveness (Fosco & Grych, 2013) and cohesion (Adrian et al., 2009) and low levels of emotionally invalidating climates (e.g., negativity, conflict, emotional neglect, and abuse; Adrian et al., 2009; Sim, Adrian, Zeman, Cassano, & Friedrich, 2009).

## Linking Emotion Regulation to Behavior

Whereas a number of family processes and relationships have been linked to the development of emotion regulation during adolescence, several investigations have studied whether emotion regulation, in turn, is related to adolescent behavior problems and adjustment. Collectively, this body of research has shown that high levels of emotion regulation are related to low levels of externalizing behavior (e.g., aggression, conduct problems; Adrian et al., 2009; Buckholdt et al., 2014; Cui et al., 2014;

Cunningham et al., 2009; Siffert & Schwarz, 2011; Walton & Flouri, 2010) and internalizing symptoms (e.g., depression, anxiety; Adrian et al., 2009; Buckholdt et al., 2014; Cui et al., 2014; Cunningham et al., 2009; Luebbe et al., 2014; Siffert & Schwarz; 2011). Moreover, several investigations have found that emotion regulation mediates the link between family processes and relationships, and adolescent behavior problems (Buckholdt et al., 2014; Cui et al., 2014; Luebbe et al., 2014; Ramsden & Hubbard, 2002; Siffert & Schwarz, 2011; Walton & Flouri, 2010). For example, using a sample of 10–18-year-old adolescents from predominantly high-risk, low-income, ethnic minority families, Cui et al. (2014) reported that youth anger regulation (but not sadness regulation) significantly mediated the links between psychological control and adolescent aggressive behavior and depressive symptoms. In addition, Siffert and Schwarz (2011) found that the association between parental negative conflict resolution and child behavior problems (i.e., internalizing and externalizing problems) was significantly mediated by adolescent maladaptive emotion regulation in a sample of 9–12-year-old Swiss youth. Moreover, the results from the study by Ramsden and Hubbard (2002) indicated that the links between family negative expressiveness and parental acceptance and child aggression were mediated by youth emotion regulation. Walton and Flouri (2010) reported that emotion-regulation difficulties mediated the link between parental warmth and conduct problems among British youth (11–18 years old). Finally, in a somewhat more complex structural equation model, Buckholdt et al. (2014) found that the links between parental invalidation of emotions and adolescent externalizing and internalizing problems were mediated by adolescent emotion dysregulation. In addition, parental invalidation of emotions was significantly predicted by parent emotion dysregulation.

## Emerging Adulthood (Ages 18–25 Years)

While obvious transformations occur during adolescence, emerging adulthood also is characterized by several critical transformations with respect to brain development and changes in the parent–child relationship. A growing body of evidence has indicated that maturity in the prefrontal cortex continues throughout the emerging adult years (i.e., 18-25 years; Eshel, Nelson, Blair, Pine, & Ernst, 2007; Gogtay & Thompson, 2010). This region has been linked to higher-order cognitive processes, such as reasoning, self-control, and decision making (Gogtay & Thompson, 2010). These advances, coupled with less activation of the amygdala region, may allow emerging adults greater resources when dealing with emotionally stressful situations (Hare et al., 2008).

In addition to brain maturation, emerging adulthood also is characterized by transformations in the parent–child relationship (Arnett, 2000; Lefkowitz, 2005). For instance, 62% of emerging adults move away from home and their parents (National Center for Educational Statistics, 2003). Perhaps in responses to this move, emerging adults often report increases in levels of closeness, mutuality, and open communication and lower levels of conflict with their parents compared to late adolescence (Lefkowitz, 2005; Morgan, Thorne, & Zurbriggen, 2010). Indeed, children who remain at home in their late teens and early 20s report having a poorer relationship with their parents (e.g., greater conflict and lower closeness) and having more adjustment difficulties in comparison to those who left home (Dubas & Petersen, 1996;

O'Connor, Allen, Bell, & Hauser, 1996). It is not surprising, thus, that families continue to have an impact on the lives of emerging adults (Arnett, 2000).

## Emotion Socialization

Research examining the impact of families on emotion regulation during emerging adulthood has focused almost entirely on convenient college student samples. Moreover, only one published investigation that we could find explicitly examined the link between emotion-related parenting practices and emotion regulation. In particular, using a sample of 18–25-year-old undergraduate students, Buckholdt, Parra, and Jobe-Shields (2009) found that high levels of negative emotion socialization (i.e., punishment, neglect, and magnification) were significantly related to poor emotion regulation. In addition to emotion socialization, other researchers have found that other forms of parenting practices were related to emotion regulation (Fischer, Forthun, Pidcock, & Dowd, 2007; Manzeske & Stright, 2009). For instance, Manzeske and Stright (2009) and Fischer et al. (2007) both found that high levels of psychological control were related to high levels of emotion-regulation difficulties.

## Emotional Climate

In addition to parenting practices, other investigators have found that the family emotional climate is linked to emotion regulation among emerging adults. As during adolescence, the evidence from this body of literature suggests that mutually responsive, supportive, and open communication in the context of various family relationships is related to high levels of emotion regulation. For example, parent–emerging adult interactions characterized by secure attachments and high levels of mutually responsive interactions have been linked to more effective emotion-regulation strategies (Fischer et al. 2007; Marganska, Gallagher, & Miranda, 2013; McCarthy, Lambert, & Moller, 2006). Moreover, adaptive emotion regulation has been significantly predicted by high levels of family cohesion, adaptability, and support and low levels of family conflict (Fosco, Caruthers, & Dishion, 2012; McCarthy, Lambert, & Seraphine, 2004). Other studies have found that high levels of positive family expressiveness and low levels of negative family expressiveness were significantly related to high levels of emotion regulation during emerging adulthood (Morelen, Jacob, Suveg, Jones, & Thomassin, 2013).

## Linking Emotion Regulation to Behavior

Similar to research conducted with adolescent samples, research focusing on emerging adulthood has indicated a significant link between emotion regulation and adjustment difficulties. Specifically, high levels of emotion regulation have been linked to low levels of externalizing behaviors (e.g., aggression, hostility, substance use; Fischer et al., 2007; Fosco et al., 2012) and internalizing problems (e.g., anxiety, depressive symptoms; Chandley, Luebbe, Messman-Moore, & Ward, 2014; Marganska et al., 2013). In addition, investigators have found emotion regulation to significantly mediate or explain the link between family processes/factors and externalizing and internalizing problems (e.g., Fischer et al., 2007; Fosco et al., 2012; Marganska et al.,

2013). For example, in an investigation conducted by Fosco and colleagues (2012), the authors reported that emotion regulation (i.e., effortful control) significantly mediated the links between family cohesion and family conflict and emotional distress (i.e., depression, anxiety) in emerging adulthood. In addition, Marganska et al. (2013) found that emotion regulation mediated the link between adult attachment and anxiety and depression among college students. Moreover, Fischer and colleagues (2007) showed that the link between parent problems (i.e., poor parenting) and alcohol problems (e.g., binge drinking) was mediated by emotion regulation.

## Conclusions and Future Directions

Consistent with the theoretical model proposed by Morris et al. (2007), the research reviewed in this chapter illustrates that families and parents can influence emotion regulation during infancy, childhood, adolescence, and emerging adulthood through observation/modeling, the emotion socialization efforts of the parents, and the emotional climate (e.g., parent–child relationship quality, marital conflict) of the family. The findings from studies conducted in adolescence and emerging adulthood are especially impressive as they suggest that families still can influence the emotional processes and regulatory skills of individuals beyond childhood, which has traditionally been viewed as a sensitive period for emotional development (Bowlby, 1988). It is possible that the plasticity of emotion regulatory skills could be attributed to the amount of brain maturation that occurs during key developmental periods such as infancy and adolescence, particularly in the prefrontal cortex (Anderson, 2002; Eshel et al., 2007; Gogtay & Thompson, 2010; Hare et al., 2008; Steinberg et al., 2006). That is, exposure to effective emotion socialization and supportive family environments may be especially important and critical during key periods of brain development.

Indeed, there are key developmental transitions where children may be particularly vulnerable to developing problematic behavior. For example, the transition from middle childhood to adolescence is characterized by many biological, cognitive, and social changes that have been associated with increased risk for psychopathology (Steinberg & Morris, 2001). Thus, developmental history and previous experiences can predispose children to future problematic behaviors; however, difficulty in developmental transitions and negative experiences also can contribute to whether children develop psychopathology even in the absence of previous maladaptive behaviors. Therefore, it is important for research to examine key socialization factors and unique challenges within each developmental period that may contribute to future psychopathology to increase understanding for prevention and intervention efforts aimed at promoting child and adolescent emotional health (Greenberg, 2006).

In infancy and early childhood, the development of emotion regulation is intimately tied to the development of close relationships, and the attachment relationship with the care-giver is a primary source of emotional support for young children. The research presented suggests a fairly strong relation between young children's attachment and emotion regulation. There is less empirical research on the ways in which attachment affects children's emotion regulation as they grow older. It could be argued that the developmental changes that occur later in a child's life (e.g., cognitive and physiological changes) weaken the association between emotion regulation and attachment. Alternatively, to the extent that the security of attachment reflects and shapes personality processes related to emotion regulation, it is likely that early attachment relations underlie the development of emotion regulation throughout the lifespan (Cassidy, 1994). Indeed, parents who are responsive and sensitive in children's early years most likely maintain those characteristics throughout a child's life.

It should also be noted that not all families may be equally influential. For instance, as children grow older, parental socialization efforts are more likely to be effective in the context of open, synchronous, and mutually responsive relationships (Criss, Shaw, & Ingoldsby, 2003; Kochanska & Murray, 2000; Maccoby, 1992). That is, having cold, distant, or even nonexistent relationships with one's family members likely lessens their collective impact on emotion regulation during the second decade of life. Likewise, the impact of families on emotion regulation in emerging adulthood may be influenced by whether individuals transitioned into full-fledged adulthood with its associated responsibilities (e.g., having children, working full-time) or attended parent-sponsored college (Arnett, 2000; White et al., 2006). Indeed, just as the role of parents in the lives of their children is often influenced by the developmental transformations and transitions during adolescence (e.g., puberty, adolescent getting a job; Paikoff & Brooks-Bunn, 1991; Steinberg, 1990), the impact of families on emotion regulation in emerging adulthood also may be shaped by comparable developmental milestones and transitions.

One noticeable gap in the literature is that few studies have examined specific emotions when studying emotion regulation and adjustment, particularly during infancy and early childhood. Some researchers have proposed an emotion specificity hypothesis arguing that children and adolescents with externalizing problems display more anger dysregulation in a negative family context, while children with internalizing problems display more sadness dysregulation (Eisenberg, Cumberland, et al., 2001; Zeman, Cassano, Perry-Parrish, & Stegall, 2006). More research is needed to support such a premise, and is important for understanding the development of psychopathology and points for intervention. Another gap in the literature is the relative lack of longitudinal investigations focused on the impact of families on emotion regulation. Longitudinal research could add to our understanding of this area of research in three major ways. First, longitudinal research would allow investigators to determine, for instance, whether families/parenting shapes emotion regulation or whether emotion regulation influences families and parenting factors. Given that numerous studies have shown reciprocal links between parenting and behavior regulation (e.g., antisocial behavior; Laird, Pettit, Bates, & Dodge, 2003; Lansford et al., 2011), it is possible that emotion regulation may be related to subsequent parenting and family factors. Indeed, two published investigations have provided support for this assertion (Eisenberg et al., 2005; Halligan et al., 2013). Specifically, Eisenberg et al. (2005) found that high levels of effortful control (assessed in early adolescence) were significantly related to high levels of parental warmth and positive expressivity four years later. Likewise, Halligan and colleagues (2013) reported that high levels of emotion regulation (assessed at 12–18 months) were significantly related to high levels of maternal sensitivity (assessed at 5 years). However, this association was not significant when controlling for continuity in both factors.

Longitudinal research also may be beneficial in examining developmental change in emotion regulation and emotion socialization. Although there likely are advances in emotion regulation through childhood, adolescence, and emerging adulthood due to the developmental transformations that were discussed earlier in the chapter, to our knowledge, there have been no published investigations studying developmental change or trajectories in emotion regulation across three or more data points. Moreover, while parents are likely to utilize different parenting techniques when recommending effective emotion regulation strategies when their children are five years old compared to 15 years old, the literature is characterized by a lack of evidence regarding this possibility. Finally, while evidence in this chapter has demonstrated that parenting and other family factors shape emotion regulation during childhood, adolescence, and emerging adulthood, longitudinal designs would allow for the investigation of critical periods regarding various aspects of emotion regulation and exploring potential reason for these critical periods.

Another area worthy of investigation in future research is exploring the interplay among genetic and environmental factors. Although there have been numerous studies examining gene X environment interactions in the prediction of different types of psychopathology (see Rutter, Moffitt, & Caspi, 2006 for a review), there have been fewer efforts to explore such processes with respect to emotional development despite some preliminary and promising findings. For example, Kochanska, Philibert, and Barry (2009) reported that among preschoolers who carried a short 5-HTTLPR allele (i.e., serotonin transporter gene), those who were insecurely attached had lower levels of self-regulation compared to securely attached children. In another study by Kim and colleagues (2011), the authors found that Americans with the GG genotype for the oxytocin receptor polymorphism (OXTR) reported significantly lower levels of emotion suppression compared to individuals with the AA genotype; Korean participants showed the opposite pattern. Thus, it is possible that the impact of families (and culture) on emotion regulation may vary by one's genotype.

In conclusion, this chapter provides evidence for the role of emotion regulation as a mechanism through which the family impacts the development of psychopathology. Research reviewed provides strong evidence for targeting emotion regulation as a point for intervention in the development of children's internalizing and externalizing behavior. Studies also suggest leveraging aspects of the family and the parent–child relationship related to the development of emotion regulation as potential points for intervention (Snyder et al., 2013). Moreover, utilizing a developmental perspective highlights the need for interventions and treatments to be sensitive to developmental changes and processes involved in emotion regulation, *and* in changes in the parent–child relationship.

## References

Anderson, P. (2002). Assessment and development of executive function (EF) during childhood. *Child Neuropsychology*, *8*, 71–82. doi:10.1076/chin.8.2.71.8724

Adrian, M., Zeman, J., Erdley, C., Lisa, L., Homan, K., & Sim, L. (2009). Social contextual links to emotion regulation in an adolescent psychiatric inpatient population: Do gender and symptomatology matter? *Journal of Child Psychology and Psychiatry*, *50*, 1428–1436. doi:10.1111/j.1469-7610.2009.02162.x

Arnett, J. J. (2000). Emerging adulthood: A theory of development from the late teens through the twenties. *American Psychologist*, *55*, 469–480. doi:10.1037/0003-066X.55.5.469

Barber, B. K., & Buehler, C. (1996). Family cohesion and enmeshment: Different constructs, different effects. *Journal of Marriage and the Family*, *58*, 433–441. doi:10.2307/353507

Belsky, J., Fish, M., & Isabella, R. A. (1991). Continuity and discontinuity in infant negative and positive emotionality: Family antecedents and attachment consequences. *Developmental Psychology, 27*, 421–431. doi:10.1037/0012-1649.27.3.421

Berk, L. (2012). *Infants and children: Prenatal through middle childhood* (7th ed.). Boston, MA: Pearson Education.

Blair, C. (2010). Stress and the development of self-regulation in context. *Child Development Perspectives, 4*, 181–188. doi:10.1111/j.1750-8606.2010.00145.x

Bosquet, M., & Egeland, B. (2006). The development and maintenance of anxiety symptoms from infancy through adolescence in a longitudinal sample. *Development and Psychopathology, 18*, 517–550. doi:10.1017/S0954579406060275

Bowlby, J. (1988). *A secure base: Parent–child attachment and healthy human development.* New York: Basic Books.

Bretherton, I., Fritz, J., Zahn-Waxler, C., & Ridgeway, D. (1986). Learning to talk about emotions: A functionalist perspective. *Child Development, 57*, 529–548.

Bretherton, I., McNew, S., & Beeghly-Smith, M. (1981). Early person knowledge as expressed in gestural and verbal communication: When do infants acquire a "theory of mind?" In M. E. Lamb & L. R. Sherrod (Eds.), *Infant social cognition: Empirical and theoretical considerations* (pp. 333–373). Hillsdale, NJ: Erlbaum.

Brumariu, L. E., & Kerns, K. A. (2013). Pathways to anxiety: Contributions of attachment history, temperament, peer competence, and ability to manage intense emotions. *Child Psychiatry and Human Development, 44*, 504–515. doi:10.1007/s10578-012-0345-7

Buckholdt, K. E., Parra, G. R., & Jobe-Shields, L. (2009). Emotion regulation as a mediator of the relation between emotion socialization and deliberate self-harm. *American Journal of Orthopsychiatry, 79*, 482–490. doi:10.1037/a0016735

Buckholdt, K. E., Parra, G. R., & Jobe-Shields, L. (2014). Intergenerational transmission of emotion dysregulation through parental invalidation of emotions: Implications for adolescent internalizing and externalizing behaviors. *Journal of Child and Family Studies, 23*, 324–332. doi:10.1007/s10826-013-9768-4

Caspi, A., Henry, B., McGee, R. O., Moffitt, T. E., & Silva, P. A. (1995). Temperamental origins of child and adolescent behavior problems: From age three to fifteen. *Child Development, 66*, 55–68.

Cassano, M. C., & Zeman, J. L. (2010). Parental socialization of sadness regulation in middle childhood: The role of expectations and gender. *Developmental Psychology, 46*, 1214–1226. doi:http://dx.doi.org/10.1037/a0019851

Cassidy, J. (1994). Emotion regulation: Influences of attachment relationships. In N. A. Fox (Ed.), *Monographs of the Society for Research in Child Development* (Serial No. 240 ed., Vol. *59*, pp. 228–249). Chicago, IL: University of Chicago Press.

Chan, S. M., Bowes, J., & Wyver, S. (2009). Parenting style as a context for emotion socialization. *Early Education and Development, 20*, 631–656. doi:10.1080/10409280802541973

Chandley, R. B., Luebbe, A. M., Messman-Moore, T. L., & Ward, R. (2014). Anxiety sensitivity, coping motives, emotion dysregulation, and alcohol-related outcomes in college women: A moderated-mediation model. *Journal of Studies on Alcohol and Drugs, 75*, 83–92. doi:10.15288/jsad.2014.75.83

Chang, H., Shelleby, E. C., Cheong, J., & Shaw, D. S. (2012). Cumulative risk, negative emotionality, and emotion regulation as predictors of social competence in transition to school: A mediated moderation model. *Social Development, 21*, 780–800. doi:10.1111/j.1467-9507.2011.00648.x

Cole, P. M., Michel, M. K., & Teti, L. O. (1994). The development of emotion regulation and dysregulation: a clinical perspective. In N. A. Fox (Ed.), *Monographs of the Society for Research in Child Development* (Serial No. 240 ed., Vol. *59*, pp. 73–100). Chicago, IL: University of Chicago Press.

Collins, W., Maccoby, E. E., Steinberg, L., Hetherington, E., & Bornstein, M. H. (2000). Contemporary research on parenting: The case for nature and nurture. *American Psychologist*, *55*, 218–232. doi:10.1037/0003-066X.55.2.218

Collins, W., Madsen, S. D., & Susman-Stillman, A. (2002). Parenting during middle childhood. In M. H. Bornstein (Ed.), *Handbook of parenting*. Vol. *1*: Children and parenting (2nd ed., pp. 73–101). Mahwah, NJ: Lawrence Erlbaum.

Cox, M. J., & Paley, B. (2003). Understanding families as systems. *Current Directions in Psychological Science*, *12*, 193–196. doi:10.1111/1467-8721.01259

Criss, M. M., Shaw, D. S., & Ingoldsby, E. M. (2003). Motherson positive synchrony in middle childhood: Relation to antisocial behavior. *Social Development*, *12*, 379–400. doi:10.1111/1467-9507.00239

Cui, L., Morris, A. S., Criss, M. M., Houltberg, B. J., & Silk, J. S. (2014). Parental psychological control and adolescent adjustment: The role of adolescent emotion regulation. *Parenting: Science and Practice*, *14*, 47–67, doi:10.1080/15295192.2014.880018

Cummings, E. M., & Davies, P. (1996). Emotional security as a regulatory process in normal development and the development of psychopathology. *Development and Psychopathology*, *8*, 123–139.

Cunningham, J., Kliewer, W., & Garner, P. W. (2009). Emotion socialization, child emotion understanding and regulation, and adjustment in urban African American families: Differential associations across child gender. *Development and Psychopathology*, *21*, 261–283. doi:10.1017/S0954579409000157

Darling, N., & Steinberg, L. (1993). Parenting style as context: An integrative model. *Psychological Bulletin*, *113*, 487–496. doi:10.1037/0033-2909.113.3.487

Davies, P. T., & Cummings, M. E. (1994). Marital conflict and child adjustment: An emotional security hypothesis. *Psychological Bulletin*, *116*, 387–411. doi:10.1037/0033- 2909.116.3.387

Davies, P. T., & Cummings, E. M. (2006). Interparental discord, family process, and developmental psychopathology. In D. Cicchetti & D. J. Cohen (Eds.), *Developmental psychopathology*. Vol. *3*. Risk, disorder, and adaptation (2nd ed., pp. 86–128). New York: Wiley.

Davidov, M., & Grusec, J. E. (2006). Untangling the links of parental responsiveness to distress and warmth to child outcomes. *Child Development*, *77*, 44–58. doi:10.1111/j.1467-8624.2006.00855.x

Denham, S. A. (1993). Maternal emotional responsiveness and toddlers' social-emotional competence. *Journal of Child Psychology and Psychiatry*, *34*, 715–728. doi:10.1111/j.1469-7610.1993.tb01066.x

Denham, S. A., Mitchell-Copeland, J., Strandberg, K., Auerbach, S., & Blair, K. (1997). Parental contributions to preschoolers' emotional competence: Direct and indirect effects. *Motivation and Emotion*, *21*, 65–86. doi:10.1023/A:1024426431247

Denham, S. A., Zoller, D., & Couchoud, E. A. (1994). Socialization of preschoolers' emotion understanding. *Developmental Psychology*, *30*, 928–936. doi:10.1037/0012-1649.30.6.928

Dubas, J. S., & Petersen, A. C. (1996). Geographical distance from parents and adjustment during adolescence and young adulthood. In J. A. Graber & J. S. Dubas (Eds.), *New directions for child development*. Vol. *71*. Leaving home: Understanding the transition to adulthood (pp. 3–19). Hoboken, NJ: Wiley.

Dunsmore, J. C., Booker, J. A., & Ollendick, T. H. (2013). Parental emotion coaching and child emotion regulation as protective factors for children with oppositional defiant disorder. *Social Development*, *22*, 444–466. doi:10.1111/j.1467-9507.2011.00652.x

Eisenberg, N., Carlo, G., Murphy, B., & Van Court, P. (1995). Prosocial development in late adolescence: A longitudinal study. *Child Development*, *66*, 1179–1197.

Eisenberg, N., Cumberland, A., & Spinrad, T. L. (1998). Parental socialization of emotion. *Psychological Inquiry*, *9*, 241–273. doi:10.1207/s15327965pli0904_1

Eisenberg, N., Cumberland, A., Spinrad, T. L., Fabes, R. A., Shepard, S. A., Reiser, M., et al. (2001). The relations of regulation and emotionality to children's externalizing and internalizing problem behavior. *Child Development*, *72*, 1112–1134. doi:10.1111/1467-8624.00337

Eisenberg, N., Guthrie, I. K., Fabes, R. A., Reiser, M., Murphy, B. C., Holmgren, R., et al. (1997). The relations of regulation and emotionality to resiliency and competent social functioning in elementary school children. *Child Development*, *68*, 295–311. doi:10.1111/j.1467-8624.1997.tb01941.x

Eisenberg, N., Losoya, S., Fabes, R. A., Guthrie, I. K., Reiser, M., Murphy, B., et al. (2001). Parental socialization of children's dysregulated expression of emotions and externalizing problems. *Journal of Family Psychology*, *15*, 183–205. doi:10.1037/0893-3200.15.2.183

Eisenberg, N., & Morris, A. S. (2002). Children's emotion-related regulation. In H. Reese & R. Kail (Eds.), *Advances in child development and behavior*, Vol. *30* (pp. 189–229). San Diego, CA: Academic Press.

Eisenberg, N., Spinrad, T. L., & Eggum, N. D. (2010). Emotion-related self-regulation and its relation to children's maladjustment. *Annual Review of Clinical Psychology*, *6*, 495–525. doi:10.1146/annurev.clinpsy.121208.131208

Eisenberg, N., Zhou, Q., Spinrad, T. L., Valiente, C., Fabes, R. A., & Liew, J. (2005). Relations among positive parenting, children's effortful control, and externalizing problems: A three-wave longitudinal study. *Child Development*, *76*, 1055–1071. doi:10.1111/j.1467-8624.2005.00897.x

Ernst, M., Nelson, E. E., Jazbec, S., McClure, E. B., Monk, C. S., Leibenluft, E., et al. (2005). Amygdala and nucleus accumbens in responses to receipt and omission of gains in adults and adolescents. *Neuroimage*, *25*, 1279–1291. doi:10.1016/j.neuroimage.2004.12.038

Eshel, N., Nelson, E. E., Blair, R., Pine, D. S., & Ernst, M. (2007). Neural substrates of choice selection in adults and adolescents: Development of the ventrolateral prefrontal and anterior cingulate cortices. *Neuropsychologia*, *45*, 1270–1279. doi:10.1016/j.neuropsychologia.2006.10.004

Fabes, R. A., Leonard, S. A., Kupanoff, K., & Martin, C. L. (2001). Parental coping with children's negative emotions: Relations with children's emotional and social responding. *Child Development*, *72*, 907–920. doi:10.1111/1467-8624.00323

Feinman, S., & Lewis, M. (1983). Social referencing at ten months: A second-order effect on infants' responses to strangers. *Child Development*, *54*, 878–887. doi:10.2307/1129892

Field, T., Diego, M., & Hernandez-Reif, M. (2009). Depressed mothers' infants are less responsive to faces and voices. *Infant Behavior and Development*, *32*, 239–244. doi:10.1016/j.infbeh.2009.03.005

Fischer, J. L., Forthun, L. F., Pidcock, B. W., & Dowd, D. A. (2007). Parent relationships, emotion regulation, psychosocial maturity and college student alcohol use problems. *Journal of Youth and Adolescence*, *36*, 912–926. doi:10.1007/s10964-006-9126-6.

Fosco, G. M., Caruthers, A. S., & Dishion, T. J. (2012). A six-year predictive test of adolescent family relationship quality and effortful control pathways to emerging adult social and emotional health. *Journal of Family Psychology*, *26*, 565–575. doi:10.1037/a0028873

Fosco, G. M., & Grych, J. H. (2013). Capturing the family context of emotion regulation: A family systems model comparison approach. *Journal of Family Issues*, *34*, 557–578. doi: 10.1177/0192513X12445889

Gaensbauer, T. J., Connell, J. P., & Schultz, L. A. (1983). Emotion and attachment: Interrelationships in a structured laboratory paradigm. *Developmental Psychology*, *19*, 815–831. doi:10.1037/0012-1649.19.6.815

Garner, P. W., & Estep, K. M. (2010). Emotional competence, emotion socialization, and young children's peer-related social competence. *Early Education and Development*, *12*, 29–48. doi:10.1207/s15566935eed1201_3

Gogtay, N., & Thompson, P. M. (2010). Mapping gray matter development: Implications for typical development and vulnerability to psychopathology. *Brain and Cognition*, *72*, 6–15. doi:10.1016/j.bandc.2009.08.009

Gottman, J. M., Katz, L. F., & Hooven, C. (1996). Parental meta-emotion philosophy and the emotional life of families: Theoretical models and preliminary data. *Journal of Family Psychology*, *10*, 243–268. doi:10.1037/0893-3200.10.3.243

Gottman, J. M., Katz, L. F., & Hooven, C. (1997). *Meta-emotion: How families communicate emotionally*. Mahwah, NJ: Lawrence Erlbaum.

Greenberg, M. T. (2006). Promoting resilience in children and youth: Preventive interventions and their interface with neuroscience. *Annals of New York Academy of Sciences, 1094*, 139–150. doi:10.1196/annals.1376.013

Halligan, S. L., Cooper, P. J., Fearon, P., Wheeler, S. L., Crosby, M., & Murray, L. (2013). The longitudinal development of emotion regulation capacities in children at risk for externalizing disorders. *Development and Psychopathology, 25*, 391–406. doi:10.1017/S0954579412001137

Hare, T. A., Tottenham, N., Galvan, A., Voss, H. U., Glover, G. H., & Casey, B. J. (2008). Biological substrates of emotional reactivity and regulation in adolescence during an emotional go-nogo task. *Biological Psychiatry, 63*, 927–934. doi:10.1016/j.biopsych.2008.03.015

Henry, C. S., Morris, A. S., & Harrist, A. W. (2015). Family resilience: Moving into the third wave. *Family Relations, 64*, 22–43. doi:10.1111/fare.12106

Hersh, M. A., & Hussong, A. M. (2009). The association between observed parental emotion socialization and adolescent self-medication. *Journal of Abnormal Child Psychology, 37*, 493–506. doi:10.1007/s10802-008-9291-z

Houltberg, B. J., Henry, C. S., & Morris, A. S. (2012). Family interactions, exposure to violence, and emotion regulation: Perceptions of children and early adolescents at-risk. *Family Relations: An Interdisciplinary Journal of Applied Family Studies, 61*, 283–296. doi:10.1111/j.1741-3729.2011.00699.x

Jaser, S. S., Fear, J. M., Reeslund, K. L., Champion, J. E., Reising, M. M., & Compas, B. E. (2008). Maternal sadness and adolescents' responses to stress in offspring of mothers with and without a history of depression. *Journal of Clinical Child & Adolescent Psychology, 37*, 736–746. doi:10.1080/15374410802359742

Katz, L. F., & Gottman, J. M. (1997). Buffering children from marital conflict and dissolution. *Journal of Clinical Child Psychology, 26*, 157–171.

Kerns, K. A., & Brumariu, L. E. (2014). Is insecure parent–child attachment a risk factor for the development of anxiety in childhood or adolescence? *Child Development Perspectives, 8*, 12–17. doi:10.1111/cdep.12054

Kidwell, S. L., Young, M. E., Hinkle, L. D., Ratliff, A. D., Marcum, M. E., & Martin, C. N. (2010). Emotional competence and behavior problems: Differences across preschool assessment of attachment classifications. *Clinical Child Psychology, 15*, 391–406. doi:10.1177/1359104510367589

Kim, H. S., Sherman, D. K., Mojaverian, T., Sasaki, J. Y., Park, J., Suh, E. M., et al. (2011). Gene-culture interaction: Oxytocin receptor polymorphism (*OXTR*) and emotion regulation. *Social Psychological and Personality Science, 2*, 665–672.

Kim, J., & Cicchetti, D. (2010). Longitudinal pathways linking child maltreatment, emotion regulation, peer relations, and psychopathology. *Journal of Child Psychology and Psychiatry, 51*, 706–716. doi:10.1111/j.1469-7610.2009.02202.x

Kim-Spoon, J., Cicchetti, D., & Rogosch, F. A. (2013). A longitudinal study of emotion regulation, emotion lability-negativity, and internalizing symptomatology in maltreated and nonmaltreated children. *Child Development, 84*, 512–527. doi:10.1111/j.1467-8624.2012.01857.x

Kochanska, G., & Murray, K. T. (2000). Mother–child mutually responsive orientation and conscience development: From toddler to early school age. *Child Development, 71*, 417–431. doi:10.1111/1467-8624.00154

Kochanska, G., Philibert, R. A., & Barry, R. A. (2009). Interplay of genes and early mother–child relationship in the development of self-regulation from toddler to preschool age. *Journal of Child Psychology and Psychiatry, 50*, 1331–1338.

Kopp, C. B. (1989). Regulation of distress and negative emotions: A developmental view. *Developmental Psychology, 25*, 343–354. doi:10.1037/0012-1649.25.3.343

Kopp, C. B. (1992). Emotional distress and control in young children. *New Directions for Child Development*, *55*, 41–56. doi:10.1002/cd.23219925505

Kramer, L., & Kowal, A. K. (2005). Sibling relationship quality from birth to adolescence: The enduring contributions of friends. *Journal of Family Psychology*, *19*, 503–511. doi:10.1037/0893-3200.19.4.503

Laird, R. D., Pettit, G. S., Bates, J. E., & Dodge, K. A. (2003). Parents' monitoring-relevant knowledge and adolescents' delinquent behavior: Evidence of correlated developmental changes and reciprocal influences. *Child Development*, *74*, 752–768. doi:10.1111/1467-8624.00566

Lansford, J. E., Criss, M. M., Laird, R. D., Shaw, D. S., Pettit, G. S., Dodge, K. A., et al. (2011). Reciprocal relations between parents' physical discipline and children's externalizing behavior during middle childhood and adolescence. *Development and Psychopathology*, *23*, 225–238. doi:10.1017/S0954579410000751

Larson, R. W., Richards, M. H., Moneta, G., Holmbeck, G., & Duckett, E. (1996). Changes in adolescents' daily interactions with their families from ages 10 to 18: Disengagement and transformation. *Developmental Psychology*, *32*, 744–754. doi:10.1037/0012-1649.32.4.744

Lefkowitz, E. S. (2005). "Things have gotten better": Developmental changes among emerging adults after the transition to university. *Journal of Adolescent Research*, *20*, 40–63. doi:10.1177/0743558404271236

Liew, J., Kwok, O., Chang, Y.-P., Chang, B. W., & Yeh, Y.-C. (2014). Parental autonomy support predicts academic achievement through emotion-related self-regulation and adaptive skills in Chinese American adolescents. *Asian American Journal of Psychology*, *5*, 214–222. doi:10.1037/a0034787

Luebbe, A. M., Bump, K. A., Fussner, L. M., & Rulon, K. J. (2014). Perceived maternal and paternal psychological control: Relations to adolescent anxiety through deficits in emotion regulation. *Child Psychiatry and Human Development*, *45*, 565–576. doi:10.1007/s10578-013-0425-3

Lundy, B., Field, T., & Pickens, J. (1996). Newborns of mothers with depressive symptoms are less expressive. *Infant Behavior and Development*, *19*, 419–424. doi:10.1016/S0163-6383(96)90003-X

Lunkenheimer, E. S., Shields, A. M., & Cortina, K. S. (2007). Parental emotion coaching and dismissing in family interaction. *Social Development*, *16*, 232–248. doi:10.1111/j.1467-9507.2007.00382.x

Maccoby, E. E. (1992). The role of parents in the socialization of children: A historical overview. *Developmental Psychology*, *28*, 1006–1017. doi:10.1037/0012-1649.28.6.1006

Malatesta, C. Z. (1990). The role of emotions in the development and organization of personality. In R. A. Thompson (Ed.), *Socio-emotional development*. Vol. *36*: Nebraska Symposium of Motivation (pp. 367–467). Lincoln: University of Nebraska Press.

Malatesta, C. Z., Grigoryev, P., Lamb, C., Albin, M., & Culver, C. (1986). Emotion socialization and expressive development in preterm and full term infants. *Child Development*, *57*, 316–330. doi:10.2307/1130587

Malatesta, C. Z., & Haviland, J. M. (1982). Learning display rules: The socialization of emotion expression in infancy. *Child Development*, *53*, 991–1003. doi:10.2307/1129139

Manzeske, D., & Stright, A. (2009). Parenting styles and emotion regulation: The role of behavioral and psychological control during young adulthood. *Journal of Adult Development*, *16*, 223–229. doi:10.1007/s10804-009-9068-9.

Marganska, A., Gallagher, M., & Miranda, R. (2013). Adult attachment, emotion dysregulation, and symptoms of depression and generalized anxiety disorder. *American Journal of Orthopsychiatry*, *83*, 131–141. doi:10.1111/ajop.12001

Martin, G. B., & Clark, R. D. (1982). Distress crying in neonates: Species and peer specificity. *Developmental Psychology*, *18*, 3–9. doi:10.1037/0012-1649.18.1.3

Masten, A. S. (2011). Resilience in children threatened by extreme adversity: Frameworks for research, practice, and translational synergy. *Development and Psychopathology, 23*, 493–506. doi:10.1017/S09545794110001

Masten, A. S., & Cicchetti, D. (2010). Developmental cascades. *Development and Psychopathology, 22*, 491–495. doi:10.1017/S0954579410000222

McCarthy, C. J., Lambert, R. G., & Moller, N. P. (2006). Preventive resources and emotion regulation expectancies as mediators between attachment and college students' stress outcomes. *International Journal of Stress Management, 13*, 1–22. doi:10.1037/1072-5245.13.1.1

McCarthy, C. J., Lambert, R. G., & Seraphine, A. E. (2004). Adaptive family functioning and emotion regulation capacities as predictors of college students' appraisals and emotion valence following conflict with their parents. *Cognition and Emotion, 18*, 97–124. doi:10.1080/02699930244000417

McHale, S. M., Updegraff, K. A., & Whiteman, S. D. (2012). Sibling relationships and influences in childhood and adolescence. *Journal of Marriage and Family, 74*, 913–930. doi:10.1111/j.1741-3737.2012.01011.x

Mezulis, A. H., Hyde, J. S., Simonson, J., & Charbonneau, A. M. (2011). Integrating affective, biological, and cognitive vulnerability models to explain the gender difference in depression. In T. J. Strauman, P. R. Costanzo, & J. Garber (Eds.), *Depression in adolescent girls: Science and prevention*. New York: Guilford Press.

Morelen, D., Jacob, M. L., Suveg, C., Jones, A., & Thomassin, K. (2013). Family emotion expressivity, emotion regulation, and the link to psychopathology: Examination across race. *British Journal of Psychology, 104*, 149–166. doi:10.1111/j.2044-8295.2012.02108.x

Morgan, J. K., Izard, C. E., & Hyde, C. (2014). Emotional reactivity and regulation in Head Start children: Links to ecologically valid behaviors and internalizing problems. *Social Development, 23*, 259–266. doi:10.1111/sode.12049

Morgan, E. M., Thorne, A., & Zurbriggen, E. L. (2010). A longitudinal study of conversations with parents about sex and dating during college. *Developmental Psychology, 46*, 139–150. doi:10.1037/a0016931

Morris, A. S., Cui, L., & Steinberg, L. (2013). Parenting research and themes: What we've learned and where to go next. In R. E. Larzelere, A. S. Morris, & A. W. Harrist (Eds.), *Authoritative parenting: Synthesizing nurturance and discipline for optimal child development* (pp. 35–58). Washington, DC: American Psychological Association. doi:10.1037/13948-003

Morris, A. S., Silk, J. S., Morris, M. D. S., Steinberg, L., Aucoin, K. J., & Keyes, A. W. (2011). The influence of mother-child emotion regulation strategies on children's expression of anger and sadness. *Developmental Psychology, 47*, 213–225. doi:10.1037/a0021021

Morris, A. S., Silk, J. S., Steinberg, L., Myers, S. S. & Robinson, L. R. (2007). The role of the family context in the development of emotion regulation. *Social Development, 16*, 361–388. doi:10.1111/j.1467-9507.2007.00389.x

National Center for Education Statistics (2003). *The condition of education*. Washington, DC: U.S. Department of Education.

O'Connor, T. G., Allen, J. P., Bell, K. L., & Hauser, S. T. (1996). Adolescent-parent relationships and leaving home in young adulthood. In J. A. Graber & J. S. Dubas (Eds.), *New directions for child development*. Vol. *71*. Leaving home: Understanding the transition to adulthood (pp. 39–52). Hoboken, NJ: Wiley.

Padilla-Walker, L. M., Harper, J. M., & Jensen, A. C. (2010). Self-regulation as a mediator between sibling relationship quality and early adolescents' positive and negative outcomes. *Journal of Family Psychology, 24*, 419–428. doi:10.1037/

Paikoff, R. L., & Brooks-Gunn, J. (1991). Do parent–child relationships change during puberty? *Psychological Bulletin, 110*, 47–66. doi:10.1037/0033-2909.110.1.47

Parke, R. D. (1994). Progress, paradigms, and unresolved problems: A commentary on recent advances in our understanding of children's emotions. *Merrill-Palmer Quarterly, 40*, 157–169.

Parke, R. D. (2004). Development in the family. *Annual Review of Psychology, 55*, 365–399. doi:10.1146/annurev.psych.55.090902.141528

Paus, T. (2009). Brain development. In R. M. Lerner & L. Steinberg (Eds.), *Handbook of adolescent psychology*. Vol. *1*: Individual bases of adolescent development (3rd ed., pp. 95–115). Hoboken, NJ: John Wiley & Sons.

Ramsden, S. R., & Hubbard, J. A. (2002). Family expressiveness and parental emotion coaching: Their role in children's emotion regulation and aggression. *Journal of Abnormal Child Psychology: An Official Publication of the International Society for Research in Child and Adolescent Psychopathology, 30*(6), 657–667. doi:10.1023/A:102081991588

Repetti, R. L., Taylor, S. E., & Seeman, T. E. (2002). Risky families: Family social environments and the mental and physical health of offspring. *Psychological Bulletin, 128*(2), 330–366. doi:10.1037/0033-2909.128.2.330

Röll, J., Koglin, U., & Petermann, F. (2012). Emotion regulation and childhood aggression: Longitudinal associations. *Child Psychiatry and Human Development, 43*, 909–923. doi:10.1007/s10578-012-0303-4

Roth, G., Assor, A., Niemiec, C. P., Ryan, R. M., & Deci, E. L. (2009). The emotional and academic consequences of parental conditional regard: Comparing conditional positive regard, conditional negative regard, and autonomy support as parenting practices. *Developmental Psychology, 45*, 1119–1142. doi:10.1037/a0015272

Rothbart, M. K., Ahadi, S. A., Hershey, K. L., & Fisher, P. (2001). Investigations of temperament at three to seven years: The Children's Behavior Questionnaire. *Child Development, 72*, 1394–1408. doi:10.1111/1467-8624.00355

Rutter, M., Moffitt, T. E., & Caspi, A. (2006). Gene-environment interplay and psychopathology: Multiple varieties but real effects. *Journal of Child Psychology and Psychiatry, 47*, 226–261.

Rydell, A., Berlin, L., & Bohlin, G. (2003). Emotionality, emotion regulation, and adaptation among 5- to 8-year-old children. *Emotion, 3*, 30–47. doi:10.1037/1528-3542.3.1.30

Saarni, C. (1999). *The development of emotional competence*. New York: Guilford Press.

Saarni, C., Mumme, D., & Campos, J. J. (1998). Emotional development: Action, communication, and understanding. In N. Eisenberg (Ed.), *Handbook of child psychology*. Vol. *3* Social, emotional and personality development (5th ed., pp. 237–309). New York: Wiley.

Sameroff, A. (2010). A unified theory of development: A dialectical integration of nature and nurture. *Child Development, 81*, 6–22. doi:10.1111/j.1467-8624.2009.01378.x

Schwarz, B., Stutz, M., & Ledermann, T. (2012). Perceived interparental conflict and early adolescents' friendships: The role of attachment security and emotion regulation. *Journal of Youth and Adolescence, 41*, 1240–1252. doi:10.1007/s10964-012-9769-4

Selman, R. (1980). *The growth of interpersonal understanding: Developmental and clinical analyses*. New York: Academic Press.

Shaw, D. S., Keenan, K., Vondra, J. J., Delliquadri, E., & Giovannelli, J. (1997). Antecedants of preschool children's internalizing problems: A longitundinal study of low-income families. *Journal of American Academy of Child and Adolescent Psychiatry, 36*, 1760–1767. doi:10.1097/00004583-199712000-00025

Siffert, A., & Schwarz, B. (2011). Parental conflict resolution styles and children's adjustment: Children's appraisals and emotion regulation as mediators. *The Journal of Genetic Psychology, 172*, 21–39. doi:10.1080/00221325.2010.503723

Silk, J. S., Steinberg, L., & Morris, A. S. (2003). Adolescents' emotion regulation in daily life: Links to depressive symptoms and problem behavior. *Child Development, 74*, 1869–1880. doi:10.1046/j.1467-8624.2003.00643.x

Sim, L., Adrian, M., Zeman, J., Cassano, M., & Friedrich, W. N. (2009). Adolescent deliberate self-harm: Linkages to emotion regulation and family emotional climate. *Journal of Research on Adolescence, 19*, 75–91. doi:10.1111/j.1532-7795.2009.00582.x

Smetana, J. G. (1989). Adolescents' and parents' reasoning about actual family conflict. *Child Development*, *60*, 1052–1067. doi:10.2307/1130779

Smetana, J. G. (2000). Middle-class African American adolescents' and parents' conceptions of parental authority and parenting practices. A longitudinal investigation. *Child Development*, *71*, 1672–1686. doi:10.1111/1467-8624.00257

Snyder, J., Low, S., Bullard, L., Schrepferman, L., Wachlarowicz, M., Marvin, C., et al. (2013). Effective parenting practices: Social interaction learning theory and the role of emotion coaching and mindfulness. In R. E. Larzelere, A. S. Morris, & A. W. Harrist (Eds.), *Authoritative parenting: Synthesizing nurturance and discipline for optimal child development* (pp. 189–210). doi:10.1037/13948-009

Sorce, J. F., Emde, R. N., Campos, J., & Klinnert, M. D. (1985). Maternal emotional signaling: Its effect on the visual cliff behavior of 1-year olds. *Developmental Psychology*, *21*, 195–200. doi:10.1037/0012-1649.21.1.195

Spinrad, T. L., Eisenberg, N., Cumberland, A., Fabes, R. A., Valiente, C., Shepard, S. A., et al. (2006). Relation of emotion-related regulation to children's social competence: A longitudinal study. *Emotion*, *6*, 498–510. doi:10.1037/1528-3542.6.3.498

Steinberg, L. (1990). Autonomy, conflict, and harmony in the family relationship. In S. Feldman & G. R. Elliott (Eds.), *At the threshold: The developing adolescent* (pp. 255–276). Cambridge, MA: Harvard University Press.

Steinberg, L. (2011). Adolescent risk taking: A social neuroscience perspective. In E. Amsel & J. G. Smetana (Eds.), *Adolescent vulnerabilities and opportunities: Developmental and constructivist perspectives* (pp. 41–64). New York: Cambridge University Press. doi:10.1017/CBO9781139042819.005

Steinberg, L., Dahl, R., Keating, D., Kupfer, D. J., Masten, A. S., & Pine, D. S. (2006). The study of developmental psychopathology in adolescence: Integrating affective neuroscience with the study of context. In D. Cicchetti, D. J. Cohen, D. Cicchetti & D. J. Cohen (Eds.), *Developmental psychopathology*. Vol *2*: Developmental neuroscience (2nd ed., pp. 710–741). Hoboken, NJ: John Wiley & Sons.

Steinberg, L., & Morris, A. (2001). Adolescent development. *Annual Review of Psychology*, *52*, 83–110. doi:10.1146/annurev.psych.52.1.83

Sroufe, L. A., Egeland, B., Carlson, E. A., & Collins, W. A. (2005). *The development of the person: The Minnesota Study of Risk and Adaptation from Birth to Adulthood*. New York: Guilford Press.

Supplee, L. H., Skuban, E. M., Shaw, D. S., & Prout, J. (2009). Emotion regulation strategies and later externalizing behavior among European American and African American children. *Development and Psychopathology*, *21*, 393–415. doi:10.1017/S0954579409000224

Termine, N. T., & Izard, C. E. (1988). Infants' responses to their mothers' expressions of joy and sadness. *Developmental Psychology*, *24*, 223–229. doi:10.1037/0012-1649.24.2.223

Thomas, A. (1984). Temperament research: Where we are, where we are going. *Merrill-Palmer Quarterly*, *30*, 103–109.

Thompson, R. A. (1990). Emotion and self-regulation. In R. A. Thompson (Ed.), *Socio-emotional development*. Vol. *36*: Nebraska Symposium of Motivation (pp. 367–467). Lincoln: University of Nebraska Press.

Valiente, C., Eisenberg, N., Spinrad, T. L., Reiser, M., Cumberland, A., Losoya, S. H., et al. (2006). Relations among mothers' expressivity, children's effortful control, and their problem behaviors: A four-year longitudinal study. *Emotion*, *6*, 459–472. doi:10.1037/1528-3542.6.3.459

Walden, T. A., & Smith, M. C. (1997). Emotion regulation. *Motivation and Emotion*, *21*, 7–25.

Walton, A. A., & Flouri, E. E. (2010). Contextual risk, maternal parenting and adolescent externalizing behaviour problems: The role of emotion regulation. *Child: Care, Health, and Development*, *36*, 275–284. doi:10.1111/j.1365-2214.2009.01065.x

Whitchurch, G. G., & Constantine, L. L. (1993). Systems theory. In P. G. Boss, W. J. Doherty, R. LaRossa, W. R. Schumm, & S. K. Steinmetz (Eds.), *Sourcebook of family theories and methods: A contextual approach* (pp. 325–352). New York: Plenum Press.

White, H. R., McMorris, B. J., Catalano, R. F., Fleming, C. B., Haggerty, K. P., & Abbott, R. D. (2006). Increases in alcohol and marijuana use during the transition out of high school into emerging adulthood: The effects of leaving home, going to college, and high school protective factors. *Journal of Studies on Alcohol*, *67*, 810–822. doi:10.15288/jsa.2006.67.810

Wilson, B. J., & Gottman, J. M. (1996). Attention – the shuttle between emotion and cognition: Risk, resiliency, and physiological bases. *Stress, coping, and resiliency in children and families* (pp. 189–228) Hillsdale, NJ: Lawrence Erlbaum.

Zahn-Waxler, C., & Kochanska, G. (1990). The origins of guilt. In R. A. Thompson (Ed.), *Socioemotional Development*. Vol. *36*: Nebraska Symposium on Motivation (pp. 183–268). Lincoln: University of Nebraska Press.

Zarling, A., Taber-Thomas, S., Murray, A., Knuston, J. F., Lawrence, E., Valles, N., et al. (2013). Internalizing and externalizing symptoms in young children exposed to intimate partner violence: Examining intervening processes. *Journal of Family Psychology*, *27*, 945–955. doi:10.1037/a0034804

Zeman, J., Cassano, M., Perry-Parrish, C., & Stegall, S. (2006). Emotion regulation in children and adolescents. *Journal of Developmental and Behavioral Pediatrics*, *27*, 155–168. doi:10.1097/00004703-200604000-00014

# Part 3

# Adverse Events and Cultural Influences

# 19

# Disasters and the Development of Psychopathology in Youth

## *An Ecological Perspective*

Carl F. Weems and Brandon G. Scott

## Introduction

This chapter provides an overview of research conducted on the impact of disasters, focusing on the development of childhood and adolescent emotional and behavioral problems. Research suggests that exposure to both human caused and natural disasters is associated with a number of post-traumatic stress reactions in youth including symptoms of several mental disorders (e.g., Aber, Gershoff, Ware, & Kotler, 2004; Eisenberg & Silver, 2011; La Greca, Silverman, Vernberg, & Roberts, 2002; Norris, Friedman, & Watson, 2002; Osofsky, Osofsky, Kronenberg, Brennan, & Hansel, 2009; Weems & Overstreet, 2008). Commonly studied reactions include symptoms of post-traumatic stress disorder (PTSD), anxiety disorders, depression, aggression, and other externalizing problems. Research findings are reviewed in this chapter within an integrative perspective drawn from contextual/ecological theories of human development (see Weems & Overstreet, 2008, 2009). Given the complexity of disaster effects on individuals, families, and communities, understanding the development of emotional and behavioral problems requires a complex integrative framework that spans multiple levels of analysis. For example, the massive scale of the Hurricane Katrina disaster raised the question, "What are the social systems that are impacted and how does context play a role in shaping adaptation following catastrophe?" (Weems & Overstreet, 2008, p. 488).

A contextual perspective emphasizes that disasters exert multiple levels of influence on emotional development through the interference of several basic human needs. Drawing from both contextual models of lifespan human development (e.g., Bronfenbrenner, 1979) and models of both risk and resilience to stress (e.g., Hobfoll, 1989; Sandler, 2001), the framework is called an ecological needs-based perspective (Weems & Overstreet, 2008). In the proceeding sections, an overview of the perspective is presented that draws upon the reviews in Weems & Overstreet (2008, 2009). The perspective is then used as a framework to review research linking natural disasters to childhood and adolescent emotional and behavioral problems. The chapter focuses primarily on research with natural disasters but research from other disasters (e.g., the terrorist attacks of 9/11) are also utilized.

*The Wiley Handbook of Developmental Psychopathology*, First Edition. Edited by Luna C. Centifanti and David M. Williams.

## An Ecological Needs-based Perspective

The perspective is based most directly upon Bronfenbrenner's ecological systems theory. This theory posits that individuals function within multiple contexts, or "ecologies," that influence each other and human development (Bronfenbrenner, 1979) and include: the macrosystem, which is the most distal ecology and includes the government, culture, cultural values and beliefs; the exosystem, which consists of processes taking place between two or more contexts, one of which does not directly involve the child, but has implications for the individual child (e.g., parent's workplace); the mesosystem, which represents the linkages between proximal ecologies (e.g., school and home, parental participation in the child's school); and the microsystem, which represents the proximal ecologies within which the child develops, including the family and school environments and peer relationships. The ontogenic level is the ecology of the individual and represents factors within the individual that influence developmental adaptation.

The perspective also posits that disasters impact emotional development by threatening basic human needs and goals. In particular, Sandler's (2001) risk and resilience model suggests that there are four basic needs relevant to adaptation to severe stress including physical safety, self-worth, control/efficacy, and a sense of social relatedness. When these needs are met, an individual is more likely to be resilient in the face of adversity (See Sandler, 2001 for expanded discussion). However, disasters threaten these basic needs and so challenge healthy emotional development and mental health. Similarly, in Hobfoll's conservation of resources model (Hobfoll, 1989) disasters can deplete the individual's financial, material, cognitive, and emotional resources. The ecological needs-based model highlights that in the case of disasters and their aftermath, threats to basic needs and the depletion of resources may come from every ecology surrounding the child, increasing the risk for negative emotional outcomes. Thus, an ecological needs-based perspective can be used to integrate data and knowledge by showing how various factors within different ecologies surrounding the child act alone and/or in conjunction with other ecologies to either impede (protect) or foster (increase the risk of) the development of psychopathology. The ecologies as well as examples of the basic needs and how they may be affected by exposure to disasters are presented in Table 19.1.

## Research Linking Disaster Exposure to Emotional and Behavioral Problems

Disaster exposure is a complex topic in that what defines exposure often varies from disaster to disaster and across research studies. Research on mental health outcomes has tended to focus on youth who were directly exposed to some disaster but also those who were in some way remotely affected. Often those directly exposed are those physically present at the disaster site or directly after the disaster and who had one or more threatening experiences. Studies have also examined the effects of "interpersonal exposure"—youth whose close friends or family members were directly exposed and youth who had a parent or other loved one die in the disaster. In general, research

**Table 19.1** Ecologies in the model and examples of how basic needs may influence disaster responses or be influenced by disaster exposure in each ecology.

| *Ecology and Definition* | *Example Needs* | |
|---|---|---|
| **Macrosystem:** the most distal ecology and includes the government, culture, cultural values, and beliefs | Physical safety | Geographic location and physical geography may be protective, thereby reducing risk of injury. |
| | Social relatedness | Community climate of support fosters social relatedness, thereby increasing levels of social support. |
| **Exosystem:** processes taking place between two or more contexts, one of which does not directly involve the child, but has implications for the individual child (e.g., parent's workplace) | Physical safety | Evacuation policies and government infrastructure, community resources decrease level of disaster exposure versus disadvantage (e.g., poverty) increasing risk of exposure. |
| | Self-worth | Parental loss of job/work decreases perceptions of self-worth. |
| **Mesosystem:** linkages between proximal ecologies (e.g., school and home, parental participation in the child's school) | Social relatedness | Having to attend new school/having to move decreases existing social relatedness. |
| | Control/ efficacy | Evacuation/relocations can foster a sense of lack of control over maintaining connections among Microsystems. |
| **Microsystem:** proximal ecologies within which the child develops, including the family and school environments and peer relationships | Physical safety | Family resources lost such as home damaged/destroyed necessitates move to more dangerous neighborhood. |
| | Control/ efficacy | Parental distress/psychopathology/ mental health decreases perception that the world is a controllable place. |
| **Ontogenic:** the individual and represents factors within the individual that influence developmental adaptation | Control/ efficacy | Perceptions of control, coping ability, pre-existing risk such as trait anxiety, negative affect, anxiety sensitivity increase risk for negative outcomes. |
| | Self-worth | Child mental health (or emotional reactions) from the disaster decrease perceptions of self-worth. |

has found a fairly consistent dose response with those with more severe or intense disaster experiences experiencing the most severe symptoms. For example, Weems and colleagues (Weems, Watts, et al., 2007) based their survey of exposures to Hurricane Katrina and its aftermath on the work of La Greca and colleagues (La Greca, Silverman, Vernberg, & Prinstein, 1996; La Greca, Silverman, & Wasserstein, 1998). Participants were asked to detail their experiences with traumatic aspects of the disaster by responding to questions such as "During the storm did you see windows and doors breaking?" and "During the storm did you get hurt?" Results indicated that level of exposure was associated with symptoms of post-traumatic stress disorder and this finding has been replicated a number of times (see Pfefferbaum et al., 2013). While the dose response finding is important there are a number of important other factors and variables which may serve as mediators and moderators of outcomes. The ecological needs model implies multiple levels of influence on the development of emotional and behavioral problems following a disaster. Thus, the following subsections discuss the influence of disaster exposure as viewed from the multiple levels of influence implied by the ecological needs based model.

## Macrosystem Influences

Disasters may impact youth emotional problems at the broadest level. These may include geographic characteristics, broad government policies, national infrastructure, cultural values as well as regional and national norms (see Bobo, 2006; Bourque, Siegal, Kano, & Wood, 2006). In particular, national infrastructure and wealth, including socio-economic and demographic characteristics, are related to disaster-related deaths and injuries (Haque, 2003) and national wealth is related to less damage and death (i.e., countries with higher income, higher educational attainment, experience fewer losses following disaster, see Toya & Skidmore, 2007). As an example of national norms, following the 9/11 attacks Gil-Rivas, Silver, Holman, McIntosh, and Poulin (2007) surveyed a large group of adults and their adolescent children; despite the distance from the attacks, links to post-traumatic stress symptoms in youth were found (see also Schlenger et al., 2002; Schuster et al., 2001).

One mechanism for finding links between distal exposure and stress symptoms is media coverage (Comer & Kendall, 2007; Pfefferbaum et al., 2003). A number of organizations have issued statements on the role of the media in disaster-related stress responses (see Hagan, American Academy of Pediatrics, Committee on Psychosocial Aspects of Child and Family Health, & Task Force on Terrorism, 2005). For example, the American Academy of Pediatrics recommends that pediatricians "Help parents recognize the potential deleterious effects of indirect disaster exposure from media…" (Hagan et al., 2005; p. 794). A mesosystem context which includes 24 hours a day/7 days a week news coverage and constant media exposure may thus broaden the effects of any particular disaster. Research suggests that watching more television (TV) coverage of a disaster is associated with more negative stress responses, including PTSD symptoms (Comer & Kendall, 2007; Hagan et al., 2005; Pfefferbaum et al., 2003). For example, following the Oklahoma City terrorist attack, youth reports of broadcast media exposure to the bombing were correlated ($r = .33$) with PTSD symptoms in youth ($n = 88$; sixth-graders; analyses excluded those with direct exposure) assessed two years post-attack (Pfefferbaum et al., 2003). Similar results have been found following the 9/11 attacks (e.g., Lengua, Long, Smith, & Meltzoff, 2005; Schuster et al., 2001); however, most past studies have either not employed prospective designs or controlled for pre-disaster symptom levels.

Theoretically, watching TV coverage may supply youth with distressing images that may foster a stress response and thus increased PTSD symptoms via increased threat perceptions (Weems, Scott, Banks, & Graham, 2012). An alternative would be that pre-existing PTSD symptoms are largely responsible for the post-disaster link between TV viewing and PTSD symptoms. For example, pre-existing symptoms prompt those to seek out or increase viewing of distressing images. In this case, controlling for pre-disaster symptoms might negate any post-disaster association between TV viewing and PTSD symptoms. Comer and Kendall (2007) have suggested that it is also possible that pre-existing conditions may potentiate distress experienced from or in reaction to media coverage. Therefore, another possibility is that TV viewing interacts with pre-existing symptoms such that TV viewing is primarily harmful to those with existing stress-related problems. Weems et al., (2012) studied a sample of 141 youth from New Orleans exposed to both Hurricanes Katrina and Gustav. Results indicated that amount of television viewing of Hurricane Gustav was associated with post-Gustav PTSD symptoms controlling for pre-Gustav PTSD symptoms (i.e., those associated with Katrina). However, pre-Gustav stress symptoms interacted with television viewing in predicting post-Gustav symptoms such that for youth with high pre-existing symptoms there was a stronger association between TV viewing and post-Gustav symptoms.

## Exosystem Influences

Exosystem influences on child adaptation originate in contexts that do not involve the child such as parent's workplace and exert their effects by creating disruptions in contexts that do involve the child (e.g., family, school). These indirect effects are potentially insidious risk factors for mental health problems. Parent's loss of work or work-related stress may translate to increased parent mental health problems or ineffective parenting, which in turn may increase risk for child mental health problems. For example, a longer work commute compared to before Hurricane Katrina was associated with PTSD symptoms in the New Orleans workforce (DeSalvo et al., 2007). Scheeringa and Zeanah (2008) found that workplace demands were the primary reason for parent–child separations during the evacuation and recovery periods following Katrina in their New Orleans sample of 70 preschool children aged 3–6 years. Scaramella, Sohr-Preston, Callahan, and Mirabile (2008) found that factors of financial strain were also related to higher child emotional and behavioral problems following Hurricane Katrina.

## Mesosystem Influences

The mesosystem represents linkages between more proximal (microsystems) ecologies. For example, parental participation in the child's school such as parent teacher association meetings is a mesosystem connection between the microsystems of school and home. Disasters may sever these mesosystem ties between the various microsystems in children's lives (e.g., a longer commute to work or increased workplace demands may make attending school-based meetings more difficult). A school-based intervention study by Salloum and Overstreet (2008) illustrates disruptions in such mesosystem connections in the post-Katrina environment but also the potential to increase those connections in a sample of 58 second- to sixth-graders. The intervention design included parent meetings, but most parents of the children receiving the intervention found it difficult to come to the school for a meeting, so the intervention incorporated a community-based parent meeting (i.e., at the parent's home or work) scheduled at the parent's convenience. This flexibility in service provision resulted in successful parent meetings for 73% of the sample, which allowed the opportunity to strengthen connections and ensure consistency between the home and school environments.

## Microsystem Influences

The microsystem represents the proximal ecologies within which the child develops, including the family/home and school environments and peer relationships. Disasters can influence child adaptation by causing stress and disruptions in the family, school, and neighborhood environments. Disaster research on the microsystems impacted by disaster has tended to focus on the family environment, with studies showing that marital stress, domestic violence, and parental psychopathology increase after disasters (Larrance, Anastario, & Lawry, 2007; Norris et al., 2002). Research by Scheeringa and Zeanah (2008) and Spell and colleagues (2008) speak to the importance of parental mental health for child functioning at two distinct developmental points. For preschool children, Scheeringa and Zeanah (2008) found that the onset of new mental health problems in preschool children was significantly correlated with the onset of new mental health problems in their caregivers. For school age children (8–16 years), Spell et al. (2008) obtained a similar finding among a sample of 260 displaced mother–child dyads recruited from primarily public schools within several of the main counties impacted by Katrina. Spell and colleagues reported that maternal psychological distress served as a significant predictor of child mental health following Hurricane Katrina. As noted by Scaramella and colleagues (2008), parental emotional distress and mental illness undermine parenting efficacy, resulting in increases in parental irritability and decreases in consistent discipline, both of which increase the risk for child mental health problems. In fact, Scaramella et al. found evidence for a mediating role of parenting efficacy in the relation between maternal depression and toddlers' internalizing and externalizing problems in Katrina-exposed families.

Although disasters create disruptions within the microsystems surrounding the child, negative developmental outcomes are not always observed in youth exposed to disasters (Kilmer & Gil-Rivas, 2010; Weems & Graham, 2014). The occurrence of negative outcomes is a function of both protective and vulnerability factors. For example, Pina et al. (2008) found that perceived helpfulness from extra-familial sources of support (e.g., teachers, friends, church members) was associated with lower post-traumatic stress reactions in youth (i.e., PTSD, anxiety, and depression). Similarly, increased risk created by disasters within the family environment can be offset by the presence of protective factors within the other microsystems surrounding the child. For example, school-based mental health services represent a protective factor within the school microsystem that can offset the negative developmental outcomes associated with disaster exposure (Abramason & Garfield, 2006; Pynoos, Goenijian, & Steinberg, 1998). Research of Salloum and Overstreet (2008) and Weems et al. (2009) demonstrate the effectiveness of school-based interventions for children in post-disaster environments. Weems et al. (2009) tested the effects of a school-based test anxiety intervention on reducing post-traumatic stress symptoms. The study used a prospective intervention design with a sample of 94 ninth-graders from New Orleans exposed to Hurricane Katrina and its aftermath. Thirty youth with elevated test anxiety completed a primarily behavioral (e.g., relaxation training combined with gradual exposure to anxiety-provoking test-related stimuli) group-administered, test anxiety-reduction intervention. Findings suggest a statistically significant effect of the intervention on test anxiety levels and academic performance, with evidence of positive secondary effects on post-traumatic stress symptoms (PTS). Moreover, change in test anxiety predicted change in PTS and there appeared to be no negative effects on natural PTS symptom decline.

## Ontogenic Influences

The ontogenic level is the ecology of the individual and represents factors within the individual that influence developmental adaptation. Theoretically, at the individual level, direct exposure to life threat in a disaster increases activity of the limbic–hypothalamic–pituitary–adrenal (LHPA) axis as part of a normative fight–flight reaction. Fear reactions are associated with elevations in the secretion of cortisol, a corticosteroid hormone produced by the adrenal cortex that can be assayed from blood, urine, or saliva samples (see Nader & Weems, 2011 for a review). The intense taxing of this system in disasters may lead to dysregulation of the system. Dysregulation in this system has been associated with a number of emotional and behavioral disorders (Gunnar, 2001; Weems & Carrión, 2009; Yehuda, 2006). Research suggests that after a period of relative cortisol hypersecretion elevated levels may reverse in trauma exposed individuals (De Bellis, 2001; Weems & Carrion, 2007) to relatively low levels of cortisol (Yehuda, 2006). This low cortisol may result from an enhanced negative feedback loop at the pituitary-adrenal level of the LHPA axis (Yehuda et al., 1995). One mechanism for this sensitization may be an increased number of glucocorticoid receptors in the LHPA axis that facilitates the negative feedback loop (Yehuda, 2006).

Changes in neural structure and function following stress (Carrión, Garrett, Menon, Weems, & Reiss, 2008; Carrión, Weems, & Reiss, 2007; Carrión, Weems, Richert, Hoffman, & Reiss, 2010) and susceptibility to dysregulation in the normative stress response may characterize individual risk for mental health problems among disaster victims. Recently, La Greca, Lai, Joormann, Auslander, and Short (2013) found molecular genetic evidence for susceptibility in that they showed that while greater exposure to hurricane stressors was related to more symptoms of PTSD and depression in a sample of 116 children, this effect was stronger for children with the Met allele of the brain-derived neurotrophic factor (BDNF). A number of other individual youth characteristics are important in shaping the developmental adaptation to disasters.

Research has suggested that pre-existing characteristics of the child can influence the impact of disaster exposure on mental health outcomes. In particular, previous research has documented that pre-hurricane trait anxiety and negative affect levels predict PTSD symptoms above and beyond exposure to the trauma (La Greca et al., 1998; Weems, Piña, et al., 2007). For example, Weems, Piña, et al. (2007) found that both pre-disaster negative affect and trait anxiety predicted post-disaster PTS symptoms even when controlling for, pre-disaster PTSD symptoms, level of exposure and demographic characteristics. Theoretically, pre-existing trait anxiety is thought to impact the way children are able to cope with and process the traumatic event (La Greca et al., 1996; Vernberg, La Greca, Silverman, & Prinstein, 1996). Those with elevated trait anxiety are theorized to be less able to positively cope and are more likely to have elevated PTS symptoms even with relatively low exposure experiences (Hensley & Varela, 2008; La Greca et al., 1998).

Youths' coping behaviors represent another potential moderator of psychological outcomes following natural disasters. For example, avoidant coping such as withdrawal is associated with greater PTSD symptoms (e.g., La Greca et al., 1996; Vernberg et al., 1996), while active coping (e.g., problem-focused coping) is associated with lower depression symptoms in youth hurricane survivors (e.g., Jeney-Gammon, Daugherty, Finch, Belter, & Foster, 1993). Pina et al. (2008) found that avoidant coping behaviors (i.e., repression, avoidant actions) predicted post-Katrina PTSD and anxiety symptoms, which is consistent with other research (Norris et al., 2002). Terranova, Boxer, and Morris (2009) examined predictors of PTSD symptoms in a sample of 152 sixth-grade school children from southeast Louisiana (neighboring Orleans parish) assessed at 1.5 months and 8 months after Katrina and found that negative coping (a combination of internalizing, externalizing, and avoidant coping) was associated with PTSD at 1.5 months. Peer victimization (i.e., being bullied) was predictive of change in PTSD (PTSD symptoms at Time 2 controlling for symptoms at Time 1) and results further indicated that negative coping interacted with level of hurricane exposure to predict change in PTSD, such that high negative coping and high exposure was associated with the highest PTSD symptoms at Time 2.

Increasingly, researchers have begun to define and identify multiple trajectories of symptoms following disasters and the importance of identifying resilient subsamples (Masten & Obradovic, 2008). For example, Bonanno, Brewin, Kaniasty, and La Greca (2010) and Bonanno, Westphal, and Mancini (2011) have identified four prototypical trajectories: chronicity, characterized by a sharp elevation in symptoms and in functional impairment leading to chronic dysfunction; resilience or healthy adjustment, indicated by transient symptoms and minimal impairment; recovery, characterized by initial elevations in symptoms and distress that gradually decrease over months; and delayed distress, exemplified by moderate elevations in symptoms and distress following a traumatic event that gradually worsen over time (see also Masten & Obradovic, 2008). Conceptually, resilience emphasizes "that some children facing adversity nonetheless do well (or return to positive functioning following a period of maladaptation)" (Sroufe, 1997, p. 256). Resilience then is defined by 1) exposure to some risk (e.g., facing disaster-related adversity), as well as 2) the relatively positive functioning of some compared to others. As a subcomponent of point 1 the "resilient" should have the same level of risk exposure as the non-resilient (for related discussion, see Luthar, Cicchetti, & Becker, 2000). Clearly exposure to a disaster represents risk, but samples of disaster-exposed youth can be very heterogeneous with regards to the level of exposure. Thus, a group with a stable low trajectory may seem "resilient" but in fact may simply be relatively less exposed to traumatic experiences. Weems & Graham (2014) report results consistent with these theoretical syntheses about the nature of trajectories post disaster (Bonanno et al., 2010; 2011) and also with models of childhood anxiety symptom trajectories more broadly (Feng, Shaw, & Silk, 2008; Weems, 2008) in that subsamples of youth with both increasing, decreasing, chronic, and stable low levels of PTSD symptoms were identified. While a relatively large group (43%) with a stable low trajectory was identified the group had significantly less exposure experiences but level of exposure was not homogeneous in this subsample. A subsample of the stable low group was defined as a resilient group according to commensurability in level of risk exposure (total sample average or higher levels of disaster experiences) as the non-resilient group (i.e., chronic/stable high). In this case a much smaller portion ($n = 16\%$) were considered resilient. Moreover, comparison of all stable low with stable high would have led to an erroneous conclusion about the use of avoidant coping strategies. It was the truly resilient (low symptoms and high exposure) who reported the lowest levels of avoidant coping strategies.

Research and theory suggests that in addition to symptoms of post-traumatic stress several other types of negative youth reactions may be associated with exposure to a natural disaster such as anxiety, depression, and somatic difficulties (e.g., Furr, Comer,

Edmunds, & Kendall, 2010; Hensley & Varela, 2008; Roberts, Mitchell, Witman, & Taffaro, 2010). In addition to anxiety, depression, and somatic problems, several studies have begun examining the link between disaster exposure and externalizing problems (e.g., conduct problems, physical aggression; Hoven et al., 2005; Madkour, Johnson, Clum, & Brown, 2011; Marsee, 2008; Reijneveld, Crone, Verhulst, & Verloove-Vanhorick, 2003; Yang et al., 2011). However, a close examination of this literature suggests there is only modest evidence to support a direct link between externalizing problems and disaster exposure (e.g., Spell et al., 2008; Yang et al., 2011). For example, Spell et al. (2008) reported a non-significant main effect of Hurricane Katrina disaster exposure on externalizing symptoms measured with the Child Behavior Checklist ($r = .09$; $p > .05$; Achenbach, 1991) among 260 youth (fourth- to eighth-graders).

One possible reason for the inconsistency between the disaster literature and maltreatment/violence literature is that "externalizing behaviors" in general may not link strongly to disaster exposure and disaster-related PTSD symptoms (Scott, Lapré, Marsee, & Weems, 2014). Among youth, peer aggression in particular may be related to the stress of disaster exposure, and aggressive behavior exhibited post-disaster may be more closely linked with PTSD symptoms than with disaster exposure (Jakupcak & Tull, 2005; Marsee, 2008; Moretti, Obsuth, Odgers, & Reebye, 2006; Ozkol, Zucker, & Spinazzola, 2011; Taft, Vogt, Marshall, Panuzio, & Niles, 2007). Theoretically, there are a number of instances where anxiety may motivate a child to act out using aggressive behavior (see Kunimatsu & Marsee, 2012; Marsee, 2008; Marsee, Weems, & Taylor, 2008). For example, anxious emotion associated with PTSD may foster aggressive acts towards peers in the context of relatively mild peer provocation (Marsee, 2008). In other words, unlike exposure to violence or maltreatment, disaster exposure may be more proximally linked to PTSD symptoms that in turn prompt aggression as part of a heightened activation of the anxiety and fear response system (Kunimatsu & Marsee, 2012). Marsee (2008) found initial support for this theoretical perspective among adolescents and the finding was recently replicated by Scott et al. (2014) in a sample of $n = 191$, fourth- to eighth-grade minority youth who experienced Hurricane Katrina with findings consistent with the theory that there is mainly an indirect link between disaster exposure and aggression and this was through PTSD symptoms.

## Conclusions

The most salient and well-researched emotional responses to a disaster are symptoms of post-traumatic stress disorder, anxiety disorders, and depression (e.g., La Greca et al.,1996; Lonigan, Shannon, Taylor, Finch, & Sallee, 1994; Silverman & La Greca, 2002; Vernberg, et al.,1996; Yule et al., 2000); however, other forms of emotional problems have also been found (e.g., Marsee, 2008; Hensley & Varela, 2008). The effects of disaster on youth mental health may stem directly from exposure to the disaster and its aftermath or from a number of factors in the broader and immediate environment changed as a result of disaster. Such an ecological perspective promotes the identification of indirect effects of disasters.

While research on disasters in youth still tends to focus on the individual child, research is emerging that identifies societal, community, and family influences on child adaptation following disaster. The positive upshot of the ecological model is that while the model points to all the many potential negative influences on youths' emotional development, it also helps to show that there are just as many areas for intervention. Applying the extant empirical knowledge within the model presented to the realm of policy (Drury, Scheeringa, & Zeanah, 2008; Osofsky, Osofsky, & Harris, 2007) suggests that efforts to prevent and minimize suffering in the wake of disaster will benefit from addressing these multiple levels of impact with interventions in each of the ecologies. From a developmental perspective, much has been learned about the cross sectional linkages between factors thought to influence emotional development. To a lesser extent, studies have also been able to examine the longitudinal course of emotional problems following disaster, but research that helps to elucidate the impact of disasters on the lifespan or long term course of emotional development are still needed.

The extant literature has identified 1) qualitative (e.g., physical presence, personal experiences, through relationships) and quantitative (e.g., distance) aspects of exposure to the disaster, that are associated with 2) a host of outcomes (e.g., PTSD symptoms, emotion dysregulation, anxiety disorders, depression, post-traumatic growth). There are also a number of correlates and predictors of outcomes in addition to aspects of exposure (e.g., coping, trait anxiety) as well as pre-disaster, pre-trauma, or otherwise pre-existing risk (e.g., pre-disaster trait anxiety, prior trauma), and 4) various intermediary processes such as mediators and moderators (e.g., parenting behavior) of exposure, and other predictors or pre-trauma risk. Disaster experience/exposure has been described according to their physical proximity to the epicenter, actual injuries suffered, witnessing death or injury to others, and suffering direct life threat, and even via interpersonal and media exposure. Studies have viewed exposure as existing on a continuum from close proximity and many experiences to distal exposure and/or few experiences. In addition, while research suggests that the larger the dose, the larger the effect on outcomes, this varies by the outcome assessed and a number of potential moderators and mediators of the effect.

The literature review in this chapter has focused on symptoms and diagnoses of mental disorders, but research has also linked disaster exposure to biological, cognitive/affective, behavioral, and social/interpersonal outcomes that may underlie risk for mental health problems. For example, research suggests that disaster exposure is associated with negative cognitions and dysregulation in emotional expression (Marsee, 2008; Sprung, 2008). Biological and physical health outcomes are also an important direction for future research in the disaster literature on youth. For example, Hensley and Varela (2008) have shown that Katrina disaster exposure was associated with somatic complaints such as headaches, gastrointestinal distress, and pain symptoms. Similarly, Leitch (2007) found physical pain (45%), sleep problems (30%) and headaches (10%) occurred following tsunami exposure and Meynard, Nau, Halbert, and Todesco (2008) reported that fever, diarrhea, skin infections, wounds and respiratory symptoms were common among their sample of tsunami-affected youth. There also appears to be an association with exposure and changes in physiological responding as indexed by cortisol activity and cardiac activity (Gump, Reihman, Stewart, Lonky, & Darvill, 2005; Pfeffer, Altemus, Heo, & Jiang, 2007). For example, Pfeffer and colleagues studied children bereaved by the 9/11 terror attacks. They found that although bereaved children had higher cortisol levels, bereaved children with PTSD showed relatively lower evening cortisol levels than bereaved children without PTSD (Pfeffer et al., 2007).

There are also numerous interpersonal effects of disaster and traumatic stress exposure; for example, Weems et al. (2010) found that 76% of the sample reported a hard time seeing friends. The immediate impact of the disasters may be that entire neighborhoods are swept away or made inaccessible. For example, in New Orleans, residents were under a forced evacuation for at least 5 weeks (DeSalvo et al., 2007) and displaced more than 2.5 million people throughout the United States (Larrance et al., 2007). Children and their families were separated from peer groups, extended family networks, neighborhoods, schools, and daycare centers, and these separations tended to be extended. For up to 9 months after the disaster approximately 85,000 people remained housed in temporary FEMA trailer communities, resulting in continued separations from their original neighborhoods, schools, and extended family groups (Larrance et al., 2007).

In addition to level of exposure, various demographic, psychosocial, family, and social variables have emerged as predictors (either simply as correlates or as longitudinal predictors or even pre-existing-before the disaster-factors) of outcomes in the child disaster literature. These include pre-existing symptoms and diagnoses of mental disorders or indices of mental health related functional impairment; biological and pre-dispositional risk factors; cognitive/affective; behavioral; social/interpersonal factors. Overall, girls appear to be at greater risk, with the exception of some studies reporting relatively more externalizing for boys (La Greca and Silverman, 2006; Weems et al., 2010). Results of age have been inconsistent (Weems, Piña et al., 2007; Weems et al., 2010). La Greca and Silverman (2006) also summarized the results of age as "inconsistent," due to developmental differences in symptom presentation, small samples, and contradictory results across the child disaster literature. For example, Hoven and colleagues (2005) found that age differences emerged in type, but not severity, of symptoms. The unique effects of disaster exposure are often difficult to disentangle from pre-existing conditions in the majority of studies conducted on disasters. However, the studies that have controlled/examined do suggest that pre-existing trait anxiety and negative affective states are potent predictors of post-disaster functioning as is prior trauma (La Greca et al., 1998; Weems, Piña, et al., 2007).

Another important take home message from the extant literature is that the effect of disaster exposure and other risks can be a function of one or more mediators or moderators. There are a number of ways to characterize both mediators and moderators conceptually and analytically. Variables that may have influenced the nature of a relationship or the conditions where a relationship exists between exposure or other predictor and an outcome are considered moderators. For example, Holmes, Creswell, and O'Connor (2007) found that intrusive imagery about 9/11 interacted with peri-traumatic stress exposure to predict relatively stable PTSD symptoms. Terranova et al. (2009) found that negative coping interacted with level of hurricane exposure to predict change in PTSD, such that high negative coping and high exposure was associated with the highest PTSD symptoms at Time 2.

Variables that serve as the putative mechanism or theoretical reason for a link between exposure or other predictor and an outcome is considered a mediator. This point is highlighted by research on the effects of disaster on academic achievement. The studies that have examined the effects of disaster related traumatic stress on academic problems point to possible difficulties arising amongst youth exposed to war/violence (Saigh, Mroueh, & Bremner, 1997), as well as pre-hurricane related disaster academic ability predicting post disaster response (La Greca et al., 1998).

While the extant literature suggests linkages between traumatic stress exposure and academic difficulties, it appears that the effect of exposure may be largely a function of emotional disorder symptoms (such as PTSD) and not a direct effect of the traumatic stress (see Saigh et al., 1997). Weems et al. (2013) found that the association of disaster-related stress to academic achievement was indirect via linkages from earlier (Time 1) post-traumatic stress disorder (PTSD) symptoms which predicted later (Time 2) test anxiety. Time 2 test anxiety was then negatively associated with academic achievement. The findings from Weems et al. (2013), as well as the findings reviewed in this chapter, highlight the importance of identifying heterotypic continuity in the mental health responses to disaster in youth.

In closing, it is important to note that effective interventions are available to youth experiencing mental health difficulties following disaster. Cognitive behavioral therapies (CBT) have extensive empirical support (e.g., Chemtob, Nakashima, & Hamada, 2002; see Silverman, Ortiz et al., 2008, for review and meta-analysis). CBT interventions are typically exposure-based, and include various additional specific techniques such as psychoeducation, cognitive coping strategies, and relapse prevention (see Silverman, Ortiz et al., 2008). The research to date for disaster-exposed youth indicate reductions in youths' post-traumatic stress symptoms from pre- to post-treatment, as well as maintenance of treatment gains at follow-up (Chemtob et al., 2002; Salloum & Overstreet, 2008). Thus far, however, relatively few studies have investigated the efficacy of school-based treatments for youth exposed to natural disasters (compared to other types of traumas) and most have taken place in the relatively recent aftermath of the disaster (e.g., earthquakes, Goenjian et al., 2005; hurricanes, Chemtob et al., 2002; Salloum & Overstreet, 2008; Taylor & Weems, 2011; and tsunami, Catani et al., 2009).

## References

Aber, J. L., Gershoff, E. T., Ware, A., & Kotler, J. A. (2004). Estimating the effects of September 11th and other forms of violence on the mental health and social development of New York City's youth: A matter of context. *Applied Developmental Science*, *8*, 111–129.

Abramason, D., & Garfield, R. (2006). *On the edge: Children and families displaced by hurricanes Katrina and Rita face a looming medical and mental health crisis* (A report of the Louisiana child and family health study). Downloadable from https://academiccommons.columbia.edu/catalog/ac:148106 Accessed January 15, 2017.

Achenbach, T. M. (1991). *Manual for the child behavior checklist/4-18 and 1991 profile.* Burlington, VT: University of Vermont Department of Psychiatry.

Bobo, L. D. (2006). Katrina: Unmasking race, poverty, and politics in the 21st century. *Du Bois Review*, *3*, 1–6.

Bourque, L. B., Siegel, J. M., Kano, M., & Wood, M. M. (2006). Weathering the storm: The impact of hurricanes on physical and mental health. *The Annals of the American Academy of Political and Social Science*, *604*, 129–151.

Bonanno, G. A., Brewin, C. R., Kaniasty, K., & La Greca, A. M. (2010). Weighing the costs of disaster consequences, risks, and resilience in individuals, families, and communities. *Psychological Science in Public Interest*, *11*, 1–49.

Bonanno, G. A., Westphal, M., & Mancini, A. D. (2011). Resilience to loss and potential trauma. *Annual Review of Clinical Psychology*, *7*, 1–25.

Bronfenbrenner, U. (1979). *The ecology of human development.* Cambridge, MA: Harvard University Press.

Carrión, V. G., Garrett, A., Menon, V., Weems, C. F., & Reiss, A. L. (2008). Posttraumatic stress symptoms and brain function during a response-inhibition task: An fMRI study in youth. *Depression and Anxiety*, *25*, 514–526.

Carrión, V. G., Weems, C. F., & Reiss, A. L. (2007). Stress predicts brain changes in children: A pilot longitudinal study on youth stress, PTSD, and the hippocampus. *Pediatrics*, *119*, 509–516.

Carrión, V. G., Weems, C. F., Richert, K., Hoffman, B., & Reiss, A. L. (2010). Decreased prefrontal cortical volume associated with increased bedtime cortisol in traumatized youth. *Biological Psychiatry*, *68*, 491–493.

Catani, C., Kohiladevy, M., Martina, R., Schauer, E., Elbert, T., & Neuner, F. (2009). Treating children traumatized by war and tsunami: A comparison between exposure therapy and meditation relaxation in North-East Sri Lanka. *BMC Psychiatry*, *9*, 1–11.

Chemtob, C. M., Nakashima, J. P., & Hamada, R. S. (2002). Psychosocial intervention for post-disaster trauma symptoms in elementary school children. *Archives of Pediatric and Adolescent Medicine*, *156*, 211–216.

Comer, J. S., & Kendall, P. C. (2007). Terrorism: The psychological impact on youth. *Clinical Psychology: Science and Practice*, *14*, 179–212.

De Bellis, M. D. (2001). Developmental traumatology: The psychobiological development of maltreated children and its implications for research, treatment, and policy. *Development and Psychopathology*, *13*, 539–564.

DeSalvo, K., B., Hyre, A. D., Ompad, D. C., Menke, A., Tynes, L. L., & Muntner, P. (2007). Symptoms of posttraumatic stress disorder in a New Orleans workforce following Hurricane Katrina. *Journal of Urban Health*, *84*, 142–152.

Drury, S. S., Scheeringa, M. S., & Zeanah, C. H. (2008). The traumatic impact of Hurricane Katrina on children in New Orleans. *Child and Adolescent Psychiatric Clinics of North America*, *17*, 685–702.

Eisenberg, N., & Silver, R. C. (2011). Growing up in the shadow of terrorism: Youth in America after 9/11. *American Psychologist*, *66*, 468–481.

Feng, X., Shaw, D. S., & Silk, J. S. (2008). Developmental trajectories of anxiety symptoms among boys across early and middle childhood. *Journal of Abnormal Psychology*, *117*, 32–47.

Furr, J. M., Comer, J. S., Edmunds, J. M., & Kendall, P. C. (2010). Disasters and youth: A meta-analytic examination of posttraumatic stress. *Journal of Consulting and Clinical Psychology*, *78*(6), 765–780.

Gil-Rivas, V., Silver, R. C., Holman, E. A., McIntosh, D. N., & Poulin, M. (2007). Parental response and adolescent adjustment to the September 11, 2001 terrorist attacks. *Journal of Traumatic Stress*, *20(6)*, 1063–1068. doi:10.1002/jts.20277

Goenjian, A. K., Walling, D., Steinberg, A. M., Karayan, I., Najarian, L. M., & Pynoos, R. (2005). A prospective study of posttraumatic stress and depressive reactions among treated and untreated adolescents five years after a catastrophic disaster. *American Journal of Psychiatry*, *162*, 2302–2308.

Gump, B. B., Reihman, J., Stewart, P., Lonky, E., & Darvill, T. (2005). Terrorism and cardiovascular responses to acute stress in children. *Health Psychology*, *24(6)*, 594–600. doi:10.1037/0278-6133.24.6.594

Gunnar, M. R. (2001). The role of glucocorticoids in anxiety disorders: A critical analysis. In M. W. Vasey & M. R. Dadds (Eds.), *The developmental psychopathology of anxiety* (pp. 143–159). New York: Oxford University Press.

Hagan Jr, J. F., American Academy of Pediatrics, Committee on Psychosocial Aspects of Child and Family Health, & Task Force on Terrorism. (2005). Psychosocial implications of disaster or terrorism on children: A guide for the pediatrician. *Pediatrics*, *116*, 787–795.

Haque, C. E. (2003). Perspectives of natural disasters in East and South Asia, and the Pacific Island States: Socio-economic correlates and needs assessment. *Natural Hazards*, *29*(3), 465–483.

Hensley, L., & Varela, R. E. (2008). PTSD symptoms and somatic complaints following Hurricane Katrina: The role of trait anxiety and anxiety sensitivity. *Journal of Clinical Child and Adolescent Psychology*, *37*, 542–552.

Hobfoll, S. E. (1989). Conservation of resources: A new attempt at conceptualizing stress. *American Psychologist*, *44*, 513–524.

Holmes, E. A., Creswell, C., & O'Connor, T. G. (2007). Posttraumatic stress symptoms in London school children following September 11, 2001: An exploratory investigation of peri-traumatic reactions and intrusive imagery. *Journal of Behavior Therapy and Experimental Psychiatry*, *38*, 474–490. doi:10.1016/j.jbtep.2007.10.003

Hoven, C. W., Duarte, C. S., Lucas, C. P., Wu, P., Mandell, D. J., Goodwin, R. D., et al. (2005). Psychopathology among New York City public school children 6 months after September 11. *Archives of General Psychiatry*, *62*, 545–552.

Jakupcak, M., & Tull, M. T. (2005). Effects of trauma exposure on anger, aggression, and violence in nonclinical sample of men. *Violence and Victims*, *20*, 589–598.

Jeney-Gammon, P., Daugherty, T. K., Finch Jr, A. J., Belter, R. W., & Foster, K. Y. (1993). Children's coping styles and report of depressive symptoms following a natural disaster. *The Journal of Genetic Psychology*, *154*, 259–267.

Kilmer, R. P., & Gil-Rivas, V. (2010). Exploring posttraumatic growth in children impacted by Hurricane Katrina: Correlates of the phenomenon and developmental considerations. *Child Development*, *81*(4), 1211–1227.

Kunimatsu, M. M., & Marsee, M. A. (2012). Examining the presence of anxiety in aggressive individuals: The illuminating role of fight-or-flight mechanisms. *Child and Youth Care Forum*, *41*, 247–258. doi:10.1007/s10566-012-9178-6

La Greca, A. M., Lai, B. S., Joormann, J., Auslander, B., & Short, M. (2013). Children's risk and resilience following a natural disaster: Genetic vulnerability, posttraumatic stress, and depression. *Journal of Affective Disorders*, *151*, 860–867. doi:10.1016/j.jad.2013.07.024

La Greca, A. M., & Silverman, W. K. (2006). Treating children and adolescents affected by disasters and terrorism. In P. C. Kendall (Ed.), *Children and adolescent therapy: Cognitive-behavioral procedures* (3rd ed., pp. 356–382). New York: Guilford Press.

La Greca, A. M., Silverman, W. K., Vernberg, E. M., & Prinstein, M. J. (1996). Symptoms of posttraumatic stress in children alter Hurricane Andrew: A prospective study. *Journal of Consulting and Clinical Psychology*, *64*, 712–723.

La Greca, A. M., Silverman, W. K., Vernberg, E. M., & Roberts, M. C. (Eds.). (2002). *Helping children cope with disasters and terrorism.* Washington, DC: American Psychological Association.

La Greca, A. M., Silverman, W. K., & Wasserstein, S. B. (1998). Children's predisaster functioning as a predictor of posttraumatic stress following Hurricane Andrew. *Journal of Consulting and Clinical Psychology*, *66*, 883–892.

Larrance, R., Anastario, M., & Lawry, L. (2007). Health status among internally displaced persons in Louisiana and Mississippi travel trailer parks. *Annals of Emergency Medicine*, *49*, 590–601.

Leitch, M. L. (2007). Somatic experiencing treatment with Tsunami survivors in Thailand: Broadening the scope of early intervention. *Traumatology*, *13(3)*, 11–20. doi:10.1177/1534765607305439

Lengua, L. J., Long, A. C., Smith, K. I., & Meltzoff, A. N. (2005). Pre-attack symptomatology and temperament as predictors of children's responses to the September 11 terrorist attacks. *Journal of Child Psychology and Psychiatry*, *46*(6), 631–645. doi:10.1111/j.1469-7610.2004.00378.x

Lonigan, C. J., Shannon, M. P., Taylor, C. M., Finch, A. J., & Sallee, F. R. (1994). Children exposed to disaster: II. Risk factors for the development of post-traumatic symptomatology. *Journal of the American Academy of Child & Adolescent Psychiatry*, *33*(1), 94–105.

Luthar, S. S., Cicchetti, D., & Becker, B. (2000). The construct of resilience: A critical evaluation and guidelines for future work. *Child Development*, *71*(3), 543–562.

Madkour, A. S., Johnson, C. C., Clum, G. A., & Brown, L. (2011). Disaster and youth violence: The experience of school-attending youth in New Orleans. *Journal of Adolescent Health*, *49*, 213–215. doi:10.1016/j.jadohealth.2011.06.005

Marsee, M. A. (2008). Reactive aggression and posttraumatic stress in adolescents affected by Hurricane Katrina. *Journal of Clinical Child and Adolescent Psychology*, *39*, 519–529.

Marsee, M. A., Weems, C. F., & Taylor, L. K. (2008). Exploring the association between aggression and anxiety in youth: A look at aggressive subtypes, gender, and social cognition. *Journal of Child and Family Studies*, *17*, 154–168.

Masten, A. S., & Obradovic, J. (2008). Disaster preparation and recovery: Lessons from research on resilience in human development. *Ecology and Society*, *13*(1), 9.

Meynard, J., Nau, A., Halbert, E., & Todesco, A. (2008). Health indicators in children from Meulaboh, Indonesia, following the Tsunami of December 26, 2004. *Military Medicine*, *173*(8), 900–905.

Moretti, M. M., Obsuth, I., Odgers, C. L., & Reebye, P. (2006). Exposure to maternal vs. paternal partner violence, PTSD, and aggression in adolescent girls and boys. *Aggressive Behavior*, *32*(4), 385–395.

Nader, K. O., & Weems, C. F. (2011). Understanding and assessing cortisol levels in children and adolescents. *Journal of Child and Adolescent Trauma*, *4*, 318–338.

Norris, F. H., Friedman, M. J., & Watson, P. J. (2002). 60,000 disaster victims speak: Part II. *Summary and implications of the disaster mental health research. Psychiatry*, *65*, 240–260.

Osofsky, J. D., Osofsky, H. J., & Harris, W. W. (2007). Katrina's children: Social policy considerations for children in disasters. *Social Policy Report*, *21*, 3–18.

Osofsky, H. J., Osofsky, J. D., Kronenberg, M., Brennan, A., & Hansel, T. C. (2009). Posttraumatic stress symptoms in children after Hurricane Katrina: Predicting the need for mental health services. *American Journal of Orthopsychiatry*, *79*(2), 212–220. doi:10.1037/a0016179

Ozkol, H., Zucker, M., & Spinazzola, J. (2011). Pathways to aggression in urban elementary school youth. *Journal of Community Psychology*, *39*(6), 733–748.

Pfeffer, C. R., Altemus, M., Heo, M., & Jiang, H. (2007). Salivary cortisol and psychopathology in children bereaved by the September 11, 2001 terror attacks. *Biological Psychiatry*, *61*, 957–965. doi:10.1016/j.biopsych.2006.07.037

Pfefferbaum, B., Seale, T., Brandt, E., Pfefferbaum, R., Doughty, D., & Rainwater, S. (2003). Media exposure in children one hundred miles from a terrorist bombing. *Annals of Clinical Psychiatry*, *15*, 1–8.

Pfefferbaum, B. J., Weems, C. F., Scott, B. G., Nitiéma, P., Noffsinger, M.A., Pfefferbaum, R. L., et al. (2013). Research methods in child disaster studies: A review of studies generated by the September 11, 2001, terrorist attacks; the 2004 Indian Ocean Tsunami; and Hurricane Katrina. *Child & Youth Care Forum*, *42*, 285–337. doi:10.1007/s10566-013-9211-4

Pina, A. A., Villalta, I. K., Ortiz, C. D., Gottschall, A. C., Costa, N. M., & Weems, C. F. (2008). Social support, perceived discrimination, and coping as predictors of posttraumatic stress reactions in youth survivors of Hurricane Katrina. *Journal of Clinical Child and Adolescent Psychology*, *37*, 564–574.

Pynoos, R. S., Goenijian, A. K., & Steinberg, A. M. (1998). A public mental health approach to post-disaster treatment of children and adolescents. *Child and Adolescent Psychiatry Clinics of North American*, *7*, 195–210.

Roberts, Y. H., Mitchell, M. J., Witman, M., & Taffaro, C. (2010). Mental health symptoms in youth affected by Hurricane Katrina. *Professional Psychology: Research and Practice*, *41*(1), 10–18. doi:10.1037/a0018339

Reijneveld, S. A., Crone, M. R., Verhulst, F. C., & Verloove-Vanhorick, S. P. (2003). The effect of a severe disaster on the mental health of adolescents: A controlled study. *The Lancet*, *362*(9385), 691–696.

Saigh, P. A., Mroueh, M., & Bremner, J. D. (1997). Scholastic impairments among traumatized adolescents. *Behaviour Research and Therapy*, *35*, 429–436.

Salloum, A., & Overstreet, S. (2008). Evaluation of individual and group grief and trauma interventions for children post disaster. *Journal of Clinical Child and Adolescent Psychology*, *37*, 495–507.

Sandler, I. (2001). Quality and ecology of adversity as common mechanisms of risk and resilience. *American Journal of Community Psychology*, *29*, 19–61.

Scaramella, L. V., Sohr-Preston, S. L., Callahan, K. L., & Mirabile, S. P. (2008). A test of the Family Stress Model on toddler-aged children's adjustment among Hurricane Katrina impacted and non-impacted low income families. *Journal of Clinical Child and Adolescent Psychology*, *37*, 530–541.

Scheeringa, M. S., & Zeanah, C. H. (2008). Reconsideration of harm's way: Onsets and comorbidity patterns of disorders in preschool children and their caregivers following Hurricane Katrina. *Journal of Clinical Child and Adolescent Psychology*, *37*, 508–518.

Schlenger, W. E., Caddell, J. M., Ebert, L., Jordan, B. K., Rourke, K. M., Wilson, D, et al. (2002). Psychological reactions to terrorist attacks: Findings from the national study of Americans' reactions to September 11. *Journal of the American Medical Association*, *88*(5), 581–588. doi:10.1001/jama.288.5.581

Schuster, M. A., Stein, B. D., Jaycox, L. H., Collins, R. L., Marshall, G. N., Elliott, M. N, et al. (2001). A national survey of stress reactions after the September 11, 2001, terrorist attacks. *The New England Journal of Medicine*, *345*(20), 1507–1512. doi:10.1056/NEJM200111153452024

Scott, B. G., Lapré, G. E., Marsee, M. A., & Weems, C. F. (2014). Aggressive behavior and its associations with posttraumatic stress and academic achievement in youth following a natural disaster. *Journal of Clinical Child and Adolescent Psychology*, *43*, 43–50. doi: 10.1080/15374416.2013.807733.

Silverman, W. K., & La Greca, A. M. (2002). Children experiencing disasters: Definitions, reactions, and predictors of outcomes. In A. M. La Greca, W. K. Silverman, E. M. Vernberg, & M. C. Roberts (Eds.), *Helping children cope with disasters* (pp. 11–34). Washington, DC: American Psychological Association.

Silverman, W. K., Oritz, C. D., Viswesvaran, C., Burns, B. J., Kolko, D. J., Putnam, F.W., et al. (2008). Evidence based treatments for children and adolescents exposed to traumatic events. *Journal of Clinical Child and Adolescent Psychology*, *37*(1), 156–183.

Spell, A. W., Kelley, M. L., Self-Brown, S., Davidson, K., Pellegrin, A., Palcic, J., et al. (2008). The moderating effects of maternal psychopathology on children's adjustment post-Hurricane Katrina. *Journal of Clinical Child and Adolescent Psychology*, *37*, 553–563.

Sprung, M. (2008). Unwanted intrusive thoughts and cognitive functioning in kindergarten and young elementary school-age children following Hurricane Katrina. *Journal of Clinical Child and Adolescent Psychology*, *37*(3), 575–587. doi:10.1080/15374410802148236

Sroufe, L. A. (1997). *Emotional development: The organization of emotional life in the early years*. Cambridge: Cambridge University Press.

Taft, C. T., Vogt, D. S., Marshall, A. D., Panuzio, J., & Niles, B. L. (2007). Aggression among combat veterans: Relationships with combat exposure and symptoms of posttraumatic stress disorder, dysphoria, and anxiety. *Journal of Traumatic Stress*, *20*(2), 135–145.

Taylor, L. K., & Weems, C. F. (2011). Cognitive-behavior therapy for disaster exposed youth with posttraumatic stress: Results from a multiple-baseline examination. *Behavior Therapy*, *42*, 349–363.

Terranova, A. M., Boxer, P., & Morris, A. S. (2009). Factors influencing the course of posttraumatic stress following a natural disaster: Children's Reactions to Hurricane Katrina. *Journal of Applied Developmental Psychology*, *30*, 344–355.

Toya, H., & Skidmore, M. (2007). Economic development and the impacts of natural disasters. *Economics Letters, 94*(1), 20–25.

Vernberg, E. M., La Greca, A. M., Silverman, W. K., & Prinstein, M. J. (1996). Prediction of posttraumatic stress symptoms in children after Hurricane Andrew. *Journal of Abnormal Psychology, 105*, 237–248.

Weems, C. F. (2008). Developmental trajectories of childhood anxiety: Identifying continuity and change in anxious emotion. *Developmental Review, 28*, 488–502.

Weems, C., & Carrion, V. (2007). The association between PTSD symptoms and salivary cortisol in youth: The role of time since the trauma. *Journal of Traumatic Stress, 20*(5), 903–907.

Weems, C., & Carrion, V. (2009). Diurnal salivary cortisol in youth: Clarifying the nature of posttraumatic stress dysregulation. *Journal of Pediatric Psychology, 34*, 389–395.

Weems, C. F., & Graham, R. A. (2014). Resilience and trajectories of posttraumatic stress among youth exposed to disaster. *Journal of Child and Adolescent Psychopharmacology, 24*, 2–8.

Weems, C. F., & Overstreet, S. (2008). Child and adolescent mental health research in the context of Hurricane Katrina: An ecological-needs-based perspective and introduction to the special section. *Journal of Clinical Child and Adolescent Psychology, 37*, 487–494.

Weems, C. F., & Overstreet, S. (2009). An ecological-needs-based perspective of adolescent and youth emotional development in the context of disaster: Lessons from Hurricane Katrina. In K. E. Cherry (Ed.), *Lifespan perspectives on natural disasters: Coping with Katrina, Rita and other storms* (pp. 27–44). New York: Springer.

Weems, C. F., Piña, A. A., Costa, N. M., Watts, S. E., Taylor, L. K., & Cannon, M. F. (2007). Pre-disaster trait anxiety and negative affect predict posttraumatic stress in youth after Hurricane Katrina. *Journal of Consulting and Clinical Psychology, 75*, 154–159.

Weems, C. F., Scott, B. G., Banks, D. M., & Graham, R. A. (2012). Is TV traumatic for all youths? The role of pre-existing posttraumatic stress symptoms on the link between disaster coverage and stress. *Psychological Science, 23*, 1293–1297. doi:10.1177/0956797612446952

Weems, C. F., Scott, B. G., Taylor, L. K., Cannon, M. F., Romano, D. M., & Perry, A. M. (2013). A theoretical model of continuity in anxiety and links to academic achievement in disaster exposed school children. *Development and Psychopathology, 25*, 729–738. doi:10.1017/S0954579413000138

Weems, C. F., Taylor, L. K., Cannon, M. F., Marino, R., Romano, D. M., Scott, B. G., et al. (2010). Posttraumatic stress, context, and the lingering effects of the Hurricane Katrina disaster among ethnic minority youth. *Journal of Abnormal Child Psychology, 38*, 49–56.

Weems, C. F., Taylor, L. K., Costa, N. M., Marks, A. B., Romano, D. M., Verrett, S. L., et al. (2009). Effect of a school-based test anxiety intervention in ethnic minority youth exposed to Hurricane Katrina. *Journal of Applied Developmental Psychology, 30*, 218–226.

Weems, C. F., Watts, S. E., Marsee, M. A., Taylor, L. K., Costa, N. M., Cannon, M. F., et al. (2007). The psychosocial impact of Hurricane Katrina: Contextual differences in psychological symptoms, social support, and discrimination. *Behaviour Research and Therapy, 45*, 2295–2306.

Yang, P., Yen, C. F., Tang, T. C., Chen, C. S., Yang, R. C., Huang, M. S., et al. (2011). Posttraumatic stress disorder in adolescents after Typhoon Morakot-associated mudslides. *Journal of Anxiety Disorders, 25*(3), 362–368.

Yehuda, R. (2006). Advances in understanding neuroendocrine alterations in PTSD and their therapeutic implications. *Annals of the New York Academy of Sciences, 1071*, 137–166.

Yehuda, R., Kahana, B., Binder-Brynes, K., Southwick, S. M., Mason, J. W., & Giller, E. L. (1995). Low urinary cortisol excretion in Holocaust survivors with posttraumatic stress disorder. *American Journal of Psychiatry, 152*, 982–986.

Yule, W., Bolton, D., Udwin, O., Boyle, S., O'Ryan, D., & Nurrish, J. (2000). The long-term psychological effects of a disaster experienced in adolescence: I: The incidence and course of PTSD. *Journal of Child Psychology and Psychiatry, 41*(4), 503–511.

# 20

# Cultural Perspectives and Influences on Developmental Psychopathology

## *Lessons about Risk, Disorder, and Wellbeing from the Study of the Indigenous Peoples of North America*

Jacob A. Burack, Ashley Reynolds, Oriane Landry, Gillian Klassen, Natalie Russo, and Stephanie A. Fryberg

"Savages we call them, because their manners differ from ours, which we think the perfection of civility; they think the same of theirs."

At the end of the 18th century, the American scientist, inventor, and statesperson, Benjamin Franklin noted the irony in the common use of the term "savages" to refer to Indigenous peoples who, ironically, were just as sure of the righteousness of their own societies and just as likely to criticize the faults, and "savagery", of the dominant European American society. In arguing against both the use of the term "savages" and the accepted notion that Indigenous ways of being were less civil than those of the mainstream society, he highlighted the intrinsic shortcoming of judging the behaviors of one culture from the perspective of another. Yet, more than 200 years later, even with a greater awareness of the vast differences across various cultural and geographic populations, mainstream European-based cultures and value systems still dominate psychological understanding and judgements of human behavior, with the role of culture often relegated to a tangential footnote (Achenbach, 2014; Weisz, McCarty, Eastman, Chaiyasit, & Suwanlert, 1997). However, when psychologists ignore culture in the study of human behavior, they ignore a basic developmental reality that all humans develop within a cultural context and express unique features of their development in accordance with their culture and unique context (Iarocci, Root, & Burack, 2009). From this perspective, the primary purpose of the developmental process is to enable the child to function adaptively within the cultural group(s) in which they live (Rogoff, 2003). This process is a transactional one in which the child is an active participant and both impacts and is impacted by the cultural context

*The Wiley Handbook of Developmental Psychopathology*, First Edition. Edited by Luna C. Centifanti and David M. Williams.

(Garcia Coll & Magnusson, 1999; Iarocci et al., 2009; Markus & Kitayama, 1991), with the end result being that the effects of culture are dependent on and experienced differently by each individual at different times in their life. This relationship between culture and psyche is consistent with Werner's (1957) orthogenetic principle that "wherever development occurs it proceeds from a state of relative globality and lack of differentiation to a state of increasing differentiation, articulation, and hierarchic integration." The older the child, the more comprehensive and nuanced their understanding of the culture, or cultures, in which they participate. The complexity of this developmental process is further underscored by the notion that cultures involve many different components that can all differentially affect and be affected by individuals over time. In this manner, cultural affiliation is a co-constitution of an ongoing process of individuals' responses to their current situation in relation to their level of developmental functioning.

Although this type of consideration of specific cultures can lead to an apparent deconstruction, or fragmentation, of a universal developmental theory (for discussions, please see Bronfenbrenner, Kessel, Kessen, & White, 1986; Kessen, 1984), we contend that the study of cultures expands and informs our conceptualizations of both development and developmental psychopathology (Achenbach, 2014). As Cicchetti and Pogge-Hesse (1982) note, cross-cultural research "can tell what developmental sequences are logically necessary, what alternate developmental pathways are possible" (p. 312). We cannot fully understand the field's essential issues related to adaptation, maladaptation, risk, resilience, disorder, and wellbeing unless we view them through the lens, or perspective, of the beholder (Kirmayer, Tait, & Simpson, 2009; Luthar & Burack, 2000; Weisz et al., 1997). Even the most basic tenet of developmental psychopathology, that "we can learn more about typical development by studying its pathology and likewise more about its pathology by studying its normal condition" (Cicchetti, 1984, p. 1) needs to be considered from the lens of culture. We can only make sense of this reciprocally informative relationship and the associated constructs of both typical and atypical development, whether due to risk or actual pathology, within the framework of societal and cultural values and expectations (Achenbach, 2014; Luthar & Zelazo, 2003; Seidman & Pederson, 2003; Wyman, 2003).

In this chapter, we provide examples from the study of Indigenous peoples (i.e., American Indian, First Nations, Inuit, and Métis) in North America to provide insights into the complexities of the notion of culture and the ways that it, and associated factors such as context and history, can both affect the adaptiveness of behaviors, development, and outcomes throughout development and color our understanding of them. For example, the study of Indigenous culture in North America must involve the consideration of multiple levels of culture and various influences on them. The collective history of the Indigenous peoples in North America with its legacy of centuries of colonization and ongoing oppression, albeit in different ways and to different extents across communities, might be seen as part of or contributing to at least some type of general, or universal, Indigenous culture (for relevant discussions of First Nations, please see Fiske, 2009; American Indians, Gone, 2009; Walls & Whitbeck, 2012; the Inuit, Kirmayer, Fletcher, & Watt, 2009; and North American Indigenous more generally, Kirmayer, Tait, & Simpson, 2009). Yet, the Indigenous cultures of North America differ so drastically from each other with regard to so many interrelated factors that reflect and impact cultural manifestations and practices, including unique histories of meeting with the European colonizers, geography, resources, economic and social opportunities and challenges, physical proximity and integration with non-indigenous peers, urbanization, sources of sustenance, language, and artwork, that the notion of an Indigenous North American culture might be considered a misnomer (Brass, 2009; Burack, Bombay, Flores, Stewart, & Pozinovsky, 2014). Thus, a basic discussion of the multiple levels of culture in this population would need to include those of: (1) Indigenous peoples in general, such as the large subgroupings of American Indian or First Nations, (2) specific tribes or communities, (3) life in Indigenous communities versus urban centers, and (4) the intersection between Indigenous cultures and that of the majority. This complexity is further compounded by the fact that Indigenous cultures, like virtually all extant cultures, are both dynamic, in that they change over time, and experienced differently across persons, even among those within the same culture.

## What is Culture?

Culture is typically considered to encompass the entire way of being that has been cultivated over time for members of a given society, including their values, beliefs, attitudes, norms, practices, language, religion, and institutions (Serafica & Vargas, 2006). However, like all constructs, culture is amorphous, rather than anything tangible, and defined by each "definer" rather than by some objective or universal meaning (Luthar & Burack, 2000). Therefore, culture is ironically itself a product of values and perspectives that are embedded in, what we could call, culture. The difficulty in conceptualizing culture is exemplified by the disparity between the common discussion of it in terms of a coherent system of meaning, institutions, and practices, and the paradoxically dichotomous representation of it as fragmented, fluid, and context-specific (e.g., Kirmayer & Ban, 2013). In the absence of contact with another culture, members of a given culture are likely to understand their culture as inherent and universal as they would know nothing else (Burack et al., 2014). Thus, the notion of culture can never be entirely captured as cultures are defined largely relative to each other. Yet, cultures clearly involve some identifiable systems. For example, Gone and Kirmayer (2010) articulated that culture involves various components in that it is (1) social, as it is shared among the members of an identified society; (2) patterned, as it is systematically organized for the understanding of both those within and from outside the society; (3) historically produced, as the society and its values continue across generations; and (4) symbolic, as it allows for the communication of meaning among the members of the society.

In this context, culture provides historical and contemporary commonalities with other members of the same group including those related to social institutions, knowledge, attitudes, and practices (Choudhury & Kirmayer, 2009). It provides the guideline for the meaning and understanding of what it means to be a child, adolescent, man, woman, or elder in relation to specific roles in society, expectations regarding behaviors as acceptable or exemplary, and parameters for beliefs and sense of belonging.

The meeting of cultures necessitates increased complexity that cannot be captured in the discussion of a single, monolithic, representative culture for each society or individual, but rather necessitates addressing culture at multiple levels. In an example from Canada, the culture of a Cree community in northern Quebec would at the very least include aspects of the culture of the specific community, other Cree communities in the region, other Cree communities throughout Canada, First Nations peoples living in rural areas (as opposed to urban or more centrally located areas), First Nations peoples throughout Canada, other Indigenous peoples of Canada (including the Métis and Inuit), North American Indigenous peoples, Indigenous peoples worldwide, oppressed minority persons at home and abroad, in addition to dominant culture that is becoming increasingly pervasive due to the developments in technology, including social media, and other aspects of the globalization process. And, just as the general culture of a society is a complex and dynamic conglomerate of multiple influences, the culture and identity of any individual is unique as cultural knowledge and practice varies across individuals in relation to many factors, including the developmental level of the individual and their relationships with family members and others in their community. As Serafica and Vargas (2006) highlight, "Cultural uniformity cannot be taken for granted. Cultural knowledge and adherence among members of an ethnic group is characterized by diversity and unity" (p. 590).

Even beyond the individual and community differences in the adherence to and practice of a culture, the specifics are impossible to delineate as cultures are dynamic and constantly changing, especially in encounters with other cultures (Serafica & Vargas, 2006). This inevitably of cultural change over time in relation to encounters with other cultures is highlighted by depictions of the efforts of Taamusi Qunaq, an Inuit activist, historian, and linguist, to found a cultural museum that included items that were either no longer in use or had been mementos of earlier members of the community (Graburn, 2006; Kirmayer, Tait, & Simpson, 2009). According to Graburn (2006, p. 145), Qunaq's work was premised on the idea that "time was like a vast river carrying everything in their culture out to sea to be lost forever. So he built a *suputik*, a weir, to catch all these things before they were lost." As Qunaq teaches, the process of change inevitably leads to loss of a culture, or many aspects of it, "as it was." However, that is not inherently problematic, since changes to culture can come with benefits. Cultures can endure even when they are modified, as notions of race, ethnicity, and culture itself undergo constant transformation due to migration, colonization, and the subsequent meetings of societies, ideologies of citizenship and national identity, and new technologies. For example, Indigenous cultures that evolved in relative isolation are now complexly influenced by numerous other Indigenous and nonindigenous cultures, many of which also influence other Indigenous and nonindigenous groups locally, nationally, and internationally. At an individual level, Indigenous persons who live in urban areas, have nonindigenous spouses, are involved in industry, work in white collar positions such as professors and accountants, or work in blue collar professions such as truck driver or factory worker, all engage in life activities emanating from culture changes due to the meeting of Indigenous and European cultures.

## The Disruption of the Cycle of Culture

The inevitable changes over time can be contextualized with regard to cycles of culture. In delineating such a cycle, Markus and Connor (2013) outline the four key elements of individuals, interactions, institutions, and ideas (See Figure 20.1). The *individuals* shape and are shaped by the cultures in which they live, including the cultural practices that in turn impact on the *interactions,* everyday social exchanges

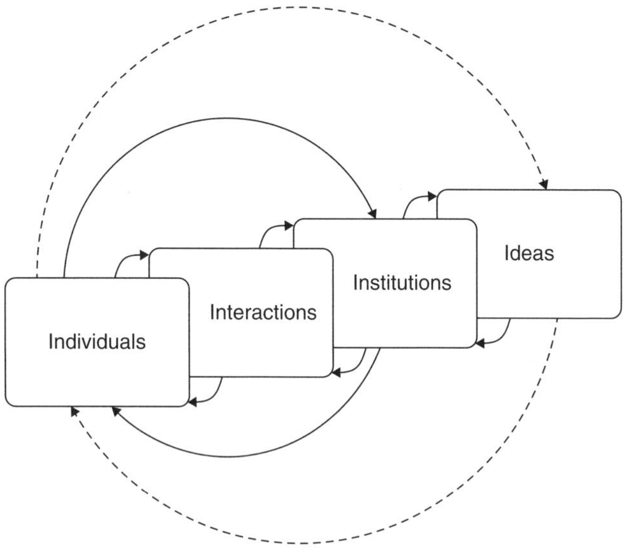


**Figure 20.1** Cycles of culture.

with others. These interactions foster and follow from the prevalent *institutions*, such as the education systems and the courts, that are essential to society and that both reflect and foster core cultural *ideas*, such as those about the essence of being a "good" person (Fryberg, Covarrubias, & Burack, in press). In traditional cultural cycles, language, parenting, and unspoken rules for social interactions are expected to be passed on in everyday social life. Thus, the natural evolution of the culture would include some changes to these practices, but not the complete break down or eradication of these cultural practices. As part of the ongoing dynamic process of the evolution of cultures, the cycle is affected by external forces such as events in history, especially encounters with other cultures. Depending on their nature, these encounters can lead to a wide range of changes from those that are minimal to those that are transformative and far-reaching, from those that are voluntary to those that are forced on the community, and from those that are seen as positive and bolster the communities in different ways to those that are catastrophic.

Small changes to the traditional cultural cycle can often be readily integrated into the culture and can eventually lead to meaningful and positive modifications while the essence and integrity of the culture is maintained. For example, the chance meeting in 1948 of an Inuit community with James Houston, a young Canadian artist, led both to the commercialization of Inuit carvings that had long been part of the culture and to the development of stone-cut printmaking and related types of art that were new, albeit based on traditional art forms (Houston, 1999). This encounter led to the introduction of new tools and technology and a new art form to many of the communities, as well as spawned a meaningful source of income for many Inuit (Houston, 1999). Although certainly not culturally transformative, the subsequent immense growth in the production of and interest in Inuit art indicates its essential role in and contribution to contemporary Inuit culture (von Finckenstein, 1999).

Abrupt and severe disruptions of the cultural cycle are often associated with deleterious, and even catastrophic, outcomes. The most compelling example is the long-term sequelae of the residential school systems, which were in operation from the late 1800s to the late 1900s in both the United States and in Canada, with more than 100,000 children in each country forced into these schools. As part of a so-called "humanitarian" reform to "civilize" and "enlighten" the Indigenous peoples of North America, both the American and Canadian governments instituted educational policies that required Indigenous children of specified ages to attend residential schools, mostly run by various Christian sects (Gone, 2009; Kirmayer et al., 2007; Miller, 1996; Milloy, 1999). For more than a century, Indigenous children were plied from their homes, sent thousands of miles away, and forced to live a life that typically involved hard physical labor and punishment, rigid routines, humiliating surveillance, and teachings that belittled their way of life in an effort to rid them of their identity and culture (Fiske, 2009). With the threat of severe punishment, they were forbidden to speak their native language, wear their native clothes, or engage in other aspects of their culture (Gone, 2009), and often suffered from inadequate health care and neglect, physical, emotional, and sexual abuse (Blacksmith, 2010; Blackstock, 2003). Even when these children were allowed to return home for the summer break from school, they were often viewed and treated as social outcasts because they brought with them a foreign language, culture, and way of living. Thus, these experiences continued to deleteriously affect the survivors throughout their lives as well as their relationships with their descendants (Blacksmith, 2010) and continue to have a lasting impact on present-day Indigenous communities (Bombay, Matheson, & Anisman, 2011; Gone, 2009).

Ironically, as the then leader of the Canadian government that had perpetuated and abetted much of the atrocities of the residential schools in North America, Prime Minister Stephen Harper (2008) articulated the essence of the legacy of the disruption of families and the cultural cycle created by the removal of children from their homes and communities in a public apology. Harper noted that,

> We now recognize that it was wrong to separate children from rich and vibrant cultures and traditions, that it created a void in many lives and communities, and we apologize for having done this. We now recognize that in separating children from their families, we undermined the ability of many to adequately parent their own children and sowed the seeds for generations to follow, and we apologize for having done this (p. 6850).

Harper's apology just touches on the extensiveness of the long-term and inter-generational sequelae of the residential school experiences to the cultural cycle of both Canadian and American communities (e.g., Burack et al., 2014; Walls & Whitbeck, 2012). As parents, the survivors of the residential schools often resorted to the only type of child-rearing they knew—the same sterile and abusive methods they had experienced in the residential schools. The intergenerational transmission of the negative effects of the residential schools were evidenced by high rates of trauma such as childhood neglect and abuse, and household dysfunction, as well as higher levels of depression, suicide and other psychiatric conditions and symptoms among the subsequent generations (Blacksmith, 2010; Bombay, Matheson, & Anisman, 2011, 2013; Evans-Campbell, 2008; Fryberg et al., in press; Stout & Peters, 2011). For Indigenous people, the dominant society's cultural idea of "kill the Indian and save the man" and resultant public policies severely interrupted the evolution process for this cultural group (Fryberg et al., in press).

## Cultural Identification

Despite histories of oppression and disadvantage, the identification with and maintenance of ancestral culture and ways of being are generally depicted as a source of resilience (Luthar, 2006; Masten, Best, & Garmezy, 1990) and promotive of wellbeing (Luthar & Burack, 2000) in the developmental outcome of minority youths. For example, Phinney (Phinney, 1989, 1991, 2000) demonstrated the importance of developing a sense of identity to culture and its association with increases in self-esteem and mental health. Cultural identity also involves the collective esteem based on positive or negative evaluation or feelings ascribed to group membership, as well as the perceptions of cohesion, commonality, and belongingness with other group members (Cameron, 2004). In one commonly used framework of cultural identity, the emphasis is on the constructs of *enculturation*, the degree to which a member of an ethnic minority group retains their culture of origin, and *acculturation*, the extent to which an individual modifies their attitudes or behavior in order to adapt to the majority culture (e.g., Berry, 1997; LaFromboise, Coleman, & Gerton, 1993). Both enculturation and acculturation vary in relation to exposure and embeddedness within the values, traditions, and practices of the distinct cultures, and may be associated with feelings of either pride or negativity about being both one's own culture and that of the dominant society. As orientation toward each culture can be independent, any combination of levels of identification with one or more cultures is possible. Thus, a person can be high in both acculturation (i.e., identifying strongly with Canadian or American dominant culture) and enculturation (i.e., well integrated within a traditional Indigenous culture). This dual identification, referred to as "bicultural," is considered by many to be the optimal cultural identity across diverse populations of minority youth, as it reflects the successful navigation of both their own and the dominant cultures, and are thereby equipped to manage cultural conflicts that arise (e.g., David, Okazaki, & Saw, 2009; LaFramboise et al., 1993; Luthar & Burack, 2000). In contrast, those who are low in both as they are not aligned with the values and ideology of either culture are thought to be the most at risk (e.g., Oetting & Beauvais, 1991; Phinney, 1989).

The history of centuries of still ongoing pervasive, profound, and ongoing challenges to the ancestral cultures of the Indigenous persons of North America from the dominant society necessitates that all Indigenous youth must navigate between at least two, often incompatible, cultures and associated ways of being—those of their culture (or cultures) and of the dominant culture in which they live. Individual differences in successfully navigating this struggle may be the reasons for the vast disparities in wellbeing at both the individual and community levels. For example, identification and affiliation with one's own ancestral Indigenous culture and people have been associated with positive mental health outcomes, despite the long history of colonization and oppression and the resultant life challenges that are faced by many (Burack et al., 2014; Wexler, 2014).

## Culture, Risk, and Wellbeing

Risk represents a challenge to the wellbeing of an individual in any one or more domains of life functioning in relation to societal or cultural developmental expectations (Burack, 1997; Fryberg & Leavitt, 2014; Luthar, 2006; Luthar & Burack, 2000;

Sroufe & Rutter, 1984). It is typically discussed within the context of the increased statistical likelihood of problematic behaviors or poor outcomes, and conversely lower levels of wellbeing in relation to contemporary cultural, societal, communal, and individual perspectives on what constitutes maladaptive or otherwise deleterious outcomes (Burack, Blidner, Flores, & Fitch, 2007; Burack et al., 2014; Iarocci et al., 2009; Kirmayer, Dandeneau, Marshall, Phillips, & Williamson, 2011). However, challenges arise when the benchmarks of success as defined by different cultures are at odds. Conceptualizations of wellbeing are virtually entirely dependent on contextual values and perspectives. As Burack and colleagues (2014) note, even the old-clichéd saying that "as long as you have your health" needs to be qualified, since notions of health and mental health vary dramatically in relation to context and culture. In some communities, just staying alive might be considered wellbeing, whereas in others, wellbeing is judged in terms of academic excellence, financial affluence, or political power. Just as indicators of wellbeing for an individual is judged in relation to societal expectations regarding the navigation of the salient developmental issues for a given age, the level of success of a community varies in relation to salient issues at a specific moment in its history. Therefore, adaptive or maladaptive development cannot be defined broadly across cultures and contexts but rather the evaluation of a given behavior is intertwined within the context in which it occurs (Luthar & Zelazo, 2003; Seidman & Pederson, 2003; Wyman, 2003). In this scenario, conflict often arises when the beliefs held by the dominant culture are discordant with those from other cultures. For example, when youths are faced with conflicting values, their ability to enculturate and acculturate are tested and come with a variety of consequences for both one's social competence and mental health (Iarocci et al., 2009). As a result of marginalization, lack of access to services, and a loss of culture, language, and spirituality arising from the conflict between their own culture and that of the dominant society, youths also face greater risk factors such as identity conflict, poor self-esteem, decreased school performance, and increased depression (Luthar & Burack, 2000; Mosley-Howard, 1995; Sameroff, Seifer, & Bartko, 1997).

As communities and individuals strive to participate and succeed in the majority culture, their ancestral cultures and ways of being are often abandoned or deemphasized by other types of persecution, necessity, or as a way of adaptation within the majority culture. In contemporary times, these challenges lead to the rather precarious survival of Indigenous languages, histories, or cultures with implications for the development of Indigenous youth (Fryberg & Leavitt, 2014). Yet, despite all the challenges faced by Indigenous communities, many communities have managed to thrive in the face of adversity (Burack et al., 2014; Gotowiec & Beiser, 1994), highlighting that adaptive or maladaptive development cannot be defined broadly across cultures and contexts but rather the evaluation of a given behavior is intertwined and transacts with the context in which it occurs (Luthar & Zelazo, 2003; Seidman & Pederson, 2003; Wyman, 2003) as the child shapes and is shaped by their cultural context (Iarocci et al., 2009).

However, conflict can arise when youth experience conflicting cultural values. For example, the beliefs held by their traditional culture may be in contrast with those from other cultures as is the case with Indigenous populations that value interdependence rather than the independence valued by Canadian and American societies. Therefore, youth development must be considered in relation to cultural conflict in order to have a full understanding of the social and emotional outcomes among Indigenous youth (Iarocci et al., 2009).

## Culture, Context, and Risk: Examples from the Study of Indigenous Youths of North America

Amid the recognition of a disparate mosaic of the Indigenous peoples of North America, the universal history of centuries of colonization and oppression (Fryberg et al., in press) suggests common sources of threats to the development of Indigenous persons (Kirmayer, Simpson, & Cargo, 2003; Kirmayer et al., 2009). One example is the considerably elevated rates of suicide among Indigenous youth, a finding that would be of concern to virtually any community but the cause of which has been linked by many to the disruption of the cultural cycle. Another example is the markedly lowered rates of academic success among Indigenous youth, that has been linked to the mismatch of cultures between the Indigenous and dominant cultures, with the latter imposed on the former. Yet, despite these increased risks for negative outcomes among Indigenous youth, we note that many Indigenous communities have continued to thrive and experience high levels of mental health and continue to pass on their culture to the subsequent generations (please also see Burack et al., 2014; Kirmayer et al., 2009). Thus, the transmission of community-specific cultures and cultural cycles in an era of increasing globalization is cited as a source of resilience for the youths in these areas of potential risk.

### Risk for Suicide and the Ameliorative Effects of Communal Cultural Continuity

The often-reported high rates of suicide among Indigenous peoples, especially among youth, are a serious problem but are also misleading as they vary dramatically across communities. Vast disparities among communities have been noted even within specific regions of Canada (Kirmayer et al., 2007). Attempts to explain these differences and others related to mental health are largely focused on community-level factors such as the history, structure, and dynamics of a given community (Chandler & Lalonde, 1998; Chandler, Lalonde, Sokol, & Hallett, 2003; Kirmayer et al., 2009).

In their attempt to explain differences in suicide rates in First Nations communities in British Columbia that ranged from 0 to 800 times the provincial average, Chandler and Lalonde (1998) argued for "cultural continuity as a hedge against suicide," in which cultural continuity is the commitment to the future and a sense of one's own continuity over time (also see Chandler et al., 2003). Consistent with the notion of the catastrophic events associated with the disruption of the cycle of culture, the risk for suicide and other deleterious outcomes is exacerbated among First Nations persons because the European colonization pervasively disrupted and undermined the ancestral cultures until contemporary times. Conversely, Chandler and Lalonde hypothesized that a community's engagement in activities aimed at maintaining or even reclaiming its culture of heritage would be associated with more positive outcomes among its youth for whom the activities would provide evidence of cultural continuity. In support of their hypothesis, Chandler and Lalonde (1998) found that lower suicide rates among Indigenous youth in British Columbia during the years 1987–1992 were associated with communities' engagement in six activities thought to reflect efforts to preserve and rehabilitate ancestral culture. These activities included attempts to (1) secure the title to their ancestral lands; (2) reclaim aspects of self-governance;

(3) take some control of education; (4) take some control of the police and fire-protection services; (5) take some control of health services; and (6) establish "cultural facilities" intended to preserve and enrich the ancestral culture. In a follow-up, Chandler and Lalonde (2009) extended their initial study (Chandler & Lalonde, 1998) by including data from adults, as well as youths, during the additional 8-year period of 1993 to 2000, and by expanding the index of cultural continuity to include both the number of council seats occupied by women and the provision of child and family services within the community. The participation of women in local government can be considered an index of cultural rehabilitation among the First Nations communities in the west coast of Canada, which were historically largely matrilineal. The information on child and family services reflects progress in gaining control of child custody and protection services following an era, known as the "sixties scoop" (Chandler & Lalonde, 2009; Kirmayer et al., 2009; Wieman, 2009) in which many children were adopted outside the community or placed in government institutions. The findings from the follow-up study indicated a clear cumulative effect of the factors on suicide rates as the more factors attained by a given community the lower its suicide rate. In addition, self-government appeared to be the only factor that never occurred in isolation, but instead was strongly correlated with a number of other factors such as control over police and fire protection, health services, and the establishment of cultural facilities.

Chandler and Lalonde (1998, 2009; Chandler et al., 2003) provide a compelling narrative of the power of cultural continuity within a community, the risks associated with its loss, and the benefits associated with the struggle for its reclamation. Even other interpretations of their indexes and findings point to the effect of the continuity of the community, through both modern and historically traditional cultural activities. In one example, Kirmayer et al. (2007) suggest that, as data from cross-sectional research is always open to alternative explanations, the reductions in suicide might have been related to other potentially covarying but unmeasured markers of generally healthy communities such as sense of empowerment, collective self-efficacy, and better infrastructure. Moreover, at least some of the factors, such as the involvement of Indigenous people in contemporary institutions like municipal government or formal school systems may not be indicators of the traditional or historical culture, and that the factors in general might better reflect cultural flexibility and adaptability rather than the maintenance of tradition. Based on these conclusions, Kirmayer and colleagues contend that "local control" better describes the factors and the reason for the decreased suicide rates than cultural continuity, but, in essence, local control reflects the ability of the community to ensure the continuity of the cultural cycle and its inevitable changes over time.

Similarly, in addressing the high rates of suicide among the Inuit, Kirmayer et al. (2007) and Kral (2012; Kral & Idlout, 2009) and colleagues highlight the empowerment of the community, especially in the delivery of mental health services, in leading to personal empowerment and wellbeing. They suggest that the social and health services of the dominant society, with their person-centered focus, have largely failed the Inuit for whom the foundation of collective wellbeing is necessary to attain personal wellbeing. Rather, greater success in preventing suicide has been evidenced among communities that have owned their own mental health and have initiated and controlled prevention projects (Kral & Idlout, 2009), especially among the youth (Kral, 2012). Due to marginalization and assimilation policies of the past, decision-making among Indigenous people has been taken away from the individual, family, and community (Kral & Idlout, 2009). Concordantly, due to the importance of the collective nature of one's wellbeing, collective control may be important for the collective wellbeing of these communities (Kral & Idlout, 2009). Although individual autonomy has always been respected within many Inuit groups, kinship and interdependence have been at the basis of their being. Therefore both collective and personal control and efficacy become intertwined and do not need to be in conflict with each other (Kral & Idlout, 2009).

## Educational Risk: The Persistent Underperformance of Indigenous Youth

The persistent problems regarding low educational attainment and high rates of school dropout among Indigenous students highlight meaningful ways that generations of youth from non-dominant cultures continue to be disadvantaged long after the initial encounter with the majority culture. As the individuals in these situations navigate between, at least two, often incompatible, cultures and associated ways of being, those who are most connected to their own culture are the most disadvantaged by the cultural mismatch. In one simple example, persons who learn and speak their own minority culture language may be delayed and less proficient in speaking the language of the majority culture, which is inevitably essential to academic success. Similarly, persons from the minority culture are often judged and assessed negatively in the case of school settings in which students are evaluated by teachers from the majority culture who, even when well-meaning, are instilled with mainstream values and guidelines for education through personal life experiences and professional training (Fryberg & Markus, 2007; Gone, 2009). These cultural discrepancies between mainstream classrooms and those from minority cultures lead to a cultural mismatch in educational settings that can lead to academic underperformance. For example, the schooling systems across both the United States and Canada continue to fail too many Indigenous people as they are based in the cultural values and notions of success of the dominant culture, in which the emphasis is on fostering and rewarding ideas of independence and assertiveness that are generally discordant with the values of the Indigenous peoples (Gone, 2009). In this manner, educational settings perpetuate the colonization of Indigenous students by disregarding or ignoring their cultural backgrounds (Fryberg et al., in press). In order to conceptualize the colonization process in the education system, we first explore the persisting problem of academic underperformance of Indigenous students in North America. Then, we discuss how promoting independence within school systems presents a cultural mismatch for Indigenous students that impacts students' interactions and individual-level experiences in the classroom (i.e., decreases performance and belonging).

The question remains of how to explain the perpetuating low rates of academic success among Indigenous students in both Canada and the United States. In one explanation, Fryberg and colleagues (Fryberg, Covarrubias, & Burack, 2013; Fryberg et al., in press; Fryberg & Markus, 2007; Stephens, Markus, & Fryberg, 2012) invoke cultural mismatching theory, in which the imposition of Western models of education advantage students from the dominant culture while disadvantaging students from other cultures, including Indigenous students. In particular North American educational systems at all levels foster and reflect specific cultural values in which independence, autonomy, individualism, and competition are esteemed, and competition is encouraged as a means of fostering learning and success (Stephens et al., 2012; Fryberg & Markus, 2007; Plaut & Markus, 2005). These values generally match the cultural models of education of the students from the dominant culture, but are likely mismatched with Indigenous students' cultural models of education (Lomawaima, 1999; Swisher & Deyhle, 1992). For example, teachers may interpret Indigenous students' reluctance to participate in a competitive classroom as a lack of motivation or as withdrawal from learning, although the origins of this behavior are more likely due to cultural values and ways of being. Indigenous cultures often explicitly discourage competition because it risks upsetting relationships between group members while encouraging harmony and cooperation within the group (Pewewardy, 2002; Sanders, 1987). The relevance of these cultural models of interdependence to the performance of Indigenous students, was highlighted by Fryberg, Troop-Gordon, et al. (2013), who found that both endorsing interdependence and establishing a trusting relationship with teachers predicted academic achievement for a group of Native American high school students from the state of Washington. In contrast, endorsing independence predicted academic achievement and having a trusting relationship with teachers did not appear to impact performance among a comparison group of European American schoolmates.

These different understandings of self also highlight differences in communication styles that affect achievement in the learning environment. Whereas quick responses to questions are rewarded by teachers in European cultures as they are considered indicative of better ability and more knowledge (Safran, Safran, & Pirozak, 1994; White & Tharp, 1988), reflection and careful thinking about the topic are more consistent with "good" communication in Indigenous cultural contexts (Littlebear, 1992; More, 1987; Pewewardy, 1998; Sanders, 1987). Teachers who lack this knowledge about Indigenous culture may misinterpret the communication style of Indigenous students and thereby erroneously attribute the style of responding to a lack of motivation or learning of classroom material.

These cultural mismatches highlight the ongoing colonization of Indigenous youths. The prominent messages of independence embedded within the American classroom, mistaken by members of the dominant culture as a culturally neutral learning space, provide both an indirect and direct method of excluding Indigenous student identities. By not incorporating Indigenous cultural backgrounds or models of education, Indigenous students receive the message that they do not belong and cannot succeed in educational contexts. These messages of independence have been shown to decrease belonging and performance for Indigenous students (Covarrubias & Fryberg, 2014; Covarrubias, Herrmann, & Fryberg, 2014; Fryberg, Troop-Gordon et al., 2013; Stephens et al., 2012).

The educational experiences of Indigenous youth are likely also affected by the complex relationship between non-educational considerations including the history of schooling of the dominant society among the Indigenous peoples. Like many oppressed minority communities, the schools have historically been places of considerable failure, while also being increasingly recognized as vital to obtaining a place in the present-day globalized economy. Yet, the educational history of the Indigenous people is even more complexly related as it is marked with painful memories of abuse and assimilation. Gone (2009) suggests that, as a result, many Indigenous individuals feel in conflict, as learning to think like a "white man" through the education system will change the available cultural experiences—once one becomes incorporated into mainstream education, one can never return to an "(ab)original state of mind" (Gone, 2009, p. 422). He notes that many Elders believe that as Indigenous cultures are essentially linked to Indigenous languages, just learning to speak English (or any other language imposed by the dominant culture) results in a different structure and knowing of experiences that can never be the same as those of the ancestors. Simply the learning of math, science, and English socializes Indigenous elementary and high school students in the dominant society's way of being to the extent that Elders often have difficulty recognizing the new individuals that emerge.

## Culturally based Perceptions of Mental Health Problems

The emphasis on European cultures in mental health is reflected in the extent to which psychiatric diagnoses and practices are based on Western views of mental disorders. For example, current clinical practices typically involve the administration of structured interviews to assess specific symptoms, behaviors, and experiences in relation to the diagnostic criteria of the World Health Organization (2010) or the American Psychiatric Association (2013). In this process, the consideration of culture-related variability is typically limited to minor differences in language, explanation, or symptom expression that are insufficient to capture the disparate ways that different cultures experience and express psychological distress (Kirmayer & Ban, 2013; Kral & Idlout, 2009). Kirmayer and Ban (2013) highlight both that "clusters of symptoms may cohere in different ways across cultures" (p. 107) and that culture affects the way people recognize and categorize mental disorders. Accordingly, the application of diagnostic categories developed in one cultural context (i.e., European culture) to another cultural context (i.e., Indigenous) inevitably detracts from the utility and validity of the process for the latter (Gone & Kirmayer, 2010).

These types of cultural differences in interpreting and coping with psychopathology are exemplified in Kirmayer and colleagues' (Kirmayer, 1994; Kirmayer et al., 2009) ethnographic study in the early 1990s of Inuit views on mental health that involved interviews with key informants from four communities in northern Quebec. The Inuit participants identified four broad causes of mental health issues including: physical or organic, emotional or psychological, spirit possession, and the consequence of rapid social and cultural change. Organically based mental health problems are those with which the child is born, such as Down syndrome, or are apparent at an early age, as in the case of epilepsy. These problems were thought to originate due to environmental factors such as the mother's drug use and practices during pregnancy, which assigned tremendous responsibility to mothers with regard to their newborns' physical and mental health. Psychological causes were associated both with individual and inter-personal factors. At the individual level, problems such as mild to moderate forms of depression and anxious mood were attributed to psychological underpinnings due to too much thinking *(isumaaluttuq)* or being unable to think due to "having no mind" (*isumaqanngituq*). Interpersonally-based problems such as family conflict were thought to underlie a wide range of mental health problems and, as a result, forgiveness was seen as essential to maintaining mental health. Spirit possession was seen as the cause of mental health problems and were described in terms of the manipulations of one's soul that could exert destructive forces on the interaction between the individual and their soul. In these cases, extreme behaviors are tolerated and explained as spirit communications. Recent social and cultural changes among the Inuit communities over the last two to three generations were described in relation to the role of the mass media as a source of cultural conflict between the youth and their parents, as it is seen as an intrusion of non-Inuit values.

This example of the northern Quebec Inuit illustrates how mental health can be conceptualized in ways that are both similar to and distinct from Western medicine (Kirmayer et al., 2009). The Inuit recognized multiple pathways to mental illness, including a biologically or bioecologically based source, a rumination-type/cognitively-based type, a psychosis-type, and environmental stressors, all of which play roles in Western medical models of psychopathology. One area of distinction is the causal attributions, such as those regarding mothers' actions during pregnancy or the individuals' ruminations. The focus on forgiveness and spiritual possession, neither of which are unique to that culture, are largely dismissed by Western medicine. In all these cases, a culturally-endorsed perspective that mental health is sometimes under one's control may also be empowering, provided the necessary supports are in place to ensure success. These disparate understandings of psychopathology necessarily lead to treatment options that are different than those utilized by mainstream practitioners.

## Cultural Influences on Intervention

The treatment of psychopathology is largely contingent on historical and cultural frameworks of meaning (Gone & Kirmayer, 2010; McCormick, 2009). This is especially the case when the power and authority is attached to cultural systems, such as the Western medical profession, that may not be relevant to individuals from communities based in other cultures (Walls & Whitbeck, 2011). For example, as colonization is seen as having led to so many physical and mental health problems among the Indigenous peoples of North America, mental health services from the dominant culture are often jettisoned as neither useful nor culturally relevant to Indigenous communities (Gone & Kirmayer, 2010; Wieman, 2009). Mainstream interventions or treatment programs have typically had little success with Indigenous populations as they are based on the dominant culture at the exclusion of cultural, historical, and sociopolitical contexts of Indigenous peoples (Kirmayer et al., 2009; Kral & Idlout, 2009). The lack of sufficient training about or sensitivity to the traditions, values, and beliefs systems of Indigenous people undermines the potential of any therapeutic success and results in situations in which Indigenous clients fear that intervention is in direct conflict with, and focused on changing, their traditional cultural values and beliefs (LaFramboise et al., 1993; McCormick, 2009).

Even when well-meaning, Western-educated mental health professionals' attempts to "help" Indigenous individuals with their struggles are undermined by the failure to consider that seeing a psychologist is not a culturally relevant approach to addressing one's problems or understanding one's behavior among Indigenous groups (Gone, 2003, 2006). Within this context, many Indigenous individuals experience their encounters with mental health professionals as coercive and are uncomfortable with the intrusion of psychology (Gone, 2009). Ironically, Indigenous individuals who have become psychologists themselves also experience discomfort with the field of psychology. Gone (2009) highlights that credentials from the dominant society are influential and can be used by Indigenous psychologists to support the community, however, those who complete the training typically complain that Western training is neither readily accessible nor culturally relevant. Rather, effective healing for the community must still be learned from within the community. This is supported by McCormick (2009) who notes that counseling is not a new phenomenon for Indigenous people who have long sought counseling from expert helpers (e.g., Elders), but those from their own communities. In that context, essential aspects of being among many Indigenous peoples such as connectedness with others, spirituality, nature, ceremonies, and tradition and/or culture can all play a significant role in promoting wellbeing.

## Conclusions

In this chapter, we provide lessons from the experience of the Indigenous peoples of North America to better understand the influences and perspectives of culture on developmental psychopathology. Culture is ubiquitous as it influences every moment of our being and every aspect of our development. Its influence is so profound, we never even notice it until we encounter a conflicting cultural perspective. And, as we learn from the study of Indigenous populations, unique risk factors present as a function of the socio-historical as well as present-day context of a community, in its resources and in its relation to other communities. Conversely, wellbeing is found in one's relationship with the cultural values of one's own heritage and community, as well as in the successful navigation of potential conflicts with other cultures, especially that of the dominant society. The perception of developmental success is culturally-defined, and therefore attempts to promote wellbeing must also occur within the appropriate cultural context.

## References

Achenbach T. M. (2014). Using multicultural research to expand the scope of developmental psychopathology. In J. A. Burack & L. A. Schmidt (Eds.), *Cultural and contextual perspectives on developmental risk and well-being*, Vol. *39* (pp. 7–38). New York: Cambridge University Press.

American Psychiatric Association. (2013). *Diagnostic and statistical manual of mental disorders* (5th ed.). Arlington, VA: American Psychiatric Publishing.

Berry, J. W. (1997). Immigration, acculturation, and adaptation. *Applied Psychology*, *46*, 5–34.

Blacksmith, G. (2010). *The intergenerational legacy of the Indian residential school system on the Cree communities of Mistissini, Oujebougamau and Waswanipi: An investigative research on the experiences of three generations of the James Bay Cree of Northern Quebec*. Montreal, QC: McGill University Library.

Blackstock, C. (2003). First Nations child and family services: Restoring peace and harmony in First Nations communities. In K. Kufeldt & B. McKenzie (Eds.), *Child welfare: Connecting research policy and practice* (pp. 331–342). Waterloo, ON: Wilfred Laurier University Press.

Bombay, A., Matheson, K., & Anisman, H. (2011). The impact of stressors on second generation Indian residential school survivors. *Transcultural Psychiatry*, *48*, 367–391.

Bombay, A., Matheson, K., & Anisman, H. (2013). Expectations among Aboriginal peoples in Canada regarding the potential impacts of a government apology. *Political Psychology*, *34*, 443–460.

Bougie, E., Kelly-Scott, K., & Arriagad, P. (2013, November). *The education and employment experiences of First Nations people living off reserve, Inuit, and Métis: Selected findings from the 2012 Aboriginal peoples survey*. Statistics Canada. Retrieved January 12, 2017 from http://www.statcan.gc.ca/pub/89-653-x/89-653-x2013001-eng.htm?fpv=10000.

Brass, G. M. (2009). Respecting the medicines: Narrating an Aboriginal identity. In L. J. Kirmayer & G. G. Valaskakis (Eds.), *Healing traditions: The mental health of Aboriginal peoples in Canada* (pp. 355–380). Vancouver, BC: UBC Press.

Bronfenbrenner, U., Kessel, F., Kessen, W., & White, S. (1986). Toward a critical social history of developmental psychology: A propaedeutic discussion. *American Psychologist*, *41*, 1218–1230.

Burack, J. A. (1997). The study of typical and atypical populations: The quest for a common science. In S. S. Luthar, J. A. Burack, D. Cicchetti, & J. R. Weisz (Eds.), *Developmental psychopathology: Perspectives on adjustment, risk, and disorder* (pp. 139–165). New York: Cambridge University Press.

Burack, J., Blidner, A., Flores, H., & Fitch, T. (2007). Constructions and deconstructions of risk, resilience and wellbeing: A model for understanding the development of Aboriginal adolescents. *Australasian Psychiatry*, *15*, S18–S23.

Burack, J. A., Bombay, A. Flores, H., Stewart, J., & Ponizovsky, V. (2014). Developmental perspectives on the role of cultural identity in well-being: Evidence from Aboriginal communities in Canada. In J. A. Burack & L. A. Schmidt (Eds.), *Cultural and contextual perspectives on developmental risk and well-being* (pp. 81–106). New York: Cambridge University Press.

Burack, J. A., & Schmidt, L. A. (Eds.). (2014). *Cultural and contextual perspectives on developmental risk and well-being* (Vol. *39*). New York: Cambridge University Press.

Cameron, J. E. (2004). A three-factor model of social identity. *Self and Identity*, *3*, 239–262.

Cicchetti, D. (1984). The emergence of developmental psychopathology. *Child Development*, *55*, 1–7.

Cicchetti, D., & Pogge–Hesse, P. (1982). Possible contributions of the study of organically retarded persons to developmental theory. In E. Zigler & D. Balla (Eds.), *Mental retardation: The developmental-difference controversy* (pp. 277–318). Hillsdale, NJ: Erlbaum.

Chandler, M. J., & Lalonde, C. (1998). Cultural continuity as a hedge against suicide in Canada's First Nations. *Transcultural Psychiatry*, *35*, 191–219.

Chandler, M. J., & Lalonde, C. (2009). Cultural continuity as a moderator of suicide among Canada's First Nations. In L. J. Kirmayer & G. G. Valaskakis (Eds.), *Healing traditions: The mental health of Aboriginal peoples in Canada* (pp. 221–248). Vancouver, BC: UBC Press.

Chandler, M. J., Lalonde, C. E., Sokol, B. W., & Hallett, D. (2003). Personal-persistence, identity development, and suicide: A study of Native and non-Native North American adolescents. *Monographs of the Society for Research in Child Development*, *68*, 1–130.

Choudhury, S., & Kirmayer, L. J. (2009). Cultural neuroscience and psychopathology: Prospects for cultural psychiatry. *Progress in Brain Research*, *178*, 263–283.

David, E. J. R., Okazaki, S., & Saw, A. (2009). Bicultural self-efficacy among college students: Initial scale development and mental health correlates. *Journal of Counseling Psychology*, *56*, 211–226.

Evans-Campbell, T. (2008). Historical trauma in American Indian/Native Alaska communities: A multilevel framework for exploring impacts on individuals, families, and communities. *Journal of Interpersonal Violence*, *23*, 316–338.

Fiske, J. (2009). Placing violence against First Nations children: The use of space and place to construct the (in)credible violated subject. In L. J. Kirmayer & G. G. Valaskakis (Eds.), *Healing traditions: The mental health of Aboriginal peoples in Canada* (pp. 140–159). Vancouver, BC: UBC Press.

Franklin, B. (1967). *Remarks concerning the savages of North-America.* In B. Franklin, *The Bagatelles from Passy.* Ed. C. A. Lopez. New York: Eakins Press. Retrieved January 12, 2017 from http://mith.umd.edu/eada/html/display.php?docs=franklin_bagatelle3.xml.

Fryberg, S. A. (2012). Cultural psychology as a bridge between anthropology and cognitive science. *Topics in Cognitive Science, 4*, 437–444.

Fryberg, S. A., Covarrubias, R., & Burack, J. A. (in press). The ongoing psychological colonization of North American indigenous people: Using social psychological theories to promote social justice. In P. Hammock (Ed.), Oxford handbook of social psychology and social justice. New York: Oxford University Press.

Fryberg, S. A., Covarrubias, R., & Burack, J. A. (2013). Cultural models of education and academic performance for Native American and European American students. *School Psychology International, 34*, 439–452.

Fryberg, S. A., & Leavitt, P. A. (2014). A sociocultural analysis of high-risk Native American children in schools. In J. A. Burack & L. A. Schmidt (Eds.), *Cultural and contextual perspectives on developmental risk and well-being*, Vol. *39* (pp. 57–80). New York: Cambridge University Press.

Fryberg, S. A., & Markus, H. R. (2007). Cultural models of education in American Indian, Asian American and European American contexts. *Social Psychology of Education, 10*, 213–246.

Fryberg, S., Troop-Gordon, W., D'Arrisso, A., Flores, H., Ponizovskiy, V., Ranney, J., et al. (2013). Cultural mismatch and the education of Aboriginal youths: The interplay of cultural identities and teacher ratings. *Developmental Psychology, 49*, 72–79. doi://dx.doi.org/10.1037/a0029056

Garcia Coll, C., & Magnusson, K. (1999). Cultural influences on child development: Are we ready for a paradigm shift? In A. S. Masten (Ed.), *Cultural processes in child development: The Minnesota Symposia on Child Psychology* (pp. 1–24). Mahwah, NJ: Lawrence Erlbaum.

Gone, J. P. (2003). American Indian mental health service delivery: Persistent challenges and future prospects. In J. S. Mio and G. Y. Iwamasa (Eds.), *Culturally diverse mental health: The challenges of research and resistance* (pp. 211–229). New York: Brunner-Routledge.

Gone, J. P. (2006). Mental health, wellness, and the quest for authentic American Indian identity. In T. Witko (Ed.), *Mental health care for urban Indians: Clinical insights from Native practitioners*, (pp. 55–80). Washington, DC: American Psychological Association.

Gone, J. P. (2009). Encountering professional psychology: Re-envisioning mental health services for Native North America. In L. J. Kirmayer & G. G. Valaskakis (Eds.), *Healing traditions: The mental health of Aboriginal peoples in Canada* (pp. 419–439). Vancouver, BC: UBC Press.

Gone, J. P., & Kirmayer, L. J. (2010). On the wisdom of considering culture and context in psychopathology. T. Millon, R. F. Krueger, & E. Simonsen (Eds.), *Contemporary directions in psychopathology: Scientific foundations of the DSM-V and ICD-11* (pp. 72–96). New York: Guilford Press.

Gotowiec, A., & Beiser, M. (1994). Aboriginal children's mental health: Unique challenges. *Canada's Mental Health, 41*, 7–11.

Graburn, N. (2006). Culture as narrative. In P. Stern & L. Stevenson (Eds.), *Critical Inuit Studies: An Anthology of Contemporary Arctic Ethnography* (pp. 139–154). Lincoln: University of Nebraska Press.

Harper. S. (2008). *Statement by ministers: Apology to former students of Indian residential schools (Official report: Hansard).* Ottawa, ON: House of Commons Debates.

Houston, J. (1999). Fifty years of thinking it over. In M. von Finckenstein (Ed.), *Celebrating Inuit art, 1948–1970* (pp. 19–38). Hull, QC: Canadian Museum of Civilization.

Iarocci, G., Root, R., & Burack, J. A. (2009). Social competence and mental health among Aboriginal youth: An integrative developmental perspective. In L. J. Kirmayer & G. G. Valaskakis (Eds.), *Healing traditions: The mental health of Aboriginal peoples in Canada* (pp. 80–106). Vancouver, BC: UBC Press.

Kessen, W. (1984). Introduction: The end of the age of development. In R. Sternberg (Ed.), *Mechanisms of Cognitive Development* (pp. 1–17). San Francisco: Freeman.

Kirmayer, L. J. (1989). Cultural variations in the response to psychiatric disorders and emotional distress. *Social Science & Medicine, 29*, 327–339.

Kirmayer, L. J. (1994). Suicide among Canadian Aboriginal peoples. *Transcultural Psychiatry, 31*, 3–58.

Kirmayer, L. J., & Ban, L. (2013). Cultural psychiatry: Research strategies and future directions. *Advances in Psychosomatic Medicine, 33*, 97–114. doi:10.1159/000348742

Kirmayer, L. J., Brass, G. M., Holton, T. L., Paul, K., Tait, C. L., & Simpson, C. (2007). *Suicide among Aboriginal peoples in Canada*. Ottawa, ON: Aboriginal Healing Foundation.

Kirmayer, L. J., Dandeneau, S., Marshall, E., Phillips, M. K., & Williamson, K. J. (2011). Rethinking resilience from Indigenous perspectives. *Canadian Journal of Psychiatry, 56*, 84–91.

Kirmayer, L. J., Fletcher, C., & Watt, R. (2009). Locating the ecocentric self: Inuit concepts of mental health and illness. In L. J. Kirmayer & G. G. Valaskakis (Eds.), *Healing traditions: The mental health of Aboriginal peoples in Canada* (pp. 289–314). Vancouver, BC: UBC Press.

Kirmayer, L., Simpson, C., & Cargo, M. (2003). Healing traditions: Culture, community and mental health promotion with Canadian Aboriginal peoples. *Australasian Psychiatry, 11*, S15–S23.

Kirmayer, L. J., Tait, C. L., & Simpson, C. (2009). The mental health of Aboriginal peoples in Canada: Transformations of identity and community. In L. J. Kirmayer & G. G. Valaskakis (Eds.), *Healing traditions: The mental health of Aboriginal peoples in Canada* (pp. 3–35). Vancouver, BC: UBC Press.

Kleinman, A. (1987). Anthropology and psychiatry: The role of culture in cross-cultural research on illness. *The British Journal of Psychiatry, 151*, 447–454.

Kral, M. J. (2012). Postcolonial suicide among Inuit in arctic Canada. *Culture, Medicine, and Psychiatry, 36*, 306–325.

Kral, M. J., & Idlout, L. (2009). Community wellness and social action in the Canadian Arctic: Collective agency as subjective well-being. In L. J. Kirmayer & G. G. Valaskakis (Eds.), *Healing traditions: The mental health of Aboriginal peoples in Canada* (pp. 315–334). Vancouver, BC: UBC Press.

LaFromboise, T., Coleman, H. L., & Gerton, J. (1993). Psychological impact of biculturalism: Evidence and theory. *Psychological Bulletin, 114*, 395–412.

Littlebear, D. (1992). Getting teachers and parents to work together. In J. Reyhner (Ed.), *Teaching American Indian students* (pp. 104–111). Norman, OK: University of Oklahoma Press.

Lomawaima, K. T. (1999). The unnatural history of American Indian education. In K. G. Swisher & J. Tippeconnic III (Eds.), *Next steps: Research and practice to advance Indian education* (pp. 3–31). Charleston, WV: ERIC Clearinghouse on Rural Education and Small Schools.

Luthar, S. S. (2006). Resilience in development: A synthesis of research across five decades. In D. Cicchetti & D. J. Cohen (Eds.), *Developmental psychopathology, Vol 3: Risk, disorder, and adaptation* (2nd ed., pp. 739–795). Hoboken, NJ: John Wiley & Sons.

Luthar, S. S., & Burack, J. A. (2000). Adolescent wellness: In the eye of the beholder. In D. Cicchetti, J. Rappaport, I. Sandler, & R. Weissberg (Eds.), *The promotion of wellness in children and adolescents* (pp. 29–57). Washington, DC: Child Welfare League of America.

Luthar, S. S., & Zelazo, L. B. (2003). Research on resilience: An integrative review. In S. S. Luthar (Ed.) *Resilience and vulnerability: Adaptation in the context of childhood adversities* (pp. 510–549). Cambridge: Cambridge University Press.

Markus, H. R., & Conner, A. (2013). *Clash!: 8 cultural conflicts that make us who we are*. New York: Penguin.

Markus, H. R., & Kitayama, S. (1991). Culture and the self: Implications for cognition, emotion, and motivation. *Psychological Review*, *98*, 224–253.

Masten, A. S., Best, K. M., & Garmezy, N. (1990). Resilience and development: Contributions from the study of children who overcome adversity. *Development and Psychopathology*, *2*, 425–444.

McCormick, R. (2009). Aboriginal approaches to counselling. In L. J. Kirmayer & G. G. Valaskakis (Eds.), *Healing traditions: The mental health of Aboriginal peoples in Canada* (pp. 337–354). Vancouver, BC: UBC Press.

Miller, J. R. (1996). *Shingwauk's vision: A history of native residential schools.* Toronto, ON: University of Toronto Press.

Milloy, J. S. (1999). *A national crime: The Canadian government and the residential school system, 1879 to 1986.* Winnipeg, MB: University of Manitoba Press.

More, A. J. (1987). Native Indian learning styles: A review for researchers and teachers. *Journal of American Indian Education*, *27*, 17–29.

Mosley-Howard, S. (1995). Best practices in considering the role of culture. *Best Practices in School Psychology*, *3*, 337–345.

Oetting, E. R., & Beauvais, F. (1991). Orthogonal cultural identification theory: The cultural identification of minority adolescents. *Substance Use & Misuse*, *25*, 655–685.

Pewewardy, C. (1998). Fluff and feathers: Treatment of American Indians in the literature and the classroom. *Equity & Excellence*, *31*, 69–76.

Pewewardy, C. (2002). American Indian and white students talking about ethnic identity in teacher education programs: Helping teacher education students know themselves as cultural beings. *Action in Teacher Education*, *24*, 22–33.

Phinney, J. (1989). Stages of ethnic identity in minority group adolescents. *Journal of Early Adolescence*, *9*, 34–49.

Phinney, J. S. (1991). Ethnic identity and self-esteem: A review and integration. *Hispanic Journal of Behavioral Sciences*, *13*, 193–208.

Phinney, J. S. (2000). Identity formation across cultures: The interaction of personal, societal, and historical change. *Human Development*, *43*, 27–31.

Plaut, V. C., & Markus, H. R. (2005). The "inside" story: A cultural-historical analysis of being smart and motivated, American style. In A. J. Elliot & C. S. Dweck (Eds.), *Handbook of competence and motivation* (pp. 457–488). New York: Guilford Press.

Rogoff, B. (2003). *The cultural nature of human development.* Oxford: Oxford University Press.

Safran, S. P., Safran, J. S., & Pirozak, E. (1994). Native American youth: Meeting their needs in a multicultural society. *Journal of Humanistic Education and Development*, *33*, 5–57.

Sameroff, A. J., Seifer, R., & Bartko, W. T. (1997). Environmental perspectives on adaptation during childhood and adolescence. In S. S. Luthar, J. A. Burack, D. Cicchetti, & J. R. Weisz (Eds.), *Developmental psychopathology: Perspectives on adjustment, risk, and disorder* (pp. 507–526). New York: Cambridge University Press.

Sanders, D. (1987). Cultural conflicts: An important factor in the academic failures of American Indian students. *Journal of Multicultural Counseling and Development*, *15*, 81–90.

Seidman, E., & Pedersen, S. (2003). *Holistic contextual perspectives on risk, protection, and competence among low-income urban adolescents.* Resilience and Vulnerability: Adaptation in the Context of Childhood Adversities, 318–342.

Serafica, F. C., & Vargas, L. A. (2006). Cultural diversity in the development of child psychopathology. *Developmental Psychopathology*, *3*, 588–626.

Sroufe, L. A., & Rutter, M. (1984). The domain of developmental psychopathology. *Child Development*, 17–29.

Stephens, N. M., Markus, H. R., & Fryberg, S. A. (2012). Social class disparities in health and education: Reducing inequality by applying a sociocultural self model of behavior. *Psychological Review*, *119*, 723–744.

Stout, R., & Peters, S. (2011). *kiskinohamâtôtâpânâsk: Inter-generational effects on professional First Nations women whose mothers are residential school survivors.* Winnipeg, MB: Prairie Women's Health Centre of Excellence.
Sue, D. W., & Sue, D. (1990). *Counseling the culturally different: Theory and practice.* Oxford: John Wiley & Sons.
Suzuki, L. A., & Kugler, J. F. (1995). Intelligence and personality assessment: Multicultural perspectives. In J. G. Ponterotto (Ed.), *Handbook of multicultural counseling* (pp. 493–515). Thousand Oaks, CA: Sage.
Swisher, K., & Deyhle, D. (1992). Adapting instruction to culture. In J. Reyhner (Ed.), *Teaching American Indian Students* (pp. 81–95). Norman, OK: University of Oklahoma Press.
US Department of Health and Human Services. (2012). *American Indian/Alaska Native profile.* Retrieved January 13, 2017 from http://minorityhealth.hhs.gov/templates/browse.aspx?lvl=2&lvlID=52
van Ommeren, M. (2003). Validity issues in transcultural epidemiology. *The British Journal of Psychiatry, 182,* 376–378.
von Finckenstein, M. (1999). The artists speak. In M. von Finckenstein (Ed.), *Celebrating Inuit art, 1948–1970* (pp. 39–50). Hull, QC: Canadian Museum of Civilization.
Walls, M. L., & Whitbeck, L. B. (2011). Distress among Indigenous North Americans generalized and culturally relevant stressors. *Society and Mental Health, 1,* 124–136.
Walls, M. L., & Whitbeck, L. B. (2012). The intergenerational effects of relocation policies on Indigenous families. *Journal of Family Issues, 33,* 1272–1293.
Wieman, C. (2009). Six Nations mental health services: A model of care for Aboriginal communities. In L. J. Kirmayer & G. G. Valaskakis (Eds.), *Healing traditions: The mental health of Aboriginal peoples in Canada* (pp. 401–418). Vancouver, BC: UBC Press.
Weisz, J. R., McCarty, C. A., Eastman, K. L., Chaiyasit, W., & Suwanlert, S. (1997). Developmental psychopathology and culture: Ten lessons from Thailand. In S. S. Luthar, J. A. Burack, D. Cicchetti, & J. R. Weisz (Eds.), *Developmental psychopathology: Perspectives on adjustment, risk, and disorder* (pp. 568–592). New York: Cambridge University Press.
Werner, H. (1957). The concept of development from a comparative and organismic point of view. In D. B. Harris (Ed.), *The concept of development: An issue in the study of human behavior* (pp. 125–148). Minneapolis, MN: University of Minnesota.
Wexler, L. (2014). Looking across three generations of Alaska Natives to explore how culture fosters indigenous resilience. *Transcultural Psychiatry, 51,* 73–92.
World Health Organization. (2010). *International statistical classification of diseases and related health problems (ICD),* 10th revision. Geneva: World Health Organization.
Wyman, P. A. (2003). Emerging perspectives on context specificity of children's adaptation and resilience. In S. S. Luthar (Ed.), *Resilience and vulnerability: Adaptation in the context of childhood adversities* (pp. 293–317). Cambridge: Cambridge University Press.

# Section IV

# DSM-5 and the Future of Developmental Psychopathology Research

# Part 1
# Psychiatric and Diagnostic Impact

# 21

# Overview of Key Changes in the DSM-5 and Clinical Implications for Child and Adolescent Mental Health Practice

Valsamma Eapen and Rudi Črnčec

## Introduction

The English writer Arnold Bennett observed "Any change, even a change for the better, is always accompanied by drawbacks and discomforts." Nearly 20 years have passed since the last major revision to the *Diagnostic and Statistical Manual of Mental Disorders* (DSM) series, DSM-IV, was published in 1994 (American Psychiatric Association, 1994). The subsequent text revision of DSM-IV, DSM-IV-TR, published in 2000 contained relatively minor changes that necessitated only modest adjustments for clinicians. The *International Statistical Classification of Diseases and Related Health Problems* (ICD) has similarly not undergone major revision during the preceding two decades. In this regard, it has virtually been a generation since we have undergone the typically somewhat anxiety- and resistance-provoking exercise of coming to learn changes within a diagnostic framework and, within the context of our particular clinical roles, thinking about and discovering how these changes affect our clinical practice. This chapter aims principally to assist the child and adolescent mental health clinician with this process.

A preface to the DSM-5 highlights that enhancements made include moves to harmonize it with the structure of the "Classification of Mental and Behavioral Disorders" chapter of ICD-11 (scheduled for release in 2018), better representation of developmental issues related to diagnosis, and integration of findings from the broad research literature, including in genetics and neuroimaging. We don't wish to overstate at the outset the magnitude of the changes within DSM-5, and several authors have already noted that most of the diagnoses and relevant criteria remain similar to those in DSM-IV (Stetka & Correll, 2013). However, clinicians will discover that there have been changes across the board including those that are conceptual, as well as new diagnoses, merged diagnoses, new names for particular disorders, and

*The Wiley Handbook of Developmental Psychopathology*, First Edition. Edited by Luna C. Centifanti and David M. Williams.

alternations to diagnostic criteria. One of the significant alterations in DSM-5 is that it has moved back to a non-axial documentation of diagnosis (formerly Axes I, II and III in DSM-IV) with separate notations for important psychosocial and contextual factors (formerly Axis IV in DSM-IV) and disability (formerly Axis V in DSM-IV). The implications of the changes to the individual clinician will undoubtedly vary depending upon a range of factors, including the types of patients typically seen, the setting in which patients are seen, training, clinical experience, and theoretical orientation, to name a few. Encouragingly, field trial data appear to suggest that a majority of users found the DSM-5 easy to use and useful in routine clinical practice (Mościcki, 2013), including in child and adolescent settings. With respect to child and adolescent related changes in the DSM-5, a notable feature is that the DSM-IV chapter "Disorders Usually First Diagnosed in Infancy, Childhood or Adolescence" (which had been evident in differing variations since DSM-II), has been deleted. Instead, a new chapter in DSM-5 describes "Neurodevelopmental Disorders" that typically manifest early in development, often before a child enters school.

We will detail in this chapter some of the implications for clinical practice arising from the changes, and while we aim to be quite comprehensive with respect to the main changes, we cannot claim to be exhaustive or as detailed in particular areas as a given reader may wish: It is hoped that clinicians may be encouraged and inspired subsequently to delve into the DSM-5 to explore nuance and specific areas that are of relevance to them. The reader will notice a mostly neutral stance as to the merit of the revisions within DSM-5 and the evidence base underpinning these, with focus instead upon how the changes may affect practice. This is done in part with the acknowledgement that given the wide scope of the changes in the DSM-5, much has already, and will no doubt continue to be published, that critiques or applauds specific changes. Moreover, given the structure of the DSM-5 is analogous to the upcoming ICD-11, clinicians working within these major nosological frameworks at this point in time may ultimately need to acquaint themselves with the changes as they are.

We are of course in good historical company, as clinicians have been making such nosological adjustments throughout the history of medicine, and within the mental health field, most obviously since the first publication of a mental disorders chapter in the ICD-6 in 1949, and the advent of the DSM-I in 1952. Most would agree that the trajectory over the intervening six decades has been toward improvement in understanding and treating patients. What seems important to observe from the outset is that the DSM-5, or any other nosological system, should not dictate how we practice. Clinicians must continue to assess individual patients, define their symptoms, make an accurate and comprehensive formulation of why they are presenting with these symptoms at this time, and then offer targeted psychological and pharmacological therapies. In a sense, perhaps we ought to consider diagnostic classification systems, especially at this time of change, with a grain of proverbial historical salt. Related to this, a difficulty for child and adolescent clinicians is that the DSM-5 would appear in general terms to have been attributed in the community with a level of certainty and comprehensiveness that it was never meant to—and cannot—have.

This chapter is organized into several sections. These will seek to cover (1) structural and conceptual changes in the DSM-5; (2) new diagnoses that have been introduced as well as merged and removed diagnoses; (3) other notable changes to diagnostic criteria and a summary of what the writers consider to be amongst the main changes with most clinical implication in the child and adolescent arena; and (4) implications for research.

It is to be noted that the DSM-5 manual itself has a section titled "Highlights of Changes from DSM-IV to DSM-5" that is useful to review (American Psychatric Association, 2013). Further, the DSM-5 website, www.dsm-5.org, contains at the time of writing a wealth of information regarding changes to specific disorders and categories of disorders in the form of "fact sheets" that may inform the reader regarding particular areas of interest.

## Structural and Conceptual Changes in the DSM-5

There have been a number of structural changes within the DSM-5. The core of the manual, the diagnostic criteria and codes, are located within what is referred to as Section II. Section II includes a major revision to the chapter structure that was present in DSM-IV and a reorganization of where particular disorders are located within these chapters. The decision to remove the "Disorders Usually First Diagnosed in Infancy, Childhood, or Adolescence" chapter would appear to be related to a general lifespan approach taken in DSM-5. In this regard, disorders of childhood and adolescence may now be found virtually throughout the manual. For example, separation anxiety now sits within the "Anxiety Disorders" chapter of the DSM-5 and pica within the "Feeding and Eating Disorders" chapter. Age-related aspects of disorders are identified by arranging each diagnostic chapter in a chronological fashion, with diagnoses most applicable to infancy and childhood listed first, followed by diagnoses more common to adolescence and early adulthood.

The chapters in DSM-5 are designed to cluster together around current understanding of antecedent, concurrent, and predictive validators. This holds the potential to aide in clinical decision-making, as related disorders are more likely to be found within the same or adjacent chapters. For instance, intermittent explosive disorder and pyromania are now located within the same chapter as oppositional defiant disorder and conduct disorder—"Disruptive, Impulse-Control, and Conduct Disorders"—as opposed to within two separate chapters in DSM-IV. As reference will be made to these diagnostic chapters throughout, and given the useful snapshot this provides to the "essence" of much of what has changed in DSM-5, the specific chapter structure is presented here:

Neurodevelopmental Disorders
Schizophrenia Spectrum and Other Psychotic Disorders
Bipolar and Related Disorders
Depressive Disorders
Anxiety Disorders
Obsessive-Compulsive and Related Disorders
Trauma- and Stressor-Related Disorders
Dissociative Disorders
Somatic Symptom and Related Disorders
Feeding and Eating Disorders
Elimination Disorders
Sleep–Wake Disorders
Sexual Dysfunctions
Gender Dysphoria

Disruptive, Impulse-Control, and Conduct Disorders
Substance-Related and Addictive Disorders
Neurocognitive Disorders
Personality Disorders
Paraphilic Disorders
Other Mental Disorders
Medication-Induced Movement Disorders and Other Adverse Effects of Medication
Other Conditions That May Be a Focus of Clinical Attention.

The decision to move from a multiaxial to non-axial system has several implications for the child and adolescent clinician that we address in turn. A great deal of child and adolescent work is, of course, couched within the context of family and relationship difficulties as well as other psychosocial factors. These relational aspects have historically been difficult to encapsulate within a framework focused, as the DSM is, upon mental disorders—that is, upon clinically significant disturbance to an *individual's* cognition, emotion, regulation, or behavior that reflects a dysfunction. The former Axis IV in DSM-IV of "Psychosocial and Environmental Problems" is essentially retained and expanded upon within DSM-5, but now under the chapter "Other Conditions that May Be a Focus of Clinical Attention." That chapter contains a list of factors that may be the focus of a young person's presentation or help to explain the need for intervention: these include relational problems, abuse and neglect, educational and occupational problems, housing and economic problems, other problems related to the social environment (where bullying is included under social exclusion or rejection) and others. These can be coded using the corresponding ICD codes. It is worth highlighting in this context that the DSM-5 authors are clear in their acknowledgement that the diagnosis of a mental disorder is not equivalent to the need for treatment. There is also no longer a specific requirement for clinicians to complete a disability rating, that is, an assessment of overall functioning as had been suggested in Axis-V of DSM-IV with the global assessment of functioning. However, DSM-5 does include, amongst a range of other useful tools, a measure in Section III of the manual that is suggested for this purpose: The World Health Organization Disability Assessment Schedule (WHODAS 2.0). The Social Occupational and Functional Assessment Scale (SOF AS) may also serve as an alternative (Goldman, Skodol, & Lave, 1992). The implication for clinicians would appear to be one of being aware of these changes and the ongoing possibility to document these important contextual factors in communication with other health professionals; and further, to retain them in a sense in one's thinking and in training the next generation of clinicians.

Related to the move to non-axial assessment, intellectual disability (intellectual developmental disorder), formerly called mental retardation in DSM-IV, and personality disorders are no longer coded on a separate axis. As an aside, the reader may notice the use of parentheses throughout the DSM-5 with a number of diagnoses. The rationale for this appears to vary. In the case of intellectual disability (intellectual disability disorder) and several other disorders, the diagnosis in parentheses will come into use in future, for example when ICD-11 is released, but the non-parenthetical diagnosis is the currently preferred term. For other diagnoses, the parentheses appear to aid in description of the condition, for example, excoriation (skin picking) disorder. Moving back to personality disorders, the specific criteria in DSM-5 have not changed from those in DSM-IV. However, an alternative model for personality disorders is proposed in Section III of DSM-5, together with other conditions for further study and potential inclusion in later versions of the main body of DSM. In other words, Section III contains content that may be clinically useful and warrants review, but which is not part of an official diagnosis of a mental disorder and cannot be used as such. While there is no requirement for clinicians to acquaint themselves with the alternative personality disorders model, the weight of discussion in this area over time does suggest that changes similar to those proposed are probable in the future. In brief, the alternative personality disorder model characterizes personality disorders using a more dimensional approach where the following are considered: (1) impairments in personality functioning, in terms of the self (identity and self-direction) and interpersonal elements (empathy and intimacy); and (2) The presence of pathological personality traits, organized in the five broad domains of negative affectivity, detachment, antagonism, disinhibition and psychoticism. Personality disorder diagnoses that can be made using this alternative system include schizotypal; antisocial; borderline; narcissistic; avoidant; and obsessive-compulsive, together with a personality disorder—trait specified (PD–TS) condition: This is several fewer than in DSM-IV and with only one diagnosis from the former Cluster A (odd–eccentric). As in the DSM-IV, only antisocial personality disorder diagnosis under the alternative criteria specifies that the individual must be at least 18 years of age, however the general criteria relate to stability across time and to onset that can be traced back to at least adolescence or early adulthood. The general theme of reluctance in making personality disorder diagnoses in young people under the age of 18 would appear to be preserved.

There is some concern that the diagnosis of personality disorders may increase given the removal of the multi-axial system. That is, following a shift from viewing personality features and pathology as underpinning primary psychiatric diagnoses to essentially no different from any other psychiatric diagnosis, clinicians might be more likely to classify them as a disorder. Clinically, a longitudinal approach to diagnosis is needed, taking into account personality as one of the factors influencing the patient's current presentation—particularly with older adolescents and adults. Any move to a cross-sectional approach to diagnosis based on current symptoms may, over time, decrease the importance of personality in mental health, which the general history of psychiatry would suggest to be a substantial loss to clinical formulation and treatment. This is not the motivation of the DSM authors. Rather it appears that the multiaxial system was originally introduced in DSM-IV, in part, to increase the research and clinical focus upon personality disorders, with the DSM-IV stating that "The coding of Personality Disorders on Axis II should not be taken to imply that their pathogenesis or range of appropriate treatment is fundamentally different from that for the disorders coded on Axis I" (American Psychiatric Association, 1994). However, the coding of personality pathology on a separate axis had arguably been a useful one structurally, and had to some extent brought the DSM into a type of alignment with alternative nosological frameworks including, as an example, the *Psychodynamic Diagnostic Manual* (PDM Task Force, 2006), which emphasize personality and developmental factors as underpinning mental health. The classification of personality remains one of the most difficult phenomenological tasks in mental health practice. We need to recognize the efforts of DSM-5 to propose a new model of personality disorder, but also acknowledge that DSM does not have a unique capacity to guide our analysis and interpretation of these complex issues.

A further conceptual shift within the DSM-5 has been toward an increasingly dimensional approach to diagnosis. That is, in addition to making a categorical diagnosis, including subtypes and/or specifiers, clinicians are also now asked to rate a number of disorders along a continuum of severity. For a number of disorders there is also a requirement to provide descriptive features such as information about the patient's level insight, and information about course, including remission status, for example. The depressive disorders have particular requirements that are useful to review. We would commend using these features over and above the making of a categorical diagnosis to clinicians, as, at heart, a diagnostic nomenclature serves to facilitate communication between professionals about the difficulties faced by patients, and an increased level of detail and specification only improves upon this.

"Not otherwise specified" (NOS) conditions have been removed completely from DSM-5 and replaced with two options for clinical use: "Other specified disorder" and "Unspecified disorder." It emerges that a large proportion, perhaps the majority, of clinical diagnoses under DSM-IV were of the NOS category, which tended to be less useful for treatment planning and for the accurate description and communication of the difficulties faced by a young person. As an example of how these new categories will work, in the case of a young person presenting with clinically significant symptoms of separation anxiety disorder lasting over four weeks but whose symptomatology fell short of the diagnostic threshold for this disorder, the clinician would record "Other specified anxiety disorder, separation anxiety with insufficient symptoms". The "Other specified anxiety disorder" aspect comes from the chapter title within which the symptoms reside, in this case "Anxiety disorders." The description that is subsequently provided for why the diagnosis is made is not prescribed, although examples are given in each chapter. If the clinician chooses not to, or is unable to, specify the reason that the criteria are not met for a specific disorder, as for example in the case of a Hospital Emergency Department, then using the example above, "Unspecified anxiety disorder" would be diagnosed. It is important to note that the differentiation between the "Other specified" and "Unspecified" disorders is the clinician's decision and is not based upon some feature of the presentation itself. In this regard, clinicians will need to familiarize themselves with some of these changes in their assessment and diagnostic practices, and also in general terms to increasingly think from dimensional and descriptive perspectives during assessment.

## New and Merged Disorders in DSM-5

DSM-5 contains 13 new diagnoses, nine of which are of particular relevance to the child and adolescent clinician. These are listed in Table 21.1 below, together with the chapter in which the new disorder is located and a brief overview. The four new disorders with less relevance to child and adolescent clinicians are not listed in the table; namely, central sleep apnea, sleep-related hypoventilation, and rapid eye movement sleep behavior disorder from the "Sleep–Wake Disorders" chapter and major neurocognitive disorder with Lewy body disease from the "Neurocognitive Disorders" chapter. It is worth noting in this context that two disorders were also eliminated from the DSM-5: sexual aversion disorder and polysubstance-related disorder.

Perhaps equally importantly, a number of disorders contained in the DSM-IV have been combined into "aggregate" disorders. There are, we believe, 22 examples of this

**Table 21.1** New disorders in DSM-5 of relevance to child and adolescent clinicians.

| *New disorder in DSM-5* | *Chapter* | *Brief description* |
|---|---|---|
| Social (pragmatic) communication disorder | Neurodevelopmental Disorders | Persistent difficulties in the social use of verbal and non-verbal communication, but without any current evidence, or history of, restricted/repetitive behaviors. |
| Disruptive mood dysregulation disorder | Depressive Disorders | Severe recurrent temper outbursts in the context of persistent irritable mood that cannot co-exist with oppositional defiant disorder, intermittent explosive disorder, or bipolar disorder. |
| Premenstrual dysphoric disorder | Depressive Disorders | In the majority of menstrual cycles, dysphoric symptoms (e.g., affective lability; irritablity; depressed mood) occur in the final week before the onset of menses, which improve within a few days of the onset of menses, and become minimal or absent in the week post-menses. |
| Hoarding disorder | Obsessive-Compulsive and Related Disorders | Persistent difficulty discarding or parting with possessions leading to an accumulation of possessions. |
| Excoriation (skin-picking) disorder | Obsessive-Compulsive and Related Disorders | Recurrent skin picking resulting in lesions. |
| Disinhibited social engagement disorder | Trauma- and Stressor-Related Disorders | Pattern of disinhibited interactions with unfamiliar adults related to extremes of insufficient care (e.g., neglect; repeated changes of primary caregivers). This diagnosis was split from reactive attachment disorder in DSM-IV. |
| Binge eating disorder | Feeding and Eating Disorders | Recurrent episodes of binge eating. |
| Restless leg syndrome | Sleep–Wake Disorders | An urge to move the legs accompanied by or in response to uncomfortable and unpleasant sensations in the legs. |
| Caffeine withdrawal | Substance-Related and Addictive Disorders | Withdrawal symptoms following prolonged daily use of caffeine. |
| Mild neurocognitive disorder | Neurocognitive Disorders | Evidence of modest cognitive decline from a previous level of performance in one or more cognitive domains (e.g., as a result in young people of traumatic brain injury or another medical condition). |

and each is of potential relevance to child and adolescent practitioners. These are presented in Table 21.2, with the DSM-5 disorder listed first, followed by the DSM-5 chapter containing the new disorder, and finally the DSM-IV diagnoses that have been merged into the aggregate DSM-5 disorder.

**Table 21.2** Disorders in DSM-5 that have resulted from the merging of two or more DSM-IV disorders.

| *DSM-5 disorder* | *Chapter* | *Constituent DSM-IV diagnoses that are therefore no longer in use* |
|---|---|---|
| Language disorder | Neurodevelopmental Disorders | Expressive language disorder<br>Mixed receptive expressive language disorder |
| Autism spectrum disorder | Neurodevelopmental Disorders | Autistic disorder<br>Asperger's disorder<br>Childhood disintegrative disorder<br>Rett's disorder<br>Pervasive developmental disorder-NOS |
| Specific learning disorder | Neurodevelopmental Disorders | Reading disorder<br>Math disorder<br>Disorder of written expression |
| Delusional disorder | Schizophrenia Spectrum and Other Psychotic Disorders | Shared psychotic disorder<br>Delusional disorder |
| Panic disorder | Anxiety Disorders | Panic disorder with agoraphobia<br>Panic disorder without agoraphobia |
| Dissociative amnesia | Dissociative Disorders | Dissociative fugue<br>Dissociative amnesia |
| Somatic symptom disorder | Somatic Symptom and Related Disorders | Somatization disorder<br>Undifferentiated somatoform disorder<br>Pain disorder |
| Insomnia disorder | Sleep-Wake Disorders | Primary insomnia<br>Insomnia related to another mental disorder |
| Hypersomnolesence disorder | Sleep-Wake Disorders | Primary hypersomnia<br>Hypersomnia related to another mental disorder |
| Non-rapid eye movement sleep arousal disorders | Sleep-Wake Disorders | Sleepwalking disorder<br>Sleep terror disorder |
| Genito-pelvic pain/ penetration disorder | Sexual Dysfunctions | Vaginismus<br>Dyspareunia |
| Alcohol use disorder<br>Cannabis use disorder<br>Phencyclidine use disorder<br>Other hallucinogen use disorder<br>Inhalant use disorder<br>Opioid use disorder<br>Sedative, hypnotic, or anxiolytic use disorder<br>Stimulant use disorder | Substance-Related and Addictive Disorders | Previously separate abuse and dependence diagnoses in DSM-IV have been combined in each case. For example, Alcohol abuse and Alcohol dependence have been combined into Alcohol use disorder. |
| Stimulant intoxication | Substance-Related and Addictive Disorders | Amphetamine intoxication<br>Cocaine intoxication |
| Stimulant withdrawal | Substance-Related and Addictive Disorders | Amphetamine withdrawal<br>Cocaine withdrawal |
| Substance/medication-induced disorders | Substance-Related and Addictive Disorders | Combination of mood (+1), anxiety (+1) and neurocognitive (–3) |

## Other Significant Diagnostic Changes and Those with Particular Implications for Child and Adolescent Practice

We have elected to organize this section following the chapter structure of the DSM-5.

There are a number of changes with substantial clinical relevance within the "Neurodevelopmental Disorders" chapter. Primary amongst these are the changes to the autism spectrum disorder classification, where a single diagnosis is now used. This change involved the removal of DSM-IV diagnoses including Asperger's disorder and PDD-NOS, which were widely applied, and the case of Asperger's disorder, a disorder with which many patients strongly identified. While the DSM-5 indicates that individuals with well-established DSM-IV diagnoses should be given an autism spectrum disorder diagnosis, clinicians may need to address this "loss" of the DSM-IV diagnosis with their patients. One approach for patients with Asperger's disorder may be to advise that they still have an autism spectrum diagnosis, and that they can continue to use the previous title if they choose.

There is ongoing debate about whether these changes mean that autism spectrum disorder will be underdiagnosed or overdiagnosed. The initial concerns about underdiagnosis appear to have softened somewhat, as the repetitive behaviors criterion can be satisfied by retrospective report. There are also data to suggest that around 91% of children with a DSM-IV pervasive developmental disorder diagnosis meet the DSM-5 criteria (Huerta, Bishop, Duncan, Hus, & Lord, 2012). There may be implications for service funding in different jurisdictions and understandable concerns from the community about the full implications of these changes, which are yet to be revealed. One final aspect of this worth commenting upon is that the earlier requirement that autism could not be diagnosed comorbidly with ADHD has been removed.

Children with social communication impairments but without restricted or repetitive behaviors are classified in DSM-5 as having social (pragmatic) communication disorder. This disorder is not intended simply to be a substitute for PDD-NOS, or indeed to apply principally to young people who have difficulties reminiscent of the autism spectrum. For example, many young people with ADHD who have significant associated social difficulties may also meet criteria for social (pragmatic) communication disorder. It is conceivable that a number of children who would have received various forms of pragmatic speech and expressive language and communication disorder diagnoses via speech pathologists will now meet the social (pragmatic) communication disorder category.

Changes to diagnostic criteria for intellectual disability (intellectual developmental disorder) now recognize that the severity of the disorder is determined more by adaptive functioning than intellectual functioning. In practical terms, this may mean that clinicians take greater steps to assess adaptive functioning in their patients alongside standardized tests of intellectual functioning. The term intellectual disability (intellectual developmental disorder) replaces the DSM-IV term mental retardation in part to reduce stigma associated with the previous term. The criteria state that onset must be during the developmental period, which suggests that a child who has, for example, a significant brain injury at age 10 may still be diagnosed with intellectual disability (intellectual developmental disorder) as they had not yet reached their developmental potential. The global developmental delay diagnosis is intended for those children aged under five years who have failed to meet expected developmental milestones in several areas, but whose age precludes standardized testing, and in this regard such a diagnosis requires reassessment after a period of time.

The criteria for ADHD have not changed substantially, with the exception that symptoms can be present prior to age 12 years as opposed to seven years in the DSM-IV. In addition, the lifespan nature and adult form of the disorder have been increasingly recognized and for young people aged 17 and older, only five of nine symptoms of inattention and hyperactivity/impulsivity are required for diagnosis. This likely means that adults will be more readily diagnosed. The terminology of ADHD *subtypes* has been altered to "current presentation" specifiers in recognition of the instability over time of the presence of symptoms of inattention and hyperactivity/impulsivity.

The collapsing of previous learning disorder diagnoses into a single specific learning disorder category reflects an understanding that a specific difficulty, such as with reading, is a symptom that in many cases points to a larger set of problems. Nonetheless, use of specifiers allow for targeting of intervention. There is also a view that given difficulties with mathematics can exert a significant influence upon adult functioning, there needs to be an increased focus upon this in addition to literacy-based difficulties.

There are some changes in DSM-5 with regard to tic disorders. The word *stereotyped* has been removed from the definition of tics with the rationale for this stemming from the fact that stereotypies, commonly encountered in autism spectrum disorder, and stereotypic movement disorder were frequently misdiagnosed as tics or Tourette's disorder. The diagnosis transient tic disorder has been replaced with provisional tic disorder because *transient* can only be defined retrospectively and is hence not particularly useful to the clinician. The term *provisional* accounts for those initially presenting with tics that may subsequently last for more than one year and thereby satisfy the duration criteria for chronic tic disorder or Tourette's disorder. DSM-5 has also added a specifier "chronic motor" or "chronic vocal" tic disorder to distinguish between vocal and motor tics that are chronic. The reference to stimulant use as a cause has been removed as there is no evidence base to support this. As with the other disorders, a new category of "Other specified" and "Unspecified" has been added to refer to tic disorders that result in significant impairment to the individual yet do not meet the full criteria for other tic disorders. Examples of these include tics with onset in adulthood, or tics triggered by other medical conditions (Eapen, Lees, Lakke, Trimble, & Robertson, 2002). We would urge clinicians to be mindful of this group of disorders, which are frequently present in clinical settings but which tend to remain underdiagnosed.

Within the "Schizophrenia Spectrum and Other Psychotic Disorders" chapter there are several changes of particular note. The traditional weight given to Schneiderian first-rank symptoms of schizophrenia has been reduced in DSM-5. Criterion A for a diagnosis of schizophrenia no longer gives any special emphasis to the bizarreness of delusions and the presence of auditory hallucinations involving a running commentary or two or more voices conversing with each other. In DSM-IV only one such symptom was required to satisfy Criterion A, while DSM-5 always requires at least two of five symptoms, of which one must be delusions, hallucinations or disorganized speech. In addition, DSM-IV subtypes of schizophrenia (paranoid, disorganized, catatonic, undifferentiated, and residual) have been eliminated from DSM-5 in part because of their limited diagnostic stability, low reliability, and poor validity. Section III of DSM-5 proposes a dimensional approach to rating the severity of the core symptoms of schizophrenia, attempting to capture the wide variations in the type and severity of symptoms expressed by people with psychotic disorders.

DSM-5 has shifted the emphasis in diagnosing schizoaffective disorder from a cross-sectional to a longitudinal approach. There is a requirement that a major mood episode be present for a majority of the disorder's total duration, after Criterion A for schizophrenia has been met. This change aims to recognize the clinical challenges in characterizing patients who have both psychotic and mood symptoms, either concurrently or at different times. Criterion A for delusional disorder no longer includes a requirement that the delusions must be non-bizarre. A new exclusion criterion distinguishes delusional disorder from psychotic variants of obsessive-compulsive disorder and body dysmorphic disorder.

DSM-5 defines the same criteria for the diagnosis of catatonia regardless of whether it occurs in the context of a psychotic, bipolar, depressive, or other medical disorder or as an unidentified medical condition. This definition contrasts with DSM-IV, in which two of five symptom clusters were required in the presence of a psychotic or mood disorder but only one symptom cluster was needed in the presence of a general medical condition. In DSM-5, three of 12 characteristic catatonic symptoms must be present.

After wide discussion, the diagnosis of attenuated psychosis syndrome has been included in Section III of DSM-5 as a condition for further study, rather than a distinct diagnosis. The syndrome requires the presence of delusions, hallucinations or disorganized speech in an attenuated form with relatively intact reality testing, but of sufficient severity or frequency to warrant clinical attention. Symptoms must be present at least once per week in the past month, and must have begun or worsened during the past year. People with the syndrome often experience anxiety and/or depression. It would appear that the majority of people who experience the syndrome, perhaps around 70%, do not go on to develop psychosis; however there may be a generally heightened risk for mental ill health. This in itself is a salutatory reminder that many young people we meet with some features of psychosis are not necessarily therefore "on track" for a diagnosis of schizophrenia.

"Bipolar and Related Disorders" contain some of the more pertinent changes in DSM-5, particularly to the practice of child psychiatrists. DSM-IV did not allow for the presence of mixed states in bipolar II disorder, and the requirement of the need for co-occurrence of threshold mania and depression in bipolar I disorder was arguably too restrictive. In DSM-5, a specifier, "With mixed features," has been added. This can be applied to episodes of mania or hypomania when depressive features are present and to episodes of depression in the context of major depressive disorder or bipolar disorder when features of mania/hypomania are present. There has been a reduction to the number of symptoms required to make a mixed-state diagnosis, namely, the presence of three or more features from the opposite pole of the illness. In fact, the presence of only one or two symptoms from the opposite pole is very common and may affect the response to treatment and the course of illness, even though this profile does not meet the DSM-5 criteria for the mixed-state specifier. A potential consequence of this change is a marked increase in the diagnosis of bipolar disorder based only on an assessment of current symptoms, and confused pharmacotherapy. The intent was to improve the early recognition of bipolar disorder, but it does remain to be seen whether the outcome will match that goal. The emphasis on increased activity and energy, as well as mood, in Criterion A for manic and hypomanic episodes is welcome. *Energy* is an important factor in clinical assessment, and has more specificity than *irritability*. Finally, a specifier "With anxious distress" can now be applied to diagnoses of bipolar and related disorders, and also depressive disorders. This allows the presence of anxiety symptoms to be recognized, even though they are not included among the diagnostic criteria for these disorders.

One aspect of change to the "Depressive Disorders" that has been much discussed, particularly in popular media, relates to the removal of the bereavement exclusion. In DSM-IV a diagnosis of a major depressive episode was excluded if the person had depressive symptoms lasting less than two months following the death of a loved one. The exclusion has been omitted in DSM-5 for a number of reasons including to remove the implication that bereavement typically lasts only two months; and in acknowledgement that bereavement is a severe psychosocial stressor that can precipitate a major depressive episode in a vulnerable individual. This change may also have service implications in terms of funding available to these individuals. Some health care professionals working predominantly in the area of grief-related psychotherapeutic work have also raised concerns about overpathologizing normal grief and the use of pharmacotherapy. Persistent complex bereavement disorder, with duration of at least 12 months (or six months in children) is included in Section III of DSM-5 as a condition for further study. Another change within this chapter involves moving premenstrual dysphoric disorder from DSM-IV Appendix B (a disorder requiring further study) to the main diagnostic category in DSM-5.

The core symptoms of major depressive episode and the required duration of at least two weeks are unchanged from DSM-IV. In DSM-5, persistent depressive disorder incorporates both chronic major depressive disorder and dysthymic disorder as defined in DSM-IV. A number of specifiers are available to describe features in an individual patient including symptoms, severity, presence of remission, and age of onset. In this regard, the new specifier "With mixed features" can be used to acknowledge the presence of at least three manic symptoms (insufficient to satisfy criteria for a manic episode). Such features increase the likelihood that the illness is within a bipolar spectrum, but a diagnosis of bipolar disorder cannot be made if the patient has never had a manic or hypomanic episode. The specifier of "With anxious distress" can be used to describe the presence of prominent anxiety symptoms. These features are an important indicator of prognosis in depression and a factor to consider in treatment decisions, even though anxiety is not itself a diagnostic criterion for depression. Of particular relevance to child and adolescent work, the previous "Post-partum" specifier has been changed to a "Peripartum" specifier in recognition that depression is common during pregnancy.

This chapter also contains the new disorder disruptive mood dysregulation disorder (DMDD). The core feature of this disorder is chronic, severe persistent irritability leading to regular severe temper outbursts in young people aged six or more years, but less than 18 years. Conceived of as well beyond developmentally normal temper tantrums, DMDD is characterized by severe and recurrent temper outbursts that are grossly out of proportion in intensity or duration to the situation. It is reasonable to anticipate that this will become a widely used diagnosis within child psychiatry as difficulties with affective regulation reflect a core issue clinically. Part of the rationale for the inclusion of the diagnosis appears to have been to reduce prepubertal children being diagnosed under the DSM-IV with bipolar disorder NOS, which was an unintended consequence of aspects of changes within the DSM-IV, and this goal is likely to be met. In distinguishing these disorders, the behavior of children with DMDD is not thought to present in an episodic fashion, as is the case with bipolar disorder. Nonetheless, in practice DMDD may carry some risk of poor diagnostic reliability and issues with differentiation from oppositional defiant disorder and conduct disorder; as well as with normal mood regulation difficulties of childhood. There are concerns as to the labeling of developmentally appropriate mood regulation difficulties and whether behavioral and emotional outbursts and irritability in adolescents will attract a label of DMDD. With regard to oppositional defiant disorder, the symptom threshold for DMDD is thought to be higher, since the condition is considered more severe. Moreover, to avoid any artificial comorbidity of the two disorders, it is recommended within the DSM-5 that children who meet criteria for both oppositional defiant disorder and DMDD should only be diagnosed with DMDD. Additional evidence is required to confirm that DMDD is associated with current or future mood or anxiety disorders as has been proposed. Clinicians need to weigh up these issues when thinking about and diagnosing this disorder. It is interesting also to reflect upon how the loss of Axis II may contribute, if we are not cognizant of it, to an inability to reflect with a developmental perspective upon young people with dysfunction of key personality areas including mood dysregulation.

It is noteworthy that the changes to mood disorders in DSM-5 remain largely descriptive and limited by their dependence on phenomenology and grouping of symptoms and signs. Clinicians should therefore continue to recognize the need to understand how the symptoms and behaviors might have arisen and assess contextual factors such as the young person's relationships, quality of care, any history of abuse, and so on.

Within the "Anxiety Disorders" chapter, the criteria for agoraphobia, specific phobia, and social anxiety disorder (social phobia) no longer include a requirement that patients older than 18 recognize that their anxiety is excessive or unreasonable. This change reflects evidence that individuals can overestimate the danger in "phobic" situations, and that older people often misattribute "phobic" fears to aging. Instead, DSM-5 requires that the anxiety be out of proportion to the actual danger or threat. The six-month duration of symptoms was previously limited to patients older than 18 years but now applies to all ages, aiming to minimize overdiagnosis of transient fears in children and adolescents. DSM-IV terminology for describing types of panic attacks (situationally bound/cued, situationally predisposed, and unexpected/uncued) has been replaced by the terms "Unexpected" and "Expected" panic attacks. Panic attacks can occur in a range of anxiety and other disorders, and can now be listed as a specifier in all DSM-5 disorders. The DSM-IV diagnoses of panic disorder and agoraphobia, panic disorder, panic disorder without agoraphobia, and agoraphobia without history of panic disorder are replaced by two diagnoses—panic disorder and agoraphobia, each with separate criteria. The wording of the criteria for separation anxiety disorder have been modified to better recognize that symptoms can also be expressed in adulthood. For example, attachment figures can include the spouse or children of adults with separation anxiety disorder, and avoidance behaviors can occur in the workplace as well as at school. The diagnostic criteria no longer specify that onset must occur before 18 years of age.

It will be interesting to observe over time whether hoarding disorder within the "Obsessive-Compulsive and Related Disorders" chapter is widely applied in child and adolescent settings, as this condition traditionally causes most clinical impairment in adulthood. We note that the diagnostic criteria for OCD now include a specifier related to whether the patient has a current or past history of tic disorder, given the high rates of comorbidity amongst these conditions. In addition, the DSM-IV "With poor insight" specifier has been refined to allow a distinction between individuals with good or fair insight, poor insight, and absent insight/delusional obsessive-compulsive disorder beliefs. Analogous insight specifiers have been included for body dysmorphic and hoarding disorders. excoriation (skin picking) disorder, one of the new disorders, is situated logically alongside trichotillomania. The placement of these disorders, together with body dysmorphic disorder within the "Obsessive-Compulsive and Related Disorders" chapter is in itself clinically useful to clinicians in reflecting upon obsessional behaviors as related to but distinct from anxiety. As with the other disorders, the structure of DSM-5 allows for substance, medication, and medical condition-related induction of these disorders—including in this context streptococcal infection.

The stressor criterion (Criterion A) for post-traumatic stress disorder (PTSD) and acute stress disorder in the DSM-5 "Trauma- and Stressor Related Disorders" chapter requires an explicit description of whether the traumatic events were experienced directly, witnessed, or experienced indirectly. Thus, the DSM-5 allows for traumatic events that the patient was not directly exposed to, which is useful clinically; however, concerns have been raised that this may lead to "vicarious" types of trauma being entertained as causing PTSD and being used in the courts and the legal system. Further, the DSM-IV Criterion A2 requiring a subjective reaction of intense fear, helplessness, or horror has been removed. The DSM-IV symptom cluster of avoidance/numbing has been divided into two distinct clusters—avoidance, and persistent negative alterations in cognitions and mood. The diagnostic thresholds have been lowered for children and adolescents, and separate criteria have been added for children aged six years or less.

Adjustment disorders have been reconceptualized in DSM-5 as an array of stress-response syndromes occurring after exposure to a distressing traumatic or non-traumatic event. In contrast, DSM-IV defined adjustment disorders as a residual category for patients who had clinically significant distress but did not meet the criteria for a more discrete disorder. Another important change has been splitting the DSM-IV reactive attachment disorder diagnosis into two parts—disinhibited social engagement disorder, a new disorder, and reactive attachment disorder. Both arise in response to a pattern of extremes of insufficient care, with reactive attachment disorder characterized by inhibited and emotional withdrawn behavior; and disinhibited social engagement disorder by a pattern of disinhibited behavior with unfamiliar adults.

The diagnosis of somatization disorder in DSM-IV was based on a count of medically unexplained symptoms, but no specific number of somatic symptoms is now required for somatic symptom disorder in the DSM-5 "Somatic Symptom and Related Disorders" chapter. In addition, "medically unexplained symptoms" are no longer a key feature, but these are relevant in conversion disorder (functional neurological symptom disorder) where it is possible to demonstrate definitively that the symptoms are not consistent with medical pathophysiology. Hypochondriasis has been eliminated as a disorder, partly because the term had become pejorative and not conducive to an effective therapeutic relationship. Most patients who would previously have been diagnosed with Hypochondriasis had significant somatic symptoms in addition to a high level of anxiety about their health, and would now receive a DSM-5 diagnosis of somatic symptom disorder. A DSM-5 diagnosis of illness anxiety disorder can be applied to patients with a high level of health anxiety but without somatic symptoms, unless their anxiety is better explained by a primary anxiety disorder. A diagnosis of pain disorder in DSM-IV assumed that some pains were associated solely with psychological factors, some with medical diseases or injuries, and some with both. DSM-5 recognizes that such distinctions cannot be made with reliability and validity, and that psychological factors influence all forms of pain. In DSM-5, some individuals previously diagnosed with pain disorder would appropriately be diagnosed as having somatic symptom disorder, using the specifier "With predominant pain". In other cases, it would be more appropriate to diagnose psychological factors affecting other medical conditions or an adjustment disorder.

In addition to the inclusion of binge eating disorder and some adjustments to anorexia nervosa, including the removal of the requirement for amenorrhea, within the "Feeding and Eating Disorders" chapter—we would also comment upon a renamed diagnosis. Specifically, avoidant/restrictive food intake disorder expands upon and replaces the DSM-IV feeding disorder of infancy or early childhood diagnosis, and reflects an eating or feeding disturbance (e.g., apparent lack of interest in eating food etc.) as manifested by persistent failure to meet appropriate nutritional and/or energy needs. This diagnosis will likely be used widely especially in those working with infants/toddlers and their families.

"Gender Dysphoria" is a new diagnostic class in the DSM-5 that will be a welcome development for many clinicians working within this area. There is a profound change in conceptualization of the defining features by emphasizing gender incongruence rather than cross-gender identification, per se. There are separate diagnostic sets for children and for adults and adolescents.

A new chapter on "Disruptive, Impulse-control and Conduct Disorders" has been included in DSM-5, including some disorders previously included in the DSM-IV chapter on "Disorders Usually First Diagnosed in Infancy, Childhood, or Adolescence." Such disorders are characterized by problems in emotional and behavioral self-control, and are frequently comorbid with ADHD. These disorders also represent a large proportion of general child and adolescent mental health work. Changes to the definitions of individual disorders include refinements to the diagnostic criteria for oppositional defiant disorder which stress that the behaviors also occur commonly in normally developing children and adolescents, and as such the frequency and persistence of symptoms must be assessed before the diagnosis is made. The criteria for ODD are now grouped into three types: angry/irritable mood; argumentative/defiant behavior; and vindictiveness. Importantly, the exclusionary criterion for conduct disorder has been removed, which may serve to improve rates of diagnosis of that disorder, which have tended to fall in recent years due perhaps to reluctance by clinicians to make the diagnosis. A diagnosis of intermittent explosive disorder no longer requires physical aggression leading to assault or the destruction of property—rather, verbal aggression and non-destructive or non-injurious physical aggression may suffice. Because of the difficulty in distinguishing these outbursts from normal temper tantrums, a minimum age of six years (or equivalent developmental level) is now required. In DSM-5, the criteria for conduct disorder are largely unchanged from DSM-IV, but a "With limited prosocial emotion" specifier has now been added. The specifier applies to those individuals with a more serious pattern of behavior characterized by a callous and unemotional interpersonal style across multiple settings and relationships. The specifier goes beyond the presence of negative behavior and reflects an individual's typical patterns in emotional and interpersonal functioning. Clinicians will need to steel themselves against therapeutic nihilism with this group, given the relatively poorer response to parent training and psychopharmacological intervention, and remain cognizant of alternative therapeutic approaches that may garner additional efficacy evidence in future, including specific empathy/theory of mind interventions.

As we note above, DSM-5 does not distinguish between substance/alcohol "dependence" needing detoxification and substance/alcohol "abuse," where misuse in in evidence, within the "Substance-Related and Addictive Disorders" chapter. Rather, a single dimension is invoked of mild, moderate, or severe use, based upon the number of symptoms present. The term *dependence* is now used only for pharmacological dependence, that is, not as a disorder, to remove any conflation of the term with drug-seeking behavior (what many people would refer to as *addiction*). The changes reflect evidence that there is not a discernable intermediate state (previously thought to be *abuse*) between substance *use* and *addiction*. This change raises clinical implications with respect to when agonist use may be appropriate, for example in opioid use disorder, and while this remains to be seen, it would appear that moderate (4–6 symptoms) or severe (7–11 symptoms) presentations will qualify. Gambling disorder is the only behavioral condition included within this chapter.

Personality disorders have been dealt with above, and we regret that a number of chapters contain changes that are beyond the scope of this manuscript to discuss in further detail. These include the dissociative disorders, elimination disorders, sleep-wake disorders, sexual dysfunctions, neurocognitive disorders, and paraphilic disorders. Of these only the Elimination disorders are entirely unchanged, apart from being moved from the DSM-IV "Disorders Usually First Diagnosed in Infancy, Childhood, or Adolescence" chapter.

We would reiterate finally that Section III of the DSM-5 lists conditions warranting more scientific research and clinical experience before they might be considered; as well as a range of other items including detailed information about cultural formulation and a glossary of cultural concepts of distress, and a range of potentially useful screening and diagnostic measures that we would suggest are worth reviewing and considering. With respect to the conditions for further study, three are particularly relevant for children and adolescents that have not yet been mentioned: non-suicidal self-injury defines self-harm without the intention of suicide; internet gaming disorder deals with the compulsive preoccupation some people develop in playing online games, often to the exclusion of other needs and interests; and neurobehavioral disorder due to prenatal alcohol exposure, which many readers will think of as fetal alcohol syndrome, is also included for further study.

## Implications for Research

We understand that the intention is for DSM-5 to be more of a "living document" than previous iterations of the DSM series. In this regard, one can expect DSM-5.1; DSM-5.2 etc. to be released in the coming years, incorporating reliable research data as these become available. This shift is largely made possible by improved access to computing and availability of the internet. Thus, there remains an ongoing need for targeted research exploring various aspects of diagnostic criteria and in this important regard the landscape of nosological research has changed—where we might otherwise have anticipated something of a hiatus in the immediate aftermath of the release of an updated classificatory system. In general terms, ongoing work in improving diagnostic biomarkers and linkages with genetics and neuroimaging will likely form an increasing part of future research efforts. That is, fulfilling the promise of moving in the direction of a mixed-dimensional and categorical approach to diagnostic classification based increasingly on neuroscience.

One diagnostic area we would identify to illustrate this point and the type of research efforts that we believe are needed is OCD. In the absence of definitive etiological markers of vulnerability or a unitary profile of pathophysiology for the vast majority of disorders, including OCD, the initial step of carefully exploring symptom dimensions merits consideration as this can be achieved using a few consistent and temporally stable symptom dimensions. In the case of OCD, these can likely be understood as a spectrum of potentially overlapping features that are likely to be continuous with "normal" worries and extend beyond the traditional nosological boundaries of OCD. Given that our understanding of the dimensional structure of obsessive-compulsive symptoms is still imperfect, this quantitative approach to phenotypic traits has the potential to advance research through identification of more robust endophenotypes, that is, groups of behavioral symptoms with a connection to genetic markers. Preliminary data suggest that these dimensional phenotypes may also be useful in studies of the natural history, neurobiology, and treatment outcomes of OCD. Indeed, through a similar process it was observed that "hoarding," for example, has a different neurobiological origin to other obsessive-compulsive symptoms, leading ultimately to the inclusion of the new diagnostic category in DSM-5. Other useful distinctions include age-of-onset of obsessive-compulsive symptoms and the individual's "tic-related" status. The later has important implications for treatment response. In addition, based on available literature, tic-related obsessive-compulsive symptoms have different putative gene(s) involvement than primary OCD, and respond better to augmentation with dopamine blocking drugs in addition to SSRIs (Robertson & Eapen, 2014).

The hope would appear to remain that diagnostic guidelines for, and treatment of, child psychiatric disorders will ultimately be informed by the wealth of clinical genetic research related to neurodevelopmental disorders. However, in spite of remarkable advances in genetic technology, this has not been the case. Candidate gene, genome-wide association, and rare copy number variant (CNV) studies have been carried out for ADHD, autism spectrum disorder, Tourette's disorder, and schizophrenia, with intriguing results, but environmental factors, incomplete penetrance, pleiotropy, and genetic heterogeneity, all of which impact on the clinical phenotype, mean that these findings have had limited clinical translation. One promising approach may be the use of developmental brain imaging measures as more relevant phenotypes. This is particularly important, as subtle abnormalities in timing and expression of gene pathways underlying brain development may well link these disorders and be the ultimate target of treatments. Neuroimaging findings in callous and unemotional traits in conduct disorder are a useful case in point (Jones, Laurens, Herba, Barker, & Viding, 2009). Moreover, the inclusion of the "With limited prosocial emotion" specifier is a further useful example of research using a developmental psychopathological framework leading to changes within DSM and treatment approaches.

We believe a similar research effort linking phenotypes to endophenotypes—to neurobiological markers, hence to treatment response, both pharmacological and psychological—is required across the family of disorders within DSM. We have articulated, as an example, the critical case for such an approach with autism spectrum disorder in a recent manuscript (Eapen, Črnčec, & Walter, 2013). It is also important to observe that much research operates within but one of these domains and coordinated multidisciplinary efforts spanning the different arenas from laboratory to clinic will be critical into the future.

It is worth noting that the National Institute for Mental Health (NIMH) has listed as a research priority the Research Domain Criteria (RDoC) project, which seeks to spur the "development, for research purposes, of new ways of classifying psychopathology based on dimensions of observable behavior and neurobiological measures" (National Institute of Mental Health, 2013). Thus, funding for mental health research by the NIMH is moving away from DSM-5 categories, per se. The RDoC project is based upon several principles, including being a fully dimensional system that is agnostic about current disorder categories. The project seeks to explore several biologically based domains including negative valence systems (i.e., aversive motivational dimensions), positive valence systems, cognitive systems, social process systems, and arousal/ regulatory systems. Within each of these domains are various constructs, for example, within negative valence systems there are constructs including acute threat ("fear"); potential threat ("anxiety") and sustained threat, for example. These constructs are then explored from various units of analysis such as genes; molecules; circuits; behavior etc. The question of whether a hybrid nosology that maps biology onto behavior is attainable remains one of the fascinating possibilities for the future (Rapin, 2014).

Notwithstanding the merits of DSM-5 across myriad areas, including as an aide to communication and a platform for service organization and delivery, and the reality that DSM-5 essentially represents that best current information we have with respect to diagnosis of mental disorders, the argument we present above does hint at the paradox whereby classificatory systems such as DSM-5 may have hindered our efforts to understand the neurobiological processes underpinning the journey from genes to clinically significant symptoms or behaviors. In the case of child and adolescent populations we have expounded this argument in a manuscript titled "Neurodevelopmental genes have not read the DSM criteria: Or, have they?" (Eapen, 2012). Put differently, in order fully to advance the field into the future, we perhaps need to avoid the temptation of proceeding from the footing that there is something inherently "true" or "complete" about the diagnostic categories as currently presented. If we take the example of tics, there appears to be a spectrum of behaviors that co-occur with tics and it would perhaps be more useful to consider these under a "tic spectrum disorder" incorporating OCD with tics, ADHD with tics and ASD with tics etc. (Eapen & Črnčec, 2014).

Following the introduction of a range of new and updated diagnostic criteria, there will also be important research questions to be resolved in the next several years regarding prevalence, as well as service and pharmacotherapy utilization. For example, it will be important to determine whether issues related to access to services in light of changes to the autism spectrum disorder criteria, including the new severity criteria, arise (Weitlauf, Gotham, Vehorn, & Warren, 2014). Similarly, it will be important to determine how the new category of disruptive mood dysregulation disorder is adopted in practice and whether this leads to a reduction of the diagnosis of pediatric bipolar disorder and prescription of antipsychotics to young people.

In perhaps more pragmatic terms, a further area for research in the near future will be the re-standardizing of questionnaires and assessment schedules against the modified diagnostic criteria – especially in instances where the clinical criteria have changed substantially. Similarly, new measures will no doubt be developed to assist in the assessment of new disorders. Finally, the DSM-5 itself outlines conditions for further study and the proposed personality disorder criteria would appear particularly fruitful in this regard.

## Concluding Comments

It is unclear how long the transition from DSM-IV to 5 will take, although it is reasonable to expect that agencies and insurance groups will have amended their data systems and forms by now and clinicians will earnestly embrace the process of adjustment in the coming years. An advantage of the DSM-5 is that both ICD-9-CM and ICD-10-CM codes are presented to facilitate the transition in differing jurisdictions. This is a time where clinicians will do well to keep their "eyes peeled" and to discuss the process of change and their clinical discoveries openly with colleagues, who will be on a similar professional path.

It must be observed that child and adolescent psychiatry did not have an especially prominent place in DSM-IV, and its position has improved little in DSM-5, notwithstanding the worthwhile attempts that have been made to include a developmental focus throughout the new manual. In particular, DSM-5 does not include the full range and nuances of early disorders recognized by child and adolescent clinicians. For example, practitioners are likely to continue using other classifications for attachment disorders, such as the DC: 0–3 system (Zero to Three, 2005) and the criteria proposed by Zeanah and colleagues (O'Connor & Zeanah, 2003).

It is impossible to predict which aspects of the DSM-5 will be most enthusiastically taken up by patients, how criteria will be interpreted by clinicians over time, and the social changes and possibly unintended consequences that will invariably follow. What we have at this early post-DSM-5 release stage is arguably the beginning of a next phase in child and adolescent mental health practice; and regardless of whether the changes within DSM-5 thrill, dismay, or have little effect on the individual reader, we would commend clinicians and researchers to engage in the process of understanding the changes so as to energize the profession and set the stage for clinically informed debate (admittedly, hopefully some years from now) about assisting our patients through the development of subsequent iterations of the DSM.

## References

American Psychiatric Association. (1994). *Diagnostic and statistical manual of mental disorders* (4th ed.). Washington, DC: American Psychiatric Association.

American Psychatric Association. (2013). *Diagnostic and statistical manual of mental disorders* (5th ed.). Arlington, VA: American Psychiatric Association.

Eapen, V. (2012). Neurodevelopmental genes have not read the *DSM* criteria: Or, have they? *Frontiers in Psychiatry*, *3*, 75.

Eapen, V., & Črnčec, R. (2014). DSM 5 and child psychiatric disorders: What is new? What has changed? *Asian Journal of Psychiatry*, *11*, 114–118.

Eapen, V., Črnčec, R., & Walter, A. (2013). Exploring links between genotypes, phenotypes, and clinical predictors of response to early intensive behavioral intervention in autism spectrum disorder. *Frontiers in Human Neuroscience*, *7*, 567.

Eapen, V., Lees, A. J., Lakke, J. P., Trimble, M. R., & Robertson, M. M. (2002). Adult onset Gilles de la Tourette syndrome. *Movement Disorders, 17*, 735–740.
Goldman, H. H., Skodol, A. E., & Lave, T. R. (1992). Revising axis V for *DSM-IV*: A review of measures of social functioning. *American Journal of Psychiatry, 149*(9), 1148–1156.
Huerta, M., Bishop, S. L., Duncan, A., Hus, V., & Lord, C. (2012). Application of DSM-5 criteria for autism spectrum disorder to three samples of children with *DSM-IV* diagnoses of pervasive developmental disorders. *American Journal of Psychiatry, 169*(10), 1056–1064.
Jones, A. P., Laurens, K. R., Herba, C. M., Barker, G. J., & Viding, E. (2009). Amygdala hypoactivity to fearful faces in boys with conduct problems and callous-unemotional traits. *American Journal of Psychiatry, 166*(1), 95–102.
Mościcki, E. K., Clarke, D. E., Kuramoto, S. J., Kraemer, H. C., Narrow, W. E., Kupfer, D. J., Ret al. (2013). Testing *DSM-5* in routine clinical practice settings: Feasibility and clinical utility. *Psychiatric Services, 64*, 952–960.
National Institute of Mental Health. (2013). Research domain criteria (RDoC). Retrieved January 13, 2017 from http://www.nimh.nih.gov/research-priorities/rdoc/index.shtml.
O'Connor, T., & Zeanah, C. (2003). Attachment disorders: Assessment strategies and treatment approaches. *Attachment & Human Development, 5*(3), 223–244.
PDM Task Force. (2006). *Psychodynamic diagnostic manual (PDM)*. Silver Spring, MD: Alliance of Psychoanalytic Organizations.
Rapin, I. (2014). Classification of behaviorally defined disorders: Biology versus the *DSM*. *Journal of Autism and Developmental Disorders, 44*, 2661–2666.
Robertson, M. M., & Eapen, V. (2014). Tourette's: Syndrome, Disorder or Spectrum? Classificatory Challenges and an appraisal of the *DSM* criteria. *Asian Journal of Psychiatry, 11*, 106–113.
Stetka, B. S., & Correll, C. U. (2013, May). A guide to *DSM-5*. *Medscape*. Retrieved January 13, 2017 from http://www.medscape.com/viewarticle/803884.
Weitlauf, A. S., Gotham, K. O., Vehorn, A. C., & Warren, Z. E. (2014). Brief report: *DSM-5* "levels of support:" A comment on discrepant conceptualizations of severity in ASD. *Journal of Autism and Developmental Disorders, 44*(2), 471–476.
Zero to Three. (2005). *Diagnostic classification of mental health and developmental disorders of infancy and early childhood* (Rev. ed., *DC:0-3R*). Washington, DC: Zero to Three Press.

# 22

# Autistic Traits in the Development of Non-Autistic Psychopathology

William Mandy

Developmental Psychopathology (DP) has been defined by two of its chief progenitors as the study of the origins and course of individual patterns of behavioral maladaptation (Rutter & Sroufe, 2000, p. 256), and described in rather more poetic terms as an investigation of the mysterious unfolding of disturbance over time (Fonagy, 2003a, p. 212). More recently, leaders in the field have been keen to emphasize an interest in the development of health, as well as psychopathology (Cicchetti & Toth, 2009). As such, developmental psychopathologists seek to identify the causes of adaption and maladaptation across the lifespan. They take a characteristic approach to the pursuit of this goal, making use of a set of powerful ideas to guide their investigations, the most important of which are described in Box 22.1.

Whilst researchers have drawn on the ideas in Box 22.1 to study a wide range of maladaptive states, it is nevertheless the case that developmental psychopathology work has tended to concentrate on a handful of partially related topics. In particular there has been a focus on antisocial behavior; the role of attachment in maladaptation and adaption; the effects of childhood maltreatment and the origins of internalizing disorders (Rutter & Sroufe, 2000).

In this chapter, it will be argued that the scope of mainstream developmental psychopathology research should be expanded to include greater consideration of traits of neurodevelopmental disturbance as risk factors for diverse forms of maladaptation. Specifically, evidence will be presented that autistic social and non-social characteristics play a role in the development and maintenance of a range of non-autistic internalizing and externalizing problems.

Initially, two recent and substantial changes to the conceptualization of autism will be described. It will be argued that the resultant reformulation of autism provides a framework for considering the role of autistic traits in the development of non-autistic psychopathology. This idea will be explored and elaborated through a review of the literature on links between, on the one hand, autistic symptomatology, and on the other, conduct problems and anorexia nervosa. The chapter concludes with a model to guide future investigation of the role of autistic traits in the development of non-autistic psychopathology.

*The Wiley Handbook of Developmental Psychopathology*, First Edition. Edited by Luna C. Centifanti and David M. Williams.

**Box 22.1** Key Ideas in Developmental Psychopathology

**Psychopathology is maladaptation**: Mental disorder and distress are not well understood simply as properties of the individual; rather, they arise from a mismatch between the capacities of the individual and the environment in which they live.

**Development is transactional**: The individual and their environment are engaged in a dynamic interaction across the lifespan, with the environment influencing the individual, and the individual shaping their environment.

**Psychopathology is multiply determined**: Maladaptation or adaption never result from a single cause; rather they emerge from the interplay of multiple interacting risk and protective factors over time.

**Multiple levels of analysis**: Developmental psychopathology aims to integrate information from multiple fields of inquiry including genetics, developmental biology, neuroscience, psychology and sociology.

**Multifinality**: A risk factor will often increase the probability of several different outcomes, dependent on the context within which it occurs.

**Equifinality**: There are often multiple developmental routes to a particular outcome such as a mental disorder. Groups that appear homogenous in cross section can turn out to be etiologically heterogeneous once they are viewed developmentally.

### A Note on Terminology

Based on the fifth edition of the *Diagnostic and Statistical Manual* (DSM-5; American Psychiatric Association [APA], 2013) the term autism spectrum disorder (ASD) is used herein to denote the phenomenon under investigation. However, reflecting the language of the previous *Diagnostic and Statistical Manual* (DSM-IV; American Psychiatric Association [APA], 1994) findings from some of the earlier papers reviewed will be described in terms of autism, autistic disorder and Asperger's disorder/syndrome, and pervasive developmental disorder—not otherwise specified (PDD-NOS). These were hypothesized autistic subtypes, which have now all been subsumed by the DSM-5 term ASD. When describing dimensional, manifestations of ASD that do not reach the clinical threshold, I use the terms autistic traits or ASD traits as exact synonyms of each other.

## Autism Spectrum Disorder (ASD): An Evolving Construct

Until the 1990s, autism was widely considered to be a categorical disorder, qualitatively distinct from normality and from other types of psychopathology (e.g., Rutter & Schopler, 1988). This idea was not based on empirical findings, but rather reflected a wider assumption in psychiatry that any valid mental disorder should be a distinct state, separated from typical development and from other disorders by a zone of rarity (Kendell & Jablensky, 2003). In the last two decades, the credibility of this idea with respect to ASD (and to other disorders) has been steadily eroded. The current consensus is that ASD as a dimensional disorder, representing the extreme end of a continuous trait distribution that extends throughout the general population (e.g., Medical Research Council, 2001).

Initial intimations of the autisms dimensionality came from family studies. These revealed that many parents and siblings of people with ASD, whilst not meeting clinical criteria, demonstrated personality traits and social difficulties that appeared to be a mild version—or *forme fruste*—of ASD (Bolton et al., 1994). For example, compared to parents of people with Down syndrome, parents of children with autism are more likely to be aloof and socially clumsy, and to have fewer high-quality friendships (Losh, Childress, Lam, & Piven, 2008). Also, parents of people with autism are more likely to show characteristics such as perfectionism, dislike of novelty, inflexibility and a detail focused style of processing, which echoes the repetitive and stereotyped behaviors of ASD (Sucksmith, Roth, & Hoekstra, 2011). This collection of subclinical social and flexibility difficulties, intermediate between typical function and ASD, is known as the broader autism phenotype (BAP).

The discovery of the BAP raised the question of whether subclinical characteristics of ASD might be found in the general population, outside of the families of people with an autistic disorder. Constantino and Todd (2003) used the Social Responsiveness Scale (SRS) (Constantino et al., 2003) to investigate this question, measuring the prevalence of autistic traits in a typically developing twin sample. This revealed a continuous distribution of SRS scores, with no evidence for a natural cut-point between elevated but subclinical difficulties, and ASD. In this sample, SRS scores showed heritability similar to that of the clinical syndrome of ASD. Constantino and Todds observation of a continuous autistic trait distribution has since been replicated several times in non-twin samples, and there are no contradictory published findings that any cut-point or zone of rarity exists between people with and without the clinical syndrome of ASD (e.g. Posserud, Lundervold, & Gillberg, 2006; Skuse et al., 2009). Further evidence for dimensionality comes from quantitative genetic analyses of data from community sample twins, which suggest that genetic influences upon ASD trait variability in the normal range are similar to those on very high, clinically severe autistic difficulties (Robinson et al., 2011). Furthermore, molecular genetic investigations have identified DNA sequence variations, called single nucleotide polymorphisms (SNPs), that are associated with both autism and variability in normal range social communication difficulties (St Pourcain et al., 2014; St Pourcain et al., 2010).

The description of ASD in DSM-5 reflects an assumption that its diverse symptoms cluster together, because they are all manifestations of the same underlying disease process. This notion of autism as a unitary disorder that necessarily combines difficulties in social (i.e. reciprocity and communication) and non-social (i.e. flexibility and sensory processing) domains has recently come under scrutiny, and may not be tenable (Happé, Ronald, & Plomin, 2006). When different social and non-social domains of autistic symptomatology are measured in the clinic and in general population samples, they tend to show only a moderate ($r \approx .3$) statistical association with each other (e.g., Mandy, Charman, Puura, & Skuse, 2014; Ronald, Happé, & Plomin, 2005). Notably, the association between the social and non-social elements of ASD is less than, for example, the association between autistic social impairments and the symptoms of attention-deficit hyperactivity disorder (ADHD) (Ronald, Simonoff, Kuntsi, Asherson, & Plomin, 2008). Twin analyses show that the different parts of the autism syndrome are likely to result from substantially distinct genetic influences

(Ronald et al., 2005). Such a finding fits with observations of the BAP, which tends to comprise parts of the autism syndrome, rather than a mild version of the full array of autistic difficulties (Pickles et al., 2000). Furthermore, clinicians often encounter individuals who have some but not all of the symptoms of ASD. Most children with PDD-NOS, the most common of the DSM-IV ASD diagnoses (Baird et al., 2006), present with severe autistic social and communication difficulties, in the absence of clinically significant levels of repetitive, stereotyped behavior or sensory abnormalities (Mandy, Charman, Gilmour, & Skuse, 2011; Walker et al., 2004). Other children show the opposite pattern, namely high levels of RSB, without autistic social problems (Greaves-Lord et al., 2013; Pooni, Ninteman, Bryant-Waugh, Nicholls, & Mandy, 2012).

I have argued that ASD is a dimensional disorder, and that its symptoms can be divided into at least two trait dimensions: a *social* domain characterized by difficulties with reciprocity and communication; and a *non-social* domain, manifesting as inflexibility and atypical sensory processing (Mandy & Skuse, 2008). By conceptualizing ASD as a dimensional, fractionated condition, rather than a categorical, unitary one, a new field of inquiry is implied, which is the investigation of autistic social and non-social traits in non-autistic psychopathology. This involves asking two questions:

1 What are the consequences in development of having subthreshold, but elevated levels of autistic traits?
2 What are the consequences of having one but not the other type of autistic traits, for example solely non-social impairments without the social ones?

With these questions in mind, I now review literature on anorexia nervosa and conduct problems, the two disorders whose links with ASD have, at the time of writing, been best and most thoroughly researched.

## ASD and Anorexia Nervosa

Anorexia nervosa (henceforth anorexia) is a severe and life-threatening disorder diagnosed when a person becomes significantly underweight due to restricted eating, reflecting an intense fear of putting on weight and a distorted body image (APA, 2013). On the surface, anorexia appears to have little in common with ASD. Its core features concern eating and weight loss, not social communication or inflexibility. Whereas ASD is more common in males than in females, anorexia shows the opposite gender ratio, with more than ten affected females for every male (Smink, van Hoeken, Oldehinkel, & Hoek, 2014). ASD is a developmental disorder that manifests in the first year of life, whereas the onset of anorexia is typically in adolescence and early adulthood (Hoek, 2006). Sociocultural factors are not thought to influence an individual's risk of developing ASD, whereas anorexia has a substantial cultural component to its etiology, reflecting a contemporary obsession with feminine thinness (Schmidt, 2003). People on the autism spectrum are at increased risk of having an intellectual disability, whereas anorexia is typically associated with average or above IQ (Kopthari, Solmi, Treasure, & Micali, 2013). Unlike ASD, which is a lifelong condition, anorexia fluctuates in severity across the lifespan, with a five-year recovery rate, defined as no longer meeting criteria for an eating disorder, of around 50% (Ben-Tovin et al., 2001).

Nevertheless, despite these differences, there is currently a burgeoning interest in the relationship between anorexia and ASD, with some even going so far as to ask whether anorexia is a female version of ASD (Oldershaw, Treasure, Hambrook, Tchanturia, & Schmidt, 2011). Such ideas stem from the observation that that many people with anorexia demonstrate inflexibility of thought and behavior as well as difficulties with social life including social anhedonia and impaired empathy (Hambrook, Tchanturia, Schmidt, Russell, & Treasure, 2008). Furthermore, children with ASD can experience a range of eating difficulties, some of which overlap with, or predispose to, those seen in anorexia (Marchi & Cohen, 1990). Researchers have sought to test the idea that at least some cases of anorexia reflect the presence of an underlying ASD, or of underlying autistic traits. The resultant studies will be reviewed below, in order to address the question, framed in the language of developmental psychopathology, of whether autistic traits are a probabilistic risk factor for the development and maintenance of anorexia.

Interest in the notion that ASD might be implicated in the etiology of anorexia was ignited by a series of papers by Christopher Gillberg and colleagues, describing a cohort of people with anorexia in Gothenburg, Sweden. Participants in this study ($n=51$, 48 females) had an adolescent-onset eating disorder, and were compared to healthy controls matched on age, IQ and educational level (Gillberg & Rastaam, 1992). At initial assessment it was estimated that four participants in the anorexia group, one male and three females, had a developmental history of ASD prior to the onset of their eating disorder (Gillberg & Rastam, 1992). When assessing the same sample at five-year follow up, the estimated rate of ASD diagnosis had risen to 20% (Gillberg, Rastam, & Gillberg, 1995), and in an 18-year follow it was reported that one-third of the anorexia cohort had received an ASD diagnosis at some point during the study (Anckarsater et al., 2012). Given that the participants in this study were mostly females with average or above IQ, amongst whom ASD is rarely diagnosed, these estimated rates of ASD prevalence are exceptionally high.

The Gothenburg finding of elevated rates of autistic symptoms amongst adults with anorexia has been replicated several times. Researchers from the Gothenburg study were involved in a separate investigation of ASD amongst 30 women (anorexia $n=21$, bulimia nervosa $n=9$) attending specialist eating disorder clinics in London. After interviewing patients using the Asperger Syndrome Diagnostic Interview (Gillberg, Gillberg, Rastam, & Wentz, 2001) they estimated that around a quarter (23%) of the sample had ASD (Wentz, Lacey, Waller, Rastam, Turk, & Gillberg, 2005). Subsequently, several studies measuring autistic traits (as opposed to an ASD diagnosis) using the self-report Autism Quotient (AQ) (Baron-Cohen, Wheelwright, Skinner, Martin, & Clubely, 2001) have suggested that adult (Hambrook, Tchanturia, Schmidt, Russell, & Treasure, 2008) and adolescent (Baron-Cohen, Jaffa, Davies, Auyeung, Allison, & Wheelwright, 2013) females with anorexia have elevated levels of autistic features, compared to typically developing controls. These findings are important as they suggest that subclinical characteristics of ASD, in the absence of a full autistic diagnosis, may be sufficient to increase an individual's risk of developing anorexia.

Further support for the ASD-in-anorexia hypothesis has come from studies of cognition. At the group level, compared to healthy controls, anorexia is associated with impaired cognitive flexibility (Lang, Stahl, Espie, Treasure, & Tchanturia, 2013), global processing difficulties (Lang, Lopez, Stahl, Tchanturia, & Treasure, 2013) and atypical social cognition including impaired theory of mind (Russell, Schmidt,

Doherty, Young, & Tchanturia, 2004). This profile of cognitive difficulties mirrors that found in samples of people with ASD (Hill, 2004; Happé & Frith, 2006; Baron-Cohen, Leslie, & Frith, 1985), and implies that the autistic-like behaviors seen in anorexia may signify underlying autistic neurocognitive characteristics.

Despite the above studies, the idea that autism and autistic traits are germane to the development of anorexia has not been universally accepted, and has, in some quarters, been dismissed outright (e.g., Pellicano & Hiller, 2013). Skepticism arises from concerns that the social problems and inflexibility seen in many people with anorexia may not be truly autistic in nature. This problem of construct validity is relevant to assessing any claim that autistic traits have played a role in the development of non-autistic psychopathology, but is especially acute in anorexia research.

The key challenge for any study seeking to assess ASD traits in anorexia is to account for the effects of prolonged periods of undernourishment (Pellicano & Hiller, 2013). Individuals with anorexia, by definition, experience starvation; and starvation in humans gives rise to a range of behavioral changes that mimic symptoms of ASD. The most famous illustration of this comes from the Minnesota Starvation Experiment, in which 36 male volunteers, selected for their physical and mental good health, were carefully observed during six months of semi-starvation during which they lost, on average, a quarter of their body weight (Keys, Brozek, Henschel, Michelsen, & Taylor, 1950). The ill effects of semi-starvation on these volunteers were wide-ranging and severe, and included an increase in rigidity, manifesting as hoarding and obsessional behavior, as well as substantial diminution of social motivation and function. If, as seems likely, such changes occur in undernourished people with restricted eating disorder, they could mimic the symptoms of ASD and grossly inflate estimates of the overlap between anorexia and ASD. Unfortunately, studies of ASD symptoms in anorexia have thus far failed to control for the effects of starvation, so the high rates of ASD diagnosis observed in the Gothenburg study, as well as the elevated AQ scores reported in other groups of people with AN, may at least partially reflect the effects of starvation, rather that the presence of genuine autistic difficulties pre-dating the onset of anorexia.

Uncertainty about whether estimated rates of ASD symptomatology in anorexia are inflated by the impact of starvation has been compounded by a tendency for researchers in this area to use non-standardized and/or suboptimal ASD measures. This mainly reflects a broader lack of reliable and valid methods for assessing ASD in adults (Brugha et al., 2012). None of the studies reported above were able to make use of parent-report using a standardized interview, which is of great value in establishing an ASD diagnosis, especially for people with severe non-autistic psychopathology that may mimic autistic traits. Furthermore, the Gothenburg studies and the investigation of Wentz and colleagues (2005) did not employ gold standard ASD assessment tools, but instead relied on the application of somewhat idiosyncratic Gillberg and Gillberg criteria, rather than the almost universally used DSM and ICD criteria for ASD. The AQ is the best available self-report ASD trait measure for adults, but never-the-less it should be treated as a screener to identify individuals for further investigation, not a definitive assessment in itself, as it has been found to lack both sensitivity and specificity in some samples (Bishop & Seltzer, 2012). Any attempt to measure autistic traits using a questionnaire, rather than an interview or direct observation, carries risks to construct validity, as non-autistic behaviors that superficially resemble ASD (e.g. avoiding social contact due to depression) can be counted as an autistic symptom

(Hobson, 2014). Thus findings of elevated AQ scores in eating disorder samples may not reflect the presence of true autistic traits, but could arise from the effects of starvation, social anxiety, low mood, and so on.

Nevertheless, a handful of investigations have been designed so as to tease apart the causes and consequences of anorexia with respect to social and non-social ASD characteristics. Taken together these offer a nuanced yet remarkably consistent picture: that it is the non-social, rather than the social, aspects of ASD that are a risk factor for the development of anorexia.

Only one investigation described in the scientific literature used a standardized, parent-report interview based on DSM ASD criteria to assess development prior to onset of anorexia (Pooni et al., 2012). As such, this study offers the most valid assessment of ASD and autistic traits in anorexia, independent of the effects of starvation, or of other aspects of the ill state such as acute anxiety. In contrast to studies using less rigorous assessment methods, elevated rates of ASD in anorexia were not found. This was because participants with anorexia did not have any more developmental social or communication impairments than typical controls. However, they did have high rates of autistic non-social difficulties with flexibility that were comparable in type and severity to those shown by controls with ASD (Pooni et al., 2012).

This pattern of findings accords with several investigations of autistic cognition in anorexia that have attempted to control for and examine the effects of starvation by comparing recovered and acutely ill people with anorexia. These show that the non-social aspects of ASD-like cognition, namely set-shifting problems and detail-focused processing, persist after recovery, whilst impairments in social cognition tend to ameliorate with a return to healthy body weight (Oldershaw, Hambrook, Tchanturia, Treasure, & Schmidt, 2010). Family studies, in which the unaffected sisters of women with anorexia are investigated, also offer insights into characteristics related to anorexia whilst avoiding the effects of starvation, including those effects that might persist after the recovery of normal body weight. Worse set-shifting and greater attention to detail have been found in the unaffected sisters of women with anorexia compared to controls (Holliday, Tchanturia, Landau, Collier, & Treasure, 2005; Roberts, Tchanturia, & Treasure, 2013).

Studies examining disordered eating in non-clinical samples, wherein starvation is by definition rare, also point towards a specific association between traits of anorexia and non-social autistic difficulties. Coombs, Brosnan, Bryant-Waugh, and Skevington (2011) examined the relationship between autistic traits, measured by the AQ and eating disorder symptoms, measured dimensionally with the Eating Attitudes Test (EAT-26) (Garner, Olmsted, Bohr, & Garkinfel, 1982), in schoolchildren aged between 11 and 14 years. The strongest AQ predictor of EAT-26 total score was the attention to detail subscale, whereas there was no significant association between social skills and eating disorder symptoms. In line with this finding of a relationship between non-social autistic characteristics and subclinical symptoms of anorexia, in a different general population sample an association was discovered between detail-focused processing, measured objectively using the Embedded Figures Task, and eating disorder traits (Carton & Smith, 2014).

In summary, research designs that are not biased by the effects of starvation suggest that initial claims that around a quarter of women with anorexia have an underlying ASD are exaggerated. Nevertheless, as the published literature on this topic has grown, a more complex picture of the relationship between autistic traits and pathological restricted eating has emerged. Current evidence shows that it is the non-social aspects of ASD, including poor set-shifting, detail-focused processing and resistance to change, that predispose to restricted patterns of eating, including anorexia. The evidence for autistic social problems as an anorexia risk factor is much weaker, as the social deficits seen in people with anorexia probably mostly arise from starvation.

The current literature on ASD and anorexia, in conjunction with the principles of developmental psychology, suggest several avenues for future research. Follow up studies of people with ASD do not find high rates of anorexia in adolescence or adulthood (Howlin & Moss, 2012). Similarly, the relationship between autistic and anorexic traits is only moderate: many people with traits of ASD do not show any tendency towards eating disorder psychopathology. This raises the question of which risk factors interact with autistic traits in the development of anorexia. The most obvious candidate is gender—it is likely that ASD traits pose the greatest risk for anorexia in females compared to males. Other risk factors that may interact with autistic traits are sociocultural influences, whereby the risk posed by ASD traits is magnified in cultural and family settings where female thinness is especially overvalued. Such hypotheses should be tested using moderation analysis in prospective designs.

It is not clear whether the relationship between anorexia and autistic non-social difficulties is direct; or whether there are intervening processes between initial autistic traits and later eating difficulties. One possibility, suggested by our clinical experience, is that neurodevelopmental difficulties in childhood may predispose to peer rejection, internalizing problems and low self-esteem, which, in our current cultural context, predispose some females to dieting and restricted eating. Mediation analyses using longitudinal data can provide a description of any such developmental cascades linking childhood traits of ASD to later eating psychopathology.

The characterization of autistic traits as a risk factor for eating disorder may help identify clinically meaningful subgroups amongst people with anorexia. This will involve the consideration of whether individuals who have anorexia and autistic difficulties have a distinct prognosis and treatment needs to people whose anorexia is the outcome of a different collection of risk factors. A related concern is whether non-social autistic traits predispose specifically to anorexia, or whether they are of relevance to other eating disorders, such a bulimia nervosa and binge eating (Roberts et al., 2013).

It will be useful to pinpoint the relative contribution of autistic traits to the development and maintenance of anorexia. Studies of teens with recent onset anorexia find fewer autistic traits than those of adults with the disorder (e.g., Fitzpatrick, Darcy, Colborn, Gudorf, & Lock, 2012; Pooni et al., 2012). This could partly reflect the less severe and chronic history of starvation in younger samples; but it could also arise because adult samples are, by their very nature, richer in patients with a chronic course of anorexia. As such, it could be that autistic traits, and especially those involving resistance to change, are implicated in the maintenance of anorexia and are especially important for understanding treatment resistance cases of the disorder.

## ASD and Conduct Problems

Within developmental psychopathology, when a young person is consistently unable to conform to society's rules and expectations they are described as having a conduct problem. There are many different ways in which a young person can misbehave, and many reasons for such behavior; which is to say that conduct problems are heterogeneous both in terms of their phenomenology and etiology. DSM-5 parses this heterogeneity by describing two main types of childhood conduct problem: (1) oppositional defiant disorder (ODD), characterized by defiance in the context of emotional and behavioral dysregulation; and (2) conduct disorder (CD), which is defined as a pattern of persistent violation of the rights of others and of important, age-appropriate societal norms for good-enough behavior. CD itself is a heterogeneous entity that can be divided in a number of ways. One distinction is between childhood- and adolescent-onset CD, with the former being marked by greater symptom severity, poorer prognosis and greater etiological load (Moffitt & Caspi, 2001). Another is between CD that primarily involves rule-breaking (e.g. playing truant and staying out late) and CD that involves direct, physical aggression. Furthermore, the DSM-5 recently acknowledged that a subgroup of children with CD can be distinguished by characteristics of psychopathy, called callous–unemotional traits (APA, 2013; Frick & Viding, 2009).

Like almost all forms of psychopathology, conduct problems emerge from the interaction of multiple risk and protective factors over time. It has long been known that in addition to parental, peer-group and cultural influences, neurodevelopmental difficulties play an important role in this process. For example, low IQ and ADHD symptomatology are amongst the most consistently demonstrated risk factors for CD (McMahon & Frick, 2007). In addition, it is widely acknowledged that impaired social cognition, for example a hostile attribution bias when making sense of other people's actions, plays an important role in the development of some conduct problems (Crick & Dodge, 1996). Recently, interest in neurodevelopmental and social risk factors has converged on several accounts of impairments that are both social and neurodevelopmental, which are implicated in the development of some conduct problems. A callous and unemotional interpersonal style, underpinned by a reduced tendency to resonate with the emotions of others, has been proposed as a key risk factor for the aggressive, antisocial behavior of some young people and adults (Blair, 2004; Fonagy, 2003b; Frick & Viding, 2009).

Whilst most recent interest in social cognition and CD has focused on the role of callous–unemotional traits, I argue here for a different, although not mutually exclusive, social neurodevelopmental hypothesis: that autistic traits are a probabilistic risk factor for the development of conduct problems. I will review the relevant literature with two specific hypotheses in mind. First, that the empathy difficulties inherent in autistic social impairments increase the risk of conduct problems by limiting the child's capacity to notice, understand and be affected by the emotional responses of other people (Mandy, Skuse, Steer, St Pourcain, & Oliver, 2013). Second, that the rigidity and insistence on sameness of the non-social ASD domain make people more likely to experience frustration, which can give rise to aggression and failure to conform to rules.

There is strong evidence for an association between autistic symptomatology and conduct problems. Children with ASD show dramatically elevated levels of ODD, and slightly raised levels of conduct disorder (Simonoff et al., 2008). Conversely, children with high levels of disruptive behavior are much more likely than controls to have an ASD diagnosis, as discovered by Gilmour and colleagues when they conducted in-depth autism assessments with conduct disordered children (Donno, Parker, Gilmour, & Skuse, 2010; Gilmour, Hill, Place, & Skuse, 2004). This association does not merely reflect ASDs association with ADHD and low IQ: the relationship between ASD diagnosis and conduct problems remains robust in analyses that control for potential confounding effects of ADHD symptoms and intellectual disability (Totsika, Hastings, Emerson, Lancaster, & Berridge, 2011).

Subclinical autistic traits, not just a full ASD diagnosis, are predictive of a wide range of conduct problems, as captured by ODD and CD diagnostic criteria. Children with conduct problems show a level of autistic traits that is intermediate between ASD and typical control groups (Cholemkery, Kitzerow, Rohrmann, & Freitag, 2014). In cross-sectional studies of community samples, children who have CD or ODD also have a tendency towards elevated levels of autistic symptomatology (Lundström et al., 2011). In fact, ASD traits may be a stronger predictor of conduct problems than ADHD traits, previously considered one of the key risk factors for disruptive behavior (Kerekes et al., 2014). Prospective studies, in which ASD traits were measured before the onset of conduct problems, have confirmed the association between autistic traits and conduct problems, and suggest that autistic traits appear prior to the onset of behavioral disturbance (Oliver, Barker, Mandy, Skuse, & Maughan, 2013; Skuse et al., 2009). This lends weight to the idea that they are a causal risk factor.

As discussed above, autistic social and non-social traits can occur independently of each other, and may have distinct relationships to different types of non-autistic psychopathology. The literature on ASD and conduct problems strongly suggests that it is social, rather than non-social (i.e. inflexibility), autistic traits that are implicated in the development of conduct problems. Children with conduct problems are distinguished from typically developing controls not by repetitive and stereotyped behavior, but by having higher levels of autistic social and communication impairment (Donno et al., 2010; Cholemkery, 2011). In community samples, it is social reciprocity (Skuse et al., 2009) and measures of the social use of language (Oliver et al., 2011) that predict conduct problems, whereas inflexibility is only a weak predictor of ODD and is unrelated to CD (Kerekes et al., 2014).

Recently, a developmental mechanism has been proposed to link autistic social impairment and conduct problems. In line with the ethos of developmental psychopathology, this has involved drawing on a model of normal development to elucidate a process underpinning maladaptation. Disruptive behaviors are almost universal during toddlerhood, and typical development in early and mid childhood is characterized by a decline in aggressive, oppositional behavior (Tremblay, 2010). This process of socialization coincides with the development of theory of mind/"mentalizing" (the ability to understand, explain, and predict others behavior in terms of underlying mental states, such as beliefs, desires, and intentions), and it is believed to rely upon the emergence of intersubjectivity (Fonagy, 2003a). The argument is that the capacity for a child to perceive and be affected by the distress or anger in others caused by their inevitable misdeeds provides powerful disincentive to the repetition of such behavior. In terms of learning theory, mentalizing makes possible the experience of socially mediated punishment for antisocial behavior (e.g. aversive experience of others' distress and disapproval) and of interpersonal reward for prosocial behavior (e.g. pleasant experience of making another happy by a prosocial act).

The corollary of this model is that individuals who struggle to understand the perspectives of others may follow a maladaptive developmental trajectory marked by levels of disruptive behavior that remain high throughout childhood. Consistent with this is the finding that, between the ages of 3 and 7 years, conduct problems in the general population decline, where as those in children with ASD escalate (Midouhas, Yogartatnam, Flouri, & Charman, 2013). Mandy and colleagues (2013) also found evidence to support the moderating role of empathy on conduct problem trajectory. They showed that traits of autistic social impairment are associated with on-going, and escalating, conduct problems between the ages of 7 and 10 years; but that they did not operate directly on the development of aggression and rule-breaking. Instead, they functioned as a moderator, tuning up the risk posed by another trait, ODD symptoms. Similarly, autistic traits appear to moderate the relationship between social anxiety and aggression, such that fears of humiliation and rejection are a risk factor for aggression amongst people with ASD, but not in those without (Pugliese, White, White, & Ollendick, 2013).

## Future Directions of the Investigation of Autistic Traits as a Risk Factor for the Development of Non-autistic Psychopathology

Figure 22.1 depicts a back-of-an-envelope model that can guide investigations of autistic traits as a risk factor in developmental psychopathology. In addition to conduct problems and anorexia, I have suggested as targets for research two other psychopathologies, obsessive compulsive disorder (OCD) and social anxiety disorder (SAD). Whilst there is less research into whether these are related to ASD traits, there is enough empirical evidence to identify them as potentially fruitful candidates for investigation.

SAD, also known as social phobia, is characterized by fear of social and/or performance situations, often linked to an acute concern about being judged negatively. Its symptoms can be reliably distinguished from autistic social impairments (White, Bray, & Ollendick, 2012), and it is diagnosable in about a third of people with ASD (Simonoff et al., 2008). Compared to controls, relatives of people with ASD have elevated rates of SAD. In the general population there is a strong ($r = .5$) cross-sectional association between traits of SAD and ASD, with social skills and attention switching being most

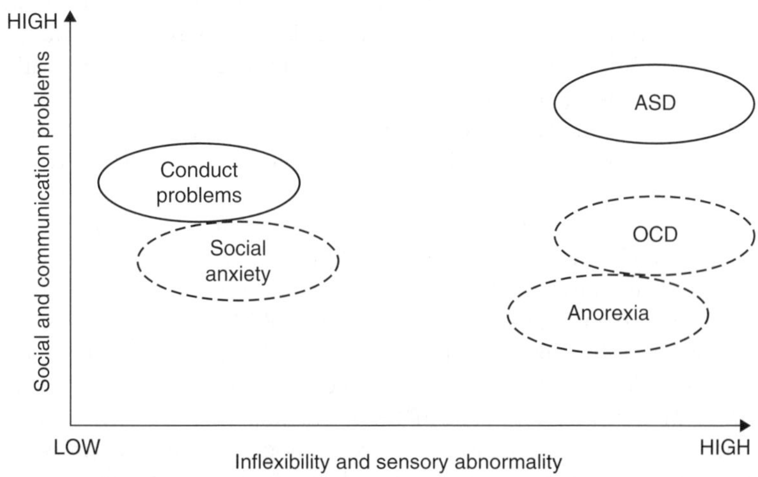


**Figure 22.1** A model of autistic traits and non-autistic psychopathology.

strongly related to social phobia traits (Freeth, Bullock, and Milne, 2012). Theoretical models of SAD add further weight to the idea that ASD traits may be implicated in its development, as these emphasize the role of social skill and empathy deficits (Bellini, 2006).

Obsessive Compulsive Disorder (OCD) is diagnosed when a person experiences unwanted, time-consuming and distressing obsessions and compulsions. It affects between one and two per cent of the population, and tends to have a chronic course, with a low chance of spontaneous remission (Skoog & Skoog, 1999). Whilst OCD is rather rare amongst children with ASD, it greatly increases in prevalence during adolescence, such that obsessional disorders are amongst the most common comorbid conditions in adults with ASD (Hutton, Goode, Murphy, Le Couteur, & Rutter, 2008). Autistic traits are found at elevated levels amongst children and adults with OCD (Anholt et al., 2010; Ivarsson & Melin, 2008); ASD and OCD traits are associated in general population samples (Wakabayashi, Baron-Cohen, & Ashwin, 2012); and rates of OCD amongst the relatives of people with ASD are high (Bolton, Pickles, Murphy, & Rutter, 1998). Relatives of ASD children with high levels of repetitive, stereotyped behavior symptoms are at particular risk of having OCD, suggesting that OCD may be associated with the non-social autism trait dimension (Abramson et al., 2005). That impression is reinforced by the phenomenology of OCD, which involves rigidity, insistence on sameness, sensory processing difficulties, detail-focused cognitive style, and difficulties set-shifting, all of which are also characteristic of autistic non-social impairment.

I finish by outlining several ways in which the principles of developmental psychopathology, in particular those outlined in Box 1, can guide future investigations of the role of autistic traits in the development of adaption and maladaptation.

In contrast to most ASD research to date, there should be consideration of the interaction between the environment and individuals with ASD traits. This would involve consideration of the characteristics of home, peer, and educational environment in which ASD traits most likely to predispose to maladaptation; and conversely what types of ecology can promote resilience for those with ASD traits. A rare example of this approach was the study described above, conducted by Midhouas and colleagues (2013), who discovered that the effects of parental warmth were protective against the risk posed by ASD for the development of conduct problems. These sorts of findings have immediate clinical implications, which could inform prevention and treatment strategies.

A related, environment-focused approach is to consider on how ASD traits influence transactions between individuals and their environment. By analogy, it is known that children predisposed to conduct problems are more likely to evoke harsh and ineffective parenting, which in turn increases their risk of developing anti-social behavior (OConnor, Deater-Dechard, Fulker, & Rutter, 1998). Children with ASD traits may evoke a range of negative experiences from their environment. For example they are more likely to be bullied, to get in trouble at school (Skuse et al., 2009), and to have parents who are feel stressed and overwhelmed (Zaidman-Zait et al., 2014). Such features of the environment are highly likely impact negatively on a child's development, and the unpicking of these sorts of transactions between the individual and the environment would identify aspects of the development of psychopathology amenable to intervention.

Another challenge will be to further map key risk factors that interact with ASD traits to increase an individual's risk of developing psychopathology. In line with developmental psychopathology, such risk factors can be conceptualized at any level, from the purely biological to the sociological. As discussed above, the risk posed for anorexia by ASD probably interacts with biological (e.g., sex), affective, cognitive, and cultural elements. The consideration of such complexes of risk will be useful for other disorders, and can help to elucidate the multifinality of ASD traits.

Current diagnostic systems for classifying psychopathology are atheoretical, and probably lack validity (Insel, 2014). The DSM and ICD systems of taxonomy have a tendency to lump together diverse difficulties, which have subtly different phenotypes and distinct etiologies. The application of an autistic traits model to the study of psychopathology will help to parse some of the heterogeneity that exists within individual psychiatric diagnoses, by delineating subgroups that have developed a disorder partly due to their autistic social or non-social traits. For example, it is very unlikely that all people with SAD have underlying autistic difficulties, but rather there may be a subgroup who do. Their SAD will require a formulation that reflects this, and which gives rise to treatments tailored to the specific etiological and maintaining factors of their difficulties. Thus, the consideration of the role of ASD traits in the development of psychopathology can serve two of the key overarching aims of psychiatry and clinical psychology: the development of a nosology based on underlying mechanisms rather than surface symptoms (Rutter, 2011); and the improvement of treatment efficacy through the introduction of bespoke interventions.

## Acknowledgments

The ideas in this paper have been influenced by several people. The overarching hypothesis that subthreshold autistic traits are risk factors for non-autistic disorders came from collaborations and discussions with Professor David Skuse. Specific concepts about the role of autistic traits in various types of psychopathology were worked out with several colleagues, in particular Dr. Beate St Pourcain and Dr. Bonamy Oliver. I also thank several students I have supervised, Caroline Barber, Josselyn Hellriegel, Aafke Ninteman, Camilla Parker, Jotti Pooni, and Lucy Wootton who worked to elaborate and test some of the ideas presented in this paper.

## References

Abramson, R. K., Ravan, S. A., Wright, H. H., Wieduwilt, K., Wolpert, C. M., Donnelly, S. A., et al. (2005). The relationship between restrictive and repetitive behaviors in individuals with autism and obsessive compulsive symptoms in parents. *Child Psychiatry and Human Development*, *36*(2), 155–165. doi:10.1007/s10578-005-2973-7

American Psychiatric Association (1994). *Diagnostic and statistical manual* (4th ed.). Washington, DC: American Psychiatric Association.

American Psychiatric Association (2013). *Diagnostic and statistical manual* (5th ed.). Washington, DC: American Psychiatric Association.

Anckarsäter, H., Hofvander, B., Billstedt, E., Gillberg, I. C., Gillberg, C., Wentz, E., et al. (2012). The sociocommunicative deficit subgroup in anorexia nervosa: Autism spectrum disorders and neurocognition in a community-based, longitudinal study. *Psychological Medicine*, *42*(9), 1957–1967. doi:10.1017/S0033291711002881

Anholt, G. E., Cath, D. C., van Oppen, P., Eikelenboom, M., Smit, J. H., van Megen, H., et al. (2010). Autism and ADHD symptoms in patients with OCD: Are they associated with specific OC symptom dimensions or OC symptom severity? *Journal of Autism and Developmental Disorders*, *40*(5), 580–589. doi:10.1007/s10803-009-0922-1

Baird, G., Simonoff, E., Pickles, A., Chandler, S., Loucas, T., Meldrum, D., et al. (2006). Prevalence of disorders of the autism spectrum in a population cohort of children in South Thames: The Special Needs and Autism Project (SNAP). *Lancet*, *368*(9531), 210–215. doi:10.1016/S0140-6736(06)69041-7

Baron-Cohen, S., Jaffa, T., Davies, S., Auyeung, B., Allison, C., & Wheelwright, S. (2013). Do girls with anorexia nervosa have elevated autistic traits? *Molecular Autism*, *4*(1), 24. doi:10.1186/2040-2392-4-24

Baron-Cohen, S., Leslie, A. M., & Frith, U. (1985). Does the autistic child have a "theory of mind"? *Cognition*, *21*(1), 37–46. doi:10.1016/0010-0277(85)90022-8

Baron-Cohen, S., Wheelwright, S., Skinner, R., Martin, J., & Clubley, E. (2001). The autism-spectrum quotient (AQ): Evidence from Asperger syndrome/high-functioning autism, males and females, scientists and mathematicians. *Journal of Autism and Developmental Disorders*, *31*(1), 5–17.

Bellini, S. (2006). The development of social anxiety in adolescents with autism spectrum disorders. *Focus on Autism and Other Developmental Disabilities*, *21*(3), 138–145. doi:10.1177/10883576060210030201

Ben-Tovim, D. I., Walker, K., Gilchrist, P., Freeman, R., Kalucy, R., & Esterman, A. (2001). Outcome in patients with eating disorders: A 5-year study. *Lancet*, *357*(9264), 1254–1257. doi:10.1016/S0140-6736(00)04406-8

Bishop, S. L., & Seltzer, M. M. (2012). Self-reported autism symptoms in adults with autism spectrum disorders. *Journal of Autism and Developmental Disorders*, *42*(11), 2354–2363. doi:10.1007/s10803-012-1483-2

Blair, R. J. R. (2004). The roles of orbital frontal cortex in the modulation of antisocial behavior. *Brain and Cognition*, *55*(1), 198–208. doi:10.1016/S0278-2626(03)00276-8

Bolton, P., Macdonald, H., Pickles, A., Rios, P., Goode, S., Crowson, M., et al. (1994). A case-control family history study of autism. *Journal of Child Psychology and Psychiatry, and Allied Disciplines*, *35*(5), 877–900.

Bolton, P. F., Pickles, A., Murphy, M., & Rutter, M. (1998). Autism, affective and other psychiatric disorders: Patterns of familial aggregation. *Psychological Medicine*, *28*(2), 385–395.

Brugha, T. S., McManus, S., Smith, J., Scott, F. J., Meltzer, H., Purdon, S., et al. (2012). Validating two survey methods for identifying cases of autism spectrum disorder among adults in the community. *Psychological Medicine*, *42*(3), 647–656. doi:10.1017/S0033291711001292

Carton, A. M., & Smith, A. D. (2014). Assessing the relationship between eating disorder psychopathology and autistic traits in a non-clinical adult population. *Eating and Weight Disorders: EWD*, *19*, 285–293. doi:10.1007/s40519-013-0086-z

Cholemkery, H., Kitzerow, J., Rohrmann, S., & Freitag, C. M. (2014). Validity of the social responsiveness scale to differentiate between autism spectrum disorders and disruptive behaviour disorders. *European Child & Adolescent Psychiatry*, *23*(2), 81–93. doi:10.1007/s00787-013-0427-5

Cicchetti, D., & Toth, S. L. (2009). The past achievements and future promises of developmental psychopathology: The coming of age of a discipline. *Journal of Child Psychology and Psychiatry, and Allied Disciplines*, *50*(1–2), 16–25. doi:10.1111/j.1469-7610.2008.01979.x

Constantino, J. N., Davis, S. A., Todd, R. D., Schindler, M. K., Gross, M. M., Brophy, S. L., et al. (2003). Validation of a brief quantitative measure of autistic traits: Comparison of the social responsiveness scale with the autism diagnostic interview-revised. *Journal of Autism and Developmental Disorders*, *33*(4), 427–433.

Constantino, J. N., & Todd, R. D. (2003). Autistic traits in the general population: A twin study. *Archives of General Psychiatry*, *60*(5), 524–530. doi:10.1001/archpsyc.60.5.524

Coombs, E., Brosnan, M., Bryant-Waugh, R., & Skevington, S. M. (2011). An investigation into the relationship between eating disorder psychopathology and autistic symptomatology in a non-clinical sample. *The British Journal of Clinical Psychology*, *50*(3), 326–338. doi:10.1348/014466510X524408

Crick, N. R., & Dodge, K. A. (1996). Social information-processing mechanisms in reactive and proactive aggression. *Child Development*, *67*(3), 993–1002.

Donno, R., Parker, G., Gilmour, J., & Skuse, D. H. (2010). Social communication deficits in disruptive primary-school children. *The British Journal of Psychiatry: The Journal of Mental Science*, *196*(4), 282–289. doi:10.1192/bjp.bp.108.061341

Fitzpatrick, K. K., Darcy, A., Colborn, D., Gudorf, C., & Lock, J. (2012). Set-shifting among adolescents with anorexia nervosa. *The International Journal of Eating Disorders*, *45*(7), 909–912. doi:10.1002/eat.22027

Freeth, M., Bullock, T., & Milne, E. (2013). The distribution of and relationship between autistic traits and social anxiety in a UK student population. *Autism: The International Journal of Research and Practice*, *17*(5), 571–581. doi:10.1177/1362361312445511

Frick, P. J., & Viding, E. (2009). Antisocial behavior from a developmental psychopathology perspective. *Development and Psychopathology*, *21*(4), 1111–1131. doi:10.1017/S0954579409990071

Fonagy, P. (2003a). The development of psychopathology from infancy to adulthood: The mysterious unfolding of disturbance in time. *Infant Mental Health Journal*, *24*(3), 212–239. doi:10.1002/imhj.10053

Fonagy, P. (2003b). Towards a developmental understanding of violence. *The British Journal of Psychiatry: The Journal of Mental Science*, *183*, 190–192.

Garner, D. M., Olmsted, M. P., Bohr, Y., & Garfinkel, P. E. (1982). The eating attitudes test: Psychometric features and clinical correlates. *Psychological Medicine*, *12*(4), 871–878.

Gillberg, C., Gillberg, C., Råstam, M., & Wentz, E. (2001). The Asperger Syndrome (and high-functioning autism) Diagnostic Interview (ASDI): A preliminary study of a new structured clinical interview. *Autism: The International Journal of Research and Practice*, *5*(1), 57–66.

Gillberg, C., & Råstam, M. (1992). Do some cases of anorexia nervosa reflect underlying autistic-like conditions? *Behavioural Neurology*, *5*(1), 27–32. doi:10.3233/BEN-1992-5105

Gillberg, I. C., Råstam, M., & Gillberg, C. (1995). Anorexia nervosa 6 years after onset: Part I. Personality disorders. *Comprehensive Psychiatry*, *36*(1), 61–69.

Gilmour, J., Hill, B., Place, M., & Skuse, D. H. (2004). Social communication deficits in conduct disorder: A clinical and community survey. *Journal of Child Psychology and Psychiatry, and Allied Disciplines*, *45*(5), 967–978. doi:10.1111/j.1469-7610.2004.t01-1-00289.x

Greaves-Lord, K., Eussen, M. L. J. M., Verhulst, F. C., Minderaa, R. B., Mandy, W., Hudziak, J. J., et al. (2013). Empirically based phenotypic profiles of children with pervasive developmental disorders: Interpretation in the light of the *DSM-5*. *Journal of Autism and Developmental Disorders*, *43*(8), 1784–1797. doi:10.1007/s10803-012-1724-4

Hambrook, D., Tchanturia, K., Schmidt, U., Russell, T., & Treasure, J. (2008). Empathy, systemizing, and autistic traits in anorexia nervosa: A pilot study. *The British Journal of Clinical Psychology*, *47*(Pt 3), 335–339. doi:10.1348/014466507X272475

Happé, F., & Frith, U. (2006). The weak coherence account: detail-focused cognitive style in autism spectrum disorders. *Journal of Autism and Developmental Disorders*, *36*(1), 5–25. doi:10.1007/s10803-005-0039-0

Happé, F., Ronald, A., & Plomin, R. (2006). Time to give up on a single explanation for autism. *Nature Neuroscience*, *9*(10), 1218–1220. doi:10.1038/nn1770

Hill, E. L. (2004). Executive dysfunction in autism. *Trends in Cognitive Sciences*, *8*(1), 26–32. doi:10.1016/j.tics.2003.11.003

Hobson, R. P. (2014). The coherence of autism. *Autism, 18*(1), 6–18.

Hoek, H. W. (2006). Incidence, prevalence and mortality of anorexia nervosa and other eating disorders. *Current Opinion in Psychiatry, 19*(4), 389–394. doi:10.1097/01.yco.0000228759.95237.78

Holliday, J., Tchanturia, K., Landau, S., Collier, D., & Treasure, J. (2005). Is impaired set-shifting an endophenotype of anorexia nervosa? *The American Journal of Psychiatry, 162*(12), 2269–2275. doi:10.1176/appi.ajp.162.12.2269

Howlin, P., & Moss, P. (2012). Adults with autism spectrum disorders. *Canadian Journal of Psychiatry. Revue Canadienne De Psychiatrie, 57*(5), 275–283.

Hutton, J., Goode, S., Murphy, M., Le Couteur, A., & Rutter, M. (2008). New-onset psychiatric disorders in individuals with autism. *Autism: The International Journal of Research and Practice, 12*(4), 373–390. doi:10.1177/1362361308091650

Insel, T. R. (2014). The NIMH Research Domain Criteria (RDoC) Project: Precision medicine for psychiatry. *The American Journal of Psychiatry, 171*(4), 395–397. doi:10.1176/appi.ajp.2014.14020138

Ivarsson, T., & Melin, K. (2008). Autism spectrum traits in children and adolescents with obsessive-compulsive disorder (OCD). *Journal of Anxiety Disorders, 22*(6), 969–978. doi:10.1016/j.janxdis.2007.10.003

Kendell, R., & Jablensky, A. (2003). Distinguishing between the validity and utility of psychiatric diagnoses. *The American Journal of Psychiatry, 160*(1), 4–12.

Keys, A., Brozek, J., Henschel, A., Michelsen, O., & Taylor, H. (1950) *The biology of human starvation* (Vols. 1 & 2). Minneapolis: University of Minnesota Press.

Kerekes, N., Lundström, S., Chang, Z., Tajnia, A., Jern, P., Lichtenstein, P., et al. (2014). Oppositional defiant- and conduct disorder-like problems: Neurodevelopmental predictors and genetic background in boys and girls, in a nationwide twin study. *PeerJ, 2*, e359. doi:10.7717/peerj.359

Kothari, R., Solmi, F., Treasure, J., & Micali, N. (2013). The neuropsychological profile of children at high risk of developing an eating disorder. *Psychological Medicine, 43*(7), 1543–1554. doi:10.1017/S0033291712002188

Lang, K., Lopez, C., Stahl, D., Tchanturia, K., & Treasure, J. (2014). Central coherence in eating disorders: An updated systematic review and meta-analysis. *The World Journal of Biological Psychiatry: The Official Journal of the World Federation of Societies of Biological Psychiatry*, 1–13. doi:10.3109/15622975.2014.909606

Lang, K., Stahl, D., Espie, J., Treasure, J., & Tchanturia, K. (2014). Set shifting in children and adolescents with anorexia nervosa: An exploratory systematic review and meta-analysis. *The International Journal of Eating Disorders, 47*(4), 394–399. doi:10.1002/eat.22235

Losh, M., Childress, D., Lam, K., & Piven, J. (2008). Defining key features of the broad autism phenotype: A comparison across parents of multiple- and single-incidence autism families. *American Journal of Medical Genetics. Part B, Neuropsychiatric Genetics: The Official Publication of the International Society of Psychiatric Genetics, 147B*(4), 424–433. doi:10.1002/ajmg.b.30612

Lundström, S., Chang, Z., Kerekes, N., Gumpert, C. H., Råstam, M., Gillberg, C., et al. (2011). Autistic-like traits and their association with mental health problems in two nationwide twin cohorts of children and adults. *Psychological Medicine, 41*(11), 2423–2433. doi:10.1017/S0033291711000377

Mandy, W., & Skuse, D. (2008). What is the association between the social-communication element of autism and repetitive interests, behaviours and activities? *Journal of Child Psychology and Psychiatry, 49*(8), 795–808.

Mandy, W., Charman, T., Gilmour, J., & Skuse, D. (2011). Toward specifying pervasive developmental disorder-not otherwise specified. *Autism Research: Official Journal of the International Society for Autism Research, 4*(2), 121–131. doi:10.1002/aur.178

Mandy, W., Charman, T., Puura, K., & Skuse, D. (2014). Investigating the cross-cultural validity of DSM-5 autism spectrum disorder: evidence from Finnish and UK samples. *Autism: The International Journal of Research and Practice, 18*(1), 45–54. doi:10.1177/1362361313508026

Mandy, W., Skuse, D., Steer, C., St Pourcain, B., & Oliver, B. R. (2013). Oppositionality and socioemotional competence: Interacting risk factors in the development of childhood conduct disorder symptoms. *Journal of the American Academy of Child and Adolescent Psychiatry, 52*(7), 718–727. doi:10.1016/j.jaac.2013.04.011

Marchi, M., & Cohen, P. (1990). Early childhood eating behaviors and adolescent eating disorders. *Journal of the American Academy of Child and Adolescent Psychiatry, 29*(1), 112–117. doi:10.1097/00004583-199001000-00017

McMahon, R. & Frick, P. (2007). Conduct and oppositional disorders. In J. Mash & R. Barkley (Eds.), *Assessment of childhood disorders* (4th ed., pp. 132–184). New York: Guilford Press.

Medical Research Council. (2001). *Review of autism research: Epidemiology and causes.* London: Medical Research Council.

Midouhas, E., Yogaratnam, A., Flouri, E., & Charman, T. (2013). Psychopathology trajectories of children with autism spectrum disorder: The role of family poverty and parenting. *Journal of the American Academy of Child and Adolescent Psychiatry, 52*(10), 1057–1065. doi:10.1016/j.jaac.2013.07.011

Moffitt, T. E., & Caspi, A. (2001). Childhood predictors differentiate life-course persistent and adolescence-limited antisocial pathways among males and females. *Development and Psychopathology, 13*(2), 355–375.

O'Connor, T. G., Deater-Deckard, K., Fulker, D., Rutter, M., & Plomin, R. (1998). Genotype-environment correlations in late childhood and early adolescence: Antisocial behavioral problems and coercive parenting. *Developmental Psychology, 34*(5), 970–981.

Oldershaw, A., Hambrook, D., Tchanturia, K., Treasure, J., & Schmidt, U. (2010). Emotional theory of mind and emotional awareness in recovered anorexia nervosa patients. *Psychosomatic Medicine, 72*(1), 73–79. doi:10.1097/PSY.0b013e3181c6c7ca

Oldershaw, A., Treasure, J., Hambrook, D., Tchanturia, K., & Schmidt, U. (2011). Is anorexia nervosa a version of autism spectrum disorders? *European Eating Disorders Review: The Journal of the Eating Disorders Association, 19*(6), 462–474. doi:10.1002/erv.1069

Oliver, B. R., Barker, E. D., Mandy, W. P. L., Skuse, D. H., & Maughan, B. (2011). Social cognition and conduct problems: A developmental approach. *Journal of the American Academy of Child and Adolescent Psychiatry, 50*(4), 385–394. doi:10.1016/j.jaac.2011.01.006

Pellicano, E., & Hiller, R. (2013). Anorexia and autism: A cautionary note. *The Psychologist, 26*(11), 780.

Pickles, A., Starr, E., Kazak, S., Bolton, P., Papanikolaou, K., Bailey, A., et al. (2000). Variable expression of the autism broader phenotype: Findings from extended pedigrees. *Journal of Child Psychology and Psychiatry, and Allied Disciplines, 41*(4), 491–502.

Pooni, J., Ninteman, A., Bryant-Waugh, R., Nicholls, D., & Mandy, W. (2012). Investigating autism spectrum disorder and autistic traits in early onset eating disorder. *The International Journal of Eating Disorders, 45*(4), 583–591. doi:10.1002/eat.20980

Posserud, M.-B., Lundervold, A. J., & Gillberg, C. (2006). Autistic features in a total population of 7–9-year-old children assessed by the ASSQ (Autism Spectrum Screening Questionnaire). *Journal of Child Psychology and Psychiatry, and Allied Disciplines, 47*(2), 167–175. doi:10.1111/j.1469-7610.2005.01462.x

Pugliese, C. E., White, B. A., White, S. W., & Ollendick, T. H. (2013). Social anxiety predicts aggression in children with ASD: Clinical comparisons with socially anxious and oppositional youth. *Journal of Autism and Developmental Disorders, 43*(5), 1205–1213. doi:10.1007/s10803-012-1666-x

Roberts, M. E., Tchanturia, K., & Treasure, J. L. (2013). Is attention to detail a similarly strong candidate endophenotype for anorexia nervosa and bulimia nervosa? *The World Journal of Biological Psychiatry: The Official Journal of the World Federation of Societies of Biological Psychiatry*, *14*(6), 452–463. doi:10.3109/15622975.2011.639804

Robinson, E. B., Koenen, K. C., McCormick, M. C., Munir, K., Hallett, V., Happé, F., et al. (2011). Evidence that autistic traits show the same etiology in the general population and at the quantitative extremes (5%, 2.5%, and 1%). *Archives of General Psychiatry*, *68*(11), 1113–1121. doi:10.1001/archgenpsychiatry.2011.119

Ronald, A., Happé, F., & Plomin, R. (2005). The genetic relationship between individual differences in social and nonsocial behaviours characteristic of autism. *Developmental Science*, *8*(5), 444–458. doi:10.1111/j.1467-7687.2005.00433.x

Ronald, A., Simonoff, E., Kuntsi, J., Asherson, P., & Plomin, R. (2008). Evidence for overlapping genetic influences on autistic and ADHD behaviours in a community twin sample. *Journal of Child Psychology and Psychiatry, and Allied Disciplines*, *49*(5), 535–542. doi:10.1111/j.1469-7610.2007.01857.x

Russell, T. A., Schmidt, U., Doherty, L., Young, V., & Tchanturia, K. (2009). Aspects of social cognition in anorexia nervosa: Affective and cognitive theory of mind. *Psychiatry Research*, *168*(3), 181–185. doi:10.1016/j.psychres.2008.10.028

Rutter, M. (2011). Research review: Child psychiatric diagnosis and classification: Concepts, findings, challenges and potential. *Journal of Child Psychology and Psychiatry, and Allied Disciplines*, *52*(6), 647–660. doi:10.1111/j.1469-7610.2011.02367.x

Rutter, M., & Schopler, E. (1988). Autism and pervasive developmental disorders. In M. Rutter, A. H. Tuma, & I. S. Lann (Eds.), *Assessment and diagnosis in child psychopathology* (pp. 408–436). London: David Fulton.

Rutter, M., & Sroufe, L. A. (2000). Developmental psychopathology: Concepts and challenges. *Development and Psychopathology*, *12*(3), 265–296.

Schmidt, U. (2003). Aetiology of eating disorders in the 21(st) century: New answers to old questions. *European Child & Adolescent Psychiatry*, *12* Suppl 1, I30–37. doi:10.1007/s00787-003-1105-9

Simonoff, E., Pickles, A., Charman, T., Chandler, S., Loucas, T., & Baird, G. (2008). Psychiatric disorders in children with autism spectrum disorders: Prevalence, comorbidity, and associated factors in a population-derived sample. *Journal of the American Academy of Child and Adolescent Psychiatry*, *47*(8), 921–929. doi:10.1097/CHI.0b013e318179964f

Skoog, G., & Skoog, I. (1999). A 40-year follow-up of patients with obsessive-compulsive disorder [see comments]. *Archives of General Psychiatry*, *56*(2), 121–127.

Skuse, D. H., Mandy, W., Steer, C., Miller, L. L., Goodman, R., Lawrence, K., et al. (2009). Social communication competence and functional adaptation in a general population of children: Preliminary evidence for sex-by-verbal IQ differential risk. *Journal of the American Academy of Child and Adolescent Psychiatry*, *48*(2), 128–137. doi:10.1097/CHI.0b013e31819176b8

Smink, F. R. E., van Hoeken, D., Oldehinkel, A. J., & Hoek, H. W. (2014). Prevalence and severity of DSM-5 eating disorders in a community cohort of adolescents. *The International Journal of Eating Disorders*, *47*, 610–619. doi:10.1002/eat.22316

St Pourcain, B., Skuse, D. H., Mandy, W. P., Wang, K., Hakonarson, H., Timpson, N. J., et al. (2014). Variability in the common genetic architecture of social-communication spectrum phenotypes during childhood and adolescence. *Molecular Autism*, *5*(1), 18. doi:10.1186/2040-2392-5-18

St Pourcain, B., Wang, K., Glessner, J. T., Golding, J., Steer, C., Ring, S. M., et al. (2010). Association between a high-risk autism locus on 5p14 and social communication spectrum phenotypes in the general population. *The American Journal of Psychiatry*, *167*(11), 1364–1372. doi:10.1176/appi.ajp.2010.09121789

Sucksmith, E., Roth, I., & Hoekstra, R. A. (2011). Autistic traits below the clinical threshold: Re-examining the broader autism phenotype in the 21st century. *Neuropsychology Review*, *21*(4), 360–389. doi:10.1007/s11065-011-9183-9

Totsika, V., Hastings, R. P., Emerson, E., Lancaster, G. A., & Berridge, D. M. (2011). A population-based investigation of behavioural and emotional problems and maternal mental health: Associations with autism spectrum disorder and intellectual disability. *Journal of Child Psychology and Psychiatry, and Allied Disciplines*, *52*(1), 91–99. doi:10.1111/j.1469-7610.2010.02295.x

Tremblay, R. E. (2010). Developmental origins of disruptive behaviour problems: The "original sin" hypothesis, epigenetics and their consequences for prevention. *Journal of Child Psychology and Psychiatry, and Allied Disciplines*, *51*(4), 341–367. doi:10.1111/j.1469-7610.2010.02211.x

Wakabayashi, A., Baron-Cohen, S., & Ashwin, C. (2012). Do the traits of autism-spectrum overlap with those of schizophrenia or obsessive-compulsive disorder in the general population? *Research in Autism Spectrum Disorders*, *6*(2), 717–725. doi:10.1016/j.rasd.2011.09.008

Walker, D. R., Thompson, A., Zwaigenbaum, L., Goldberg, J., Bryson, S. E., Mahoney, W. J., et al. (2004). Specifying PDD-NOS: A comparison of PDD-NOS, Asperger syndrome, and autism. *Journal of the American Academy of Child and Adolescent Psychiatry*, *43*(2), 172–180. doi:10.1097/00004583-200402000-00012

Wentz, E., Lacey, J. H., Waller, G., Råstam, M., Turk, J., & Gillberg, C. (2005). Childhood onset neuropsychiatric disorders in adult eating disorder patients. A pilot study. *European Child & Adolescent Psychiatry*, *14*(8), 431–437. doi:10.1007/s00787-005-0494-3

White, S. W., Bray, B. C., & Ollendick, T. H. (2012). Examining shared and unique aspects of social anxiety disorder and autism spectrum disorder using factor analysis. *Journal of Autism and Developmental Disorders*, *42*(5), 874–884. doi:10.1007/s10803-011-1325-7

Zaidman-Zait, A., Mirenda, P., Duku, E., Szatmari, P., Georgiades, S., Volden, J., et al. (2014). Examination of bidirectional relationships between parent stress and two types of problem behavior in children with autism spectrum disorder. *Journal of Autism and Developmental Disorders*, *44*, 1908–1917. doi:10.1007/s10803-014-2064-3

# 23

# A Brief History of the Diagnostic Classification of Childhood Externalizing Disorders

Paul J. Frick and Laura C. Thornton

## Introduction

Symptoms of common mental disorders in children and adolescents have been conceptually organized into two broad dimensions. One dimension, which is the focus of the current chapter, has been labeled as *undercontrolled* or *externalizing*, and it includes various impulsive, hyperactive, disruptive, and aggressive behaviors. The second dimension has been labeled as *overcontrolled* or *internalizing* and it includes such behaviors as social withdrawal, anxiety, and depression. The distinction between internalizing and externalizing problems is well supported by a number of factor analytic studies (Lahey et al., 2008).

Externalizing problems are the most common reasons leading children and adolescents to be referred for mental health treatment (Kimonis & Frick, 2012). This is likely due to several factors. First, externalizing behaviors lead to significant distress in the child, often being associated with many other problems in the child's social, academic, and emotional adjustment. Further, these behaviors lead to significant disruption and distress to people around the child, such as family members, peers, and school personnel. Externalizing behaviors are also highly associated with illegal and criminal behavior, leading to significant costs associated with serving these youth in the juvenile justice system and to financial and emotional costs to the victims of their criminal behavior (Cohen & Piquero, 2009). Finally, these behaviors are highly predictive of problems later in life, including mental health, medical, legal, occupational, and social problems (Odgers et al., 2008).

Given this substantial risk for both current and future impairment in multiple life domains, it is not surprising that the Diagnosis and Statistical Manual of Mental Disorders has included externalizing disorders in their list of mental disorders in each of its most recent revisions (DSM; American Psychiatric Association [APA], 1980; 1987; 1994; 2000; 2013). Specifically, the DSM has typically provided criteria for three externalizing disorders: attention deficit hyperactivity disorder (ADHD), oppositional defiant disorder (ODD), and conduct disorder (CD). Although factor analyses generally support the distinction among these different types of externalizing behaviors (Lahey et al., 2008), it is important to note that they overlap considerably

*The Wiley Handbook of Developmental Psychopathology*, First Edition. Edited by Luna C. Centifanti and David M. Williams.

in samples of children and adolescents. For example, approximately half of children with ADHD have a co-occurring conduct problem diagnosis (Waschbusch, 2002) and between 65% and 90% of children with either ODD or CD have a co-occurring ADHD diagnosis (Abikoff & Klein, 1992). Recognizing this overlap is important for designing studies and interpreting research findings on these disorders, so that one can distinguish between correlates that are common across externalizing disorders and correlates that are specific to only one disorder. Identifying general and specific correlates are critical for causal theories of how these disorders develop (Lilienfeld & Waldman, 1990; Waschbusch, 2002). Further, children with both ADHD and CD show a more persistent course of ADHD (Lynam, 1996) and the presence or absence of comorbidity influences the effectiveness of different interventions (Frick, 2012). Thus, the overlap among these disorders has both theoretical and clinical implications.

Despite this overlap, the current chapter will chart the evolution of these diagnoses in the DSM separately. The major changes across the most recent revisions are summarized in Table 23.1. However, before discussing each disorder and the changes in how they have been defined, it is important to note that prior to the most recent edition of the DSM, ADHD, ODD, and CD were grouped together within a class of disorders labelled "Disorders Usually First Diagnosed in Infancy, Childhood, or Adolescence" (American Psychiatric Association, 1980; 1987; 1994, 2000). Besides these externalizing disorders, this section of the manual included such diverse diagnoses as mental retardation, learning disorders, eating disorders, pervasive developmental disorders, and tic disorders. Thus, this grouping was not based on any consideration of shared etiology or any evidence for the frequency of co-occurrence but was solely based on the presumed typical timing of onset.

This method of grouping externalizing disorders changed in the DSM-5 based on several overarching goals of the revised manual (American Psychiatric Association, 2013). First, one goal of the DSM-5 was to improve the manual's attention to important developmental considerations in diagnostic criteria (Frick & Nigg, 2012). Specifically, the new edition of the manual attempts to promote a lifespan view of mental disorders, whereby continuities and changes in manifestations across development are considered for all disorders. Thus, a chapter grouping disorders based on timing of onset was not consistent with such a goal in a number of respects. Specifically, it ignored the fact that many disorders not included in this category often first manifested in childhood and adolescence, such as specific phobia (Kessler et al., 2007). Further, it minimized the importance of certain disorders included in this section when making diagnoses in adults, such as ADHD (Barkley, Murphy, & Fischer, 2008).

A second overarching goal of the DSM-5 was to foster a more dimensional approach to diagnosis. One way it attempts to do this is to organize disorders in ways that take into account common dimensions, such as shared risk factors or common symptom clusters (Frick & Nigg, 2012). For example, there are rather extensive data to suggest that ODD, CD, and one of the core symptom clusters of ADHD (i.e., hyperactivity/impulsivity) cluster around an overarching externalizing dimension that seems to share substantial genetic influences that are potentially reflective of shared problems of self-control (Lahey, Van Hulle, Singh, Waldman, & Rathouz, 2011; Markon & Krueger, 2005). However, there is also evidence to suggest that some symptoms of ADHD, especially the inattention symptoms, cluster strongly with autistic symptoms, motor coordination, and reading problems both within individuals and across siblings (Couto et al., 2009). Further, in terms of etiology, ADHD is associated

**Table 23.1** A summary of major changes in the diagnostic criteria for externalizing disorders in the most recent editions of the *Diagnostic and Statistical Manual of Mental Disorders* (DSM).

| *Edition* | *Disorder name* | *Placement in manual* | *Key symptom clusters* | *Major subtypes* | *Major changes from previous edition* |
|---|---|---|---|---|---|
| III (APA, 1980) | Attention deficit disorder (ADD) | "Disorders Usually First Evident in Infancy, Childhood, or Adolescence" | Inattention, impulsivity, and hyperactivity | attention deficit disorder with hyperactivity (ADD/H); attention deficit disorder without hyperactivity (ADD/W) | Name changed to emphasize attention deficits; explicit symptom list provided to make diagnosis. |
| | Oppositional disorder (OD) | "Disorders Usually First Evident in Infancy, Childhood, or Adolescence" | Single symptom list of disobedient, negativistic, and provocative opposition to authority figures. | None | Not included in previous edition |
| | Conduct disorder (CD) | "Disorders Usually First Evident in Infancy, Childhood, or Adolescence" | A repetitive and persistent pattern of aggressive or non-aggressive conduct in which the basic rights of others or major age-appropriate societal norms or rules are violated. | undersocialized aggressive; undersocialized nonaggressive; socialized aggressive; socialized nonaggressive. | Explicit symptom list provided to make diagnosis; no longer conceptualized as being a reaction to negative environmental factors; previous subtypes were runaway reaction, unsocialized aggressive reaction, and group delinquent reaction. |
| III-R (APA, 1987) | Attention deficit hyperactivity disorder (ADHD) | "Disorders Usually First Evident in Infancy, Childhood, or Adolescence" | Single symptom list of inattention, impulsivity, and hyperactivity. | Severity specifiers of mild, moderate, and severe. | Name changed to provide equal emphasis on attention and hyperactivity; symptoms put into single list; severity specifier included based on number of symptoms; subtype without hyperactivity eliminated. |

(*Continued*)

**Table 23.1** (Continued)

| *Edition* | *Disorder name* | *Placement in manual* | *Key symptom clusters* | *Major subtypes* | *Major changes from previous edition* |
|---|---|---|---|---|---|
| | Oppositional defiant disorder (ODD) | "Disorders Usually First Evident in Infancy, Childhood, or Adolescence" | Single symptom list of disobedient, negativistic, and provocative opposition to authority figures. | Severity specifiers of mild, moderate, and severe. | Name changed to include defiance; severity specifier added based on number of symptoms. |
| | Conduct disorder (CD) | "Disorders Usually First Evident in Infancy, Childhood, or Adolescence" | Single symptom of list of conduct in which the basic rights of others or major age-appropriate societal norms or rules are violated. | Severity specifiers of mild, moderate, and severe; group type, solitary aggressive type, undifferentiated type. | Subtypes changed to focus on whether or not antisocial behavior displayed as a group activity; severity specifier added based on number of symptoms and degree of harm caused to others. |
| IV (APA, 1994) | Attention deficit hyperactivity disorder (ADHD) | "Disorders Usually First Evident in Infancy, Childhood, or Adolescence" | Inattention; hyperactivity-impulsivity | ADHD-combined type (ADHD-CT); ADHD-predominantly inattentive type (ADHD-PIT); ADHD-predominantly hyperactive-impulsive type (ADHD-PHIT) | Symptoms divided into two clusters; subtype without hyperactivity added; severity specifier removed. |
| | Oppositional defiant disorder (ODD) | "Disorders Usually First Evident in Infancy, Childhood, or Adolescence" | Single symptom list of disobedient, negativistic, and provocative opposition to authority figures. | None | Severity specifier removed. |
| | Conduct disorder (CD) | "Disorders Usually First Evident in Infancy, Childhood, or Adolescence" | Aggression to people and animals; destruction of property; deceitfulness or theft; serious violations of rules | Severity specifiers of mild, moderate, and severe; childhood-onset and adolescent-onset types. | Symptoms divided into four clusters; subtypes changed to focus on timing of onset. |

| | | | | | |
|---|---|---|---|---|---|
| 5 (APA, 2013) | Attention deficit hyperactivity disorder (ADHD) | "Neurodevelopmental Disorders" | Inattention; hyperactivity and impulsivity | Severity specifiers of mild, moderate, and severe; ADHD-combined presentation (ADHD-CP); ADHD-predominantly inattentive presentation (ADHD-PIP); ADHD-predominantly hyperactive-impulsive presentation (ADHD-PHIP) | Disorder placed with neurodevelopmental disorders; symptoms reworded to be appropriate across the lifespan; minimum age of onset raised to 12 years; severity specifiers based on number of symptoms included; subtypes changed to presentation specifiers; exclusionary criteria for autism spectrum disorders removed. |
| | Oppositional defiant disorder (ODD) | "Disruptive, Impulse-Control and Conduct Disorders" | Angry/irritable mood; argumentative/defiant behavior; vindictiveness | Severity specifiers of mild, moderate, and severe. | Symptoms divided into three clusters; severity specifiers included based on number of situations in which the person displays symptoms; exclusionary criteria for CD eliminated. |
| | Conduct disorder (CD) | "Disruptive, Impulse-Control and Conduct Disorders" | Aggression to people and animals; destruction of property; deceitfulness or theft; serious violations of rules | Severity specifiers of mild, moderate, and severe; childhood-onset, adolescent-onset, and unspecified onset; with limited prosocial emotions. | Specifier for those who show significant levels of callous–unemotional (CU) traits added. |

with early-appearing alterations or immaturities in neural development (Frick & Nigg, 2012). This led to a difficult decision as to how to group the externalizing disorders. In terms of high levels of co-occurrence and their shared problems in self-control, ADHD could be placed with the other externalizing disorders, such as ODD and CD. However, in terms of high levels of co-occurrence and shared associations with alterations in neurological development, it seemed to be better placed with other neurodevelopmental disorders, such as learning disorders, motor disorders, and autistic spectrum disorders.

The DSM-5 adopted the latter conceptualization, with the overriding consideration of ADHD being viewed more as a neurodevelopmental condition rather than primarily or solely a behavioral condition (American Psychiatric Association, 2013). Thus, in the DSM-5, the three externalizing disorders for the first time are split into two separate chapters. That is, ADHD is placed in the chapter "Neurodevelopmental Disorders," whereas ODD and CD are placed in the chapter labelled "Disruptive, Impulse Control, and Conduct Disorders" along with the disorders of intermittent explosive disorder, pyromania, and kleptomania. It is important to note that this placement in different categories is inconsistent with a long history of grouping these disorders together. Further, the defining features of the neurodevelopmental disorders that they "manifest early development, often before the child enters grade school, and are characterized by developmental deficits that produce impairments of personal, social, academic, and occupational functioning" (American Psychiatric Association, 2013, p. 31,) could easily apply to ODD and CD as well. Similarly, the defining feature of all the disruptive, impulse control, and conduct disorders involves "problems in the self-control of emotions and/or behaviors" (American Psychiatric Association, 2013, p. 461), which could easily apply to ADHD as well. In summary, the DSM has never had a category specific to externalizing disorders and, in the current classification system, the disorders traditionally considered externalizing are grouped in separate sections.

## Attention Deficit Hyperactivity Disorder

ADHD has been recognized as a mental health disorder in medical and psychological classification for well over 100 years (Smith, Barkley, & Shapiro, 2007). However, there have been a number of changes in how the disorder is conceptualized and what core symptom domains define the disorder. Early conceptualizations were often split as to whether they (a) emphasized deviations in neurological development, leading to the diagnostic labels of "minimal brain dysfunction" or "minimal brain damage," or (b) emphasized the behavioral manifestations, leading to terms like the "hyperactive child syndrome" (Clements & Peters, 1962). The first time this diagnosis was included in the DSM, the criteria focused on the latter, with the label "Hyperkinetic Reaction of Childhood (Adolescence)", and the description of the disorder included problems with overactivity, restlessness, distractibility, and short attention span (American Psychiatric Association, 1968). Like all diagnoses included in the DSM-II, the term "hyperkinetic reaction" reflected a model of mental illness in which the disorder was considered a reaction to an intrapsychic conflict and the definition avoided explicit symptom lists for defining the disorder. Further, this early definition presaged two important sources of debate that have continued across later revisions of the manual.

First, it defined the disorder as one primarily of childhood and adolescence. Second, it defined the disorder as requiring both hyperactivity and inattention, although hyperactivity was given prominence in the name given to the disorder.

In the DSM-III and subsequent revisions of the manual, the assumption of an intrapsychic etiology was eliminated and the DSM began to include explicit symptom lists with clearly defined diagnostic thresholds (e.g., four or more symptoms of hyperactivity). Further, the DSM-III adopted the term "attention deficit disorder," reflecting a conceptual belief that the primary or core dysfunction in this syndrome had to do with attention, particularly problems in vigilance and sustained attention (Frick & Nigg, 2012). It defined the disorder by three behavioral dimensions: inattention, hyperactivity, and impulsivity. It also specified two primary subtypes: attention deficit disorder with hyperactivity (ADD-H) that required significant symptoms from all three dimensions and attention deficit disorder without hyperactivity (ADD-W) that specified that the child did not show significant levels of hyperactivity. The name that clearly emphasized attention deficits, the specification of subtypes, and the inclusion of a subtype without hyperactivity all became immediate sources of controversy. Thus, the next revision published 7 years later (DSM-III-R; American Psychiatric Association, 1987) renamed the disorder attention deficit hyperactivity disorder (ADHD) to put attention deficits and hyperactivity on equal footing. Further, it used a single behavioral dimension including symptoms of inattention, impulsivity, and hyperactivity; and removed any subtypes.

Since the publication of the DSM-III-R, one of these controversies has garnered a significant amount of research and the consistency of findings has led to a generally accepted conclusion. Namely, research has consistently supported a two-dimensional structure for the symptoms of ADHD that includes both an inattention–disorganization dimension and an impulsivity–hyperactivity dimension (Frick & Nigg, 2012). As a result, both of the most recent versions of the DSM (DSM-IV and DSM-5; American Psychiatric Association, 1994; 2013) included these two symptom domains in their definition. The only remaining controversy in terms of the core symptom domains is whether impulsivity should be separate from hyperactivity in adulthood, when the importance of impulsivity as a defining feature seems to increase (Barkley et al., 2008).

## Subtypes of Attention Deficit Hyperactivity Disorder

In contrast to this relative consensus on the core symptom dimensions of ADHD, the issue of whether and how one should define subtypes of the disorders has remained quite controversial. As noted above, the DSM-III created a subtype called attention deficit disorder without hyperactivity. This was done largely to reflect the fact that some children present with inattention but without hyperactivity and to reflect research suggesting that those with attention deficits without significant levels of hyperactivity often show a different pattern of attention deficits (e.g., a sluggish cognitive style) and different pattern of comorbidity (e.g., more internalizing and learning disorders; Milich, Balentine, & Lynam, 2001; Penny, Waschbusch, Klein, Corkum, & Eskes, 2009). After the subtypes were eliminated in the DSM-III-R, they were again added in the DSM-IV definition of Attention Deficit Hyperactivity Disorder (ADHD). Specifically, similar to subtypes used in the DSM-III, the DSM-IV included a subtype defined primarily by symptoms of inattention and disorganization, ADHD-predominantly inattentive type (ADHD-PI), as well as a subtype defined by elevated rates of both inattention–disorganization symptoms and impulsivity–hyperactivity symptoms, ADHD-combined type (ADHD-CT). The DSM-IV also added an additional subtype that was not included in previous versions of the manual defined primarily by elevated rates of impulsivity and hyperactivity, ADHD-predominantly hyperactive-impulsive type (ADHD-PHI).

Subsequent research on these subtypes called into question their validity for a number of reasons. First, the definition of ADHD-PI allowed children to have above-average levels of impulsivity–hyperactivity (or hyperactivity/impulsivity), as long as they did not reach the threshold of six symptoms. As a result, this subtype led to a heterogeneous grouping of children who varied greatly on the amount of impulsivity and hyperactivity they displayed (Diamond, 2005; Milich et al., 2001). Second, a meta-analysis of five longitudinal data sets by Willcutt et al. (2012) reported a high degree of instability in these subtypes over time, with the majority of children changing subtypes when reassessed at later time points. Third, the Willcutt et al. (2012) review also reported that there were few consistent unique neuropsychological or cognitive problems associated with the different subtypes specified in the DSM-IV, and most of those that were found could be explained by children with ADHD-CT showing more symptoms than those with ADHD-PI. However, in studies that used a more restrictive definition of ADHD-PI that significantly limited the degree of hyperactivity that could be present, some differences did emerge, such as those with attentional problems without hyperactivity showing an atypical attentional blink response (a measure of early stage gating of information; Carr, Henderson, & Nigg, 2010) and showing a sluggish cognitive tempo (Derefinko et al., 2008) relative to those with ADHD-CT.

Based on this available research, it was clear that there were some major limitations in how the DSM-IV subtypes were defined. Unfortunately, there was not an alternative method that had been used in research sufficiently to warrant its adoption in the DSM-5 (Frick & Nigg, 2012). As a result, the DSM-5 chose to rename the different symptom patterns as "presentations" rather than "subtypes" to document the very different symptom presentations that can occur but to be more consistent with the instability shown across time in these presentations. Further, the definition included a severity rating based on the number of symptoms displayed by the child, irrespective of whether the symptoms were inattention–disorganization or impulsivity–hyperactivity. However, this issue of whether there are important subtypes of ADHD remains unsettled and it will be important for future research to determine if there are alternative methods for defining subtypes that might implicate distinct etiological factors across subtypes, especially those with attention deficits and no hyperactivity, and lead to more stability in the presentations over time (Frick & Nigg, 2012).

## Classifying Attention Deficit Disorder across the Lifespan

Another critical issue in the classification of ADHD is how to adequately capture its manifestation across the lifespan. As mentioned above, the early DSM-II definition viewed this disorder as limited to childhood and adolescence, and in later editions it was viewed as being first evident in childhood with a minimum age of onset. Specifically, the DSM-IV specified a minimum age of onset of 7 years for ADHD (American Psychiatric Association, 1994). Research has called into question this requirement because children who show enough symptoms to meet criteria for

ADHD but whose symptoms emerge after age 7 have the same symptom profile, course, impairment, severity, treatment response, and neurobiological findings as those identified as having an onset prior to age 7 (Kieling et al., 2010). The limited validity for this age of onset seems to be particularly problematic for people who show the predominantly inattentive presentation, whereby the majority do not show an onset by age 7 (Applegate et al., 1997). As a result, it is clear that the requirement of onset by the age of 7 lacks validity for designating a clinically distinct group of persons with symptoms of ADHD. Importantly, prospective studies following samples of children with ADHD in adulthood suggest that nearly all persons identified with ADHD over the lifespan could have been identified by age 12 to 14 based on the symptoms they showed at that time (Kieling et al., 2010). As a result, the DSM-5 chose to place the minimum age of onset for a diagnosis of ADHD as being prior to age 12.

Another developmental issue for classifying persons with ADHD relates to the fact that the vast majority of research on its validity has been conducted with school-age children (Frick et al., 1994). Although there is evidence that symptoms of ADHD often emerge in preschool and diagnostic criteria designate an impaired group of preschool children (Lahey et al., 2004), more research is needed in this age group to determine the optimal method for differentiating normative manifestations of inattention-disorganization and impulsivity-hyperactivity from symptoms indicative of a mental health condition (Frick & Nigg, 2012).

Similarly, concerns have been raised about the diagnosis of ADHD in adults including: (a) whether the symptoms currently used to diagnose ADHD are worded in ways that make them applicable to adults (e.g., runs about or climbs on things); (b) whether other symptom domains not included in the current diagnostic criteria may be important for diagnosing adults (e.g., problems in executive functioning, problems in emotional regulation); and (c) whether the diagnostic cut point for the number of symptoms to make the diagnosis should be the same for children and adults (Barkley et al., 2008; Frick & Nigg, 2012). The DSM-5 chose to address two of these issues in their criteria for ADHD. First, the wording of symptoms was revised to include examples that are more relevant across the lifespan. For example, the symptom "Often has difficulty organizing tasks and activities" includes the examples of difficulty managing sequential tasks; difficulty keeping materials and belongings in order; messy and disorganized work; has poor time management; and fails to meet deadlines (American Psychiatric Association, 2013). Second, the diagnostic cut-point for adults was lowered to five (but remained at six for persons ages 16 and younger) based on longitudinal research suggesting that this cut point identified more adults who had been identified with ADHD in childhood (Barkley et al., 2008; Mannuzza et al., 2011).

## Summary of Key Issues

In summary, in recent years there has been a growing consensus as to the core symptoms of ADHD, at least in childhood and adolescence when the disorder is most often first diagnosed (see Table 23.1). Specifically, two clusters of symptoms seem to emerge as key to the diagnosis: inattention–disorganization and impulsivity–hyperactivity. Further, although the majority of persons with ADHD show elevated rates of both symptom clusters, there is a substantial minority who primarily show problems inattention–disorganization but the importance of this subgroup for guiding treatment, causal research, and the optimal method for defining this group is still in need of more research. Finally, although there is general agreement that ADHD is a developmental disorder that starts in childhood and often causes impairment throughout the lifespan, there is still disagreement as to the optimal methods for defining the disorder early in development (i.e., preschool) and in adulthood.

## Oppositional Defiant Disorder

The second externalizing disorder that has been included the DSM since 1980 is oppositional defiant disorder (ODD). As noted in Table 23.1, the key components to the diagnostic criteria for ODD have not changed much since they were introduced in the DSM-III (American Psychiatric Association, 1980) and include a recurrent pattern of negativistic, defiant, disobedient, and hostile behavior toward authority figures that persists for at least 6 months (American Psychiatric Association, 2013). Despite this rather lengthy history in diagnostic classification, ODD has been one of the more controversial of the externalizing disorders for at least two major reasons (Frick & Nigg, 2012; Moffitt et al., 2008). First, the oppositional and argumentative behaviors that form the criteria for this disorder are commonly displayed in normally developing children, especially at certain developmental periods, such as early in preschool years (i.e., the terrible twos) and in adolescence (Wakschlag et al., 2007). Second, ODD and the behaviors which form the criteria for this disorder are frequently comorbid with a host of other disorders (Rowe, Maughan, Pickles, Costello, & Angold, 2002). As a result, there are concerns that ODD overpathologizes a normative behavior pattern and that, unless it is accompanied by another disorder (e.g., ADHD, CD), it is transient and benign and should not be considered as a separate disorder.

To begin to address the first issue, the DSM-5 includes in their diagnostic criteria for ODD several forms of guidance in determining when the severity and frequency of symptoms is enough to indicate the presence of a disorder. First, as in previous editions, the symptoms must either (a) cause distress in the person with ODD or in others in his or her immediate social context or (b) impact the person negatively in important areas of functioning (e.g., social, educational, occupational). Importantly, while impairment is required in only one area to make the diagnosis, the DSM-5 recognizes that the pervasiveness of the symptoms is an important indicator of severity (Frick & Nigg, 2012). Specifically, a specifier of "mild" is given if the symptoms are confined to only one setting (e.g., at home, at school, at work, with peers), whereas a specifier of "moderate" is given if some symptoms are present in at least two settings and a specifier of "severe" is given if some symptoms are present in three or more settings. Second, the symptoms must be more intense and frequent than is normative for persons of the same developmental level, gender, and culture. Further, the DSM-5 provides guidance as to what is normative at the ages at which ODD is most often first diagnosed. For children under age 5, the behavior must occur on most days for 6 months and for children 5 and older, the behavior must occur at least once per week for 6 months. The only exception to this frequency requirement is for the symptom of "spiteful and vindictive", which must have occurred at least twice in the previous 6 months.

To address the issue of whether ODD is associated with impairment separate from other mental health disorders, Frick and Nigg (2012) reviewed research suggesting that ODD is related to problems in adjustment *independent* of the various comorbidities that are often associated with it. For example, controlling for co-occurring ADHD, children with ODD are more likely to show greater levels of CD, substance use, and emotional disorders concurrently (Garland & Garland, 2001; Harpold et al., 2007) and later in development (Biederman, Petty, Dolan, et al., 2008; Biederman, Petty, Monuteaux, et al., 2008; Burke, Waldman, & Lahey, 2010). Importantly, this incremental predictive utility of ODD relative to ADHD is found in children as young as ages 3 to 5 (Gadow & Nolan, 2002). Also, in an epidemiological sample of 1,420 children and adolescents ages 9 to 16, ODD predicted risk for diagnoses of anxiety and depression in adulthood (ages 19 to 21), even in the absence of CD (Rowe, Costello, Angold, Copeland, & Maughan, 2010).

This predictive link to emotional disorders highlights a final important issue in the classification of ODD. That is, several recent factor analyses have supported a multidimensional conceptualization of the criteria for ODD that separates the emotional and behavioral symptoms (Burke Hipwell, & Loeber, 2010; Rowe, Costello et al., 2010). Although the items on the factors vary somewhat across the samples, these analyses are consistent in suggesting that the angry–irritable mood dimension forms a separate factor from the defiant–headstrong behavior dimension. What is less clear from these analyses is the appropriate placement of the symptom "is often spiteful and vindictive," which does not consistently load with the other symptom dimensions (Burke, Hipwell, et al., 2010; Rowe, Costello et al., 2010) and which may be more related to the severe conduct problems associated with CD (Stingaris & Goodman, 2009). Importantly, although the symptom dimensions tend to be highly correlated, with correlations ranging from .62 to .78 (Burke, Hipwell, et al., 2010; Rowe, Costello, et al., 2010; Stingaris & Goodman, 2009), they tend to differ in their predictions of other problems in adjustment. For example, in a cross-sectional study of 18,415 participants in a national mental health survey in the United Kingdom (ages 5 to 16), all three dimensions of ODD were related to CD (Stringaris & Goodman, 2009). However, the angry–irritable dimension was also related to emotional disorders, the defiant–headstrong dimension was related to ADHD, and the spiteful–vindictive symptom was related to indicators of callous and unemotional traits. Similar divergent predictions from the different ODD dimensions have been found longitudinally, with most studies finding that all three dimensions predict risk for later CD but the angry–irritable dimension specifically predicts risk for later emotional disorders (Burke, Hipwell, et al., 2010; Rowe, Costello, et al., 2010). Based on this research, the DSM-5 chose to group the symptoms of ODD into three clusters that explicitly recognize the different symptoms types: angry/irritable mood, argumentative/defiant behavior, and vindictiveness (American Psychiatric Association, 2013).

## Summary of Key Issues

In summary, despite the behaviors associated with ODD being highly prevalent to some degree in normally developing children, oppositional and defiant behaviors that are persistent, frequent, and severe seem to designate a group of children at risk for multiple problems in adjustment. This risk is apparent even after controlling for common co-occurring conditions. Current diagnostic criteria for ODD in the DSM-5 provide some guidance in distinguishing between normative behaviors and symptoms of an impairing disorder and it recognizes that the pervasiveness of symptoms tends to be a strong indicator of severity. Finally, the DSM-5 criteria recognize that ODD is defined not only by problems in behavioral regulation, but also by problems in emotional regulation.

## Conduct Disorder

The third and final externalizing diagnosis is conduct disorder (CD). CD is defined as a repetitive and persistent pattern of behavior that violates the rights of others or in which major age-appropriate societal norms or rules are violated (American Psychiatric Association, 2013). There are four types of symptoms that define this disorder: aggression to people and animals (e.g., fighting, bullying), destruction of property (e.g., fire-setting, vandalism), deceitfulness, or theft (e.g., conning, shoplifting), and serious violations of rules (e.g., truancy, running away from home). Thus, CD focuses on more serious conduct problems than those forming the criteria for ODD. Importantly, the diagnostic criteria recognizes that the severity of CD, in terms of both the number of symptoms displayed and the amount of harm caused to others, can vary from "mild," in which there are few symptoms in excess of those required to make the diagnosis and the conduct problems cause minor harm to others (e.g., lying, truancy), to "severe," in which the persons shows many symptoms in excess of those required for the diagnosis and the conduct problems cause considerable harm to others (e.g., forced sex, use of a weapon; American Psychiatric Association, 2013).

CD was first recognized as a mental health disorder in the second edition of the Diagnostic and Statistical Manual of Mental Disorders (DSM-II; American Psychiatric Association, 1968). This early definition of CD in the DSM-II was conceptualized as being a reaction to negative environmental factors and three distinct reactions were described: runaway reaction, undersocialized aggressive reaction, and group delinquent reaction. Thus, from its very first definition, there has been recognition that there are many distinct subgroups of persons with CD who can be differentiated by the behaviors they display and by the causes leading to these behaviors. As noted in Table 23.1, this heterogeneity within persons who received the diagnosis of CD has been the major source of change in the diagnostic criteria over the past four decades. Specifically, in the DSM-III (American Psychiatric Association, 1980), a different method for subtyping persons with CD was introduced which differentiated among those who were a) aggressive or not and b) those who were considered "socialized" (e.g., has lasting friendships, feels guilt/remorse) or not. Research on the undersocialized subtype of CD supported its validity, in that adolescents who were classified as such tended to have poorer adjustment in juvenile institutions and were more likely to continue to show antisocial behavior into adulthood compared to other adolescents with CD (Frick & Loney, 1999; Quay, 1987). The undersocialized group was also more likely to show several neurophysiological correlates to their antisocial behavior, such as low serotonin levels and autonomic irregularities (Lahey, Hart, Pliszka, Applegate, & McBurnett, 1993; Quay, 1993; Raine, 1993).

Despite these promising findings, the name given to this group, undersocialized aggressive, resulted in considerable confusion as to the core features of this subtype and as to the best way to operationalize these features (Lahey, Loeber, Quay, Frick, & Grimm, 1992). Some definitions focused on the child's ability to form and maintain social relationships, whereas others focused primarily on the context (alone or as a group) in which the antisocial acts were typically committed. Very few definitions focused directly on the interpersonal and affective characteristics that were central to the clinical descriptions of psychopathic individuals on which this method of sub-typing was purportedly based (Quay, 1987). In an attempt to address this definitional confusion, the next revision of DSM revised its criteria for subtyping conduct disorder (DSM-III-R; American Psychiatric Association, 1987). As noted in Table 23.1, the criteria for the undersocialized subtype were changed to focus solely on whether the antisocial acts were committed alone and whether the pattern included aggressive symptoms, both of which were judged to be more easily assessed than the features defining the undersocialized type. It was renamed the solitary–aggressive subtype. The criteria for the second subtype focused solely on whether the antisocial acts were committed with other antisocial peers, and this subtype was assumed to be primarily nonaggressive in nature. It was renamed the group subtype.

## Childhood-onset and Adolescent-onset Conduct Disorder

The method of subtyping was changed yet again in the next edition of the manual (see Table 23.1). It was replaced by a distinction based on when the severe conduct problems first onset, with a childhood-onset group showing severe conduct problems well before the onset of adolescence (i.e., before age 10) and an adolescent-onset group showing the onset of severe conduct problems coinciding with the onset of puberty (American Psychiatric Association, 1994). This distinction was chosen based on (a) extensive research showing that the two groups had very different outcomes (e.g., the childhood-onset being more likely to persist into adulthood); (b) evidence that the childhood-onset group was more likely to be aggressive and thus, it largely subsumed the aggressive subtypes in the previous edition of the DSM; and (c) minimal evidence supporting the validity of the solitary–group distinction (Moffitt, 2006).

Support for this distinction based on the timing of onset has continued to grow (Frick & Viding, 2009; Moffitt et al., 2008) and this research led to this method of specifying unique subgroups of persons with CD to be continued in the most recent DSM-5. However, it is important to note that several issues related to this method of subtyping still must be resolved. First, it is not firmly established what should be the exact age to differentiate childhood- and adolescent-onset groups. In an early test of the differential predictive utility of different age cut-offs, Robins (1966) found that youth who were 11 years or younger at the onset of their serious conduct problems were over twice as likely to be diagnosed with antisocial personality disorder (APD) as adults. Since this study, cut-offs for defining childhood-onset have ranged from 10 to 14 for the onset of the first serious conduct problem (Patterson & Yoerger, 1997; Tibbetts & Piquero, 1999). This difficulty in defining a clear cut-point for the age of onset has led some researchers to suggest that this distinction should be used more dimensionally, as opposed to a categorical distinction (Lahey, Waldman, & McBurnett, 1999). Another problem with establishing the age of onset for CD relates to difficulties in persons' retrospective recall of past behaviors, especially for older adolescents, which makes accurately pinpointing the age at which a child first showed severe conduct problems often difficult to establish (Moffitt et al., 2008). Third, this approach to subtyping within the diagnosis of CD does not make a distinction within the childhood-onset group about those who are most likely to continue to show problems into adolescence and adulthood (i.e., lifecourse-persistent) and those who show problems that are limited to childhood. Specifically, a significant proportion of children within the childhood-onset group show relatively mild and transient conduct problems (Odgers et al., 2007; Tremblay, 2003). Thus, it is important to consider additional ways to distinguish important subgroups within the broader category of childhood-onset CD.

## Callous-Unemotional Traits and Conduct Disorder

One method for distinguishing an important subgroup within those youth with childhood-onset CD is based on the presence of callous-unemotional (CU) traits, characterized by a lack of guilt/remorse, a callous lack of empathy, a failure to put forth effort on important tasks, and a shallow and deficient affect. These characteristics were part of the DSM-III definition of the "undersocialized" subtype of CD that was characterized by "a failure to establish a normal degree of affection, empathy, or bond with others" (American Psychiatric Association, 1980, p. 45). However, in the DSM-III definition, these emotional factors were combined with other social factors, such as loyalty to a deviant peer group, which did not always form a coherent pattern of socioemotional functioning and made it difficult to determine the core dimension(s) on which to define subgroups (Frick, 2009). CU traits, on the other hand, were based more explicitly on the affective components that have been used to define the construct of psychopathy, as well as being defined by emotions (e.g., lack of empathy and guilt) that have been critical to developmental models of the emergence of conscience (Frick, Ray, Thornton, & Kahn, 2014a). This refined conceptualization led to an extensive body of research suggesting that these traits could be reliably assessed and that they differentiated clinically and etiologically important subgroups that were not adequately captured by the childhood/adolescent onset distinction.

A comprehensive review of over 200 studies of CU traits and their importance for designating a distinct group of children and adolescent with severe conduct problems made several conclusions relevant for the use of these traits in the classification of CD (Frick, Ray, Thornton, & Kahn, 2014b). First, CU traits are predictive of a more severe, stable, and aggressive pattern of behavior in antisocial youth. Specifically, children and adolescents with CD who are also elevated on CU traits exhibit a particularly severe, aggressive, and persistent form of the disorder that is not captured by current diagnostic criteria. For example, McMahon, Witkiewitz, Kotler, and The Conduct Problems Prevention Research Group (2010) reported that CU traits in grade 7 predicted adult arrests, number of APD symptoms, and an APD diagnosis two years post high school, even after controlling for number of CD symptoms, number of ADHD symptoms, number of ODD symptoms, and childhood onset of CD.

Second, Frick et al. (2014) reviewed over 100 studies suggesting that CU traits designate a group of children with CD who show a number of distinct emotional, cognitive, personality, and social characteristics relative to other antisocial youth that seems to implicate different causal processes leading to CD in those with and without elevated rates of CU traits. For example, children with both serious conduct problems and elevated CU traits show reduced responding to signs of fear and distress in others, whether this is assessed through self-report measures of physiological arousal (Marsh et al., 2011), cognitive tasks assessing attentional orienting to emotional pictures (Kimonis, Frick, Cauffman, Goldweber, & Skeem, 2012; Kimonis, Frick, Fazekas, & Loney, 2006), psychophysiological responses to emotionally evocative films (de Wied, van Boxtel, Matthys, & Meeus, 2012), or amygdala responses to fearful faces (Viding et al., 2012). In contrast, children with serious conduct problems without elevated CU traits typically show an enhanced emotional response to fear and distress in others, again across different domains of assessment (Kimonis et al., 2006; Viding et al., 2012).

Third, Frick et al. (2014) reviewed 24 studies that investigated the response to treatment of children and adolescents with CU traits and they reported that, of the 20 studies that compared outcomes for those with and without elevated CU traits, 18 (90%) reported results suggesting that the group high on CU traits showed poorer treatment response. Thus, research suggests that youth with CD and elevated CU traits present quite a treatment challenge. However, there is also evidence that these youths can respond positively to certain intensive treatments (Kolko & Pardini, 2010; Waschbusch, Carrey, Willoughby, King, & Andrade, 2007; White, Frick, Lawing, & Bauer, 2012) and to interventions that are tailored to the unique emotional, cognitive, and motivational styles of children and adolescents with CU traits (Caldwell, Skeem, Salekin, & Van Rybroek, 2006; Hawes & Dadds, 2005; Somech & Elizur, 2012).

As a result of this extensive research on CU traits, the DSM-5 chose to include in the criteria for CD a specifier to designate those youth with serious conduct problems who also show elevated rates of CU traits (see Table 23.1). The specifier of "With limited prosocial emotions" is given if the individual (a) meets criteria for CD and (b) shows two more of the following CU traits persistently over 12 months in more than one relationship or setting:

- lack of remorse or guilt;
- callous-lack of empathy;
- unconcern about performance at school, work, or in other important activities; and
- shallow or deficient affect.

These four criteria and the diagnostic cut-off were chosen based on extensive secondary data analyses of CU traits across large samples in different countries. These analyses indicated that these four criteria consistently were the best indicators of the overall construct of CU traits and the presence of two symptoms, if shown persistently, designated a more severely impaired group of antisocial youth (Kimonis et al., 2014).

Subsequent research has supported the validity of these criteria. For example, in a population-based sample ($n = 5{,}326$) of children and adolescents ages 5 to 16, Rowe, Maughan, and colleagues (2010) reported that children and adolescents with both CD and the specifier were five times more likely to continue to have a diagnosis of CD three years later, compared to youths with CD with less than two CU symptoms. Similarly, Kahn, Frick, Youngstrom, Findling, and Youngstrom (2012) studied both community ($n = 1{,}136$) and clinic-referred ($n = 566$) samples and reported that those children who met the criteria for the specifier were more severe than those with CD only, especially by being more aggressive and cruel. Pardini, Stepp, Hipwell, Stouthamer-Loeber, and Loeber (2012) tested the new specifier in a community sample of 1,862 girls ages 6 to 8 and reported that the 25% of girls who met criteria for CD and who also met criteria for the specifier showed more bullying, more relational aggression, and more global impairment both at baseline and across a 6-year follow-up period compared to girls with CD alone. Finally, McMahon et al. (2010) reported that CU traits assessed in the seventh grade significantly predicted adult antisocial outcomes (e.g., adult arrests, adult antisocial personality symptoms) and that the combination of a CD diagnosis and the specifier showed greater positive predictive power for adult antisocial outcomes than the diagnosis of CD alone.

### Summary and Key Issues

Conduct Disorder is defined by a pattern of serious behavior problems that can cause significant problems for both the person with the disorder and others who are affected by his or her antisocial and aggressive behavior. Persons with this diagnosis can vary greatly on the severity and stability of their antisocial behavior and on the most likely causes of their behavior problems. As a result, the primary issue in classifying CD has been attempts to define meaningful subgroups of persons with the disorder that reduce this heterogeneity and provide important information to guide both etiological theories and treatment. Currently, the major methods for distinguishing subtypes within CD focus on when the serious conduct problems first onset (i.e., childhood-onset vs. adolescent-onset) and whether or not the person with CD also shows elevated levels of CU traits (i.e., with Limited Prosocial Emotions).

## Conclusions

In summary, externalizing behaviors have been recognized as a serious mental health concern, at least for children and adolescents, for the past several decades. Further, the three main types of externalizing disorders (i.e., ADHD, ODD, and CD) and the core symptoms that define them have remained relatively unchanged in the most recent revisions of the DSM (see Table 23.1). Current controversies that await additional research include investigating the best methods for grouping these disorders with other mental health diagnoses and how to best capture the natural course of these disorders across the lifespan. With respect to the latter, the vast majority of research conducted on externalizing disorders has been conducted with children and adolescents. Thus, much more research is needed to determine how these disorders are expressed in adults. Another issue requiring additional research is on how best to capture the heterogeneity within persons with these disorders. The most recent DSM-5 now includes specifiers that allow for persons with each disorder to be differentiated in terms of the severity of the disorder, with severity within both ADHD and CD being primarily defined by the number of symptoms present and with severity defined for ODD being defined by the number of situations in which the symptoms are displayed. However, there remains considerable controversy over whether other specifiers are needed to define differences in the course of the disorder, differences in etiology, and differences in response to treatment. Research providing data to resolve this controversy will be critical for guiding future definitions of externalizing disorders.

## References

Abikoff, H., & Klein, R. G. (1992). Attention-deficit hyperactivity and conduct disorder: Comorbidity and implications for treatment. *Journal of Consulting and Clinical Psychology*, *6*, 881–892. doi:10.1037/0022-006X.60.6.881

American Psychiatric Association. (1968). *Diagnostic and statistical manual of mental disorders* (2nd ed.). Washington, DC: American Psychiatric Association.

American Psychiatric Association. (1980). *Diagnostic and statistical manual of mental disorders* (3rd ed.). Washington, DC: American Psychiatric Association.

American Psychiatric Association. (1987). *Diagnostic and statistical manual of mental disorders* (3rd ed., rev.). Washington, DC: American Psychiatric Association.

American Psychiatric Association. (1994). *Diagnostic and statistical manual of mental disorders* (4th ed.). Washington, DC: American Psychiatric Association.

American Psychiatric Association. (2000). *Diagnostic and statistical manual of mental disorders* (4th ed., text rev.). Washington, DC: American Psychiatric Association.

American Psychiatric Association. (2013). *Diagnostic and statistical manual of mental disorders* (5th ed.). Washington, DC: American Psychiatric Association.

Applegate, B., Lahey, B. B., Hart, E. L., Biederman, J., Hynd, G. W., Barkley, R. A., et al. (1997). Validity of the age-of-onset criterion for ADHD: A report from the DSM-IV filed trials. *Journal of the American Academy of Child & Adolescent Psychiatry, 36*, 1211–1221. doi:10.1097/00004583-199709000-00013

Barkley, R. A., Murphy, K. R., & Fischer, M. (2008). *ADHD in adults: What the science says.* New York: Guilford Press.

Biederman, J., Petty, C. R., Dolan, C., Hughes, S., Mick, E., Monuteaux, M. C., et al. (2008). The long-term longitudinal course of oppositional defiant disorder and conduct disorder in ADHD boys: Findings from a controlled 10-year prospective longitudinal study. *Psychological Medicine, 38*, 1027–1036. doi:10.1017/S0033291707002668

Biederman, J., Petty, C. R., Monuteaux, M. C., Mick, E., Parcell, T., Westerberg, D., & Faraone, S. V. (2008). The longitudinal course of comorbid oppositional defiant disorder in girls with attention-deficit/hyperactivity disorder: Findings from a controlled 5-year prospective study. *Journal of Developmental Behavioral Pediatrics, 29*, 501–507. doi:10.1097/DBP.0b013e318190b290

Burke, J. D., Hipwell, A. E., & Loeber, R. (2010). Dimensions of oppositional defiant disorder as predictors of depression and conduct disorder in girls. *Journal of the American Academy of Child & Adolescent Psychiatry, 49*, 484–492. doi:10.1016/j.jaac.2010.01.016

Burke, J. D., Waldman, I., & Lahey, B. B. (2010). Predictive validity of childhood oppositional defiant disorder and conduct disorder: Implications for DSM-V. *Journal of Abnormal Psychology, 119*, 739–751. doi:10.1037/a0019708

Caldwell, M., Skeem, J., Salekin, R., & Van Rybroek, G. (2006). Treatment response of adolescent offenders with psychopathy features: A 2-year follow-up. *Criminal Justice and Behavior, 33*, 571–596. doi:10.1177/0093854806288176

Carr, L., Henderson, J., & Nigg, J. T. (2010). Cognitive control and attentional selection in adolescents with ADHD versus ADD. *Journal of Clinical Child and Adolescent Psychology, 39*, 726–740. doi:10.1080/15374416.2010.517168

Clements, S. D., & Peters, J. E. (1962). Minimal brain dysfunctions in the school-age child: Diagnosis and treatment. *Archives of General Psychiatry, 6*, 185–197. doi:10.1001/archpsyc.1962.01710210001001.

Cohen, M. A., & Piquero, A. R. (2009). New evidence on the monetary value of saving a high risk youth. *Journal of Quantitative Criminology, 25*, 25–49. doi:10.1007/s10940-008-9057-3

Couto, J. M., Gomez, L., Wigg, K., Ickowicz, A., Pathare, T., Malone, M., et al. (2009). Association of attention-deficit/hyperactivity disorder with a candidate region for reading disabilities on chromosome 6p. *Biological Psychiatry, 66*, 368–375. doi:10.1016/j.biopsych.2009.02.016

de Wied, M., van Boxtel, A., Matthys, W., & Meeus, W. (2012). Verbal, facial and autonomic responses to empathy-eliciting film clips by disruptive male adolescents with high versus low callous-unemotional traits. *Journal of Abnormal Child Psychology, 40*, 211–223. doi:10.1007/s10802-011-9557-8

Derefinko, K. J., Adams, Z. W., Milich, R., Fillmore, M. T., Lorch, E. P., & Lynam, D. R. (2008). Response style differences in the inattentive and combined subtypes of attention-deficit/hyperactivity disorder. *Journal of Abnormal Child Psychology, 36*, 745–758. doi:10.1007/s10802-007-9207-3

Diamond, A. (2005). Attention-deficit disorder (attention-deficit/hyperactivity disorder without hyperactivity): A neurobiologically and behaviorally distinct disorder from attention-deficit/hyperactivity disorder (with hyperactivity). *Development and Psychopathology*, *17*, 807–825. doi:10.1017/S0954579405050388

Frick, P. J. (2009). Extending the construct of psychopathy to youths: Implications for understanding, diagnosing, and treating antisocial children and adolescents. *Canadian Journal of Psychiatry*, *54*, 803–812.

Frick, P. J. (2012). Developmental pathways to conduct disorder: Implications for future directions in research, assessment, and treatment. *Journal of Clinical Child and Adolescent Psychology*, *41*, 378–389. doi:10.1080/15374416.2012.664815

Frick, P. J., Lahey, B. B., Applegate, B., Kerdyck, L., Ollendick, T., Hynd, G. W., et al. (1994). DSM-IV field trials for the disruptive behavior disorders: Symptom utility estimates. *Journal of the American Academy of Child and Adolescent Psychiatry*, *33*, 529–539. doi:10.1097/00004583-199405000-00011

Frick, P. J., & Loney, B. R. (1999). Outcomes of children and adolescents with conduct disorder and oppositional defiant disorder. In H. C. Quay & A. Hogan (Eds.), *Handbook of disruptive behavior disorders* (pp. 507–524). doi:10.1007/978-1-4615-4881-2_24

Frick, P. J., & Nigg, J. T. (2012). Current issues in the diagnosis of attention-deficit/hyperactivity disorder, oppositional defiant disorder, and conduct disorder. *Annual Review of Clinical Psychology*, *8*, 77–107. doi:10.1146/annurev-clinpsy-032511-143150

Frick, P. J., Ray, J. V., Thornton, L. C., & Kahn, R. E. (2014a). Annual research review: A developmental psychopathology approach to understanding callous-unemotional traits in children and adolescents with serious conduct problems. *Journal of Child Psychology and Psychiatry, and Allied Disciplines*, *55*(6), 532–548. doi:10.1111/jcpp.12152

Frick, P. J., Ray, J. V., Thornton, L. C., & Kahn, R. E. (2014b). Can callous-unemotional traits enhance the understanding, diagnosis, and treatment of serious conduct problems in children and adolescents? A comprehensive review. *Psychological Bulletin*, *140*, 1–57. doi:10.1037/a0033076

Frick, P. J., & Viding, E. M. (2009). Antisocial behavior from a developmental psychopathology perspective. *Development and Psychopathology*, *21*, 1111–1131. doi:10.1017/S0954579409990071

Gadow, K. D., & Nolan, E. E. (2002). Differences between preschool children with ODD, ADHD, and ODD+ADHD symptoms. *Journal of Child Psychology and Psychiatry*, *43*, 191–201. doi:10.1111/1469-7610.00012

Garland, E. J., & Garland, O. M. (2001). Correlation between anxiety and oppositionality in a children's mood and anxiety disorder clinic. *Canadian Journal of Psychiatry*, *46*, 953–958.

Harpold, T., Biederman, J., Gignac, M., Hammerness, P., Surman, C., Potter, A., et al. (2007). Is oppositional defiant disorder a meaningful diagnosis in adults? *Journal of Nervous and Mental Disease*, *195*, 601–605. doi:10.1097/NMD.0b013e318093f448

Hawes, D. J., & Dadds, M. R. (2005). The treatment of conduct problems in children with callous-unemotional traits. *Journal of Consulting and Clinical Psychology*, *73*, 737–741. doi:10.1037/0022-006X.73.4.737

Kahn, R. E., Frick, P. J., Youngstrom, E., Findling, R. L., & Youngstrom, J. K. (2012). The effects of including a callous-unemotional specifier for the diagnosis of conduct disorder. *Journal of Child Psychology and Psychiatry*, *53*, 271–282. doi:10.1111/j.1469-7610.2011.02463.x

Kessler, R. C., Amminger, G. P., Aguilar-Gaxiola, S., Alonso, J., Lee, S., & Ustun, T. B. (2007). Age of onset of mental disorders: A review of recent literature. *Current Opinion in Psychiatry*, *20*, 359–364. doi:10.1097/YCO.0b013e32816ebc8c

Kieling, C., Kieling, R. R., Rohde, L. A., Frick, P. J., Moffitt, T., Nigg, J. T., et al. (2010). The age at onset of attention deficit hyperactivity disorder. *The American Journal of Psychiatry*, *167*, 14–16. doi:10.1176/appi.ajp.2009.09060796

Kimonis, E. R., Fanti, K., Goldweber, A., Marsee, M. A., Frick, P. J., & Cauffman, E. (2014). Callous-unemotional traits in incarcerated adolescents. *Psychological Assessment*, *26*, 227–237. doi:10.1037/a0034585

Kimonis, E. R., & Frick, P.J. (2012). Externalizing disorders. In J. E. Maddux & B. A. Winstead (Eds.), *Psychopathology: Contemporary issues, theory, and research* (3rd ed., pp. 443–472). Mahwah, NJ: Erlbaum.

Kimonis, E. R., Frick, P. J., Cauffman, E., Goldweber, A., & Skeem, J. (2012). Primary and secondary variants of juvenile psychopathy differ in emotional processing. *Development and Psychopathology*, *24*, 1091–1103. doi:10.1017/S0954579412000557

Kimonis, E. R., Frick, P. J., Fazekas, H., & Loney, B. R. (2006). Psychopathy, aggression, and the emotional processing of emotional stimuli in non-referred girls and boys. *Behavioral Sciences & the Law*, *24*, 21–37. doi:10.1002/bsl.668

Kolko, D. J., & Pardini, D. A. (2010). ODD dimensions, ADHD, and callous-unemotional traits as predictors of treatment response in children with disruptive behavior disorders. *Journal of Abnormal Psychology*, *119*, 713–725. doi:10.1037/a0020910

Lahey, B. B., Hart, E. L., Pliszka, S., Applegate, B., & McBurnett, K. (1993). Neurophysiological correlates of conduct disorder: A rationale and a review of research. *Journal of Clinical Child Psychology*, *22*, 141–153. doi:10.1207/s15374424jccp2202_2

Lahey, B. B., Loeber, R., Quay, H. C., Frick, P. J., & Grimm, J. (1992). Oppositional defiant disorder and conduct disorders: Issues to be resolved for DSM-IV. *Journal of the American Academy of Child and Adolescent Psychiatry*, *31*, 539–546. doi:10.1097/00004583-1992 05000-00023

Lahey, B. B., Pelham, W. E., Loney, J., Kipp, H., Ehrhardt, A., Lee, S. S., et al. (2004). Three-year predictive validity of DSM-IV attention deficit hyperactivity disorder in children diagnosed at 4–6 years of age. *The American Journal of Psychiatry*, *161*, 2014–2020. doi:10.1176/appi.ajp.161.11.2014

Lahey, B. B., Rathouz, P. J., Van Hulle, C., Urbano, R. C., Krueger, R. F., Applegate, B., et al. (2008). Testing structural models of DSM-IV symptoms of common forms of child and adolescent psychopathology. *Journal of Abnormal Child Psychology*, *36*, 187–206. doi:10.1007/s10802-007-9169-5

Lahey, B. B., Van Hulle, C. A., Singh, A. L., Waldman, I. D., & Rathouz, P. J. (2011). Higher-order genetic and environmental structure of prevalent forms of child and adolescent psychopathology. *Archives of General Psychiatry*, *68*, 181–189. doi:10.1001/archgenpsychiatry.2010.192.

Lahey, B. B., Waldman, I. D., & McBurnett, K. (1999). Annotation: The development of antisocial behavior: An integrative causal model. *Journal of Child Psychology and Psychiatry*, *40*, 669–682. doi:10.1111/1469-7610.00484

Lilienfeld, S. O., & Waldman, I. D. (1990). The relation between childhood attention-deficit hyperactivity disorder and adult antisocial behavior reexamined: The problem of heterogeneity. *Clinical Psychology Review*, *10*, 699–725. doi:10.1016/0272-7358(90)90076-M

Lynam, D. R. (1996). The early identification of chronic offenders: Who is the fledgling psychopath? *Psychological Bulletin*, *120*, 209–234. doi:10.1037/0033-2909.120.2.209

Mannuzza, S., Castellanos, F. X., Roizen, E. R., Hutchison, J. A., Lashua, E. C., & Klein R. G. (2011). Impact of the impairment criterion in the diagnosis of adult ADHD: 33-year follow-up study of boys with ADHD. *Journal of Attention Disorders*, *15*, 122–129. doi:10.1177/1087054709359907

Markon, K. E., & Krueger, R. F. (2005). Categorical and continuous models of liability to externalizing disorders: A direct comparison in NESARC. *Archives of General Psychiatry*, *62*, 1352–1359. doi:10.1001/archpsyc.62.12.1352

Marsh, A. A., Finger, E. C., Schechter, J. C., Jurkowitz, I. T. N., Reid, M. E., & Blair, R. J. R. (2011). Adolescents with psychopathic traits report reductions in physiological responses to fear. *Journal of Child Psychology and Psychiatry*, *52*, 834–841. doi:10.1111/j.1469-7610.2010.02353.x

McMahon, R. J., Witkiewitz, K., Kotler, J. S., & The Conduct Problems Prevention Research Group. (2010). Predictive validity of callous unemotional traits measures in early adolescence with respect to multiple antisocial outcomes. *Journal of Abnormal Psychology, 119*, 752–763. doi:10.1037/a0020796

Milich, R., Balentine, A. C., & Lynam, D. R. (2001). ADHD combined type and ADHD predominantly inattentive type are distinct and unrelated disorders. *Clinical Psychology: Science and Practice, 8*, 463–488. doi:10.1093/clipsy.8.4.463

Moffitt, T. E. (2006). Life-course persistent versus adolescence-limited antisocial behavior: Research review. In D. Cicchetti, & D. J. Cohen (Eds.), *Developmental Psychopathology, Vol 3: Risk, disorder, and adaptation* (2nd ed., pp. 570–598). New York: Wiley.

Moffitt, T. E., Arseneault, L., Jaffee, S. R., Kim-Cohen, J., Koenen, K. C., Odgers, C. L., et al. (2008). Research review: DSM-V conduct disorder: Research needs for an evidence base. *Journal of Child Psychology and Psychiatry, 49*, 3–33. doi:10.1111/j.1469-7610.2007.01823.x.

Odgers, C. L., Caspi, A., Broadbent, J. M., Dickson, N., Hancox, R. J., Harrington, H., et al. (2007). Prediction of differential adult health burden by conduct problem subtypes in males. *Archives of General Psychiatry, 64*, 476–484. doi:10.1001/archpsyc.64.4.476

Odgers, C. L., Moffitt, T. E., Broadbent, J. M., Dickson, N., Hancox, R. J., Harrington, H., et al. (2008). Female and male antisocial trajectories: From childhood origins to adult outcomes. *Development and Psychopathology, 20*, 673–716. doi:10.1017/S0954579408000333

Patterson, G. R., & Yoerger, K. (1997). A developmental model for late-onset delinquency. In D. W. Osgood (Ed.), *Motivation and delinquency* (pp. 119–177). Lincoln: University of Nebraska Press.

Pardini, D., Stepp, S., Hipwell, A., Stouthamer-Loeber, M., & Loeber, R. (2012). The clinical utility of the propose DSM–5 callous-unemotional subtype of conduct disorder in young girls. *Journal of the American Academy of Child & Adolescent Psychiatry, 51*, 62–73. doi:10.1016/j.jaac.2011.10.005

Penny, A. M., Waschbusch, D. A., Klein, R. M., Corkum, P., & Eskes, G. (2009). Developing a measure of sluggish cognitive tempo for children: Content validity, factor structure, and reliability. *Psychological Assessment, 21*, 380–389. doi:10.1037/a0016600

Quay, H. C. (1987). Patterns of delinquent behavior. In H. C. Quay (Ed.), *Handbook of juvenile delinquency* (pp. 118–138). Oxford: John Wiley & Sons.

Quay, H. C. (1993). The psychobiology of undersocialized aggressive conduct disorder. *Development and Psychopathology, 5*, 165–180. doi:10.1017/S0954579400004326

Raine, A. (1993). *The psychopathology of crime: Criminal behavior as a clinical disorder.* San Diego, CA: Academic Press.

Robins, L. N. (1966). *Deviant children grown up.* Baltimore, MD: Williams & Wilkins.

Rowe, R., Costello, E. J., Angold, A., Copeland, W. E., & Maughan, B. (2010). Developmental pathways in oppositional defiant disorder and conduct disorder. *Journal of Abnormal Psychology, 119*, 726–738. doi:10.1037/a0020798

Rowe, R., Maughan, B., Moran, P., Ford, T., Briskman, J., & Goodman, R. (2010). The role of callous unemotional traits in the diagnosis of conduct disorder. *Journal of Child Psychology and Psychiatry, 51*, 688–695. doi:10.1111/j.1469-7610.2009.02199.x

Rowe, R., Maughan, B., Pickles, A., Costello, E. J., & Angold, A. (2002). The relationship between DSM-IV oppositional defiant disorder and conduct disorder: Findings from the Great Smoky Mountains Study. *Journal of Child Psychology and Psychiatry, 43*, 365–373. doi:10.1111/1469-7610.00027

Smith, B. H., Barkley, R. A., & Shapiro, C. J. (2007). Attention-deficit hyperactivity disorder. In E. J. Mash & R. A. Barkley (Eds.), *Assessment of childhood disorders* (4th ed., pp. 53–131). New York: Guilford Press.

Somech, L. Y., & Elizur, Y. (2012). Promoting self-regulation and cooperation in prekindergarten children with conduct problems: A randomized controlled trial. *Journal of the American Academy of Child & Adolescent Psychiatry, 51*, 412–422. doi:10.1016/j.jaac.2012.01.019

Stringaris, A., & Goodman, R. (2009). Three dimensions of oppositionality in youth. *Journal of Child Psychology and Psychiatry*, *50*, 216–223. doi:10.1111/j.1469-7610.2008.01989.x

Tibbetts, S. G., & Piquero, A. R. (1999). The influence of gender, low birth weight, and disadvantaged environment in predicting early onset of offending: A test of Moffitt's interactional hypothesis. *Criminology*, *37*, 843–878. doi:10.1111/j.1745-9125.1999.tb00507.x

Tremblay, R. E. (2003). Why socialization fails. In B. B. Lahey, T. E. Moffitt, & A. Caspi (Eds.), *Causes of conduct disorder and delinquency* (pp. 182–226). New York: Guilford Press.

Viding, E., Sebastian, C. L., Dadds, M. R., Lockwood, P. L., Cecil, C. A. M., De Brito, S. A., et al. (2012). Amygdala response to preattentive masked fear in children with conduct problems: The role of callous-unemotional traits. *American Journal of Psychiatry*, *169*, 1109–1116. doi:10.1176/appi.ajp.2012.12020191

Wakschlag, L. S., Briggs-Gowan, M. J., Carter, A. S., Hill, C., Danis, B., Keenan, K., et al. (2007). A developmental framework for distinguishing disruptive behavior from normative misbehavior in preschool children. *Journal of Child Psychology and Psychiatry*, *48*, 976–987. doi:10.1111/j.1469-7610.2007.01786.x

Waschbusch, D. A. (2002). A meta-analytic examination of comorbid hyperactive-impulsive-attention problems and conduct problems. *Psychological Bulletin*, *128*, 118–150. doi:10.1037/0033-2909.128.1.118

Waschbusch, D. A., Carrey, N. J., Willoughby, M. T., King, S., & Andrade, B. F. (2007). Effects of methylphenidate and behavior modification on social and academic behavior of children with disruptive behavior disorders: The moderating role of callous/unemotional traits. *Journal of Clinical Child and Adolescent Psychology*, *36*, 629–644. doi:10.1080/15374410701662766

White, S. F., Frick, P. J., Lawing, S. K., & Bauer, D. (2012). Callous-unemotional traits and response to functional family therapy in adolescent offenders. *Behavioral Science & the Law*, *31*, 271–285. doi:10.1002/bsl.2041

Willcut, E. G., Nigg, J. T., Pennington, B. F., Solanto, M. V., Rohde, L. A., Tannock, R., et al. (2012). Validity of DSM-IV attention deficit/hyperactivity disorder symptom dimensions and subtypes. *Journal of Abnormal Psychology*, *121*, 991–1010. doi:10.1037/a0027347

# Part 2
# Legal, Societal, and Policy Impact

# 24

# How can Developmental Psychopathology Influence Social and Legal Policy? Adolescence, Mental Health, and Decision Making

Kathryn L. Modecki and Bep Norma Uink

The cornerstone of developmental psychopathology is that all pathology is a process (Cicchetti, 1984). Through this lens, youthful antisocial behavior is the result of a developmental process, and the focus is not on the static representation or diagnosis of behavior in adolescence, for instance, but instead the focus is on the developmental pathways that lead youth to engage in psychopathological behaviors. As a result, social and legal policy that is influenced by developmental psychopathology should reflect two key ideas. First, youth behaviors represent a snapshot of individuals at one point in time. Because behavior is the result of a dynamic, longitudinal process, policy to prevent, treat, and legislate these behaviors must necessarily look to their origins (Loeber & Farrington, 2000; Shirk, Talmi, & Olds, 2000). Second, youth behaviors are the outgrowth of a dynamic process in which individual's liabilities interact with internal and external contexts. Youthful behavior and decisions cannot be pinned to a single internal liability. Rather, internal liabilities interact with other internal contexts such as emotional and cognitive functioning and external contexts such as family functioning and peer norms, in order to determine behavioral outcomes. As a result, to effectively prevent and treat antisocial behavior, social and legal policy must grasp its broad origins.

Developmental psychopathology is a particularly useful lens for adolescence research, as this is a stage of major transition, in which cognitive, emotional, and psychosocial abilities are measurably altered (Cauffman & Steinberg, 2000; Modecki, 2008). During this transition, previous liabilities such as susceptibility for low emotional regulation, externalizing difficulties, or depressed mood often take ascendance. Indeed, youths' externalizing (including defiance, impulsivity, aggression, and antisocial features) and internalizing (including depression, anxiety, and withdrawal symptoms) problems often escalate during the teenage years, and this increase combined with greater amounts of time with peers and more extensive interactions with social institutions

*The Wiley Handbook of Developmental Psychopathology*, First Edition. Edited by Luna C. Centifanti and David M. Williams.

interact to render adolescent psychopathology an issue of social and legal import. Put another way, youthful externalizing and comorbid problems not only apex during adolescence, but this combines with greater personal freedoms and more intensive contact with schools, youth programs, and neighborhood streets, so that youthful psychopathology is often dealt with within education systems, community-based programs, and juvenile justice policy.

Given the impact of adolescents' psychopathology on social and legal systems, it is worth considering how policy currently legislates adolescents' youthful externalizing, and its legal outgrowth, juvenile delinquency. In fact, the legal system has already signaled interest in research that connects development and legal treatment of juvenile offenders. Specifically, developmental research findings have permeated legislative dialogues surrounding juveniles' criminal culpability and sentencing for capital crimes committed by individuals under the age of 18. Although such progress, as described below, is encouraging, further insights may be gleaned by taking a developmental psychopathology perspective, and a "second wave" of policy-focused research is needed to inform questions of juvenile culpability and capacity for decision making in legally relevant contexts (e.g. police interrogation, courtroom) Specifically, because juvenile crime and psychological disorders are interrelated and because externalizing youths nearly always present with a broad swath of contextual and interpersonal liabilities, developmental psychopathology should be informing juvenile treatment and policy on a much broader scale.

## Impact of Recent Developmental Research on Criminal Legal Policy for Adolescents

To provide perspective on how a psychopathology focus might add to the calculus of legislating youths' antisocial behavior, it is helpful to consider how developmental research has already impacted legal treatment of adolescents. This work has indicated that normative development makes adolescents particularly susceptible to engaging in risky and antisocial behaviors, but has not generally focused on psychopathology that emerges during the teenage years, per se. Rather, most previous policy-focused research has focused on normative developmental differences between children, adolescents, and adults and not on mental health issues that manifest during adolescence. Thus, policy continues to invoke a "snapshot" perspective on adolescents' behavior, and has not yet engaged with research that highlights early childhood origins of psychopathology, including externalizing disorders. Youths with externalizing disorders are, of course, manifesting symptoms of psychopathology, by definition. Nonetheless legal policy tends to reflect the notion that externalizing adolescents are merely choosing a problematic course, and that crime is simply a matter of decision making, rather than a matter of decision making interacting with antecedent risk factors, including a comorbid psychological disorder. This same assumption presumes that youths with and without mental health issues will invoke similarly competent decision capacities during their adjudication.

Social and legal policy around juvenile offending in non-capital cases has progressed over the last decade to better reflect developmental understanding of adolescent decision-making capacities in antisocial contexts. This legislative headway has been propelled by a body of research that has operationalized and tested legally relevant and developmentally salient dimensions of adolescents' decision making, and helped to explain adolescents' heavy antisocial behavior involvement. Namely, researchers have argued that risky and antisocial decision-making capacities among normative, healthy adolescents are immature relative to adults (e.g. Cauffman & Steinberg, 2000; Modecki 2008; 2009; 2016; Shulman & Cauffman, 2013). Specifically, relative to adults, adolescents are developmentally disadvantaged in settings that are marked by thrills, excitement, or peer influence, or in situations that offer the potential for these types of emotional or social rewards. Youths focus disproportionally on the psychosocial benefits of risky or antisocial behavior in these contexts, and often fail to consider the long-term implications of their choices (Modecki, 2016; Scott, Repuucci, & Woolard, 1995). Thus, adolescents are not developmentally equipped to make the same decisions within antisocial settings as are individuals who have reached full maturity. As a result, scholars argue that youths should not be held equally as responsible or culpable as adults for their crimes.[1]

Have these research findings impacted legal policy? There are some indications that the Supreme Court has considered adolescents' deficits in decision making in its treatment of juvenile crime. For instance, in 2005, in *Roper v Simmons* the Supreme Court deemed the death penalty for crimes committed by juveniles constituted cruel and unusual punishment, and in 2012, in *Miller v Alabama* ruled that non-capital offenses committed by juveniles could not be punished by life in prison without the possibility of parole. Despite these rulings though, the US juvenile justice system remains highly punitive in its orientation. Illustratively, in response to the Court's less retributive decisions, US state policies have not signaled a more rehabilitative shift and youth continue to be transferred to adult court at very high rates (Slobogin, 2013). What scholars might infer from this example is that there is room for research using a developmental psychopathology lens to influence social and legal treatment of externalizing youth. However, a critical mass of evidence is likely required and progress may be small at first and may build incrementally.

## A Second Wave of Policy Research?

One area where developmental psychopathology is especially relevant to policy and thus holds the potential to impact legislation is around corrective penalties and legal processes for crimes committed by juveniles with a psychological disorder. Delinquent adolescents have a much greater rate of psychological disorders relative to the general adolescent population (Abram, Teplin, McClelland & Dulcan, 2003; Teplin, Abram, McClelland, Dulcan & Mericle, 2002). For example, diagnostic-specific impairment prevalence rates among detained juvenile offenders, even after excluding conduct disorder diagnoses, are estimated at roughly 60 % for boys and more than 65 % for girls (Teplin et al., 2002). Teplin and colleagues report that 17 % of detained male adolescents and 26 % of detained females adolescents suffer from depression disorders. Further, 50 % of male youth and 47 % of female youth meet criteria for a substance use disorder. These psychological disorders are also linked to early contextual liabilities within a child's life—including maladaptive parenting and dysfunctional families. Thus the presence of mental health issues among adolescent offenders works as a double jeopardy, in which risk factors for psychological disorders also represent liabilities for youths (Grisso, 1999; 2004). As a result, those youths most in need of protective buffering from their behavioral choices are less likely to have contextual supports to ameliorate adolescents' risk.

Further, a growing literature also indicates that impaired decision making is implicated in at least some of these psychological disorders, including depression, anxiety, and schizophrenia, and subfactors of disorders such as callous-unemotional traits. Thus youths with a diagnosis of a psychological disorder likely suffer from even greater decision impairments than the typical adolescent. But it remains to be understood how decision impairments linked to psychopathology impact youthful culpability. Further, these decision deficits among youths with psychopathology almost certainly influence their choices in legally relevant contexts—from understanding Miranda warnings (e.g., the right to consult an attorney) to confessing to crimes. Despite growing understanding of the links between developmental psychopathology and poor decision making, there has been very little consideration to date of how adolescents' psychopathology affects their culpability and legal capacities.

In the following sections, we briefly outline some of the contextual elements that are both risk factors for psychopathology in childhood and adolescence and may represent hindrances to adolescents' beneficial choices. We next discuss how adolescents with psychopathology, and externalizing in particular, may be especially ill-equipped for decision making both in antisocial contexts and in the adjudication process. We then provide some starting points for future research in relation to psychopathology and juvenile criminal culpability and legal treatment.

## Early Risk Factors for Adolescent Psychopathology, and Double Jeopardy

A developmental psychopathology perspective identifies factors which place individual youth at risk for abnormal development (Cicchetti & Rogosh, 2002). We provide a brief consideration of some of the known familial and parental risk factors in the development of child and adolescent psychopathology, to underscore how these contextual risks place youth with mental health issues in a double bind in terms of problematic outcomes. Contextual liabilities predispose children to a psychological disorder during adolescence, and because these liabilities mean youths have fewer protections, they also place youths with a psychological disorder at even greater risk for legal system involvement during adolescence. We focus our discussion on common psychological disorders of childhood and adolescence including mood disorders, substance use disorders, conduct disorder and delinquent behavior, although risks for other disorders are discussed where appropriate.

### Economic Hardship

Low family economic status can serve as a marker for stressful micro and macro level contexts associated with poverty and economic strain. Such stressors stemming from low economic status of the family have been found to be associated with child and adolescent diagnoses of depression (both major and dysthymia disorder), conduct disorder (CD), oppositional defiant disorder (ODD), anxiety disorders, as well as delinquency, and somatic complaints (Wadsworth, Raviv, Reinhard, Wolf, DeCarlo Santiago, & Einhorn, 2008).

Poverty can compound risks of maladaptive parenting practices, and diminished parenting is often coupled with economic hardships (Conger et al., 1993; Modecki & Wilson, 2009). Furthermore, familial economic hardship in and of itself predicts youths' internalizing symptoms (Gerard & Buehler, 1999). Combined with having parents who are low in acceptance and monitoring, and high in strict or inconsistent discipline, this economic hardship is also associated with children's externalizing behaviors. All told, family economic stress increases the likelihood of developmental psychopathology, and also limits the family's prospects for buffering youth with mental health issues from experiencing adverse outcomes that result from these problems (Loeber & Farrington, 2000).

## Maladaptive Parenting

Even without the burden of economic strain, maladaptive parenting is tied to youth psychopathology (Modecki, Hagan, Sandler, & Wolchik, 2015). For instance, maladaptive parenting behavior directed at a child has been found to explain as much as 60 % of the variance in that child's antisocial behavior and as much of 37 % of the variability in that child's depressive symptoms (Reis et al., 1995). In fact, there is a large body of evidence demonstrating that family contexts that include conflict and aggression put youth at increased risk for mental health issues such as internalizing and externalizing and conduct problems (See Repetti, Taylor, & Seeman, 2002 for an excellent review). These findings speak to the pervasiveness of the family environment in influencing child and adolescent psychopathology. As an example of how maladaptive parenting may further contribute to difficulties within the legal system, research has shown that youth who belong to "bad families" or who are seen as having poor parents are especially likely to receive unusually harsh dispositions in juvenile court (Sanborn, 1996). Treatment resources are also less likely to be diverted to these adolescents whom are most in need of services. Thus, risk factors for psychopathology in childhood are perpetuated in adolescence when the youth has contact with the juvenile justice system.

## Parental Psychopathology

Maladaptive parenting can also be the result of parental psychopathology, and parental psychopathology is itself another well-established contextual risk factor for youth psychopathology. For example, children who have a parent with a diagnosis of schizophrenia are more likely to receive a future diagnosis of schizophrenia (Elrlenmey-Kimiling et al., 2001); parental anxiety increases children's risk for depression (Woodhouse, Ramos-Mercuse, Ehlrich, Warner & Cassidy, 2009); and parental early maladaptive schemas are associated with offspring's depression and externalizing behaviors (Van Vlierberghe, Timbremont, Braet & Basile, 2007).

Goodman and Gotlib (1999) propose four risk mechanisms through which maternal psychopathology specifically may operate to increase offspring's risk of developing a psychological disorder. Although they limit their discussion to maternal depression, the proposed risk mechanism can be applied to transmission of other parental disorders, including externalizing disorders. First, genetic vulnerabilities that have predisposed the mother to depression may be inherited by the child. Second, abnormal development of the child's regulatory systems *in utero* may confer risk for affective disorders. Third, a mother's negative cognitions which perpetuate the depressive disorder may be learned by the child through social learning processes. Last, maternal depression may expose the child to environmental stress, creating risk for other psychological disorders. These proposed risk mechanisms may be equally salient to the transmission of other predisposing factors from parent to child. For example, a cognition that is seen as central to both anxiety and to aggression—perceiving a hypothetical ambiguous situation as threatening—is positively correlated between mothers and their child (Cresswell, O'Connor, & Brewin, 2006). Moreover, a mother's anticipated distress to the hypothetical situation is predictive of the child's incorrect threat perception, suggesting either a role for social learning of threat perception or an inherited vulnerability toward aggressive cognitions (e.g. Brookmeyer, Henrich, & Schwab-Stone, 2005; Dix & Lochman, 1990).

## Compounding Effects of Contextual Deficits

These contextual deficits—economic hardship, maladaptive parenting, and parental psychopathology—confer an increased risk for psychopathology on children and adolescents but also transmit a "compounding effect" whereby youth who are in need of support due to mental health problems will be less likely to receive support due to insufficient functioning in their parental and familial systems. For instance, parents in families of low socioeconomic status know less about their children's rights in the context of police interrogations (Woolard, Cleary, Harvell, & Chen, 2008). As a result of these knowledge deficits, low-SES families are less able to protect their child's long-term interests in legal contexts. In addition to helping their offspring navigate their legal rights, parents must also ensure that youths adhere to their court-mandated treatment and monitor their child within community-based supervision settings. Thus, it not surprising that maladaptive parenting and parental psychopathology increase youths' likelihood for out-of-home placements within secure facilities (O'Donnell & Lurigio, 2008). As one example, first-time offenders are at increased risk for out-of-home placement when maternal psychopathology is present, such as history of substance abuse (Fader, Harris, Jones, & Poulin, 2001).

It is these compounding effects that need to be highlighted for policy and programs. Rather than viewing low SES and family dysfunction as indicators of youths' poor prospects for treatment or as signs of likely recidivism, contextual risks could be viewed in terms of developmental barriers that have handicapped youths' chances for avoiding delinquency. Policy makers could also consider these barriers as impediments to fair treatment, given that they increase the likelihood that youths will receive especially punitive sentencing (Grisso, 2004). As a result, these risk factors for psychopathology should signal youths' rehabilitative needs and a corresponding legal and social responsibility to provide therapeutic intervention (Grisso, 2004). Within this developmental psychopathology framework, social and legal policy would construe risk factors as markers for youths' remediation needs. Risk factors for psychopathology would signal a need to build and repair emotional, social, and behavioral skills deficits among youths' who may have been deprived these opportunities at an earlier age (Guerra, Modecki, & Cunningham, 2014; Modecki & Wilson, 2009; Williamson, Modecki, & Guerra, 2015).

Beyond the compounding effects of risk factors that foretell psychopathology in adolescence and which exacerbate negative outcomes from adolescents' mental health issues, there are also potential shortfalls in decision making among youth experiencing a psychological disorder. Importantly, risk factors described above likely interact with decision deficits to render youths particularly ineffectual in making responsible, informed decisions within risky and antisocial contexts (e.g. Goodnight, Bates, Newman, Dodge, & Pettit, 2006). These deficits may further impact adolescents' legally relevant decisions such as waving Miranda rights, following advice offered by their attorney, and making a confession (Kassin et al., 2010; Oberlander & Goldstein, 2001; Redlich, Summers, & Hoover, 2010). Thus, we now turn our attention to some of these shortfalls in executive function (EF) that have been identified among youths with a psychological disorder and which may underscore some of their decision deficits.

## Decision Making Deficits among Adolescents with Psychopathology

We begin this section with an overview of decision-making skills captured under the umbrella term of executive function. We describe how EF skills develop across the course of adolescence among normative youth and highlight a burgeoning literature linking deficits in EF to adolescent psychopathology broadly. We then narrow our discussion to links between EF deficits and externalizing disorders and consider whether these deficits should be considered in relation to mitigated criminal culpability and in relation to diminished decision making capacity in legally relevant environments.

### Executive Functioning

Executive functioning is a key aspect of decision making and refers to a collection of neurocognitive processes that allow for the top-down control of impulses and behavior, as well as for the conscious planning of goal-directed behavior (Miyake et al., 2000; Weyandt, 2009). The term also encompasses cognitive skills such as strategic planning, cognitive flexibility (or attention shifting), working memory and response inhibition. EF skills are typically associated with conscious regulation of thoughts and behavior (Kerr & Zelazo, 2004). Importantly, these skills also form the basis of successful problem solving (Ellis, Weiss, & Lochman, 2009). For example, selectively attending to cues, planning, shifting cognitive sets, and recalling and holding information in working memory are all EF tasks that allow for successful decision making.

*Development of EF* Executive functioning develops rapidly during childhood, but continues to develop incrementally during adolescence. Underlying EF is the prefrontal cortex, the cognitive control center of the brain, which continues to mature into young adulthood in the form of system refinement and increased networking. Such system refinement is reflected in incremental progression during adolescence on cognitive tasks that tap EF functions including working memory, inhibitory control, and attention shifting (Luciana, 2013; Romer, 2010).

Although the literature broadly indicates that EF continues to improve during adolescence, there is some variability depending on the task and aspect of EF it purports to measure. For example, previous research has documented a surge in attentional capacity and cognitive processing speed around age 15 and gradual increases in planning across adolescence (Anderson, Anderson, Northam, Jacobs, & Catroppa, 2001). Cognitive control capacities in the form of temporal discounting tasks also continue to increase across adolescence with a sharp surge between ages 15 and 16 (Water, Cillessen, & Scheres, 2014).) Likewise, long-term memory and working memory incrementally increase across adolescence, as measured by informed versus uninformed Iowa Gambling Tasks (Van Duijvenvoorde, Jansen, Bredman, & Huizenga, 2012). By contrast, cognitive flexibility appears to be relatively stable by adolescence (Anderson et al., 2001). Not surprisingly given this variation in EF skills, tasks used to measure various aspects of EF performance tend to correlate only modestly among adolescents (Anderson et al., 2001).

All told, developmental differences in EF among typically developing youths tend to be most evident in tasks that have a strong motivational component, when rewards and losses result from decisions, and when there is affective information to process. In other words, "cool" EF skills—functions that guide behavior in emotionally neutral situations—appear to mature before "hot" EF skills—functions that guide behavior within emotionally and motivationally salient situations (Hooper, Luciana, Conklin, & Yarger, 2004; Prencipe et al., 2011; Zelato & Carlson, 2012). In fact, affective decision making—decisions made under conditions of heavy emotion or potential for rewards—does not reach adult levels until young adulthood (early twenties).

There is also considerable variation in the progression of both cold and hot EF across adolescence. As discussed below, the presence of a psychological disorder can contribute to individual differences in both "cold" and "hot" EF skills. Importantly, deficits in *either* "cool" or "hot" EF skills indicate possible shortfalls in real-world decision making, because regulation of behavior relies on an integration of motivational drives as well as deliberative processes (Luciana, 2013). These decision shortfalls would arguably emerge in situations driven by affect and which occur in peer contexts (e.g. antisocial settings) or in contexts that are stressful (e.g. legal settings).

In fact, the brain areas responsible for integration of both types of information—affective and cognitive—is the prefrontal cortex and its underpinning neural systems. Because this cognitive control network continues to improve in its capacity to direct information during adolescence, it can become overburdened by poor functioning in either cold or hot domains (Luciana, Conklin, Hooper, & Yarger, 2005). Processing demands are heightened during adolescence, as youths must navigate social relationships and also wrestle with strong internal arousal and motivational, approach drives (Luciana, 2013). Thus adolescents are a work in progress, and are maturing in their ability to handle information processing demands that engage hot and cold brain systems (Luciana, Conklin, Hooper, & Yarger, 2005).

*EF Deficits among Youths with Psychopathology* Youths with psychopathology appear to have even greater processing demands on their cognitive control system than normative youths. Illustratively, youths with psychopathology tend to have difficulties with adult and peer relationships which create added affective burdens and few external supports to help regulate themselves (Telzer, Fuligni, Lieberman, & Galván, 2013). These youths already tend to be disregulated and emotional upheavals may act as an ongoing source of internal stress for the brain's control systems (Luciana, 2013; Luciana & Collins, 2012). These existing demands mean that youths with psychopathology are poorly equipped to handle new inputs arising either in highly arousing and social situations (antisocial contexts) or in situations marked by stress and heavy information processing requirements (legally relevant contexts). These EF deficits may render youths with psychopathology particularly ill-prepared to handle novel situational demands, cope with emotions and stressors, and solve problems.

Importantly, Deficits in EF have been implicated in a variety of child and adolescent psychological disorders. Although there is some research to suggest that EF impairments may be more tightly linked with level of psychopathology, rather than with specific diagnoses, certain patterns of deficits track meaningfully with adolescent maladjustment (Cassidy, 2015; Stordal et al., 2005). Illustratively, youth with either childhood onset or adolescent onset schizophrenia (including diagnoses of schizophreniform and schizoaffective disorders) perform worse on EF tasks and verbal memory tasks compared to non-psychiatric controls (Kravariti et al., 2003). Adolescents who have been diagnosed with Major Depressive Disorder also show decreased speed in mental processing (Favre et al., 2008) and showed biased processing toward negative stimuli (Kyte, Goodyer, & Sahakian, 2005).Working memory, attention and processing speed deficits have also been found in youth with Bipolar Mood Disorder (Doyle et al., 2005), and working memory deficits are associated with a continued ADHD diagnosis from childhood into adulthood (Halperin, Trampush, Miller, Marks, & Newcorn, 2008). Impaired EF also increases the risk of substance abuse in adolescence (Blume & Marlatt, 2009). Taken together, these findings suggest that some form of neuropsychological functioning tends to be compromised in youth exhibiting mental health issues, and that impaired EF is a key risk factor for youth psychopathology. This is important because, as described earlier, youths who have contact with the juvenile justice system often have a psychological diagnosis comorbid with their externalizing behavior (Teplin et al., 2002).

*EF and Externalizing Disorders* In addition to EF deficits associated with other psychological disorders, there is a growing literature linking EF shortfalls to adolescent externalizing. This literature points to the possibility that EF processes may be especially important in the etiology of externalizing. One possible role for EF in the etiology of externalizing is that youths are not able to effectively recruit planning, goal-setting, and self-organization skills in contexts where they are most needed. Thus, shortfalls in EF point to deficiencies in how youth process and direct emotional and social information, and shortfalls in how they problem solve when considering potential choices (Luciana, 2013). Importantly, decision making among externalizing youths may be further handicapped because these youths also generate excessive demands on their executive control system, which, as described below suffers from impairments. Because externalizing youths tend to be disregulated, their executive control system must work to create stasis, regardless of other happenings or stressors (Luciana & Collins, 2012). On top of this, externalizing youths tend to seek out novel situations which entail intensive processing of social cues, and unexpected stressors. Thus, relative to healthy adolescents, externalizing adolescents place greater demands on their executive systems. These heavy inputs likely enervate their executive control system, which is already lacking (Luciana & Collins, 2012; Luciana, 2013). As a result, externalizing youths may have difficulties effectively coping with heavy emotional inputs or stressors and make poor decisions across a variety of contexts and situations.

*Which Executive Functions are Impaired in Youth with Externalizing Disorders?* As described above, deficits in externalizing adolescents' EF are arguably indicative of a system that cannot effectively direct the flow of information from different sources. As a result, the literature describes a range of EF deficits in relation to externalizing, aggression, and other forms of antisocial behavior. For the most part, the literature emphasizes executive functions underpinning cognitive control (Morgan & Lilienfeld, 2000), but in meta-analytic work, some of the strongest effects between externalizing and EF are in processes of working memory, spatial working memory, and attention (Ogilvie, Stewart, Chan, & Shum, 2011).

There is a fairly robust link in the literature between deficits in EF related to cognitive control and adolescent externalizing disorders. Illustratively, a 'behavioral disinhibition' factor, referring to a youth's inability to inhibit socially inappropriate or personally damaging behaviors, has been proposed as a common underlying factor in all externalizing disorders (Tarter et al., 2003; Young et al., 2009). Young and colleagues (2009) demonstrated that a range of externalizing problems, including substance use, ADHD, conduct disorder and novelty seeking, loaded onto a latent factor of behavioral disinhibition. Importantly, the behavioral disinhibition factor negatively correlated with a range of EF measures including response inhibition, moving attentional focus (set shifting) and working memory. Not surprisingly, the strongest of these relationships was between behavioral disinhibition and response inhibition, suggesting that the ability to inhibit responses is a key deficit in youth with externalizing symptomology.

Consistent with the idea that deficits in response inhibition are implicated in externalizing, externalizing youths also show EF deficits in the form of response perseveration, or responding with a default or dominant response rather than a correct one that is based on the information at hand (Séguin, Arseneault, Boulerice, Harden, & Tremblay, 2002). Likewise, rates of development in effortful control skills, which involve the ability to inhibit cognitive and behavioral responses, develop in parallel with rates of externalizing symptoms throughout middle childhood (Zhou, Hofer, & Eisenberg, 2007). Behavioral "under-control" is also associated with preschoolers' externalizing behaviors (Eisenberg et al., 2001).

However, other aspects of EF, beyond behavioral disinhibition or cognitive control, are tied to youthful externalizing. As stated earlier, some of the strongest effect sizes linking EF to antisocial behavior appear to be for "cold" aspects of EF such as working memory, spatial working memory, and attention (Ogilvie et al., 2011). Illustratively, youth who score high on the Child Behavior Checklist (CBCL) externalizing subscale have been shown to have impaired speed of processing (Brunnenkreef et al., 2007). Also in support of this idea, Cassidy (2015) recently used latent variable modelling to demonstrate that externalizing is uniquely paired with deficits in working memory and verbal fluency in both children and adolescents. Other research has reported that conceptual flexibility (ability to engage in flexible thinking and behavior), but not monitoring (ability to actively monitor and assess information in working memory) or inhibition (ability to intentionally inhibit an automatic response), is associated with youthful externalizing (Latzman, 2009).

Deficits in these cold aspects of EF are often found in psychological disorders that are comorbid with externalizing, as well. Illustratively, working memory and response inhibition deficits are found in youth with a diagnosis of ADHD (Barkley,1997; Young et al., 2009), with comorbid ODD and CD (Hobson, Scott, & Rubia, 2011), and substance use disorders (Chambers, Taylor, & Potenza, 2003; Young et al., 2009). Youth with diagnosis of ADHD and CD also exhibit poorer ability to shift attention between tasks and in forming abstract concepts (Ernst et al., 2004). As with the EF research generally presented here, comorbidities make it difficult to directly tie EF to externalizing per se. But this comorbidity is precisely what courts and policy makers need to consider in terms of youthful culpability and their ability to navigate the legal environment.

*What do EF Impairments among Youths with Externalizing Disorders Mean for Legal Policy?* Most EF tasks are designed to capture clinically significant impairments in laboratory settings. As a result, EF tasks highlight only some of the decision impairments found among youths with psychopathology. Even if deficits described here are subclinical, EF deficits found among externalizing youths certainly still impact regulation of everyday behavior and decisions (Ogilvie et al., 2011; Rinsky & Henshaw, 2011). Daily life requires youth to perceive, evaluate, and respond to information; and far more research is needed to understand how shortfalls in both "hot" and "cold" EF contribute to antisocial choices and decisions made by youth once they are engaged with the legal system. The deficits described here indicate reduced capacity for decision making in antisocial contexts (potentially invoking "hot EF") and also reduced competence to make informed, planned choices in the legal environment ("cold EF"). Some examples of "cold" choices youths might face include whether to confess, whether to communicate honestly with lawyers, and whether to implicate friends and acquaintances (Schmidt, Reppucci, & Woolard, 2003).

Research that elucidates how development and psychopathology contribute to juvenile offending could help shape the courts' conceptualizations of culpability for youth with psychopathology. More specifically, research is sorely needed on how, among adolescents with externalizing psychopathology, EF deficits interact with antisocial contexts that have heavy social and affective inputs. Because these youths manifest information processing deficits, they are arguably particularly ill-equipped to "cope" with decision demands in contexts that lead to antisocial behavior. By highlighting how internal liabilities contribute to antisocial choices, such research could work to "tip the scales" towards treatment for psychopathology rather than punishment for punishments' sake for young offenders. As Mulford and colleagues explain in their comprehensive synthesis of legal issues influencing youth with psychopathology (2004): "Delinquency jurisdiction is invoked by a juvenile's actions, yet those same actions may often be seen as part of a larger constellation of mental health problems. There is no theoretical bright line indicating when the conceptualizations of mental illness are more or less appropriate than the law's rubric of delinquency." In fact, legal and psychological frameworks rest on different assumptions about the causality of behavior. The legal system views delinquency and by extension, externalizing, as an act of free will. Psychologists view externalizing as an outgrowth of conscious and unconscious processes governed by an executive control system that is not yet fully functional. Juvenile justice policy is likely to shift only when lawmakers become convinced that delinquency goes beyond simply choosing to break the law (Woolard, Reppucci, & Redding, 1996). By highlighting the dynamic biological, social, and contextual processes that contribute to aberrant decision making during adolescence, a developmental psychopathology perspective could help apprise this debate.

There is also good reason to believe that youths with psychopathology may have difficulties making informed decisions within novel and stressful contexts which characterize the legal environment. As described above, youth who are involved with the justice system are also likely to have diminished cognitive control and working memory capacities, as well as diminished ability to sustain attention. Though these results are apparent in the laboratory setting, such deficits may have manifold consequences in the legal environment—where stakes are far higher (Grisso, 1997; Grisso et al., 2003). In fact, a growing body of work has called for more attention to decision deficits in legal environments among youthful offenders (Kassin et al., 2010). While not fully reviewed here, they highlight the need to place psychopathology within the broader conversation of youthful capacity to make informed legal decision. Youths with a psychological diagnosis are arguably more likely to be detained and charged for their offenses, given their problem-solving and decision-making deficits in legally relevant contexts (Grisso, 2004). Among adult populations, researchers have also highlighted the link between psychological disorders and poor decision making—for instance in the form of poor understanding and reasoning around Miranda rights (Cooper & Zapf, 2007; Rogers, Harrison, Hazelwood, & Sewell, 2007). Table 24.1 includes further examples of the types of risks youth with mental health problems face within the juvenile justice systems. What a developmental psychopathology framework can bring to this conversation is clearer understanding of the links between developmental stage, origins of deficits, and incapacity.

## How can Developmental Psychopathology Influence Policy for Adolescent Offenders with a Psychological Disorder?

Adolescents who engage in juvenile delinquency present with a range of contextual and individual risk factors that place them in a double bind for poor legal outcomes. Not only do family and social risk factors predispose youths to psychological disorders, these risks also signal to judges and court personnel an increased risk for recidivism, which corresponds with more punitive legal treatment. In the same vein, young offenders with a psychological disorder are at heightened risk for EF deficits that likely contribute to reduced capacity for decision making in antisocial contexts. Such EF deficits also have important implications for capacity to make informed choices within the legal system.

Courts in the United States still maintain a punitive orientation towards juveniles who offend, many of whom have mental health symptoms. For youths with mental health issues, the legal system does not take into account contextual liabilities that put them at risk for psychopathology and also for more punitive treatment. Many of these offenders come from low-SES backgrounds with parents who also experience psychopathology. Often, offenders evidence problems that can result in their involvement in other service systems, including child welfare (Herz, Ryan, & Bilchik, 2010). These risk factors influence sentencing, because courts consider these youths to have few social supports to avoid recidivism. Further, presence of a psychological disorder can also place youths at increased risk for antisocial decision making. Psychopathology also puts youths at risk for making poor decisions once they are in contact with the legal system—particularly in relation to police interrogation and Miranda warnings.

**Table 24.1** Examples of the types of risks youth with mental health problems face within juvenile justice systems.

| *Stages of justice system involvement* | *Potential liabilities for youth with mental health problems* |
|---|---|
| **Arrest** Case can be dealt with informally through diversion or be handled formally and proceed through juvenile justice system | Failure to show respect to police-resulting in arrest (Worden & Myers, 1999); risk of false confession to police (Redlich, Summers, & Hoover, 2010); poor understanding of Miranda rights (Kassin et al., 2010) |
| **Diversion**:<br>**Non-law-enforcement sources**<br>**Law-enforcement sources** | Difficulties complying with demands of low-risk diversion, behavior misinterpreted as poor attitude (e.g. Burrell & Warboys, 2000) |
| **Prosecution** Case either processed through juvenile court, possible diversion, or possible transfer to adult court through statutory exclusion or prosecutorial discretion | Less apt to make favorable impressions at intake which would allow for diversion rather than prosecution (Mulford et al., 2004) |
| **Juvenile court intake** Charges filed or dismissed, possible diversion, or proceed to formal processing | More likely to be detained and charged for offenses (Grisso, 2004) |
| **Formal processing** Case proceeds to adjudication, case dismissed, or case waived to adult court | Poor presentation and lack of involvement in making decisions about diversion may increase risk for formal processing (Mulford et al., 2004); when mental health screening takes place prior to adjudication, formal entry into the juvenile justice system may be a requirement for mental health services eligibility (Mears & Kelly, 1999; Mulford et al., 2004) |
| **Adjudication** Adjudicatory hearing is equivalent to a criminal trial—where facts are established for the case at hand; youth may be found delinquent (e.g., guilty), case may be dismissed (e.g. not guilty), or case may be continued in contemplation of dismissal (e.g. awaiting youth's fulfilment of set requirements prior to dismissal) | More likely to waive their right to counsel (Viljoen, Klaver, & Roesch, 2005); diminished capacity to communicate with counsel Viljoen & Roesch, 2005); less likely to follow advice offered by counsel; increased likelihood of making a false confession (Redlich, Summers, & Hoover, 2010); mental health factors (e.g. serious substance use and poorer quality home environments) put youth at risk for more punitive disposition outcomes (Campbell & Schmidt, 2000; Sanborn, 1996) |
| **Placement** | More likely to be recommended for out-of-home placement (DeGue, Scalora, Ullman, & Gallavan, 2008) |
| **Aftercare** | Likely increased need for aftercare (Mulford et al., 2004) |
| **Probation** | Increased risk for recidivism (McReynolds, Schwalbe, & Wasserman, 2010) |

Thus, there is a critical need for second wave research, focused on tenets of developmental psychopathology to inform policy. This work might further emphasize how youths experiencing economic hardship and maladaptive parenting are more deserving of treatment, not less. This work might further emphasize the role of psychological disorders in antisocial decision making and make clear that treatment not punishment is a better approach to redirect offending youths towards more positive developmental trajectories. Finally, developmental psychopathology research can highlight how decision liabilities among adolescents with psychological disorders interact with legal contexts to make these youths susceptible to poor choices and outcomes within the court system.

## Note

1 Of course, the question of *when* responsibility should be considered equivalent remains a pressing one for legal policy. Through the early–mid twenties, young adults undergo psychosocial growth (Modecki, 2009) and neural development within the brain continues (Sowell, Thompson, Holmes, Jernigan, & Toga, 1999). Yet even though young adults do have some psychosocial and physiological vulnerabilities, they are more mature than adolescents and their antisocial decisions are likely mediated by a more fully developed identity, character, and capacity for coping and problem solving (Modecki, Zimmer-Gembeck, & Guerra, 2017). Thus, science and policy are on firmer ground maintaining adolescents' developmental immaturity, rather than delineating a later age when reasoning and decision making are certain to be "adult-like," at least at present.

## Acknowledgments

Portions of this research were funded by a grant from the Australian Institute of Criminology through the Criminology Research Grants Program to Kathryn Modecki, Bonnie Barber, and Wayne Osgood. The views expressed are the responsibility of Kathryn L. Modecki and are not necessarily those of the AIC.

## References

Abram, K. M., Teplin, L. A., McClelland, G. M., & Dulcan, M. K. (2003). Comorbid psychiatric disorders in youth in juvenile detention. *Archives of General Psychiatry,60*, 1097–1108. doi:10.1001/archpsyc.60.11.1097

Anderson, V. A., Anderson, P., Northam, E., Jacobs, R., & Catroppa, C. (2001). Development of executive functions through late childhood and adolescence in an Australian sample. *Developmental Neuropsychology, 20*(1), 385–406. doi: 10.1207/S15326942DN2001_5

Barkley, R. A (1997). Behavioral inhibition, sustained attention, and executive functions: constructing a unifying theory of ADHD. *Psychological Bulletin, 121*(1), 65–94.

Blume, A. W., & Marlatt, G. A. (2009). The role of executive cognitive functions in changing substance use: what we know and what we need to know. *Annals of Behavioral Medicine, 37*, 117–125. doi: 10.1007/s12160-009-9093-8

Brookmeyer, K. A., Henrich, C. C., & Schwab-Stone, M. (2005). Adolescents who witness community violence: Can parent support and prosocial cognitions protect them from committing violence? *Child Development, 76*(4), 917–929. doi: 10.1111/j.1467-8624.2005.00886.x

Brunnekreef, J. A., De Sonneville, L. M. J., Minderaa, R. B., Oldehinkel, A. J., Verhulst, F. C., & Ormel, J. (2007). Information processing profiles of internalizing and externalizing behavior problems: evidence from a population-based sample of preadolescents. *Journal of Child Psychology and Psychiatry, 48*(2), 185–193 doi:10.1111/j.1469-7610.2006.01695

Burrell, S., & Warboys, L. M. (2000). *Special education and the juvenile justice system* (pp. 1–15). US Department of Justice, Office of Justice Programs, Office of Juvenile Justice and Delinquency Prevention.

Campbell, M. A., & Schmidt, F. (2000). Comparison of mental health and legal factors in the disposition outcome of young offenders. *Criminal Justice and Behavior*, *27*(6), 688–715.

Cassidy, A. R. (2015). Executive function and psychosocial adjustment in healthy children and adolescents: A latent variable modelling investigation. *Child Neuropsychology*, *22*(3), 292–317.

Cauffman, E., & Steinberg, L. (2000). (Im)maturity of judgement in adolescence: why adolescents may be less culpable than adults. *Behavioral Sciences & the Law*, *18*(6), 741–760. doi: 10.1002/bsl.416

Chambers, R. A., Taylor, J. R., & Potenza, M. C. (2003). Developmental neurocircuitry of motivation in adolescence: a critical period of addiction vulnerability. *American Journal of Psychiatry*, *160*(6), 1041–1052. http://dx.doi.org/10.1176/appi.ajp.160.6.1041

Cicchetti, D. (1984). The emergence of developmental psychopathology. *Child Development*, *55*(1), 1–7.

Cicchetti, D., & Rogosh, F. A. (2002). A developmental psychopathology perspective on adolescence. *Journal of Consulting and Clinical Psychology*, *70*(1), 6–20. doi: 10.1037/0022-006X.70.1.6

Conger, R. D., Conger, K. J., Elder, G. H., Lorenz, F. O., Simons, R. L., & Whitbeck, S. B. (1993). Family economic stress and adjustment of early adolescent girls. *Developmental Psychology*, *29*(2), 206–219.

Cooper, V. G., & Zapf, P. A. (2008). Psychiatric patients' comprehension of Miranda rights. *Law and Human Behavior*, *32*(5), 390. doi:10.1007/s10979-007-9099-3

Cresswell, C., O'Connor, T. G., & Brewin, C. R. (2006). A longitudinal investigation of maternal and child "anxious cognitions." *Cognitive Therapy Research*, *30*, 135–147. doi: 10.1007/s10608-006-9021-1.

DeGue, S., Scalora, M., Ullman, D., & Gallavan, D. (2008). In-home or out-of-home?: Predicting long-term placement recommendations for juvenile offenders. *International Journal of Forensic Mental Health*, *7*(1), 15–27.

Dix, T., & Lochman, J. E. (1990). Social cognition and negative reactions to children: A comparison of mothers of aggressive and nonaggressive boys. *Journal of Social and Clinical Psychology*, *9*(4), 418–438.

Doyle, A. E., Wilens, T. E., Kwon, A., Seidman, L. J., Farone, V., Fried, R., Swezey, A., Snyder, L., & Biederman, J. (2005). Neuropsychological functioning of youth with bipolar disorder. *Biological Psychiatry*, *58*, 540–548. doi:10.1016/j.biopsych.2005.07.019

Eisenberg, N., Cumberland, A., Spinrad, T. L., Fabes, R. A., Shepard, S. A., Reiser, M., … & Guthrie, I. K. (2001). The relations of regulation and emotionality to children's externalizing and internalizing problem behavior. *Child Development*, *72*(4), 1112–1134. doi:10.1111/1467-8624.00337

Ellis, M. L., Weiss, B., & Lochman, J. E. (2009). Executive functions in children: Associations with aggressive behavior and appraisal processing. *Journal of Abnormal Child Psychology*, *37*(7), 945–956. doi: 10.1007/s10802-009-9321-5

Erlenmeyer-Kimling, L., Rock, D., Roberts, S. A., Janal, M., Kestenbaum, C., Cornblatt, B., … & Gottesmen, I. I. (2000). Attention, memory and motor skills as childhood predictors of schizophrenia-related psychoses: the New York high rise project. *American Journal of Psychiatry*, *157*, 1416–1422. doi: 10.1176/appi.ajp.157.9.1416

Ernst, M., Grant, S. J., London, E. D., Contoreggi, C. S., Kimes, A. S., & Spurgeon, L. (2003). Decision making in adolescents with behavior disorders and adults with substance abuse. *American Journal of Psychiatry*, *160*, 33–40. doi: 10.1176/appi.ajp.160.1.33

Fader, J. J., Harris, P. W., Jones, P. R., & Poulin, M. E. (2001). Factors involved in decisions on commitment to delinquency programs for first-time juvenile offenders. *Justice Quarterly*, *18*(2), 323–341. doi: 10.1080/07418820100094921

Favre, T., Hughes, C., Emslie, G., Stavinoha, P., Kennard, B., & Carmody, T. (2008). Executive functioning in children and adolescents with major depressive disorder. *Child Neuropsychology, 15*(1), 85–99. doi:10.1080/09297040802577311

Gerard, J. M., & Buehler, C. (1999). Multiple risk factors in the family environment and youth problem behaviors. *Journal of Marriage and the Family, 61 (2)*, 343–374.

Goodman, S. H., & Gotlib, I. H. (1999). Risk for psychopathology in children and adolescents of depressed mothers: a developmental model for understanding mechanisms of transmission. *Psychological Review, 106*(3), 458–490.

Goodnight, J. A., Bates, J. E., Newman, J. P., Dodge, K. A., & Pettit, G. S. (2006). The interactive influences of friend deviance and reward dominance on the development of externalizing behavior during middle adolescence. *Journal of Abnormal Child Psychology, 34*(5), 573–583. doi: 10.1007/s10802-006-9036-9

Grisso, T. (1997). The competence of adolescents as trial defendants. *Psychology, Public Policy, and Law, 3*(1), 3.

Grisso, T. (1999). Juvenile offenders and mental illness. *Psychiatry, Psychology and Law, 6*(2), 143–151.

Grisso, T. (2004). *Double jeopardy: Adolescent offenders with mental disorders.* Chicago: University of Chicago Press.

Grisso, T., Steinberg, L., Woolard, J., Cauffman, E., Scott, E., Graham, S., & ... Schwartz R. (2003). Juveniles' competence to stand trial: A comparison of adolescents' and adults' capacities as trial defendants. *Law and Human Behavior, 27*(4), 333–363. doi: 10.1023/A:1024065015717

Guerra, N., Modecki, K., & Cunningham, W. (2014). *Developing social–emotional skills for the labor market: the PRACTICE model.* World Bank Policy Research Working Paper, (7123). Wahington DC: World Bank.

Halperin, J. M., Trampush, J. W., Miller, C. J., Marks, D. J., & Newcorn, H. (2008). Neuropsychological outcome in adolescents/young adults with childhood ADHD: Profiles of persisters, remitters and controls. *Journal of Child Psychology and Psychiatry, 49*(9), 958–996. doi:10.1111/j.1469-7610.2008.01926.x

Herz, D. C., Ryan, J. P., & Bilchik, S. (2010). Challenges facing crossover youth: An examination of juvenile-justice decision making and recidivism. *Family Court Review, 48*(2), 305–321.

Hobson, C. W., Scott, S., & Rubia, K. (2011). Investigation of cool and hot executive function in ODD/CD independently of ADHD. *Journal of Child Psychology and Psychiatry, 52*(10), 1035–1043. doi:10.1111/j.1469-7610.2011.0

Hooper, C. J., Luciana, M., Conklin, H. M., & Yarger, R. S. (2004). Adolescents' performance on the Iowa Gambling Task: implications for the development of decision making and ventromedial prefrontal cortex. *Developmental Psychology, 40*(6), 1148–1158. doi: 10.1037/0012-1649.40.6.1148

Kassin, S. M., Drizin, S. A., Grisso, T., Gudjonsson, G. H., Leo, R. A., & Redlich, A. D. (2010). Police-induced confessions. *Law and Human Behavior, 34*(1), 3–38. doi: 10.1007/s10979-009-9188-6

Kerr, A., & Zelazo, P. D. (2004). Development of "hot" executive function: the children's gambling task. *Brain and Cognition, 55*(1), 148–157. doi: 10.1016/S0278-2626(03)00275-6

Kravariti, E., Morris, R. G., Rabe-Hesketh, S., Murray, R. M., & Frangou, S. (2003). The Maudsley early onset schizophrenia study: cognitive function in adolescents with recent onset schizophrenia. *Schizophrenia Research, 61*, 137–148. doi:10.1016/S0920-9964(02)00291-8.

Kyte, Z. A., Goodyer. I. M., & Sahakian, B. J. (2005). Selected executive skills in adolescents with recent first episode major depression. *Journal of Child Psychology and Psychiatry, 46*(9), 995–1005. doi: 10.1111/j.1469-7610.2004.00400.x

Latzman, R. D. (2009). *Interrelations among youth temperament, executive functions, and externalizing behaviors.* PhD (Doctor of Philosophy) thesis, University of Iowa, 2009. http://ir.uiowa.edu/etd/306

Loeber, R., & Farrington, D. P. (2000). Young children who commit crime: Epidemiology, developmental origins, risk factors, early interventions, and policy implications. *Development and Psychopathology, 12*, 737–762.

Luciana, M. (2013). Adolescent brain development in normality and psychopathology. *Development and Psychopathology, 25*, 1325–1345. doi: 10.1017/S0954579413000643

Luciana, M., & Collins, P. F. (2012). Incentive motivation, cognitive control, and the adolescent brain: Is it time for a paradigm shift? *Child Development Perspectives, 6*(4), 392–399. doi: 10.1111/j.1750-8606.2012.00252.x

Luciana, M., Conklin, H., Hooper, C., & Yarger, R. (2005). The development of nonverbal working memory processes in adolescents: Different maturational trajectories for recall versus executive control. *Child Development, 76*, 697–712. doi: 10.1111/j.1467-8624.2005.00872.x

McReynolds, L. S., Schwalbe, C. S., & Wasserman, G. A. (2010). The contribution of psychiatric disorder to juvenile recidivism. *Criminal Justice and Behavior, 37*(2), 204–216.

Mears, D. P., & Kelly, W. R. (1999). Assessments and intake processes in juvenile justice processing: Emerging policy considerations. *Crime & Delinquency, 45*(4), 508–529.

Miller v. Alabama and Jackson v. Hobbs, 132 S. Ct. 2455 (2012). Retrieved December 18, 2016 from https://www.supremecourt.gov/opinions/11pdf/10-9646g2i8.pdf

Miyake, A., Friedman, N. P., Emerson, M. J., Witzki, A. H., Howerter, A., & Wagar, T. (2000). The unity and diversity of executive functions and their contributions to complex "frontal lobe" tasks: A latent variable analysis. *Cognitive Psychology, 41*, 49–100. doi:10.1006/cogp.1999.0734

Modecki, K. L. (2008). Addressing gaps in the maturity of judgment literature: Age differences and delinquency. *Law and Human Behavior, 32*(1), 78–91. doi: 10.1007/s10979-007-9087-7

Modecki, K. L. (2009). "It's a rush": Psychosocial content of antisocial decision making. *Law and Human Behavior, 33*(3), 183–193.doi: 10.1007/s10979-008-9150-z

Modecki, K. L. (2016). Do risks matter? Variable and person-centered approaches to adolescents' problem behavior. *Journal of Applied Developmental Psychology, 42*, 8–20. doi:10.1016/j.appdev.2015.11.001

Modecki, K. L., Hagan, M., Sandler, I., & Wolchik, S. (2015). Latent profiles of non-residential fathers six years after divorce: Predicting long term offspring outcomes. *Journal of Clinical Child & Adolescent Psychology, 44*(1), 123–126.

Modecki, K. L. & Wilson, M. N. (2009). Associations between individual and family level characteristics and parenting practices in incarcerated African American fathers. *Journal of Child and Family Studies, 18*(5), 530–540. doi:10.1007/s10826-009-9255-0

Modecki, K. L., Zimmer-Gembeck, M., & Guerra, N. (2017). Emotion regulation, coping and decision-making: Three linked skills for preventing externalizing problems in adolescence. *Child Development, 88*(2). doi:10.1111/cdev.12734

Morgan, A. B., & Lilienfeld, S. O. (2009). A meta-analytic review of the relation between antisocial behavior and neuropsychological measures of executive function. *Clinical Psychology Review, 20*(1), 113–136. doi:10.1016/S0272-7358(98)00096-8

Mulford, C. F., Reppucci, N. D., Mulvey, E. P., Woolard, J. L., & Portwood, S. L. (2004). Legal issues affecting mentally disordered and developmentally delayed youth in the justice system. *International Journal of Forensic Mental Health, 3*(1), 3–22. doi: 10.1080/14999013.2004.10471193

Oberlander, L. B., & Goldstein, N. E. (2001). A review and update on the practice of evaluating Miranda comprehension. *Behavioral Sciences & the Law, 19*(4), 453–471. doi: 10.1002/bsl.453

O'Donnell, P. C., & Lurigio, A. J. (2008). Psychosocial predictors of clinicians' recommendations and judges' placement orders in a juvenile court. *Criminal Justice and Behavior, 35*(11), 1429–1448. doi: 10.1177/0093854808324061

Ogilvie, J. M., Stewart, A. L., Chan, R. C., & Shum, D. H. (2011). Neuropsychological measures of executive function and antisocial behavior: A meta-analysis. *Criminology*, *49*(4), 1063–1107. doi: 10.1111/j.1745-9125.2011.00252.x

Prencipe, A., Kesek, A., Cohen, J., Lamm, C., Lewis, M. D., & Zelazo, P. D. (2011). Development of hot and cool executive function during the transition to adolescence. *Journal of Experimental Child Psychology*, *108*(3), 621–637. doi:10.1016/j.jecp.2010.09.008

Redlich, A. D., Summers, A., & Hoover, S. (2010). Self-reported false confessions and false guilty pleas among offenders with mental illness. *Law and Human Behavior*, *34*(1), 79–90. doi: 10.1007/s10979-009-9194-8

Repetti, R. L., Taylor, S. E., & Seeman, T. E. (2002). Risky families: family social environments and the mental and physical health of offspring. *Psychological Bulletin*, *128*(2), 330–366. doi: 10.1037//0033-2909.128.2.330

Rinsky, J. R., & Henshaw, S. P. (2011). Linkages between childhood executive functioning and adolescent social functioning and psychopathology in girls with ADHD. *Child Neuropsychology*, *17*(4), 368–390. doi: 10.1080/09297049.2010.544649

Rogers, R., Harrison, K. S., Hazelwood, L. L., & Sewell, K. W. (2007). Knowing and intelligent: A study of Miranda warnings in mentally disordered defendants. *Law and Human Behavior*, *31*(4), 401–418. doi: 10.1007/s10979-006-9070-8

Romer, D. (2010). Adolescent risk taking, impulsivity, and brain development: implications for prevention. *Developmental Psychobiology*, *52*(3), 263–276. doi: 10.1002/dev.20442

Roper v. Simmons, 125 S.Ct. 1183 (2005). Retrieved December 18, 2016 from https://www.supremecourt.gov/opinions/04pdf/03-633.pdf

Sanborn, J. B. (1996). Factors perceived to affect delinquent dispositions in juvenile court: Putting the sentencing decision into context. *Crime & Delinquency*, *42*(1), 99–113.

Schmidt, M. G., Reppucci, N. D., & Woolard, J. L. (2003). Effectiveness of participation as a defendant: The attorney–juvenile client relationship. *Behavioral Sciences & the Law*, *21*(2), 175–198. doi:10.1002/bsl.532

Scott, E. S., Reppucci, N. D., & Woolard, J. L. (1995). Evaluating adolescent decision making in legal contexts. *Law and Human Behavior*, *19*(3), 221–244.

Séguin, J. R., Arseneault, L., Boulerice, B., Harden, P. W., & Tremblay, R. E. (2002). Response perseveration in adolescent boys with stable and unstable histories of physical aggression: The role of underlying processes. *Journal of Child Psychology and Psychiatry*, *43*(4), 481–494. doi: 10.1111/1469-7610.00039

Shirk, S., Talmi, A., & Olds, D. (2000). A developmental psychopathology perspective on child and adolescent treatment policy. *Development and Psychopathology*, *12*(4), 835–855.

Shulman, E. P., & Cauffman, E. (2013). Reward-biased risk appraisal and its relation to juvenile versus adult crime. *Law and Human Behavior*, *37*(6), 412.

Slobogin, C. (2013) Treating juveniles like juveniles: Getting rid of transfer and expanded adult court jurisdiction. *Texas Tech Law Review*, *46*, 13–37.

Sowell, E. R., Thompson, P. M., Holmes, C. J., Jernigan, T. L., & Toga, A. W. (1999). In vivo evidence for post-adolescent brain maturation in frontal and striatal regions. *Nature Neuroscience*, *2*(10), 859–861.

Stordal, K. I., Mykletun, A., Asbjørnsen, A., Egeland, J., Landrø, N. I., Roness, A., Rund, B. R., Sundet, K. S., Lundervold, A. J., & Lund, A. (2005). General psychopathology is more important for executive functioning than diagnosis. *Acta Psychiatrica Scandinavica*, *111*(1), 22–28. doi: 10.1111/j.1600-0447.2004.00389.x

Tarter. R. E., Kirisci, L., Mezzich, A., Cornelius, J. R., Pajer, K., Vanyukov, M., Gardner, W., Blackson, T., & Clarke, D. (2003). Neurobehavioral disinhibition in childhood predicts early age at onset of substance use disorder. *The American Journal of Psychiatry*, *160*(6), 1078–1085. doi: 10.1176/appi.ajp.160.6.1078.

Telzer, E. H., Fuligni, A. J., Lieberman, M. D., & Galván, A. (2013). Meaningful family relationships: Neurocognitive buffers of adolescent risk taking. *Journal of Cognitive Neuroscience*, *25*(3), 374–387. doi:10.1162/jocn_a_00331

Teplin, L. A., Abram, K. M., McClelland, G. M., Dulcan, M. K., & Mericle, A. A. (2002). Psychiatric disorders in youth in juvenile detention. *Archives of General Psychiatry, 59*(12), 1133–1143. doi:10.1001/archpsyc.59.12.1133.

Van Duijvenvoorde, A. C., Jansen, B. R., Bredman, J. C., & Huizenga, H. M. (2012). Age-related changes in decision making: Comparing informed and noninformed situations. *Developmental psychology, 48*(1), 192–203. doi: 10.1037/a0025601

Van Vlierberghe, L., Timbremont, B., Braet, C., & Basile, B. (2007). Parental schemas in youngsters referred for antisocial behavior problems demonstrating depressive symptoms. *The Journal of Forensic Psychiatry and Psychology, 18*(4), 515–533. doi: 10.1080/14789940701515442

Viljoen, J. L., Klaver, J., & Roesch, R. (2005). Legal decisions of preadolescent and adolescent defendants: predictors of confessions, pleas, communication with attorneys, and appeals. *Law and Human Behavior, 29*(3), 253.

Viljoen, J. L., & Roesch, R. (2005). Competence to waive interrogation rights and adjudicative competence in adolescent defendants: cognitive development, attorney contact, and psychological symptoms. *Law and Human Behavior, 29*(6), 723.

Wadsworth, M. E., Raviv, T., Reinhard, C., Wolf, B., DeCarlo Santiago, C., & Einhorn, L.(2008). An indirect effects model of the association between poverty and child functioning: the role of children's poverty related stress. *Journal of Loss and Trauma, 13*, 156–185. doi: 10.1080/15325020701742185

Water, E., Cillessen, A. H., & Scheres, A. (2014). Distinct age-related differences in temporal discounting and risk taking in adolescents and young adults. *Child Development, 85*(5), 1881–1897. doi:10.1111/cdev.12245

Weyandt, L. L. (2009). Executive functions and attention deficit hyperactivity disorder. *The ADHD Report, 17*(6), 1–7.

Williamson, A. A., Modecki, K. L., & Guerra, N. G. (2015). SEL programs in high school. In J. Durlak, T. Gullotta, C. Domitrovich, P. Goren, & R. Weissberg (Eds.), *Handbook of social and emotional learning. Research and practice.* New York: Guilford Press

Woodhouse, S. S., Ramos-Marcuse, F., Ehrlich, K. B., Warner, S., & Cassidy, J. (2009). The role of adolescent attachment in moderating and mediating the links between parent and adolescent psychological symptoms. *Journal of Clinical Child & Adolescent Psychology, 39*(1), 51–63. doi: 10.1080/15374410903401096

Woolard, J. L., Cleary, H. M., Harvell, S. A., & Chen, R. (2008). Examining adolescents' and their parents' conceptual and practical knowledge of police interrogation: A family dyad approach. *Journal of Youth and Adolescence, 37*(6), 685–698. doi: 10.1007/s10964-008-9288-5

Woolard, J. L., Reppucci, N. D., & Redding, R. E. (1996). Theoretical and methodological issues in studying children's capacities in legal contexts. *Law and Human Behavior, 20*(3), 219.

Worden, R. E., & Myers, S. M. (1999). Police encounters with juvenile suspects. *Report to the National Research Council's Panel on Juvenile Crime: Prevention, Treatment and Control.* Washington, DC: National Research Council.

Young, S. E., Friedman, N. P., Miyake, A., Willcutt, E. G., Corley, R. P., Haberstick, B. C., & Hewitt, J. K. (2009). Behavioral disinhibition: liability for externalizing spectrum disorders and its genetic and environmental relation to response inhibition across adolescence. *Journal of Abnormal Psychology, 118*(1), 117–130, doi: 10.1037/a0014657

Zhou, Q., Hofer, C., & Eisenberg, N. (2007). The developmental trajectories of attention focusing, attentional control and behavioral persistence, and externalizing problems during school age years. *Developmental Psychology, 43*(2), 369–385. doi.org/10.1037/0012-1649.43.2.369

# Index

Page references to Figures or Tables will be in **bold**, while references to Notes will be followed by the letter 'n' and Note number.




*The Wiley Handbook of Developmental Psychopathology*, First Edition. Edited by Luna C. Centifanti and David M. Williams.